Warehousing and Transportation Logistics

Systems, planning, application and cost effectiveness

Heinrich Martin

KoganPage

First published in German as *Transport- und Lagerlogistik* 1995–2016
by Springer Fachmedien Wiesbaden GmbH
First published in Great Britain and the United States in 2018 by Kogan Page Limited

2nd Floor, 45 Gee Street	c/o Martin P Hill Consulting	4737/23 Ansari Road
London	122 W 27th Street	Daryaganj
EC1V 3RS	New York, NY 10001	New Delhi 110002
United Kingdom	USA	India

© Heinrich Martin 2018

ISBN   978 0 7494 8220 6
E-ISBN   978 0 7494 8221 3

British Library Cataloguing-in-Publication Data

A CIP record for this book is available from the British Library.

Library of Congress Control Number

2017001497

Typeset by Integra Software Services Pvt. Ltd., Pondicherry
Print production managed by Jellyfish
Printed and bound in Great Britain by Ashford Colour Press Ltd.

CONTENTS

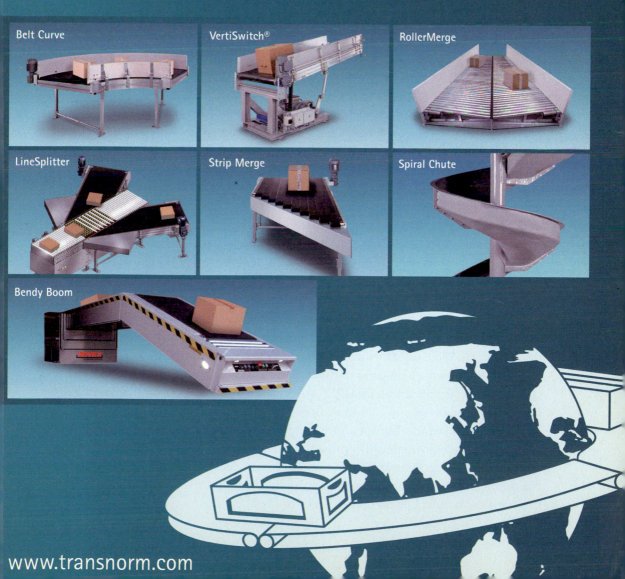

FOREWORD

Transport and Warehousing Logistics offers an overview of all logistics functions within internal business logistics, as well as intra-logistics, with a particular focus on transport, warehousing and assembly logistics. You can find interfaces such as unit creation, material flow or goods storage as well as systems and management for planning or information to identify objects, control and processing of orders.

This book does not just contain specialist knowledge for students of technical subjects, particularly logistics, but it also serves as a practice-oriented book for the planning of bachelor and master degree theses, with a multitude of useful information and ideas. It is also a workbook for professional practitioners, production, planning and industrial engineers, who are specifically concerned with the planning side of this specialist area.

The key focus in the creation of this book was on the management techniques in transport and warehousing together with any necessary pre-dimensioning, and not on calculations related to engineering and construction. It is looking first and foremost at the transmission of comprehensive and detailed knowledge in the relevant areas. This is done by means of demonstrating the constructive and functional structure of the individual pieces including advantages and disadvantages, application areas and important planning-related figures – as well as presenting their connections and interdependencies. This logistics-focused perspective runs through the entire book, even if it is not always directly visible. There are many economic considerations and calculations through the book, to determine the amortization period for an investment. This is supported by statements on cost based on present day values. Examples and questions help to complement and consolidate the content. A wealth of Figures, technical drawings, structural models and Tables will help recognize different options during the creative phase of planning and to find alternative answers.

The examples at the end of almost every chapter are not just there to help clarify the content but they also serve to deepen and complement the content of each chapter. Answers to these questions can be found in the relevant chapter.

The notes shown with Figures or examples offer further information on the topic.

Sources are identified with the URLs under each Figure, so that additional detailed information can be accessed quickly. I would like to express my sincere thanks to the companies involved for their support with information and material for publication.

This book has been translated from the German version, *Transport-und Lagerlogistik: Systematik, Planung, Einsatz und Wirtschaftlichkeit*, which was published by Springer Nature. I would like to thank Kogan Page Publishing for their support and hard work in bringing about the English translation of this book.

Linde Material Handling

OPTIMIZING MATERIAL FLOW

Providing solutions for productivity, reliability and safety

Digital connectivity, automation and ever more individualized products are the main drivers of change in intralogistics. This change affects each company in different ways.

That is why we at Linde do not simply sell standard products and only implement new technologies when they achieve added value.

This ensures we provide intelligent solutions that meet our customers' needs 100 %. As a result, we are looking for people who do not only understand their business but are also eager to listen to customers.

Find out more about us at   → www.linde-mh.com

ABBREVIATIONS

ATS	Automated transport system
ATV	Automated transport vehicle
CAM	Computer aided manufacturing
CCD	Charge coupled device
CEN	Comitée Européen de Normalisation
Cf.	Confer/refer to
Ch.	Chapter
CIM	Computer integrated manufacturing
CIP	Continuous improvement processes
DIN	German Institute for Norming
DC	Distribution centre/direct current
EAN	European Article Number
ERP	Enterprise resource planning system
FIFO	First-in-first-out
GI	Goods issue
GPS	Global positioning system
GR	Goods receipts
I-point	Identification point
ISO	International Organization for Standardization
JIS	Just-in-sequence
JIT	Just-in-time
LAN	Local area network
LCD	Liquid crystal display
LU	Load unit
LIFO	Last-in-first-out
MDS	Mobile data storage
MF	Material flow
M	Million
Pal	Pallet
PF	Periphery
PPS	Production planning and management
RAM	Random-access memory
RFID	Radio frequency identification
ROI	Return on investment

TMS	Transport management system
TM	Means of transport
UVV	Accident prevention regulations
VBG	Association of Professional Societies
VDI	Association of German Engineers
VDMA	Association of German Machine Engineering Institutions
WAS	Warehouse administration system
WMS	Warehouse management system
TU	Time unit

GLOSSARY

ABC-analysis   an inventory method dividing items into three categories – A, B and C – in order to show their relative importance and value. A items are the most important and valuable, C the least

ABY-XYZ-analysis   a method used to classify material with regard to its value and quantity based on the Pareto principle, which expects that a small number of cases has a disproportional impact. This can also be referred to as the 80/20 principle

Ackermann steering   a geometrical arrangement of links for steering vehicles to help address the problem of wheels placed on the inside and outside needing to trace diverging circles

CAM – computer-aided manufacturing   using software to manage operations in a manufacturing environment

CEN (Comité Européen de Normalisation)   the EU committee for standardization, whose aim is to foster the EU economy and who published public standards

CIM – computer integrated manufacturing   using computers to control the entire manufacturing process, allowing for information exchange between individual processes

crossdocking   unloading material from one means of transport and directly loading them in to another outbound one with little or no storage in between

DIN standards   published by the German Institute for Standardization (Deutsches Institut für Normung) after collaboration at national, EU or international level. They provide an agreed set of rules for procedures

EAN code   a barcode – the most commonly used code has thirteen digits, a superset of the original 12-digit Universal Product Code (UPC-A) developed in the 1970s

EN – European standards   passed by one of the three European standards organizations: CEN, CENELEC and ETSI. They are designed and agreed in a collaborative process by all interested parties

ERP – enterprise resource planning   the integrated management of key business processes, often aided by software and technology in real time

FEU – forty-foot equivalent unit   a term often used in ocean freight to describe cargo in a container equal to forty-foot (40x8x8 feet), equalling about 25 metric tons or 72 cubic metres

FIFO – first in first out   an approach to dealing with stock, which ensures that those items stored first are also removed from storage first

information flow   the management of information in supply chains between customers and suppliers, as well as internally

input-output analysis   a quantitative economic method representing the interdependencies between different sectors at national or regional level and their impact on the economy

I-point – identification point   used in logistics to describe a specific location in the Goods receipts area. When passing this point, products are scanned for certain information such as type, item number, quantity, weight

ISO container   a container constructed in line with ISO standards for freight transportation

JIS – Just In Sequence   an inventory strategy matching JIT with relevant sequences in the production/assembly line

JIT – Just In Time   a production method aimed at reducing flow times and response times from customers and suppliers

Kanban system   a scheduling approach for Lean manufacturing and just-in-time manufacturing. Can be used for inventory control to manage the supply chain

key performance indicator (KPI)   a performance measurement to evaluate the success of an activity or process

land use plan   a document that helps ensure the judicious utilization of available land through activities and functions in line with the overall land development objectives of a municipality

LIFO – last in first out   the last items stored are the first to be removed or retrieved

Lean production   a systematic approach to prevent wastage in a manufacturing or production environment – material waste as well as inefficient processes and methods

MF – material flow   the transport of raw, part-finished, pre-fabricated materials as well as components and final products through the relevant production processes

MTM – methods time management   A pre-determined motion time system utilized mainly in industrial environments for the analysis of methods for performing a manual task or operation. The result of the analysis is the expected time in which the task should be performed

one-container system   part of the Kanban system, material flow is managed through the pull principle, whereby once the container is emptied the relevant material ticket is used to order a new, filled container

order picking (or order preparation)   a logistics process in warehouses whereby items are retrieved and collated in a specific quantity in order to fulfil customer orders

order processing time   the expected length of time from placement of an order to shipping. It can be influenced by stock availability, errors during order picking, weather and other external conditions for transport

Pareto principle (or the 80/20 rule)   the principle that, in many cases, about 80 per cent of the impact results from 20 per cent of the causes

pick and pack   a process in order picking where components of an order are retrieved from their source (picked) and directly placed into a shipping container addressed to the recipient (packed)

pick-by-balance   each item retrieved is registered through change to the overall weight and a relevant confirmation slip printed

pick-by-voice   using voice commands and speech recognition technology in warehouses to aid picking items

pull principle   a system whereby production orders are triggered by stock levels reaching a certain pre-determined point

push principle   a system where order production is demand-based (forecast or actual)

quality management   organizational systems and processes to ensure a consistent level of quality in products or services with four key parts: planning, assurance, control and improvement

RFID (radio frequency identification) technology   uses electromagnetic fields for automatic identification and tracking of tags containing stored information fixed to items

Sankey plan   in material flow analysis a diagram depicting the relationship between resources, including arrows to show their direction

TEU – twenty-foot equivalent unit   a unit of cargo in freight shipping containers equal to twenty-foot ($20 \times 8 \times 8$ feet)

top-down principle   an organizational approach whereby strategic direction is determined by top management and cascaded down through the organization

turntable steering   a simple steering mechanism composing a single pivot in the middle of the front axle with both front and rear axle being solid

two-container system   in this Kanban approach two containers are filled with the same item and items are always retrieved from the container in front. Once that one is empty an order for refill is automatically triggered, and the back container is moved to the front, ensuring a constant supply

VDI guidelines   standards issued by the Association of German Engineers (Verein Deutscher Ingenieure – VDI)

VDMA   German Mechanical Engineering Industry Association (Verband Deutscher Maschinen und Anlagenbau – VDMA)

warehouse management system   software used for support and optimization of warehousing processes and management

Business and logistics 01

1.1 Business interfaces

A business is an open, socio-technical system with the objective of offering services to third parties while making a profit. As an open system, there are dependencies and relationships with its environment, which can be expressed as interfaces (see Figure 1.1).

The *sales market* is the most important interface, as no business is viable without the sale of products. Whether the products are in line with the requirements, wishes and ideas of the customers, can be seen in the number of orders, ie the sale of products. Orders, as well as positive and negative information about the products from customers, will feed back to the business via sales professionals.

The *source market* interface provides information on the conditions for purchasing capital, materials and personnel in the marketplace.

The *authorities* interface highlights the regulations and legislation that have to be adhered to as well as applicable requirements when using machinery and employing personnel.

The *technology* interface indicates which processes, methodology, machinery or services are offered by the market for those areas that are important to the business in order to run production, transport, warehousing and information transmission at low costs.

A business that doesn't continuously observe and monitor these interfaces, in order to be able to economically produce, transport, control and inform in line with state of the art processes, will inevitably be left behind. This is why head offices and planning departments (see Example 1.12) analyse the business environment and compare the findings with their internal situation. Hence, the transformation of the market from a seller's to a buyer's market is a good example of the buyers' requirements on delivery service, compliance with schedules, quality and product diversification influencing manufacturing, transport and warehousing systems, having a real impact and, eventually, leading to the development of new systems. A business can also be represented as a control cycle (see Figure 1.2).

Figure 1.1   Business interfaces

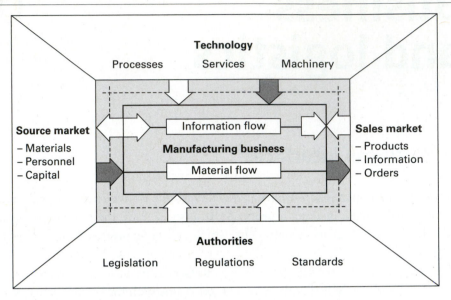

Figure 1.2   The business as control cycle

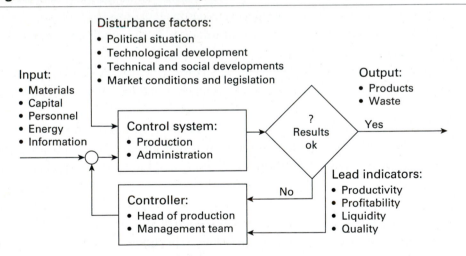

1.2 Logistics goals and functions

For production to be economical, materials or goods have to be provided at the workplace or for the end user – and they have to be:

- the right materials and goods;
- the right quantities;
- the right quality;

- at the right time;
- at the right place;
- at minimal cost.

These are the objectives that logistics is concerned with. Logistics is the science of the planning, creation, management and control of material and information flows in systems, and is based on:

- technology (manufacturing, transport and warehousing technology components of material flow);
- information technology (elements of the information flow);
- business and economics (economic component).

The terminology of logistics encompasses a cross-cutting systems approach – thinking in terms of overall costs. Logistics components include goods, merchandise, materials, pieces of work and information. Technical, information-related and business functions, which are continuously improved and optimized, serve to fulfil the above-mentioned guiding principles of logistics.

The operational functions are as follows:

- the flow of goods and materials: transportation, storage, order picking, packaging and management;
- the flow of data and information: recording, storage, transferring, processing and distribution;
- leadership functions: planning, assessment, decision-making, controlling and monitoring.

The objectives of logistics are to reduce costs for operational material flow and the related information flow, as well as increase performance. Logistics costs (see Example 1.5; Figure 12.30) can be divided into costs for storage (see Chapter 9.6), for transport and handling (the costs of external and internal transport, freight charges to the service provider, packaging costs), as well as into costs for systems and management, such as product programme planning and order processing. Logistics performance is shown by the quality of reliability, delivery time, loyalty, flexibility and precision.

Logistics operates in a cross-function and cross-business, holistic as well as user- and service-oriented way.

Logistics is the key to improving and optimizing business infrastructure with the goal of increasing market performance, uncovering streamlining potential and guaranteeing a high-quality delivery service. Logistics is also a planning tool in order to design internal and inter-business processes. When considering any action, it takes into account the performance potential of producers and service providers, on both the procurement and the sales side.

1.3 Business logistics

The goal of business logistics is to achieve the optimal interaction between humans, technology, management and information. Its task is to plan, design, manage and control the flow of material, goods and production as well as the related flow of information in an economic way, from the supplier to the business, within the business and from the business to the end customer.

This results in a horizontal structure of task areas within business logistics for a producing company in (see Figure 1.3):

- procurement logistics;
- production logistics;
- distribution logistics;
- waste disposal logistics.

A *retail business* uses procurement and distribution logistics, whereas a *service business* generally only uses distribution logistics. Business logistics also has a vertical interface function, which can be structured into an administrative, dispositive and operational level and which is concerned with the areas of technology, information technology and business management (see Figure 1.4).

Thus, business logistics encompasses the operational flow of materials and goods along with the related dispositive and administrative functions required for the fulfilment of all business tasks. Business logistics takes into account both elements of internal logistics as well as elements of external logistics directed by the business, such as warehousing, order picking and provision of goods in line with the just-in-time (JIT) principle via the haulier.

Intra logistics is used to describe the internal material flow in a system, together with the related information flow, and aims to achieve improvement, increased performance as well as cost reduction within internal logistics. Intra logistics is concerned with cargo, bulk and liquids and describes the interplay of technical and information factors, such as warehousing, order picking, transport, packaging, handling and management. Intra logistics represents a demarcation to external logistics.

1.3.1 Procurement logistics

The customization of requirements has resulted in a great many versions of this model. The result has been an incredible increase in items and quantities. For a car manufacturer, the number of individual items for the entire production programme

Figure 1.3 Business logistics structure

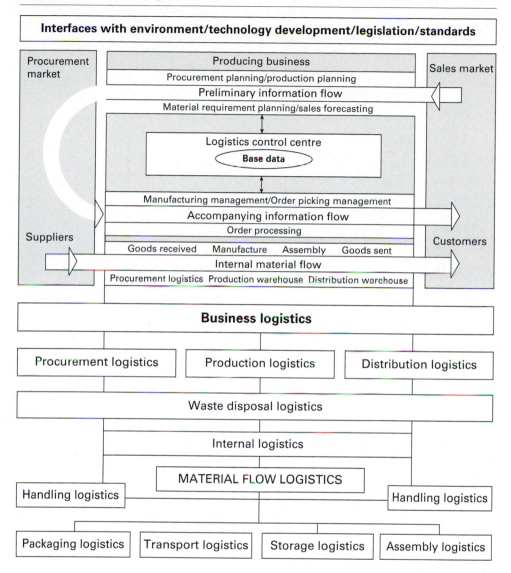

increased from 30,000 items in 1965 to approximately 90,000 items in 2000. For a business, this means anw enormous increase in transport, warehousing, provision, administration and procurement of materials. This clearly demonstrates the importance of procurement logistics.

In order to limit the number of items despite the diversity in types (see Figure 1.5), businesses reduce the extent of *in house production*, create manufacturing centres focused on technology and production, and work with modular systems or component manufacturing. The procurement activities resulting from the diversity in items and

Figure 1.4   Interface functions of logistics

		Business logistics		
		Procurement logistics	Production logistics	Distribution logistics
Business management	Administrative level	⊘	⊘	⊘
	Dispositive level	⊘	⊘	⊘
Technology	Administrative level	⊘	⊘	⊘
	Dispositive level	⊘	⊘	⊘
	Operational level	⊘	⊘	⊘
Information technology	Administrative level	⊘	⊘	⊘
	Dispositive level	⊘	⊘	⊘
	Operational level	⊘	⊘	⊘
		External logistics	Internal logistics	External logistics

Figure 1.5   Development of diversity in types and items

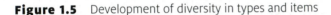

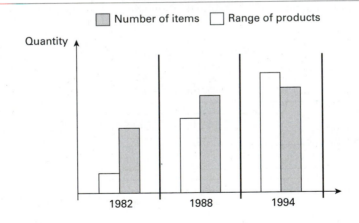

materials received a new organizational structure by means of procurement logistics, as well as altered ways of working in order to ensure the provision of materials for manufacturing and assembly.

When required, procurement occurs through individual order or service level agreements, using external warehousing, such as the buyer's or the supplier's, using consignment stores or depots, or as consumption-based procurement, eg container principle, JIT or e-procurement (see Chapter 9.1).

It is the *goal of procurement logistics* to prepare and implement all logistical tasks in the goods and materials flow, along with the relevant information flow with regard to planning, design, managing and controlling. This means that procurement logistics is responsible for the business's requirement-based supply from the suppliers to the provision in production via transport, receipt of goods and procurement depot. It takes into account measures and actions, eg the hauliers and their depots, and it also enacts specifications and regulations about the condition, timing and location of goods to be delivered. (Tasks and goals of procurement logistics: see Example 1.1).

One opportunity for procurement logistics to reduce stock levels and order processing times (see Figures 2.22 and 2.23) is *just-in-time supply* for manufacturing and assembly. JIT is a supply strategy in line with needs-based material supply, whereby the materials or goods are provided immediately before processing, without the need for interim storage. A result of this strategy is the change from central goods receipt to decentralized delivery locations.

Procurement logistics is a process-related form of logistics for purchasing goods required for service provision, such as raw materials and machinery, but also information, money, energy, personnel and services on the relevant markets.

In an economic sense, procurement is part of the market economy. Systems, machinery and resources related to the material flow are counted as capital goods and are usually bound to a decision on investment.

1.3.2 Production logistics

Production logistics is part of business logistics and encompasses the operational flow of materials and goods along with the accompanying flow of information and related dispositive and administrative functions required for the fulfilment of production tasks.

The *goal of production logistics* is the timely and cost-effective provision of the right materials, in the right place, at the right time and in the right quantities. It is production logistics' task to supply material at the production locations by means of the internal material flow. It has to optimize and carry out transport to and from resources and workplaces. Production logistics designs and directs the flow of materials and information in production right up to the distribution depot via different manufacturing and assembly stages with the relevant production depot.

1.3.3 Distribution logistics

Distribution logistics stems from business logistics, and can be seen as complementary to procurement. Distribution logistics encompasses the flow of goods and materials as well as the related flow of information from the end of production with the creation of loading units (see Chapter 3.3) over the distribution depot right up to the end customer. Distribution logistics is logistics related to the process of distribution, and makes use of a variety of transport measures to distribute goods to customers.

It is the *task* of distribution logistics to ensure provision of the right type and quantity of products and/or merchandise for customers and buyers. Part of distribution logistics is also the choice of the location for distribution depots, planning for storage and transport as well as the order picking and packing of goods. As a result of the consumption-based supply of materials and often prescribed packaging rules, the challenges for distribution logistics are on the increase.

The goal of distribution logistics is the timely and cost-effective supply of goods for customers, by planning, designing, directing and controlling the flow of materials and information from the business to the customer. Hence, distribution logistics takes care of supplying customers with the company's products. The functions displayed in Figure 1.6 are assigned to it and it is its job to optimize these. Influencing factors on the design of distribution logistics are:

- range of products: quantity, measurement, weight etc;
- manufacturing method: order-based or serial production;
- customer structure: wholesale, retail;
- distribution principle: central and/or regional depots;
- production site: one factory, multiple factories, production programme (see Figure 1.7);
- Order picking and distribution concept: see Example 7.17.

The importance of distribution logistics can be judged by the amount of costs and by its suitability to strengthen competitiveness (for more on distribution logistics costs, see Example 1.5).

Figure 1.6   Distribution logistics functions

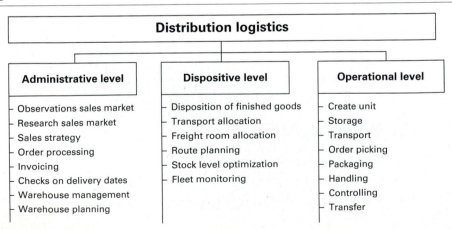

Figure 1.7 Possible distribution structures with central depot

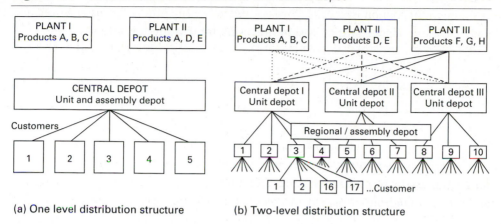

(a) One level distribution structure   (b) Two-level distribution structure

1.3.4 Waste disposal logistics

Companies in all sectors are obliged to take back packaging they distributed after use by customers and to recycle these for re-use. The accountability for disposal of packaging waste has been transferred from public waste disposal to industry. Waste from packaging material must not be stored nor may it be used in thermal recycling. Rather, it has to be sorted according to type of material and rendered recyclable (see Example 1.10). Such regulations exist for a great number of materials that occur as residual or waste materials in a business (see Figure 1.8). The cost of disposal for all waste occurring in a business represents a significant fraction in operational budgeting. Waste disposal logistics takes care of this issue by monitoring disposal processes as a separate business area. Here, the logistical chain of residual materials is looked at from their creation to their disposal and recycling possibilities, as well as determining influencing factors on quantities, type and treatment of the waste material flow. The tasks of waste disposal logistics show parallels and similarities to production and distribution logistics (material flow functions, fleet disposition). Disposal costs for waste can be reduced by:

- waste prevention, cessation of use of non-recyclable packaging;
- reduction of waste;
- re-use, such as containers for multiple use (see Example 3.8);
- re-use, such as waste paper, scrap metal (see Example 1.10);
- re-use, such as building material, incineration.

Supply and disposal logistics can be seen as a cycle, and attempt to work as follows: prevention before recycling, and recycling before disposal. By using economic waste collection systems and depending on the amounts of waste with complementary container, storage and transport systems, it can achieve an additional reduction in disposal costs.

Figure 1.8   Disposal structure for recyclable and valuable materials

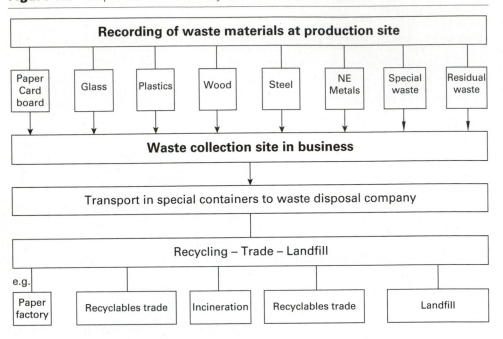

1.4 Internal logistics

Internal logistics (see Figure 1.3) forms part of business logistics, and encompasses the operational site-specific task areas of procurement and distribution, as well as production logistics. The most important operational functions of internal logistics are handling, storage, transport, assembly and packaging. These functions are functions of the material flow (comp. Chapter 2.1). From a logistical perspective of the operational, dispositive and administration levels of these functions, and while taking into account the related information flows, there are:

- transport logistics (see Chapter 4.2), handling logistics (see Chapter 7.1);
- warehousing and order picking logistics (see Chapters 9.5 and 11.1);
- waste disposal logistics (see Chapter 1.3.4);
- information logistics (see Chapter 13).

1.5 Business management logistics

Business management is responsible for the economic aspects of transport and warehousing systems. This is so that the relevant decisions are not only technically correct but also economically sound, and to ensure this, business management will:

- create economic conditions by use of key indicators;
- determine the best answer from alternative planning by developing a business case and carrying out a cost–benefit analysis;
- influence the organizational structure by deploying a key logistics department.

The short-, medium- and long-term logistics strategies have to be developed and written based on business aspects. Relevant business management tasks are:

- analysis and planning: preparation of investment calculations;
- strategy development: determining key indicators and assessment of alternatives;
- building organizational structure, processing and controlling.

The goal of *controlling* is to maintain logistical processes by providing information and data, often in graphic format, to the decision-makers at strategic/operational level for evaluation.

Controlling takes care of planning, monitoring and coordination tasks. It works with processes and methods, eg input–output analysis, product cycle analysis, break even analysis and key indicator analysis. This data is based on accounting figures, derived using information technology (IT) and prepared evaluation.

Business management logistics is also concerned with delivery services. This is about the results of a logistical system. The output should meet the customers' expectations. The following components are part of delivery service/efficiency:

- *delivery time,* or service time (for more on order processing time, see Figure 2.23), period of time from receipt of order to delivery at the customer's location;
- *delivery reliability,* or timeliness, delivery capacity: probability (percentage) of actual compliance with delivery confirmations;
- *integrity of deliveries,* or delivery quality: condition of deliverables in terms of type and quantity;
- *delivery flexibility:* meeting of customer wishes with regards to delivery.

1.5.1 Key performance indicators

A key value is the definition of a specific condition without numerical value. Only when quantified, will this result in a key performance indicator. Key indicators can be absolute numbers or ratios. They can be dimensionless or have a related dimension and quantify actuals or desired operational conditions Key indicators are used to compare, assess, plan and represent a significant basis for information and planning for managing directors, departmental heads and planning staff. They are also used in controlling and management to demonstrate facts and issues. All key indicators in a function area are combined in a key indicator system and, if maintained continuously, can help with management and decision-making in this area (see Example 1.2).

Indicator groups:

- Absolute figures are arrived at by adding up, subtracting or averaging.
- Ratios are relative figures, always based on a comparison and that can be divided up into subordinate numbers, related numbers and index numbers.
- Subordinate numbers are different values that are subordinate to one another. Subsets are related to the relevant total quantity, such as an item's turnover to the turnover of the entire range of items.
- Related numbers represent the relationship of two values that are related to each other generally but differ from one another with regard to content, such as business turnover to number of employees.
- Index numbers express average changes of certain values that are similar but chronologically separate, such as turnover in Quarter 2 to Quarter 1.

Basic logistic key indicators are:

- For management:
  - liquidity, productivity, profitability;
  - delivery readiness, service efficiency;
  - return on investment (ROI);
  - logistics costs;
  - order processing times;
  - waste disposal costs;
  - inventory range.
- In the area of material flow:
  - efficiency in use of height, space and premises;
  - stock/empties and inventory costs;
  - handling frequency, storage reach;
  - storage and handling costs;
  - use of fleet;
  - order processing times, availability.

Key indicators and key indicator determination for warehousing and order picking: see Examples 1.7; 11.3; 11.4; 11.21, for forklift trucks: Chapter 6.6.7.8.

1.5.2 Goals, strategies

Goals represent a future objective to be maintained (see Chapter 1.2). This immediately raises the question what means and approach are needed to achieve the goals.

Strategies are the approaches taken to reach a goal. Goals give direction in choosing between alternatives. Strategies describe the method deployed to achieve the goal. The connection between goal and strategy is inevitable, with the goal determining 'what' should be achieved, while the strategy states the 'how' or 'in what way' the goal will be reached. There are logistics strategies for procurement, production and distribution logistics (see Chapter 12.1.5):

- just in time strategy (see Chapters 1.3.1 / 9.1);
- first in – first out (FIFO) strategy (see Chapter 9.8);
- double game strategy (see Chapter 9.7);
- Kanban strategy (see Chapter 9.7);
- push or pull strategy (see Example 2.15);
- just-in-sequence (JIS) strategy (see Example 2.15).

1.6 Logistics and organizational structure

The perceived value of logistics in a business depends on many factors, such as the size of the business, openness of the management team, and the business situation. In principle, logistics can be included in the organizational structure in a centralized or decentralized way. Centralized means that logistical tasks are combined into one department, whereas decentralized means that logistical tasks are distributed amongst several function areas. Depending on the business's organizational structure (line, functional, line and staff, matrix or divisional organization), the implementation of logistics can be centralized or decentralized (see Figure 1.9).

Figure 1.9   Logistics concept for a centralized and a decentralized business structure

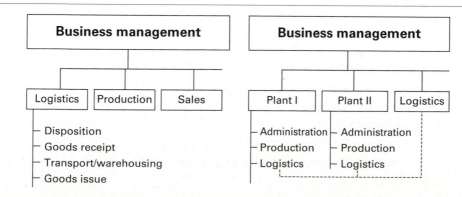

1.7 VDI guidelines

2520	Introduction of business logistics; workplan	12.90
2523	Project management for logistics systems for MF and warehousing technology	07.93
2525	Logistics key indicators for small and medium-sized enterprises	07.99
4400	Logistics key indicators for production (Bl 2)	12.04
4402	Benchmarking	11.00
4405	Process-oriented cost analysis for internal logistics (Bl 1)	10.03
4414	Reorganization and expansion of logistics systems	12.95

1.8 Examples and questions

Example 1.1: Procurement logistics

a) What are the goals of procurement logistics?

Answer: The goals of procurement logistics can be deduced from the business goals to ascertain success potential. Thus, procurement logistics encompass:

- ensuring supply security;
- improving goods and material flow with related information flow and control systems;
- avoiding supplier dependency;
- securing supplier potential;
- minimizing stock;
- reducing costs of working capital, supply and provision;
- ensuring quality of purchased materials;
- achieving adaptability in procurement even in case of minimal forecast accuracy.

b) Which tasks are met by procurement logistics?

Answer: Procurement logistics tasks range from the supplier to the provision by production and, thus, expand across external transport, delivery including receipt of goods and quality checks, releasing goods for storage in the procurement warehouse, manufacturing of storage units, warehousing, storage administration and disposition, assembly of orders for production, including relevant internal transport and the information flow including planning, design, management and control of these tasks.

In summary, procurement logistics encompasses the supply process from procurement (source) to provision (drain) in production, created by:

Material flow, process organization and information flow.

The ranking and perceived value of the tasks in a business depends on its size, its structure and the importance of procurement.

c) Procurement logistics – example: garment industry

In the garment industry, outer fabrics, components like, eg, buttons, thread, zippers as well as finished parts come from many different companies worldwide, ie there is a physical and information network in procurement. Global procurement processes are, depending on the perspective and including distribution, called either value or supply chain. For these cross-company procurement streams, fast and accurate information is decisive for the management and control of production processes. A jacket, for example, consists of 40 different parts, trousers of approximately 30 and a blouse of approximately 15 parts. A garment manufacturer requires approximately 25,000 parts. For large clothing manufacturers around 20,000 deadlines have to be administered and, including suppliers, producers, hauliers and agents, there are up to 200 companies who participate in the supply chain management. This flood of information can only be managed with IT. A procurement logistics professional receives his/ her information via the phone, e-mail, fax or IT. Here, interfaces represent potential sources of disturbance, and IT is required to integrate the different media. Intelligent tools must record, process and manage all information centrally, and this creates transparent processes for the procurement delivery.

Example 1.2: Key indicator system for distribution centres

How could a consistent key indicator be structured for internal logistics in a distribution centre?

Answer: According to Chapter 1.5.1, a range of key indicators can be combined in a system for the assessment of performance and costs. With representative key indicators related to costs, time and service, it is possible to assess a distribution centre (DC). The representative key indicators are (see Figure 1.10):

- cost per delivered item: total DC cost divided by number of items to be delivered per time unit;
- shipping value factor: quotient from total costs and sales value of goods per time unit;
- order cycle fulfilment: quotient from intended and actual order processing time;
- delivery quality: as a function of supply readiness and factor as well as failed delivery quota and factor.

Figure 1.10   Key indicators for a distribution centre (www.Klaus-Heptner.com)

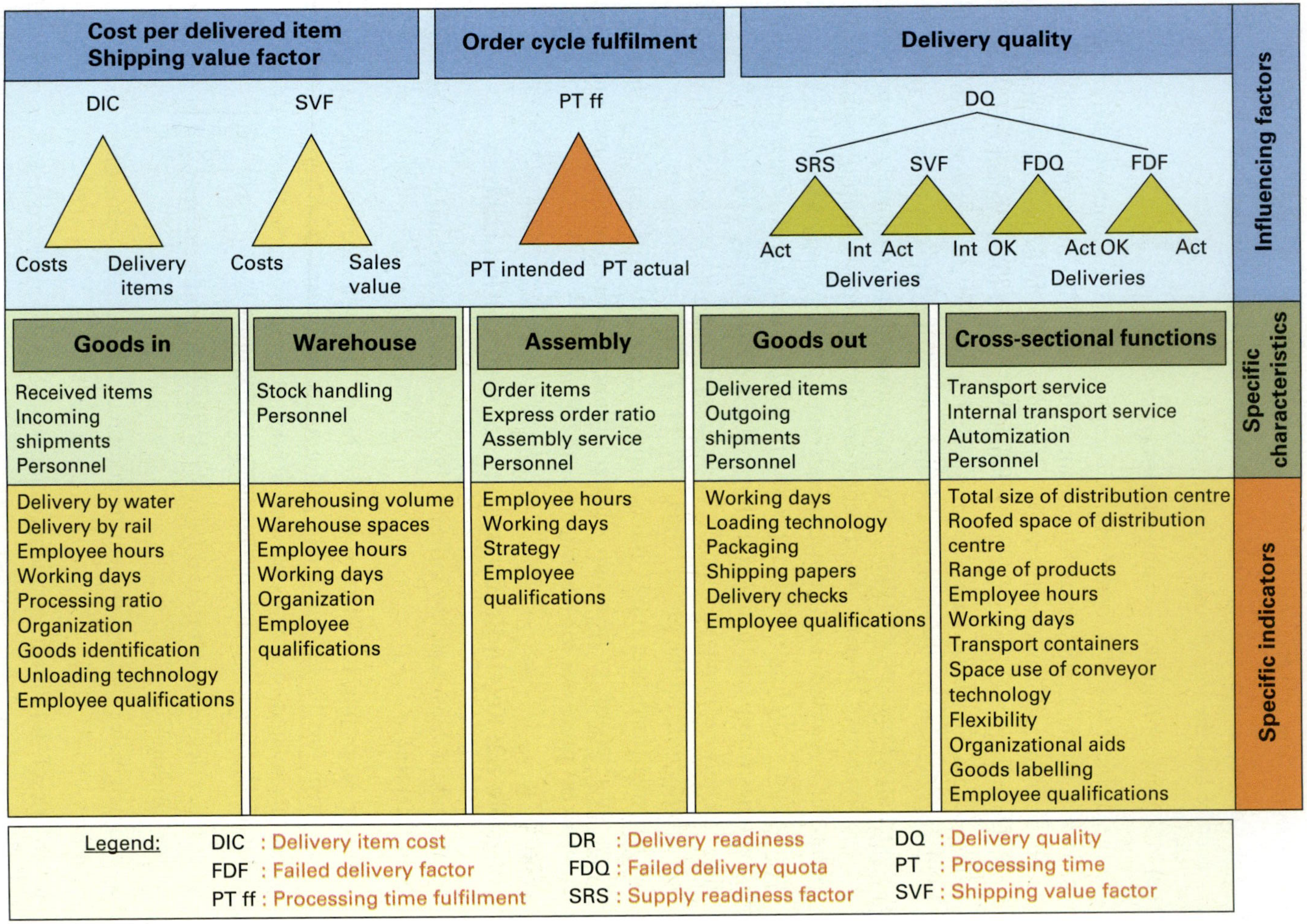

Influencing factors		

Cost per delivered item
Shipping value factor

DIC

SVF

Costs   Delivery items

Costs   Sales value

Order cycle fulfilment

PT ff

PT intended   PT actual

Delivery quality

DQ

SRS   SVF   FDQ   FDF

Act   Int Act   Int OK   Act OK   Act
Deliveries   Deliveries   Deliveries

Specific characteristics		

Goods in	**Warehouse**	**Assembly**	**Goods out**	**Cross-sectional functions**
Received items	Stock handling	Order items	Delivered items	Transport service
Incoming shipments	Personnel	Express order ratio	Outgoing shipments	Internal transport service
Personnel		Assembly service	Personnel	Automization
		Personnel		Personnel

Specific indicators		

Goods in	**Warehouse**	**Assembly**	**Goods out**	**Cross-sectional functions**
Delivery by water	Warehousing volume	Employee hours	Working days	Total size of distribution centre
Delivery by rail	Warehouse spaces	Working days	Loading technology	Roofed space of distribution centre
Employee hours	Employee hours	Strategy	Packaging	Range of products
Working days	Working days	Employee qualifications	Shipping papers	Employee hours
Processing ratio	Organization		Delivery checks	Working days
Organization	Employee qualifications		Employee qualifications	Transport containers
Goods identification				Space use of conveyor technology
Unloading technology				Flexibility
Employee qualifications				Organizational aids
				Goods labelling
				Employee qualifications

Legend:

DIC : Delivery item cost
FDF : Failed delivery factor
PT ff : Processing time fulfilment

DR : Delivery readiness
FDQ : Failed delivery quota
SRS : Supply readiness factor

DQ : Delivery quality
PT : Processing time
SVF : Shipping value factor

A survey of approximately 30 businesses (in the spare parts trade) came up with the following results:

- cost of delivery item: approx. €2.50–4/item; shipping value factor: 4–8 per cent;
- process time fulfilment: 97–99 per cent; delivery quality: 95–99 per cent.

Example 1.3: Benchmarking

What is benchmarking?

Answer: there is a difference between internal, business-related benchmarking and external benchmarking. External benchmarking is a management method to find the best answer to a problem by comparing different businesses in a sector or market. The process is based on identifying improved methods and best practice in other businesses and then adapting them into one's own business.

Example 1.4: Supply chain management

What is the definition of supply chain management?

Answer: Supply chain management describes a holistic and process-oriented approach to improve business processes by engaging with all suppliers, service providers and customers. Supply chain management starts with the raw material sources and carries on to the delivery of the finished product to the end customer. This means that business logistics with its basic process in planning, managing, providing, producing and distributing, is a main component of supply chain management, as shown in Figure 1.11.

Figure 1.11 Structure diagram of a supply chain management system

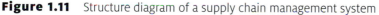

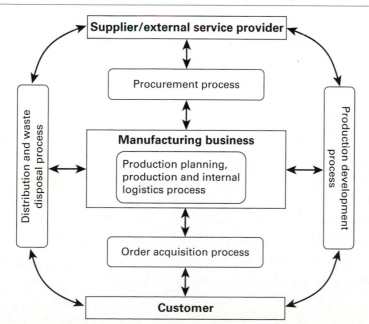

With regard to adding value to the individual activities in a supply chain, the term *value chain* is also used, which considers the individual activities and workings of a business from the perspective of creating value; this uses resources. Activities and resources are connected through processes.

Example 1.5: Business logistics costs

What are the logistics-related costs in different sectors?

Answer: The answer is presented in examples in Figure 1.12 (survey by Professor Dr Baumgarten, 2002, TU Berlin, see Figure 12.30) in relation to manufacturing costs.

Figure 1.12   Division of business logistics costs in different sectors

Sector	Business logistics costs %**	Procurement logistics %	Production logistics %	Distribution logistics %	Development costs %	Disposal costs %	Other costs %
Automobile industry	8.2	thereof: 23.4 =1.92	thereof: 27.2 =2.23	thereof: 26.8 =2.2	thereof: 7.8 =0.64	thereof: 2.8 =0.23	thereof: 12 =0.98
Consumer goods industry	12.8	6.5 0.83	4.1 0.52	64.1 8.21	3.2 0.41	2.0 0.26	7.7 0.99
Retail	27.6	10.3 2.84	17.7 4.89	53.4 14.74	0.3 0.08	5.3 1.46	12.9 3.56

Example 1.6: Outsourcing

a) What is meant by outsourcing?

b) How are outsourcing and key competencies connected?

Answer:

a) Outsourcing is a strategy to improve the business situation by awarding business contracts for services delivered by the business to date to other companies or service providers. Causes and reasons for outsourcing of business areas could be, for example, avoiding future investment, focusing on key competencies for the business and the utilization of specialists in other companies.

b) A key competency is the strength of a business in one particular area. The answer to question b) is provided by way of a portfolio matrix (see Figure 1.13).

Figure 1.13 Decision-making matrix for choosing an outsourcing strategy

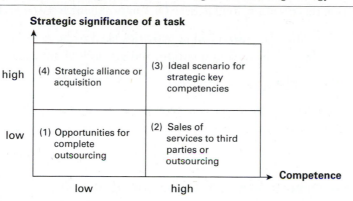

Strategic significance of a task

	low	high
high	(4) Strategic alliance or acquisition	(3) Ideal scenario for strategic key competencies
low	(1) Opportunities for complete outsourcing	(2) Sales of services to third parties or outsourcing

Competence

Example 1.7: Outsourcing costs for a distribution depot

Nowadays, hauliers tend to be service providers, too, and take on distribution depots including order-picking functions for companies. The basis for offers to take over a distribution depot is a key indicator for static and dynamic services. Which key indicators are required for a takeover offer, in relation to DIN pallets 1,200 × 800 mm?

Answer (see Example 11.15):

- **Costs for pallet space approximately €5/month.**
- **Incoming goods and storage approximately €2.50/pallet.**

Unloading lorries with forklift truck/set down pallet/IT entry with storage space determination/place label on pallet/pick up pallet/take to storage space/placing on shelf or on the floor.

- **Outsourcing/prepare for shipping/outgoing goods approximately €2.50/pallet.**

a) Moving those pallets from shelf or floor/transport to shipping preparation location/IT record/putting label on/pick up pallet/load onto lorry.

b) Activities *after* individual order picking and packaging (as in a)/pick up pallet/transport to shipping preparation location/IT record/put on label/pick up pallet/load onto lorry.

- **Order picking including packaging, eg stretching.**

Depending on the type of order picking, on weight, volume, measurements, type of packaging, specific characteristics etc.

a) Repacking cardboard from lattice box into KLT-containers **approximately €1.50/repacked KLT.**

b) Repacking cardboard from pallet to customer's heavy load carrier or from larger individual parts into heavy load carrier GLT **approximately €6/repacked GLT.**

These values for different order picking activities need to be determined for each company, depending on the time in question, and are decisive for the relevant costs.

- **Administrative outlay**

This includes conducting customer conversation, leadership (overhead costs), profit margin, excluding processing costs: disposition; delivery papers; export, customs duty etc.

Example 1.8: Opportunities for achievement of goal

The value creation process is made from raw material and semi-finished products using a certain method or procedure with the aid of tools and results in raw parts, semi-finished products or finished products. It requires a combination of resources which, seen from a business management side, are critical factors:

- space, personnel, machinery and furnishings.

An optimized value creation process can be achieved by reducing these critical resources and, specifically, by minimizing non-value-creating periods.

A fishbone diagram should show opportunities on the strategic and operational level to achieve the above objectives.

Answer: The fishbone diagram is a cause-and-effect-diagram presenting an analytical overview of problem areas or influencing factors, which are entered as 'fishbones' on an axis. The objective here is represented by the fish head (see Figure 1.14, the reduction of order processing times).

Example 1.9: Comparison of achievements by means of a network diagram

The network diagram (performance radar) focuses on objectives that are decisive competitive factors and is a strategic management tool to simultaneously show the achievements of many objectives. The result of 12 objectives in a company's warehousing logistics for 2009 should be shown in comparison to 2008 (100 per cent).

Answer: Figure 1.15.

Example 1.10: Disposal of card and cardboard

A high volume of empty cardboard boxes (space requirements) is the result of unpacking and repacking, as well as the order picking of goods in retail and

Figure 1.14 Opportunities to achieve an objective on different levels

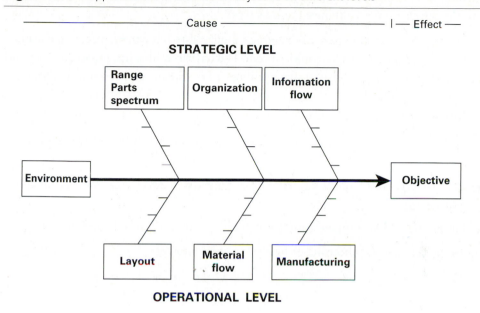

Figure 1.15 Success radar for achievement of logistics objectives

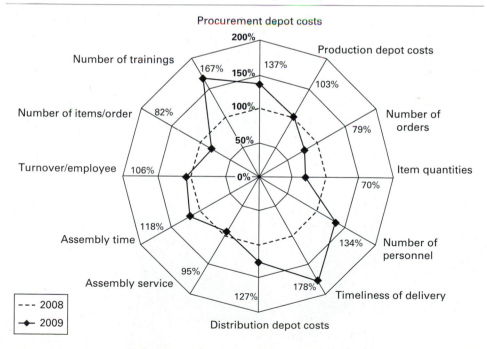

production businesses, and a huge amount of time is spent on their disposal. What are the opportunities to reduce these factors?

Answer: A horizontal or vertical baler (see Figure 1.16). It can be placed in a central location or at the site where empties occur. The baler requires little space, and should have a large opening so that empty cardboard boxes can be thrown in without the need for cutting up.

Key characteristics of a baler:

- Measurements: 2,000 × 1,300 × 3,000 mm; opening: 1,200 × 600 mm; pressure force: 550 kN.

- Bale weight: 400 to 500 kg; bale measurements: 1,200 × 800 mm; production: 1–2 bales/h.

- Cycle time: 45 s; compensation for bales: depending on supply and demand.

- Disadvantage: warehousing of bales (possible outside).

Figure 1.16   Vertical baler for cardboard (www.hsm.eu)

A comparison of expenses and income without taking into account energy, internal transport and storage costs:

- Expenses:
  * rental costs baler/month €230/month;
  * external transport: 1x/month pick up €60/month;
  * costs for binding materials: 6 bales/month €20/month.
- Savings:
  * personnel costs: 2h/workday at €15/h and 22 wd/month €660/month;
  * compensation: 3t/months = 6 bales €90/month approx.
- Economics:
  * Savings – expenses = €440/month.

Example 1.11: What does vertical integration mean?

Answer: Vertical integration is a key indicator to show how many of all required processes and activities as well as components needed for production are actually manufactured within the business itself, or bought in. The lower the vertical integration, the fewer processes exist, the more the business has focused on its key competencies. This could mean that parts of the value creation chain have been given to suppliers. Vertical integration of 0 is a retail business – no value is added. If a business has a vertical integration of 35 per cent, it means that 65 per cent of parts or production steps are bought in. In the automobile industry, independent areas are created within the business, eg forwarding warehouses for procurement parts.

Example 1.12: Lean production/lean management

What features and objectives are pursued by 'lean production' and 'lean management'?

Answer: Lean production is a business strategy and is applied in production logistics planning in order to simplify complex organizational types, and to achieve lean production. People are at the centre of this perspective. Humans and machines are matched up and this leads to higher performance and higher productivity. Some features of lean production are:

- customer focus;
- focus on key competencies;
- demand-based resource deployment and focus on quality;
- preventing waste of any kind, continuous improvement processes;

- fault detection/debugging;
- part production in small flexible teams (team work);
- reduction of hierarchical structuring, strengthening individual accountability and reduction of vertical integration.

Lean management is defined by methods and processes that optimize the planning of technical processes in the value creation chain. Tools for the introduction of lean management include: continuous improvement processes, Kaizen, standardization, Kanban, pull management, Just-in-time and value stream analysis.

Example 1.13: Logistics system costs

Which system costs are required in logistics and what benefits do they bring?

Answer: The investments made in a logistics system result in added value and are summarized under warehousing costs (see Chapter 9.6). Naturally this also includes transport costs (factory traffic, freight costs), management costs (disposition, manufacturing management, production programme planning) and the planning costs. As a result, the delivery service components listed in Chapter 1.5 are improved. Figure 12.30 shows components that may influence logistics expenses.

Example 1.14: Logistics structure

How can logistics be structured in detail?

Answer: Logistics can be structured on the following levels:

1 Macro logistics level: macro/micro logistics.
2 Micro logistics level: military, business and hospital logistics.
3 Business logistics level: industry, retail and services logistics.
4 Industry logistics level: procurement, production, distribution and disposal logistics.

Questions

1 What are the interfaces of a business with its environment?
2 What pillars is logistics based on?
3 What are logistics' objectives and tasks?
4 What functions are used to achieve logistics goals?
5 What is the structure of business logistics?

6 Describe the functions of procurement and distribution logistics.

7 What factors influence distribution logistics design?

8 How can disposal costs be reduced?

9 What does internal logistics encompass?

10 What are the tasks of business management logistics as part of business logistics?

11 What are key indicators?

12 What is the definition of 'objectives' and 'strategies'?

13 How can logistics be integrated into the organizational structure?

14 What is supply chain management?

15 What can be achieved with outsourcing?

16 When is a 'benchmark' used?

17 What is the structure of network and fishbone diagrams and what are they used for?

18 What are value creation chain, vertical integration and key competency?

19 What are the objectives of lean production and what are its features?

Material flow logistics

2.1 Material flow functions

The term 'material flow' can be understood in quite a wide sense. In line with VDI guideline 3300, material flow is the *spatial, chronological and logistical interconnection* of all processes in the production, processing and distribution of goods within defined areas. Thus, there is a difference, from the company's perspective, between an external goods flow and an internal material flow (MF). The technologies applied in cargo and bulk transport can be seen in Figure 2.1.

Hence, the material flow encompasses all internal object flow processes to do with the tasks concerning procurement, production and distribution. Its objects include raw, supplementary and operational materials, semi-finished and finished products, and tools. It is the material flow's task to connect production and assembly units, as well as guarantee supply and disposal. This happens with the help of the basic functions (for symbols see Figure 2.4):

- produce with processing and checking;
- move with transport and handling;
- rest with warehousing and involuntary stop.

The material flow is created as a result of a succession of processes aimed at achieving the end product, such as processing, handling, checking, transporting, assembling, storing and loading. The physical manifestation of the internal material flow can be seen in the applied transport and warehousing systems or, for the external goods flow, in the transit technology applied. It is the task of material flow logistics (see Figure 1.3) to holistically approach the material flow on its administrative, planning and operational levels. This task consists of the physical and informative provision of materials within the framework of the internal material flow (also see Figure 2.3).

Material flow control can be carried out according to the push or pull principles (see Example 2.15). In the case of the push principle, the material is taken by the transport worker or means of transport from the procurement or storage area to the production sites *based on demand*. In the case of the pull principle the workers in the production or assembly sites have to pick up the required materials from the relevant

Figure 2.1   Transport structure

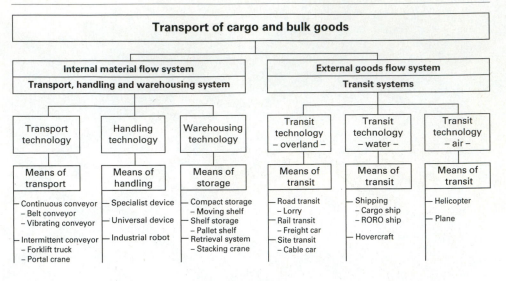

storage areas themselves *based on use*. For the pull principle, there is a distinction between the one-bin system and the two-bin system. In the *one-bin system* (for more on the Kanban system, see Example 2.4) each bin is allocated a material card that is taken from the empty bin and serves as a request or order card for a new, full bin.

In the *two-bin system* two bins of a material are placed at a workplace, often in line with the principle of continuous storage. When the first bin is empty, a new bin is brought to the consumption site as a result of transporting back the empty bin with its material card. The consumption site can continue to work with the second bin without any interruption.

2.2 Division, allocation

The traffic connections of a site using city streets, country roads and highways, railroads and airports to a company's procurement and market sites are a deciding factor when deciding on the means of transport to ship procured goods and to distribute the company's products to the consumer.

Traffic connections are also an important location factor and help when finding a location (see Chapter 12.10.3). The external flow of goods can be divided into the following:

- local;
- regional;
- nationwide.

viastore

WE PROVIDE THE

„WOW!"

We provide our customers with total peace of mind – and above all we ensure their customers feel it, too. Thanks to our integrative intralogistics systems and warehouse management software, they are supplied with exactly what they ordered, at the right time, in the right quantity and in the right place. Guaranteed.

If you would like to join us in providing plenty of "Wows", we look forward to receiving your application at career.de@viastore.com.

The internal material flow, the transport of materials within the company site and property boundaries, can be divided into:

- *Internal area – company*

  This is responsible for the functionally correct design of the plan to use the land (see Example 12.2) for the effective allocation of buildings, which includes storage areas according to material flow-based points of view. The internal area is also responsible for determining the thoroughfares on the site, the separation of material and personnel flow, and for the transport between halls and buildings.

- *Internal area – building*

  This is concerned with the allocation of divisions, such as in halls and buildings, with a facility layout of the different divisions based on the material flow, and with the required handling, transport, storage and commissioning systems (see Figures 2.16 and 2.18).

- *Workplace area*

  This area is tasked with designing a workplace based on a material flow, ergonomic and physiological perspectives, choosing handling systems, optimizing work processes and humanizing the workplace (see Figures 9.16, 9.17, 11.11 and 12.35).

The material flow system handles the supply and disposal of production by means of fulfilling the functions of transport, handling, warehousing and assembling for:

- workpiece flow: workpieces, assembly parts and finished products;
- tool flow: tools, devices and test equipment;
- excipients, shavings and waste.

Hence the material flow system has to be integrated in to the production system (see Figure 2.2).

It represents a component of computer-aided manufacturing (CAM). CAM itself is integrated as a component in computer-integrated manufacturing (CIM).

CIM can be considered a potential way to implement production logistics, and thus it is understandable that material flow and material flow logistics have to fulfil interface tasks.

A process diagram of the administrative, information-related and physical process in a production system can be created by chronologically comparing information, document, data and material flow. An example of this is shown in Figure 2.3. A horizontal model conveys the information that is required or provided by IT, who receive, print or provide documentation simultaneously, and which functions or activities are carried out in the material flow.

Figure 2.2 Integrated perspective on production system

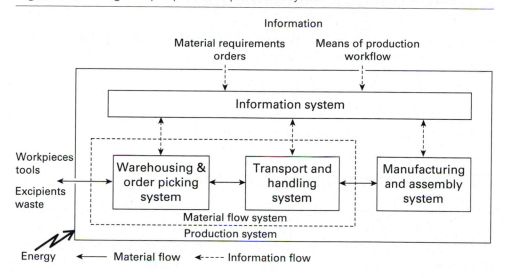

Figure 2.3 Process diagram of material, information, data and document flow. Additional columns could be used to enter times of activities, responsibilities, etc

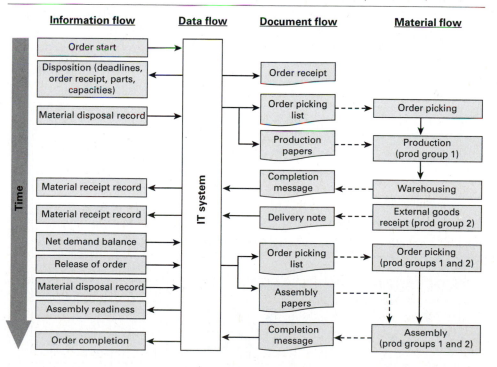

2.3 Material flow components

The *internal* material flow encompasses all material movements within a self-contained area. It can be described by its:

- technical and spatial component;
- quantitative component;
- chronological and organizational component.

2.3.1 Technical and spatial component

The technical and spatial design of the material flow can be identified by the existing means of warehousing, order picking, handling and transport. In order to analyse and assess a material flow, it must be represented graphically with simple abstract and general, often basic, structures, often on a geometric basis (see Figure 2.4).

The actual lines and design of the material flow are based on a number of factors and depend on many different elements. These factors and elements can be existing, business-specific influence factors that may or may not be affected (see Figure 2.5). In practice, these factors and elements don't have impact individually but only in combination. Their level of influence and impact on material flow and its costs can vary, depending on the business and the situation.

Figure 2.4   Basic structures and symbols for material flow

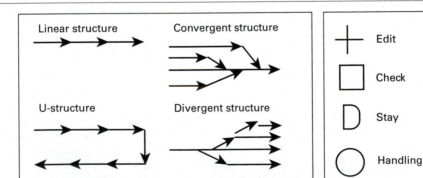

Figure 2.5 Influencing factors on the material flow and the level to which they can be influenced. Column 1: short term; column 2: medium term; column 3: long term

Influencing factor	Impact on MF through	1	2	3
Premises	Location: retail, industrial park Shape of premises: rectangular			X
Building	Building type: storeyed, hall Building features: support grid; load-bearing capacity ceiling		X	X
Manufacture	Principles of manufacture: workshop (job-shop principle); island (group principle); flow (construction site principle) Product: range, number of items Manufacturing method: individual/lot-size production; external workbench	X	X	X
Transport	Cargo: general cargo, loading unit Means of transport: continuous/non-continuous conveyor Transport path: line management; cargo stream: m, mSt	X	X	
Warehouse	Stored goods: storage unit Type of storage: floor, shelf storage Means of storage: pallets, continuous shelf	X	X	
Management	Central, decentralized Level of automation Data transfer; IT	X	X	
Operational structure	Administrative requirements Dispositive requirements Strategies		X	
Allocation	Building allocation Department allocation Allocation of work tools		X	

The technical and spatial material flow components are determined, improved and optimized by engineering plans.

2.3.2 Quantitative component

The quantitative representation of the material flow is achieved through specifying the cargo stream as volume stream V, mass stream m and cargo item stream $m_{St.}$. The cargo is either general or bulk (Chapter 3.1) and there is a difference between means of transport that operate continuously and those that don't.

1 Cargo stream continuous conveyors $\dot{V}$

1.1 Bulk transport

eg Sand transport with conveyor belts (see Chapter 5.2.2)

- Volume stream $\dot{V}$ $\dot{V} = 3,600\, A\, v$ (m³/h)   (2.1)
- Mass stream $\dot{m}$ $\dot{m} = \dot{V}\, \Phi_S$ (t/h)   (2.2)

A	m²	Goods cross Chapter
v	m/s	Speed of transport
Φ_S	t/m³	Bulk density of movement

eg Transport of flour with bucket elevator (see Chapter 5.4.2)

- Volume stream $\dot{V}$ $\dot{V} = 3{,}600\ V f v / a$ (m³/h)   (2.3)

V	m³	Single container volume (bucket)
f		Filling level of single bucket
a	m	(Median) distance of containers (buckets)

1.2 General cargo transport

eg Package transport using a conveyor belt

- Mass stream $\dot{m}$ $\dot{m} = 3{,}600\ m\ v/a$ (t/h)   (2.4)
- Cargo stream $\dot{m}_{St}$ $\dot{m}_{St} = 3{,}000\ v/a$ (St/h)   (2.5)

a	m	(Median) distance of cargo (packages)
v	m/s	Speed of transport
m	t	(Average) mass of individual cargo (package)

2 Cargo stream non-continuous conveyor

2.1 General cargo transport

eg Pallet transport with forklift truck in warehouse (in/out of warehouse)

- Mass stream of a vehicle $\dot{m}$ $\dot{m} = 60\ \dot{m}_e/t_s$ (t/h)   (2.6)
- Cargo stream of a vehicle $\dot{m}_{St}$ $\dot{m}_{St} = 60\ /\ t_s$ (St/h)   (2.7)

t_s	min	Median session for individual activity (see Chapter 9.7)
$\dot{m}_e$	t	(Average) mass of a transport unit

2.2 Calculation of fleet number (see Chapter 9.7)

Number of vehicles z for given bulk/cargo transport task:

$$\dot{m}_{Sch} = \dot{m}\ n \quad m_{StSch} = m_{St}\ n \tag{2.8}$$

$$z = \sum \dot{m} / \dot{m}_{Sch} = \sum \dot{m}_{St}/\dot{m}_{StSch} \tag{2.9}$$

n	h/shift	Number of hours in one shift
$\dot{m}_e$	t	(Average) mass of a transport unit
ts	min	(Median) session (loading, unloading, journey time)
$\sum \dot{m}$	t/shift	Total mass stream in one shift
$\sum \dot{m}_{St}$	St/shift	Total cargo stream in one shift
$\dot{m}$	t/h	Mass stream of one vehicle per hour
$\dot{m}_{Sch}$	t/shift	Mass stream of one vehicle per shift

$\dot{m}_{St}$ St/h   Cargo stream of one vehicle per hour

$\dot{m}_{StSch}$ St/shift   Cargo stream of one vehicle per shift

z   Number of vehicles, eg forklifts

Example: 420 pallets must be moved in and out of a warehouse in one session (shift duration: 7 hours; session: 3 minutes). How many forklift trucks are needed?

$$\text{Calculation}: \dot{m}_{St} = 60 : 3 = 20 \text{ Pal/h equals } \dot{m}_{StSch} = 20 \times 7 = 140 \text{ Pal/shift};$$

$$z = 420 : 140 = 2 \text{ forklift trucks}$$

2.3.3 Time and organizational component

The time and organizational component of the material flow is the value of the order processing time, made up in manufacturing of:

- order time (processing time including set-up and distribution time);
- control time; wait and rest time; transport time.

The wait and rest time can generally comprise up to 85 per cent of the order processing time and is divided into:

- workflow-related rest time;
- storage time;
- rest time due to disturbances;
- people-related rest time.

Approximately 75 per cent of wait and rest time are allocated to workflow-related rest time.

The aim is to reduce these timings, by organizational measures such as synchronous assembly and manufacture or a combination of production synchronous procurement and synchronous assembly and manufacture. A reduction in the order processing time can result in:

- reduced manufacturing costs;
- increased productivity;
- decrease in committed current asset;
- decrease in required human resources for transport and warehousing tasks;
- increased capital turnover;
- improved capital yield;
- increased use of machinery;

- faster delivery to market;
- shortened delivery times.

An exact detailed perspective on the order processing time encompasses both administrative timings – ie the time used in work preparation and in the office, and material flow times. The order processing time begins with the receipt of the order and ends with the arrival of the goods. A reduction in order processing time can be achieved by changing non-value-creating periods into value-creating periods. A reduction at interfaces, in particular, through process-oriented manufacture can provide significant improvements; often, the interface time between two departments can take one workday (see Examples 2.14; 2.19 and Chapter 2.5.3.2).

2.4 Material flow costs

The material flow's significance can be seen in the internal costs of material flow, which can, depending on sector and product, represent a share of 50 per cent or more of production costs. The operation cost calculation does not record material flow costs sufficiently. The costs for material flow can be divided into four main cost types:

- material flow-related personnel costs;
- input costs for transport and set up of depots;
- material flow-related space and transport expenses;
- material flow-related working capital costs.

Internal material flow costs result from the influencing factors (see Figure 2.5) on the material flow. If costs are examined according to these cost types, this will provide a pretty accurate idea of the material flow costs in the business. Those transport costs accounted for in operational cost calculations often only record part of the actual material flow costs. Lost time due to bad transport conditions, expenses for interim storage and transport labour costs of specialist personnel are not captured. The material flow's significance and assessment can only be recognized sufficiently if all costs caused by the material flow are determined.

2.5 Material flow analysis

The terms of material flow analysis, material flow process analysis or actual recording of material flow, also called vulnerability analysis, all describe the recording of the transport procedure and processes, as well as all planned and unplanned storage periods of material within the internal business.

The material flow processes are captured by on site observation and record the personnel, materials, space, transport and storage that form part of the material flow.

2.5.1 Causes

Causal instances for internal material flow analysis are as follows:

- mechanization and automation of the transport and/or storage areas;
- low utilization levels of means of transport;
- high transport and storage costs;
- obsolete transport and warehousing technology;
- extension of production quantities and product range;
- bottlenecks, accidents, disturbances, high order processing times;
- high personnel costs, complex process organization.

These causes (see Example 12.1) make an analysis and assessment of the existing conditions obligatory and result in optimization and management of the material flow.

2.5.2 Goal, task, process

The goal of any material flow analysis is to identify weak points, to find their causes, and to determine and divide up the costs of the material flow in order to then manage to achieve an optimal material flow with minimized material flow costs.

Material flow analysis can deliver the required base data to determine:

- the allocation of the individual production departments or the correct site for the depot within the business;
- which means of transport to choose for a pending transport task;
- how to minimize order processing times;
- how to prevent accidents and downtime in the transport;
- how to improve the use of space or increase transport means utilization.

It is the task of material flow analysis to gain information and data in order to assess and manage material flow, to determine (see Chapter 12.2):

- data on the product range: item structure;
- details for transport and storage cargo:
  - characteristics, according to Figure 3.2; transport units, storage units;
  - cargo streams, in line with Chapter 2.3.2; transport frequency (see Figure 2.7);
  - transport structure, management, stock administration;

- data on transport and storage aids: according to Chapter 3.1.4; handling (see Example 3.2);
- information data:
  - management of material flow (see Chapter 2.1);
  - warehousing administration system (see Chapter 13.3);
  - data transfer (see Chapter 13.3);
  - order processing times (see Figure 2.23);
- data on means of transport and storage types:
  - capacities, services, throughput, capacity use, availability (see Example 12.5);
  - space and room sizes, heights;
  - speed, routes; order picking system, order picking times and services;
  - warehousing figures, capacity, handling, organization and management;
- business data:
  - operational costs (personnel costs, maintenance);
  - material flow costs, warehousing costs (for more on working capital costs, see Chapter 9.6);
- data on buildings, halls, premises.

The material flow analysis is carried out in line with the procedures shown in Figure 12.5.

2.5.3 Capturing the material flow

The material flow can be captured directly (see Figure 12.8) on site, or indirectly at a desk (static analysis) using operational documents such as manufacturing schedules, stock card files, cost listings and IT files. Both methods are used in practice, in order to reduce the time needed for analysis.

The methods for capturing data have to be chosen based on the type, level of detail required and objective. The easiest and most effective aids are surveys, questionnaires, tables and forms. When drafting and developing such lists, the material flow manager must always consider the following questions:

1 *Why* does transport or storage occur? (Transport or storage reason)
2 *What* and *how much* is being moved or stored? (Cargo, finished goods, raw materials, waste, volume or mass stream, quantity, volume, weight)
3 *From where* and *to where* does the transport go? (From depot to manufacturing, from goods received to depot, from one workplace to the next)

4 By *what means* and *how* does the transport occur? (With lift equipment, continuous conveyors, industrial trucks, in bundles, stacked, on pallets, by means of warehouse or transport workers, qualified or unskilled workers)

5 *When* and *for how long* does the transport or storage occur? (Time of day, length of time)

2.5.3.1 Multi-moments

The multi-moment analysis serves to determine time-related or proportional aspects of operational processes, such as:

- use of machinery;
- means of transport;
- workers;
- use of space;
- to measure storage periods for materials, transport routes or resources deployment.

It is divided into the *multi-moment time measurement* method and the *multi-moment frequency* method.

This is a static method, capturing the time proportion through sample observations. If the required level of accuracy for an investigation isn't too high and the determined time proportions of individual procedures are not too small (from 2 per cent), the multi-moment method can be simple, quick and economical.

Once the objective, observation objects, observable activities and a suitability check of the method for the task in question have been determined, these are the steps of the process (REFA multi-moment standard programme):

- Determine the path of observation.
- Determine the time a tour takes through sample records.
- Establish the required number of observations N by using the multi-moment formula:

$$N = [3.84\ p\ (100 - p)]/\ f^2 \quad \text{Number of Observations} \qquad (2.10)$$

3.84   Factor for statistical certainty of 95%

p in %   Proportion as part of the total of determined quantities

        $p = [n\ (\text{observations per quantity})/N\ (\text{total observations})]100$

f in %   Degree of divergence (absolute divergence) of n related to N

In practice, for sufficient accuracy, it can be assumed that $N = 1,600$ to $2,500$ and f between ±1.0 per cent to ±2.5 per cent. This equation (2.10) only strictly applies to normally distributed values. The distribution frequency must resemble a bell curve.

- calculation of total time effort;
- determining observation times with the help of random numbers (hour and minute random numbers, from VDI 2492);
- execution of observation, recording in table (for a list, see Example 2.3);
- determining percentage part p of the values;
- conclusions, measures, decisions (see Example 2.2).

To analyse the activities in the shipping area of a depot, and to help with reorganization, the percentages of depot workers' individual activities were determined using the multi-moment method and are displayed in Table 2.1.

Routes, transport work, movements into and out of storage come to 63 per cent, which means that reorganization needs to implement transport measures. It is worth considering whether the use of IT or better storage lists could reduce the 17 per cent of documentation time. The multi-moment method thus delivers the base data for management and provides a focus for streamlining measures.

2.5.3.2 Gantt charts

A Gantt chart is an easy, quick and effective method of depicting processes. Figure 2.6 shows the process of passivating welding seams. Passivation is a surface technique to achieve a protective layer on a metal material in order to reduce corrosion. The chart illustrates a compensation time of 4 hours (= 12 per cent) and a radiation time of 8 hours (= 24 per cent). The preparation and post work without shunting time is the biggest time proportion at 22 hours. This is the streamlining approach to reduce this time (see Example 2.21).

2.5.3.3 From–to–matrix

A from–to–matrix, or material flow matrix, serves to capture transport frequency (number of transport units per time unit between source and sink or vice versa), transport

Table 2.1   Time percentages in shipping

Activities	Proportion of time (p in %)
Inspection work	3
Routes and transport work	43
Documentation	17
Into and out of storage	20
Distribution work and dead time	15
Clean-up work	2
Total shipping work	100

Figure 2.6 A Gantt chart

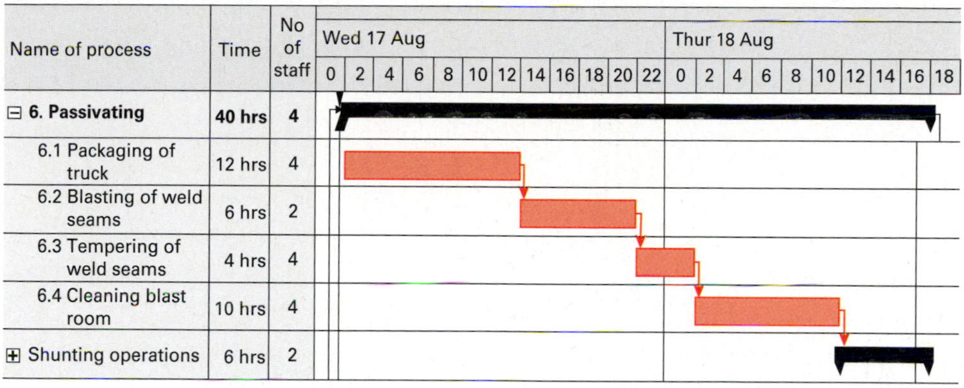

Name of process	Time	No of staff	Wed 17 Aug												Thur 18 Aug								
			0	2	4	6	8	10	12	14	16	18	20	22	0	2	4	6	8	10	12	14	16	18
⊟ 6. Passivating	40 hrs	4																						
6.1 Packaging of truck	12 hrs	4																						
6.2 Blasting of weld seams	6 hrs	2																						
6.3 Tempering of weld seams	4 hrs	4																						
6.4 Cleaning blast room	10 hrs	4																						
⊞ Shunting operations	6 hrs	2																						

Figure 2.7 A 'from–to' transport matrix (x_n = number of transport units per time unit)

Nr	TO / FROM	GI	M	PD	A	DD	GO	Total
	1	2	3	4	5	6	7	8
1	Goods in (GI)		x_1LE	x_2LE	x_3LE			
2	Manufacturing (M)			x_2LE	x_5LE	x_4LE		
3	Production depot (PD)		x_6LE					
4	Assembly (A)		x_5LE	x_7LE		x_8LE		
5	Distribution depot (DD)						x_9LE	
6	Goods out (GO)							
7	Totals							

weight, transport volume, transport routes, transport costs or means of transport. A square matrix occurs when all sources are sinks at the same time (Figure 2.7).

2.5.3.4 Surveys

A survey developed by the person dealing with a material flow analyses is a written aid, specifically tailored to capture data about the observation object. Thus, a survey of industrial trucks may collect data such as: cost code, name, type, manufacturer, year built, style of build, quantity, motor type, load capacity, lift height, speed and lift speed, weight, wing loading, measurements, turning radius, aisle width, capacity, annual running and repair costs, application area. Depending on the task, only certain values are required so that a specific survey is created (Figure 2.8).

Figure 2.8 Survey form for the registration of industrial trucks

Nr	Vehicle type Inv. Nr	Manufacturer	Year built	Load capacity [t]	Stack height [m]	Load area [m²]	Traction [t]	Degree of use [%]	Capacity used [%]	Operating time [h]	Location	Notes
1	2	3	4	5	6	7	8	9	10	11	12	13
1												
2												

Company:

PROJECT: Transport optimization

Sheet no.::
Of   sheets

Department:
Responsible staff:

Analysis: Registering industrial trucks

Date:

2.5.4 Analyse and depict material flow recordings

The aim of the analysis is to organize and summarize the structure along certain themes, or classify the collected data and information. If possible, IT programs should be used, and for this reason the survey should be tailored to IT requirements. One method of analysis is the *ABC analysis* (Figure 2.9).

The collected data are depicted in accordance with specific criteria such as turnover, profit, transport costs, space and in relation to a product or product groups (classification of products or product groups). They are arranged in either decreasing or increasing order and shown in percentages.

Based on the percentages of turnover in relation to the relevant group of products, Figure 2.9 shows that group A encompasses 20 per cent of products, which represent 80 per cent of turnover, group B at 30 per cent represents 15 per cent of turnover and group C, while including 50 per cent of all products, represents only 5 per cent of turnover. Items in group A have, in general, a high handling frequency, groups B and C a lower frequency. The ABC analysis also allows conclusions to be drawn about the warehousing systems used for the products and the prevalent level of mechanization.

The proportion of products that are classified as large, medium and small can be determined using ABC analysis.

Once analysed, the material flow recordings often result in a confusing amount of data. Thus, it makes sense to visually represent this data in graphics (see

Figure 2.9   An ABC analysis chart

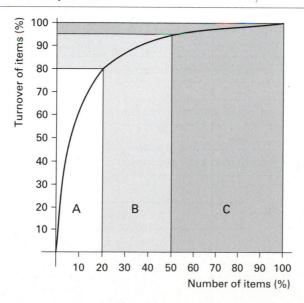

Chapter 12.9.5). The goal of representing the material flow recordings is to facilitate a visual positive and negative review of the prevalent state of things.

The choice of graphic representation depends on the goal of the analysis, on the material flow manager and the recipient of the finished document. The use of colours plays an important part, in order to highlight different material flow streams or other special features. Options (see Figure 12.12) include tables, charts, drawings, process maps, adhesive plans, flat and 3D models. Graphic depiction has the advantage of being clear and the essential parts will be easily identifed. Qualitative (see Figure 2.10) and/or quantitative material flow (see Figure 2.14) are the most common representations.

Figure 2.10 A qualitative material flow process map for a mail order company

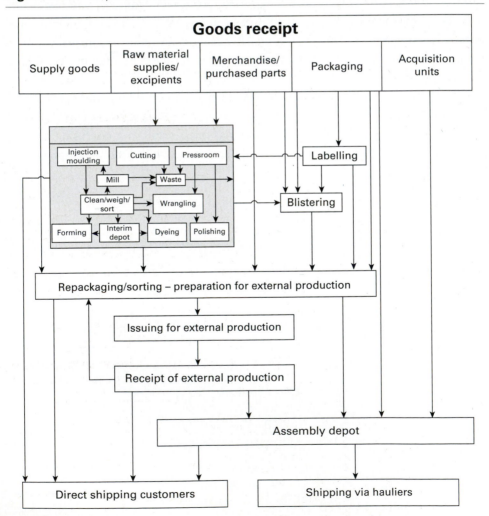

2.5.5 Value stream design

Value stream design is a method to depict the MF and information flow across the entire value creation chain, which serves to show up non-value-creating processes. This method is used in the manufacture of a product family in order to reduce stock and unnecessary material movements, to decrease order processing times, manufacturing faults and processes, as well as waiting times, transport and repairs. Thus, it is about eliminating waste (Kaizen). In value stream design, data for the material and information flows are represented by symbols (see Figure 2.11). Analysis starts at the customers' requirements and moves 'upstream' from goods out to the supplier – number of transport units/time units, type and weight of load units, means of transport and transport routes in m.

After the entire process, the sub-processes are represented in detail. The value stream design of the current situation turns (see Figure 2.12) – after the elimination of non-value-creating times and stocks – the value stream design of the desired state (see Figure 2.13). In depicting the value stream design, the information flow is shown in addition to the material flow. The aim of this method is to optimally connect related processes.

2.5.6 Identifying weaknesses and assessment

The identification of weaknesses and the assessment of the situational analysis of the material flow can be facilitated through graphic representation. In this way, bottlenecks, opposed traffic, junctions and unwanted storage can be spotted easily.

Figure 2.11   Examples of material and information flow symbols

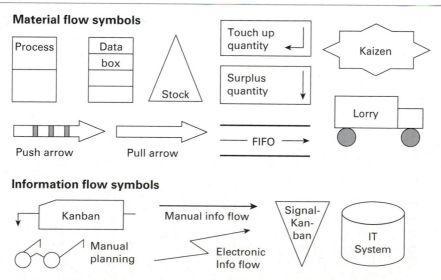

Figure 2.12 Example 1: Representation of the current situation of business processes by using value stream design (www.awf.de)

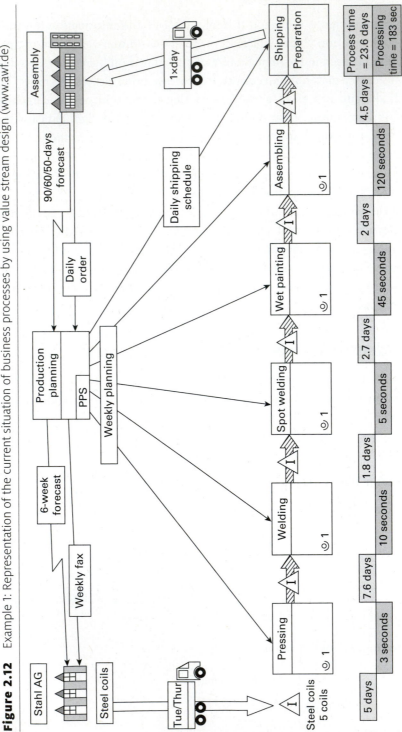

Figure 2.13 Example 2: Graphic of current situation in a business via value stream design to reduce order processing times: areas and individual functions (www.awf.de)

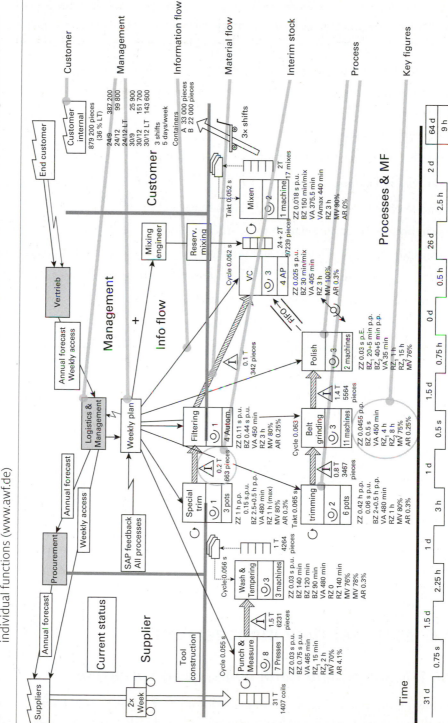

Indicators can be used to discuss the prevalent conditions, they serve to compare, assess and document the success of operational processes and data before and after the material flow management and during a material flow analysis (see Chapter 1.5.1 and Figure 12.27). Amongst a wealth of possible material flow indicators are:

- manual labour to machine-aided work;
- material flow costs of order processing time (equals the degree of performance power);
- warehousing costs in relation to space;
- number of entries to depot in relation to time unit.

Additional indicators:

- degree of use of space, room and height (see Chapter 9.7);
- warehousing space in relation to production space;
- transport space in relation to storage space;
- personnel costs in MF area in relation to overall staff costs;
- employee resources in material flow in relation to total staff;
- value of warehouse stocks in relation to capital.

The results of the material flow analysis have to be assessed in line with technical and economic criteria. Criteria may include:

- building allocation to departments; structural building design;
- order processing time of material and receipts; use of machinery and means of transport;
- costs in transport area; capital committed in warehouse and MF;
- expansion potential; flexibility of premises;
- clarity of transport conditions; transport by qualified personnel;
- measuring and conditions of traffic areas; degree of mechanization and automation.

Data cleared of weaknesses represent the current situation of the material flow (see Figure 12.5). During a material flow analysis and prior to management of the material flow, the solutions can be summarized in a catalogue of preliminary measures.

2.6 Material flow management

2.6.1 Management data, goals, design principles

Following the material flow analysis, a decision must be taken about whether material flow management should be introduced. Often, this decision takes time, to allow for a longer period of time passes.

Hence, it is necessary to once again check the data recorded in the material flow analysis when commencing material flow management. After the checks, data reflecting the actual situation must be updated for the desired state. This data for the desired state is, essentially, actual data aligned with the future by using estimated or forecast values. They are in line with the desired management data that is to be achieved (see Chapter 12.5.2).

The objective of every material flow management is to achieve a material flow with minimized costs. It is about working on a solution that is technically functional, economical and easy to organize. The following design principles can help the material flow manager in finding an appropriate solution:

- avoid manual transport; aim for flexible solutions;
- plan for expansion, consider future factors;
- sensible mechanization or automation of transport and use to full capacity;
- increase use of space capacity;
- avoid junctions and opposing traffic in material flow;
- create a functional transport unit based on the principle: manufacturing unit = transport unit = storage unit;
- aim for short paths, high transport speed, means of transport at full capacity;
- if possible, make use of gravity;
- pay attention to pre- and post-MF activities (follow on values to external transport);
- aim for short order processing times;
- avoid storage if possible, save storage space;
- connect transport with manufacturing (cooling, heating, mixing, sorting).

One of the most important things in a solution for material flow management is the type of management – whether it is working on a new design on a greenfield site (moving the operations) or on a restructuring of the material flow with a multitude of limitations. For multi-storey construction, some of the conditions are room height, floor load capacity, column spacing, measurements and elevator load capacity.

The material flow is of greatest importance in the management of factories, transport, warehousing or streamlining. It must not be managed in isolation but has to be considered holistically with:

- *Information flow*: This encompasses all communication in oral and written form between operational staff via phone, fax, internal mail, couriers or e-mail.
- *Person flow*: This includes the paths of staff and visitors in a business in time and space-related dependency to and from the factory entrance (parking lot) and on the factory premises.

- *Energy flow:* This encompasses the provision of individual operational parts with the required type and amount of energy, such as gas, water, electricity, stream, air pressure etc.

2.6.2 Approach

The material flow management process might follow these steps (see Chapter 12.5):

- Work on management data with conditions and restrictions.
- Develop an ideal plan for function processes.
- Plan for alternative solutions with transport and warehousing systems.
- Compile rough costings.
- Assess alternatives and determine the optimum option.
- Describe the layout of the chosen option.

Depending on the scope, there is a difference between rough planning and fine-tuned planning. A detailed representation of the layout can simultaneously serve as a tender document for providers. The tender and execution process up to the commissioning and takeover of the material flow system results from Chapter 12.6. The planning phase for the material flow can be based on conventional and/or computer-aided methods.

2.6.2.1 Conventional material flow management

This happens in line with the process described in the previous chapter as a static management approach (VDI 2498, Figure 12.3; Approach to find alternative systems).

2.6.2.2 Computer-aided material flow management

For complex material flow relations with many conditions, the layout of a manufacturing workshop can be created with the help of a PC coupled with relevant software. The following information is required:

1 A spatial structure of all operational resources.
2 Space values.
3 Shapes of space are known.
4 The transport matrix (Figure 2.7) exists (see Chapter 12.10.5, material flow simulation see Chapter 12.9.3.2).

Under these circumstances, material flow management has great advantages because it is possible to carry out the necessary calculations when determining dimensions, and to draw up representations of alternative layouts, within a short time. The computer prevents planning mistakes, reduces expensive planning time and increases planning quality. However, the initial creation can take time in order to build the tools for objects, as 3-D representations are often used in order to simulate the journey of a loaded forklift truck (see Example 2.13, Chapter 12.9.3.2, Example 12.25).

2.6.2.3 Material flow simulation

MF simulation can be deployed in extensive MF planning with the aim of determining the performance capacity of the MF management and its alternative with the aid of a computer, to identify weak points and to check data specification.

2.7 VDI guidelines

2339	Operating unit for material flow systems	05.99
2492	Rated-activity sampling in material flow	06.68
2498	Procedures in material flow planning Bl. 1 and 2	08.11
2523	Project management for logistical systems in MF and storage technology	07.93
2689	Manual of material flow investigations	1.74/05.10
2693/1	Investment estimation for planning of material flow with dynamic calculation procedures	1.96
3628	Automated material flow systems; interfaces between various function levels	10.96
3634	Quantitative measurement in material flow	06.91
3961	Operating unit for material flow in plants	09.89

2.8 Examples and questions

Example 2.1

How many documents (letters, faxes, delivery notes, order notes, e-mails, etc) are distributed between business departments in one day?

Answer: Data recording is carried out via the from–to matrix (Table 2.2). Departments are entered as criteria in a vertical and horizontal direction and the related number of shipments are entered. The admin office sends 1 document to the workshop, 10 to the archive and 15 to the sales office. The admin office receives 3 documents from the lab, 2 from the workshop, 3 from the archive and 25 from the sales office.

Table 2.2   A from–to-matrix for documents sent per day (administration)

To From	Lab	Workshop	Archive	Sales office	Admin office	Total
Lab		0	4	0	3	7
Workshop	0		0	7	2	9
Archive	0	0		10	3	13
Sales office	2	7	5		25	39
Admin office	0	1	10	15		26
Total	2	8	19	32	33	94

Example 2.2: Execution of a multi-moment analysis

Here, the level of utilization of 20 presses is to be checked in a business with a small production area. The causes of interruptions in use, in particular, need to be examined. The *median* level of utilization of *all* presses is to be determined.

Answer: Once established as a suitable method, the task is resolved via the multi-moment method. The best way to proceed is to determine an accurate median value and then work backwards to the number of required records. The resultant proportion must be estimated and corrected once the records have been captured. For small percentages of 1 per cent to 5 per cent, which also require a higher accuracy, a large number of observations will be necessary – which in turn results in higher costs and longer recording periods. The limitation of this method lies in these small proportions.

Procedure:

1 Determining the number of required observations N (equation (2.10)) based on the estimated resulting proportion for the individual activity and based on sensibly estimated degrees of divergence f in line with Table 2.3 (result: maximum N).

2 Establishing total time required for the multi-moment analysis (observations). Once the route has been determined, trial rounds can come up with a median length of time required of $t_R = 15$ minutes. The number of required rounds R for $N = 2,380$ observations and $n = 20$ presses.

Total observation time

$R = N/n = 2,380 / 20 = 120$ rounds

$R \times t_R = 120 \times 15$ minutes $= 30$ hours

Table 2.3   Type and quantity of observed activities

Activity	Estimated proportion of time $\bar{p}$	Required divergence $\bar{f}$	Number of observations N	
Production	$\bar{p_1}$ = 55%	± 2.0%	2,380	Largest N value
Disruption:				
Set up	$\bar{p_2}$ = 10%	± 1.5%	2,540	
Repair	$\bar{p_3}$ = 5%	± 1.5%	810	
Missing material	$\bar{p_4}$ = 5%	± 1.0%	1,830	
Missing personnel	$\bar{p_5}$ = 15%	± 1.5%	2,180	
Undefined	$\bar{p_6}$ = 10%	± 1.5%	1,540	

Given 10 rounds a day, an observer would have to complete 12 days of observations. The observation times are taken from the general random tables (random hours table, random minute table, VDI 2492).

3 Recording and analysis: A multi-moment survey (see Example 2.3) collates the activities of each press for all rounds in a tally per day and can also be used for analysis. The individual result proportions p can be derived as a percentage from the number of observations per day divided by the total number of observations. These percentages correspond to the time proportions of the relevant activities. The actual divergence f (absolute divergence) will now be calculated based on the actual number of observations N and the determined resulting proportion p in line with f in formula 2.10.

$$p = n'/N \times 100$$

In Table 2.4, the estimated and calculated proportions are compared and this results in, for the example mentioned, an effective production time of all 20 processes. This is based on a statistical accuracy of 95 per cent of $p_1 \pm f_1 = 57.4 \pm 1.98$, so a range of 55.4 per cent to 59.4 per cent.

Example 2.3: Observation sheet

Design an observation sheet for a multi-moment analysis based on Example 2.2 for five presses. The analysis should be done as a tally. The resulting proportions p can be calculated via the survey sheet.

Answer: Table 2.5.

Table 2.4 Results of multi-moment records for N = 2,380 observations (cutting or neckline)

Activity	Time proportion p		Divergence f	
	Estimated	Determined	Desired	Achieved
Production	55%	57.4%	±2.0%	±1.98%
Set up	10%	12.4%	±1.5%	±1.32%
Repair	5%	6.7%	±1.5%	±1.00%
Material missing	5%	4.2%	±1.0%	±0.8%
Personnel missing	15%	17.1%	±1.5%	±1.51%
Undefined	10%	2.2%	±1.5%	±0.6%
Total	100%	100%	–	–

Table 2.5 Observation sheet for multi-moment analysis

Survey sheet No.: 1						Observer: Meyer	
Tasks for analysis: Press workloads							
Number of rounds: 12						Day of observations: 4.3.04	
		Observation objects					$p = \frac{n'}{N}$
No.	Processes	Press 1	Press 2	Press 3	Press 4	Press 5	Total $1 - 5 \triangleq n'$	%
1	Production	///// /	/////	///// //	///// ////	///// /	33	55
2	Set up	/	///	//			6	10
3	Repair			/		///	4	7
4	Material missing				///		3	5
5	Personnel missing	/////	//	//			9	15
6	Undefined		//			///	5	8
	Total	12	12	12	12	12	60 = N	100

Example 2.4: Kanban management

Which elements/components belong to Kanban management?

Answer: Kanban management is based on usage, and facilitates a reduction of stock provisions. Its aims are to manage the value creation chain at optimal cost, to reduce the planning efforts and capital commitment without additional transport or guarantee of delivery readiness.

Elements are (see Figures 2.14 and 2.15):

Figure 2.14 A sample Kanban card

	Item no. 742–746–02	Production kanban P
Customer	Item name: Flange sleeve, prepared	Quantity/loading unit 1000 (approx. 84 pieces/small loading container)
Card no. 1/3		Loading unit: 12 small load containers 6428 on Euro pallet
Reportable quantity 2	Loop no. 3	
Producing site: Preparation		Buffer storage 102/3/1

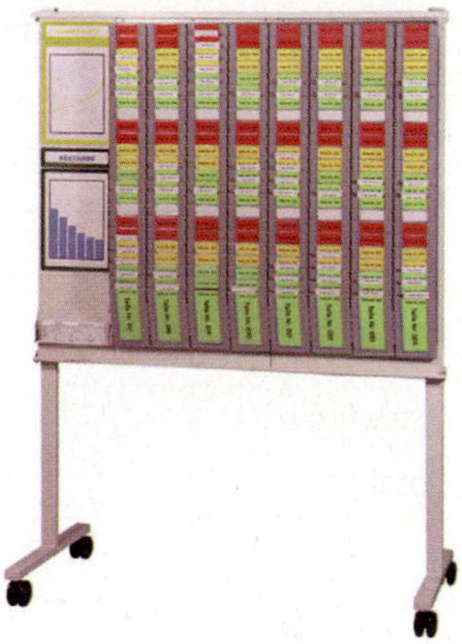

Figure 2.15 A Kanban board (www.orgatex.com)

- The Kanban card: The transport Kanban, with information such as article number, identity code, source – sink, Kanban card number, operating instructions, quality information and filling capacity of the bin.

- Kanban board: Information and statistics.

- Kanban insertion board.

Example 2.5: Material flow formats

Possible material flow structures for an industrial business must be sketched in relation to the location of the premises and road and rail links. The expansion direction should be included.

a) Premises are located on a road.

b) Premises are located at the intersection of two roads.

c) Premises are located between two roads.

The material flow procedure has to be structured for manufacture and assembly.

Answer: Figure 2.16.

Example 2.6: Quantitative material flow process plan

The transport frequency between the departments of an industrial enterprise is derived from the MF analysis as a result of a from–to matrix (see Table 2.6). The matching MF process plan has to be drawn up.

Answer: The result of the analysis can be found in Figure 2.11.

Figure 2.16   The material flow procedure is dependent on premises allocation and transport links
Legend: Internal material flow (MF): departmental allocation GI: Goods in
GO: Goods out   D: Depot   P: Production   E: Extension

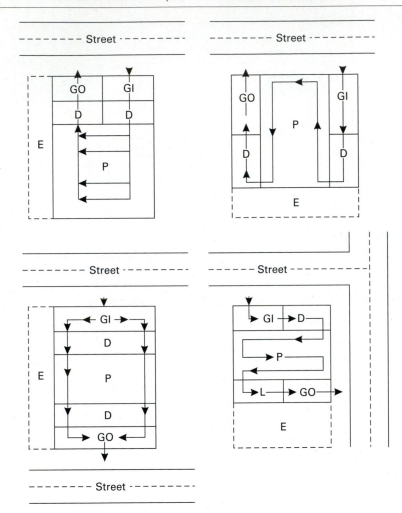

Example 2.7: From–to–matrix

An analysis of factory management, with a graphic representation of the personnel flow between departments.

Answer: The personnel flow is represented with the help of a from–to–matrix in triangular shape (see Figure 2.17).

Table 2.6 Transport frequency of a business in tons per day listed in a from–to matrix

No.	To From	1	2	3	4	5	6	7	8	9	10	11	12	13	14
1	Goods in		3.5	4.5											
2	Moulding depot				3.5										
3	Raw materials depot				4.5										
4	Order picking					4.5	2.5	1							
5	Cutting						1.5	3							
6	Metalworks							2.5							
7	Manufacture						1.5		8						
8	Assembly depot									3	3	S		2	
9	Pre-assembly								3						
10	E-workshop														
11	Main assembly												8		
12	Painting													8	
13	Packaging														8
14	Shipping														

Figure 2.17 From–to matrix for personnel flow

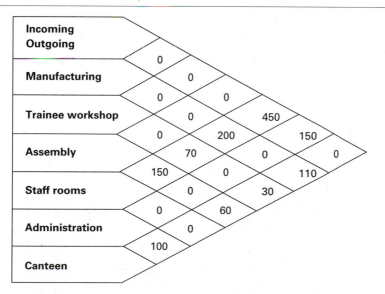

Example 2.8: Material flow block layout

The material flow must be drawn in a facility layout.

Answer: The layout should distinguish between a qualitative or a quantitative MF.

In Figure 12.16 a block layout contains a qualitative MF roughly represented by arrows. A quantitative MF is shown in Figure 2.11 with different arrow strengths depending on size. The legend shows the standard size.

Example 2.9: Material flow shapes

Draw sketches of manufacturing and order picking-related material flow shapes as well as material flow oriented building arrangements.

Answer: see Figures 2.18 and 2.19.

Figure 2.18   Manufacturing and order picking-oriented material flow shapes (resource allocation)

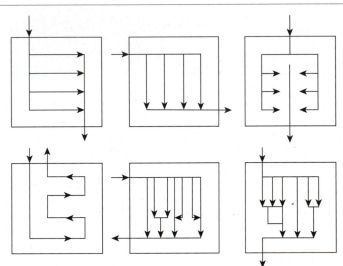

Figure 2.19   Material flow-oriented building allocation

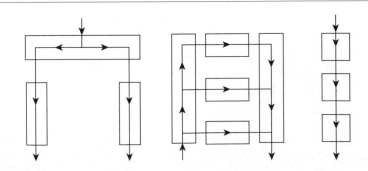

Example 2.10: Material flow representation

Figure 2.10 represented the MF of a retail business with its own plastic production and third party manufacturing of assembly parts. This was represented as a quantitative MF process plan. For organizational purposes it can make sense to structure the material flow in line with functional aspects, in order to combine departments with similar functions. The task is to transform the MF into an MF with a functional structure.

Answer: The structure of the MF process map is in two columns in line with the functions: goods coming in / goods going out, warehouse, order picking, manufacture and third party manufacture. The activities are entered and connected as in a computer-based chart.

Example 2.11: Actual data assessment

An ABC analysis allows for the comparison of two dependent factors. How can the figure of the two dependencies be increased?

Answer: The structure of an ABC–XYZ analysis (Figure 2.20) in a matrix allows for categorization, such as of items with certain characteristics. The entire spectrum of these items will be divided up in to 'fields', enabling the analysis of focal points.

Figure 2.20   An ABC–XYZ analysis

	A	B	C
X	High consumption value (CV) High forecast accuracy (FA) Consistent consumption (C)	Medium CV High FA Consistent consumption C	Low CV High FA Consistent consumption C
Y	High CV Medium FA Semi-consistent consumption C	Medium CV Medium FA Semi-consistent consumption C	Low CV Medium FA Semi-consistent consumption C
Z	High CV Low FA Stochastic C	Medium CV Low FA Stochastic C	Low CV Low FA Stochastic C

Example 2.12: Material flow in assembly

The material flow in the workplace is characterized by a physiological, ergonomic and psychological design of technical and organizational means of work and transport. The principle of non-independent chaining with workpiece carriers has proved to be advantageous. The order of workplaces plays a big role in this. It distinguishes linear, square and asymmetrical material flow structures. Which structures are available for assembly conveyors?

Answer: Figure 2.21 shows possible MF structures in the assembly area, built from components to form a complete set-up.

Figure 2.21 a) Compact assembly system with horizontal and vertically running mobile desks. b) Complete assembly system with workpiece carrier, transverse transport, turntables, lift, belt and chain roller conveyor, separator, hoist and positioning device (www.minitec.de)

a)

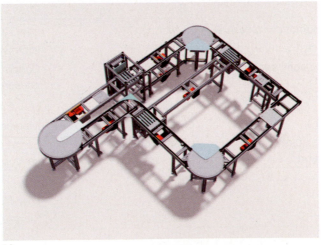

b)

Workpiece carriers can be transported through:

- One-belt conveyor: Workpiece carrier is picked up on one side by a moving belt and dropped off on the other side by static rollers.

- Double-belt conveyor: Workpiece carrier is powered by a narrow belt on either side.

- Accumulating roller-chain conveyor: Workpiece carrier moves on two powered accumulating roller chains.

- Accumulating roller conveyor: Workpiece carrier runs over accumulating roller conveyors with adjustable friction clutch, powered by chain and sprocket (at assembly spots, use of special rolls due to stops and separating).

- Electro pallet conveyor: Motor-powered vehicle in profile construction with four wheelsets running on rails (current collectors glide over rail grinding lines); track width 500 to 2,000 mm, capacity load up to 1,000 kg; structure and details (see VDI 4422) deployed for pallets of relevant cargo transport.

Example 2.13: Computer-aided material flow management

What are the application areas for computer-aided material flow management, what is the methodology, which prerequisites have to be met and what structure does the software require?

Answer: Computer-aided management is used in:

- complex material flow systems in order to record dependencies;

- high calculation input in order to save management time and to increase management quality:

  - a large number of possible alternatives to obtain visual layout representations (also in 3D) within a short time;

  - frequently re-occurring calculations, as a computer can complete these in the minimum time.

The methodology of computer-aided management can be represented roughly. First of all, the requirement profile has to be determined, then the computer can execute the following:

- choice of system alternatives;

- system dimensioning and calculation;

- choice of alternative arrangements;

- representation of management results.

This is what the assessment of the management result is based on. If it is still unsatisfactory, the computer will iteratively start a new optimization with the already calculated data. One prerequisite for computer-aided management is to list and approve a requirement profile containing specified basic data, indicators and restrictions.

Software for such a material flow management system has to be modular-based, to resolve subtasks and, on the other hand, to continuously and holistically resolve a management task. It is important that each module contains system libraries as tools, so that it can refer back to components and base data at any time; in order to calculate the maximum performance for each component for a transport route made up of various means of transport, and to indicate the weakest link.

Example 2.14: Order processing times

a) How can a reduction in order processing times, determined by the analysis and calculated by the management system, be represented graphically?

b) Which components form the order processing time in industrial enterprises, with approximate percentage values?

Answer: a) Figure 2.22; b) Figure 2.23 and with value stream design Figure 2.13.

Example 2.15: Provision of material/material flow management

Which types (strategies) of provision of material are deployed in the material flow?

Answer: The type of material flow management is dependent on the type of manufacturing/assembly. MF management types deployed include *consumption-based* and *requirements-based* processes in line with the push–pull principle (see Chapter 2.1), the Kanban system and the push–pull system. In push processes, the goods streams are managed by a push–pull system tool; in pull processes, it is the next workspace or customer who does the pulling.

JIT purchasing follows the goal of receiving the materials requirement-based and timely, but as late as possible, in order to prevent rest times and to commence production once the requirement has been notified. In order to prevent stocks building up, the pull principle can be introduced, with the Kanban system being one example (see Example 2.4).

The JIS (just in sequence) principle is the timely delivery of parts in the right quantities to an assembly line. This happens without storage and might merely allow for an interim buffer near the production. However, the frequent retrieval of materials requires a standardization of retrieval processes, as, otherwise, the fixed order costs would increase and the cost advantage of JIS would be lost.

C-parts tend to be stored in a depot and transported to the consumption site in larger quantities.

Figure 2.22 Representation of the actual versus the desired order processing time depending on improvement measures
Legend: In the brackets are savings in percentage in respect to the order processing time (OPT) a (5%): Amalgamation of departments b (10%): Introduction of manufacturing management c (5%): Reduction of dead and base times in order picking: introduction of item-oriented order picking d (3%): Optimization of documentation; changes to process organization e (5%): Introduction of CNC machinery f (10%): Introduction of process-oriented manufacture and team work g (2%): Consequence of f: optimal allocation h (10%): Changes to means of storage and order picking in line with the 'goods to man' principle i (2%): Optimization of packaging through semi-automation k (2%): New contracts with hauliers

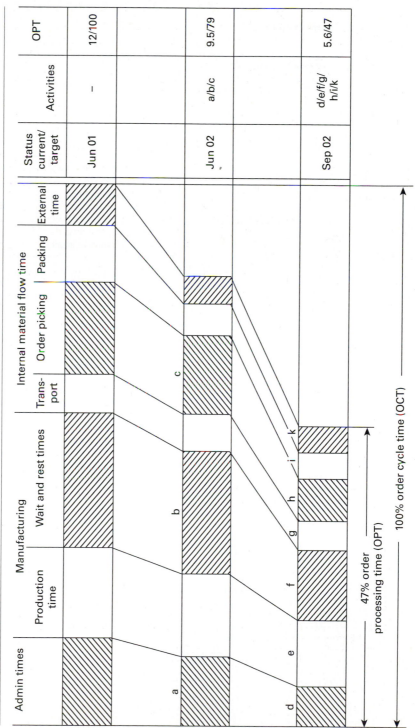

Figure 2.23   Components of order processing times

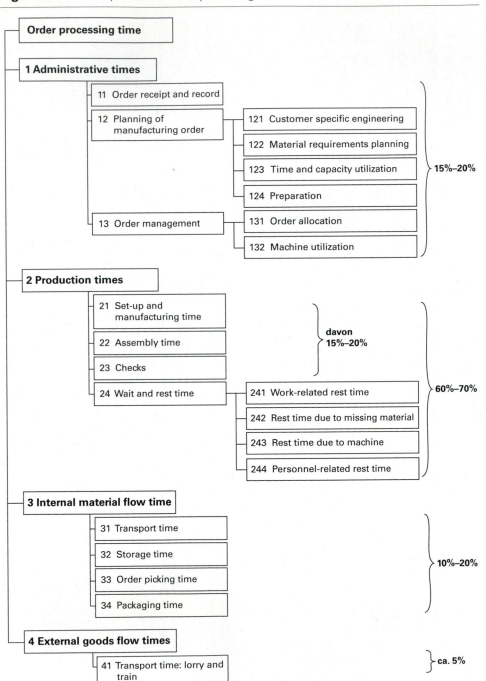

Figure 2.24   Above: Difference of push process (top) and pull process (bottom). Below: Effects of the push–pull process

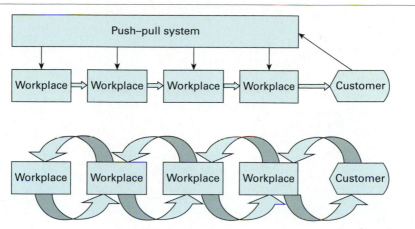

Example 2.16: Material flow with continuous and non-continuous conveyors

Present examples of applications of continuous and non-continuous conveyors in visual form.

Answer: Dip coating plants can be structured in different ways, as shown in Figure 2.25a as a cycled dip system with a power and free conveyor, in Figure 2.25b as flow through dip coating system with a circular conveyor (see Chapter 5.3.3) or in Figure 2.25c as a cycled dip system with an electric monorail (see Chapter 6.3).

Figure 2.25a   Graphic representation of a cycled dip system with a power and free conveyor (www.eisemann.com)

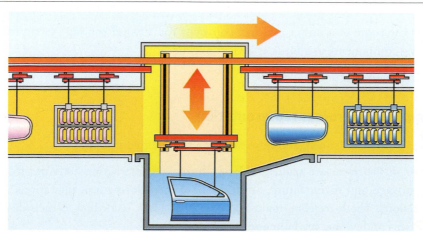

Figure 2.25b   Graphic representation of a flow through dip system with a circular conveyor (www.eisemann.com)

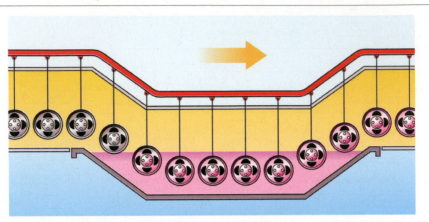

Figure 2.25c   Graphic representation of a cycled dip system with an electric monorail as a feeding machine (www.eisemann.com)

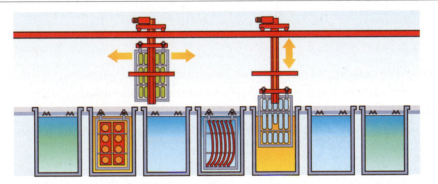

Example 2.17: Material flow with continuous conveyors

Sketch the route of a power and free conveyor for a wood coating system for large window components in a bird's eye view outline.

Answer: Figure 2.26.

Example 2.18: Process representation

How is a process defined, and how can it be represented visually?

Answer a: Processes are sequential procedures and interacting activities for transport, storage and manufacture, and they describe information, operations as well as decisions. There are core, main and part processes. According to their deadlines, processes can be long, medium and short term.

Figure 2.26   Route of a power and free conveyor system for a wood coating system for large window components (www.eisemann.com)

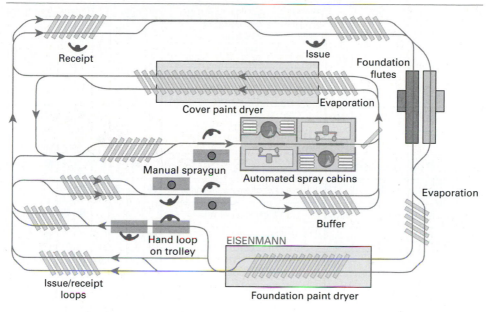

Answer b: Processes can be represented based on different aspects and in different formats. See Figures 2.3, 2.6 and 2.13; and Examples 12.18 and 12.19.

The process of putting together a catalogue can be divided into five areas; these are shown in Table 2.7:

- classification: shown by symbols;
- time required: duration in minutes or hours;
- activities: verbal description;
- organization unit/tool;
- responsibility: department or employee.

Example 2.19: Order processing time, stock levels/representation order processing time

a) How can stock levels, and thus interest costs on stock, be reduced if the order processing time is decreased, such as through streamlining goods in, order picking and quality checks, by 2.5 days? The average stock level is €1.4 m and the average order processing time is 10 days – calculated interest rate: 8 per cent.

Answer: The average stock level/order processing time cycle is €140,000 per day. By decreasing order processing time by 2.5 days, the interest cost is reduced by €28,000.

Table 2.7 Process map of making a catalogue

Activities	Throughput time [min]	Waiting time [min]	Processing time [min]	Individual activity description	Mail with attachments	Free hand	Adobe Photoshop	Sample photos	Product dvlt team	Dept head	Design studio	Photographer	Layout team
Process: Catalogue creation · **Frequency:** 1x per Season · **Costs:** 25 €/hour · **responsible:** Herr x · **Date** 05.04.2002 10:20 am													
1	0		600	Shipping of sample photos to design studio	●			●	●				
2	600		3000	Forwarding comments on samples to design studio	●			●	●				
3	3600	4800		Creation of drawings in design studio		●					●		
4	8400			Receipt of catalogue drawings	●			●	●				
5	8400		1800	Checking drawings					●	●			
6	10200		600	Inform design studio about amends if applicable	●						●		
7	10800		450	Receipt of sample photos from design studio					●	●			
8	11250			Taking photo samples					●	●			
9	11250		540	Photographer briefing for sample photos					●	●	●	●	
10	11790		300	Photo session for catalogue					●		●	●	
11	12090		0	Receipt of photos from photographers							●		
12	12090		480	Photo selection							●		
13	12570		5	Forwarding photos and drawings to layout team				●			●		
14	12575		0	Finalizing and sending to printers									●
Total (min)	12575	4800	7775										
Hours	209.6	80	129.6										
Working days	26.2	10	16.2										

Total catalogue creation p.a.	2
Personnel costs p.a.	ca. €6,000
Costs of one catalogue creation	ca. €3,000

Sample representation of a catalogue creation process

Calculation: Reduction of stock level costs by: €1.4m × 0.25 = €350,000
Reduction of stock interest costs by: 2.5 days is 25% of the order processing cycle 8% of €350,000 = €28,000 per annum or €1,400,000 × 0.08 = €112,000 per annum; reduction by 25% 112,000 €/annum × 0.25 = €28,000 p/a.

b) Representation order processing time: *Answer*: Figure 2.27; see also Figures 2.22 and 2.23.

Figure 2.27 Order processing times with proportion of processing and rest times during order processing (www.awf.de)

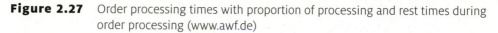
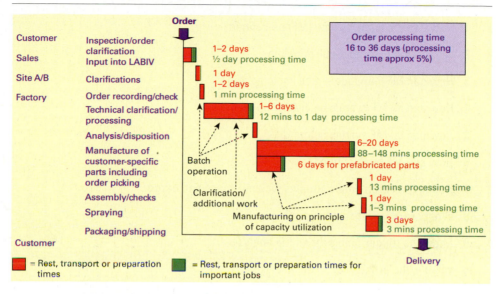

Example 2.20: Material flow simulation

What is a material flow simulation?

Answer: MF simulation is used to validate extensive MF management with the aim of determining MF management performance capacity and its alternatives, identifying weak points and checking provided data. See Chapter 12.9.3.2 for methodology.

Example 2.21: Order processing time

Create a representation of the order processing time of loading and unloading a lorry with pallet loading units.

Answer: Figure 2.28.

Figure 2.28 Assembled order processing times for loading and unloading a lorry
Legend from left (time in minutes): lorry arrival in lane – 2; opening lorry – 4; waiting time – 2; unloading – 16; loading – 29; closing lorry – 5; leaving lane – 2

Questions

1 How can the material flow (MF) be defined?

2 What is the push-and-pull principle?

3 How can MF management be implemented?

4 How can an MF system be divided up?

5 How can an MF system fit into CIM?

6 How can MF be described?

7 Define the cargo goods streams (volume, mass and cargo).

8 What are MF costs made up of?

9 Show the trigger points for an MF analysis.

10 What is the process of an MF analysis?

11 What are the methods and processes used to carry out an MF analysis?

12 What are the values to be determined by an MF analysis?

13 What is the structure of a Gantt chart?

14 What is the structure of a from–to matrix and what is it used for?

15 What are the visual representations that can be used to assess an MF?

16 What indicators serve to assess and compare an MF?

17 What is the definition of a process and how can it be divided up?

18 What is the objective of MF management?

19 What is material design and what is it used for?

Cargo, packaging, loading unit 03

3.1 Cargo and storage goods

3.1.1 Division

The type of cargo is a deciding factor when determining a means of transport for a given task. This also goes for planning a storage space. Cargo and storage goods in internal material flows can be solid, liquid and gaseous materials.

The transport of liquids and gasses in pipes does not form part of transport technology; rather this falls under process technology. However, if liquids are filled in vessels with no pressure or gasses by using a certain amount of pressure then they are treated like solid materials and in line with relevant transport and storage regulations. Liquids and gasses are used in transport technology as carriage media for hydraulic or pneumatic transport systems for sand, granulate, pneumatic capsules and wood shavings. Solid cargo is divided into bulk and general cargo.

3.1.2 Bulk cargo

Bulk cargo is a lumpy, granular or dusty mass bulk product with a flow-ability, which ordinarily changes its shape during transport and cannot be held together as one unit without the use of aids. Typical bulk cargos are ore, coal, waste, sand, cement, gravel, grain, coffee.

In order to determine a means of transport or ways of storage, the characteristic physical and chemical features of bulk cargo must be established (see Figure 3.2).

These features serve to classify materials:

- *Cargo texture*

  Division into grain size and shape, such as sharp or rounded edges, fibrous, threaded. Depending on the level of the composition's uniformity, we talk of *sorted* (ratio of maximum to minimum grain size *smaller* than 2.5) or unsorted (ratio *bigger* than 2.5) general cargo. Grain size is diagonally the biggest distance between the edges.

Figure 3.1 Division of cargo

Bulk cargo divided by:

Quantity:	Part
– Single cargo	Machine part
	Package
– Mass cargo	Post package
	Moulded parts
	Sacks
Function:	
– Transport, storage	Vessel, box
or loading aid	Pallet, loading frame
– Loading unit	Pallet + cargo
	Box + transport
	goods
Shape:	
– Flat	Sheet metal
	Chipboard
	Glass panels
– Long	Profiles
	Pipes
	Poles
– Wound	Paper rolls
	Wire bundles
	Coils

- *Cargo cohesion*

  The flow behaviour can be characterized as flowing easily or flowing with diffi-culty, and this is expressed by the embankment angle. The embankment angle β_R at rest is the cargo's tilt angle after it has been emptied onto a horizontal ground. This is dependent on the cargo's grain size, temperature and water content.

  The embankment angle β_R is the decisive factor when planning and determin-ing the stockpile area for storing cargo on the ground. In order to move cargo by means of transport, such as belt conveyors, the embankment angle in motion is decisive (see Table 3.1).

- *Cargo behaviour*

  The physical, mechanic and chemical features must be described: grinding (coke, quartz); attacking (sodium chloride); explosive (coal dust); flammable (sawdust); dusty (cement); sticky (clay); hygroscopic (plaster); smelly (refuse).

  Other characteristic features are moisture content, sensitivity to pressure and/ or light.

Figure 3.2 General cargo features

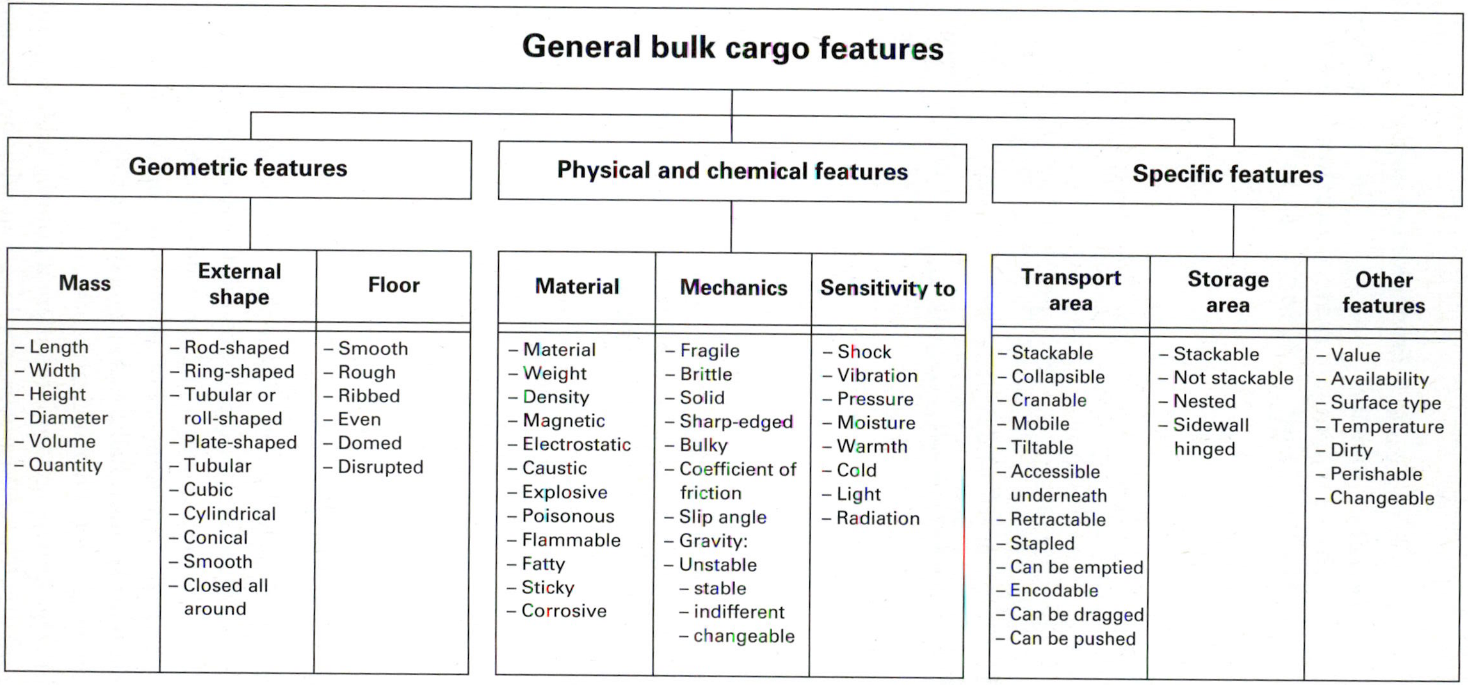

General bulk cargo features

Geometric features

Mass	External shape	Floor
– Length	– Rod-shaped	– Smooth
– Width	– Ring-shaped	– Rough
– Height	– Tubular or	– Ribbed
– Diameter	roll-shaped	– Even
– Volume	– Plate-shaped	– Domed
– Quantity	– Tubular	– Disrupted
	– Cubic	
	– Cylindrical	
	– Conical	
	– Smooth	
	– Closed all	
	around	

Physical and chemical features

Material	Mechanics	Sensitivity to
– Material	– Fragile	– Shock
– Weight	– Brittle	– Vibration
– Density	– Solid	– Pressure
– Magnetic	– Sharp-edged	– Moisture
– Electrostatic	– Bulky	– Warmth
– Caustic	– Coefficient of	– Cold
– Explosive	friction	– Light
– Poisonous	– Slip angle	– Radiation
– Flammable	– Gravity:	
– Fatty	– Unstable	
– Sticky	– stable	
– Corrosive	– indifferent	
	– changeable	

Specific features

Transport area	Storage area	Other features
– Stackable	– Stackable	– Value
– Collapsible	– Not stackable	– Availability
– Cranable	– Nested	– Surface type
– Mobile	– Sidewall	– Temperature
– Tiltable	hinged	– Dirty
– Accessible		– Perishable
underneath		– Changeable
– Retractable		
– Stapled		
– Can be emptied		
– Encodable		
– Can be dragged		
– Can be pushed		

Table 3.1   Bulk density and embankment angle of cargo

Cargo	Density ρ in t/m³	Bulk density ρ_s in t/m³	Embankment angle At rest β_R in°	Embankment angle In motion β_B in°	For bucket elevators Filling factor φ	For bucket elevators Conveyor speed in m/s
Coal	0.9	0.7	50	35	0.5	1.9
Ash (Slag)	2.5	0.9	45	35	0.7	2.5
Barley	0.9	0.7	35	25	0.8	3.0
Gravel (wet)	2.5	0.7	50	35	0.7	2.5
Plastic pellets	1.3	0.7	25	5	0.7	2.0
Flour	0.7	0.5	55	50	0.9	3.5
Sand (dry)	2.5	1.6	35	20	0.7	2.5
Sawdust	0.4	0.25	35	5	0.8	3.0
Cement	2.8	1.2	45	20	0.8	2.5

- *Bulk density ρ_s*

  This is the weight of volume in t/m³ (see Table 3.1). This measurement is an important factor to determine the mass stream and performance of a transport system. We distinguish the bulk density of *loose* (rest) and *compacted* (motion) cargo. The ratio of the two bulk densities is called the degree of density.

- *Temperature*

  This feature is particularly important because the means of transport has to match the relevant required transport temperature. At room temperature, cement acts like flour, but at 80°C coupled with emulsified air during manufacturing processes, it acts like fluids.

3.1.3 General cargo

Solid transport goods that do not change shape during transport and can be handled individually as one unit are called general cargo. Cargo can be packaged or unpackaged, have small or large measurements, and can consist of one or multiple materials.

Typical general cargo consists of: manufacturing or assembly parts; packets; boxes; tins; bottles; rings; balls; sacks; containers; trays; loading units; machines; vehicles; outer garments (hanging garments).

General cargo can be divided into different criteria, such as quantity, function or form (Figure 3.1). General cargo that is long and wide but not very thick may be called *sheet*. General cargo that is small in diameter but is long (> 2.5 m, often 6 m, bundled – see Figure 11.24 for more) may be called *long* or *oversized* goods. Large quantities of general cargo, such as screws or postal packages, may also be called *mass cargo*. The garment industry distinguishes between *hanging* and *boxed* garments. As is the case for bulk cargo, transporting general cargo requires an understanding of the geometric, chemical and physical features, and obligatory and necessary prerequisite for planning functional and economic transport and storage systems.

3.1.4 Transport, storage and loading equipment

Transport, storage and loading equipment are load carriers (DIN 30 781) and include tools that are used to put together uniform logistical units. They create the conditions for mechanization and automation in the flow of materials and goods. The terms for transport, storage and loading equipment and load carriers are often used as synonyms. They can be divided according to level of floor clearance (see Example 3.4):

- transport and loading equipment without floor clearance;
- transport and loading equipment with floor clearance.

3.1.4.1 Transport and loading equipment without floor clearance

These are small load carriers (up to a loading area of 400 × 600 mm), crates, boxes and small containers. Some of these are normed or standardized; often they have a modular system to accommodate different sizes. They are made of cardboard, wood, galvanized steel sheets or coloured plastic. Crates and small containers may have particular features and can be stackable, nested, impact and shock proof, foldable and often with smooth floors. They may have carrier handles, covers, inserts, compartments or include devices for identity (ID) storage and encoders in order to ensure traceable transport. Transport and storage aids without floor clearance (see Figure 3.3) include:

- stacking and viewing boxes (can be lifted with special lift trucks – see Figure 6.6.4e);
- grid, wire and full-wall containers (1 m³ content: small containers);
- stack nest, foldable and collapsible containers;
- special containers: tray, basket, sack, barrel, bin, box, crate, toolbox.

Developments in the means of transport without floor clearance are continually taking place. As an example, small cargo containers were developed in collaboration between VDMA and the automobile industry that can be used for manual, mechanical and automated handling, as well as in exchange (pooling capability). They ensure vertical closure like a stackable crate and also a horizontal closure by means of feet on the bottom, which result in a secure fit through cross-stacking.

Protected strips can be placed on the small cargo container. It also has surfaces from which water can easily run off and handles. It can be emptied mechanically or automatically. It has grooves for the driving pin of rack storage and retrieval devices

Figure 3.3   Transport and storage aids without floor clearance (a–e: www.ssi-schaefer.com)

a) Viewing and stackable crates

b) Shelf with storage boxes, heavy crates on roller tracks

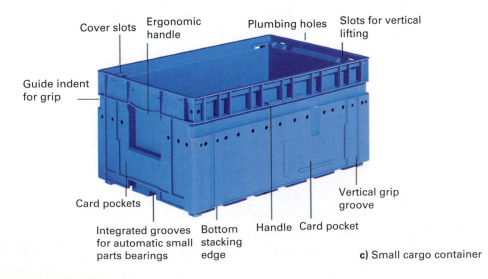

c) Small cargo container

Figure 3.3   *(Continued)*

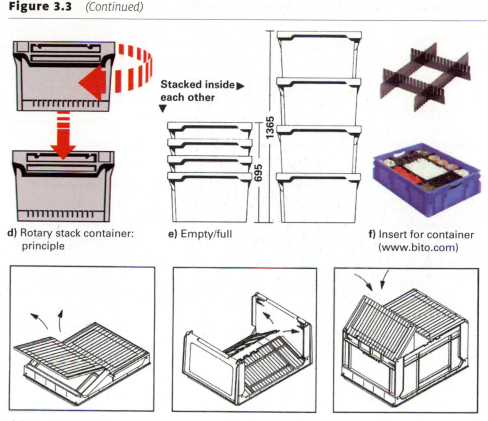

d) Rotary stack container: principle

Stacked inside ▶ each other ▼

695   1365

e) Empty/full

f) Insert for container (www.bito.com)

g) Collapsible container for multi-use (www.mauser-group.com)

with automated small part bearing (see Chapter 11.6). The small cargo container's measurements are 600 × 400 mm or 400 × 300 mm, based on the Euro-pallet. It is given the name 6428, ie this container is 600 mm long, 400 mm wide and 280 mm high (see Figures 3.3c and 3.24).

3.1.4.2 Transport and storage aids with floor clearance

Large load carriers (> 400 × 600 mm) are pallets, large containers and loading frames with a supporting, enclosing or closed platform (Figure 3.4). On the one hand, they are used to collate general cargo such as crates, small containers, boxes and packages into larger loading units and, on the other hand, they enable non-floor clearing goods to clear the floor, resulting in streamlined transport and storage. Storage aids are made from a variety of different components such as chipboard, wood, plastic, sheet metal or aluminium and are sometimes standardized and partly adapted to the transport goods. Loading equipment may be stackable, collapsible and nested.

Figure 3.4   Classification of loading equipment with floor clearance

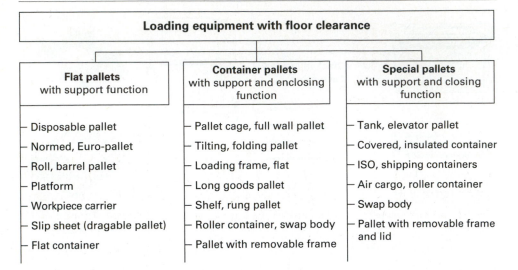

The classification of loading equipment can be based on a variety of criteria,

- level of floor clearance: two-way/three-way pallet;
- type of use: disposable, pool, multiple use pallet;
- standard: DIN-flat pallet, non-standard pallet.

The most important types of loading equipment *with floor clearance* are (see Figures 3.5a–t):

1 Flat pallets (DIN 15 141 and DIN 15 146). The following lists the different names that apply (see Example 3.1):

- *Disposable pallet*: Disposable pallet, pallet for one-off use, often made of low-quality wood, flat pallet used as assembly carrier for ovens, fridges or washing machines.
- *Two-way, four-way pallets*: Named due to the ability to get under the pallet with the forks of a forklift truck from two or four sides, entry height of 100 mm for pallets (see Figure 3.5).

Types of flat pallets are:

- *DIN pallet*: Euro pool or swap pallet of the European Pallet Pool (see Figure 3.5) with measurements (L × W × H) 1,200 × 800 × 150 as a flat pallet. This pallet is made of wood and fulfils specific requirements, such as consistent dimensions, so that it can be utilized in automated high shelving warehouses. It has a

Figure 3.5 Loading equipment with floor clearance

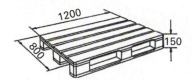

a) Four-way pallet (DIN pallet) **b)** Steel flat pallet **c)** Two-way pallet

d) Flat pallet with side frame (stackable) **e)** Flat pallet with removable frame (stackable) **f)** Flat pallet with removable mesh frame (stackable)

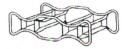

g) Barrel pallet **h)** Mesh box pallet **i)** Full wall box pallet

k) Foldable mesh box pallet **l)** Stackable frame **m)** Box pallet for warm goods

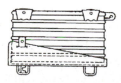

n) Box pallet with floor discharge **o)** Box pallet with discharge wall **p)** Roller container

(continued)

Figure 3.5   *(Continued)*

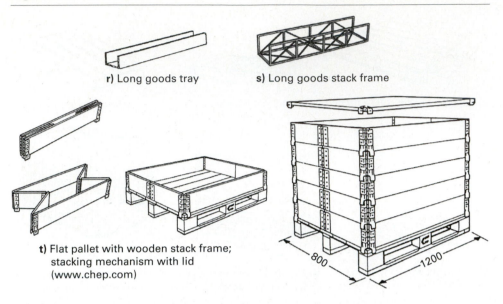

r) Long goods tray

s) Long goods stack frame

t) Flat pallet with wooden stack frame;
stacking mechanism with lid
(www.chep.com)

load capacity of 1 tonne. The International Union of Railways' Pallet Pool was founded in 1961 and pursues that aim of deploying the standardized flat pallet, called a pool pallet, in an exchange system (empty for full loaded), in order to achieve an uninterrupted transport chain. The prerequisites for membership in the Pallet Pool are determined by the DG AG Central Transport Management Department, in Mainz.

Pool flat pallets are labelled:

- EUR branding on right corner leg by the European Pallet Pool.
- DB branding on middle leg by the European Railway Association as well as the country and manufacturer codes.
- EPAL on the left leg: branding with the quality label of the European Pallet Association.

The standardized loading areas of the flat pallet are:

- 800 × 1,200 mm, deployed in all sectors;
- 800 × 1,000 mm, deployed in the drinks industry;
- 1,000 × 1,200 mm: deployed in the chemical industry and breweries;
- 600 × 400 mm (Düsseldorf pallet): deployed in many sectors.

• A *roller pallet* is a flat pallet with four fixed castors that run in special grooved rails.

- A *barrel pallet* will hold two or three barrels. It is structured either as a tube frame or as bent sheet metal and has fork shoes to guide the fork tines.

- *Flat pallets with braces, stack on or push on frames* are used for non-stackable, pressure-sensitive goods, so that these can be stacked five times (see Figures 3.5 d and f). A stacking frame is foldable, with a height of up to 1.6 m, and is also available on the market as mesh construction.

- *Flat pallet with foldable wooden stacking frame* in different heights is used for loose cargo. A collapsible frame secures it during transport (Figures 3.5t and 3.30).

2 **Box pallets:** They serve both transport as well as provision at the workplace and storage of goods, have floor clearance, are often stackable and sometimes have side flaps or openings for loading and unloading.

Box pallets come as:

  - *Mesh box pallets*: Features a usable inside space of 800 × 1,200 × 800 mm (0.75 m³) with a load capacity of 1 t. Fivefold stacking is possible up to full load capacity. Form fitting stacking through angled frames and the goods can be seen from outside. One half-wall is foldable and can be picked up by fork tines or lifted by the corner legs. The mesh box pallet runs on chain and roll conveyors.

  - *Disposable box pallet*: The flat pallet is inextricably connected with crates or large cardboard boxes and provides one-off use for bulk and liquid transport. It is often used in a reusable container, but is then made more carefully and of better quality wood.

  - *Full wall box pallet*: May have foldable side walls, has a profile frame for form-fitting stacking with or without corner supports and can be transported with lifting devices if eye hooks are available. Capacity load 1 is made for fivefold stacking in which special designs are available as a bulk container with retractable floor or hopper and is made from perforated sheet metal for wet or hot goods (see Figure 3.5i).

  - *Rung or stacking frame* for bulky goods and long goods (see Figure 3.5l).

  - *Long goods pallet*: Available as a long goods tray (see Figure 3.5r) and in a stackable version as a long goods stacking frame (see Figure 3.5s). When used for automated outsourcing of long goods (includes residual lengths), it is often shaped as a self-supporting cassette (see Figures 11.24 and 11.25).

  - *Roller container*: (Figure 3.5p) Special use, for food transport between the order picking depot and retail. Made up of a platform with rotating castors (guide castors) and two or three mesh side panels.

3 **Special pallets** are available in a great variety. Examples of special pallets are silo or tank containers mounted on a steel pallet (slip-sheet: see Example 3.14).

4 **Loading frames** are un-normed loading tools, usually to an internal standard and tailor-made for the relevant goods to be transported. They meet requirements for safeguarding and are stackable and can be deployed directly at the workplace (see Figure 6.6.18).

5 **Platforms** are loading tools with floor clearance to pick up loads as part of the internal material flow. The loading platform has four feet (up to 400 mm high) made of steel and can be lifted with a forklift or platform truck. It is not stackable, nor is it suitable for all storage equipment due to loss of volume as a result of the four feet. An advantage for a working pallet is less bending down for employees. By replacing two fixed feet with castors, it turns into a roller platform, which can be steered easily with a *roller lever* (see Figure 6.6.4c) and is also available as an electro-hydraulic towbarless truck.

3.1.4.3 Containers

Containers are standardized large vessels with a loading volume of 10 to 80 m³, used for direct shipping from manufacturer to customer. Advantages are cost saving through streamlining handling, fast transport via ship, rail or road, through stacking containers and weather protection for the transported goods. They can be utilized for general cargo, bulk cargo, liquids and gasses (tank/cooling container). At Hamburg harbour, 90 per cent of general cargo is handled in containers and the rest is loose cargo. The onward transport of the containers happens with rail (approximately 20 per cent), feeder ships (approximately 30 per cent) to the Baltic sea and lorries (approximately 50 per cent). Containers can be accessed by forklift trucks and are transported using forklifts, cranes and loading bridges equipped with spreaders (Chapter 7.3.4, Figures 7.10, 7.11, 7.16 and 7.17). There are different types of containers:

- ISO *container* (DIN ISO 668)

  These shipping containers can be deployed internationally (Figure 3.6) and are 10, 20, 40 and 45 foot long (approximately 3, 6, 12 and 13.7 m); they have a maximum load of approximately 11, 21, 26 and 29 t. The biggest disadvantage is that they are not compatible with Euro-pallet measurements (inner width: 2.33 m). Loading usually happens via the container's back gate and they can be stacked tenfold on a ship, but only up to threefold stacking outside when at full load, or five-/sixfold when empty due to wind pressure.

  A ship's load is made up of: approximately 30 per cent are 20 foot; 65 per cent are 40 foot; 2 per cent are special containers. The same applies for lorries

Figure 3.6a   Container (1 fork pocket, 2 corner fittings, 3 two-winged doors)

Figure 3.6b   Container on rail carriage, showing container names (www.hhla.de)

(see Examples 3.7 and 7.6). Abbreviations that are valid internationally are: TEU (20 foot equivalent unit) for a 20 foot container; and FEU (40 foot equivalent unit) for a 40 foot container. As an example, the ship MSC Zoe can transport; 11,000 TEU on deck, and 8,000 TEU below deck, with ship measurements of 400 m in length, 59 m in width and a depth of 16 m. Transporting a 20 foot container from Singapore to Hamburg costs – depending on demand – between €700 and

Table 3.2   Main data for inland containers

Container name	External/internal measurements			Gross weight max. kg	Own weight steel/ aluminium kg
	Length mm	Width mm	Height mm		
B12	12.192	2.500	2.600	30,480	3,500
	12.000	2.440	2.400		2,600
B9	9.125	2.500	2.600	25,400	3,000
	8.900	2.440	2.400		2,200
B6	6.058	2.500	2.600	20,320	2,300
	5.900	2.440	2.400		1,800

€1,500 and takes around four weeks; it increases the price of a bottle of wine by only 10 cents from Australia to Hamburg! (For handling equipment, see Chapter 7.3.4, Transport safe container with twist lock, similar to a T-head bolt). Costs for a new 20 foot container are around €2,500. The largest container ship has a TWU capacity of 18,000, whereby 22 containers are lined up side by side.

• *Deutsche Bahn inland container*

This transport unit for inland traffic allows for threefold stacking, and rear and side loading, and is aligned with Euro pallet measurements (Table 3.2).

• *Exchange container*

Mainly deployed in the disposal sector for residual materials, waste and rubbish. Exchange principle: full against empty (model: see Chapter 2.3.2).

• *Swap containers* (lorry)

In line with ISO 6346, each container worldwide can be identified by:

• four letters, prefix ZCSU: owner identification, usually a shipping company or leasing company;
• six-digit number 226669: container number, 0: verification number;
• maximum total weight in kg and lb;
• tare in kg and lb;
• cargo load in kg and lb;
• volume in m³ and ft³.

A 40" container with a maximum weight of 30 t has a tare of 3.6 t and at a volume of ca. 68 m³, a cargo load of 26.2 t (load safety: see Chapter 3.3.6).

3.2 Packaging

3.2.1 Package, multi-pack

Packaging items and multi-packs are general cargo.

A *packaging item*, also called a package, is created by packaging the goods, ie packaging encompasses all activities to create a packaging item.

Packaged goods can be bulk cargo, general cargo, liquids or gas.

Packaging can be paper, foil, boxes, crates, tins, bottles, tubes, sacks, bags, etc.

Packaging aids are divided into sealing and padding materials. Sealing aids are tapes, straps and staples. Passing materials or fillers are foam, excelsior, paper chips, polystyrene, paper mats/padding and air cushions.

Packaging materials can consist of paper, cardboard, glass, carton, aluminium, steel, plastic and wood.

Packaging fulfils a range of functions, as outlined in Figure 3.7. The creation of packaging items has to occur based on minimizing packaging costs. For general and bulk cargo, liquids and gas it is done with specialized filling, packing and wrapping machines. The result is usually a consumer package representing a sales unit, such as a bar of chocolate, a bag of coffee or a can of beer. Packaging machines automatically pack products into a box – cigarettes and wine bottles would be a couple of examples.

A *multi-pack* is a larger unit, in which several of the same packaging items are collated, with examples such as 20 × 500 g coffee filters in one 10 kg multi-pack, or canned beer in a tray. This requires packaging materials and packaging aids.

For different packing tables and cardboard trolleys, see Example 9.10.

Figure 3.7   Packaging functions

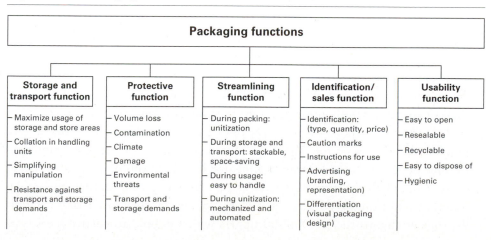

3.2.2 Packaging types

These are divided into the following.

Packaging for shipping is used to protect the goods during transport.

In cases of *transport damage* there are checks to ascertain whether the transport packaging should have withstood the relevant forces. VDI standard 2700 assumes a mass force of 0.8 FG for brake incidents and 0.5 FG for a start-up process (FG = fighting gravity, see Example 3.13).

Product packaging is used to ensure longevity and to protect the goods until they arrive with the end consumer. It is the immediate product wrapping. Often, additional packaging is used, such as wrapped sweets in a packet.

Outer packaging is additional packaging on top of sales packaging. It does not have any immediate protective function and loses significance once the goods are being used. It can be difficult to differentiate between outer packaging and sales packaging, as the lines can be blurred. For foodstuffs, around 6 per cent of the product value is created by outer packaging (for more on packaging research, see Figure 3.15).

3.2.3 Waste and packaging disposal

Waste created within a business is removed by container systems (see Figure 1.8). There is a differentiation between tipping systems and exchange systems:

- *Tipping system*

  Large waste containers are utilized, which are emptied directly at the waste or waste collection location by special equipment. The empty containers remain there. The tipping system is used for small and medium amounts of rubbish. Container sizes range from 0.12 to 0.6 m³ as household and large waste bins and from 0.8 to 5.0 m³ as large refuse containers.

- *Exchange system*

  In the exchange system, waste is removed by use of large refuse containers. The full containers are replaced with empty ones during pick-up. Depending on the size, design and intake system of the removal vehicles, these can be roll-off containers, skips or containers with integrated press function (see Figure 3.8).

  Roll-off containers (see Figure 3.9a to c) are rolled onto the relevant site via suitable vehicle structures. There are different designs of roll-off containers. Roll-off tippers are used for transporting and handling roll-off containers. These possess rope or chain structures as well as a lift function, which initially tips up the container while on the vehicle. The roll-off container is then lowered down with the rope or chain structure. Roll-off tippers with a double-articulated hook-arm

Figure 3.8   Classification of exchange containers

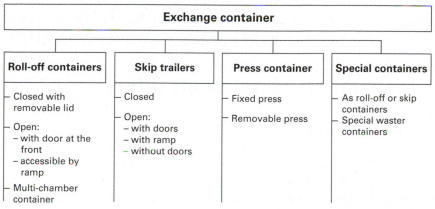

Exchange container			
Roll-off containers	**Skip trailers**	**Press container**	**Special containers**

– Closed with removable lid
– Open:
  – with door at the front
  – accessible by ramp
– Multi-chamber container
	– Closed
	– Open:
	  – with doors
	  – with ramp
	  – without doors
		– Fixed press
		– Removable press
			– As roll-off or skip containers
			– Special waster containers

lower the container directly to the ground by using the hydraulic hook system (see Chapter 7.3.4).

Skip trailers, also called skips, are lowered to the ground with cranes integrated into the vehicle. Skips come in multiple designs. Skip lorries are used to transport and handle skips, with integrated cranes to pick up and lower down skips (see Figure 7.12).

Press containers compress the waste with inbuilt pressing equipment that is either fixed or connected to the container via a removable joint (see Figure 3.9c).

Figure 3.9   Roll-off containers

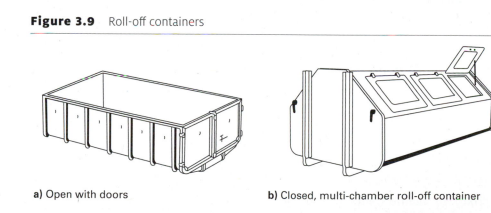

a) Open with doors   b) Closed, multi-chamber roll-off container

c) Press container with roll-off tipper

Packaging waste, such as boxes or cartons, are often compressed on-site in a *baler* (see Figure 1.16) into different sized balls in order to keep the waste volume as small as possible and to create cargo units that can be easily transported and handled (repackaging expenses for semi-finished products, see Figure 12.14).

3.3 Load unit, load, transport safety

3.3.1 Logistical unit, load unit

Each piece of cargo with a sufficient weight, volume and measurements constitutes a unit, and it can be moved, stored or assembled with mechanic, automatic transport or storage aids. These logistical units are workpieces, tools, boxes, crates or small containers.

Larger logistical units are created by collating general cargo in small logistical units via loading aids, into standardized transport or storage units. By determining the shape and measurements, the internal material flow can be simplified, the efficient use of storage space can be increased and the material flow costs can be reduced. In particular, the creation of load units has the following advantages:

- saving reloading processes;
- reducing handling times;
- protecting transported goods;
- increasing handling performance;
- cost savings as a result of matching means of transport with the load unit size;
- creating transport systems and transport chains;
- reducing accident potential;
- facilitation of mechanization and automation;
- reducing storage space requirements as a result of stackable load units;
- achieving economic goals: load unit equals production unit, transport unit, storage unit and sales unit;
- saving on packaging costs;
- protecting against theft;
- reducing times required for stocktake and material flow costs;
- mechanization of load assembly;
- reducing insurance costs;
- optimal match between load unit and load;
- simplified identification.

The creation of a load unit can result in disadvantages due to the costs of loading aids as well as storage, space required for empties and administration of loading aids and means of security. Additional costs are caused by: the surplus weight of loading aids (tare), as well as the need to transport these back; plants and devices to create load units, such as palletizers; means of transport, such as forklift trucks, tugs or wagons required for handling and transport of load units; along with relevant personnel at the loading as well as unloading site. Low transport costs can only be guaranteed if there is a match between general cargo or packages, and transport aids, loading aids and loading space (Figure 3.10).

If possible, there should be an attempt to ensure:

Assembly units = transport unit = shipping unit = sales unit

Figure 3.10   Load unit creation system

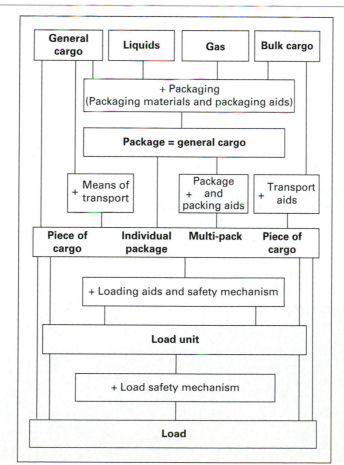

This should apply to certain products, such as fridges, freezers, washing machines and dishwashers. A fridge is mounted on a disposable pallet, covered in shrink-wrap for secure transport and transported as a unit to the customer via distribution and regional depots (multi-cycle system, see Example 3.8).

Transport units are containers, swap bodies, trailers etc.

3.3.2 Load unit creation

Transport and empties have the greatest influence on the type and creation of load units, with the shape and measurements dependent on:

- type, shape and measurements of the general cargo or packages;
- transport and loading aids;
- modular / non-modular packaging unit;
- measurement of loading space (see Examples 3.3 and 3.4).

Depending on how many goods are to be packaged or collated within a time unit, the process for creating load units can be manual, mechanized, part-automated or fully automated, or carried out by industrial robots (Figure 3.11). An industrial robot as a line, portal or articulated-arm robot is able to stack load units of varying types, or of single or multiple origin on a pallet or any other required packing base. Depending on the type of general cargo, the grab function has to be operational to grab a closed box with suckers (see Chapter 8.2.1).

Figure 3.11   Robot with articulated arm for creation of mixed pallets (www.dematic.com)

3.3.3 Palletizing, packing patterns, palletizer

A pallet unit, consisting of the load and loading aids (eg a pallet), is a current prevalent load unit. The process of creating a load unit is called palletizing. Here, the general cargo consisting of crates, boxes, sacks, buckets or packages are layered and stacked in a prescribed pattern.

The *packaging patterns* (packing scheme) and the *stacking pattern* have to utilize the available surface as efficiently as possible, and to achieve load security. If layers are stacked in an uneven pattern, a *bonded stack* is created (Figure 3.12a). Layers with an even pattern that are stacked identically create a *column stack* (Tower stacks, Figure 3.12b). This involves stacking crates or plastic crates used for drinks, the column has a vertical form fit, and the stack has to be horizontally secured with, for example, a rubber band. The optimal use of the packing surface is only possible with a modular division of package measurements (Figure 3.13a).

Depending on the composition of the palleted goods (identical, disparate, surface finish, shape) and on the quantity of general cargo per hour, the palletizing process can be carried out manually, or be part or fully automated. Palletizers and portal robots with palletizing capabilities of up to 5,000 general cargo pieces per hour can be deployed to create load units. For automatic processes, the packing and stacking pattern are selected on the palletizer. The machines are divided into the following designs:

Figure 3.12   Stacking types

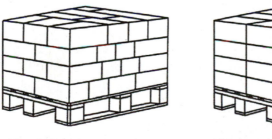

a) Bonded stack   b) Column stack

Figure 3.13   Packing scheme (pattern, layer pattern) on a DIN pallet

a) With a modular package unit

b) With a non-modular package unit

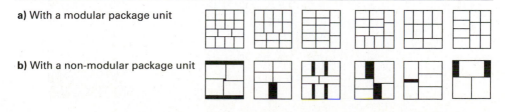

- *alignment station* with stops, turning and rotating functions and chuters to achieve a defined position for the general cargo (packing scheme);
- *layer collection station*, with rakes in order to create the position for the entire general cargo in line with the packing scheme;
- *delivery station* for the layers on the pallet unit in line with *thrust principle* (pulling out the sheet underneath the layer) or in line with *put down principle* (using a grabbing system, which is a bottom-up principle, eg a sucker, clamp or hook);
- *lift station* to align the pallet unit with the approximate height of the layer collection station – the *top-down principle*.

The palletizer also has a feeding device for general cargo, such as roller conveyors, belt conveyors as well as an empty pallet dispenser and unloading mechanisms for the complete pallet unit, in the shape of a heavy load roller conveyor.

There are:

- *Full palletizers* (Figure 3.14), which completely palletize a pallet load in *a single attempt*. These are used for large quantities per hour and a limited number of items. The full palletizer requires long feeding runs, as long as the length of all packages of a pallet load.

Figure 3.14   Palletizer: Full palletizer, palletizing according to top-down principle with empty pallet dispenser (www.beumer.com)

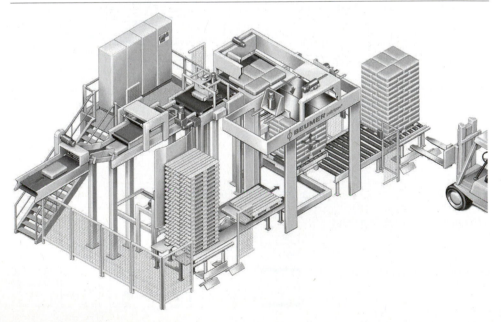

- *Layer palletizers*, which simultaneously palletize multiple pallet loads *in layers*. These are utilized for fewer packages per hour and a larger number of items as well as for different performance levels of filling machines or to create *made to order pallets* and *mixed pallets (selection pallets)* with a variety of items. The layer palletizer requires short feeders with the length of all packages in a layer. For layer palletizers, there are two working principles:
  - mobile palletizer and stationary pallet position;
  - vice versa.

The created pallet unit must have a right-angled stacking structure, an even outer edge and a level stack surface and the palletizing process must ensure that goods are protected throughout (see Figure 3.28).

Palletizing can also be carried out by palletizing robots, where general cargo can be grabbed by the robot individually or as a full layer to create a mixed pallet (see Example 3.12; Figure 3.11; Chapter 8.2.1).

To *depalletize* the load unit, several methods can be used depending on the loaded goods, such as tipping the load unit for bags, robots with grabbing systems such as suckers, clamps or lifts for boxes, crates or cases as well as line, articulated or portal robots for a variety of goods (see Figure 8.1).

3.3.4 Transport safety for load units

Each transport and storage unit, each packaging and load unit must be secured in line with the estimated *demands of transport, handling and storage* (for more on transport and storage demands, see VDI-R2700; Figure 3.29).

3.3.4.1 Packaging requirements

Figure 3.15 can be used as a guide to determine the relevant required packaging for a transport, handling and/or storage process. Result: Packaging regulation.

3.3.4.2 Pallet safety

There are a variety of possibilities and methods to secure pallet load units, which can be applied either during or after palletizing. Load safety materials such as paper, rubber, plastic straps and glue can be used.

Safety methods include:

- During the palletizing process:
  - bonded stacking;
  - paper, friction mats in between layers;
  - lubricants;

Figure 3.15   Process for determining required packaging

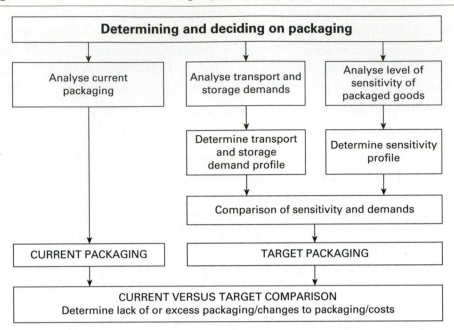

- spot gluing of layers;
- tray creation.
- After palletizing:
  - nets, stacking frames;
  - rubber bands;
  - straps;
  - shrink wrap;
  - stretch film.

The nature of the securing method depends on the number of load units to be secured per time unit, the transport and storage demands and the shape of loading goods. These processes can be applied manually, part- or fully automated.

3.3.4.3 Shrinking

For shrinking, a plastic film (thickness from 25 to 150 µm) is placed over or around a load unit and heated up to 180 to 220 °C. The film will soften when heated and shrink when it cools down, tightening around the loaded goods, thereby stabilizing them. It also creates a connection between the pallet load unit and the pallet.

Plastic film is made of PE or PP and on offer as wrap, in tubular form to slip over or as covers. The film is heated in a shrinking oven, tunnel or frame with heated air or gas flame. Although shrink-wrap offers an excellent degree of safety for transport and against theft, thanks to its strength, has the advantage of being transparent and can be used universally (advertising, barcode, presentation, protection against dust and moisture), its market share against stretch film is decreasing. This, in comparison to stretch film, is due to:

- high cost – shrinking film per pallet load is €1.10 to €1.30;
- large amount of waste, high disposal costs (approximately 500 to 1000 g/load unit);
- energy costs of approximately €0.30 / pallet load (approximately 2.6 KWh/load unit);
- large space requirements;
- time intensive.

It is used mostly for pallets with heavy, stackable goods or for small and light goods (Figure 3.16). Pallet load units can be rendered watertight by covers, such as for outdoor storage (possible condensation). It is also worth considering whether the packaged goods can be heated up and whether they might get fused to the shrink wrap, examples being film bags or plastic sacks (the solution here would be to powder the packaged goods).

If load units are only shrunk every now and again, the use of film covers and manually operated hot air devices can be used to shrink.

3.3.4.4 Stretching

There are two ways of stretching: stretch wrap and stretch hoods.

Stretch wrap process The pallet load is placed on a turntable and wrapping itself is a one-layered film wrap from a film roll. This film roll (500, 750 and 1,000 mm wide) moves upwards as a column so that a spiral wrapping motion is created.

Figure 3.16 Shrinking process of a small package, film thickness 15–25 μ, heating time approximately 10 minutes, temperature approximately 150 °C

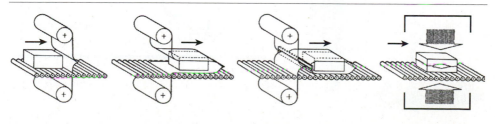

A distinction should be made between:

- The stretching of film without pre-stretching occurs exclusively through the pull of the rotation of the pallet load on the turntable, whereby the film roll is slowed down (Figure 3.19). The width of the film decreases.

- The stretching and lengthening of the film is independent of the pallet load turning and occurs through a frame with two rolls turning at different speeds – this is the pre-stretching. This can be up to 200 per cent and then the film is wrapped around the packaged goods without stretch. The film width is maintained.

Load safety occurs through the restorative forces of the film with a residual tension of less than 30 per cent. The upper half of the load is more wrapped than the bottom. Features of the stretch wrap process:

- not heating the packaged goods, which means no impact on quality;

- negligible energy costs;

- film costs are less than for shrinking: stretch wrap 17–23 μm film strength, for 1.80 m high pallet load as well as 3 foot and two heat wraps with 50 per cent overlap, approximately €0.50, little waste per usage approximately 200–250 g;

- little space requirements, damage and theft protection less than with shrinking;

- high package performance: 60 to 80 pallet units/h.

The disadvantages include:

- limited transparency with milky film (hard to read barcode);

- hand film is manually wrapped around the load unit (pre-stretched foil);

Figure 3.17   a) Load safety with stretch film: pallet load via hand pallet truck on stationary turntable, film roll on column. b) Self-driving stretch wrap machine v = 1.4 m/s, film approx. 17–23μ, pre-stretching 150/200/300% (www.packen-wir-es-ein.de)

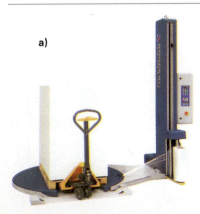

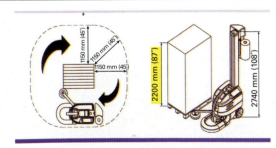

Figure 3.17 (*Continued*)   c) Process for the stretch cover method: once the film hood has been stretched and fastened over the bars, the film sleeve is measured for the height of the stack and sealed closed. The film sleeve is stretched at the four corners with the help of the bars, and slipped over the load while simultaneously being stretched vertically (biaxial stretch). Finally, the bottom stretch is created (www.beumer.com)

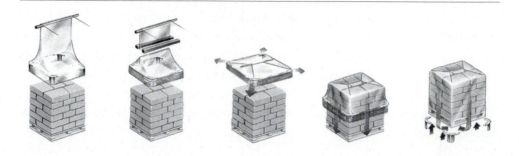

- stretching without turntable: satellite stretch method (see Example 3.6);
- sample calculation and comparison waste amount and costs of stretch film (see Example 3.9).

Stretch cover method   A film sleeve with side folds is stretched and slipped over the load unit, as in Figure 3.17c.

Features of the stretch cover method include:

- no heating of packaged goods or film, so no adverse impact on quality;
- negligible energy costs;
- little space required;
- low film costs compared with shrinking (approximately €0.70/pallet load);
- stretch sleeves 60 to 150 μm film strength, sleeves cost around €0.50 for pallet load height of 1.80 m;
- small quantity of waste, use approximately 300 to 700 g;
- damage and theft protection higher than for stretch wrap method;
- film cover safety higher than stretch wrap method;
- waterproof;
- high packaging performance: up to 170 load units/h;
- 30 per cent less film used compared to stretch wrap method;
- anti-theft protection;
- accurate cost calculation through exact film usage;
- clear, transparent film, enables product presentation.

3.3.5 Pallet-free load unit

The advantage of palletized goods lies in the easy pick-up, transport and delivery of a unit with the help of forklift trucks. Disadvantages are the cost of loading aids, the return of empties and the space required for empty pallets, especially when transporting overseas.

In order to reduce or eliminate these disadvantages, pallet-free load units with ground clearance were developed with shrink film. The last layer is built – either in the palletizer or by hand – so that recesses on the right and left layer edge are created for fork pick-up. Immediately after the shrinking process, a fork gap is created in the shrink film and the unit turned 180°, so that the forklift can get under and pick up the unit. By using an additional shrink cover, the pallet-free unit with ground clearance can also be made waterproof. Depending on the good, it can be stackable without equipment.

3.3.6 Load assembly and safety

The creation of load units, just like the structure of the load in a lorry, container or rail carriage, is always carried out with the aim of having as little loss in volume as possible. This is possibly through matching unit measurement to the loading area of the transport vehicle.

Based on the prerequisite that the loading area's dimensions are fine to take the weight of the load and the weight of the trucks required for loading (or unloading), a stowage plan (stowage pattern, loading concept, loading list) is drawn up to distribute weight evenly. The stowage plan for motor vehicles with a trailer usually assumes side loading (see Chapter 7.3.2). The location of a load unit, in cases where the load is not of single-origin, has to be determined accurately for unloading. This is important for JIT delivery, for keeping to a certain order when unloading, for the unloading side and in case of a tight unloading window. The unloading is carried out by forklift trucks, equipped with a telescopic or long fork. With regard to the Euro-Pallet, the stowage pattern for a width of 2.45 m to 2.50 m in lorries, containers or rail carriage is either three pallets lengthwise (3 × 0.8 m = 2.4 m) or two pallets across (2 × 1.2 m = 2.4 m).

For lorry loading, the following pallet numbers apply for Euro-Pallets (Figure 3.18 a to d) and for loading frames (Figure 3.18 e):

- Motor vehicle, loading area of 7 m in length:
  - Loaded cross-wise: 16 pallets (17 if pallets 15 + 16 are stowed lengthwise).
  - Loaded lengthwise: 17 pallets.
  - Mixed stowage: 14 pallets.
  - Articulated lorry: 33 pallets (platform length 13.6 m).

Figure 3.18   Stowage pattern of DIN pallet loads on lorries

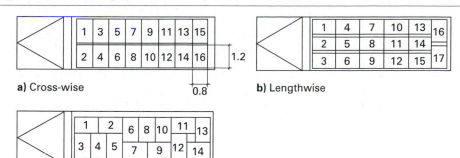

a) Cross-wise

b) Lengthwise

c) Mixed stowage

d) Articulated lorry

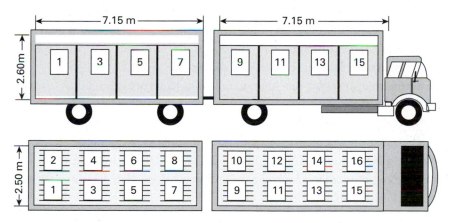

e) DIN pallet loads in lorries

The entire length of an articulated lorry with trailer is 16.5 m. The maximum vehicle height is 4 m, the height of pallets and load up to 3 m, the additional load is 22.5 t.

For load and transport safety, one has to distinguish:

- Force-locking safety mechanism: friction that can be increased through suitable surfaces and/or through pressure using lashing straps, ropes and chains.

- Interlocking safety mechanism: Front and side panels, support posts, chocks, gap-free stowage through foamed material, air cushions and frames (see Figure 3.19 a to c).

Figure 3.19 Load safety mechanisms for transport goods in a container

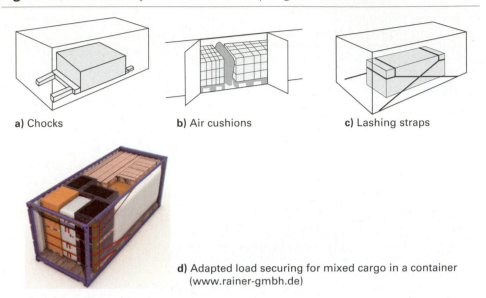

a) Chocks   b) Air cushions   c) Lashing straps

d) Adapted load securing for mixed cargo in a container
(www.rainer-gmbh.de)

If neither the load units nor the lorry have lashing straps, or if the load is heavy (stone slabs, large crates), head lashing with two loops and anti-slip mats are required as well as two straps for lashing (Figure 3.19 d); $\alpha = 20 - 65°$; $\beta = 6 - 55°$.

Fully automated strapping machines are utilized to secure other units, from boxes to large cartons.

Loading and unloading a lorry can be carried out manually, mechanized or auto-mated, depending on whether it is side or back loading (see Chapter 7.3.3, Loading and unloading times for load units; Figure 2.28). Usually, a loading ramp is used for back loading, but loading from the ground for side loading is also suitable, if no loading ramp is available.

3.4 Planning of packaging and creation of load units

Before it is possible to start the proper planning of packaging or the creation of load units, the transport aids and/or loading aids have to be determined. When searching for a suitable transport or loading aid, a number of questions have to be analysed and answered, such as:

- What *features* are required for the transport aid (open, closed, air, water or odour tight, dismountable, stackable or multi-use)?

- What *material* must the transport aid be made of (paper, wood, cardboard, metal, textile or plastic)?

- What should the *type and measurements* of the transport aid be (container, pallet; DIN measurements, loading weight, loading height or container volume)?

- How will the transport aid *fit into* the means of transport (lengthwise, cross-wise, from both sides, from the top or from the bottom)?

- What *environmental influences* will the transport aid be subject to (temperature, moisture levels, dust or weather)?

- Does the transport aid need *cleaning* (disinfection in hospital, food processing facility, pharmaceutical industry)?

These days, the planning of packaging and the creation of load units is increasingly carried out by computer. Expert systems, for instance, help make choices for packaging materials – with simulation programs testing features as well as transport and storage demands on packages. The creation of load unit, package design and optimization of load units as well as transport safety mechanisms are determined and decided by using relevant software programs (see Example 3.10).

3.5 VDI guidelines, DIN standards

VDI	2415	04.96	Handling pallets with industrial trucks
	2698	03.95	Storage and transport of coils
	2700	00.04	Load safety in road vehicles

DIN	536–1	09.91	Crane rails; Form A (with foot flange); measurements
	1301–1	10.10	Units, unit names, unit symbols
	1304–1	03.94	General formula symbols
	15 147	08.01	Wooden flat pallets; quality conditions
	15 190–101	04.91	Freight containers, inland containers, nominal sizes

3.6 Examples and questions

Example 3.1: Pallet designs

A pallet is a platform with ground clearance for a variety of general cargo. It can turn non-stackable goods into stackable goods by use of collars or frames and, by use of mountable side panels, it can take loose cargo or protect the goods – as a mesh box pallet – and make it stackable. What are the different designs a pallet can have?

Answer: The pallet can be made of different materials (see Chapter 3.1.4.2) as a two-way or four-way design and have different shapes:

- with six or nine feet stackable into one another (mostly made of particle board, plastic or steel sheet);
- with continuous runners or joists and blocks (usually of wood or steel sheet), the fixed runners/joists lengthwise or crosswise on the underside of the platform play a very significant role for transport with continuous conveyors and for the pick-up by forklift trucks.

Hence, the choice of transport aids depends on the cargo goods: type, build and design of a pallet, material, storage method and access opening for forklift need to be considered.

Example 3.2: Container management

What do we mean by container management and what goals does it pursue?

Answer: Container management (load carrier) is a concept that administers, organizes and finances the great variety of loading aids in a company to achieve:

- transparency of the container cycles;
- discovery of optimization potential;
- reduction of container stock and loss;
- increase in availability and plan ability, usage-based invoicing.

This results in these tasks for a container management system:

- container analysis including type, name, ID number, material, maximum additional load, measurements, stock, stackable when loaded/unloaded, price and other features;
- container control, computer support, container identification, such as RFID;
- deployment in procurement logistics: outsourcing of container management;
- container invoicing, organizational container management;
- matching product to loading aid type.

In practice, container management is responsible for the organization, administration and provision of loading aids. A number of service providers offer the function of container management and work in line with the system shown in Figure 3.22.

Example 3.3: Creation of load units

What factors should be considered when planning a load unit holistically and what principles should be utilized?

Answer: Based on the questions asked in Chapter 3.4, the following, often interrelated, factors appear to influence the creation of a load unit:

- *Cargo, handling, features*: see Figure 3.2 (Differentiation: General cargo and bulk).
- *Deployment condition:*
  - weight limitations: ceiling load capacity, lift load capacity, stacking height, type of means of transport;
  - building restrictions: lift measurements, gate access, corridor width, room height, column distance, type of ramp and loading gates;
  - environment: temperature, moisture, internal/external deployment, noise, fumes and lighting;
  - internal and external transport, handling at destination.
- *Transport aid type* (loading aids): see Figure 3.5.
- *Costs of:*
  - means of transport, transport aids;
  - packaging, transport safety mechanisms;
  - time;
  - personnel;
  - space requirements;
  - transport.

Principles:

- low creation costs;
- quick and simple manufacture;
- simple identification;
- maximum space usage;
- simple operation and transport;
- stackable;
- pallet-free transport unit;
- secure against transport and storage demands;
- little maintenance of equipment;
- low weight;
- optimal (standardized) measurements;
- exchangeable, reusable transport aids;
- high protection against theft and optimal protection against damage.

Example 3.4: Loading aids

What features can be used to distinguish loading aids?

Answer: They can be distinguished as follows:

- ground clearance: direction, as in two-way and four-way pallets;
- size: small load carrier and large load carrier;
- form stability: stable like pallets and containers, or unstable like sacks and nets;
- design: carrying, enclosing and closed;
- material: wood, plastic, steel; function: rigid, nested and stackable;
- standardization: standard and non-standard.

Example 3.5: Packaging with boxes/types of boxes

What types of boxes are there and what has to be considered when packaging goods in boxes?

Answer: Boxes (or cartons) come in many varieties: folding boxes, chute boxes, trays and assembly boxes with lid such as telescope box or without lid, made of one piece, to set up with or without floor bonding with tape. Another way to distinguish between them is through material thickness: single or double wall cardboard. In order to save space for transport and storage, boxes are delivered folded up.

Task and function of packaging: see Figure 3.7. A box should ideally fit on a loading aid in a modular manner. A telescope box ensures quick closure, prevents anyone reaching in (theft) and must be picked up by palletizing robots with automatic suction cups: expensive, only feasible for large quantities.

Example 3.6: Stretch film wrapper

How is a load unit secured with stretch film without using a turntable?

Answer:

a) By using the satellite stretch method.

An articulated arm, which can circle the ground freely, is fixed on a wall, column or stand. Without losing the width, the film is pre-stretched up to 400 per cent in a frame and then wrapped, tension-free, around the package, usually a pallet. If the wrapping machine is not used, the work surface is empty, as there is no turntable or ramps. The elastic properties of the film ensure that the load unit retains a stable form, for heavy or light goods (see Figure 3.20).

b) By using an automated film wrapper for ensuring a pallet will transport safely with stretch film. The wrapper can be integrated into a roller conveyor on the transport path (see Figure 3.17b).

Figure 3.20   Stretch film wrapping in line with satellite method

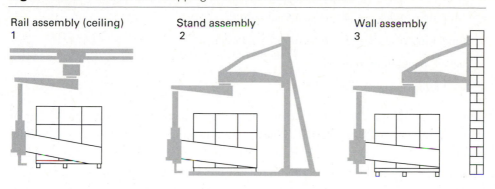

Example 3.7: Pallet pool system

What is the procedure for a pallet pool system?

Answer: The procedure is: empty pallets storage pool; empty pallets delivery; full pallets transport; handover industry/trade; empty pallet pick up, transport to storage pool. The only chargeable time is the time of use: quick loading and unloading (Figure 3.22).

Example 3.8: One-off and multi-use systems

What is a one-off and a multi-use (packaging) system? What are the relevant processes and what tasks are taken over by the pool?

Answer: Packaging regulations are about *prevention, reduction, recycling* and *re-use* of packaging. Reduction of packaging consists of reduced use of materials. This is usually possible if the packaging is larger than required. If material thickness is reduced, such as for cardboard, to below the required thickness for transport safety, the loss of stability can only be compensated for by constructive measures, which often results in increased packaging costs.

Recycling of packaging for one-off packaging can be achieved by only using homogeneous materials, or by replacing non-recyclable materials. An example of the former option is the use of cardboard made of corrugated cardboard, produced without closing agents such as glue, tape or staples. The latter can see film or polystyrene replaced by corrugated cardboard. *One-off packaging* is packaging that is used only once, and has the advantage of not requiring the return of empties. For the manufacture and use of one-off packaging, the following procedure applies:

- production of raw material;
- production of packaging material (corrugated cardboard);
- manufacture of means of packaging (box ≙ one-off packaging);

- packaging of goods in one-off packaging;
- shipping of package ($\triangleq$ one-off packaging);
- unpacking of package from one-off packaging;
- recycle packaging materials;
- production of raw materials.

Re-use of packaging consists of the multiple, repeated use of the same packaging or transport aid in a *multi-use system*. This has the advantages of reducing raw materials, energy and waste. Packaging has to be picked up from the recipient, has to be sorted according to type and size, cleaned and reconditioned. Following storage, there will be further transport to another recipient. In order to be aware of how much packaging is available where and in what condition, relevant bookkeeping of the multi-use packaging is required. All the costs can decrease or use up the entire cost advantage of re-use.

There are two systems for multi-use packaging:

- a *closed* or *self-operated system*;
- an *open* or service-*operated multi-use system*.

With a closed-cycle system, the crate, container, special pallet or load carrier only moves between the sender and the recipient, such as between the supplier and the automobile factory (Figure 3.21). There is a difference between step-by-step exchange systems and exchange systems with a reservation period.

In an open-cycle system, the packaging (crate, container) will always have a new sender or recipient, because the packaging (loading aid) is taken from a pool. The returns management (returns logistics) is tasked with administering, retrieving, sorting, cleaning, storing, delivering and, if necessary, disposing of the multi-use packaging (Figure 3.22).

If applied in the following combinations, multi-use packaging can be seen as economic:

- industrial plant to industrial plant;
- industrial plant to wholesale;
- industrial plant/wholesale to retail trade.

Figure 3.21 Self-operated multi-use system (closed multi-use cycle)

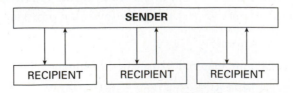

Figure 3.22   Service-operated multi-use system (open multi-use-cycle system): Cycle
of a pallet in the pallet pool system (www.chep.com)
Pool tasks: retrieval, de-label, clean, check, store, possibly dispose of,
bookkeeping

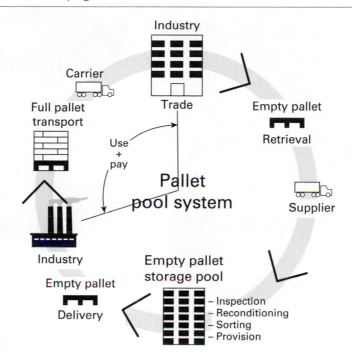

There are a number of different multi-use packaging systems between service providers and manufacturing/trade businesses as goods recipients for full and empty goods.

In comparison with a cardboard folding box, a plastic container has the advantages of robustness, sealing options, significantly higher circulation – and resulting prevention of packaging waste – and time saving for repackaging. Multi-use containers have a hinged lid, smooth walls (Figure 3.23), can be stacked inside one another when empty and can be stacked on top of the lid when full (multi-functional container).

There are pallet pool systems for DIN pallets, specifically, in which only the time of use is charged, from taking over of the pallet until this is no longer required by the customer (industry/trade, Figure 3.23b). This system has short usage time, modest costs for the users, and higher capacity use of the pallets – which, in turn, means a smaller number of pallets in the pallet pool.

Figure 3.23a   Multi-use container, small load carrier with hinged lid. Below: individual. Above: stacked in empty and full state (www.bito.com)

Figure 3.23b   Multi-use container, large load carrier in empty state and open (www.auerdirect.de)

Figure 3.24   Modular structured load unit with large load carrier container on DIN pallet, 800 × 1200 with cover (strapping in mid-section guiding slots) (www.ssi-schaefer.com)

Example 3.9: Stretch film: waste calculation, costs, comparison

What is the amount of waste and what are the costs for DIN pallet transport safety with different stretch films, and how can the cost comparison between stretch and shrink film be calculated? The load on the DIN pallet (800 × 1200 mm) is 1.65 m high. Normal stretch films are between 0.017 and 0.023 mm thick, pre-stretched films are between 0.008 and 0.011 mm, whereas shrink film is between 0.08 and 0.150 mm thick.

Answer: We assume 11 wraps for transport safety.

a) With normal stretch film (0.017 mm) and 0 per cent pre-stretch with a film width of 0.5 m and a price of €1.20/kg (prices can vary significantly: up to €1.80/kg the method for calculation is decisive here), and a film density of 920 kg/m³, the required film weight FW is to be calculated as follows:

FW = film thickness × film density × film length × film width

Film length: $(1.2 + 0.8) \times 2 \times 11 = 44$ m

Film weight FW: 17×10^{-6} m × 0.5 m × 44 m × 920 kg/m³ = 0.344 kg

Costs are: 0.344 kg × €1.20/kg = €0.41

Result: Securing 1 pallet load with **normal stretch film** costs **€0.41**.

b) In reality, the film is stretched by around. 30% (to 130%), ie instead of 0.344 kg only 0.344:1.30 = 0.265 kg are required. This results in a median film thickness for the pallet load of: 0.265 : (0.92 × 44 × 0.5) = 0.0131 mm

Result: To secure 1 pallet load with **pre-stretched film (30%)** only costs 0.265 kg × €1.20/kg = **€0.32**.

c) By using pre-stretched film of 0.008 mm thickness the film weight per pallet is: 0.008 × 0.92 × 44 × 0.5 = 0.162 kg

The stretch is now 10% (110%), so the real weight is: 0.162 : 1.10 = 0.147 kg/pallet.

The costs (price for pre-stretched film: € 1.87/kg): 0.147 kg/ pallet × €1.87/kg film = €0.27.

Result: Securing 1 pallet load with **pre-stretched film (10%)** costs **€0.27**.

d) What percentage saving is achieved by pre-stretching to 30% in comparison with the normal film?

The saving is: (0.32 × 100) : 0.41 = 78%, ie **22% cost reduction**.

What percentage saving is achieved by pre-stretching to 10% in comparison with the normal film?

The saving is: (0.275 × 100) : 0.41 = 67%, ie **33% cost reduction**.

What percentage saving is achieved by pre-stretching to 10% in comparison with pre-stretch film (30%)?

The saving is: $(0.275 \times 100) : 0.32 = 0.86$, ie **14% cost reduction**.

The ratio of shrink film to stretch film can be determined through the film thickness.

Example 3.10: Computer-aided optimization of stowage space and packaging

What are the advantages of computer-aided optimization of stowage space and packaging with heterogeneous goods, and how can a pallet load be automatically created?

Answer: See Figure 3.25. With a modular software program, it is possible to determine stowage plans for optimizing the stowage of heterogeneous goods (pallets, barrels, boxes etc) in a lorry or container by taking into account related problems. In doing so, loading time can be shortened and load safety increased, packaging volume and material minimized, layer patterns for pallets and mixed pallets can be generated and optimized – so costs can be saved. The automatic generation of a mixed pallet can be carried out with an articulated arm or a portal robot (Figure 3.26).

Figure 3.25   *Multimix* stowage plan editor: interactive insertion of packaged goods (www. multiscience.com)

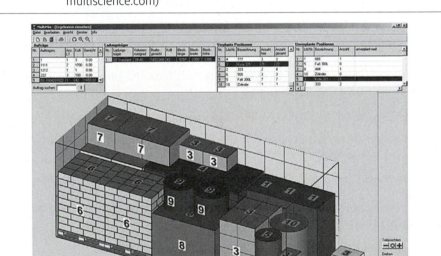

Figure 3.26 Generating a pallet load (*Multipack*). a) Using an articulated arm.
b) Using a portal robot (www.multiscience.com)

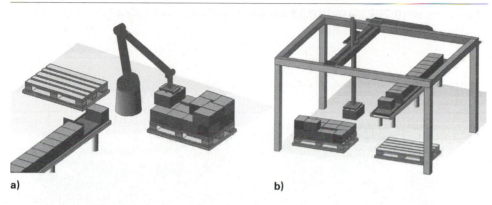

a)   b)

Example 3.11: Coding system for packaging

What are inkjet coders used for? What inkjet technology is there?

Answer: Inkjet coders can label products and packaging and can be put on cardboard, trays, sacks and film. We distinguish between thermal (HP ink cartridge technology) and pierzo-electrical (Pierzo technology) inkjet methods.

Figure 3.27 Left: Labelling packaging with ink. Right: Printing or labelling two adjacent
sides of a pallet while resting or moving (around 7 pallets/minute) using a
swivel arm (www.bluhmsysteme.com)

Example 3.12: Layer palletizer

Describe an automated layer palletizer, depalletizer or repalletizer.

Answer: Figure 3.28 shows a palletizer, whose automation is achieved with the following components: robot; vacuum-multifunction-grabber; conveyor technology for feeding and removal; control technology. The grab action is based on vacuum suckers and chambers as well as additional mechanic grab support. Cardboard boxes, bottles, tins, glasses, trays and sacks can all be palletized in this way. The measurements go up to 1,600 × 1,400 × 1,000 mm, the product height from 50 mm to 500 mm at a layer weight of up to 300 kg. The maximum performance of the machine is 300 layers per hour.

Figure 3.28 a) Layer-wise palletizing of trays with different items. b) Layer pallet (www.schmalz.com)

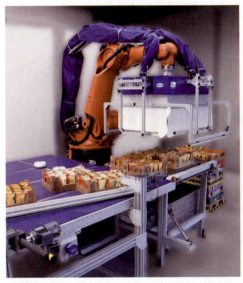
a)

b)

Example 3.13: Load safety on a lorry

What mass forces are impacting on a load during different driving manoeuvres?

Answer: According to VDI guidelines 2700: see Figure 3.29; F_G = weight load = $m \times g$. For goods prone to tipping over, the ratio of mass forces, acting transversely to travel direction, increases to 70 per cent of the weight load (see Figure 3.19).

Forces during brake manoeuvres have to be absorbed at the front wall via the friction between loaded goods and the loading area, whereby friction Friction = $\mu \times F_G$ and for braking = $0.8 \times F_G$.

For chipboard floors with artificial raisin and wooden Euro-pallet: $\mu \approx 0.2$ to 0.25. The load weight should be 22 t, then $F_G \approx 22 \times 10 = 220$ KN. The friction $F_{Friction} = 0.2 \times 220 = 44$ KN.

The safety force $F_S = 0.8 \times F_G - F_R = 0.8 \times 220 - 44 = 132$ KN.

Figure 3.29 a) Forces that need to be considered for load safety when driving (VDI 2700). b) Load safety for heavy goods by using lashing straps (www.zurrpack.eu)

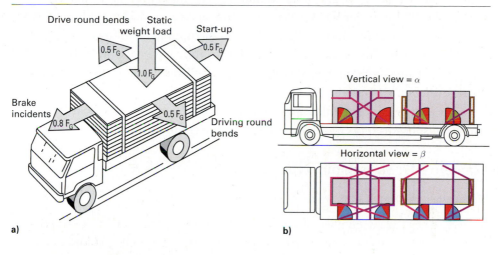

Example 3.14: Slip-sheet method

What does the slip-sheet method look like, what is it for and what are the method's advantages?

Answer: The method's components are: forklift truck; push–pull attachment; slip sheet.

The slip-sheet is a pull pallet of approximately 1 mm thickness with the load weight of a DIN pallet. It consists of waterproof, tear-resistant and fully recyclable strong liners (weight of up to 2.5 t) and, depending on design, costs between €0.80 and €2.00. The push–pull attachment of the truck serves to pull off, put down, pull up or push off the pallet.

Using a slip-sheet as pallet-free transport aid is suitable for long transport journeys (overseas), where a return is not feasible for economic reasons. The slip-sheet's advantages are better space utilization of the container, lower load weight (freight cost saving), no maintenance costs and modest storage space requirements (1,000 slip sheets take up 1 m³).

Example 3.15: Export shipping of packages

What are the problems that can occur due to changes in climate when shipping packages on lorries, ships or rail in a container? What precautions can be taken?

Answer: When transporting through different climate zones, but also due to differences in temperature from day to night, temperatures can go below dew point and condensation can occur. This can lead to corrosion damage and/or mould. Preventative measures are plastic covers over metal parts or the use of drying agents.

Example 3.16: Pallet checks

Why are pallet checks necessary and what needs to be checked?

Answer: Defective or damaged pallets can cause accidents, delays, additional work and machine downtime. In fact, 70 per cent of disruptions in automated high rack shelving are due to unusable pallets. In order to fully eliminate the economic and safety risk, pallets for automated storage layers and mechanic transport machines undergo checks.

These checks concern pallet measurements, cover and running board damage, visible nails, headroom, chocks as well as cleanliness on the outside.

Example 3.17: Stretch film types

What types of stretch film are there and what are their features?

Answer: There are a number of different film types on the market, with different features such as transparent, adhesive on the inside, smooth outside, coloured, printed, pre-stretched, anti-static, UV-stabilizing, food-safe.

Example 3.18: Container designs

What are the standard and special containers used by industry?

Answer: Containers are deployed in all areas of the economy and industry for storage and transport tasks, in agriculture, on building sites or with special functions, such as for energy production. Designs include: standard containers for general and bulk cargo; thermal containers (also called Reefer, a cooling container); special containers such as open top containers, platform containers, flat and tank containers.

- Open top containers are used especially for tall general cargo that has to be transported by crane during loading and unloading.

- Flat containers (DIN 668 / 20 foot) have folding as well as fixed side panels.

- Platform containers (20 foot) are used for a variety of transport goods that are extra-long, extra-wide or extra high.

Example 3.19: Container labelling

What is important when labelling containers?

Answer: Depending on shape, material and size (Eurobox, small load carriers, large load carriers, plastic crates, mesh boxes etc), there are different ways of affixing labels for Kanban cards (Figure 2.14), shipping papers or container identification. Fixing methods are self-adhesive or magnetic for hanging clear pockets, covers of all kinds, label and receipt pockets. Often, containers already have card pockets. We can distinguish between temporary, flexible or permanent labels (Figures 3.30, 3.31 and 3.32 a–c).

Figure 3.30   Clear pockets on different containers (www.orgatex.com)

Figure 3.31   Pushing a Kanban card into a self-adhesive label pocket (www.orgatex.com)

Figure 3.32   Labels on a variety of equipment (www.orgatex.com). a) Affixing a pallet-brace. b) and c) Storage spot labels

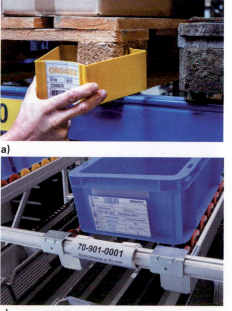

a)

b)

c)

Example 3.20: Components of an automated handling system

What are the main components of a handling system?

Answer: The main components are:

- structural design of goods in and goods out or relevant means of handling (see Chapter 7.3);

- loading and unloading system (see Figure 7.9; Figure 3.33);

- lorry and trailer system;

- load safety (see Example 3.13, Figure 3.34).

Figure 3.33   Loading an assembled pallet load using a conveyor carpet (www.westfaliaEurope.com)

Figure 3.34   Securing an assembled paper roll load with adjusted safety elements (www.westfaliaEurope.com)

Questions

1   What are the criteria to classify bulk cargo?

2   How can general cargo be divided up?

3   What is a small load carrier?

4   How can loading aids with bottom clearance be classified?

5   What are loading frames? What are platforms?

6   Which containers match Euro-Pallet measurements?

7   What does packaging consist of?

8   What functions are fulfilled by packaging, and by packaging regulations?

9   How can transport, sales and repackaging be defined?

10   Explain the difference between the tipping system and the exchange system.

11 What means of transport are used for roll-off containers and skip trailers?

12 What are the advantages of creating a load unit, and what are the disadvantages?

13 What is palletizing, packaging pattern and stacking pattern?

14 Sketch out the method of load creation.

15 What different types of palletizing machines are there?

16 What are the different load securing measures for pallets?

17 What are the advantages and disadvantages of shrinking and painting?

18 What planning data is required for determining transport aids for the internal material flow?

19 What is an open multi-use packaging system?

20 What are the advantages of computer-aided stowage space optimization?

21 What is container management and what goals are pursued by its use?

22 What mass forces impact on a load during different driving actions?

Transport logistics basics
04

4.1 Internal transport

The primary task of internal transport is to bridge the distances between transport origin, the source and the transport destination, the so-called sink. Bridging the distances equals the transport function (synonymous with conveying for this purpose) as logistics function of the material flow (see Chapter 2.1).

Transport can be carried out horizontally, sloping or vertically. Transport processes also include the logistics functions of stacking, handling, handing over, taking in, passing on, distributing, collating, sorting and picking. As transport does not provide any value added to the transport goods, but rather adds expenses, the transport goods should, ideally, be subject to a work process during transport – for example: warming, cooling, moistening, drying, mixing, painting, assembling.

Transport can be carried out by people, manned technology (hand pallet trucks) or automated processes (FTS). The transport quantity is described as volume stream ($\dot{V}$), mass stream ($\dot{m}$) and/or cargo stream ($\dot{m}_{St}$) by the transport good stream (see Chapter 2.3.2).

4.2 Transport logistics

Transport logistics is the holistic view of all procedures and information channels that are required for a transport process. This is the interaction between (Figure 4.1):

- administration, personnel management, transport, vehicle administration;
- disposition, transport strategies, transport management;
- operations, transport technology, data transmission technology.

It is transport logistics' task to distribute and provide goods within the internal production processes at the lowest cost possible. Due to more efficient utilization of transport capacities, transport costs will decrease when the value per

Figure 4.1 Operational transport logistics building blocks

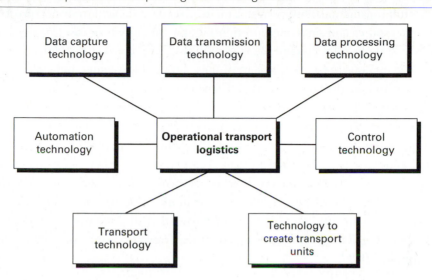

weigh or the value per volume unit increases. Transport logistics aims to optimize transport with regard to loading, unloading, capacity utilization, handover and identification.

4.3 Transport system, transport technology, transport chain

A system consists of elements that are related to each other and their environment. Thus, a transport system (Figure 4.2) consists of the components transport unit (Chapter 3.3), transport technology (Chapter 4.4) and transport organization (Chapter 13).

Figure 4.2 Transport system components

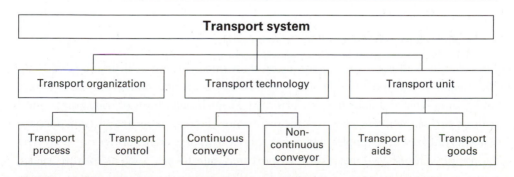

A *transport system* can consist of the same or different means of transport, which together fulfil an internal transport task. This involves describing the transport procedure mentioning source and sink, transport time and the quantity flow (see Chapter 2.3.2). Transport systems fulfil tasks of the material flow. They connect functionally related areas, link manufacturing and assembly sites, help with loading and unloading in production and are the interface between procurement depots and production.

The *transport process* contains the performance demands for each transport task.

A *transport chain* is an order of transport processes, matched and connected based on technical and organizational aspects, from an external source to an internal sink and vice versa. The transport chain can be structured on one or on multiple tiers. In a one-tier structure, the transport occurs without a change in means of transport. A multi-tiered structure includes one or more changes in means of transport. As long as the transport unit is maintained during a change in means of transport, it is called *combined traffic* (for more on container transport with ship, rail and lorry, see Example 7.9).

4.4 Internal means of transport

Means of transport help implement the logistical functions of transporting, handling, stacking, storing and picking. They can be structured according to a number of characteristics and criteria:

- power type;
- load capacity;
- transport area (line, surface, room);
- transport good (general cargo, bulk);
- transport direction (horizontal, sloping, vertical);
- mobility (fixed location, guided, free);
- degree of mechanization (manual, mechanized, automated);
- work principle (continuous, non-continuous);
- transport level (floor, underfloor, above floor).

However, it is also possible to use more than one criterion at a time to divide up the means of transport (see Figure 4.3). The terms ground-bound and floor-based, and ground-free and floor-free, are identical. Floor-based means of transport require a floor surface whereas floor-free means do not. Floor-free means of transport are usually rail-based, examples being circular conveyors, crane bridges and electric monorails. Floor-based means of transport may be rail-free, such as forklift trucks, roller conveyors, tractors, or they can be rail-based, such as portal cranes, storage

Figure 4.3   Classification of means of transport

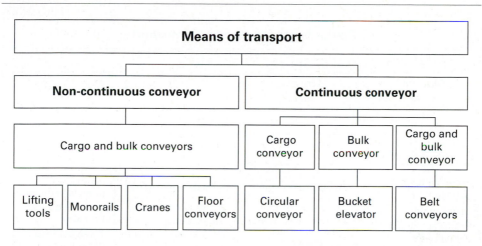

and retrieval systems and transfer cars. Based on the different operating techniques, a driverless transport system can be rail-based or rail-free (see Chapter 6.7).

4.5 Power types

The power type describes a certain type of energy conversion, to create motion energy for the means of transport. The term 'power' also encompasses its modules, such as motor (energy converter), gears, transmission elements and controls. There is a distinction between manual drive, gravity drive and motor drive (Figure 4.4). The transport motion occurs through force or friction via tyres, wheels, belts or form circuits, examples such as chains, gears or carrier.

4.5.1 Manual drive

Features: for non-continuous conveyors only is power for travel and lift motions created manually by the operator via shaft or fixed handle. Pulling or pushing together with additional steering is used for hand pallet trucks, carts, wagons, lifting rollers, etc. These are suitable for short distances with light loads, without significant gradients, on good ground and for low frequencies. Manual drive is not applicable to continuous conveyors.

4.5.2 Gravity drive

Features: only available for continuous conveyors, such as roller conveyors, wheel conveyors, chutes and in warehousing technology for continuous shelves; cheapest

Figure 4.4   Structure of power types for means of transport

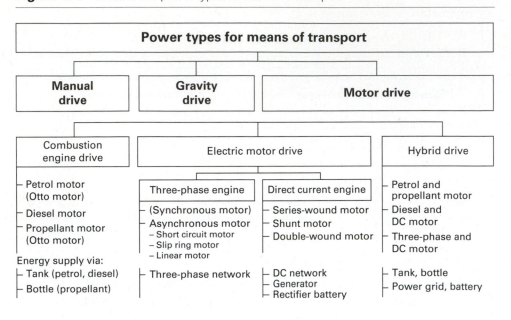

energy type; not used in automated plants as it is difficult to reach a constant speed with continuous acceleration.

4.5.3 Combustion drive

Combustion engines transform the warmth created by the burning of a fuel within a cylinder into mechanical energy. Fuels are petrol, diesel and propellants (butane, propane) that come in liquid form and store a great deal of energy at low volume. As a result of their compact build, combustion engines have a high performance weight but a short lifespan in comparison with the electric motor (operating hours ratio 5,000 to 10,000 h).

Designs include:

- petrol (Otto) engine and propellant motor as Otto engine;
- diesel engine.

For petrol engines, the gas/air mix is compressed to 7–10 bars and then ignited. The speeds are higher than for a diesel engine. The diesel engine is mainly applied in transport technology. Diesel fuel is added to the combustion chamber via an injection pump under high pressure and then it ignites itself independently as a result of the air that has been compressed to 50 bars and heated to 600°C.

Energy transmission can occur mechanically, hydro-dynamically or hydro-statically – mechanically through the type clutch and gears (high operational effort, many wear parts but simple and good effectiveness), hydro-dynamically through variable torque conversion (high build effort, expensive, bad effectiveness but best approximation of the demanded torque process) and hydro-statically power conversion (see Chapter 4.5.7).

Advantages of combustion engines are: fast operational readiness; high drive and lift performance; large driving range; good economy; can manage steep inclines; high drive power and transport performance; compact unit; large energy store; can be deployed outside in bad weather conditions.

Disadvantages are: low load-bearing capacity; load adjustment through gears; high operational efforts through mechanic power transmission; no direct reversibility; start-up only neutral; noise pollution; driver subject to bumpy rides; air pollution; hazardous fumes (not applicable to propellants); emission control through catalysts for Otto and propellant engines and through particle filters for diesel engines; only limited deployment in enclosed spaces.

4.5.4 Electromotive drive

Features: the electric motor is a machine for converting electrical work into mechanical. Three-phase and DC motors are used in transport technology.

4.5.4.1 Three-phase engines

Three-phase is a type of alternating current, created by a specific chain of their different alternating currents. They work with a tension of 400 (230) V and are deployed specifically in places where there are no great requirements for work speed regulation. A change in direction can be achieved by switching two stand connectors. Three-phase engines source electricity from the ubiquitous public grid (net frequency 50 Hz). Three-phase energy cannot be stored but can be transformed using a transformer.

Three-phase engines come as synchronous and asynchronous engines. For transport technology, only asynchronous engines play a role. There is a distinction between the *short-circuit*, *slip-ring* and *linear* engines. Asynchronous engines have approximately 5–10 per cent slippage compared to the synchronous engine speed. Synchronized torque:

$$n_s = \frac{60\,f}{p} = \frac{60 \times 50}{1} = 3000 \text{ min}^{-1} \tag{4.1}$$

f in [Hz]   net frequency
p pole pairs

Slippage s in %:

$$s = \frac{n_s - n}{n_s} \times 100 \tag{4.2}$$

For $s = 8\%$ and $p = 1$ equals $n = n_s - s \times n_s = 2760 \text{ min}^{-1}$

Pole-changeable engines are created by adding several; these engines have n_s = 3,000 – 1,500 – 1,000 – 750 min^{-1}.

- *Short-circuit engines*

The anchor has a short-circuit coil through which streams flow as a result of induction, which in connection with the stator's rotating field, create a torque. The engine is structured in a simple way (no slip rings, no brushes), is robust, low in maintenance, operationally safe, easy to control and good value. Disadvantages include the high start-up current (minimized by starting up with start delta switch) and no way to regulate the speed. Short-circuit engines are standard drives for continuous conveyors.

- *Slip-ring engine*

This has upstream resistance to the running circuit, which reduces the high start-up current, and also results in different start-up features. At nominal speed (series resistance zero) the engine has the features of a short-circuit engine. Through gradual switching of the engine's series resistance, a good torque adjustment in line with the start-up condition can be achieved. The engine contains slip-rings and brushes, is expensive and more sensitive than the short-circuit engine. It can be deployed in case of high gear changes, soft start-up and higher speed, making it suitable for lift machines.

- *Linear engine*

This has a special structure, in which the rotating field is replaced by an electro-magnetic field vertically along a guide track (rotor and stator have infinite diameters). A part of the engine shifts in a straight line in opposition to the other engine part as a result of the influence of electro-magnetic forces. This leads to a forward motion. The linear engine creates thrust and is, thus, suitable for driving devices. The engine does not require maintenance, has no mechanic parts, is wear-free, quiet, has a low effectiveness and low heat generation. It is becoming increasingly important.

4.5.4.2 Direct current engines

Direct currents that always flow in one direction cannot be transformed, but can be transported over long distances (with only little loss) and can be stored in chemical energy. Direct current engines work with 230 (460) V of tension and can control the work speed quite accurately. They source direct current from:

- A direct current net, which is fed by a direct current generator or a rectifier. The generator transforms mechanical into electric energy, the rectifier transforms alternate current into direct current.

- Directly from a direct current generator or rectifier belonging to a diesel-electric vehicle engine.

- From a battery that stores electric energy in the form of chemical energy.

Direct current engines are usually deployed in non-continuous conveyors. Depending on the coil placement, there is a distinction between series motors and shunt motors.

- *Series motor*

Anchor and field coil are placed behind one another. The motor has a high start-up torque, the speed is strongly dependent on the load. By pole-changing the anchor coil a reversal in the rotation direction can be achieved. Due to automatic speed adjustment to the respective load and due to the high start-up moment, the series motor is used in floor conveyors.

- *Shunt motor*

Rotor and stator coils are placed in parallel. The speed is relatively independent of load, it has a low start-up moment, but has sensitive speed regulators. It is used in lifts and shaft hosting systems, but also floor conveyors, although these are increasingly equipped with a frequency converter and alternate current motors.

4.5.4.3 Current supply

Current supplies for electric motors in non-continuous conveyors with limited motion, such as cranes, shelf operating systems and monorails, can be conductor lines or movable cables, which must fulfil VBG 8c safety regulations.

Conductor line designs include:

- *Wire conductor lines:* These consist of round copper wires that are supported by isolators approximately every 8 cm. The current collectors, made of rolls or contact strips, lift up the round wire from the isolators in the process.
- *Rail conductor lines*: These consist of fixed rails and are used especially for high vehicle performance and high driving speeds. The current collectors are spring-loaded. For compact conductor lines, rails are housed in a sheet metal or plastic casing (touch guard) in which runs the current collector trolley.

Flexible cable designs:

- *Trailing cable*: Often designed as flat cables, it is used for short and medium/long distances. The cable is supported via a cable trolley running in steel profiles with the cable clamped in its saddles and hanging down in loops.
- *Cable drum*: This is used for medium/long distances. The cables are wound on a drum, which is powered either by a spring or by an electric motor.
- Contactless energy transmission for electro-hydraulic brake systems (see Example 6.6–15), for driverless transport systems (see Example 6.7–10).
- Battery concept (see Figure 6.7.13).

4.5.5 Hybrid drive

This form of drive enables the changeover from one drive method to another, so is a combination of two different drive methods. The changeover happens without disruption to the drive, as it can change from electric battery drive inside to combustion engine drive outside. Another form of hybrid drive is the changeover from alternating current in the shelving aisle to direct current outside the shelving aisle.

4.5.6 Electrical battery drive unit

An electric battery drive is an electric motor fed by a battery. It would be more accurate to call it an electric battery drive unit. It consists of a battery as direct current supplier, the direct current motor, the gears, steering and accessories, such as a battery charger and a battery charging display.

There are *non-rechargeable* and *rechargeable* batteries, so-called accumulators. These can be divided into *starter batteries* to start up combustion engines and *drive batteries* to drive traction and lift engines. Starter batteries can also be used as drive batteries for lower performance.

A battery stores the electric energy as chemical energy. It delivers direct currents for floor conveyors without connection to the electric grid. The energy storing process is called charging and the energy transfer is called discharging. The battery cell is the battery's smallest enclosed energy-giving unit consisting of positive and negative electrode plates, micro-porous separators in between (the poles) and the electrolyte. The nominal voltage per cell is between 1.2 V and 2 V. Through the *series connection* of cells, the voltage increases, whereas the capacity grows through *parallel connection*.

The usual battery voltage is 24 V, 48 V and 80 V, and the capacity goes from 100 Ah to 1,000 Ah. As electrolyte (see Figure 4.5a), lead accumulators, with diluted sulphuric acid (2 V / cell) can be distinguished from alkaline batteries with diluted ammonia solution (1.2 V /cell).

Lead batteries can be found in mesh plate technology and in the prevalent armour plate technology (see Table 4.1). Mesh plate batteries are a good value option for easy usage, with an average lifespan of around 700 charge and discharge cycles.

Armour plate batteries are suitable for normal and heavy use. Their lifespan encompasses around 1,500 charge and discharge cycles. This, given a single shift operation and 300 charges per year, equals a lifetime of five years. Figure 4.5a displays current and future designs for lead batteries.

The *performance-enhanced* armour plate battery, with 25 per cent higher performance, is created through a different cell structure with more active mass and increased acid density.

Table 4.1   Battery type data

Battery type	Voltage [V]	Operating temp. [°C]	Energy density [Wh/kg]	Performance density [W/kg]	Effectiveness [%]
Lead acid	2.0	30	30	100	72
Alkali	1.2	30	40	90	70

Figure 4.5a   Division of drive batteries for floor conveyors

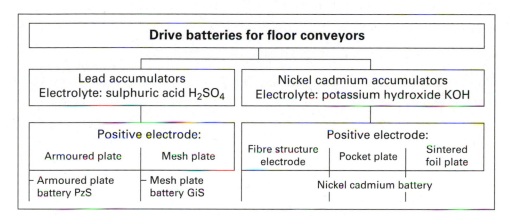

Figure 4.5b   Electrolyte circulation (www.hoppecke.com)

Batteries with *electrolyte circulation* (Figure 4.5b) guarantee an optimal mixing of electrolytes during charge and an even electrolyte density in the battery through ambient air being pumped into the lower part of the battery and rising air bubbles, which create a circular stream within the electrolyte.

This has the following advantages:

- shortened charge time: reduced to 6–8 hours instead of 8–12 hours;
- lower energy use: reduced to 12A/100 Ah instead of 20–25A/11Ah;
- lower temperature development when charged;
- less maintenance: after approximately 12 months or 200 charging cycles;
- higher life expectancy;
- for three shift operations: only two batteries required.

The chemical reactions in a lead-acid-battery follow the following equation for both charging and discharging:

$$Pb + PbO_2 + H_2SO_4 \text{ Discharge} \Rightarrow / \Leftarrow \text{ Charge } 2PbSO_4 + 2H_2O$$

Another prerequisite for a long battery cell lifespan is the regular provision of cleaned water to balance the water loss during the charging procedure. An automated solution is the water refill system, which requests the required water amount from a reservoir and which allows for the measurement of acid density. It prevents the electrolyte overflowing when the battery is refilled with water.

Since 2015, industrial trucks have been increasingly using lithium ion accumulators for powering electric motors (approximately 700 to 1,000 charging cycles, highly specific energy). These accumulators have no memory effect and can be charged with current less than the nominal current. They are sensitive to over and deep discharge.

For the use of floor conveyors in spaces where there is a danger of explosions, there is an *ex-protected* battery.

In this *maintenance-free* battery, the sulphuric acid is bound in a gel, so that there is no need to refill the battery, or to carry out other maintenance activities. Other *advantages* are:

- no electrolyte pollution of the environment;
- electrolyte checks are not necessary;
- charging stations are not separate;
- no obligatory ventilation, as no oxyhydrogen leaks.

These clean gel batteries require 20–40 per cent remaining capacity, have a lifespan of approximately 900 to 1,000 charges, a long charging duration of 11 to 14 hours and are only modestly resilient. The problem occurs when charging: heating up and the inability to discharge the heat quickly enough.

Nickel-cadmium batteries (NiCd batteries) are particularly useful in cycle operations, as they can be recharged continuously. approximately 25 per cent of the available time is lost to charging. Out of a capacity of 80 Ah, only around 25 per cent can be utilized, so 20 Ah. They are expensive and can only be used for small vehicles.

The DIN designation of an armour plate battery is 80 V 6 apb 600. So, this is an 80 V battery with six positive electrodes (lead plates) per cell. Apb stands for standard armour plate battery (mpb = mesh plate batteries). The nominal capacity is 600 Ah. The nominal capacity is the capacity during an uninterrupted five-hour discharge with contact discharge current, in this case 120 A per hour.

Batteries can be used for one or two shifts, with current research being carried out into three-shift deployment using interim charges. An armour-plated battery may not be discharged to under 20 per cent of stored energy's remaining capacity, because the lifespan will decrease by frequent deep discharge.

Aside from lead accumulators, there are other electro-chemical systems, such as the nickel-cadmium battery, which can be used for floor conveyors. These batteries have a greater energy and performance density (approximately 80 W/kg, 90 Wh/kg), longer service life, higher mechanic and thermal strength and cause lower environmental impact during manufacturing, use and disposal. Nickel-cadmium batteries have the advantages that they can be quickly charged at any time and contain the non-corrosive electrolyte potassium hydroxide. As a result of the low cell voltage of 1.2 V, a 24 V battery consists of 20 cells; nevertheless the space requirements are no larger than for a 24 V lead battery (see Example 4.4 for cell structure and circuit).

The energy of a battery used for an electric floor conveyor is (U × K × 0.8): 1,000 in kWh. To charge an empty battery the following is required (see VDI-2695, and Chapter 6.6.7.8):

$$E = \frac{U \times K \times 0.8 \times 1.5}{1000} \tag{4.3}$$

E	kWh	Energy requirement
U	V	Battery voltage (Operating voltage)
K	Ah	Battery capacity (K5 value)
0.8	≙	80% battery discharge
1.5	≙	Charge factor: loss in charger and in battery; for electrolyte circulation factor is only 1.15.

The lifespan of a battery decreases as a result of incorrect discharging, too low acid levels, too frequent deep discharge and bad maintenance. The choice of charger is a function of the number of existing floor conveyors, the battery voltage and the time available for charging.

The charging time can be roughly determined by:

$$t_1 = \frac{1000 \times E_5}{I \times U} \quad [h] \tag{4.4}$$

t_1	h	Charging time
E_5	kWh	Energy amount (5-hour capacity $\triangleq K_5$)
I	A	Load current
U	V	Load voltage

To protect the battery, charging the current from unregulated chargers should not be more than 200 per cent of five-hours' worth of discharge current. Charging options are *charge mode* and *sequencing mode*. The sequencing mode consists of exchanging for a new battery. The charging mode occurs by using an individual charger or a collection station. It is also possible to integrate a charger in to the floor conveyor (see Example 4.5). Interim charges for lead batteries via electrolyte circulation is also possible; however, the charging time has to be a minimum of 30 minutes. Battery and charger have to match exactly.

Advantages of battery operation electric drive: independent of electric grid; loaded start-up; easily regulated; odour free; noise free; low wear; easy operation; unproblematic change of direction; particularly economic when charged at night; no clutch; no gears; long lifespan.

Disadvantages: limited capacity; battery maintenance (contacts upkeep, check acid density and cell voltage); lost time through battery charging or exchange; low maximum speed (maximum 18 km/h); relative high initial investment; decrease in performance over usage time; loading regulations; deep discharge; space for battery; battery weight (in parts).

4.5.7 Hydraulic drive unit

Hydraulic drives (pneumatic drives) use pressured energy inflowing liquids (gas) to transmit performance, which are received by the respective media through transformation of mechanic energy. The performance can be transformed at any time into the factors power and speed, or moment and angular velocity, through control and regulation. A labour motion in a straight line is enabled through the use of work cylinders (thrust motor), whereas a rotary engine enables a circular motion.

For hydrostatic performance transmission, we usually distinguish between the primary part (pressure creation; electric (diesel) motor and pump), steering and control components and the secondary part (for more on work cylinder or rotary engine, see Figure 4.6). The hydraulic circuit is represented in a simplified way with the help of circuit symbols (DIN 24 300); see Figure 4.7. The symbols for oil hydraulic and pneumatics only differ in the marks on the connections and the types of outlets.

Figure 4.6   Hydrostatic performance transmission. a) For straight motions. b) For rotary motions

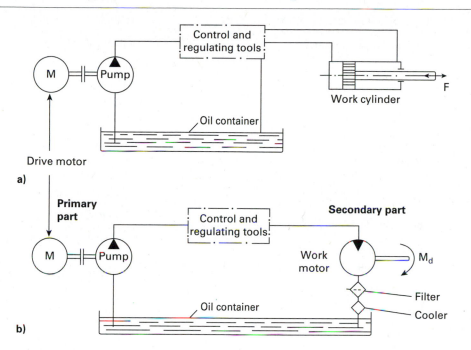

Hydro-pumps, hydro-motors and hydro-valves are all components of hydraulic drives. Pumps and motors are positive displacements, which can deliver a constant or variable stream of oil depending on design type (operational pressure for cog pumps up to 120 bars, for piston pumps up to 300 bars). This hydraulic power transmission is expensive and is not very effective in comparison with mechanical power transmission, but the operational effort is slower and it guarantees sensitive regulation of the labour motions.

A great number of non-continuous conveyors (mobile crane, forklift truck, cranes) use hydraulic drive units to power lift, drive, rotary and swivel tools, to tilt lifting equipment and to power forklift attachments (Figure 4.16).

4.6 Wheel, tyres, roadway

The wheel converts a circular motion into a translational motion and transmits power between its footprint and the roadway. It consists of hub, rims and tyre, of hub and tyre, or of a homogeneous material only, such as a steel wheel or plastic wheel. The roadway can be a road or track. The tyre is a wear element and must be replaceable.

Figure 4.7   Symbols for oil hydraulic elements in line with DIN 24 300

Symbol	Name and description	Symbol	Name and description
Hydro valves (general)		Hydro-current valves	
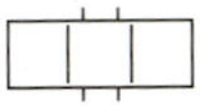	Valves are represented by a rectangle. Number of fields = switching positions; cables are pulled towards neutral positions		Throttle valve, with variable constriction and effective in both directions
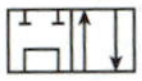	Within the fields, arrows point in the direction of the throughflow; barriers are shown as horizontal lines	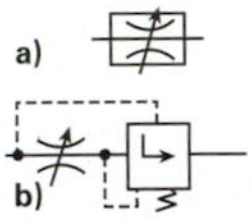 a) b)	Current regulation valve (2-way) a) summary b) functional diagram
		Hydro-pumps	
	Symbols for the activity areas are placed at right angle to the connections outside of the rectangle	a) b)	Pump with constant displacement a) with one conveyor b) with two conveyors
Hydro-way valves			Pump with variable displacement a) with one conveyor b) with two conveyors
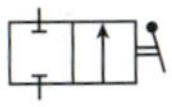	2/2-way valve in barred in neutral, manually operated by lever	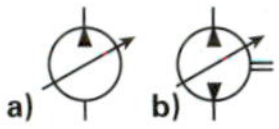 a) b)	
	4/2-way valve magnet-operated – pre-controlled, with spring reset	Hydro engine	
Hydro-stop valves		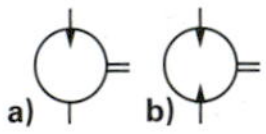 a) b)	Engine with constant displacement a) with one flow direction b) with two flow directions
	Stop valve, spring-loaded, barring pressure flow in one direction		
Hydro-pressure valves			Swing motor (with limited angle of rotation)
a) b)	Pressure valve (general) a) one-edge valve with closed neutral position b) one edge-valve with open neutral position	Hydraulic cylinders	
			Cylinder (single effect) Backwards motion through external force
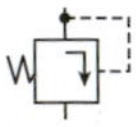	Pressure relief valve limits pressure by opening the outlet against spring force	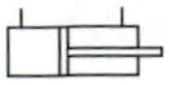	Cylinder (double effective) with one-sided piston rod

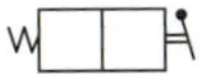

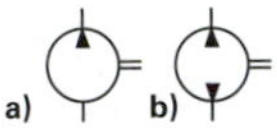

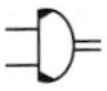

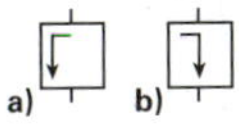

4.6.1 Tyres and roadway

The tyre for a floor conveyor must be chosen depending on the operating conditions. These conditions include:

- floor surface;
- roadway conditions;
- operating site, such as inside or outside deployment;
- environmental conditions: dust, temperature, moisture;
- floor pollution: oil, fat, alkalis, acid, sawdust, glass;
- type of floor conveyor: forklift, wagon, tractor;
- speeds.

Depending on the deployment, different features may be required, including:

- high load capacity and friction;
- high degree of elasticity, suspension and toughness;
- low rolling resistance and abrasion;
- good curve ratio and low noise levels;
- good surface pressure;
- long lifespan;
- low costs;
- high operating safety and puncture resistance;
- low level maintenance.

The selected type is the connection between the floor conveyor and roadway, has to transmit and take in power, absorb shocks and fulfil the requirements of the deployment conditions. Tyres come in different designs, such as *air tyres*, *super elastic tyres*, *full tyres* and *plastic tyres*.

4.6.1.1 Air tyres

The body of the tyre consists of the wheel tread and the substructure. The wheel tread is distinctive. The tread is for better manoeuvrability and traction on wet surfaces. Depending on the structure of the material layers, there is a distinction between *cross-ply (belt) tyres* and *radial tyres*. The cross-ply tyre has better stability as a result of more solid side panels and beneficial shock-absorbing properties, but has higher rolling resistance. The radial tyre has better suspension.
   Advantages: good suspension; low floor pressure; possibility to re-tread; tread.
   Disadvantages: puncture prone; regular air pressure checks; large measurements.

Too high or low air pressure negatively impacts the tyre lifespan as a result of high strain (bulging tread or flexing of side panel).

Deployment: inside and outside.

Air tyres come in different designs, as radial and cross-ply tyres:

- *normal* and *wide tyres* (ratio of side panel height to tyre width 1:1, for wide tyres by 0.7);

- *low pressure* and *high pressure tyres* (internal tyre pressure for low pressure tyres up to 3.5 bars, high pressure tyres from 5 bars).

4.6.1.2 Super elastic tyres

Super elastic tyres are full tyres with different, radially spaced rubber mixtures. They combine the advantages of air and full tyres. The treaded surface consists of wear-resistant rubber, the intermediate part is made of highly elastic rubber, guaranteeing good shock and vibration absorption and has approximately 80 per cent of an air tyre's suspension.

Steel wire cores – embedded in the tough rubber of the wheel base – guarantee a solid rim fit.

Advantages: puncture safe; maintenance free; shock and vibration absorbent; stable; highly resilient; long lifespan; same rims as in air tyres; treaded.

Disadvantages: expensive; sensitive to oil and grease.

Deployment: suitable for touch deployment and difficult environmental conditions.

4.6.1.3 Full tyres

Usually, the surface of a full tyre made of tough rubber is not treaded (see Example 4.6).

Advantages: puncture safe; large capacity load; small measurements; maintenance free; low rolling resistance.

Disadvantages: little suspension; high point load; licensed for up to 16 km/h driving speed.

Deployment: suitable for solid floors and tough environments.

4.6.1.4 Plastic tyres

The plastic tyre consists of tough plastic (polyurethane) and can be structured as follows:

- plastic bandage permanently bonded to steel ring;
- tyre with steel wire core in tyre base (base in cylindrical and conical design);
- solid plastic tyre.

Advantages: high capacity load; high abrasion resistance; long lifespan; puncture safe; maintenance free; small measurements; resistant to oil, grease, petrol and diesel.

Disadvantages: limited driving speed up to 10 km/h; sensitive to acid and alkali.

Deployment: almost exclusively in buildings.

4.6.1.5 Wheel rims

Wheel rims are made of pressed, cast or forged steel or light metal. Air and super elastic tyres use rims that are split down the middle and sides. A side split rim can have two, three or four parts. Super elastic tyres also have special one-part rims. Full and plastic tyres use one-part, cylindrical and two-part conical rims that are split in the middle or down the side. Usually, special devices and presses are required to put on the tyre body.

4.6.2 Wheels for tracks

There is a distinction between non-drive impellers and drive wheels. Usually wheels are made of steel castings with cylindrical, ball-shape or conical surface design and with two-sided, one-sided or without flange, depending on guiding responsibility and track profile.

The friction for the wheel–track combination steel on steel is about 0.1 to 0.35 (Table 4.2). Resistance for steady-state at full load can be accurately determined through the journal friction, rolling resistance, flange friction, hub end face friction and the resistance for potentially installed guide rolls on the side.

In practice, a quick and approximate calculation of the drive resistance F_{wf} is carried out by using the overall driving resistance w_{ges} in per cent:

Table 4.2 Friction value for wheel/tyre and roadway/tracks

Wheel-/ roadway combination	Friction μ_0
Steel/steel	0.1 – 0.35
Rubber/asphalt iced	0.1 – 0.2
Rubber/asphalt dry	0.6 – 0.8
Air tyres/concrete	
wet	0.7
dry	0.9
Air tyres/cobblestones	
wet	0.5
dry	0.7

$$F_{wf} = w_{ges}G \quad N \tag{4.5}$$

w_{ges}	$\approx 20\%$	for impeller-track made of steel for plain bearing
w_{ges}	$\approx 5\%$	for impeller-track made of steel for roller bearing
G	in N	weight force of wheel load

For more on the calculation of drive resistance for floor conveyors see Chapter 6.6.3.

4.6.3 Roadway, track

A roadway is the floor surface on which vehicles like wagons, tractors, trucks or picking vehicles move. The type and condition of the roadway are decisive for the type of tyres on the conveyor vehicle. Outside the following applies for air tyres:

- high pressure tyres have a small volume;
- a high surface pressure;
- low rolling resistance;
- they require well maintained roads.

For low-pressure tyres the large footprint results in lower surface pressure. They can be deployed in unpaved terrain (higher rolling resistance). Double tyres can also reduce surface pressure. In buildings with asphalt, concrete, plastic or industrial flooring, full tyres can be chosen. For screed flooring, the thickness and load capacity of the screed have to be considered.

Tracks are an option to guide transport vehicles. They come in pairs for transfer cars, or on their own, for storage and retrieval systems. A large variety of track designs are available for circular, slow circular or drag chain conveyors, which can either consist of thermally rolled finished products (eg I-carrier) or of track profiles manufactured through chipless reshaping of sheet metal. For monorails, one or double-sided bead profiles are used (see Figures 4.8, 6.3.1 and 6.3.2).

Tracks of circular conveyors and monorails are subject to particularly high level demands as a result of pints, junctions and bends.

For floor-based means of transport, flat and crane tracks are utilized (see Figure 4.9). Friction for wheel–roadway combinations is between 0.1 and 0.8 (see Table 4.2).

4.7 Dimensioning basics

The planning for transport and warehousing technology should only consider mechanical and technical key figures that are important in understanding the means of transport and their pre-dimensioning.

Figure 4.8 Impellers of continuous conveyors and monorails with different track profiles

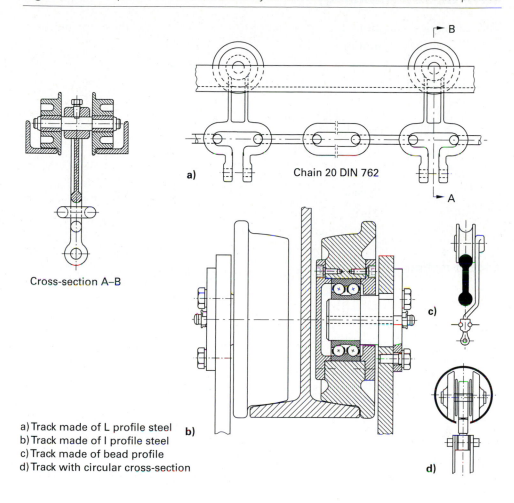

a)

Chain 20 DIN 762

Cross-section A–B

c)

a) Track made of L profile steel
b) Track made of I profile steel
c) Track made of bead profile
d) Track with circular cross-section

b)

d)

Figure 4.9 Crane tracks according to DIN 536

 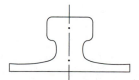

a) Flat track profile shape F   **b)** Foot flange track shape A

4.7.1 Basic terminology

The calculation equations for performance can be divided into those for uniform, straight and circular motions.

Straight motion

$$P = \frac{F \times v}{1000} = \frac{mv^2}{1000\,t} \quad [\text{kW}]$$ (4.6)

P	in kW	Performance
F	in N	Force $[F = ma = m \times (v/t)]$
v	in m/s	Speed
m	in kg	Mass
t	in s	Time

Circular motion

$$P = \frac{M \times \omega}{1000}$$ (4.7)

And with $\omega = 2\pi n$

P	in kW	Performance
M	in Nm	Moment ($M = J\,\alpha$)
ω	in rad/s	Angular speed ($\omega = \alpha\,t$)
n	in 1/min	Nominal torque
J	in kgm^2	Moment of inertia
α	in s^{-2}	Angular acceleration

An engine's constant performance results in the torque run using the number of revolutions as hyperbole (see Figure 4.10).

Figure 4.10   Representation of the torque formula at constant performance

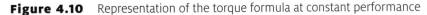

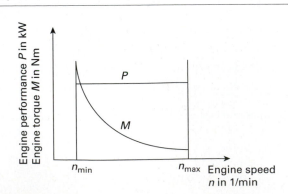

The *stability v* of a means of transport or storage means that the sum of the stability moment M_{St} related to the tilting edge is larger than the sum of the tilting moments M_K.

$$v = \frac{M_{St}}{M_K} > 1 \qquad (4.8)$$

The tilting behaviour has to be examined for forklift trucks, cranes, wagons and racking.

The *gradeability p* of a vehicle is a key measure and is a percentage. It is a measure for the gradient on a tilting plane.

$$P = \frac{h}{l} \times 100 \ [\%] \qquad (4.9)$$

l in m Length of the inclined plane

Gradeability is achieved when the wheels are not yet spinning.

A dead load (mass) is all the masses of a means of transport, that have to be moved during any kind of motion (lift, sink, drive) along with the respective payload. The dead load ratio v0 is defined as:

$$v_0 = \frac{\text{Payload}}{\text{Payload} + \text{dead mass}} \qquad (4.10)$$

Continuous conveyors are characterized by small dead loads compared to non-continuous conveyors, resulting in a lower drive performance.

4.7.2 Force transfer through form and friction

The force (peripheral form) is transferred by *form fit* between chain and cogwheel, between cogs, and between carriage and cam.

Force or *friction* transfer of the peripheral force exists between rubber band and drum, between rope and sheave, between fan belt and pulley, between wheel and road, for the brand brake and the Capstan winch (see Example 4.7).

Wheel and roadway: During the braking process of a vehicle (mobile crane, forklift truck and electric wagon) the structure of the brake is only of secondary significance to the length of the brake delay. What is significant is the amount of friction between the vehicle's heel and the road. This is also true for the start-up process: excessive acceleration results in the spinning of the wheels. The biggest possible delay (acceleration) is shown in the following equation (4.11):

$$F_a = ma \qquad and \ F_W = G \mu_0 \qquad (4.11)$$

$$F_a \leq F_W \qquad or \ ma < mg\mu_0$$

$$a \leq g\mu_0 \qquad in \ m/s^2$$

Figure 4.11   Force transfer on traction discs

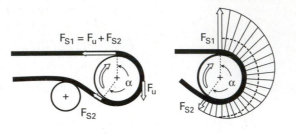

F_a	in N	Acceleration (delay) force
F_W	in N	Resistance (friction) force
m	in kg	Mass to be accelerated
G	in N	Weight force (normal force)
a	in m/s^2	Acceleration/delay
g	in m/s^2	Acceleration of gravity
μ_0		Friction between wheel and road

The friction between wheel and road is subject to many influencing factors (road material, road surface, wheel material) and can, therefore, vary significantly. In line with the values shown in Table 4.2, the achievable delay is 1–8 m/s^2.

Traction discs: If the rope (band, belt) wraps around the disc (drum) at wrap angle α (Figure 4.11), the torque impacting the disc will try – via the wrapping friction and if there is existing tension – to move the rope and take it with it accordingly.

The forces within the rope are described by the laws of rope tension (Eytelwein equation):

$$\frac{F_{S_1}}{F_{S_2}} = e^{\mu_0 \alpha} \tag{4.12}$$

$$F_u = F_{S_1} - F_{S_2} \quad \text{[N]} \tag{4.13}$$

F_u	in N	Peripheral force resulting from the resistance; based on the moment M to be transferred or decelerated: $F_u = M/r$, r in M; radius of rope, belt or brake disc, drum
M	in Nm	See equation
F_{S_1}	in N	Ingoing rope force (large)
F_{S_2}	in N	Outgoing rope force (small)
α	in °	Wrapping angle
μ_0		Friction value between rope and rope disc
e		Euler's number $e = 2.718$

For better representation, the pulling forces in the rope are drawn in turned by 90° in their attack point (see Figure 4.11).

Figure 4.12   Drive factors k_1 and k_2 in dependency of μ_0 and α

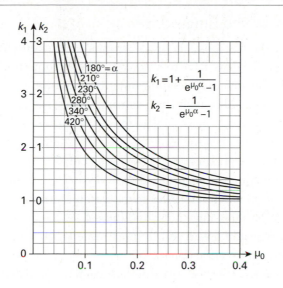

By using equation (4.13) in equation (4.12), we get the following formulae for rope pulling forces:

$$F_{S_1} = F_u \frac{e^{\mu_0\alpha}}{e^{\mu_0\alpha}-1}\, F_u\left(1 + \frac{1}{e^{\mu_0\alpha}-1}\right) = F_u k_1 \ \ [N] \tag{4.14}$$

$$F_{S_2} = F_u \left(\frac{1}{e^{\mu_0\alpha}-1}\right) F_u k_2 \tag{4.15}$$

The formed driving factors k_1 and k_2 can be read in dependency of friction μ_0 and wrapping angle α (as parameter) shown in Figure 4.12. The friction force transfer from the driving side (disc, drum) on the elastic means of pulling (rope, band, belt) of the driving side is dependent on:

- the size of the wrapping angle α;

- the friction μ_0;

- the rope pulling force F_{S_2} in the outgoing rope (pre-tensional force).

4.7.3 *Transport good streams*

You will find the following calculations in Chapter 2.3.2:

- volume stream $\dot{V}$;

- mass stream $\dot{m}$;

- cargo stream $\dot{m}_{St}$.

4.7.4 Engine design

4.7.4.1 Aspects for choosing a drive

In order to choose the best possible option from all of the different types of drive, the requirements for the drive have to be known. These requirements already constitute selection criteria, such as: operating time (rarely, continuous, one or multiple shifts); speed (low, high and controllable); starting torque; full load torque; overload; acceleration; operational readiness; replaceability; operation; maintenance; controllability; space requirements; noise level; exhaust gas composition; odour nuisance; energy use; effectiveness; purchase price; operating costs.

To choose a drive, the following should be known: deployment area (outside and in a building); environmental influences (temperature, moisture, dust and threat of explosion); permissible emissions (noise and fumes).

The condition, type and length of transport route (horizontal transport, vertical transport) are important section criteria.

The planner or builder must be aware of the advantages and disadvantages as well as the torque-speed process of the individual drive types. There are drive machines that deliver nearly constant torque, such as electric motors or those that deliver a periodically changing torque, such as piston motors. Machinery may demand a constant torque, such as continuous conveyors, or require a periodically changing torque, such as piston pumps for pneumatic transport.

Lift equipment, on the other hand, experiences alternate strains. When choosing a suitable drive, it is always the operating behaviour of drive and machinery that is decisive. The start-up process and the steady state have to be examined, and considerations made whether the start-up happens with load or on empty.

4.7.4.2 Inertia and acceleration

Drive engines of non-continuous conveyors are subject to high demands by large start-up torques, frequent gear changes, braking and changes in rotation direction. They work on intermittent duty. Drive engines in continuous conveyors ordinarily operate permanently and are switched off less often. The engine design is based on the relative length of the duty cycle DC, as in the following example:

$$DC = \frac{\Sigma \text{Duty cycle}}{\Sigma \text{Duty cycle + breaks}} \times 100 \ [\%] \tag{4.16}$$

For non-continuous conveyors, the DC value is between 20 per cent and 60 per cent, for continuous conveyors at 100 per cent. Where asynchronous three-phase motors are used, such as a squirrel cage, it is often sufficient to design them according to full load inertia P_V, as its start-up moment is temporarily at least 1.5 times as large as the nominal moment.

The following applies:

$$P_n = \frac{P_{An}}{1.6 \text{ to } 2.0} \geq P_V \text{ [kW]} \tag{4.17}$$

The nominal performance P_N is the performance mentioned on the type label for the drive motor. The start-up performance P_{An} is the performance required for start-up and results from the sum of the full load inertia performance and the acceleration performance P_B.

$$P_N \geq P_{An} = P_V + P_B \tag{4.18}$$

The full load inertia performance P_V is the required drive performance at full load in stationary mode. P_B is the percentage of performance to accelerate the mass from inertia in a straight or circular motion.

$$P_B = P_B \text{ straight} + P_B \text{ circular} \tag{4.19}$$

$$P_B = m \times a \times v + M_B \times \omega \tag{4.20}$$

m	kg	mass – accelerated straight
$a = v/t_A$	m/s^2	straight acceleration (v: speed, t_A: start-up time)
M_B	Nm	acceleration moment for mass in circular motion
ω	rad/s	angular speed

4.7.4.3 Drive and lift motors

We distinguish between performance calculations for drive and lift motors as well as traction motors for load handling tools, such as a telescopic fork. The dimensioning equation for full load inertia performance P_V is:

$$P_V = \frac{F \times v}{1000 \times \eta_{ges}} \text{ [kW]} \tag{4.21}$$

In this case, v is the traction or lift speed in m/s and η_{ges} is the total effectiveness of the traction or lift tool. The force F in N for the drive corresponds to the resistance (mainly friction resistance), which is made up of the nominal capacity load of the means of transport and all tare, that have to be lifted alongside, such as the load carrying tool. To calculate the motor for the load carrying tool's motion, the type of motion (horizontal, vertical) is crucial.

For electro-motor drive the traction, lift and additional motors are single motors (separate drives). Lift and additional motors are powered by an electro-hydraulic single drive. For combustions motor drive, traction, lift and additional motions are achieved through the entire drive, with lift and additional motion occurring hydraulically.

4.8 Economy, investment, operating costs

Transport, handling and warehousing processes cause costs without generally generating added value. In order to minimize these material flow costs, a rational movement of goods should be aimed for. The result of planning depends on the right choice of means of transport, the transport system or the entire transport chain, because the choice of means of transport determines the ongoing costs (operating costs). Following checks whether the transport of the goods can be avoided, the following aspects are important to design economic transport measures:

- Aim for short transport routes and design appropriate transport and warehousing units.
- Avoid reloading transport goods.
- Aim to use means of transport to full capacity.
- Prevent empty journey and waiting times by organized and well-planned deployment.
- Combine production processes such as sorting, heating, moistening or cooling with the transport processes.
- Utilize standardized building blocks and modular systems.
- Check/deploy continuous conveyors, which may transport small measurements or small dead loads at high speed.
- Ensure accessibility to enable exchange of modules.
- Pay attention to peripheral conditions: connect internal and external transport system where possible.

There are always multiple solutions when searching for the most suitable and most economic means of transport for a transport problem. The best solution can be determined by using an *evaluation matrix* with weighted criteria (see Chapter 12.9.4.2) and must be arrived at through using an *efficiency comparison*. This will take into account a certain lifespan, in order to convert investments (purchasing costs) into interest and amortization, and to differentiate between fixed, transport-dependent and variable costs. Key figures (see Chapter 1.5.1) can be used to compare means of transport and transport times.

The process for an efficiency comparison calculation is as follows:

1 Determination of fixed and variable costs for each means of transport.

2 Calculation of operating costs per time unit.

3 Comparison of operating costs.

4 Determination of optimal means of transport.

The operating costs for a means of transport (transport machinery) are made up of fixed costs divided into capital costs, amortization, fixed repair costs and fixed wage costs, and of variable costs divided into running and repair costs (maintenance costs), energy and personnel costs (see Chapter 6.6.7.8 and Example 4.8).

The invested capital (investment amount made up of purchasing costs of the machinery, build and assembly costs, costs for training of personnel, planning costs, financing costs) incurs interest and has to be written off in amortization:

$$\text{Annual capital costs} = \frac{\text{Investment amount}}{2} \times \text{interest rate} \qquad (4.22)$$

This formula applies:

- to average calculations: a consistent interest rate is applied for all years, which does not correspond to the actual annual interest costs;
- without taking into account compound interest.

The amortization corresponds to the effective value decrease and is, in linear amortization:

$$\text{Annual amortization} = \frac{\text{Investment amount}}{\text{economic lifespan}} \qquad (4.23)$$

- For economic lifespan = technical lifespan, with the economic lifespan being a function of the usage, technical advancement and the production programme.
- For economic lifespan, which is different from the lifespan accepted for tax purposes: fixed annual repair costs have to be considered for periodic checks that are carried out regardless of the number of operating hours. Fixed personnel costs apply when considering an entire transport system. Maintenance and repair costs include costs for wages, materials and spare parts for repairs and maintenance. Energy costs include charging costs for battery operation, electricity costs for electric drive and devices, fuel costs for combustion engines and also amortization and interest for spare batteries and tyres, as their lifespan is always shorter than that of the means of transport.
- At inflation rate equals zero.

The variable costs also include wage costs of operation staff (Figure 4.13).

When looking at this cost perspective it has to be taken into account that the profit (performance) is the same for all investment objects. The choice of a means of transport is often a result of the deployment time, because efficiency, production programme, costs and performance are time-based functions. Figure 4.14 shows the deployment area for manual transport, floor conveyor and continuous conveyor in dependence on costs and operating time (level of use). The simplified methods depicted here for an efficiency or cost comparison calculation are sufficient in most

Figure 4.13   Cost structure for means of transport

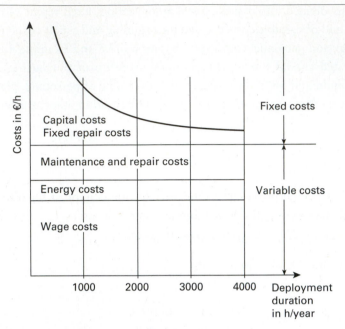

Figure 4.14   Deployment area of manual transport, floor conveyor and continuous conveyor in dependence

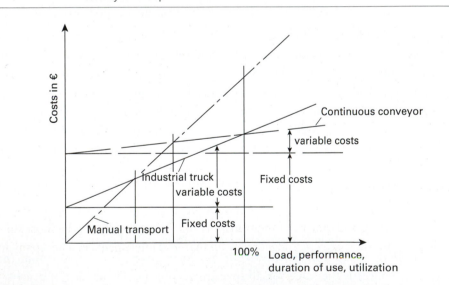

cases for a rough decision based on indicated quotes, in order to choose means of transport and transport or warehousing systems.

If it is not just about the choice or purchase of a means of transport, but about something like building a new warehouse, then all costs must be justified. These investments include:

- premises costs including purchase costs, additional costs (such as land transfer tax) and the costs of development in order to make the land ready for building on;
- building costs for buildings with heating, ventilation, sanitary areas and lights;
- costs for external areas including loading and unloading, lights and fencing;
- costs for special equipment, such as sprinkler systems;
- costs of warehouse furnishings, such as shelving and pallets;
- costs for transport machinery with purchase price, freight, assembly materials and assembly costs;
- planning and financing costs.

In order to get the operating costs, the new warehousing system must be known. The cost calculation has to be done with sensibly selected figures; see Table 11.4 in Example 11.4 as well as Table 11.6 in Example 11.21.

To determine an optimal warehousing system out of the respective alternative/ options, a comparison can be made between the respective *operating costs* on the one hand, and the static (see Example 4.8) or dynamic (see Example 12.10) *amortization periods*. For the calculations, it is necessary to determine any times for savings, which can then be converted into monetary units.

An *investment* is the investing of monetary means in investment goods. Investments can be distinguished by:

- utilization time: short, medium or long-term investments;
- objects: production, rationalization, extension and replacement units.

4.9 Transport planning

4.9.1 Aspects of transport planning

Over the last few years, there has been a realization that only a holistic and decision-focused perspective of transport options can lead to optimal transport planning. It is the task of planning and dimensioning transport machinery to choose the most suitable and appropriate means of transport for all material movements in a company in respect of transport goods, transport route, mass and cargo stream. This will then lead to good efficient use at optimal performance. Transport problems are multi-faceted and varied and, in order to manage a transport programme, technical, economic and organizational problems have to be considered and resolved. In order to implement the planning and dimensioning of a transport task it is not enough to apply purely functional thinking, but instead taking a holistic, logistical system approach is required. Planning figures and peripheral conditions have to be determined using a precisely worded remit:

- *type of transport good* and its mechanical, physical and chemical features;
- *transport goods stream* as mass stream in t/h or volume stream in m³/h. Maximum and minimum transport, even, changing or intermittent delivery of transport goods;
- *type of transport route*, distance in m with information about the shape, tilt, gradient (line guidance), vertical and horizontal transport, local requirements without blocking other existing means of transport;
- *type of drive*, such as gravity, manual operation, electric drive, combustion motor drive, pneumatic or hydraulic drive (see Chapter 4.5), adjustable speed, reversibility and automatic controls;
- *type of energy supply*, such as battery, trailing cable, conductor lines and air pressure;
- *length of operating duration*, such as interrupted, continuous, one or multiple shift operation;
- *type of loading and unloading,* manually, mechanical, automated, interim discharge and adjustable intake/output;
- *type and number of delivery points*;
- *type of operation and maintenance*, fool proof operation, easy replacement of consumption parts;
- *type of environmental influence* depending on deployment outside, in building, in the tropics, room temperature, moisture, wind, ice, threat of fire and explosion, dust, aggressive fumes, environmental conditions, round conditions and environmental protection;
- *type of safety measures* against fire, theft, protection from touch and operating safety;
- *type of constructive design* as modular system, lightweight construction, transport, assembly and extension options;
- *amount of investment*, *savings* and *operating costs*, efficiency calculation, eg ROI calculation (see Chapter 4.8);
- *type of connection* to existing means of transport, transport aids or transport systems with regard to connection measurements (doors, gates, room height, floor coverings, ceiling load capacity), goods intake and delivery, speed, extension devices and interfaces;
- *knowledge* of legislation, especially regulation and orders on noise, dust development, CO levels, accident prevention, work protection, safety regulation and packaging regulations.

4.9.2 Approach and implementation

The approach to choosing a means of transport is first and foremost to investigate, process and establish the above key figures. Then suitable means of transport for the respective task can be determined and, by means of an efficiency calculation, the optimal means of transport can be chosen. Whether it is about a change or extension of production or a redesign of the material flow, thorough planning is required in any case, with the goal of obtaining reliable planning and dimensioning data. The planner or engineer must have knowledge in the area of machine engineering, electric technology, material sciences and control technology, in order to offer an economic and cost-effective solution for a transport task, and in order to be able to achieve the shortest building times possible by using modular units. They must have an insight into packaging technology and be familiar with the material flow and warehousing technology, as well as with the features of using continuous and non-continuous conveyors in connection with automated control mechanisms. The planner must have the ability to estimate the transport demands during the transport process and to implement the transport planning exercise in line with these criteria.

4.10 VDI guidelines, DIN standards, recommendations

For all operations and business areas, a number of standards, regulations, guidelines and legislation, some with international significance (DIN-EN, ISO standards) have been created in order to aid the planner and engineer in designing building blocks and machine parts, to advise them on safety, take some responsibility, determine holistic and sensible figures, enable the keeping of spare parts stock but minimize spare part warehousing.

Although these regulations are not required by law and are merely recommendations they form part of most contracts and, in court cases, are seen as generally applicable technical regulations. Therefore, it is necessary and required to obtain the relevant standards and regulations for the respective field prior to planning, construction and implementation. Standards and regulations are continuously updated, amended, added to or revoked in line with technical developments.

A technical guideline is worked up jointly by experts from industry and business and describes the state of technology. The Society of German Engineers (Verein der Deutschen Ingenieure – VDI) publishes VDI guidelines as single sheets for conveyor technology, material flow and logistics. Both the Society of German Machine Engineering Institutions (Verein Deutscher Maschinenbau-Anstalten – VDMA) and the Committee on Economic Manufacturing (Ausschuss für Wirtschaftliche Fertigung – AWF) publish guidelines for a number of different areas.

DIN, short for Deutsches Institut für Normung e.v. – or German Institute for Standards – develops DIN standards to support rationalization, quality assurance, safety as well as communications in sciences and technology. The European standard DIN-EN has become significant as a result of the common European market. ISO, short for International Organization for Standardization, creates standards beyond Europe at international level for all countries willing to cooperate.

The UVV accident prevention regulations include rules on how to avoid accidents at work. They show employers' and employees' obligations to fulfil and achieve safety at work. Trade associations have been given the task by law to develop UVV guidelines and enact them. The development of the UVV guidelines occurs in technical committees.

The European technical committee for standardization, CEN (Comité Européen de Normalisation), presents standards under the name European Norm, EN (these are European Pre-standards ENV, technical specification TS and harmonizing documents HD) in German, English and French. The EN either encompasses international standards such as ISO, or national standards such as the German standard DIN are adopted. This leads to names such as DIN EN 27 023, meaning the European standard 'EN 27 023: 1992' is recognized as a German standard. DIN EN 27 023 is the German version of EN 27 023: 1992.

VDI guidelines, DIN standards:

VDI	2700	11.04 Securing of loads on road vehicles
	3617	02.10 Disposable/returnable packaging
	3968 Bl. 4	01.94 Safety of load units; shrinking
	3968 Bl. 5	08.07 Safety of load units; stretching
	3960	03.98 Determination of service hours of industrial trucks
	3975	03.02 Storage of hazardous substances
	3978	08.98 Achievement and cycle time of piece good conveyor systems
DIN	1301-1	10.10 Units, unit names, unit symbols

4.11 Examples and questions

Example 4.1: Criteria for deployment of a means of transport

What are the criteria that the deployment of a means of transport for a given transport task depends on?

Answer: The answer to this question can be very wide reaching. Here, we only want to list some of the overarching criteria:

- requirements and demands of the transport task;
- features, characteristics and quantities of the transport goods;

- figures relating to the means of transport;

- deployment and environmental conditions;

- figures relating to regulations (for more on selection criteria for forklift trucks, see Chapter 6.6.2).

Example 4.2: Forklift hydraulic system

Using hydraulic symbols, sketch out a schematic representation of a forklift hydraulic system with lift and tilt cylinder.

Answer: Figure 4.15.

Figure 4.15 Hydraulic circuit diagram of a forklift without attachment with 4/3-way valve, manually operated with spring reset

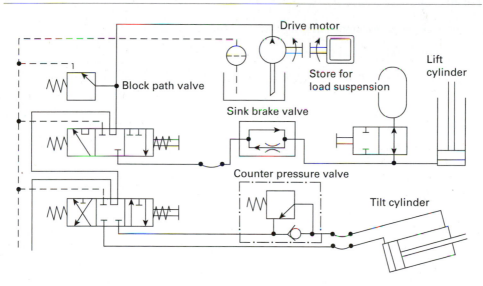

Example 4.3: Drive batteries

Sketch out the circuit options for a 24 V drive battery for floor conveyors.

Answer: Figure 4.16.

Figure 4.16 Standardized circuits for a 24 V battery

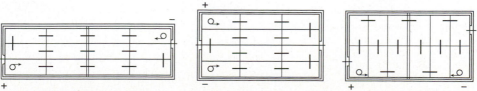

Example 4.4: Battery concept

a) What figures are important for the planning of a battery concept?

b) What direction is the development of drive batteries evolving into?

Answer:

For a): The battery concept depends on:

- operation hours and deployment conditions;
- battery type and battery voltage;
- degree of automation and level of demand;
- charging type: exchange battery and charging operations.

For b):

- energy and performance density and duration of use, capacity;
- mechanic and thermal strength;
- ability to be stored when charged;
- safety;
- easy disposal;
- accurate display of remaining charge.

Reduction of:

- maintenance efforts;
- measurements;
- weight;
- environmental pollution during manufacture, use and disposal;
- dependency on high or low temperatures.

Example 4.5: Choice of battery

Sketch out a process plan for choosing a battery and charger.

Answer: Figure 4.17.

Figure 4.17 Process map for choosing a battery

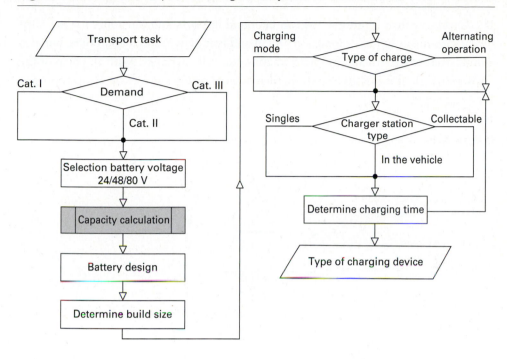

Example 4.6: Bandage on forklift wheel

Pressing an elastic bandage on a wheel, such as a forklift wheel, occurs by using a hydraulic press. How is this process structured?

Answer: Figure 4.18.

Figure 4.18 Pressing and pulling a bandage on/from a wheel body

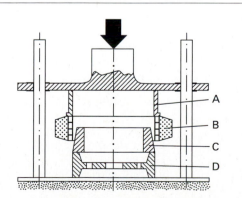

a) Press ring   b) Bandage   c) Expansion ring   d) Wheel body

Example 4.7: Calculation of manual pulling force for a Capstan winch

The Capstan winch (Figure 4.19) can be found in ports and harbours for the horizontal movement of heavy loads, to pull in and manoeuvre ships and boats, but also in industrial environments to move wagons and rail carriages. With the help of the Capstan winch, it is possible to strengthen manual pulling power by using appropriate wrap angles.

Figure 4.19   Capstan winch

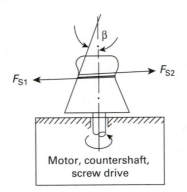

Motor, countershaft,
screw drive

Principle: force transfer by friction based on the law of belt friction (see Equation 4.12). There is a motor in the base of the winch, which powers the winch accordingly.

The pulling of the rope by hand (pre-tension F_{S_2}), with a given friction and selected wrap figure, results in the load force F_{S_1} for:

$$F_{S_1} = F_{S_2} e^{\mu_0 \alpha}$$

$\mu_0 = 0.14$ for wire ropes
$\mu_0 = 0.2$ for hemp ropes

What wrap coefficient n ($\alpha = n \times 2\pi$) must be chosen in order for a manual pulling force of 150 N to turn into a load pulling force of 3000 N using a wire rope? What peripheral force is required of the motor at the head of the winch?

Answer:

$$e^{0,14n\ 2\pi} = \frac{3000}{150} = 20$$

$$n = 1.14 \times \frac{\ln 20}{\ln e} \times \frac{1}{0.14 \times 2\pi} = 3.4$$

This means four wraps are required.

The peripheral force is: $F_U = F_{S_1} - F_{S_2} = 3000 - 150 = 2850$ N. A Capstan winches possesses a hollow core. Its task is to ensure that the rope keeps sliding into the hollow core when moving up. This is the case when the tilting angle ß is larger than the friction angle φ.

Example 4.8: Static amortization calculation

In order to help make a decision on rationalization, the pay-off period for a rationalization plan for a distribution depot should be determined in a static amortization calculation. For this exercise, the energy costs are not taken into account, but the amount for contingencies is increased. The savings are made up by freeing up resources and reducing labour. The amortization is only captured for up to 80 per cent.

Answer: by using a table calculation we determine the following:

Amortization period (a) = investment (€): savings (€/a)

As it is shorter than 2 years, the implementation of the plan is recommended.

The proceeds are determined as amortized cost = purchase price – amortization. The rough amortization calculation did not take into account profit tax, subsidies or subsidized staffing costs.

1.	Purchasing expenses €	
1.1	Purchase value (PV) resources	
	1 reach truck	– 30,000
	1 vertical order picker	– 30,000
	Approx. 35 m roller conveyors	– 5,000
	Pallet shelving €13.000,– / Shelving €42.000,–	– 55,000
	Warehousing admin system (soft and hardware)	– 15,000
1.2	Building measures (estimated)	
	2 door aperture incl. doors	– 7,000
	2 wall openings for roller conveyors	– 2,000
	Identification point	– 5,000
1.3	Revenues of freed up resources (residual value)	
	Roller conveyors (2002: €18.250,–), AFA = 8 years	+ 6,850
	Forklifts (2005: €14.000,–), AFA = 10 years	+ 11, 200
	Pallet shelving (2002: €48.500,–), AFA = 8 years	+ 18,200
1.4	Total amount:	– 112,750
1.5	Contingency (Risk premium): 15%	–16,912
1.6	One-off purchasing expense	– 129,662

2.   Annual excess payments   [€/a]

2.1   Operating cost resources

      New roller conveyors (5% of PV)   − 250

      Reach truck (10% of PV)   − 3,000

      Vertical order picker (10% of PV)   − 3,000

      Replacement forklift   + 3,000

      Replacement roller conveyor   + 1,000

2.2   Wage costs

      9 staff in goods in, warehouse and goods out areas   − 315,000

      5 staff freed up for other tasks   + 175,000

2.3   Interest from 1.1 und 1.2 (8%)   − 5,960

2.4   Amortization

      Resources (1.1) 20% /a linear   − 27,000

      Building measures (1.2) 3.4% /a   − 476

2.5   Annual excess payments   − 175,686

3.   Amortization calculation: pay off period (amortization period) =

$$\frac{\text{One-off procurement expenses}}{\text{annual income surplus}} = \frac{\text{Investment} - \text{freed up resources}}{\text{Annual income} - \text{annual operating costs}} =$$

$$\frac{\text{Investment}}{\text{Operating costs old} - \text{planned operating costs}} = \frac{-129,662 \text{ €}}{-175,686 \text{ €}/a} = 0.74 \text{ years}$$

Freed up resources equal the liquidation value.

An investment is only successful if the amortization period is shorter than the period of use. The amortization calculation equals the return on investment calculation.

Asset turnover = net turnover/investment capital.

Return on sales = profit/net turnover.

Capital interest (= return on investment = asset returns) = return on sales/investment capital and is called ROI (return on investment). ROI = return on sales x asset turnover.

Figure 4.20 shows an overview of the investment calculation process and its examples.

Figure 4.20 Structure of important investment calculation processes

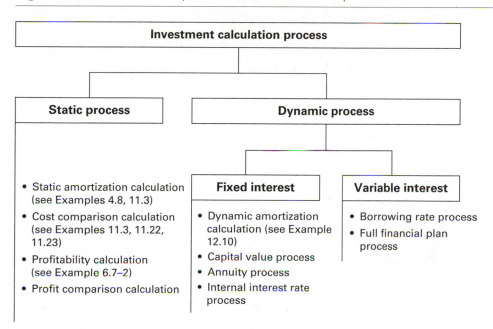

Example 4.9: Comparison of battery types

What are the features of lead batteries as opposed to NiCd batteries?

Answer: The features of a lead-acid-battery are described in Chapter 4.5.6, and include a high number of cycles, strong reliability and long usage periods. NiCd batteries have long rest times in discharged and partly discharged modes as well as good storage capacity. They have a higher energy density at lower weight, deep discharge is non-problematic, they possess high stability in the face of mechanical demands and the electrolyte does not freeze up at low temperatures. They are, however, more expensive than lead accumulators.

Questions

1 What is the task of internal transport?

2 What is the task of transport logistics?

3 What is a transport system, a transport chain and transport technology?

4 What are the criteria to structure internal means of transport?

5 What are the advantages and disadvantages as well as the deployment areas for combustion and electric motor drives?

6   What is the structure of a battery?

7   What is the lifespan of an armour-plated battery?

8   What are the advantages and disadvantages of a battery-fed electric drive?

9   Draw a systematic structure of the types of drive for means of transport.

10   What drive batteries are there for floor conveyors?

11   What is the structure of hydro-static performance transfer for a straight motion?

12   What deployment conditions are used to choose tyres for floor conveyors?

13   What are the features to look for in tyres?

14   What types of tyre are there?

15   What are the advantages and disadvantages of super elastic tyres?

16   List the types of steel wheels for circular and drag conveyors.

17   What is the Eytelwein equation and what does it describe?

18   Deduce the drive factor k_1.

19   How do you calculate the nominal performance P_N of a drive motor?

20   What are the different processes for investment calculations?

21   What aspects should be considered for transport planning?

22   What is the definition of the amortization period?

Continuous conveyors

05

5.1 General

5.1.1 Definition, advantages and disadvantages, deployment

A continuous conveyor creates a continuous transport goods stream. It works uninterrupted across a longer period of time so that the drive has to be designed for permanent operation. Usually, a continuous conveyor only has one drive and is characterized by low energy requirements, high operating safety and simple structure. Loading and unloading can occur during operation and often at all points along the transport route. Floor-based continuous conveyors transport the goods horizontally, tilted and vertically, they have a fixed transport route and require a lot of floor space. Floor-free continuous conveyors tend to be on tracks. Continuous conveyors do not require operating staff for the transport process. Their automation is easily achieved in comparison to non-continuous conveyors. Difficulties can occur when extending the performance levels, adjusting the set-up or changing the task.

For mass good conveyance such as coal, ore, sand etc, continuous conveyors are the most effective means of transport while having a relatively low drive performance as a result of avoiding dead times and a good dead load ratio (Formula 4.10). Continuous conveyors can be mobile, driveable or fixed. They can be subject to a production process quite easily, such as heating, cooling, moistening, sorting, assembling or mixing. Usually, transport does not lead to an increase in value but only in price. As a result of the continuous or variable speed, or cycles, and via a control set-up (targeting), continuous conveyors are extremely suitable for automate transport processes in internal material flow. They can also be deployed in automated processes in production and warehousing.

Fixed machines require a lot of floor space and additional expenses, on top of the already high investment, are required for gateways and crossings. Other disadvantages are:

- fixed transport route;
- difficulties when changing production;
- very limited deployment areas in terms of transport good.

Continuous conveyors are used for cargo and/or bulk goods for the smallest and largest mass streams (belt conveyors up to 20,000 t/h) and for short, medium and large distances for (external) fixed transport routes. Operating staff are not required for the transport process. Based on these deployment possibilities, continuous conveyors can be deployed across all industry sectors.

By using modular systems and by changing speed, the capacity and machinery can be expanded. Continuous conveyors can be found to bring in and transport out materials and products in the chemical industry, mining, open-cast mining, metal processing industry, power stations, manufacturing processes, warehousing, car assembly and to connect production processes.

5.1.2 Division and sub-division

Continuous conveyors can be divided according to different aspects. On the one hand, the construction can be based on type of power transmission and the operating principle (Table 5.1); on the other hand, they can be divided by type of transport good (see Chapter 4.4):

- continuous conveyors for bulk cargo;

- continuous conveyors for general and bulk cargo;

- continuous conveyors for general cargo.

In line with the division in Table 5.2, continuous conveyors' structure, advantages/disadvantages, deployment and calculation must all be considered. Aspects for efficient transport planning are summarized in Chapter 4.9.1.

Table 5.1 Division of continuous conveyors according to constructive and functional aspects

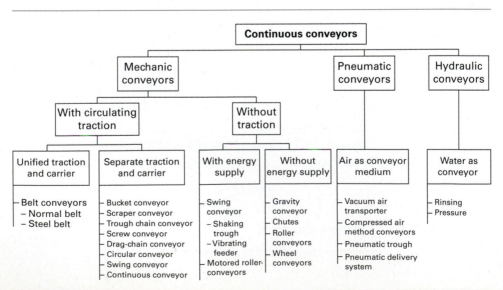

Table 5.2 Division of continuous conveyors according to transport good type

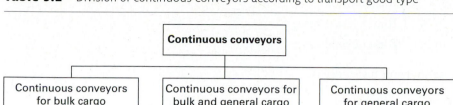

Continuous conveyors

Continuous conveyors for bulk cargo	Continuous conveyors for bulk and general cargo	Continuous conveyors for general cargo
– Bucket conveyors	– Belt conveyors	– Drag chain conveyors
– Scraper conveyors	– Link conveyors	– Circular conveyors
– Trough chain conveyors	– Chutes	– Continuous conveyors
– Screw conveyors	– Pneumatic conveyors	– Roller conveyors
– Screw pipe conveyors		– Suspension chain conveyors
– Swing conveyors		– Sorting conveyors
– Hydraulic conveyors		

5.1.3 Dimensioning basics

For dimensioning planning for continuous conveyors the following is necessary:

- transport good streams for bulk or general cargo (volume, mass or piece stream, see Chapter 2.3.2);

- inertia and acceleration (moments, performance, see Chapter 4.7.4.2).

The total resistance is calculated from the lift and friction resistance. If the mass stream reaches level H, the lift resistance is:

$$F_{wh} = \frac{\dot{m}\, g\, H}{3.6 \times v} \ [N] \tag{5.1}$$

F_{wh}	in N	Lift resistance
$\dot{m}$	in t/h	Mass stream
g	in m/s^2	Acceleration of gravity
H	in m	Lift height
v	in m/s	Transport speed

If the height difference between the goods entry and goods exit is zero (horizontal transport), then $F_{wh} = 0$.

For the purpose of dimensioning it is sufficient to calculate the total friction resistance. The required total f_{ges}, dependent on the transport good and construction of the means of transport, results from:

$$f_{ges} = \frac{F_R}{F_N} \tag{5.2}$$

f_{ges} Total friction

F_R in N   Total friction force

F_n in N   Total normal force

The total friction resistance is:

$$F_{WR} = f_{ges} L \left(m_1 g + \frac{\dot{m} g}{3.6 v} \right) \ [\text{N}]$$
(5.3)

F_{wR} in N   Total friction resistance
f_{ges} Total friction
L in m   Transport distance
m_1 in kg/m Length-related tare of means of transport
g in m/s²   Acceleration of gravity
$\dot{m}$ in t/h   Mass stream
v in m/s   Transport speed

The first item in the bracket considers the friction cause by tare, the second item the friction cause by the mass stream. The total friction resistance of a continuous conveyor is F_w and, for continuous conveyors with a pulling device (belt, rope and chain), it corresponds to the circumferential force F_u:

$$F_W = F_u = f_{ges} L \left(m_1 g + \frac{\dot{m} g}{3.6 v} \right) \pm \frac{\dot{m} g H}{3.6 v} \ [\text{N}]$$
(5.4)

For units, see Equations (5.1) and 5.3). '+' applies to upwards and '−' to downwards conveyance. The motor design occurs in line with the equations (4.2.1) ($ED = 100\,\%$).

5.2 Continuous conveyors for bulk and general cargo

5.2.1 General

The group of continuous conveyors for bulk and general cargo can be divided into:

- belt conveyor;
- link belt conveyor;
- chutes.

Belt conveyors are used for horizontal or tilted bulk and general cargo transport, where the belt is both pulling and carrying device. The belt conveyor can be split into:

- belt conveyor (rubber, textile and wire belt);
- steel belt conveyor.

Link belt conveyors are means of transport that consist of covered individual or flexible linked plates. They are powered by endless, two-stranded chains. If the plates are equipped with side panels, *trough belt conveyors* are created. If there are cross and side panels, they are called *box belt conveyors*.

Chutes are gravity conveyors and are divided into straight and curved disposal and reusable chutes as well as spiral chutes.

5.2.2 Belt conveyors

The most significant representative of the group of belt conveyors is the *rubber belt conveyor*, which comes in portable, mobile and stationary design. For transporting bulk goods, the belt operates in a troughed shape to achieve an increased level of filling. For general cargo, the flat belt is run scraping over a surface. The size of the bulk good mass stream results is calculated in dependency of the *belt width*, the *trough depth* and the *transport speed*.

The rubber belt conveyor can be found outside and in buildings, for transporting waste, stones, brown coal, ores, salts, sand, gravel, cement, cereals, packages, cartons, sacks, boxes, containers, letters, piece works or for harbour handling, in flow production or for bunkering bulk goods.

The *advantages* are:

- simple construction, high speed and low energy use;
- few drives for long transport routes, even material flow;
- suitable for short to long transport routes, universal deployment;
- little need for staffing as a result of low operating requirements and maintenance;
- quiet operation and gentle transport;
- possibility of slopes and inclines depending on transport route.

Disadvantages include:

- additional costs for elevation of means of transport in passages and crossings;
- wear of rubber belt depending on transport good;
- expensive rubber belt, limited by temperature and scraping transport good;
- fixed transport route, straight for bulk goods and large drum diameter.

Figure 5.1a   Basic structure of a rubber belt conveyor

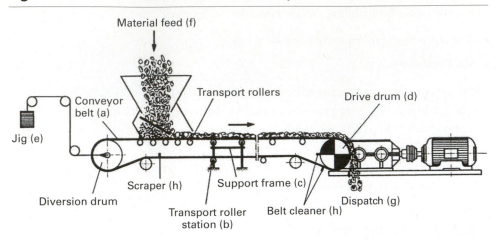

Figure 5.1a shows the *basic structure* of a rubber belt conveyor. The labels on the rubber belt show the following functions: (a) runs over moulded roller stations; (b) which are fixed on a frame. (c) The drive from the motor via clutch, brakes, gears impacts on the drive drum. (d) Through frictional connection between belt and drum, force transmission only happens when the clamping device creates pre-tension in the belt via the deflection drum. Bulk goods are fed via slides, chutes or funnels, the ejection of goods happens via dispatch head. (g) Cleaning devices (h) ensure the belt is kept clean, guidance devices ensure straight running and monitoring devices ensure secure operation.

The belt runs at speeds of up to 10 m/s (chain conveyors up to 1.5 m/s) for belt widths of up to 3.6 m. Depending on transport goods, it can get over inclines of up to +20° and can normally be deployed in up to 100 °C (180°).

A rubber belt of 3.2 m width (mould 30°) runs at a transport speed of 8 m/s and transports volume stream of 34,000 m – for the conveyance of brown coal ($\rho_s = 0.7$ t/m³) this means approximately 1,000 freight wagons.

In the copper mine of Los Pelambres (see Figure 5.1b), three machines are connected in series at 8 km in length each, contain a steel rope belt of 1.80 m in width each with cross arms in line with DIN EN 10 027-1 and transport ore upwards while crating up to 25 MW.

The *support structures* consist of lengthways beams with posts (distance 2–2.5 m) and cross connections and are manufactured for carrying and mobile rubber belt conveyors made of round or square steel, or they are welded together as segments of rolled profiles for fixed machines. Long machines are created by bolting together segments. The carrying frames are there to carry the transporting rollers. Here, we

Figure 5.1b Cross section of a conveyor machine for ore made of three steel rope belts (www.conitech.de)

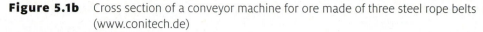
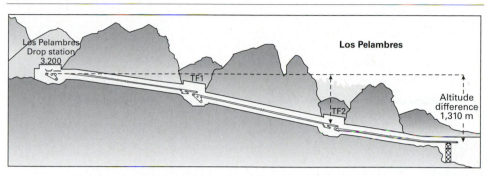

distinguish between rigid arrangements of the internal transporting rollers and flexible designs with garland transporting rollers. Shiftable means of transport are used for large earthwork projects such as brown coal and phosphate mining. They can be shifted crossways to the transport direction irrespective of their length.

Transporting rollers – often combined in transporting roller stations (troughed roller station) – carry the rubber belt. The distance between transport rollers is 0.8 to 1.5 m (and more) for the top belt and 1.6 to 4.0 m (and more) for the bottom belt. In order to minimize the drive performance and the start-up torque, the rotating mass and the friction of the transport rollers have to be small. This is why they incorporate deep groove ball bearings with low seal friction, which have to be particularly protected against dust and moisture. Nowadays, transport rollers are made in serial production. The arrangement of transport rollers leads to a flat or troughed top belt through a flat, two- or three-part troughed roller station (for DIN 22 107, see Figures 5.2 and 5.73). A 100 m long rubber belt conveyor has a three-part troughed top belt (transport roller stations 1 m apart) and for a flat bottom belt (2 m distance between the straight transport rollers) has a total of 700 deep groove ball bearings.

The transport rollers with fixed axis (for more on internal storage, see Figure 5.3) are preferred (as opposed to cap storage: external storage). The chamfered edges of the internal transport rollers lie in plain slits. The most used transport roller diameters are 63.5, 88.9, 108, 133 or 159 mm (DIN 15 207). If the transport rollers are connected through chain, cross, eyelet, rope or hook joints, they become transport roller garlands, which come closest to the ideal line of the troughed curve and, thus, the best filling cross section (see Figure 5.3).

Drive drums have standardized diameters of 200 to 2,000 mm and are made in cast steel or welded construction. The drum is 100 to 200 mm longer than rubber belt width. The size of the force to be transmitted from the drum to the rubber belt

Figure 5.2   Possible arrangement of transport rollers for top belt. a) Flat. b) 3-part troughed

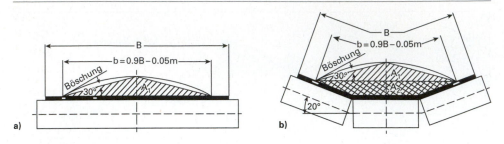

Figure 5.3   Structure and arrangement of different transport roller designs

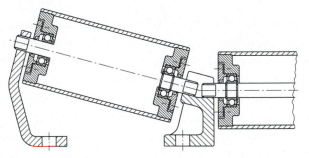

a) Transport roller station of a conveyor belt

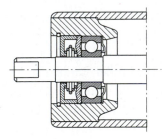
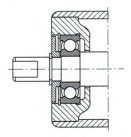
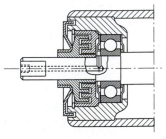

b) Transport roller of a
   sorting plant

c) Transport roller of a
   mining conveyor belt

d) Transport roller of a coal
   large belt plant

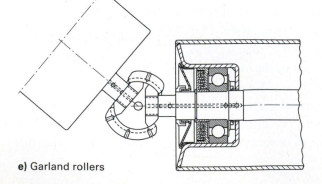

e) Garland rollers

Table 5.3 Friction between belt and drum for different operating conditions

Operating conditions	Blank steel drum	Rubber with herringbone grooves	Ceramic top layer
Dry operation	0.35–0.4	0.4–0.45	0.4–0.45
Clean operation	0.1	0.35	0.35–0.4
Wet operation with clay or loam pollution	0.05–0.1	0.25–0.3	0.35

(Drum top layer material)

is, according to equation 4.12, dependent on a wrap angle that is as large as possible, on a high friction between drum and belt (see Table 5.3) and on the pretension force. Besides the cylindrical design, there are spherical drums (good at straight runs through self-centring features) and drums made up of rods (cleaning effect). The larger the drum diameter, the lower the strain on the rubber belt.

Drives are usually arranged on the head side (goods dispatch) of the machine, for small portable or mobile belt conveyors or for multiple drum drives at the end (goods feed). This is called a pushed belt.

Possible arrangements for drives are (Figure 5.4a to f):

- for single-drum drive:
  - with head drive and direct dispatch (as shown in 'a');
  - for head drive and built-on dispatch (as shown in 'b').
- For multiple-drum drive:
  - with two-drum drive and built-on dispatch (as shown in 'd');
  - with two-drum head drive (as shown in 'e');
  - with head and end-drive (as shown in 'f').

The single-drum drive is structured as:

- *drum motor* (see Figure 5.5). It represents a compact build and is designed from 0.05 kW to 140 kW performance (see Example 5.8);
- *gear motor* with drive drum, deflection pulley, gears, short circuit or slip ring rotor motor, elastic clutch, brakes with braking fan and backstop;
- *twin drive* (two-sided).

Jigs are required because only the right pre-tension force (see Chapter 4.7.2) can enable a power transmission between belt and drum. The deflection pulley or

Figure 5.4   Possible arrangements of drives for rubber belt conveyors

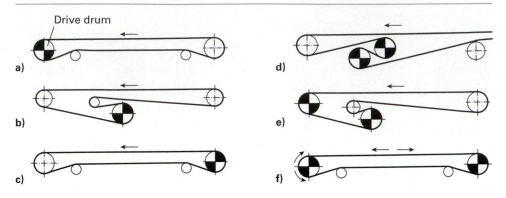

Drive drum

a)

b)

c)

d)

e)

f)

Figure 5.5   Electric drum motor

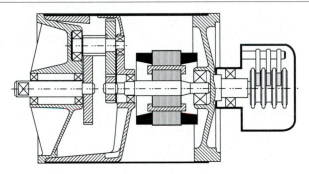

tensioning drum is flexibly mounted in lengthwise direction of the means of transport and can be shifted by the jig. We distinguish (see Figure 5.6 a to e):

- rigid tensioning devices with tensioning winch or screw spindle (as shown in 'a') for smaller rubber belt conveyors, where retensioning is necessary due to plastic belt expansion;

- independent tensioning devices with weight tensioning station (as shown in 'b'), with weight-loaded clamping loop (as shown in 'c'), with pneumatic, hydraulic (as shown in 'd'), electric (as shown in 'e') or hydraulic tensioning devices.

As the operating expansion of belts with textile insert make up 1.5 per cent for steel rope machines but only 0.1 per cent lengthwise, tensions can be interpreted differently.

Guiding devices support the straight running of a belt. This is achieved through:

- *tilted position* of 1 ° and 3 ° of the outside transport rollers of a three-part troughed roller set in transport direction;

Figure 5.6 Tensioning devices

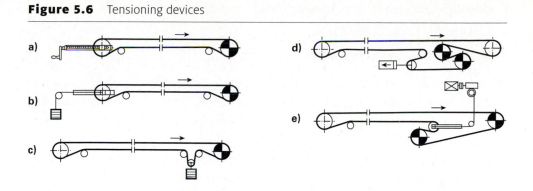

Figure 5.7 Castor set. a) Bars. b) Pivot point. c) Starting roller

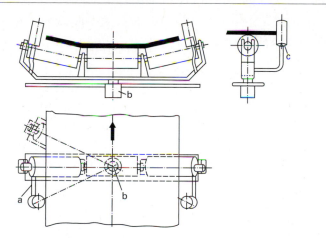

- independent *set of castors*, approximately 40 m apart (see Figure 5.7). The belt runs on the side rollers in tilted operation, creating torque, which results in the tilted position of the set of castors around the middle axis. The resulting tilted position created a realignment of the belt through side forces directed at the middle of the belt.
- *spherical* drums.

The sideways running of the belt can be caused by:

- one-sided loading of transport goods;
- insufficient cleaning of drums and transport rollers following sticky transport goods;
- different tension in the rubber belt across the belt width in the tension carrier;

Warehousing and Transportation Logistics

- side forces, caused by rain, wind or snow;

- kinks in the endless connection;

- badly aligned support structure.

Cleaning devices are there to remove sticky goods, in order to specifically prevent dirt build-up on the transport rollers for the bottom belt, the entire belt and, for multiple drums, the drive drum. Cleaning mechanisms can include: weight-bearing wipes, circulating brushes, pressured water, bar drum and belt curves for long machines.

Special attention must be given to the feeding and dispatch facilities. At the feeding point of bulk goods and general cargo, the rubber belt has to constantly do away with the drop energy of the transport good and ensure it gets to transport speed via friction. For the lowest wear on the belt one must ensure:

- short drops and feed into the transport facilities;

- the feed happens at transport speed, such as via an acceleration conveyor and dependent on the transport good.

Depending on the size of these factors, a cost-effective feeding funnel (chute) with a grid and padded rollers (see Figure 5.1a) or a small acceleration conveyor will be used. The dispatch usually occurs directly through the drive drum, via a built-on or variable jig.

Conveyor belts are simultaneously providing traction and support. The tension devices consist of several *textile inserts* for small to medium pulling force and of *steel rope inserts* for high traction. For protection from physical and chemical attack (wear, impact strain, moisture) the tension carrier is covered on all sides with an elastic material such as rubber or PVC (only for textile inserts) (see Figure 5.8a).

Natural and artificial fibres of cotton B, fibre wool Z, rayon R, polyamide P or polyester E are available as tension carriers. The lengthwise thread in fibre manufacturing is called *warp* and the cross thread is called *weft*. For fibre combinations

Figure 5.8a Rubber belt cross section a) Fabric belt. b) Steel rope belt

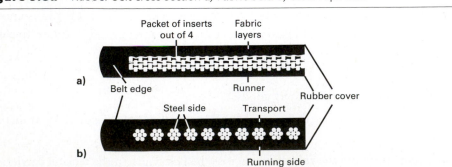

Figure 5.8b Steel rope belt structure (www.conitech.de)

this means that the first letter is the warp and the second letter the weft direction. The break resistance k_Z of the tension carrier is then given after the fibre abbreviation EP 160/65. This means this fibre has a break resistance per layer of 160 N/mm lengthwise and 65 N/mm crosswise.

While textile conveyor belts usually have a multi-layer design, a steel rope belt has one layer only (see Figure 5.8b).

Tables 5.4–5.6 list details on structure, label and calculation values, as well as the quality of cover panels for rubber conveyor belts with textile or steel rope insert. The conveyor belt lies endlessly over the drum of the transport machine. Its endless connection is particularly significant for the straight running of the belt. Nowadays single-belt conveyors are built with a distance between axis of 4,000 m, requiring 8,000 m of belt, which are put together in pieces of 100 m length (transported to deployment site: 80 connections).

The known designs for connection points of rubber belts are:

- for *textile inserts*:

  - mechanized connection in fixed or hinged form (hooks, rods or joint-connections);

  - cold glued or hot vulcanized connections as diagonal connections (see Figure 5.9a) or as zigzag connection (overlapping connections);

  - finger connection for one or two layered belts with PVC coating; this is known as a dull connection of belts, whose ends are cut into and so look like 'fingers';

- for *steel inserts*:

  - one, two or three level connections (see Figure 5.9b; DIN EN 15 236-4).

The decrease in conveyor belt firmness is balanced out by an appropriate safety number.

If you enter the forces of an endless rubber belt vertically to its direction (running direction), this creates the *belt pulling plan* (Figure 5.10).

Table 5.4   Rubber cover panel quality

Quality of cover panels	M	N	P	Q
Tensile strength lengthwise N/mm²	25	20	15	10
Elongation at break lengthwise in %	450	400	350	300
Abrasion mm³ max.	150	200	250	300

Table 5.5   Technical data for rubber belts with textile inserts

Fibre	Fibre type	Break resistance		Thickness of fibre in finished belt mm	Belt weight without cover panels kg/m²
		Chain N/mm	**Weft** N/mm		
Cotton (B)	B18	18	15	0.7	0.85
	B35	35	20	1.0	1.15
Cotton-fibre wool (BZ)	BZ50	50	30	1.2	1.44
	BZ80	80	45	1.65	1.97
Fibre wool (Z)	Z90	90	40	1.3	1.58
Polyester (E)	E100	100	40	1.0	1.70
Polyester-fibre wool (EZ)	EZ100	100	40	11	1.65
	EZ125	125	50	1.15	1.85
Polyester polyamide (EP)	EP160	160	65	1.30	1.97
	EP200	200	80	1.40	2.13
	EP250	250	80	1.60	2.31
	EP315	315	80	1.85	2.40
	EP400	400	1000	2.15	2.98

In relation to the equations (4.12) to (4.15) in Chapter 4.7.2 ($F_{S1} \triangleq F_{T1}$), the following applies:

$$F_{T1} = e^{\mu\alpha} F_{T2} = F_{T2} + F_{wo} + F_{wu}$$
$$F_{u} = F_{T1} - F_{T2}$$
$$F_{u} = F_{T2} + F_{wu}$$
$$G = 2 F_{V}$$

F_{wu}	in N	Required force to overcome motion resistance in bottom belt
F_{wo}	in N	Required force to overcome motion resistance in top belt
G	in N	Tension weight force
F_{V}	in N	Preload force, created at the redirection drum

Table 5.6 Technical data for rubber belts with steel rope inserts

Belt type	Break resistance k_z per mm Belt width in mm	Rope diameter max in mm	Rope division in mm	Break force of rope F_B in N	Min. cover thickness		Belt weight without cover in kg/m² [1]
					Transport side in mm	Running side in mm	
St 1000 [2]	1,000	4.3	12	13,250	4	4	9,5
St 1250	1,250	4.3	10	13,750	4	4	10,5
St 1600	1,600	6.0	15	26,500	5	5	14,0
St 2000	2,000	6.0	12	26,500	5	5	16,0
St 2500	2,500	7.5	15	41,250	6	6	20,0
St 3150	3,150	8.5	15	52,000	6	6	25,0
St 4000	4,000	9.5	15	66,000	7	7	30,0

1) For each mm of cover add approx. 1.15 kg/m²
2) V-DIN 22 131 Sheet 1

Figure 5.9 Connection types for rubber belts. a) Diagonal connection (textile inserts), vulcanized. b) 2-level connection (steel rope inserts)

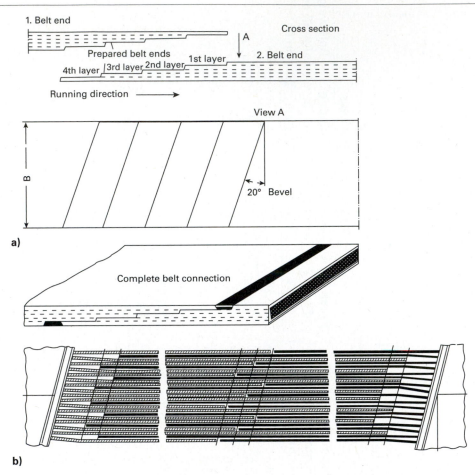

1. Belt end

Cross section

A

Prepared belt ends

4th layer / 3rd layer / 2nd layer / 1st layer

2. Belt end

Running direction

View A

B

20° Bevel

a)

Complete belt connection

b)

Figure 5.10 Belt pulling plan for horizontal conveyor with head drive

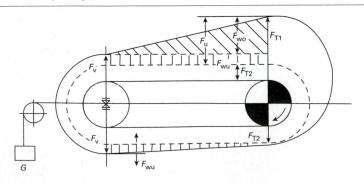

F_u F_{wo} F_{T1}

F_v F_{wu} F_{T2}

F_v F_{T2}

G F_{wu}

By equating the external forces on the belt and its internal forces, and taking into account an appropriate safety value and choosing a belt width, you arrive at the number of inserts in a belt.

$$F_{T1}v = zBk_z$$

$$z = \frac{F_{T1} \times v}{B \times k_z} \tag{5.5}$$

F_{T1}	in N	Maximum belt pulling force
k_z	in N/mm	Break strength of material, *per inserts per mm width*
z		Number of inserts
v		Safety number (Table 5.7)
B	in mm	Belt width (standard widths in DIN 22 101)

For a steel rope belt $z = 1$. The number of steel ropes is calculated as follows:

$$z_s = \frac{F_{T1} \times v}{F_B} \tag{5.6}$$

z_s		Number of steel ropes
F_B	in N	Break strength of a steel rope (see Table 5.6)

The high safety number takes into account:

- loss in strength at connection points;
- loss in strength due to age;
- additional strain as a result of belt curving;
- different level of strain in individual layers;
- acceleration force at start-up;
- high quantity of connection points;
- inserts transporting unevenly across belt width.

Usually, a belt has at least three inserts for up to 800 mm width and four inserts for over 800 mm. It is recommended to avoid more than six inserts, because this would

Table 5.7 Safety numbers for rubber belts

Number of inserts z	3 to 5	6 to 9	10 to 14
Safety number v	11	12	13

render the belt too stiff to curve. The elongation of cotton inserts is at about 15 per cent, for artificial fibres at 10 per cent and for steel ropes at 2 per cent.

The drum diameter is a function of the number of inserts, the elongation of inserts, the type of endless connection and its break strength as well as the permitted surface pressure between drum and belt. For textile inserts, the drum diameter can be calculated in line with DIN 22 101 (minimum drum diameter for finger connection, one layer: 40 mm; two layers: 60 mm; for overlapping diagonal connection one layer: 60 mm; two layers: 80 mm). For steel rope inserts, select D_{Tr} 800 to 1,400.

Calculation: The transport good stream of bulk goods depends on:

- transport speed v in m/s;
- bulk density p_s in t/m^3 (see Table 3.1, see Chapter 3.1.2);
- tilt angle δ in ° of the rubber belt conveyor;
- transport cross section A in m^2, which in return is a function of the rubber belt width B in m, the troughing shape of the belt and the flow behaviour of the bulk goods.

The volume stream $\dot{V}$ is calculated according to equation (2.1).

$$\dot{V} = 3,600 \ A \ vk \ [\text{m}^3/\text{h}] \tag{5.7}$$

k Reduction factor dependent on the tilt of the rubber belt conveyor (see Table 5.8), for other units see equation (2.1).

In line with DIN 22 101, the volume stream for medium flow behaviour with an even feed can be given depending on the rubber belt width B and the trough shape:

Flat (see Figure 5.2a) $\dot{V} = 240 \ v \ (0.9 \ B - 0.05)^2$
Troughed 20° $\dot{V} = 465 \ v \ (0.9 \ B - 0.05)^2 \ [\text{m}^3/\text{h}]$ (5.8)
Troughed 30° $\dot{V} = 545 \ v \ (0.9 \ B - 0.05)^2$

These equations, given a transport good speed of 1 m/s, arrive at a theoretical volume stream in m^3/h, listed in Table 5.9.

The mass stream is calculated according to equation (2.2).

$$\dot{m} = \rho_s \ \dot{V} \quad [\text{t/h}] \tag{5.9}$$

When determining measurements for the rubber belt conveyor for a given bulk good type and volume stream per time unit, variations can be achieved by changing:

Table 5.8 Reduction factor k

δ in °	4	10	14	16	18	20	21	22	23	24
k	0.99	0.95	0.91	0.89	0.85	0.81	0.78	0.76	0.73	0.71

Table 5.9   Volume stream in m³/h for v =1 m/s. a) Flat belt. b) Belt troughed 20°

a)

B in m	0.4	0.5	0.65	0.8	1.0	1.2	1.4	1.6	1.8	2.0
$\dot{V}$ in m³/h	23	38	69	108	173	255	351	464	592	735

b)

B in m	0.4	0.5	0.65	0.8	1.0	1.2	1.4	1.6	1.8	2.0
$\dot{V}$ in m³/h	42	70	126	197	318	467	645	850	1085	1350

- rubber belt width;
- trough shape;
- transport good speed.

$$F_\text{u} = f_\text{ges} L \left(m_1 g + \frac{\dot{m}}{3.6v}\right) \pm \frac{\dot{m} g H}{3.6v} \ [\text{N}] \qquad (5.10)$$

F_u	in N	Peripheral force at the drive drum
$F_\text{ges} = f_\text{N} f_\text{H}$		Total friction
f_N		Coefficient, whose size is dependent on the transport length; it takes into account *shunts* such as redirection resistance of the belt at the drums, drum bearing friction, friction resistance at belt entry location (see Table 5.10)
L	in mm	Length of the rubber belt transport plant (Axis distance)
f_H		Friction, takes into account *main resistance*, consisting of flex resistance of the belt and goods as well as the transport roller friction

$f_\text{H} = 0.017$ for well set-up machines with smooth running transport rollers and for transport goods with little internal friction

$f_\text{H} = 0.020$ for normally set-up machines

$f_\text{H} = 0.023$ for unfavourable operating conditions, dusty operations, transport goods with large internal friction

$\dot{m}$	in t/h	Mass stream
m_1	in kg/m	Length dependent mass of rubber belt and the rotating roller portions in the top and bottom of the machine

$m_1 = 2\,m_\text{g} + m_\text{ro} + m_\text{ru}$

m_g	in kg/m	Belt weight per m
m_ro	in kg/m	Circulating roller weight top belt per m
m_ru	in kg/m	Circulating roller weight bottom belt per m
H	in m	Lift or sink height of belt conveyor

Table 5.10   Coefficient f_N as function of transport length L

L in m	3	5	10	20	50	100	200	500	1000
f_N	9	6.6	4.5	3.2	2.2	1.8	1.45	1.2	1.1

The member '±' of the equation (5.10) gives the required peripheral force for the lift height as '+' and as '−' for the gradient, and equals zero for horizontal transport.

The steady performance at full load can be calculated in line with equation (4.21):

$$P_V = \frac{F_u v}{1{,}000 \eta_{ges}} \; [\text{KW}] \tag{5.10a}$$

The start-up performance P_{an} is given by the equation (4.18)

$$P_{an} = P_V + (1.1 \text{ to } 1.2)\, P_g \; [\text{kW}] \tag{5.11}$$

Acceleration performance for straight acceleration of masses; factor 1.1 to 1.2 means a 10 to 20 per cent addition for the acceleration performance of the rotating mass.

$$P_g = \frac{L\left(m_1 + \frac{\dot{m}}{3.6 v}\right) v^2}{1.000\, t_a \eta_{ges}} \; [\text{kW}] \tag{5.12}$$

t_a in s   Start-up time of an asynchronous motor is (equation (4.17))

$$P = \frac{P_{an}}{1.7 - 2.0} > P_V \; [\text{kW}] \tag{5.13}$$

Belt conveyor types *Steep incline conveyor belts* were developed in order to transport goods up as steep an angle as possible. The safe transport of bulk goods with troughed rubber belt or of general cargo with a flat belt, fails depending on the transport goods at an incline angle of between 10° and 20°. In order to still overcome steeper inclines, troughed belts can be used with a special cleat design such as humped belts, V-trough belts or flat belts with cold, glued, straight or slanted T-cleats, often in connection with vulcanized or glued on waved edges on both sides. This creates a box belt (see Figure 5.11 and Example 5.3). The return and cleaning of these belt constructions causes problems. For the steep angle transport of general cargo, the cover plates of the rubber belts (transport side) are treaded to achieve better adhesion (μ value!) of the transport goods on the belt, such as fish bone, cross profile, wart or studded belt.

Figure 5.11   Steep angle conveyor belt. a) Box belt of cleats and wave edge. b) Cross section of a box belt conveyor

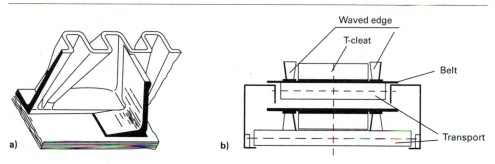

Sliding belt movement: If the transport rollers of a belt conveyor are replaced by a base of sheet metal, wood or plastic (slide track) and if a conveyor belt with minimal rubber coating (or PVC coating) on the running side (μ value!), a sliding movement of the belt will create a transport conveyor for general cargo. It is particularly characterized by a quiet, non-slacking and tremor-free operation. The entry or transfer of goods occurs on tables, chutes, roller tracks, using ejectors, such as deflectors, drivers, wipers or air pressured drivers (eg Figure 5.83).

Small conveyors with belts are used as handling devices for: assembly and manufacturing workshops to connect assembly sites; levelling; provision to workplaces; cushioning; separation; connecting machines; sorting; transport of small items.

They can be driven with variable speed, can be timed and are mobile and height adjustable. They use belts coated with rubber or PVC, or wire mesh belts, dependent on the transport goods. *Special designs* of rubber belt conveyors play a significant role in the internal material flow and exist as centrifugal belt conveyors for bulk and telescopic or curved good conveyors for general cargo.

Centrifugal belt conveyors (see Figure 5.12) consist of a short endless rubber belt that is rotated at high speed (8 to 25 m/s). The fine or medium grain bulk cargo is thrown upwards tangentially, up to 22 m wide and 10 m high (mass streams of up to 1,000 t/h). The centrifugal belt conveyor is used for large bunkers, at storage sites and to feed ship-loading areas (see Figure 5.12).

Telescopic belt conveyors are loading and unloading devices for lorries, wagons or ships and for general cargo such as sacks or cardboard boxes. High handling rates can be achieved with this means of transport as a result of short distances for stowage and modest levels of manipulation (see Figure 7.6a).

Curved belt conveyors offer the possibility to guide general cargo around bends (20° to 180°). They are used for automatic systems, such as luggage transport at large airports. The guided belt slides and runs over conical drums. A force directed at the middle of the bend is created by tensing the belt, and this is usually transmitted by the reinforced outer edge as pulling force on rollers of ball bearings (see Figure 5.13).

Figure 5.12   a) Centrifugal belt conveyor, principal sketch b) Centrifugal belt conveyor, loading of ship holds

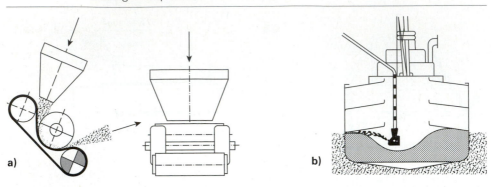

a)   b)

Figure 5.13   Curved belt conveyor a) 90° with side guidance, high speed, for luggage or mail pieces; without edge for protruding goods, low speed (see Example 5.22) b) 2 × 90° curves in S shape (a: www.transnorm.com; b: www.habasit.ch)

Basic structure

Observation perspective: generally in the curve centre

❶ Drive position outside left
❷ Drive position outside right
❸ Drive position inside right
❹ Drive position inside left

1. Redirection drum
2. Belt slider
3. Conveyor operation
4. Drive drum
5. Lower belt cover
6. Supports

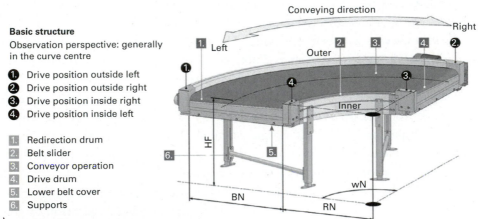

a)

b)

Figure 5.14 a/b a) Helix spiral stack made of 180° belt curve conveyors (www.transorm. com) b) Hose bag belt conveyor (www.beumer.com)

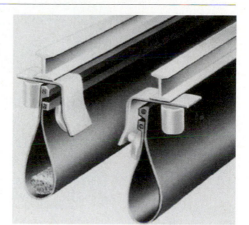

b)

a)

Curved belt conveyors include 360° spiral belt conveyors made up of 180° bends (Figure 5.14a; Figure 5.16c), special constructions such as the hose bag conveyors (see Figure 5.14b) and pipe conveyors (see Figure 5.14c); the latter two serve to transport fine grained bulk cargo that mustn't be exposed to environmental influences, or which, in the case of dusty foods, should not harm the environment. With the hose bag belt conveyor, the goods are put into the bag, which then closes automatically.

The pipe or roller belt conveyor (see Figure 5.14c) consists of a steel rope or textile belt, which is rolled up after the goods are inserted. The rollers are contained in transport and guide stations, which have to be placed short distances apart. This results in an expensive transport device. The ability to overcome inclines of up to 30° results from a larger contact area.

Strap conveyors (Figure 5.14d) are used for general cargo of different measurements, such as for flat, large goods, such as glass panels. Straps can be: toothed belt, round belt and fan belt. Lift belt conveyors are used to discharge goods from one conveyor onto another (Figure 5.14e). The lift occurs pneumatically, mechanically or hydraulically.

Figure 5.14c   Pipe conveyor (www.beumer.com)

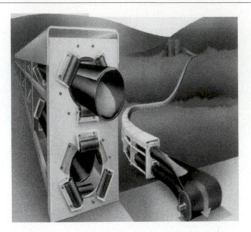

Figure 5.14d/e   Strap conveyors during discharge (www.dematic.com). e) Lift belt conveyor (www.transnorm.com)

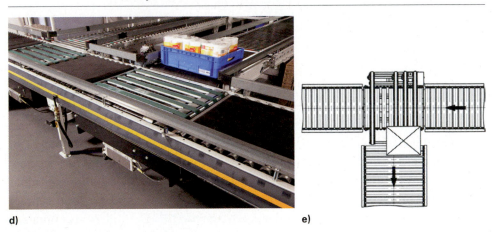

d)   e)

Wire belt conveyors Wire belt conveyors are used for the transport of hot or even glowing general cargo or large grained bulk cargo, or if cargo should be drained, dried, baked or cooled. There are different designs:

- *Wire link belts* made of flat wire with s-edges and round wire in wide spiral shape with welded edges (see Figure 5.15).

- *Wire mesh belts* made of round spiral wire and flat spiral wire.

- *Wire cloth belts* made of rods with smooth or waved crossbars or made of wire.

Figure 5.15 Round wire link belt in wide spiral design

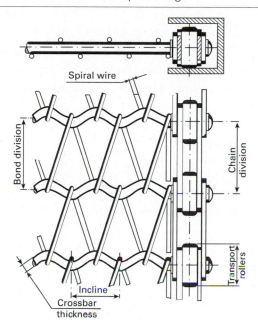

We are confronted with wire belt conveyors everywhere, which also exist as curve conveyors for all kinds of redirection angles. Places where we are likely to find one could be for drying rubber bands, cardboard, veneers, soap, tobacco or when transporting machine parts through paint spraying equipment, for screen-printing machines, in manufacturing corrugated cardboard, asbestos or rubber. They are also used to transport through baking, glass, ceramic, tempering or annealing furnaces and for manufacturing processes such as annealing, hardening, brazing, branding etc.

Steel belt conveyors are continuous conveyors for general and bulk cargo that consist of a drive and tension drum with modest width but large diameter, and which are equipped with an endless steel belt made of cold rolled carbon or stainless steel. This is supported by slide tracks or straight transport rollers. The thickness of the steel belt varies between 0.4 and 1.6 mm and depends on the belt width (up to 4.0 m), belt length (distance between axis up to 300 m) and on the cargo.

The endless connection is held together by recessed bolts. It has a high stability, a hard and smooth surface, low strain, heat, cold and rust resistance. The smooth surface allows for easy cleaning, dirt cannot cling onto anything and it is resistant to wear and tear. Scrapers can directly interact with the steel belt and a discharge of goods is easily facilitated by different scraping devices at any point on the transport route. With low speeds, the steel belt conveyor can also be used in flow manufacturing. Other deployment areas are transport of mass general cargo, with examples being packet distribution conveyors (v up to 2.5 m/s), but also transport of sticky goods such as clay, for hot goods up to 550 °C, for continuous oven and drying plants, especially in food manufacturing. Other examples include meat processing or sausage production factories due to the good cleaning ability with hot water. Special designs are perforated belts for drying and draining machines, rubber belts for people transport or magnetized belts for automated sorting systems.

5.2.3 Link belt conveyors

If plates, troughs or boxes are linked together endlessly and connected with a double-stranded chain serving as a pulling device, this creates, depending on the transport means, a *plate, trough, or box belt conveyor, as well as a spiral link belt conveyor*.

The two chains are powered by two fixed sprockets. The means of transport also includes a tension device for the chain, which is made up of either springs or weights. The chains can be: a steel bolt chain with a fixing device for the plates; a link chain in line with DIN 8175; a bushing chain (DIN 8165 Bl. 1; Figure 5.16a).

Trough and box belt conveyors are usually used for sharp edged (scrap metal), wearing (coke, slag) and hot (sinter) bulk cargo, as well as for mass goods and heavy piece goods. They are suitable for transport good streams of up to 1,000 t/h, transport lengths up to 400 m, plate or box width of 0.2 to 4.0 m and transport speed from 0.1 to 1.0 m/s. The calculation principles for plate and box belts can be found in DIN 22 200.

The spiral link belt conveyor (see Figure 5.16b) – or spiral conveyor – consists of a spiral endlessly circulating chain with specially formed plastic plates. It can continually transport goods upwards and downwards but can also be used to store. Thanks to its vertical build, it requires little space (Figure 5.16c).

Figure 5.16a   Link belt conveyor. 1) Double bushing chain with flange roller and fixing mechanism for plates. 2) Underside of link belt from Figure 5.16b: plate chain with transport rollers and guide channel (www.denipro.com)

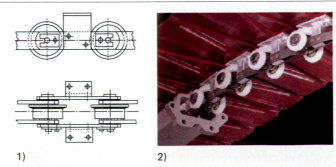

1)   2)

Figure 5.16b Spiral conveyor for packages (www.denipro.com)

Figure 5.16c Space comparison for vertical transport (www.ambaflex.com)

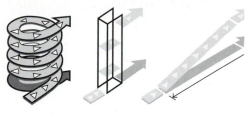

Figure 5.16d Link belt conveyor for bag transport (www.denipro.com)

5.2.4 Slides or downward pipes

Slides, chutes or downward pipes (see Figure 5.17) are used for tilted or vertical downward transport of piece general and bulk cargo. These can be straight, bent or built in single or branched design.

A slide is based on the principle of the oblique plane. If the tilt angle is larger than the friction angle between good and slide, the transport good will glide down thanks to gravity. At a constant friction coefficient mg, the good will accelerate during transport. The good's final velocity *ve* upon exiting the slide is calculated from the energy relationship on the oblique plane (see Figure 5.18):

$$GH = \frac{mv_e^2}{2} + F_R L$$

with $F_R = \mu_g \, G \cos \delta, \, L = \dfrac{H}{\sin \delta}$

results in $v = \sqrt{2gH \, (1 - \mu_g \cot \delta)}$ [ms] (5.14)

Figure 5.17   Slide designs. a) Downward pipe with points. b) Falling steps with adjustable cross bars. c) Design example of spiral slide (www.dematic.com)

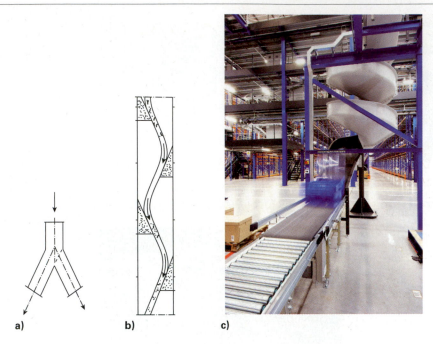

a)   b)   c)

Figure 5.18   Forces on the oblique plant for gravity transport

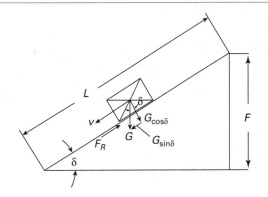

v_e	in m/s	Transport good speed at slide exit
g	in m/s^2	Earth acceleration
G	in N	Transport good weight force
H	in m	Height difference
δ	in °	Tilt angle
μ_g		Friction coefficient
L	in m	Length of oblique plane

Table 5.11 Minimum tilt angle of slides

Transport goods	Tilt angle α of slides in°
Cereal	30 to 35
Coal	30 to 40
Ore	≈45
Salt	≈50
Atomized goods	≈60
Postal packages	≈28

A given earth acceleration can be achieved for an existing height difference H through:

- alternation of μ_g on the transport path;
- inclusion of elements to slow speed;
- alteration of tilt angle δ of the slide along the transport path.

Equation (5.14) provides the tilt angle δ

$$\tan \delta = \frac{\mu_g}{1 - \dfrac{v_e^2}{2gH}} \qquad (5.15)$$

Tilt angles for straight slides made of sheet metal can be found in Table 5.11 for a variety of bulk and general cargo.

Spiral slides are open slides with a circular, elliptical or rectangular slide base winding around a pillar in helical shape. They are used to transport general cargo, such as packages, onto lower levels or sacks for the continuous loading of ships. The goods' centre of gravity follows a helical line. Bulk goods such as coal, ore and salts are transported in downwards pipes, telescopic downward pipes, closed spiral slides or in vertical gullies. These gullies' cross-bars are placed at intervals on different sides in steps (Figure 5.17b) in order to slow the cargo's speed and to destroy the kinetic energy. By including flaps or points in the pipes or spiral slides, the transport goods can be diverted into different directions. The slide or pipe can have feeds at any point. Often these means of transport are also used as buffers.

5.3 Continuous conveyors for general cargo

5.3.1 General

Continuous conveyors that are exclusively used for transporting general cargo tend to be *chain conveyors*, ie the pulling mechanism is an endless chain, the transport vessels being different trolleys or wagons, which are fixed to the chain and pulled along by drivers. These continuous conveyors include:

- drag chain conveyors (below floor conveyors);
- transport chain conveyors (chain conveyors);
- circular and drag circular conveyors;
- swing conveyors/rotating conveyors/travelling tables;
- roller conveyors with force- and form-fitting drive.

5.3.2 Drag chain and transport chain conveyors

Drag chain conveyors are mostly used for horizontal or slightly tilted transport of general cargo and consist of:

- single or double stranded chains above or, usually, under the floor (floor conveyors, underfloor conveyors).

For underfloor conveyors (for more on circular floor conveyors and floor conveyors, see Figures 5.20 and 5.77), the wagon transport occurs through a drag chain (a) laid into the floor sliding through a track profile (b). The driver (c) on the wagon provides the linkage to the chain using the driver sprocket (d).

- Slider or roller tracks, wagons.
- Driving devices that are either fixed to a chain or on the wagon (for more on principal sketches, see Figure 5.19).

Figure 5.19   Principal sketch of a drag chain conveyor with: a) Smooth sliding track b) Troughed sliding track c) Flat roller track d) Troughed roller track e) Roller wagon (f= driver)

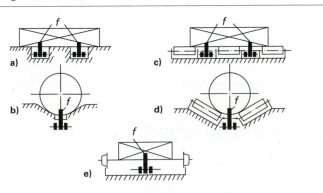

Figure 5.20   Underfloor conveyor with wagon. a)–e) See text

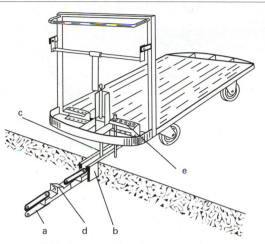

Equipped with a cost-effective, mechanic target controller (e), the underfloor conveyor can be used for automation of internal material flow and can effectively adapt to the local conditions and tasks. The wagons can be locked in and removed at any point on the route. The running lines of the drag chain conveyor are flexible but will be a circular run overall. Two separate rounds can be connected through a transfer conveyor.

Drag chain conveyors are used to transport general cargo in many different guises, including light and heavy goods conveyors for: slabs, bundles, metal sheets, rings, platins, pallets (see Figure 5.21a), crates, barrels, paper rolls.

The correct deployment depends on the right choice of the transport chain, which is simultaneously *load carrying* and *load moving* (the transport good and purpose determine the chain design). Heavy load drag chain conveyors are often moved on support frames to ensure low wear and tear and small power requirements. For transport chain conveyors with small loads, chains with sliding motion are suitable. Different uses within mechanized and automated pallet transport are shown in Figures 5.21a – as elements see Figures 5.32, 5.33 and 5.34c.

Another design for drag chain conveyors is the grid belt conveyor (Figure 5.21b) with a rubber block chain as carrier (single vulcanized steel ropes). The grid consists of corrosion-free polyester bars. Its advantages are the joint-free, noiseless and wear-resistant rubber block chain. Deployment is in coolers, water baths and in the food industry.

5.3.3 Circular conveyors, power and free conveyors

Circular conveyors (see Figures 5.22 and 5.23) and power and free conveyors (see Figure 5.25) are some of the most important continuous conveyors for general

Figure 5.21   a) Drag chain conveyor and rotating tables for pallets (www.dematic.com).
b) Grid belt conveyor (www.nerak.de)

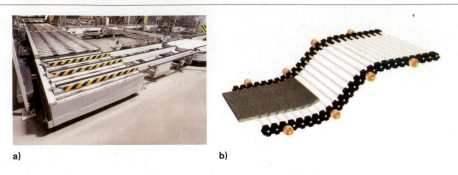

a)   b)

Figure 5.22   Circular conveyor moving up and down (www.schierholz.de)

cargo in the internal material flow and are universally used. The pulling device is an endless moving chain with fixed drives. These run on a variety of tracks. Trolleys whose design is based on the nature of the transport good are agile (sometimes rotating) and fixed on the load-bearing drives. The variable route of the track is usually placed under the ceiling of a building and fixed with bars using clamping or bolted connections on the ceiling, although it can also be held up with c or t shaped support columns. The drive tracks have I-profiles (see Figure 4.8a), with wheels running on the bottom flange, or they can be specially designed, as shown in Figures 4.8c and d. In addition to the round steel chain (see Figure 4.8d) there is also a plug-in chain.

Pairs of rollers that are spaced out at alternate 90° angles and connected by loops form cardan joint chains that can move through the room. Such cross-joint

Figure 5.23 Example of a datasheet for circular conveyors (www.schierholz.de)

Technical data Circular conveyor systems						
System	Monomatic 230	Monomatic 234	Monomatic 232	Invermatic 730	Monomatic 280	Monomatic 270
Material	Steel	Steel	Steel	Steel	Steel	Steel
Track view	⊐	⊐	⊏	⊏	I	I
Nominal route load	100 kg	100 kg	100 kg	100 kg	100 kg	230 kg
Nominal load per chain part	100 kg	100 kg	100 kg	50 kg	70 kg	230 kg
Max. chain load	7,500 N for steel chain, 5,500 N for stainless steel chain				6,500 N	18,000 N
Max. incline	4,000 N for steel chain, 5,500 N for stainless steel chain				6,500 N	8,000 N
Max. Steigung	90°	90°	90°	90°	60°	60°
Chain type	Cardan link chain partition 400 or 500 mm				Plug-in chain partition 80 mm	Plug-in chain partition 100 mm

Figure 5.24 Structure of a cardan joint chain

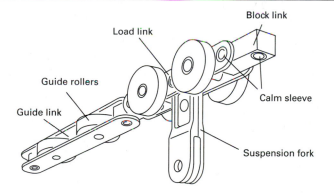

chains run sideways in the chain channel (Figure 5.24) and do not require any diverting devices. The chain channel absorbs all forces created by the pulling of the chain. Otherwise, this task is fulfilled by horizontal and vertical redirection devices, such as sprockets, arc shaped roller batteries or sheets. As the circular conveyor uses spaces such as paths, manufacturing sites and workplaces, safety measures like protection nets are required. The chain needs a drive and tensioning station. Types of drives include the *rear drive*, which occurs form-fitting via a sprocket or force-fitting via a friction wheel. On the other hand, the distance drive (drag chain drive, Figure 5.26) is used, which transfers the force on a straight piece. A short, endless drive chain

Figure 5.25   a) Power and free conveyor, cross section (www.schierholz.de) b) Case transport with P&F conveyor as well as diversion of free strand (www.schierholz.de)

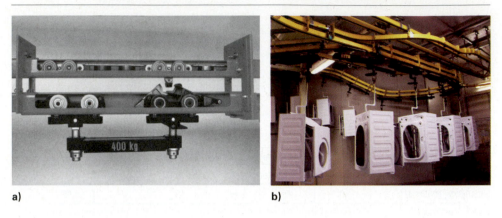

a)   b)

Figure 5.26   Drag chain drive using drivers

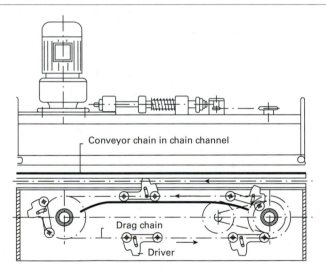

Conveyor chain in chain channel

Drag chain

Driver

interacts with the load chain via drivers. The often variable drive is most effectively placed just after large resistance, such as inclines or goods dispatchers. If the chain hoist is too high, the required drive power is distributed across two or more motors. The tensioning mechanism consists of weight or spring tensioning devices.

The circular conveyor is particularly suitable for automated transport in the internal material flow, thanks to its targeting and coding devices, and through independent feed and dispatch stations. Thus, these means of transport can often be found in:

- large serial production centres of automobile plants;
- fridge, freezer, washing machine and television manufacturing;
- paint shops;
- mail order firms;
- slaughter houses;
- the cigarette industry;
- food processing plants;
- dip procedures;
- cooling and drying rooms;
- flowing storage;
- buffers for manufacturing and assembly processes.

The *advantages* are:

- three-dimensional line;
- automation capabilities of the plant;
- low energy use;
- bridging of height differences and large distances;
- savings in floor space;
- multiple deployment possibilities;
- noiseless operation;
- good adaptability to internal material flow;
- low wear and tear of tracks and chain.

The mass stream $\dot{m}$ can be calculated in equation (2.4):

$$\dot{m} = 3.6 \frac{v}{a} \times m \tag{5.16}$$

$\dot{m}$	in t/h	Mass stream
m	in kg	Mass of transport good per trolley
v	in m/s	Chain speed = transport speed
a	in m	Trolley distance

The quantity per hour of transported goods equals the piece stream $\dot{m}_{St}$ in line with equation (2.6):

$$\dot{m} = 3{,}600 \frac{v}{a} \times z \quad \text{[pieces / hour]} \tag{5.17}$$

z Number of pieces per trolley; other units see equation (5.16).

Guiding values for circular conveyor speeds during feed and dispatch of transport goods are:

- manual $v_{max} \leq 12\text{m/min} = 0.20$ m/s
- automated $v_{max} \leq 18\text{m/min} = 0.30$ m/s

Feeder speeds for drag chain conveyors are $v_{max} \leq 24$ m/min $\triangleq 0.40$m/s. The drive performance and chain hoist force can be determined through the single resistances, such as driving resistance, redirection resistance, the roller curves, vertical bends and the incline resistance. One-motored drives power circular conveyors up to approximately 500 m, those with multiple motors up to 2,000 m transport length.

Power and free conveyors (see Figure 5.25) are made up of two separate track strands:

- Within the top part, the endless and continuously rotating chain with drivers is moving with the relevant running gear (power cord, pulling device).
- The lower strand contains load running gears (free strand).

The load running gear is connected to the chain drivers through controllable cams and can be transported to and separated from the chain at any location through discharging mechanisms. Rotating disks, points, transfer chains, lift and lowering stations allow for the stowing, storing, organization, sorting (see Figure 5.25b), de-queuing of trolleys or changing over into other transport systems. This circular drag conveyor is more suitable for being programmed through targeting controls. Another important device for the load running gear is an independent release from the power cord during buffering.

Whether an electric monorail or a power and free conveyor is utilized for a given transport task is dependent on the length of the transport route, the number of trolleys and the sequence of trolleys per time unit (see Figure 5.27).

The main disadvantage of the circular drag conveyor is the inevitable transporting of all trolleys. The *power and free conveyor* no longer has this disadvantage and

Figure 5.27   Deployment area of monorails and power and free conveyors

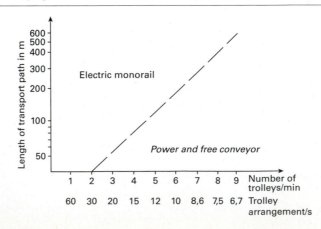

resembles the monorail in terms of flexibility (see Chapter 6.3). Only the trolleys in use are transported.

5.3.4 Roller conveyors, ball transfer tables

If transport rollers are placed a short distance apart back to back in flat or angled frames, and if these are equipped with height-variable trestles, roller conveyors are created. They come as *roller conveyors*, which *are powered*; and *roller tracks*, which are *not powered*. In both cases, we have to differentiate whether the means of transport carry heavy or light general cargo.

If the rollers are of a modest width, they are called *disk rolls* or *small rolls*. Several of these small rolls can be placed next to each other on an axis and multiple axes placed behind each other, and can be created in disk roller or small roller tracks.

Light cargo roller conveyors: Powered roller conveyors (horizontal transport) for light cargo have, depending on deployment site and load, simply built rollers made of steel or plastic, which are connected to the key areas via thread axes or by simple placement of a round axis. The division of the rollers is dependent on the shortest length of the cargo, which must have a level bottom or be placed on bars or plates (transport aids). The load area must equal 2.5 times the roller division. The transport roll must be approximately 100 mm wider than that of the cargo and be set up for a load of 70 per cent of the maximum cargo weight (see Figure 5.3).

The drive for transport rollers can be:

- friction fitting force transfer using a *rubber belt* (see Figure 5.28a) or *fan belt* (see Figure 5.28b), which run underneath the rollers against the transport direction;

Figure 5.28   Drive design for roller tracks (cross section)

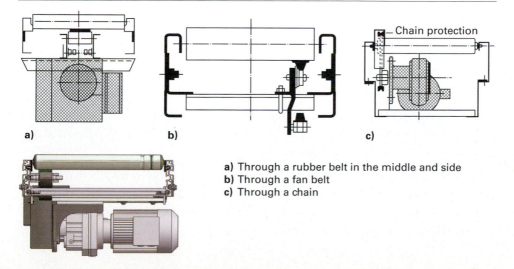

a)   b)   c)

a) Through a rubber belt in the middle and side
b) Through a fan belt
c) Through a chain

Figure 5.29   Transport rollers. a) With a sprocket. b) With a double sprocket
(www.nerak.de)

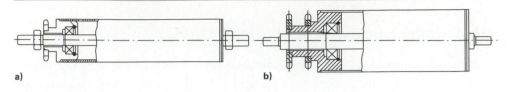

a)   b)

- form fitting force transfer with the aid of *chains* (see Figure 5.28c) and the relevant transport rollers (see Figure 5.29).

Roller conveyors can be adjusted relatively easily to the operational conditions (modular system) through the following:

- *Roller curves*

  As a result of the increasing radius, the transport speed of the goods also has to be increased radially to the outside. This occurs at the powered rollers, either through conical or divided cylindrical transport rollers with low sliding of the transport cargo (30° to 180°).

- *Discharge and transfer equipment* (VDI 3618; Examples 5.13 and 5.23)

  These are for sorting and it is hard to imagine automated internal transport without them. Systems can be found in Example 5.11, design types are:

  – *Belt transfer* (see Figure 5.30): A small powered belt protrudes to the middle of the main conveyor at a 45° angle and, in repose, lies approximately 2 mm beneath the rollers' top edge. The discharge process is achieved through lifting the belt by approximately 5 mm above the rollers' top edge. The transport cargo is necessarily brought along. Different arrangements are possible. The transport performance is a function of the speed of the main conveyor and the discharge distance, as well as the transport length, and can be seen in Table 5.12.

  – *Chain transfer* (see Figure 5.31): Two discharge chains that run crosswise to the roller conveyor are equipped with drivers, which grab the transport cargo and push it in a right angle to the means of transport. Instead of drivers, it can also be the entire chain conveyor (lift chain) getting lifted.

  – *Deflectors*: The discharge of transport cargo on roller or belt conveyors by 90° while maintaining the lengthways motion. This process is supported and accelerated by a rotating belt within the deflector.

  – *Drivers* are abruptly functioning ejectors that eject cargo vertically in the transport direction. Rotating pushers are gentler (for more on rotating arm sorter, rotary push sorter, see Figure 5.83), and discharge the cargo by 90° to the transport direction through rotating motion.

Figure 5.30a Belt transfer, discharge of general cargo at 45°

Figure 5.30b Roller transfer at under 45°. Right: discharge station general cargo transport in house up to 32 kg (www.transnorm.com)

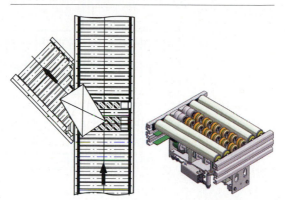

Table 5.12 Transport performance of belt transfer

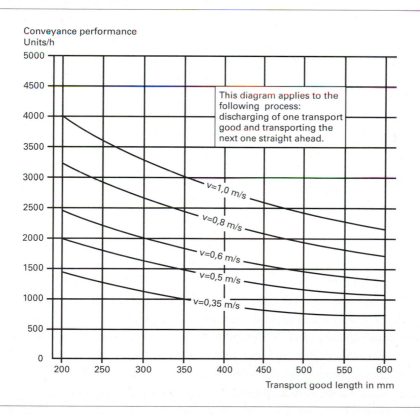

Figure 5.31   Chain transfer, discharge of general cargo at 90°

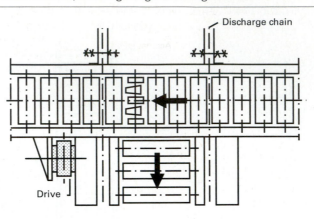

Accumulating roller conveyors enable the balance between time and quantity of general cargo, transport these over horizontal distances, allow for unpressurized stowage under low pressure and achieve a separation of transport cargo. Hence, this means of transport for general cargo is deployed in the following: warehouses; for buffering; ahead of branches; before non-continuous conveyors; ahead of palletizing machines or manufacturing machines; on collating devices.

We differentiate between unpressurized stowage and stowage at low pressure of goods.

If a container, carton, crate or package is blocked by a barrier, the weight force of the transport cargo impacts on a switch roll or a ruler, which switches off the friction between belt and transport roller at the subsequent stowage space through a linkage system.

There are other possibilities to construct low-pressure accumulating roller conveyors, such as the chain-powered accumulating *conveyor roller with slip clutch* (see Figure 5.74 for adjustable back pressure and drag force). For unpressurized accumulation, multiple roller conveyors can be connected in series, or the accumulating roller conveyor is divided into segments.

The accumulating chain conveyor utilizes a different operation method. It consists of two non-powered roller tracks that are divided by an endless chain (see Figure 5.32). The chain is divided into fully automated lift and lowering segments, creating accumulating and buffering stretches. The pneumatic chain lift makes contact with the load unit, such as a pallet, and transports it to the next free space.

Small accumulating roller tracks for small items such as tins, packages or boxes consist of rollers with ball-bearings (diameter: 20 mm, work width up to 400 mm; transport length 1 to 6 m; transport speed approximately 0.15 m/s; materials: steel,

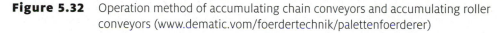

Figure 5.32   Operation method of accumulating chain conveyors and accumulating roller conveyors (www.dematic.vom/foerdertechnik/palettenfoerderer)

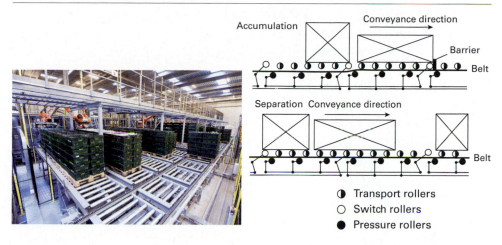

aluminium, plastic) that are hooked into two rotating chains with modes division (roller distance 25 mm). The accumulating rollers operate like rotating chain conveyors and carry the transport cargo like a belt. If there are jams, then the rollers keep rolling under the transport cargo (only suitable for horizontal transport).

Roller conveyors have other equipment such as *foldable roller tacks* for passageways, *two-way barriers* for *junctions, points, branches* and *turning opportunities*, one example being for pallets (see Example 5.25).

Heavy load roller conveyors are produced for pallet transport in the most varied of designs, in line with their function and task, and in conjunction with a control system, they allow for building an automated transport system in the internal material flow. The building components required for straight transport routes, angle changes, crossings, branches and differences in height, are represented in Figures 5.33 and 5.34 (transfer lift cars, see Chapter 6.5.1).

For non-powered roller and small roller tracks, the transport of the cargo occurs in horizontal position through external forces (through moving by *hand*) or in a slightly tilted (2° to 5°) position of the track through *gravity*. As the cargo speed is constantly increasing in heavy load systems (see Chapter 5.2.4), brakes in the form of alteration of the tilt angle, centrifugal, stream or eddy current brakes are installed.

For direct deceleration, the centrifugal brake roller is located approximately 1 to 3 mm above the rollers or small rollers of the transport track.

The small rollers (see Figure 5.35a) can also be put together in rails to form a track. Moreover, one-sided rollers with or without flange can be used to build a flow rack for crates or cartons with low weight (see Figure 5.35b/5.36).

Figure 5.33 A variety of powered roller conveyors for pallet transport (www.dematic.com)

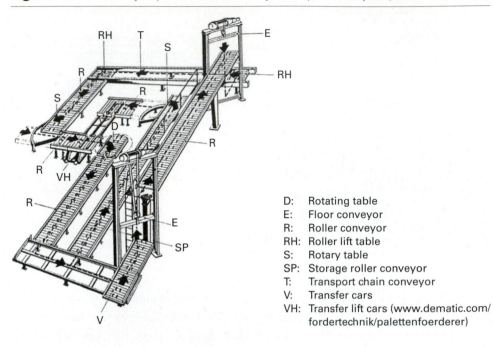

D:	Rotating table
E:	Floor conveyor
R:	Roller conveyor
RH:	Roller lift table
S:	Rotary table
SP:	Storage roller conveyor
T:	Transport chain conveyor
V:	Transfer cars
VH:	Transfer lift cars (www.dematic.com/fordertechnik/palettenfoerderer)

Figure 5.34 Components for pallet transport (www.dematic.com)

a) Rotary table

b) Roller lift table for right-angled feed and discharge of pallets (slits for transport chain conveyors)

c) Pallet check equipment, profile control via scanner

To distribute, sort or collate heavy or light general cargo using roller or small roller conveyors/tracks the following are used:

- *Transfer tracks* (for more on transfer cars, see Chapter 6.5.1).

- *Points* as roller conveyors (see Figure 5.37a) or small roller track points.

Figure 5.35 a) Small rollers. b) One-sided rollers with flange

Figure 5.36 Flow rack construction with: 1 Small roller track 2 Roller track 3 Flange rollers (see Chapter 10.3.3.2)

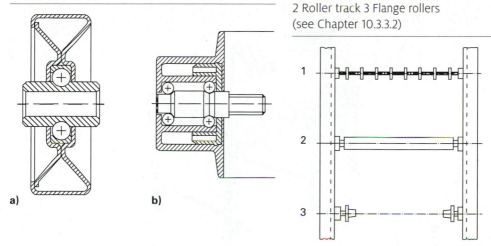

a) b)

Figure 5.37a/b a) Roller track point for three directions. b) Omniwheel

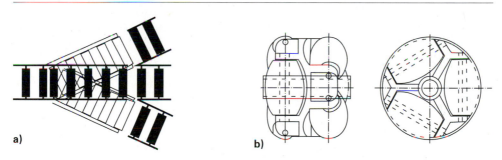

a) b)

- *Omniwheels* (see Figure 5.37b) to push cargo off by hand or air pressurized pusher equipment (pusher ≙ cross slide). The normal rollers contain double staggered small barrel rollers, rotating crossways to the transport direction.

- *Ball roller tracks* or *ball roller tables* facilitate the movement of general cargo on the horizontal plane by balls that rest on smaller balls in little pots.

- *Scissor lift roller conveyors* (Figure 5.37c) for which the length l and roller distribution t is variable by extension, the height can be altered by a telescopic pipe and any shape of curve can be achieved. Powered by gravity, and also by motor.

- Varied accessories for different tasks in a system such as manual or motor-powered *barriers, passageway pieces, diversion equipment, counters* and more.

Figure 5.37c Height variable, extendable and pliable scissor roller track (www.bestconveyors.co.uk)

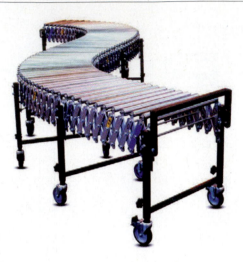

Advantages of the non-powered roller and small roller tracks (gravity conveyors):

- simple assembly;
- flexible modification and extension;
- good adaptability to tasks;
- low maintenance;
- low levels of wear;
- no energy costs;
- low investment;
- small weight;
- possibilities to combine with other means of transport.

5.3.5 *Circulating conveyors*

For general cargo such as pallets, containers and workpieces, there are circulating conveyors that work horizontally and vertically. Vertical conveyors are structured as continuous conveyors on the paternoster principle (see Figure 10.80) and on the elevator principle as non-continuous conveyors (see Chapter 6.6.2). Vertical conveyors include swing conveyors, S and C vertical conveyors, paternoster conveyors as well as special designs.

Swing conveyors consist of parallel endless two-stranded chains between which free-hanging swings or buckets are fixed on connection bars. Depending on the transport good, the swings come in different shapes. The swings always remain horizontal due to gravity and the rotating hangers.

S and C vertical conveyors both have upwards and downwards conveyance; for the S conveyor the feed and discharge points are opposite one another, for the C conveyor they are on the same side. Considerations are the transport with cargo of the same or different measurements as well as the product make-up of the transport good. The conveyancing performance for the S conveyor is up to 2,800 pieces/h, for heavy goods up to 300 pieces/h and for the conveyor up to 1,300 pieces/h. The transport good must be fed at intervals. The drive component is a rubber chain with steel rope inserts, running over plastic wheels (see Figures 5.38a and b, 5.39a and b).

Horizontal circulating conveyors include different design shapes of *conveyor tables*. Figure 5.40a is a conveyor table – rotating verticals – with tables that can be tilted and lowered. Figure 5.40b represents a horizontal conveyor table with fixed tables. Tables and wagons are usually run on tracks. Tensioning and driver stations are required for the chains that are on the side or horizontal. (see Figure 2.21).

Conveyor tables are divided in to constructive designs – horizontally (see Figure 5.40b) and vertically running conveyor tables. These general cargo conveyors

Figure 5.38a   Principle S and C vertical conveyors for small load transport. Comparison space requirements vertical conveyor/tilted belt conveyor (www.nerak.de)

Figure 5.38b   Principle C vertical conveyor for general cargo (www.nerak.de)

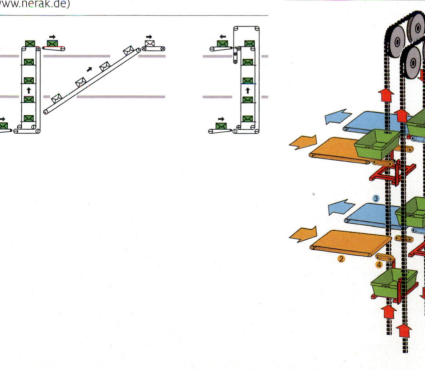

Figure 5.39a S vertical conveyor for container transport (www.nerak.de)

Figure 5.39b S vertical conveyor for pallet transport (www.nerak.de)

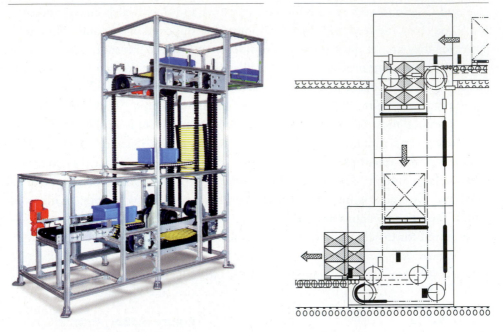

Figure 5.40 Basic representation. a)–b) See text

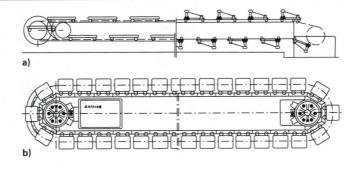

a)

b)

are deployed in flow manufacturing and assembly and operate continuously or at intervals, and are most often built into tables. Horizontally running conveyor tables are powered by chains in the centre or on the side and are connected with individual chains that are fixed to the tables or wagons. Other conveyor tables have scale-like elements that lie on top of or abutting one another, and which run around tensioning or driver stations. Tables and wagons usually run on tracks. Vertically running conveyor tables represent a compact build and are created with tables that can either be tilted or lowered.

5.4 Continuous conveyors for bulk cargo

5.4.1 General

The continuous operation of the continuous conveyors makes possible large transport good streams. Means of transport have been particularly developed in line with different operating principles for bulk goods in horizontal, tilted and vertical directions. These can be divided into:

- *bucket conveyors*: chain bucket conveyors, belt bucket conveyors and a bob bucket conveyor;
- *scraper* and *trough chain conveyors*;
- *means of transport with screws*: screw conveyors and screw pipe conveyors;
- *swing conveyors*: chutes and vibrating conveyors;
- *means of transport with air*: pneumatic conveyors, pneumatic troughs, tubular post machines and air tables.

5.4.2 Bucket conveyors

A *bucket chain conveyor* has one or two rotating chains to pull; a bucket conveyor belt has a belt. Buckets are fastened onto the belt or chain in regular intervals as load carriers. In line with the means of pulling, the drive and redirection occur via rollers, chain sprockets or drums. Bucket conveyors (elevators) are used for vertical transport of different powdery, granular or small-sized bulk cargo, such as cereals, flour, sand, cement, gravel, clinker, chemicals, coal or soot. The deployment areas include: food processing factories; mills; in the chemical industry; building material companies; foundries; coking plants.

Large conveyance height of 40 m, in exceptional cases 80 m and modest floor space requirements are the main advantages of bucket conveyors. In recent years, the chain has been mostly replaced as a pulling mechanism by the rubber belt with mesh or steel rope inserts.

The *advantages* of the bucket conveyor belt as compared to the bucket chain conveyor are:

- higher transport speed (chain: 0.3 to 1.2 m/s; belt: 1.0 to 3.5 m/s);
- quieter, noise-free operation;
- impervious to dust;
- low levels of wear;
- smaller motion resistance.

Figure 5.41   Constructive structure of a bucket conveyor belt

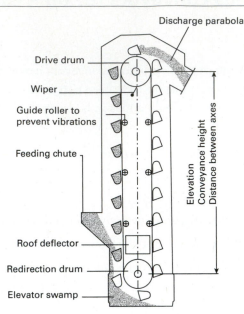

Disadvantages can be observed in the tilted operation of the belt, the fastening of the buckets and the cleaning of the drums.

Bucket conveyor belt: The constructive structure of the bucket conveyor belt can be seen in Figure 5.41. The force transfer occurs, as it does for the belt conveyor, through the friction between the belt and the drive drum. The shapes of the buckets (flat, flat round or medium deep, with even, profiled or rounded backwall) are standardized. Material can include steel sheet metal, cast steel or plastic.

Fixing the back wall of the bucket to the belt happens in line with DIN 15 236 T1 (= DIN CEN/TS), with differences according to insert. The most common bucket fastening methods on the belt are plate screws (for more on DIN 15 237, see Figure 5.42a) or bolting strips (Figure 5.42b). Because transport goods can get between the belt and the back of the bucket, and as a result of redirecting the buckets around the drum, a protective base of rubber mesh or full rubber is placed in between. To counteract the potential weakening of the belt due to the screw holes and in order to improve the redirection around the drums, elastic hangers made of rubber brackets have been developed.

The bucket strands are housed in a closed case, consisting of the *foot* (tensioning station), the *shaft* (segments) and the *head* (drive station). We differentiate the box funnel, in which both strands are housed in a common shaft and the double funnel (separation of the ascending and descending strand). The feed of the cargo

Figure 5.42   Bucket fastenings on belt with a) plate screws b) bolt strips

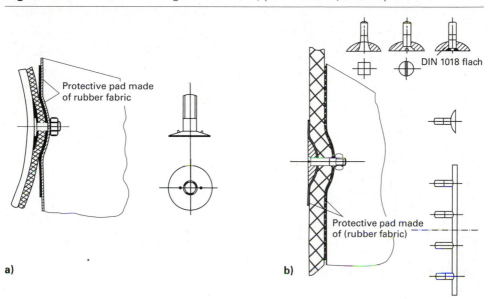

requires special attention. For light bulk cargo and low speed, the intake of the transport cargo is possible through a scooping action with higher energy requirements (Figure 5.43a), or through direct emptying of the transport cargo into the buckets, whereby the cargo that falls into the swamp is drawn away by conveyor conveying screw.

Emptying the buckets (goods transfer) is achieved through gravity (for more on bucket chain conveyors, see Figure 5.45) or centrifugal force (mostly bucket conveyor belt) (Table 5.13).

When calculating the discharge angle α (cargo lifting off bucket), the borderline case is observed, in which the centrifugal force F_f and the gravity component $G \cos \alpha$ cancel each other out in radial direction (Figure 5.43b). The following applies:

$$F_f - G \cos \alpha = 0$$

$$\cos \alpha = \frac{F_f}{G} = \frac{mr\omega^2}{mg} = \frac{v^2}{rg} = 0.00112\, n^2 r \qquad (5.18)$$

v	in m/s	Transport speed
r	in m	Radius $\approx D_{Tr}/2$
g	in m/s^2	Earth acceleration
n	in 1/min	Rotation speed of drum

Figure 5.43a Filling the bucket via scooping action

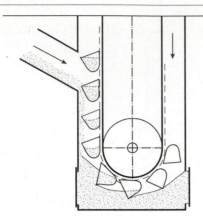

Figure 5.43b Determination of the transfer angle at bucket emptying stage

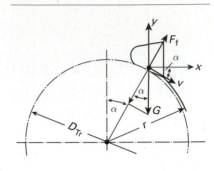

Table 5.13 Possibilities for emptying of bucket conveyors

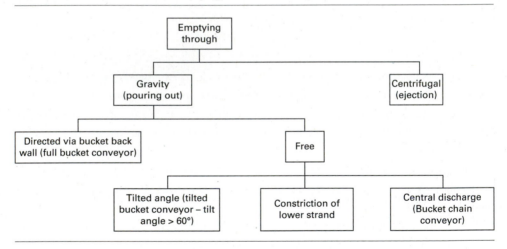

When α has been reached, the transport cargo will move – neglecting internal friction and air friction – along a throwing curve. The path equation can be calculated with the path components in the direction x and y.

$$x = v \times t \times \cos\alpha \quad \Rightarrow$$

$$t = \frac{x}{v \times \cos\alpha}$$

$$y = -v \times t \times \sin\alpha - \frac{g \times t^2}{2}$$

$$y = -x \times \tan\alpha - \frac{g}{2v^2 \times \cos^2\alpha} \times x^2 \tag{5.19}$$

The mass stream in t/h is a function of the transport cargo /characteristics, grain size, bulk density ρ_s in t/m³), the bucket contents V_B in m³, the transport speed v in m/s, the fill level 0 and the distance between buckets (bucket separation) a in m, in line with equation (2.3).

$$\dot{m} = 3{,}600\, V_B\, \varphi\, \rho_s\, \frac{v}{a}\ [\text{t/h}] \tag{5.20}$$

Values for φ, ρ_s in Table 3.1, for V_B depending on chosen bucket from DIN standard.

For calculating the belt and the transfer forces between the drum and the belt, equations in Chapter 4.7.2 are decisive. The required circumferential force F_U consists of the lift resistance F_{wh}, the *scoop force*, *discharge force* and the force to bend the bucket belt during operation around the drive and redirection drum. The ball bearing friction and the resistance of the guiding rollers can be neglected. The largest proportion is the lift resistance. This, together with the elevation H in m, results from equation (5.1).

$$F_{wh} = \frac{\dot{m}gH}{3.6v}\ [\text{N}] \quad \text{(for units, see equation (5.1))} \tag{5.21}$$

The other values are hard to determine. The force required for scooping is dependent on the following:

- the speed with which the bucket meets the resting cargo;
- the friction of the bucket within the cargo;
- the acceleration forces of the scooped cargo.

These values are determined experimentally and taken into account by additions.

The circumferential force F_u within the means of traction (chain or belt) equals the total resistance F_w and can be calculated analogous to equation (5.4), with a value added for the scoop resistance F_{ws} (f_{ges} lies between 0.04 and 0.07).

The full load inertia P_v of the bucket conveyor is calculated like this:

$$P_v = P_h + P_z\ [\text{kW}] \tag{5.22}$$

P_h	in kW	Lift performance
P_z	in kW	Additional performance requirements from feed, scoop and redirection resistances

If the buckets are arranged close to each other, a *full bucket conveyor* is created, whose lines are usually in S-shaped designs (see Figure 5.44).

Bucket chain conveyor: The buckets of the bucket chain conveyor are connected to the chain on the bucket back wall or on the side (Figure 5.45). The performance levels required can be determined in the same way as for bucket conveyor belts, but

Figure 5.44 a) Feed station. b) Discharge station. c) Full wall bucket conveyor in S-shape (www.nerak.de)

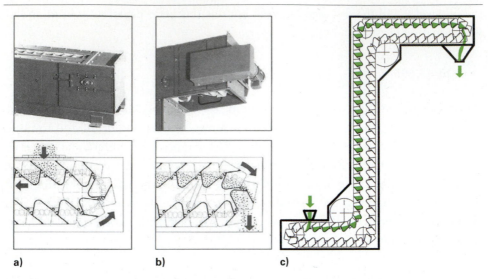

a)   b)   c)

Figure 5.45 Bucket conveyors, gravity based emptying through constriction

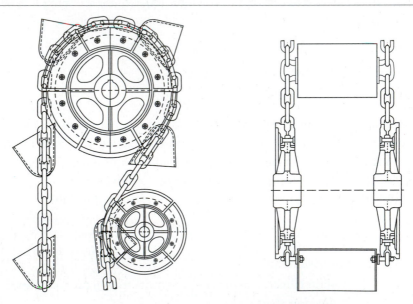

can also be taken from the equations of DIN 22 200. The sprockets of the chain star-shaft (drive shaft) are smaller than corresponding drums in the belt elevators. There are hardly any problems with guiding the chains compared to the lopsided running of the belt (deployment particularly for large mass stream of wet or muddy cargo). The bucket conveyors are equipped with backstops.

Figure 5.46 Pendulum bucket conveyor

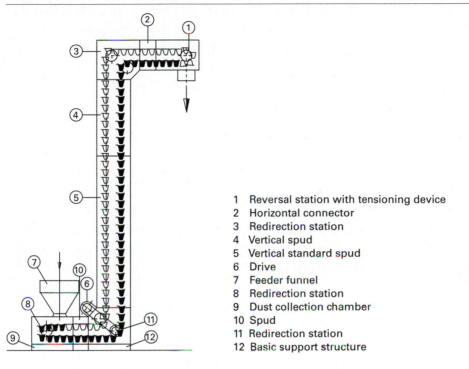

1 Reversal station with tensioning device
2 Horizontal connector
3 Redirection station
4 Vertical spud
5 Vertical standard spud
6 Drive
7 Feeder funnel
8 Redirection station
9 Dust collection chamber
10 Spud
11 Redirection station
12 Basic support structure

Pendulum bucket conveyors: Pendulum bucket conveyors are chain conveyors for all types of bulk cargo for horizontal and vertical transport (any transport lines), in which the bulk cargo is transported with swinging hanging buckets (bucket content 0.03 to 0.5m³, Figure 5.46) at speeds of between 0.15 and 0.5 m/s.

The buckets moving over the rollers in runners are placed at regular intervals between two endless chains. The transport cargo feed has to occur at a precise place and in doses such as defined, over the feeder drum or feeder wheel. The cargo discharge occurs through tilting the bucket; for this, levers or removable curve tracks move against cams or rollers, which are placed on the front of the buckets (tracks and size-based bucket allocation DIN 15 256 = DIN CEN/TS). Deployment: in power stations as coaling system; for bulk transport in the chemical and process technology industry; in agriculture for transport of cereals.

5.4.3 Scrapers and trough chain conveyors

Scraper conveyors, which are deployed for horizontal and slightly tilted transport through scrapers (drivers fixed to one- or two-stranded chains), are often used underground due to their sturdy build. The scrapers push the transport cargo forward in the transport trough. In long machines, they are supported by rollers that run along and the backwards strand can lie above or below the transport strand. *Advantages*, such as cheap production, manifold deployment possibilities and simple cargo feed and discharge compare to the following disadvantages:

- high energy requirements;
- high level wear;
- value reduction of transport cargo due to destruction and squashing;
- high maintenance cost due to dirt in the chain;
- low transport speed (0.3 to 0.9 m/s).

At transport lengths of up to 100 m underground, coal conveying of 80 to 300 t/h can be achieved, depending on construction size. For transporting powdery or small granular cargo, a capsuled scraper conveyor with rubber transport chains (steel rope inserts) and driver made of plastic is used. The transport chain is not jointed and the build is corrosion-free (Figure 5.47).

Push-bar conveyors are used for transporting metal shavings in a mechanic processing workshop. Hydraulically powered push-bars (lift approximately 1.5 m; transport speed approximately 10 m/m) slide over sliders in sheet metal ducts and possess arrow-like drivers, which are open in the transport direction (force and form

Figure 5.47   Scraper conveyor with closed build and rubber conveyor chain for powdery cargo

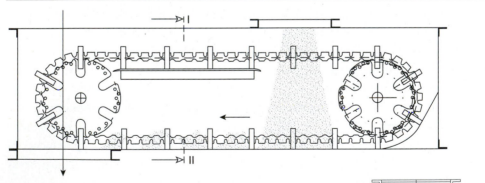

Cross section I – II

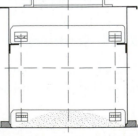

Figure 5.48 Trough chain conveyor cross-section with one- and two-stranded chain

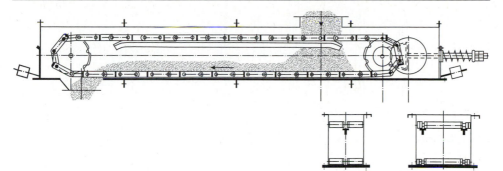

fitting drive). For the backwards motion of the push-bar, the unbroken shavings and metal shavings (at least 10 cm in length) stick to the wall hook. The fuller the duct is, the better the transport effect. It can also be deployed for manure removal with closable driver in backwards lift.

The decisive difference of the trough chain conveyor (see Figure 5.48) to the scraper conveyor lies in the transport of not just a partial amount, but an entire layer, although the one- or two-stranded chain only has narrow drivers.

The principle can be seen in the internal resistance in the cargo and at the drivers being larger than the resistance between the cargo and the smooth trough walls. The trough chain conveyor has a closed trough in which the endless chain is running so that dusty and powdery, granular and small-sized cargo in predominantly dry, non-sticky conditions such as cereals, flour, sugar, cement or chemicals can be transported.

The trough chain conveyor can also be utilized as infeed or discharge conveyor for silos. It enables horizontal, tilted, and both horizontal and tilted lines.

Shape and measurements of the chain (loop, block, fork chain) are determined. Flat cross bars or transverse bars (Figure 5.49) are used. These standardized chains include drive and diverter chain stars. The drive occurs from the drive engine onto the chain star, to the chain, which is tense through the screw spindle or pressure springs. Transport lengthens up to 60 m.

The transport good stream (up to 160 m³/h for trough width of up to 560 mm) depends on the width of the trough, the possible layer depth and the transport speed, which is based on the make-up of the cargo.

Advantages of a trough chain conveyor include:

- feed and discharge of cargo at any point;
- gentle transport, no rolling around;
- no dust emission due to closed build;
- cargo temperatures of up to 500 °C;
- modest space requirements;
- uninterrupted cargo stream.

Figure 5.49   Chain and drive designs

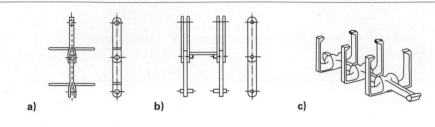

a)   b)   c)

Figure 5.50   Trough chain conveyor for vertical transport

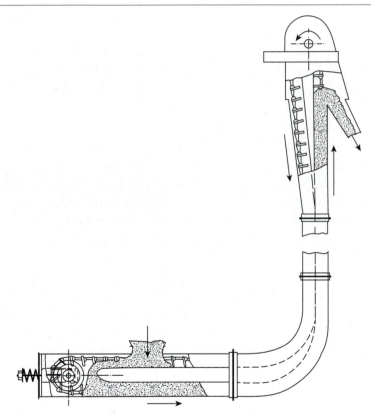

Disadvantages are:

- low speed (0.1 to 0.3 m/s);
- chain strand maintenance;
- determined transport route, hard to adjust;
- wear of trough floor and chain;
- limited types of bulk cargo.

Vertical transport can be achieved for the trough chain conveyor (Figure 5.50) by using a material column through:

- supporting the separate upwards transport strand;
- shaped cross bars (shape dependent on cargo type);
- large internal cargo friction and low external friction (friction between trough wall and cargo);
- horizontal cargo feed.

The mass stream can only be altered by increasing or reducing the chain speed. A certain cargo compression occurs during transport. The vertical trough chain conveyor can only be completely emptied by using pushers in the bottom part. Transport heights are possible up to 30 m. The volume stream $\dot{V}$ is determined in line with equation (2.1).

$$\dot{V} = 3,600 \; c_1 c_2 \nu A \; [\text{m}^3/\text{h}]$$

c_1 Reduction factor for remainder of cargo compared to chain motion for fine to large granular cargo:

- horizontal, slightly tilted: $c_1 = 0.6$ to 0.9
- vertical: $c_1 = 0.5$ to 0.7

c_2 Reduction factor for the transport cross section loss through the chain ≈ 0.95 (often neglected due to compression):

ν in m/s Chain speed
A in m² Cargo-cross section

The mass stream $\dot{m}$ is calculated in line with equation (2.2).
For the calculation of the drive performance (equation (4.21)) insert $f_{ges} \approx 0.2$ to 0.5 for drivers supported by rollers and $f_{ges} \approx 0.5$ to 1.0 for scraping drivers in equation (5.4).

5.4.4 Transport with screws

For horizontal or lightly tilted (in special cases also vertical) transport of bulk cargo, transport screws can be utilized. These can be divided into:

- screw conveyors;
- screw pipe conveyors.

The very simple structures of screw conveyors consist of a trough with cover as transport organ, the screw in different designs consists of a pusher, the drive and the cargo feeder and discharge.

The rotating screw pushes the cargo along without the cargo rotating for a horizontal transport. The cargo friction along the trough walls, the gravity and the screw shape (full screw) prevent a potential rotation. The movement of the cargo can be compared to the straight motion of a travelling nut that has been secured against turning on a rotating screw spindle. Transport occurs in the closed trough (up to 50 m transport length), which can be dust, gas or odour-proof, depending on the cargo type.

Troughs with heating and cooling mechanisms are used in order to expand the kinds of dusty, granular, small-sized, semi-wet, fibrous or pulpy cargo that can be transported by screw conveyors. This means of transport is not suitable for large grain, easily crushing, abrading as well as sticks, baking or adhesive cargo. Depending on the screw design, work procedures can also be connected to the transport process such as mixing, stirring, heating, cooling, washing or sifting.

Screw conveyors are particularly suited to deployment over short distances as feeder or interim conveyors.

Advantages are:

- simple construction;
- easy maintenance;
- small transport cross section;
- feed and discharge at any point;
- transport in closed trough (dust-free);
- good integration in automated manufacturing plants;
- small space requirements;
- low breakdown susceptibility;
- mixing effect with ribbon screw or stirring screw.

Disadvantages include:

- relatively high energy usage (Table 5.14);
- wear of screw and trough;
- danger of cargo getting stuck (jam threat);
- cargo value reduction due to crushing or abrading.

The most important component of a screw conveyor is the conveyor's screw, which is structured as:

- *full screw*: perforated round metal blanks are cut open lengthwise along the radius, pressed into a screw shape and welded onto the tubular shaft (Figure 5.51a);
- *ribbon screw*: spiral made of flat steel with bars, welded to tubular shaft (Figure 5.51b);
- *stirrer*: tubular shaft with shovels or paddles for stirring – often adjustable – representing an interrupted screw surface (Figure 5.51c).

Table 5.14   Performance comparison for continuous hourly conveying of 40 t of cement via rubber belt conveyor and pneumatic trough conveyor depending on the means of transport

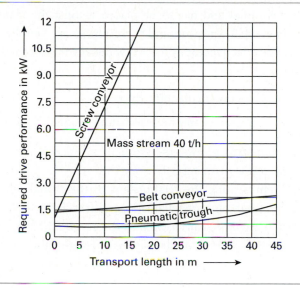

Figure 5.51   Conveyor screws: a) Full screw b) Ribbon screw c) Stirrer (paddle screw) d) Screw with right and left thread on a shaft

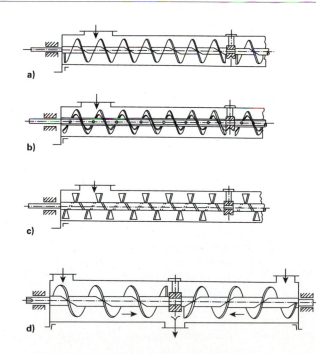

The transport direction depends on the type of thread (right or left) and the rotation directions. If right and left threads are arranged on a tubular shaft, there are different combinations available for cargo feed, distribution and cargo discharge (Figure 5.51d).

The screw shaft is radial and has to be placed against the transport direction. It requires supports every 2.5 to 3 m and these places are simultaneously used to connect the waves. The effectiveness of the screw conveyor is a function of the gradient angle of the screw:

- Large gradient angle means smaller effectiveness.
- Smaller gradient angle necessitates multiple turns, also with less effectiveness.

For small and medium-sized screws, the gradient $s \approx 0.9\ D$ and for large screws $s \approx (0.5\ to\ 0.8)\ D$ (D: screw diameter).

The fill level φ, representing the relationship of the actual and the theoretical transport volume, is a function of the diameter, gradient and length of the screw, the number of supports and connections as well as the cargo (Table 5.15).

Depending on the transport good, the conveyor trough gains movement of about 5 to 10 mm to the screw conveyor. To prevent jams, the screw shaft is either placed in the trough off centre or the trough becomes wider at the top. A long conveyor is made up of rounds of 3 to 6 m in length. Measurements for the screw conveyor and possible rotation speed (n = 140 to 16 1/min) are determined in DIN 15261-1/-2 in dependency on the screw diameter (D = 100 mm to 1,250 mm).

The mass stream $\dot{m}$ is determined by the full screw in line with equations (2.1) and (2.2):

$$\dot{m} = 60\ \frac{\pi D^2}{4}\ s\varphi n k \rho_s\ \text{[t/h]} \tag{5.24}$$

D	in m	Screw diameter
s	in m	Screw gradient
φ		Fill level
n	in 1/min	Rotation speed of the screw
k		Reduction factor for tilted transport (for $5° = 0.9$; $10° \approx 0.8$; $15° \approx 0.7$; $25° \approx 0.5$)
ρ_s	in t/m³	Bulk density (see Table 3.1)

Table 5.15   Fill level and total loss for screw conveyor

Cargo	Features	Fill level φ	Total loss f_{ges}
Sand, ash, coke	Heavy and abradent	0.125	4.4
Rough salt, sawdust, cement	Light and slightly abrasive	0.3	3.1
Flour, beans, cereal	Light and non-abrasive	0.4 to 0.5	1.8

The transport speed v is between 0.2 and 0.4 m/s and can be calculated as follows:

$$v = \frac{sn}{60} \text{ [m/s]}$$

The drive occurs via gear engines. The actual performance is hard to measure as the individual resistance values cannot be calculated accurately. We have to fall back on empirical values and work with total loss value f_{ges}. The full load inertia performance P_v of equation (5.24) produces:

$$P_v = \frac{\dot{m}g}{3,600}(Lf_{ges} \pm H)\frac{1}{\eta_{ges}} \text{ [kW]} \qquad (5.26)$$

L	in m	Transport length of screw
f_{ges}		Total loss (see Table 5.15)
H	in m	Transport height ('+' increasing and '–' decreasing)
η_{ges}		Drive efficiency
$\dot{m}$	in t/h	Mass stream

In addition to trough screw conveyors, different special constructions are used:

- *Pipe screw conveyors*: for short distances without centre bearing; fill level $\varphi = 1$; screw gradient is increased slightly after transport goods feed in order to avoid jams.

- *Press screw conveyors*: for easily flowing goods, to avoid a 'shooting through' of transport cargo when there are pressure differences; the screw pipe is designed with different gradients.

- *Mixing screw conveyors*: equipped with paddle screw, whose paddles may be adjustable in its tilted position.

- *Sifters*: for sifting out foreign objects or large pieces of cargo; screw runs within a sifting box, the screw wings are covered in sieve screens.

- *Vertical screw conveyors*: suitable for freely-flowing cargo; vertical screw run with high rotation speed (check for speed with regard to risk of bending). The transport effect occurs when the friction of the cargo on the pipe walls caused by the centrifugal force is bigger than the friction between the cargo and the screw wings. The cargo is either fed in through a funnel (Figure 5.52), or through a feeding screw. In the lower end of the screw conveyor, the screw is double-stranded and conically designed.

Flexible conveyor screws are made of a pliable wire spiral of up to 100 mm diameter, which rotates in a flexible hose. The wire spiral protrudes from the end of the hose by about 10 cm and is dipped into the cargo such as sugar, cereals, plastic granulate etc. This pliable transport screw is also suitable for vertical transport for the mass stream of granular products of up to 18 t/h and for short transport distances (up to 20 m).

Figure 5.52 Vertical conveyor screw with feeding funnel

Figure 5.53 Pipe screw conveyor b: Width of the welded in sheet metal spiral D: Pipe diameter s: Spiral gradient

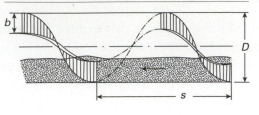

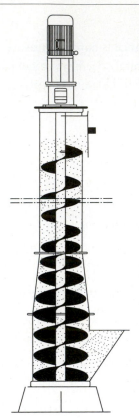

If a spiral made of flat steel is welded into a pipe in the shape of a screw, and if the pipe resting on the roller is rotated, then a pipe screw conveyor (Figure 5.53) for horizontal and vertical transport is created. As there is no bearing inside the pipe, and the power occurs along the circumference of the pipe through a sprocket, this pipe screw conveyor is particularly suited to transporting hot cargo. The rotation speed for the cargo has to be small due to the centrifugal force, as otherwise the cargo just moves around without being transported. The condition $\omega^2 r < g$ has to remain fulfilled.

This results in:

$$\omega^2 r = \left(\frac{2\pi n}{60}\right)^2 \frac{D}{2} < g$$

$$n_{\text{kritisch}} = \frac{42.7}{\sqrt{D}}\,[1/m] \tag{5.27}$$

Figure 5.54   Transport concrete mixer with two-way screw

Due to the low rotation speed and the small gradient ($s = 0.5$ D), the transport speed is between $v = 0.07$ to 0.15 m/s. With a modest radial wrap height b of the spiral ($b = 0.3$ D), and thus small values for s and v, the mass stream is at a maximum of 50 t/h. Calculations based on equation (5.24) with $\varphi = 0.25$ (maximum diameter of the screw conveyor $D = 0.8$ m; transport length L up to 50 m).

The pipe screw conveyor has the advantages of: transporting hot, abrasive and small-sized cargo; achieving a good level of mixing; offering the possibility of ventilating, warming, cooling or drying cargo with a cold or warm air stream; no pollution with grease (no bearing); avoiding crushing cargo that tends to break up.

The use of this principle can be found in the rotating ovens of the cement industry, in the transport concrete mixer (Figure 5.54), which has a two-stranded screw welded into its pear-shaped container, which – depending on the rotation direction – either works as a mixer or transport screw.

5.4.5 Vibrating conveyors

There are two ways of using vibrations to achieve the transport of cargo in horizontal, tilted or vertical lines. On the one hand, asymmetrical to-and-fro motions of a trough floor are used to equip cargo with a total of impulses in the transport direction larger than in the opposite direction, while simultaneously taking advantage of the difference between the coefficients of adhesive sliding friction – *vibrating chutes*. The other way is offered by the *vibrating trough conveyor*, where the trough floor moves up at a tilted angle. In order to achieve the cargo leaving the trough floor, the vertical acceleration has to be larger than the earth acceleration. The cargo performs a throwing motion. If this process is repeated periodically, transport occurs.

Vibrating conveyors can be used to transport non-sticky or baking bulk goods, and only allow for low layer height for dusty cargo. Work procedures can be carried out during the transport process, such as sifting, washing, draining, moistening, cooling or heating. Special deployment areas are bin discharge, the dosage and allocation for processing machines and the classification of cargo through sifting.

Figure 5.55 Vibrating chute

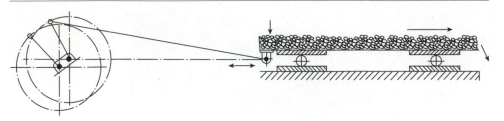

For the vibrating chute (see Figure 5.55), there is friction between the trough and the cargo, and it works in line with the *acceleration procedure*. The trough is loaded with cargo and resting on rollers, and moves slowly in a horizontal direction and back at fast speed. Due to mass inertia, the cargo keeps moving in the transport direction during the backwards motion until the friction between the cargo and the trough has used up all kinetic energy. In order to maintain the moving along of the cargo during the forward motion, the trough acceleration must not exceed $a \leq \mu r\, g$, resulting from the development of equation (4.11).

Vibrating chutes work with large amplitudes (stroke = 120 to 130 mm) and small frequencies of 50 to 100 double strokes per minute. An uneven to-and-fro motion is required, achieved through a crank mechanism with a:

$$\text{push bar ratio of} \quad \lambda = \frac{r\;(\text{crank radius})}{l\;(\text{push bar})} = 0.2 \text{ to } 0.5$$

and with cams or elliptical wheel transmission. The strands of vibrating chutes consist of rounds of up to 3 m. Mass streams are possible up to 200 t/h. The volume stream $\dot{V}$ is determined in line with equation (2.1):

$$\dot{V} = 3,600\, A\, v_m \,[\text{m}^3/\text{h}] \tag{5.28}$$

A in m²   Cargo cross section
v_m in m/s   Medium transport speed (0.1 to 0.3 m/s)

$$v_m = \frac{s_u n}{60} \,[\text{m/s}] \tag{5.29}$$

s_u in m   Distance travelled by the cargo in one to-and-fro motion of the chute
n in 1/m   Rotation speed of the cam (chute frequency)

The full load inertia performance ($\triangleq$ drive performance) is calculated using DIN equation (4.21)

$$P_v = \frac{F \times v_m}{1,000 \times \eta} \,[kW] \tag{5.30}$$

F in N   Exciting forces (trough force) $F = m_N a_r$ in kg correlate to the working load (Cargo and dead mass), a_r = chute acceleration in m/s²

v_m in m/s   Engine efficiency

η Engine effectiveness

In line with equation (5.4) about the total friction f_{ges}, the full load inertia performance is:

$$P_v = \frac{\dot{m} g L}{3{,}600} \times (f_{ges} \pm \sin \alpha) \text{ [kW]} \qquad (5.31)$$

$\dot{m}$ in t/h   Mass stream

g in m/s²   Earth acceleration

L in m   Transport length

f_{ges} Total friction $f_{ges} \approx 1.0$ to 1.5

α in °   Gradient or tilt angle

$+, -$ Upwards (+) or downwards (−) transport

In order to calculate $\dot{V}$, s_u must be determined. If the time (t) is entered in a coordinate system on the horizontal axis and the distance (s), speed (v) and acceleration (a) of the cargo (Index g) and the chute (Index r) on the vertical axis, this results in s_u as shown in Figure 5.56.

Figure 5.56   Distance, speed and acceleration curves in dependence of the time for a vibrating chute with cargo

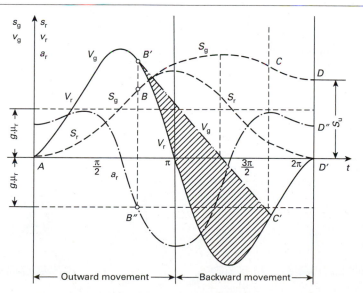

For given stroke, speed and acceleration of the crank mechanism and the friction μ_r, the cargo starts to slide forward on the chute with a delayed motion when $\mu_r g$ is reached at point B, and then executes a delayed straight motion to point c (change from adhesive to sliding motion). At this point, the trough and cargo have the same speed, so the motion happens together again from hereon. Between B and C the path of the cargo is relative to the chute and its size is the sum of su for a to-and-fro motion. This value is represented by the hatched area (integration).

Due to the high drive performance level (in order to move the mass), the high level of wear of the chute floor and the demands placed on the foundations thanks to the great amplitudes as well as the machine noise, the vibrating chute is replaced more and more by the vibrating trough.

Vibrating troughs operate in line with the throwing process (micro throw). It moves upwards in the forward phase and downwards in the backwards phase. Thus, the cargo is 'thrown' from the vibrating trough in transport direction during the initial part of the vibrating motion, creating small hopping movements. Contrary to the vibrating chute the transport procedure occurs with small amplitudes and great frequency at a nearly sinusoidal speed curve, requiring uniform acceleration during the to-and-fro motion. The vertical component of the acceleration is decisive and it has to be bigger than earth acceleration (equation (5.36)). The cargo friction with the trough is only temporary, so that we talk of a 'visibly' sliding transport. The vibrating conveyor consists of an open (trough) or closed (pipe) pan, which – depending on the drive – is supported through tilted leaf springs (steering) or compression springs on a solid or sprung counter frame, or hung up on tension springs (Figure 5.57).

The trough floor is built for the purpose of transporting lumpy cargo in either domed or beaded shape to ensure stiffness. Depending on the cargo, the trough can be covered in either rubber, plastic or special steel. Figure 5.58 represents the trough and cargo motion for a sinusoidal vibration curve.

$$s_r = r(1 - \cos \alpha) \quad \text{with } \alpha = \omega t \text{ and } \omega = 2\,\pi f$$

Figure 5.57   Vibrating conveyor with balancing mass drive a) Supported with compression springs b) Hung up on ropes and springs c) Equipped with vibrating counter frame

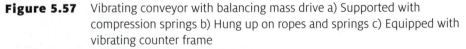
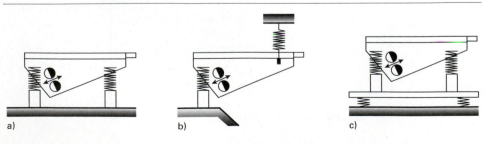

a)   b)   c)

becomes

$$s_r = r(1 - \cos(2\pi f t)) \; [m] \tag{5.32}$$

Trough speed

$$\dot{s}_r = v_r = 2\pi f r \sin(2\pi f t) \; [m/s] \tag{5.33}$$

Trough acceleration

$$\ddot{s}_r = a_r = 4\pi^2 f^2 r \cos(2\pi f t) \; [m/s^2] \tag{5.34}$$

The vertical component of the trough acceleration is the deciding factor for the transport process.

$y_r = \ddot{s}_r \sin\beta$, whose maximum size is calculated for:

$\cos(2\pi f t) = 1$ for

$$y_{rmax} = 4\pi^2 f^2 r \sin\beta \tag{5.35}$$

In creating the relationship between the maximum vertical acceleration to the earth acceleration, then you get the throw value Γ

$$\Gamma = \frac{4\pi^2 f^2 r \sin\beta}{g} \tag{5.36}$$

This means:

$\Gamma \leq 1$ no throwing motion $\rightarrow$ vibrating chute
$\Gamma > 1$ Throwing motion $\rightarrow$ vibrating trough

The theoretical transport speed v is dependent on:

- trough frequency f in 1/s
- amplitude r in m
- angle of attack β in °
- trough gradient α in °

and is calculated from the following:

- the median horizontal trough speed when moving the cargo between 0 and t_s (Adhesion time);
- the horizontal cargo speed during the throwing period t_s and t_a (Figure 5.58).

$$v = \frac{g n^2 \cot\beta}{2f} \tag{5.37}$$

Figure 5.58 Principle representation of cargo motion in vibrating troughs

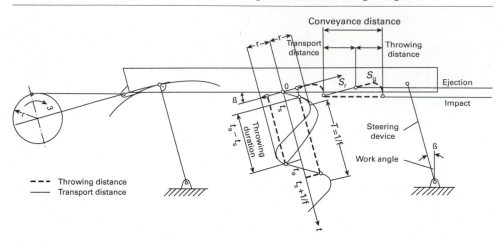

v in m/s   Transport speed

$$n = \frac{t_a - t_s}{T}$$

The equation (5.37) applies to $0 \le n \le 1$ and $1 \le \Gamma \le 3.3$ for the maximum throwing time $t_a - t_s$. If the time value is $n = 1$, then this means that one or more trough movements are skipped by the cargo.

The machine identification number K, which is a measurement for the wear of the trough parts (limitation as a result of the occurring mass forces) is used to determine the transport speed and represents the relationship between largest exciting force F_{max} for an empty trough and the trough weight force. K is dependent on the frequency f and the amplitude r.

$$K = \frac{F_{max}}{G_r} = \frac{a_{r_{max}}}{g} = \frac{4\pi^2 f^2 r}{g} \qquad (5.38)$$

G_r in N   Trough weight force

The weight force of the cargo is taken into account by increasing G_r by 20 per cent. $K < 5$ for vibrating trough in normal use; $K = 5$ to 10: limit (highly dynamically used vibrating troughs). The real transport speed is also influenced by the cargo characteristics and the transported layer height.

T	in s	Vibration length	s_g	in m	Cargo path
f	in Hz	Frequency	v_r	in m/s	Trough speed
r	in m	Amplitude	v	in m/s	Cargo speed
t	in s	Time	α	in °	Rotation angle

t_s	in s	Time of transfer	β	in°	Angle of attack (20° to 40°)
t_a	in s	Time of impact			Angle of the trough vibration
$0 - t_s$	in s	Adhesion time			against the trough floor
$t_a - t_s$	in s	Throwing time	s_r	in m	Trough path
			γ	in°	Trough tilt, angle of trough floor
					against horizontal plane

The mass stream $\dot{m}$ in t/h for horizontal transport is:

$$\dot{m} = 3{,}600 \, A \, v \, \rho_s \; [\text{t/h}] \tag{5.39}$$

A	in m²	Cargo cross section
ρ_s	in t/m³	Bulk density
v	in m/s	Transport speed

Cargo streams for bunker discharge up to 2,000 t/h and for feeds up to 1,000 t/h (width up to 2,500 mm) are possible. The use of vibration conveyors occurs:

- for transport of fine to lumpy cargo (piece size up to 1,000 mm);
- for transport of wearing and chemically aggressive cargo;
- for hot cargo in steelworks;
- to take bulk cargo out of bunkers;
- in the stone and soil industry for gravel, sand, shingle and limestone;
- to feed belt conveyors or ovens;
- in the chemical industry as allocator and compressor;
- in forges for the processing of form sand and to separate old sand from forged goods.

Advantages of the vibration trough include:

- low levels of wear, as not immediate touching of metal parts during transport;
- gentle cargo transport;
- easy maintenance;
- long lifetime;
- low noise levels, especially for padded troughs;
- safe operation, even under extreme conditions like dust and heat;
- lower energy use than for vibrating chutes;
- transport stream can be regulated through changing the amplitude, vibration number or throwing angle, especially for vibrators.

Figure 5.59   Vibrating trough with thrust crank drive

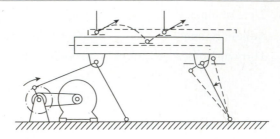

Figure 5.60   Balancing mass motor

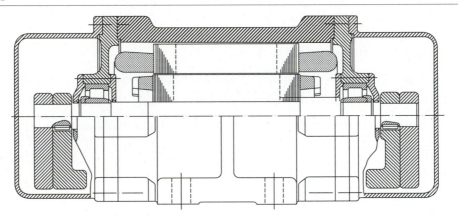

Disadvantages are stronger vibrations, the energy use is higher than that of the belt conveyor and vibrations have to be isolated from the surroundings. The drive aggregates are the most important differentiator for vibrating troughs. They are divided into trough vibrators with: thrust crank drive (forced drive); unbalanced drive (balancing mass drive); electromagnetic drive (vibrator).

Vibrating troughs with thrust crank drive (Figure 5.59) are mostly used for medium to large cargo streams (up to 200 m³/h) for transport over large distances. The transport speed is from 0.3 to 0.7 m/s.

Vibrating troughs with balancing mass drive (Figure 5.57): Balancing mass motors (Figure 5.60) are asynchronous motors with unbalancing segments on their wave ends. An increase or decrease of the unbalance means a change to the centrifugal force, and occurs through individual or multiple or differently formed disc segments or through filling up the drill-holes.

There are two possible drive designs: integration of one or two balancing mass motors. If a single balancing mass motor is used to create vibrations, it has to be connected to the trough through a torsional flexible joint, otherwise only a circular

Figure 5.61 Circular exciter

Figure 5.62 Directional exciter, unbalanced position for resulting centrifugal force

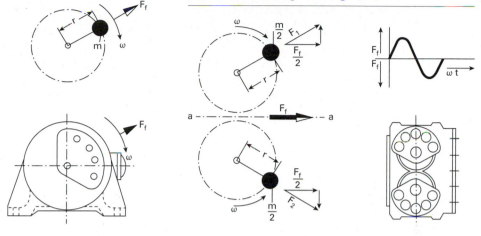

vibration will occur. This is because for a circular exciter (a balancing mass motor), the centrifugal force Ff created by the unbalance rotates with the speed of the motor (Figure 5.61).

Usually two synchronous balancing mass motors running in opposite directions are arranged as a drive (Figure 5.62) and the result is a directional centrifugal force F_f, which works along the line a-a (known as a *directed exciter*).

The same result can be achieved through a drive motor and two waves equipped with unbalancing masses, which are powered by a gear drive. Figure 5.62 shows that the components of the centrifugal forces F_1 and F_2 are added to the resulting centrifugal force F_f. Under the condition of two equal sized unbalanced masses that are staggered by 180°, and which run in opposite directions, the components placed vertically on a-a cancel each other out. The amplitudes are 5 to 0.5 mm, the frequencies are 15 to 30Hz and the transport speed is 0.05 to 0.4 m/s.

This two-mass vibration system of working load m_G and the springs c works close to the natural frequency w_E (for more on resonance range, see Figure 5.63). The relationship between operating frequency w to natural frequency w_E is called *detuning ratio*. It can be set so that the vibration amplitude of the working mass r_N does not decrease under the load of the cargo and, thus, the transport stream is also not reduced. As can be seen in Figure 5.63 the amplitude of the *basic frame* r_G can change depending on absorption D and are nearing 0.

In order to minimize the dynamic strain on the foundation by the vibration exciter and in order to undo the influence of the trough strain on the transport stream

Figure 5.63 Amplitude curve of two-mass vibration systems in dependency of detuning ratio

ω Operating angle speed

$\omega E = \omega_t$ Natural angle speed

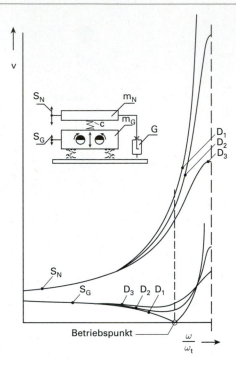

caused by the cargo, *the resonance balancing conveyor* was developed. It consists of a conveyor trough (pipe) and a counter-frame, which are connected by springs (Figure 5.57c)

Electronic magnet vibrator (Figure 5.64): a vibrating conveyor with an electro-magnetic drive, it uses the power of a magnet fed by alternating current to create vibrations. The principal build can be seen in Figure 5.64. The trough (with bulk cargo) and the anchor of an electromagnet are connected solidly with each other (working mass ≙ working side) and, together with the free mass and the bobbin (counter mass, connected via pre-tensed compression springs: storage springs), forms a two-mass vibrating system, working in the resonance area.

An alternating current of 50 Hz leads to a trough frequency of 100 Hz, which is only suitable for small troughs. Via a half-wave rectifier, the trough vibrates with 50 Hz. It is possible to change the amplitude of the vibrator through regulating the tension, so that the transport speed can also be controlled (dosage). The amplitudes are between 0.05 and 1 mm, the transport speed between 0.01 and 0.15 m/s and the frequency is between 50 and 100 Hz. Due to noise protection legislation

Figure 5.64   a) Vibrating trough with electromagnetic drive m_N: Working mass m_F: Free mass A: Anchor s: Air gap b) Vibrating conveyor: finger cascade sieve to separate and sort difference mixtures, eg stones, rubbish, etc (www.joest.com)

a)   b)

Figure 5.65   Spiral vibrational trough for vertical conveying with simultaneous air cooling of cargo (www.joest.com)

development of vibrating troughs with high performance is moving towards the balancing mass motor drive.

For vertical conveying, *spiral vibrating troughs* (Figure 5.65) are used, which are constructed from a trough that runs like a spiral around a pipe. The unbalance drives are at the foot. If the rotation direction of both unbalance drives is the same, then

Figure 5.66   Parts conveyor (sorting pan). a) Cylindrical. b) Stepped

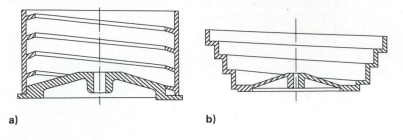

a)   b)

torsion vibrations can be achieved (torsional vibrations: forward-upwards rotation; backwards-downwards rotation). Depending on the trough width (50 to 400 mm), transport heights up to 10 m can be achieved. Outer diameter 200 to 1,600 mm, mass stream up to 30 t/h. Special deployment area: cooling and drying of bulk cargo during transport (hot sand).

Parts conveyors are used for work or packaging machines and for magazines or assembly sites; these sort, separate, order, feed or align bulk, non-directional small parts such as bolts, screws, discs etc. The parts conveyor has a pan (Figure 5.66), which creates torsional vibrations through an electric vibrator (similar to the spiral vibrating trough) and feeds the small parts through specifically shaped troughs, deflectors or chicanes into the machine in directional form. Parts conveyors are used in flow manufacturing and take on storage functions, creating a rationalizing tool for handling technology.

5.4.6 Transport with air

For these continuous conveyors, a gas stream – mostly air as carrier gas – is used as fuel in pipelines. The following means of transport can be distinguished:

- pneumatic conveyors (suction and pressure conveyors);
- pneumatic trough conveyors;
- air tables, air cushion transport;
- pneumatic tube systems.

Categorization can occur according to:

- the method of materials feed (suction or pressure conveyors);
- the operating pressure (low, medium or high-pressure conveyors);
- the transport principle (flight or flow conveyors).

The cargo concentration is decisive for the transport principle. If the air speed is higher than the floating speed, it is called *lean phase conveying* (see Figure 5.67a) or flight conveying (speeds of 10 to 40 m/s). Floating speed is the air speed at which parts are floated in the vertical airstream. The floating speed depends on the form, size and density of the parts. The pipeline is only loosely filled with cargo during flight conveying. This method is used for powdery or small sized, non-baking bulk cargo.

For *dense phase conveying*, the cargo concentration is very high, but the speed low (0.5 to 5 m/s). It is split into plug conveying (see Figure 5.67b) and thrust conveying (see Figure 5.67c). In the latter, a closed material stream is pushed through the pipeline slowly (with little air, high pressure; low wear; transport of wet cargo possible). For plug conveying, the closed material stream is divided along the transport path in individual plugs by blowing air into it. The line of the pipes can be adapted to the surroundings and installed easily.

Space requirements are low and, usually, it uses the dead space below the building ceiling. Additional *advantages* include: quiet operation; complete emptying of the machine; no loss of cargo; ventilation and cooling of cargo on the transport path; dust-free operation; no operating staff required; possibility of automatic control.

Disadvantages are: particularly high performance demands, strong wear of abrasive cargo.

As the vacuum generator is located at the end of the machine with *suction conveyors* (see Figures 5.68a and b), transport can occur *from multiple* feed stations *to one* collection site. The problem with this procedure lies in the division of cargo through air and in the discharge of cargo from the separator (cyclone) into the atmospheric area. Suction conveyors work with a vacuum of up to 0.6 bar, which is usually created by rotary blowers. These conveyors can be used to good advantage for distances up to 150 m, a transport stream up to 100 t/h, conveyor heights up to 30 m and a grain size of up to 15 mm.

Figure 5.67   Stream types for pneumatic conveying. a) Flight conveying. b) Plug conveying. c) Thrust conveying

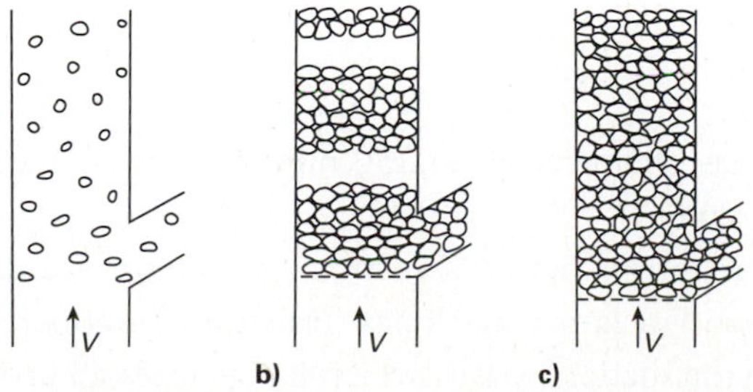

Figure 5.68a   Suction conveyors. Emptying of bulk cargo from lorry into silo and transport to the consumer (pressure conveying system)

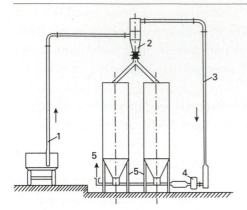

1 Suction pipe and suction hose
   (siphoning out of tanker)
2 Suction cyclone with rotary feeder,
   filter, y-pipe with flap
3 Clean air pipe
4 Blower
5 Silo battery with throughput and
   pressure conveyor pipe

Figure 5.68b   Suction conveyors extraction from multiple silos

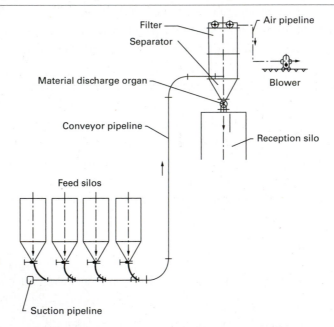

The transport pipelines (diameter 50 to 250 mm) consist of steel, glass or plastic – depending on the cargo type.

The cargo intake is carried out by a suction nozzle (hose). It is then transported on with the air stream. For larger machines (transport cargo stream up to 400 t/h) the material is fed to the suction nozzle, which hangs from an articulated, telescopic pipeline on a crane arm, through rotating distribution discs (eg when unloading cement from ships).

The separator principle consists of a significant decrease of air speed through an enlargement of the cross-section area, so that cargo parts can be separated through centrifugal force and gravity (the cyclone effect: air stream enters the separator tangentially, destruction of cargo energy through friction on the cyclone wall) and fall down. Downstream dust separators (filters) have the task of not letting any dust into the vacuum chamber. The cargo gets to its destination through container or rotary valves, which close off the vacuum chamber to the atmospheric pressure.

Pressure conveyors (Figure 5.69) are divided into low, medium and high pressure conveying. These means of transport have the problem of feeding the cargo into a pressure chamber. As the pressure generator is placed before the transport path, air pressure conveyors can transport bulk cargo *from one* feeder *to multiple* discharge stations (bunker or silo).

As the separation of cargo and air occurs in atmospheric conditions, only a few difficulties are prevalent in this part of the machine.

Figure 5.69 Pressure conveyors with different feeders. a) Using a rotary valve allocation b) Through an injector effect (nozzle and diffuser) c) Using a conveyor screw

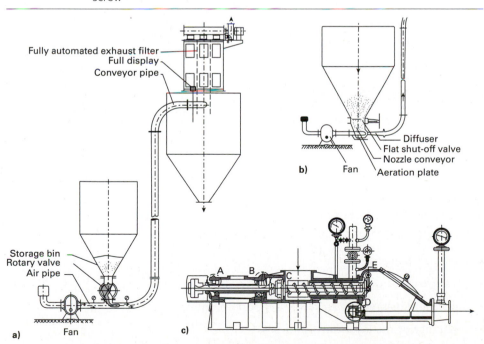

Low pressure conveying is approximately 0.1 bar for distances up to 100 m and can be used for light cargo. A fan creates the air.

Rotary blows create air pressure for medium pressure conveying (pressure 0.2 to 0.6 bars). Rotary valves (Figure 5.69a) or nozzles with diffusers (injector principle, Figure 5.69b) serve as feeders for the cargo. The transport length is up to 200 m.

For high pressure conveying (0.6 to 2.5 bars, in special cases up to 6 bars), the air pressure is created with rotation compressors, rotary blowers, screw compressors or reciprocating compressors. Large transport heights (up to 100 m) and long transport lengths (up to 2,000 m) can be achieved. The feeding of the cargo into the pressure pipeline can happen continuously thanks to high pressure screw pumps (Figure 5.69c), or pressure containers. Due to the high drop in pressure, causing problems with sealing, the performance capabilities of this kind of machine is great. Often suction and air pressure conveyors are combined in order to take advantage of both systems (simultaneous intake at multiple places and discharge at different locations) and to cover the air requirements with one drive (Figure 5.68a).

When calculating pneumatic machines, this has to be based on the given values, such as the mass stream, the cargo characteristics, the pipeline length and the determined line. The following have to be calculated and selected:

- floating speed;
- mix ratio of air and cargo;
- reduced transport length;
- pipeline diameter;
- air pressure in the pipeline;
- carrier air flow rate;
- required drive performance.

The pneumatic conveyor trough (see Figure 5.70a) is built from a conveyor trough (rectangular cross section), separated by a porous layer of textile or plastic fibres. A fan blows air into the lower part, which travels through the porous layer into the top chamber. If fine grained, powdery or dust-like cargo is put in there and if the conveyor trough has a light gradient, cargo transport is achieved through the loosening and fluidizing effect of the air. The size of the trough gradient (3 to 15°) and the required amount of air are first and foremost depending on:

- transport material;
- pressure in the air chamber;
- choice and distance of air feeder support columns;
- resistance of the layer during air passage.

Figure 5.70 a) Pneumatic conveyor trough b) Air cushion transport of a 250 t injection moulding machine (www.solving-gmbh.de)

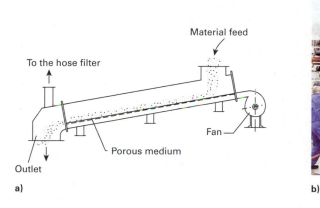

a)   b)

The transport lengths are up to 60 m, the mass streams for loosened mass cargo such as cement, aluminium oxide, or phosphate up to 1,800 t/h (normal 120 to 200 t/h). The trough width is up to 1,000 mm (normal 300 to 500 mm) and the air pressure is 20 to 50 mbar. The pneumatic troughs are connected to filters for dust removal. This closed build is complemented by open pneumatic conveyor troughs for flat silo constructions to feed the cargo from silos.

Advantages of the pneumatic conveyor troughs can be summarized as follows:

- economic transport of loose mass cargo;
- no loss of cargo and no pollution of space;
- low energy requirements (Table 5.14), low wear, maintenance and repairs;
- small measurement and easy assembly.

Air cushion transport With this principle non-dusty bulk cargo such as plastic granulate, cereals and especially general cargo of the most different shapes (round or square) with smooth floors such as boxes, cartons, bottles, tins and so on can be transported in open cargo streams. Low pressure fans – usually with controls for the amount of air – transport air in an air channel, whose topside is equipped with a metal sheet cover with nozzles and a guiding frame, and which represents the transport track. The nozzles – the shape depends on the cargo type – ensure a directional stream and thus create an air carpet, which slightly lifts the cargo and moves it with only low contact across the transport area.

Advantages of air cushion transport are:

- low maintenance operation;
- accident safety;
- no moving machine parts (other than capsuled fan);
- no joints at crossings;
- cargo feed and discharge at any point;
- adaptable to task at hand through modular system with a range of building blocks such as bends, gradients and forks;
- even cargo stream;
- simple cleaning of the transport paths (especially with food transport);
- transport with simultaneous drying and cooling possible;
- fully automated transport in gentle execution.

Air cushion transport of heavy general cargo: Figure 5.70b (see Example 6.7–3).

5.5 Standards, guidelines, recommendations

DIN standard for continuous conveyors:

DIN	15 201 1	04.94	Continuous conveyors, names, images, symbols
	15 207 2	10.00	Continuous conveyors, transport rollers for belt conveyors, key measurements
DIN	15 236 Bl. 1	04.80	Continuous conveyors, bucket conveyors, bucket fixation on belt
	22 101	12.11	Belt conveyors for bulk cargo, calculation basics
	22 107	08.84	Continuous conveyors, transport roller arrangements for belt conveyors
	22 200	05.94	Link chain conveyors, calculation basics

ISO standards for continuous conveyors:

| ISO | 703 | 06.07 | Conveyor belts, mouldability, cargo values and test methods |

The following VDI guidelines apply to continuous conveyors.

Continuous conveyors for bulk cargo:

| 2322 | Belt conveyors for bulk cargo | 10.03 |
| 2324 | Bucket conveyors (U) | 12.01 |

3602	Belt conveyors for bulk cargo	01.01
3603	Belt conveyors for bulk cargo: tensioning, diverting and return stations	11.02
3608	Belt conveyors for bulk cargo: conveyor belt	10.90
3622	Belt conveyors for bulk cargo: belt pulleys	02.97
3971	Steep and vertical conveyors for bulk cargo: designs	12.94
3972	Stockyards for bulk cargo	05.11
4436	Measurements of mass and volume flows of bulk solids	02.07

Continuous conveyors for general cargo:

2339	Operating unit for material handling systems	05.99
2340	Systematic of transfers – merges and diversions of unit loads	03.97
3584	Flow storage systems for piece goods	09.03
3618	Transfer systems for general cargo: pallets, containers and frames	10.94
3638	Palletizers	07.95
3643	Suspended trolley system, load 500 kg	11.98
3649	Calculation of availability in handling and storage systems	01.92
3978	Achievement and cycle time of piece good conveyor systems	08.98
3979	Guideline for inspection of unit load conveying systems	07.92
4420	Automated loading and unloading of lorries by piece goods	11.96
4421	Driving systems for piece goods conveying	10.00
4422	Electrical pallet conveying track, electrical conveying track	09.00
4443	Electrical pallet conveying track, electrical conveying track	12.08

FEM recommendation:

| 2.562 | Questionnaire for planning bulk cargo conveyors |

5.6 Examples and questions

Example 5.1: Drive performance of a belt conveyor with two-pulley drive

For a rubber belt conveyor with front built discharge and two-pulley drive (see Figure 5.4d), determine the spread of the motor performance across the two drive motors. To solve this task, you can assume the following:

Index 1 for pulley 1, index 2 for pulley 2

$D_{Tr1} = D_{Tr2}$ Pulley diameter

$\mu_1 = \mu_2$ Same friction by belt cleaning

$\alpha_1 = \alpha_2$ Wrap angle

$e^{\mu(\alpha/2)} = 2$ Actual value: equals $(\alpha/2) = \pi$, $\mu = 0.22$

Answer: According to Figure 5.71, the following applies to the total drive:

$$\frac{F_{T_1}}{F_{T_2}} = e^{\mu\alpha} \qquad \text{Total wrap angle } \alpha = \alpha_1 + \alpha_2$$

$$F_{uges} = F_{T_1} - F_{T_2} = F_{u1} + F_{u2}$$

Figure 5.71   Representation to determine performance spread for two-pulley drive

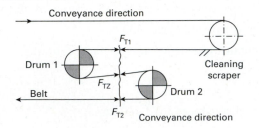

For pulley 1

$$F_{T_1} = F_{Tz}e^{\mu_1\alpha_1} = 2F_{Tz}$$
$$F_{u_1} = F_{T1} - F_{Tz}$$

For pulley 2

$$F_{T_2} = \frac{F_{T_z}}{e^{\mu_2\alpha_2}} = \frac{F_{T_z}}{2}$$

$$F_{u_2} = F_{T_z} - F_{T_2}$$

The circumferential forces behave like performance.

$$\frac{F_{u_1}}{F_{u_2}} = \frac{F_{T_z}}{1/2F_{T_z}} = 2 \triangleq \frac{P_1}{P_2}$$

Afterwards, the performance spread is 2:1.

Example 5.2: Determining transferable belt force F_{T1}

In incoming goods, a steel rope conveyor belt without name and with a width of 1,200 mm is found. What is the belt pulling force it can transmit?

Answer: Removing the rubber cover, measure the steel rope and the rope division. You get a rope diameter: 4.3 mm and a rope division of 10 mm. According to Table 5.6, these values go with belt type St 1250. For an assumed safety number $v = 10$ the transmittable belt pulling force F_{T1} according to Equation (5.5) is:

$$F_{T_1} = \frac{zBk_z}{v} = \frac{1200 \times 1250}{10} = 150 \; kN$$

(for a steel rope z = 1)

Example 5.3: Design of a cleated belt

Sand and gravel (grain 0 to 30 mm; bulk density ρ_s = 2.0 t/m³; angle of repose β_B = 20°) shall be transported over a height difference of 8 m. The required volume stream is 180 m³/h and the belt speed is 1.68 m/s.

Answer: The solution of this task is to:

- choose a conveyor design;
- choose a belt design (wave edge, cleats);
- calculate the required volume stream;
- determine the number of fibre inserts;
- determine the pulley diameter.

Figure 5.72a   S conveyor with diverting stations and belt design

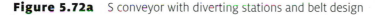

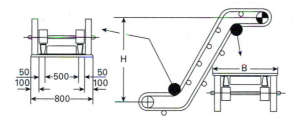

Conveyor design: In order to enable horizontal feed and discharge of the cargo, choose an S conveyor design with α = 45° gradient in line with Figure 5.72a.

Belt design: As this is steep conveying, choose a chest belt (see Figures 5.72a and 5.11) with the following measurements:

- belt width B = 800 mm;
- free edge zones for diverting rollers, 100 mm each;
- wave-edge installed on both side, 50 mm each;
- working width B_n = 500 mm;
- cleat height 140 mm;
- cleat distance 250 mm (so 4 'boxes' per m).

Checking the volume stream: You can either determine a median value of the transport volume per m (volume content in four boxes) through experiments, or you can determine the theoretical transport volume per box and per *m* via angle of repose β_B

Figure 5.72b   Cross-section of a loaded chest belt with angle of repose β

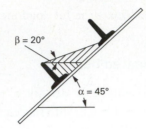

and the geometric measurements of working width, cleat height and cleat distance (Figure 5.72b). Experiments help determine a volume of 0.038 m³/h.

Equations (5.7) and (5.9) allow the calculation. According to them, the transport volume is:

$$V = \frac{\dot{V}}{v} = \frac{180}{3600 \times 1.68} = 0.03 \, \text{m}^3/\text{m}$$

The comparison from trials and the calculation results in sufficient construction. *Number of layers in belt*: Based on the given speed, the mass stream, the transport length and the transport height, equation (5.10) can determine the peripheral force F_u and equation (4.13) with Figure 4.12 can determine the maximum belt pulling power FT_1 which is 18 kN. Equation (5.5) with the selected tissue type BZ 80 determines the number of layers from Table 5.4:

$$z = \frac{F_{T_1}v}{Bk_z} = \frac{18,000 \times 10}{800 \times 80} = 2.8$$

A belt with 3 BZ 80 inserts is chosen.

Pulley diameter: the minimum pulley diameter cannot be calculated based on DIN 22101 but must be determined by using Table 5.16.

Table 5.16   Minimum pulley diameter dependent on the height of the wave edge

	Minimum pulley diameter in mm		
Wave edge height in mm	Quality: black: normal	Quality: black: oil and grease resistant, flame retardant, heat resistant	Quality: white: oil and grease resistant
60	160	200	250
80	200	250	320
100	250	315	400
120	315	400	500
160	400	500	630
200	630	800	1,000
300	800	1,000	1,250

Example 5.4: Full load inertia performance

What equation can be used to calculate the full load inertia of different continuous conveyors?

Answer: See equations (4.21), (5.4) and (5.10a).

$$P_v = \frac{F_u v}{1,000 \; \eta_{ges}} (Lf_{ges} \pm H) \; [kW]$$

Example 5.5: Transport roller station

Sketch a three-part troughed transport roller station with rubber belt in two views.

Answer: Figure 5.73.

Figure 5.73   Three-part transport roller station

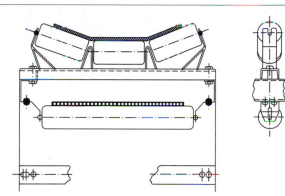

Example 5.6: Accumulation roller

Sketch and describe an accumulating roller, which is built with slip clutch and whose accumulating pressure and drag can be adjusted. The roller, consisting of steel or plastic, should be powered from roller to roller by a chain.

Answer: Figure 5.74.

Figure 5.74   Accumulating roller with slip clutch

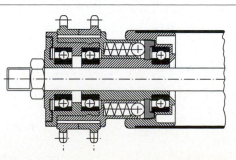

Example 5.7: Wire belts

Using sketches, show the difference in construction for wire links, wire mesh and wire fibre belts.

Answer: For more on wire link belts: Figures 5.15 and 5.75a; wire mesh belts: Figure 5.75b; wire (bar-) mesh belts: Figures 5.75c and d.

Figure 5.75   a) Wire eyelet link belt b) Wire mesh belt with hollow pin chain made of cross-spiral mesh c) Bar mesh belt with smooth crossbars d) Wire fibre belt

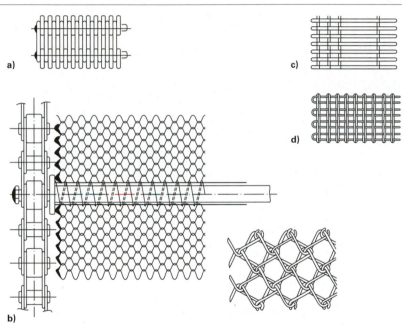

Example 5.8: Pulley motor

Motors are not just built into a pulley (for more on pulley motors, see Figure 5.5) but also into transport rollers. Where are these transport roller motors used?

Answer: Figure 5.76. Built into non-powered roller tracks, each fifth transport roller is designed as a transport roller motor. They are used in continuous gravity shelves to stabilize speed as well as horizontal transport of containers.

Example 5.9: Underfloor conveyor

How can a hand pallet truck be transported continuously?

Answer: Figure 5.77.

Figure 5.76 Example of a transport roller motor

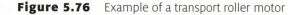

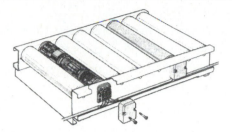

Figure 5.77 Underfloor chain conveyor (underfloor conveyor) with drag for hand pallet trucks (www.jungheinrich.de)

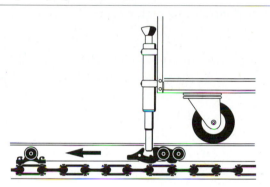

Example 5.10: Safety equipment for belt conveyors

List a number of different safety monitoring devices for belt conveyors.

Answer: Safety equipment includes: electronic speed monitor; belt operation monitor; emergency cable switch to switch off the machine; rope tear monitor; metal search device; metal cutter (eg magnetic drum).

Example 5.11: Sorting conveyor for general cargo

Sorting through general cargo discharge equipment can be shown through the use of a belt transfer (Figure 5.30) and the transfer table (Figure 6.5.1), or an entire machine for container sortation (Figure 5.88).

How can sorting conveyors be structured, and what principle do they work on? Which automatic medium and high-performance sorting conveyors are there?

Answer:

- Structure of sorting conveyors:
  - Sorting performance: sorting by hand is under 1,000 pieces/h. Sorting performance between 1,000 to 5,000 p/h is considered low and between 5,000 and 10,000 p/h is considered a medium performance. High performing sorting conveyors achieve over 10,000 p/h.
  - Structure of a sorting conveyor: The structure can be line, round, ring or circular. Sorters with line structure have low sorting performance. Sorters with ring structure can be designed very flexibly, with inclines, declines, right and left bends as well as multiple discharge points. Ring sorters can achieve the highest sorting performance. For sorters with a circular structure, the number of terminals is low, they have a compact build, which is usually made up of a rotating disk and have medium sorting performance.

- High performance sorting conveyors:

1 *Transport plate belt with transfer shoes (shoe sorters)*: The circulating slatted transport belt serves as the transport line to one side (Figure 5.78) or both sides. Between the transport plates, there are linear-guided transfer shoes, whose number is determined depending on the length of the cargo via controls. The sorting occurs at an angle of 20° or 30°. The precisely controlled, diagonal discharge process through a series of transfer shoes guarantees a gentle discharge of items with solid, smooth bottoms, with examples being boxes, packages, cartons or containers (see Example 5.16).

2 *Tilt tray sorters*: An endless powered chain with transport trays, or wagons with tilting trays powered by linear motors, they can be moved three-dimensionally (up to 15° = 27 per cent gradients for always horizontal trays) and transport the cargo to the destinations. Once arrived, the cargo is discharged to the left or right through gravity by tilting of the trays by 35°. Sorting performance of tilt trays can be 15,000 p/h. Speed can be up to 2.5 m/s with fully automated allocation and a maximum cargo weight up to 50 kg. Larger items are placed on multiple trays. Figures 5.79a and b show the top view and layout of such a machine.

3 *Cross-belt sorters (Cross-sorters)*: As for the tilt tray sorter, the cross-belt sorter consists of an endless wagon chain. The wagons are connected to each other spherically and are moved with rollers with a PU cover, with low levels of wear and noise. Instead of tilt trays, belt conveyors are installed crosswise to the transport direction, which are powered with DC motors (for discharge, contactless energy transfer, see Figure 6.63). The allocation of general cargo (packages, containers) occurs through a transfer conveyor installed at a 45° angle to the sorter, whereas the cargo has to be placed on the transfer conveyor at under 45°. Sorting performance up to 17,000 units/h for $v = 2.5$ m/s and general cargo up to 50 kg is possible (see Figures 5.80 a to c).

Figure 5.78 Transport plate conveyor: discharge of package with discharge shoes to one side (www.dematic.com/automatischesortiersysteme)

Figure 5.79a Tilt tray sorter (www.dematic.com/kippschalensorter)

Figure 5.79b Layout tilt tray sorter, round with left-sided destinations (v = 2m/s) (www.dematic.com/kippschalensorter)

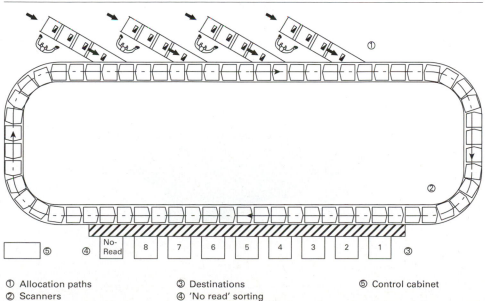

① Allocation paths ③ Destinations ⑤ Control cabinet
② Scanners ④ 'No read' sorting

Figure 5.80a   Cross-sorter (www.dematic.com)

Figure 5.80b   Modular build of a cross-belt element (www.beumer.com)

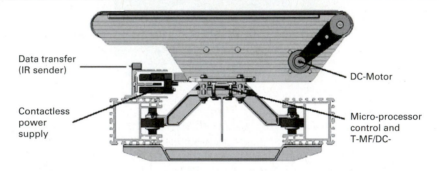

Data transfer
(IR sender)

DC-Motor

Contactless
power
supply

Micro-processor
control and
T-MF/DC-

Figure 5.80c   Cross-belt element of a cross-sorter (www.dematic.com/de/
crossbelt-sorter)

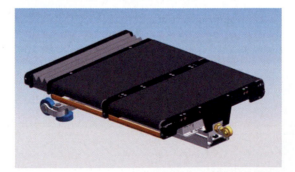

4 *Ring sorter (circular sorter)*: The cargo is transported through a transfer belt onto a circulating, self-rotating storage belt or into the segments of a rotating disc, which transport the cargo into containers or by centrifugal force (see Figure 5.81). Performance is 4,000 to 7,000 pieces per hour.

5 *Push sorter*: As shown in Figure 5.82a in cross section, this sorter works with a pusher, which pushes the cargo onto a feeding flap vertically to the distribution belt. The cargo, such as textiles, is discharged into a box by opening the flap. This is suitable for a few destinations with performance of up to 8,000 pieces per hour.

Figure 5.81   Ring sorter (www.psb-gmbh.de)

6 *Split-tray sorter*: A chain conveyor trays with foldable bottom between the links (Figure 5.82b). If a book or shirt is placed in the tray and this is located above the destination, such as a box underneath, then the tray, which is split down the middle, opens up and the cargo is discharged in a controlled manner (as with the pusher sorter). There are single, dual and quadruple split trays (Figure 5.82d).

Example 5.12: Sorters/transfer equipment

What is the difference between sorters and transfer equipment?

Answer: To sort general cargo, sorters or transfer equipment can be used.

The sorter has an integrated transfer device which cannot be disconnected. The basic means of transport for it can be a transport chain conveyor, a belt conveyor or a roller conveyor, such examples would be for the transport plate belt with transfer shoes (Figure 5.78), for the tilt tray sorter (Figure 5.79a) or for the cross-belt sorter (Figure 5.80a). Transfer devices (feeders and dischargers) can be integrated or built in retrospectively. This depends on which means of transport are to be combined (Example 5.13).

Figure 5.82a Push sorter
(push tray): Cross section
(www.dematic.com)

Figure 5.82b Split-tray sorter with single
split tray (www.distrisort.com)

Figure 5.82c   Split-tray sorter side view

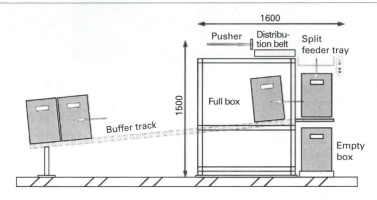

Figure 5.82d   Different versions of split trays for split-tray sorters (www.distrisorter.com)

Example 5.13: Discharge and transfer equipment

Transfer equipment is used for sorting, picking, redirecting, rotating, distributing, assembling, feeding or discharging general cargo with continuous conveyors. The equipment is dependent on the characteristics and features of the cargo, the throughput and the basic means of transport. What transfer equipment is there (see Chapter 5.3.4)?

Answer: The equipment works on the push, guide and carry principle, the push – sometimes thrust – transfer crosswise to the transport direction often incorporates:

- a thrust motion of the cargo;
- an empty motion when returning to the original position;
- a frontal change that can be built in retrospectively depending on design.

The guiding transfer occurs through sideways redirection along a sheet or along a powered strap. This means:

- no frontal change of the cargo;
- insignificant thrust effect;
- can be built in retrospectively.

The carrying transfer grabs the cargo on its running side. Hence, the make-up of the cargo bottom is of particular importance for the use and performance. Features are:

- no thrust;
- no cargo frontal change;
- retrospective integration is not possible.

The transfer equipment can be distinguished into whether:

- they can be integrated or built in retrospectively;
- they are powered or not (gravity);
- they work in a horizontal or vertical way;
- they have a linear or rotating structure;
- they have transfer equipment that is carried along.

Rotating transfer equipment (deflector, rotating pusher) is shown in Figure 5.83. It can be built onto a belt conveyor and achieves a tailored, gentle discharge of the cargo through a sinusoidal speed curve of the discharge arm. It is used for cargo with a weight of up to 30 kg and measurements of up to $1000 \times 800 \times 800$ mm. The performance can be up to 6,000 pieces per hour. The transfer equipment operates noiselessly, is easily installed and has a high functional reliability.

Figure 5.83   Rotating deflector (rotating arm sorter) (www.lippert.de)

Transfer equipment (see VDI 2340) includes:

- feeding and discharging means of transport, such as lift tables (Figure 6.2.1), pivot and turntables (Figure 5.33), points, transfer cars (Figure 6.5.1), belt transfer (Figure 5.30);

- deflectors, such as insertable, rotating and pivoted deflectors (pushers), plate belt conveyors with sliding shoes, chain transfer (Figure 5.3.1), tilt tray sorter (Figure 5.79a and b), cross-sorter (Figure 5.80a), transport plate belt with discharge shoes (Figure 5.78).

Example 5.14: Hinged belt conveyors

Show two different hinged belt conveyors in a sketch.

Answer: Figure 5.84. For conveyor tables, see Figures 5.40 and 2.21.

Example 5.15: Sorting of bulk cargo mixtures with air classifiers

What principles do air classifiers work on and what procedures are there?

Answer: With air classifiers, light bulk cargo mixtures can be separated by air flow. The physical principle is based on the stationary sinking speed of the particles and it is depicted in Figure 5.85. There are a number of designs, with Figures 5.86a and b representing two important types. Other types include cross-stream sifters, cyclones, light cargo cutters and zigzag air classifiers.

Examples 5.16 and 5.17: Shoe sorters and tilt tray sorters

Pick one picture each of a shoe sorter and a tilt tray sorter.

Answer: Figures 5.87a and b and Figure 5.79a.

Figure 5.84   Hinged belt conveyor. a) Vertically rotating. b) Horizontally rotating

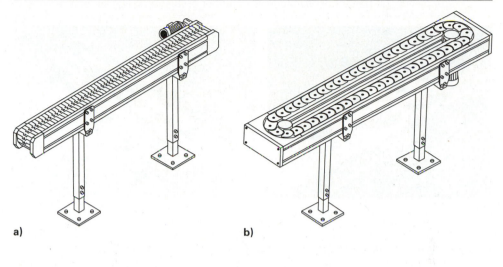

a)

b)

Figure 5.85   Sorting principle (www.venti-oelde.de)

Figure 5.86   a) Expansion air classifier b) Counter flow sifter (www.venti-oelde.de)

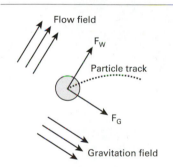

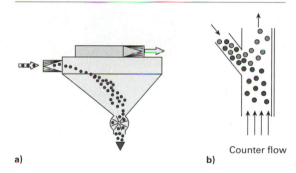

Example 5.18: Underfloor conveyors

Show the design for an underfloor conveyor.

Answer: Underfloor conveyors are drag chain conveyors whose guiding systems are in the floor. Figure 5.88 shows a machine in a furniture factory, whose design is tailored to the cargo and which simultaneously serves to sort and pick orders.

Example 5.19: Drag chain conveyors

Show an example of a drag chain conveyor with floor-free tracks system.

Answer: The drag system (Figure 5.89) consists of an electric monorail with double undercarriage, with a hand pallet truck connected with a pull bar. Advantages

Figure 5.87   Sorters. a) Shoe sorter (www.dematic.com/automatische-sortiersysteme).
b) Tilt tray sorter (www.dematic.com/kippschalensorter)

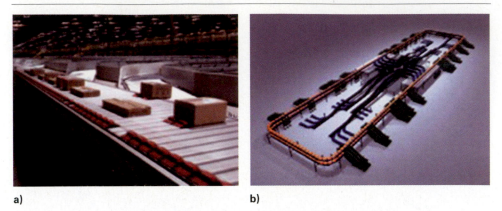

a)   b)

Figure 5.88   Underfloor conveyor in a furniture factory (www.eisemann.com)

include: the floor is uninterrupted by grooves; flexible deployment; bridging of long transport paths; avoiding transfer equipment.

Example 5.20: Cross-sorter (cross-belt sorter)

Show a picture for a cross-sorter.

Answer: Figure 5.90.

Example 5.21: Gravity roller track

What gradient does a non-powered roller track need in order to transport an empty box (600 × 400 cm) without problems?

Answer: The roller trach must have a gradient of 5 to 6 per cent; this equals 3.5° to 4.5°.

Figure 5.89 Drag system with hand pallet trucks (www.eisenmann.com)

Figure 5.90 Cross-sorter (www.dematic.com/de/cross-belt sorter)

Example 5.22: Curved belt conveyor

Show different drive and guide concepts for a curved belt conveyor.

Answer: Figure 5.91.

Example 5.23: Merging and discharging examples

Use pictures to show possible constructions for merging or discharging cargo.

Answer: Figure 5.92a to d.

Figure 5.91   Drive and guide concepts for curved belts (www.transnorm.com)

Drive concept		Guiding concept	
Form closure	Force closure	Fixed guiding	Moving guiding
Chain	Friction wheel $F_R = \mu \times F_N$	Roller	Wedge
Toothed belt	Drive pulley $e^{\mu\alpha} = T1/T2$ $T1$ $T2$	Chain	Belt beading

Figure 5.92   a) Merging of boxes. b) Belt discharge. c) Line crossing. d) Possibilities of 45° and 90° dischargers (www.transnorm.de)

a)   b)   c)

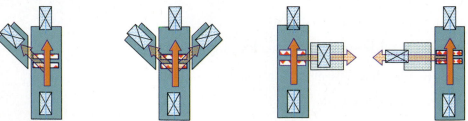

d)

Example 5.24: Pneumatic tubes

What does a pneumatic tube consist of and where are they still used today?

Answer: A pneumatic tube uses pipelines as transport paths, usually with a diameter of 10 to 15 cm, in which small containers with a minimally small diameter are moved as transport aids through suction or air pressure (0.3 to 0.5 bars) at up to 30 km/h.

Pneumatic tubes are used in industry and trade, such as in steel forges, paper factories, chemical plants, hospitals, banks and warehouses in order to transport steels or blood samples to the lab, or books, forms, workpieces and items quickly and gently to their destination.

Example 5.25: Rotating options for pallets

What are the rotating options for pallets?

Answer: We distinguish horizontal and vertical rotation.

- Horizontal: Roller conveyors with lift chain (Figure 5.31); roller plate (Figure 5.21b); turntable with rollers (Figures 5.33 and 5.34a); Figure 5.93 shows different rotating and swivel options for roller conveyors for pallets.

- Vertical: Swivel bracket (roller, ball bracket) (Figures 6.36 and 8.5), as well as pallets with load stabilizer and rotation set (Figure 6.36).

Figure 5.93 Rotation and swivel conveyor with roller conveyors for pallet transport (www.westfaliaEurope.de)

Example 5.26: System components of chain and roller conveyors

Pictorial representation of system components

Answer: Figures 5.94 to 5.99 show system representations, as well as their practical deployment.

Figure 5.94a/b Corner solution with turntable, without redirection of pallet; throughput performance approximately 200 load units/h (www.kardex-mlog.com)

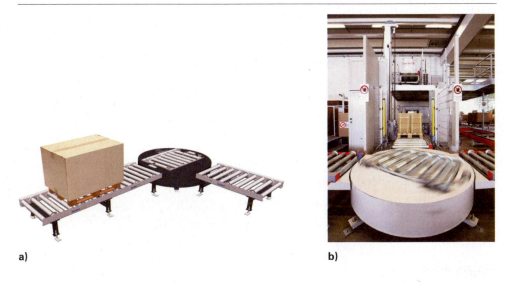

a)   b)

Figure 5.95a/b Corner solution with four-way turntable, without redirection of pallet; entry and exit without interim rotation; throughout performance approximately 249 load units/h (www.kardex-mlog.com)

a)   b)

Figure 5.96a/b   Corner solution with lift table and redirection of pallet; throughput
performance approximately 240 load unit/h (www.kardex-mlog.com)

a)   b)

Figure 5.97a/b   Converter roller-chain conveyors with redirection of pallet from roller to
chain conveyors or vice versa (www.kardex-mlog.com)

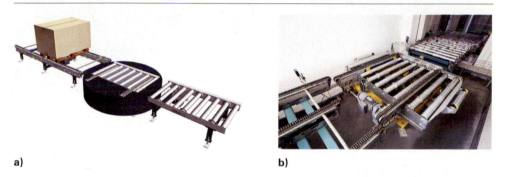

a)   b)

Figure 5.98a/b   Vertical converter of pallet with chain or roller conveyor; lift height
up to 25 cm; throughput performance at 5 m height, approximately
180 load units/h (www.kardex-mlog.com)

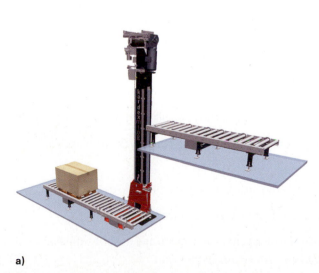

a)   b)

Figure 5.99a/b   Transfer car: horizontal transport of pallet; load intake with chain or roller conveyor as well as telescopic fork; car with stationary or accompanying drive; throughput performance depends on the transport path length and route approximately 180 load units/h (www.kardex-mlog.com)

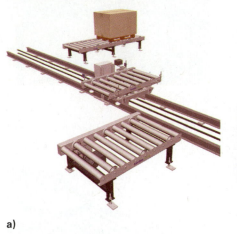

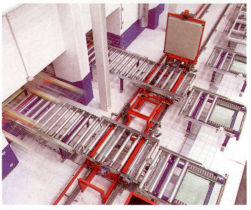

a)   b)

Questions

1   What divisions and categorization are there for continuous conveyors?

2   What are the advantages of rubber belt conveyors and where are they used?

3   Sketch both a single pulley and a two-pulley drive for belt conveyors.

4   Why are tensioning devices required for belt conveyors?

5   What can cause a sideways slip of the belt?

6   What is the structure of a rubber belt and how can the number of inserts be calculated?

7   How is the mass stream for a rubber belt conveyor calculated?

8   What can achieve a steep conveying of general and bulk cargo?

9   What are the features of a telescopic and curved belt conveyor and where are they used?

10   How can the end speed of the cargo be influenced for chutes?

11   What is the structure of an underfloor conveyor system?

12   Sketch out tracks for circular and drag chain conveyors and describe the basic distinguishing features between both means of transport.

13   What sorters are there for general cargo and what principle can they operate on?

14   List continuous conveyors for bulk cargo.

15   What is the difference between a chain and a belt bucket conveyor?

16   Describe the advantages and disadvantages of a troughed chain conveyor.

17   How do you calculate the mass stream of a bucket conveyor?

18   What are the prerequisites for a vertical transport of bulk cargo via troughed chain conveyors and what limits the conveying height?

19   What is the structure of a screw conveyor, which values must be known to calculate the mass stream and how is the full load inertia performance P_v calculated?

20   Name different construction designs of screw conveyors.

21   What conveying principle is the screw pipe conveyor based on and how far is the speed limited?

22   What is the difference in the process of a vibrating chute and a vibrating conveyor?

23   Using a diagram, explain how the cargo transport path on the vibrating chute is determined for going to and fro.

24   What does the throwing value of a vibrating conveyor consist of?

25   What are vibrating conveyors divided into and how does an imbalance motor work?

26   What is the structure of an imbalance motor as circular exciters or exciters?

27   What is the main use of vibrating conveyors?

28   What is the difference between suction and air pressure conveying?

29   What are the feeder options for cargo for air pressure conveyors?

30   Sketch out the stream forms for suction and air pressure conveyors?

31   What is a transport chain conveyor, and where is it used?

32   Explain the air cushion principle for bulk and general cargo, as well as their use in transport technology.

33   Name five sorters. What principles do they operate on?

34   How does contactless energy provision work for cross-belt sorters?

35   How does the tilt tray sorter work? How does the cross-belt sorter work?

Discontinuous conveyors

06

6.1 Features, deployment, division

Discontinuous conveyors are a means of transport that transport bulk and general cargo from on (task) site to a point of delivery in a discontinued manner. Their discontinuous method of operation often occurs in work cycles. Their work processes are further characterized by the alternation of load and empty runs, by downtime for loading and unloading and by exclusion runs. This is how drives can be set up for intermittent or short-term operation. Loading and unloading happens during downtime and the load can only be fed on or discharged at certain points with the load receiving means.

Discontinuous conveyors are floor-bound or floor-free, track-bound or track-free means of transport. Operation is often done manually, which is why the operating costs are high. Automatic operation can be achieved with a greater effort compared to continuous conveyors. The specific advantages of the discontinuous conveyors lie in the high level of deployment flexibility, such as for changing the transport task or the set-up layout, as well as the increase in performance.

Bulk cargo has to be filled in large containers, general cargo can be transported as individual goods or as a load unit. There are usually separate drives for each motion, such as driving, lifting and load intake.

Discontinuous conveyors are deployed in all areas of a business. Their categorization is in line with Figure 6.1. The most important discontinuous conveyors for the internal material flow are included in the following representation.

6.2 Lifting devices

As part of the business material flow, cranes and elevators are used to overcome differences in height in the workplace (see Figure 6.27) to load lorries, to fill a two-level shelving rack (see Figure 10.9) or to work across two floors. Freight elevators, which are not subject to the strict regulations for passenger lifts, are used for pure vertical transport, as are lift tables, pallet and container stackers and special vertical conveyors.

Figure 6.1   Discontinuous conveyor systematics

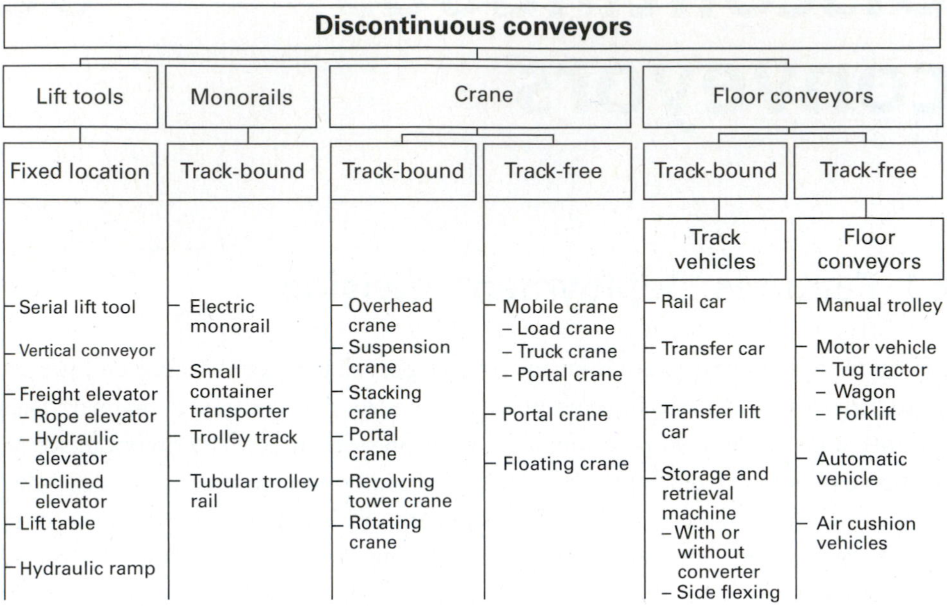

Discontinuous conveyors					
Lift tools	Monorails	Crane		Floor conveyors	
Fixed location	Track-bound	Track-bound	Track-free	Track-bound	Track-free
				Track vehicles	Floor conveyors

– Serial lift tool	– Electric monorail	– Overhead crane	– Mobile crane
			  – Load crane
			  – Truck crane
			  – Portal crane
				– Rail car	– Manual trolley

– Vertical conveyor	– Small container transporter	– Suspension crane	– Portal crane	– Transfer car	– Motor vehicle
					  – Tug tractor
					  – Wagon
					  – Forklift

– Freight elevator
  – Rope elevator
  – Hydraulic elevator
  – Inclined elevator
	– Trolley track	– Stacking crane	– Floating crane	– Transfer lift car	– Automatic vehicle

– Lift table	– Tubular trolley rail	– Portal crane		– Storage and retrieval machine
				  – With or without converter
				  – Side flexing
					– Air cushion vehicles

– Hydraulic ramp		– Revolving tower crane			
		– Rotating crane			

6.2.1 *Hydraulic ramps*

Hydraulic lifts are divided into hydraulic ramps for *load* and hydraulic ramps for *work*. Wherever level compensation is required, such as at a loading ramp or to facilitate the operation of a machine, hydraulic ramps for loads can be used, which are constructed as scissor lifts. They consist of a basic frame, scissor systems, top frame with cover, electro-hydraulic drive as well as the required controls and circuits. The lift height for a single scissor system is about 60 per cent of the platform length (platform length up to 3,000 mm), for a double scissor system it is 100 per cent. The electro-hydraulic drive, which can be integrated separately or as part of the ramp, consists of a cage motor with a high-pressure sprocket pump. Overload protection is provided by a pressure relief valve. The electric control happens via a hand or foot switch. Hydraulic ramps are usually stationary, but can also be mobile. The table can be designed as a roller conveyor, with a turntable or rotating plate (see Figure 6.2). Figure 6.3 depicts a special design.

Hydraulic lift ramps can achieve heights of up to 6.5 m with multiple scissor systems, up to 25 m with telescopic cylinders and can be used as assembly ramps in large apparatus engineering, or for maintenance of halls and cranes. A hydraulic ramp for work can be fixed, pivoted, adjustable or telescopic. It is built as a mobile or self-driving device. The telescopic columns have notched lengthwise cylinders to prevent the turning of the ramp. When deployed outside, the ramp has to be switched off at a wind strength of 6 (10 km/h).

Figure 6.2 Scissor hydraulic ramps with additional functions

Figure 6.3 Hydraulic tandem scissor lift ramp with 4 t load capacity (www.wtt-foerdersysteme.de)

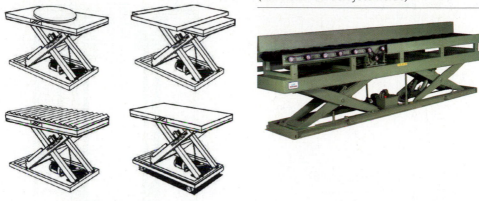

6.2.2 *Vertical conveyors*

Vertical conveyors for pallets or containers are constructed as lifts (see Figure 6.4) or portal lifts (elevators) according to the elevator principle with a rope or chain lift device, or with a vertical belt conveyor (see Example 6.6–26).

Figure 6.5 shows a portal lift for up to 200 kg, using a direct drive with a drawbar mounted gear motor and interlocking drive wheels. The lift speed can be up to 2 m/s for up to 200 cycles. A rubber block chain with steel inserts acts as the tensioning member. The depicted frame takes on the construction element and the cladding. The carriage is connected with the rubber block chain.

6.3 Electric monorails

Electric monorails exist for small machines with manual operation; they are usually motor-powered. In contrast to circular and P&F conveyors, each trolley is independent and has its own drive (for more on deployment area, see Figure 5.27).

An electric monorail (single track rail) transports cargo above floor level, mostly horizontally, and consists of tracks fixed to the ceiling or to supports, and the trolley. Along the running track (= carrying rail) there are electric rails (conductor line: 400 V; 50 Hz) and the trolley (friction wheel) (see Figures 6.6 and 6.7).

Depending on the arrangement of rail and trolley we distinguish between:

- electric monorail with external runners, current collector and rail unprotected on the outside;

Figure 6.4 Console lift for pallets (www.dematic.com)

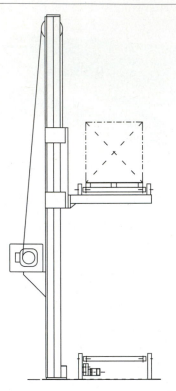

Figure 6.5 Portal lift for individual loads (www.nerak.de)

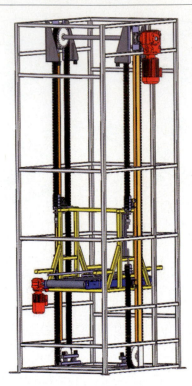

Figure 6.6 U-section of an electric monorail with internal electric rail for enclosed runner system

Figure 6.7 Bead section of an electric monorail with external electric rail for external runner system

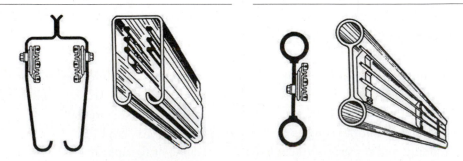

- electric monorail with enclosed runners, current collector and rail protected on the inside of the drive rail;
- electric monorail with a combination of internal and external runners.

The number of runner wheels on the trolley depends on the load capacity of the trolley (see Figures 6.8 and 4.8c and d).

Figure 6.8 Trolley types for electric monorails (www.eisenmann.com)

Single trolley

Double trolley

The individual transport units can be operated by hand, via reel drive, electrically with floor control (up to 63 m/min), automatic or with cabin control, and will aim for their destination automatically if circular. The speed is between 10 m/min and 100 m/min. The line can be adjusted to the production process through straight pieces, bends, points, swivel discs, drop sections and horizontal offset station (Figure 6.9). We can distinguish between rail crossing via hub, two-way and three-way points (Figure 6.10), as well as trolley transfer through a rotating disc and parallel points. The lifting gear can be an electric hoist with load hook, or a load receptor aligned with the cargo type in the shape of a fork, trough, container, hook or table. A circular route with forks (see Figure 6.11) can be used for cargo distribution, assembly and sorting, and its load intake and discharge can occur automatically (transfer points, transfer car, pivoting or quadruple point). Monorail trolleys move automatically and are equipped with crash buffers. Points are changed automatically in line with a programme and buffer zones are designed as hanging depots. The vertical transport occurs via elevators or, for modest gradients up to 5 per cent, through momentum, as well as climbing support through sloping transfer (for more on contactless energy transfer, see Example 6.6–15).

Trolley systems were developed for modest loads; these operate on different principles and represent different track cross sections. In Figure 6.12, a trolley system is shown with a transfer conveyor (inclined conveyor) to bridge a difference in height (floors). The horizontal transport is carried out manually, motor-driven by chains, or through gravity.

Figure 6.9 Electric monorail transport for flowers (www.eisenmann.com)

Figure 6.10 Fork elements (www.dematic.com)

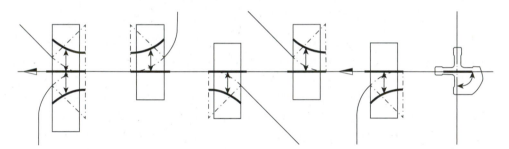

Figure 6.11 Deployment of an inclined monorail for pallet transport in the drinks industry (www.eisenmann.com)

Figure 6.12 Trolley system in textile mail order company with hanging items in inclined transport (www.mekomeier.com)

Figure 6.13 Trolleys can be connected together, or run separately (www.mekomeier.com)

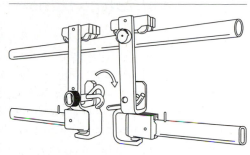

Advantages of the electric monorail include:

- flexible lines and large area of deployment;
- easy adaptation to the material flow and the business requirements;
- floor-free transport and noise-free operation (environmentally friendly);
- saving of operational costs (intermittent operation, only those trolleys in use are running, each trolley has its own drive);
- automation of machine via target control: instructions mechanically to trolley, such as cam settings electronic or electro-magnetic/magnets;
- simple extension options;
- load capacity up to 6.3 t;
- curved with small radius r > 1.2 m;
- combination with suspension cranes (line and area operation);
- change in direction of individual trolleys is possible;
- equipped with lifting tools.

It is also an advantage that, when motor-powered, handling tasks, such as lifting, lowering, turning, sorting or combinations of these motions are possible. This allows for the separation of trolley and load. While the load (= production piece) is stored or processed, the trolley can carry out other transport tasks.

For horizontal transport over a modest distance and low frequency, manual monorails can be used for cargo up to a load of 1.6 t/m of track, ie the operation of the monorail is by hand through pushing or pulling. Usual deployment is at workplaces. (For more on electric monorails see Figure 2.25c and Example 6.6–16; for technical data see Figure 6.54b.)

6.4 Cranes

6.4.1 General, categorization

The advantages of a crane are the vertical and horizontal movements, in any direction, and the motions can happen simultaneously. Cranes are suitable for transporting general cargo and bulk cargo, bulky loads, long cargo or mass cargo. Certain designs, such as *travelling cranes* (see Figure 6.14) do not need any floor space (floor-free operation), and the transport space is located above the workspace. The *suspension crane* allows for transverse transport of the trolley from one hall area to another. The *stacking crane* is used in storage to operate high shelves, and the *mobile crane* is used in open depots.

On the other hand, they have the following disadvantages:

- limited deployment area (track-bound);
- not suitable for continuous conveying;
- uneconomical for moving light cargo (large dead load).

When choosing the crane design for a given transport, many factors come into play, such as:

- type of cargo: general/bulk cargo (see Example 6.6–23);
- deployment location: inside, outside, at a construction site;
- deployment area: in a warehouse, manufacturing, assembly;

Figure 6.14 Travelling crane, 80 t in printing plant (left); processing crane in aeroplane construction assembly area (www.demagcranes.com)

- measurements and dimensions of the building footprint, size of storage location;

- maximum load size;

- distance of hooks to wall/crane track;

- median cycle length and maximum number of cycles per time unit;

- required height of hooks and the distance between support columns.

The passage profile of the crane working area is determined based on: span; height of the hook; specific dimensions of the crane design, eg for the bridge crane; type of head carrier connections to the crane bridge; design of the relevant trolley with electric hoist or winch (running on bottom and top belt); type of load intake tool.

The dimensions for the trolley approach and for the crane should be kept as small as possible in order to increase the efficient use of the space. Accident prevention measures have to be implemented through installation of walkways with bannisters and ladders for maintenance of the machine parts.

Power supplies can be designed as open or protection conductor lines with wires or tracks, and are implemented as mobile connection cables using cable drums, or as trailing, flat or hanging cables for cranes, trolley and storage and retrieval machine (see Chapter 4.5.4.3; for more on contactless energy transfer, see Example 6.6–15).

Cranes can be built with a fixed location or movable on tracks, can be used in mobile deployment, or built on ships. This variety of deployment possibilities is also expressed in the name of cranes. DIN 15 001 T 2 provides a categorization of cranes according to their purpose or deployment location and distinguishes between 16 main types of crane with numerous sub-categories. These types of crane include:

Figure 6.15 Travelling crane designs from above: single girder travelling crane made of rolled and box sections; double girder travelling crane (www.demagcranes.com)

workshop crane, assembly crane, warehouse crane, port crane, steel mill crane, forge crane, construction crane, wharf crane, ship crane, container crane.

This is not the complete identification of a crane. It also requires information on the crane design. The categorization of cranes according to design is contained in DIN 15 001. It divides designs into wall-mounted and pillar-mounted jib cranes, which can be built up to 8 t of load capacity.

Crane designs include:

- jib cranes and rotating cranes;
- bridge cranes;
- portal cranes;
- overhead cranes;
- tower cranes;
- vehicle cranes;
- swimming cranes;
- cable cranes.

Vehicle cranes can be built as:

- mounted crane of serial lorry drive with load capacities up to 80 t;
- telescopic vehicle crane with load capacity up to 500 t;
- lattice boom vehicle crane with load capacity up to 1,000 t;
- all-terrain crane with load capacity up to 1,600 t (rough terrain crane up to 160 t);
- lattice boom caterpillar crane with load capacity up to 1,600 t (rotating top car on caterpillar drive).

6.4.2 *Travelling cranes (bridge cranes)*

The most utilized type of crane in assembly, manufacturing and warehouse environments is the travelling crane, which can run along or on top of tracks. We distinguish (Figure 6.15):

- single girder travelling crane: built from t-girder or box girder, up to 10 t load capacity and 24 m span, usually floor operation, with effective dimensions and modest own weight;
- double girder travelling crane (see Figure 6.14): built from t girder, plate girder, truss box girder, up to 80 t load capacity and 35 m span, floor or cabin operation ($v = 63$ m/s) for fixed location operation with radio control;
- special cranes, such as process cranes, automatic care, cranes with load capacity up to 560 t and cranes with a span of up to 60 m.

Travelling cranes can be combined with a host of different trolley designs and can, thus, adapt to the transport task at hand in the best possible way (see Figure 11.24).

Suspension and *ceiling* cranes are travelling cranes in single or double girder design (Figure 6.16), whose tracks are suspended via tension rods on ceilings and roof constructions.

The lifting device consists of an electric chain or rope hoist. An electric drive is used from a crane girder length of 6 m and 500 kg load capacity. If the ceiling or roof construction has sufficient load capacity, then suspension cranes can be used for loads up to 10,000 kg, and their *advantages* include:

- retrospective integration into buildings or rooms (depending on ceiling load capacity);
- modest own weight;
- quick assembly;
- modest build height, so efficient use of ceiling height;
- easy motion, manually movable, motor-powered, works in combination with a monorail;
- cross connection of adjacent bays;
- large crane track length thanks to multiple suspension points;
- compensation for different track distances through inclined motion;
- no jamming of crane bridge, crane easy to guide.

Figure 6.16   Bay with suspension cranes to operate in assembly (www.demagcranes.com)

Figure 6.17 Suspension crane/monorail combination

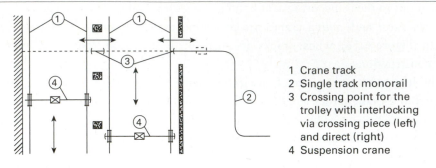

1 Crane track
2 Single track monorail
3 Crossing point for the trolley with interlocking via crossing piece (left) and direct (right)
4 Suspension crane

Decisive for the integration of a suspension crane are the load capacity, necessary span of the girders, suspension distance for the crane tracks and the load capacity of the ceiling.

For adjacent areas, there is the possibility to create cross-transport of the trolley (see Figure 6.17) without discharging the load through relevant mechanic interlocking. This uses direct interlocking in columnless bays, otherwise crossing pieces are used.

A combination with a monorail (see Chapter 6.3) does not pose any difficulties (see Figure 6.17).

6.4.3 Portal cranes

Cranes with a portal-shaped frame are called portal cranes and are different in:

- their operation (analogue bridge cranes);
- their bridge build (analogue bridge cranes);
- their support designs: one or two supports;
- their option to have cantilevers: the crane bridge can be equipped with fixed or foldable cantilevers at one or both ends.

Cranes can move lengthwise or crosswise, are fixed or drive on tracks. For *full portal cranes* (see Figures 6.18, 7.17, 7.19 and 6.75a and b), the bridge is supported by two portal supports on ground level crane tracks; for half portal cranes (Figure 6.19a and b) there is a high crane track instead of a support. Both crane types can be equipped with a top and bottom belt trolley, or take on fixed job or rotating cranes. Full portal cranes can also be called *gantry crane* or *loading bridge*.

Full portal cranes are used in a building when the ceiling or support structure cannot take any additional load. The main deployment areas for these cranes are in outside storage areas. They have to be secured against wind with holding brakes or rail tongs. Portal cranes have been particularly useful in container handling on tracks or track-free together with straddle carriers (see Figure 7.10g), portal stackers (see Figure 7.10e) and container loading bridges (see Figure 7.17).

Figure 6.18 Full portal crane with fixed cantilevers on both sides and two-track-winch trolley (statically determined system)

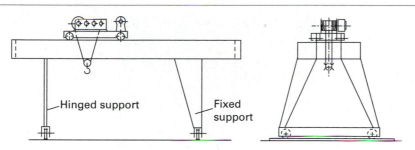

Figure 6.19 a) Semi-portal crane as lattice girder construction with one-sided cantilever and traverse trolley for handling general cargo in port area. b) Semi-portal crane for operating a sheet metal warehouse with magnet traverse (www.demagcranes.com)

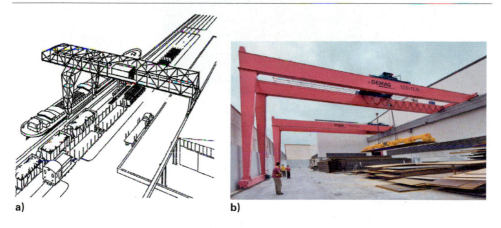

Storage and retrieval machines have been developed as drive-over machines for bar storage in the shape of full portal cranes and bridge cranes (see Figures 10.14, 11.24) which only require modest floor space and which operate the store either semi- or fully automatically. Here, the material is stored in troughed pallets in cantilever shelves, built as shelf warehouse with little aisle width. The portal stacker drives on a high track. The lifting travers for stacking the troughed pallets is moved with an electric hoist.

6.4.4 Stacking crane

Mechanization and good use of space can be achieved by using the stacking crane (see Figures 6.20, 11.32), which is a combination of a forklift truck frame and bridge crane. It only requires a little space for the moving of pallets, containers, packages or long goods.

Figure 6.20   Stacking crane in double-girder design with rotating column, floor operation (www.demagcranes.com)

Its *advantages* are: modest aisle width (approximately 1.4 m without cabin, 1.7 m with cabin); high stacking heights up to 10 m; load capacity up to 5 t; good use of storage space; no change in means of transport when altering shelves.

Designs include double-girder travelling crane or suspension crane, rotating column (360°), telescopic mast for overcoming obstacles, floor controls, control from a cabin fixed to the mast (good observation of work processes), or automatic (see Figure 10.16).

The floor in the shelving aisles is not broken up by tracks.

6.5 Track vehicles

Track vehicles are floor conveyors belonging to the class of non-continuous conveyors. Tracks are used for forced guidance of the vehicles and these are also load carriers (see Chapter 4.6.3; see Figure 4.9). Tracks are paired for cars, but for storage and retrieval systems only one track is required.

Track-bound floor conveyors include track cars (see Figure 6.21), transfer cars for storage and retrieval systems, and shifting trolleys for storage and retrieval systems. Stationary lift devices can be made into track vehicles by integrating a drive, such as track-lifting ramps.

Figure 6.21   Heavy load track vehicle for transporting coils (www.mafi.de)

6.5.1 *Transfer and transfer lift cars*

Transfer cars (distribution cars) are used for distributing and sorting cargo, usually pallets at head ends or along transport routes (see Figure 6.22) between defined transfer points. The cargo intake and discharge occurs independently. The process is carried out by a powered car, set onto the tracks, which is equipped with a roller or chain conveyor.

The transfer lift car carries out intake and discharge functions in the pre-storage zone in order to provide a connection between roller conveyor and storage and retrieval system transfer point. The transfer and transfer lift cars are provided with energy through a trailing cable. The transfer lift car drives under the pallet, the lifting device takes up the pallet with two or three bars and moves it to the transfer point. The side of the roller conveyor has gaps at the points where 'the bars' are (Figure 6.23).

Transfer and transfer lift cars connect dead ends, allow for staggered and parallel discharge as well as 90° redirection.

Figure 6.22   Transfer car (www.dematic.com)

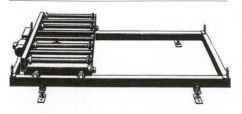

Figure 6.23   Transfer-lift car (www.dematic.com)

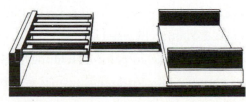

6.5.2 *Storage and retrieval machines*

Storage and retrieval machines as shelf dependent track vehicles are described in Chapter 10.4.2 as stack and picking machines.

In addition, transfer possibilities for storage and retrieval machines for picking are shown here. If a storage and retrieval machine has to serve multiple shelving aisles due to low levels of cargo handling, there are two options to transport the track-guided storage and retrieval machine to other shelving aisles:

1 Using a shifting trolley (shifting bridge, shifter): see Figure 10.35.

2 Design as curved track storage and retrieval machine: see Figure 10.36.

A shifter trolley resembles a transfer car, with a track to drive on for transporting the storage and retrieval car. The storage and retrieval car still has to be guided at the top. Contrary to the transfer car, which conveys cargo, the shifting trolley transports means of transports. It is provided with energy through a trailing cable. For curved track storage and retrieval machines, the chassis is designed to drive over points and can follow curved tracks.

6.6 Industrial trucks

6.6.1 *Advantages and disadvantages, division*

Floor conveyors are part of the group of floor-level conveyors. They are a track-free means of transport for horizontal and vertical transport. Industrial trucks are used for internal transport for irregular required transport and lifting work of general and bulk cargo. Hand pallet trucks manage the pallet transport between workplaces, tug tractors pull mobile stairs at airports, electric cars connect manufacturing departments with warehousing, forklift trucks store pallets in shelves, and stackers equipped with a shovel accessory transport sand on building sites.

Advantages of industrial trucks:

- deployment in all business areas, neither fixed location nor track bound;
- high level of mobility and manoeuvrability (turning on the spot);
- varied use of the same device;
- can drive up narrow passages and around tight bends;
- no disruption by fixed tracks (less risk of accidents);
- low operating costs for high lifting heights, load capacities and traction;
- when used for load units, savings in reloading processes;

- low initial investment, easy adjustment to changing circumstances;
- good use of high spaces by using stacker;
- extended area of deployment with accessories.

Disadvantages of industrial trucks:

- limited load capacity;
- not suitable for continuous conveying;
- larger drive resistance of wheels compared to track vehicles;
- requires lifts with high load capacity and large dimensions for storied buildings;
- each vehicle must have trained personnel.

Industrial trucks can be categorized based on different criteria, such as:

- horizontal or vertical transport motion;
- type of drive;
- steering or operating method;
- designs.

A basic division occurs in the group of *non-motor-powered* industrial trucks, such as carts, rollers or wagons, as well as the group of *motor-powered* industrial trucks, such as tug tractors, wagons or stackers (see Example 6.6–13).

6.6.2 Selection criteria

To select an industrial truck for a given transport, storage or handling task, it is useful to compare profiles of requirement for the task with the performance profile of the relevant industrial trucks. The selection criteria are divided into vehicle-based, deployment-based and regulation-based criteria:

- Vehicle-based selection criteria are:
  - type of drive: electric motor, combustion engine, hybrid drive (see Chapter 4.5);
  - design: three or four-wheel design, for stackers self-supporting or wheel-supported;
  - steering system: turntable or Ackermann steering;
  - steering mode: short or long; folding drawbar, steering wheel;
  - wheels: air, super elastic, full rubber or plastic tyres (see Chapter 4.6);
  - rough terrain truck: low pressured air tyres, building deployment: high pressured air tyres (10 bar);

- load and gradient capacity, performance, drive speed, ergonomics, maintenance;

  - specific to forklifts: lifting frame (see Chapter 6.6.7.4), lifting height, lifting and lowering speeds;

  - accessory options, lifting load, self-supported lift, build height, working aisle width;

  - costs: investment, fixed and variable costs, operational costs.

- Deployment-based selection criteria:

  - cargo: bulk, general, characteristics, texture, loading characteristics;

  - deployment site: indoors or outside;

  - deployment conditions (working environment): roadway conditions, floor make-up, ceiling load capacity, screed load capacity, permissible speed, head-room, gradient;

  - efficient use of industrial trucks;

  - financing: purchase, hire, leasing;

  - specific to forklifts: working aisle width, stackability of cargo, nature of warehouse.

- Regulation-based selection criteria:

  - accident prevention regulations, standards, guidelines, regulations;

  - safety:

    * vehicle: protective roof, overload protection grid, visibility;

    * operator: impact protection, corner protection, exclusive transport route, oncoming traffic;

    * driver: driving licence, physical condition.

6.6.2.1 Design

An industrial truck can be built as *three* or *four-wheel design* (see Figure 6.24). The three-wheel design allows for shorter wheelbase and has greater manoeuvrability, leading to smaller working aisle width. The four-wheel build has larger wheelbase, larger working aisle width and a larger turning radius.

Furthermore, we can distinguish between wheel-supported and self-supported industrial trucks (forklifts). Self-supported vehicles pick up, lift and transport the load outside of the wheel-base, wheel-supported versions do this within the wheel-base. Another design form is the combination of wheel-supported and self-supported designs. We distinguish narrow and wide gauge designs.

Figure 6.24   (Left) Electric three-wheel forklift. (Right) Electric four-wheel forklift (www.jungheinrich.de)

6.6.2.2 Steering system, steering mode, steering

An industrial truck's steering system can be designed as turntable steering or Ackermann steering. For the turntable steering, two fixed impellers are placed on a drawbar, which are connected to the steering axle via a u-shaped stool. This creates a very manoeuvrable vehicle. For the Ackermann steering, the wheels are articulated by axle stubs. The choice of chassis has to be done based on the given deployment conditions, because the chosen system influences the manoeuvrability, the turning radius, the height of the loading area, load capacity and the working aisle width.

For the steering on non-powered industrial trucks (wagons, trailers) the choice depends on:

- type, dimensions and weight of the cargo;
- loading height;
- make-up of roadway;
- bend radius for single vehicle and for trailer operation.

Four-wheel Ackermann steering (Figure 6.25a) is protected against overturning and runs like on tracks. It has a small turning radius, low loading height and an adjustable drawbar. It can be deployed in narrow halls with up to 15 t load capacity.

Turntable steering comes in single, two- and four-wheel steering. *Single axle turntable steering* (Figure 6.25b) is very manoeuvrable for a single vehicle, but does not run like on tracks, has a high loading height and, when turned completely is at risk of falling over. It can be used with a single trailer for up to 15 t load capacity. Double-axle turntable steering (Figure 6.25c) has tilt-protection (steering block, adjustable drawbar) and runs like on tracks, but has a large turning radius and high loading height. It can be deployed with up to 15 t loading capacity.

Figure 6.25   Steering systems for trailers (www.linde-mh.com). a) Four-wheel Ackermann steering. b) Single-axle turntable steering. c) Double-axle turntable steering. d) Four-wheel turntable steering

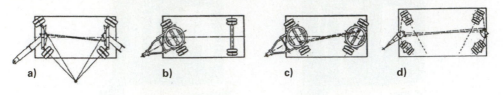

Four-wheel turntable steering (Figure 6.25d) features a low loading height, small turning radius and adjustable drawbar. It runs like on tracks and is tilt-protected. It can be used up to 30 t load capacity in narrow spaces.

For steering powered industrial trucks, either turntable steering or Ackermann steering can be used. Despite the longer wheelbase (axle distance) for an industrial truck with turntable steering, and as a result of the possible 90° small turning radius, a smaller working aisle width compared to the Ackermann steering is possible, while maintaining the load capacity is possible. The bigger the wheelbase, the larger the turning radius. Figure 6.25a shows the different angles of the individual wheels on an axle when the steering wheel is turned. This means pushing wheels and, thus, wear (especially when driving backwards). Hence steering wheels are limited to be either less than or equal to 80 per cent. Steering aids are meant to minimize the force required to turn the steering wheel. We distinguish between electric and hydraulic steering aids (Servo steering).

The steering mode can be: *manual* steering through the operator via the steering wheel or drawbar; *automatic* steering without an operator with the help of guidance systems; or a combination of *manual* and *automatic* steering. Manual steering (steering control) equals driver-operated steering. We distinguish pedestrian operation or stand-on operation, as well as a combination of both (see Figure 6.77).

6.6.2.3 Pedestrian operation

For pedestrian operation, all steering and operative functions are carried out by operators walking next to the vehicle – usually steering occurs via the drawbar. The operation elements for driving and lifting, as well as stopping, are located in the head of the drawbar. Steering and braking happens by moving the drawbar up or down. Deployment for battery-operated electric industrial trucks, that can be used in pedestrian operator mode, such as three-wheel tug tractors, low forklift/platform trucks, hand pallet cars. For motor-powered vehicles, the speed is limited to pedestrian speed of 3 km/h (see Figure 7.18a and b).

6.6.2.4 Stand-on operation

For stand-on operation the industrial truck can be operated from the driver's platform (see Figure 7.18c and 6.6.32) or the driver's seat. The latter is divided into front and side seat steering. The front seat is ergonomic and makes sense for mostly driving forward, such as for tug tractors or E-wagons. The side seat (see Figures 7.18e and 6.6.19) is fixed at a right angle to the load intake direction. It is enough to turn the head slightly when driving forward or backward to view the driving area. For frequent backward motion, manoeuvring, and limited visibility through load units, side seats are preferable, as they have a smaller wheelbase. This is deployed for reach trucks, high rack forklifts and low lift trucks. For forklifts, a steering button on the steering wheel allows, if required, one-hand-steering with the left hand. The right hand operates the lifting, lowering and tilt movements of the vehicle (for more on tilted seats, see Figure 6.43).

For both pedestrian and stand-on operation, the steering and operative functions can be carried out by either walking next to or standing on the vehicle. For stand-on operation, there is a foldable platform (see Figure 7.18c).

6.6.3 *Drive resistance*

The drive resistance F_{wf} of an industrial truck consists of the:

- rolling resistance F_{wr};
- acceleration resistance F_{wst};
- climbing resistance F_{wa};
- air resistant: neligible.

$$F_{wf} = F_{wr} + F_{wa} + F_{wst} \, [\text{N}] \tag{6.1}$$

The rolling resistance is dependent on the wheel bearing, the roadway surface and the type of tyre in use. In order to simplify the rolling resistance calculation, we assume the unit rolling resistance w_r. The rolling resistance F_{wr} is calculated by:

$$F_{wr} = mgw_r \tag{6.2}$$

m	in kg	Total vehicle mass (own weight + load + driver)
g	in m/s²	Earth acceleration (average value g = 9.81 m/s²)
w_r	in ‰	Unit rolling resistance
w_r	= 12–14‰	For good roadway and full rubber tyres
w_r	= 14–16‰	For good roadway and air tyres (high pressure tyres)
w_r	= 20–25‰	For good roadway and air tyres (low pressure tyres)

The acceleration resistance F_{wa} encompasses the accelerated vehicle and load masses F_{wag} and the accelerated rotating mass F_{war} of the drive motor, gears, clutch, wheels etc, relevant to the drive wheel diameter (rotating mass acceleration can usually be neglected).

$$F_{wa} = F_{wag} + F_{war} \ [N] \tag{6.3}$$

$$F_{wag} = ma \ [N] \tag{6.4}$$

$$F_{war} = J_{red} \frac{a}{r^2} \ [N] \tag{6.5}$$

m	in kg	Total vehicle mass
a	in m/s^2	Vehicle acceleration (a = 0.1 to 9.5m/s^2)
J_{red}	in kgm^2	Mass inertia, reduced to drive wheel axle
r	in m	Drive wheel radius

The climbing resistance F_{wa} of industrial trucks can either be calculated via the downhill force, the unit climbing resistance w_{st}, or via the gradient itself by giving the gradient p.

$$F_{wst} = m \ g \ \sin \alpha = mgw_{st} = mgp \ [N] \tag{6.6}$$

m, g		See Formula (6.2)
α	in	Climbing angle: $\sin \alpha = p$ in %/100
p	in %	Gradient
w_{st}	in ‰	Unit climbing resistance

Electric tug tractors and forklift with load drive on ramps up to 15 per cent gradient – see Example 6.6–8.

For the total weight m = 2,750 kg of a vehicle (load, driver, own weight) this arrives at a drive resistance when neglecting the acceleration resistance with full rubber tyres (w_r = 15‰)

- For horizontal roadway:

$$F_{wf} = F_{wr} = 2{,}750 \times 9.81 \times 0.015 = 404.7 \ N$$

- For a roadway with 5 per cent gradient ($\hat{=} \ \alpha$ = 2.87°):

$$F_{wf} = F_{wr} + F_{wst} = 404.7 + (2{,}750 \times 9.81 \times 0.05) = 1{,}754 \ N.$$

To calculate the drive motor performance, we have to distinguish between the electric battery and the combustion engine drive. As the electric motor can be overloaded temporarily, the motor is usually designed based on the rolling resistance F_{wr}, the diesel motor, which cannot be overloaded, on the total drive resistance F_{wf}.

$$P = \frac{F_{wr} \, v}{1.000 \ \eta_{ges}} \ [kW] \tag{6.7}$$

P	in kW	Drive motor performance
F_{wr} or F_{wf}	in N	Rolling or drive resistance

v	in m/s	Driving speed
η_{ges}		Engine effectiveness

Forklifts are designed on the drive motor performance P and the lift motor performance P_h.

The lift motor performance P_h is calculated by:

$$P_h = \frac{F_h \, v_h}{1.000 \, \eta_{ges}} \; [kW]$$ (6.8)

F_h	in N	Lift load (load capacity and cargo to be lifted)
v_h	in m/s	Lifting speed

For tug tractors, the traction transfer from wheel to roadway (slipping of wheels) has to be checked: compare equation (4.11) (tug tractor performance = traction).

6.6.4 Manually operated industrial trucks

If the transport distance is no longer than 25 m, without any gradients, and if transport only occurs occasionally, then manual operation can be quite economical. These non-powered industrial trucks include, aside from a large number of carts specifically designed for certain cargo: trolleys, rollers, carts, hand trucks, trailers.

Possible wheel arrangements are shown in Figure 6.26.

Trolleys are usually equipped with push handles and have one or two wheels, such as the flat trolley, push cart and stacker trolley. The push cart can be equipped with sliding aids or a third wheel for transport over steps (Figure 6.26).

Rollers are manual vehicles that have three or more fixed or steering castors, such as triangle or quadrangle rollers, dollies and box trolleys.

Figure 6.26   Arrangements of steering and/or fixed castors (fixed roller/wheel) for transport aids and manually operated industrial trucks

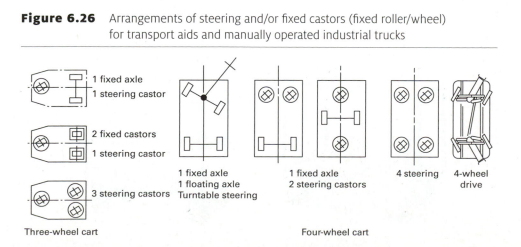

The lifting roller (for more on trolley jacks, see Figure 6.27b) has a separate lever with two rollers and a ball-shaped head for driving under and lifting a rolling platform (see Chapter 3.1.4). In doing so, the trolley jack's ball-shaped head fits into the spherical shell on the platform. When the lever is pressed down and the safety catch has snapped in place, both parts are fixed to one another. The load can be transported and manoeuvred easily.

Figure 6.27a Trolleys. (Left) Stair rolling stacking trolley. (Right) Stacking trolley (www.fetra.de)

Figure 6.27b Lifting roller (www.planindustrie.de)

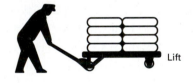

Figure 6.27c Hand trolley (www.fetra.de)

Trucks consist of at least three fixed and/or flexible castors and have an open, partially or fully closed load platform. A great variety of trucks can be found on the market such as table, shelf and picking trucks.

Hand trucks have no steering system but two or four steering rollers (Figure 6.27c) or are equipped with a steering lever or push handle (Figure 6.27d). They have at least three wheels, one of which can be steered. Examples are a platform or box cart. If the hand truck is equipped with a low lifting device, this creates a platform or low lift truck for picking up from the floor by driving around the stacking box (Figure 6.27e), or lifting over the lower side edge.

No business nowadays can do without the hand pallet truck (see Figures 6.27f and 7.18a) for load units with floor clearance (pallets, containers). The lift is about 100 mm, the load capacity up to 1/2 t. The load can be lifted and lowered hydraulically through manual up and down movements of the lever.

Figure 6.27d Hand truck with push handle (www.fetra.de)

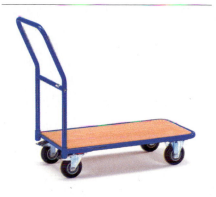

Figure 6.27e Lift truck for picking up one or more boxes off the floor (www.ssi-schaefer.com)

Figure 6.27f Hand pallet truck for pallets (www.ssi-schaefer.com)

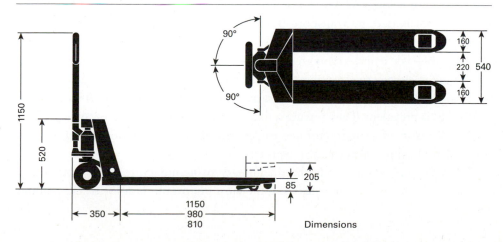

Dimensions

Figure 6.27g Scissor lift for pallets (www.toyota-forklifts.de)

A truck that lifts above 1 m is a *high lift truck*, which is subject to specific safety regulations (railings). The *scissor lift* (lifts up to 1 m, Figure 6.27g) allows for ergonomic working (for motor drives, see Figure 6.48a), as the load can always be at optimal working height thanks to the adjustable lift device. Stability is achieved through automatic supports.

Trailers are non-powered trucks with a clutch and hoist device for tug tractors (Figure 6.28b).

6.6.5 Tug tractors

The tug tractor belongs to the group of motor-driven industrial trucks. It is a means of traction for horizontal transport of loads on trailers or other load carriers, such as roller platforms. We distinguish between single axle, semi-trailer and double-axle truck. Double-axle trucks are of greatest significance for internal material flow – they can be built as electric tugs for up to 15 t trailer loads and as a diesel tug tractor for up to 75 t of trailer load. For electric tug tractors, the three-wheel design (Figure 6.28a and 6.28b) is prevalent. They feature a fixed rear axle and steered front wheel.

A tow consists of a tug tractor and trailer. Instead of a conventional trailer, pallet trucks or roller containers can also be used.

VDI 2198 presents a standardized summary of manufacturer information and design features for industrial trucks and the most important data for trucks and tug tractors.

Figure 6.28 Electric tug tractors in three-wheel design

a) Design with driver´s seat (www.linde-mh.com)

b) Design with driver´s platform (www.toyota-forklifts.com)

6.6.6 Carts

Carts are part of the group of motor-powered industrial trucks. They are divided into carts:

- *without lift*:
  – platform carts, tipper, electric carts, horizontal picking carts;
- *with low lift devices* to drive under loads:
  – approximately 100 to 200 mm for platform and forklift trucks;
  – approximately 600 mm for portal lift carts;
  – approximately 100 mm lift for carrier vehicles and horizontal picking carts;
- *with low lift devices* for driving under and lifting of loads and people:
  – up to 1 m lift height for horizontal picking carts;
- *with high lift devices* – high lift carts (lift > 1 m) = wheel supported stacker (see Chapter 6.6.7);
- *with scissor lift* (lift up to 1.6 m, in special cases up to 5.50 m; see Figure 6.27 g).

Carts are used for horizontal transport of loads, eg using a platform or fork. Usually they are built in a four-wheel design and equipped with battery-electric for interior use and battery-electric or combustion engine drive for outside deployment.

Steering in pedestrian mode is implemented using a lever; in driver mode the steering can happen through a *foldable* lever, or with a *steering wheel*. In automatic operation, the cart can be steered through *induction* (see Chapter 6.7). The loading area can be fixed platform, a roller track, a telescopic fork, a chain conveyor or a lift table.

Cart designs include:

- *Electric carts* (see Figure 6.29): These have a fixed platform as loading area and are equipped with a driver's platform or seat. The battery-powered cart is used for transport of non-palletized cargo and to pull trailers. When driving outside, platform carts have a driver's cabin for protection and can be equipped with a variety of special structures, such as loading crane, water tank or spreading device. Front and side panels can make up a box cart in open or closed design. VDI sheet 2198 describes the design features.

- *Electric low lift cart* (see Figure 6.30): These have a lifting device for 100 to 150 mm, a fork or platform as load carrier to take on pallets, mesh boxes, etc, and are used for the horizontal transport of cargo. Support wheels increase the side stability. Low lift carts are battery-operated (one-wheel drive). They place high demands on the floor (evenness, load capacity, cleanliness). As they only have low floor clearance, gradient routes, such as for loading or unloading using ramps, have to be checked in order to avoid the fork scraping on the floor (for more on gradient kink, see Example 6.7– 4). Cargo sledges and load carriers (concave fork, platform) form one unit in low lift carts.

Design variations have differences in steering the vehicle in pedestrian mode, such as the electric lever forklift in driver mode with driver's platform or seat, as well as in combined mode with foldable lever (short lever) and foldable driver's platform (see Figure 7.18c). The low lift cart comes in broad gauge design as a lever-led

Figure 6.29   Electric cart (www.still.de)

Figure 6.30 Low lift carts

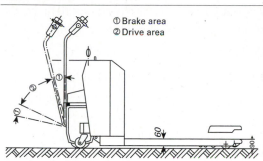
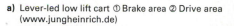

① Brake area
② Drive area

a) Lever-led low lift cart ① Brake area ② Drive area
(www.jungheinrich.de)

b) Low lift cart in pedestrian mode
(www.jungheinrich.de)

c) Low lift cart in driver mode with side
seat (www.Stoecklin.com)

d) Low lift cart in driver mode (driver's platform)
picking for two lengthways pallets via
wheel-support long fork (www.linde-mh.com)

electric pallet truck. Low lift carts also include the specially designed horizontal picking cart (see Chapter 11.4.1).

- *Straddle carriers* are a means of transport for bulky cargo and cargo with large measurements, such as containers (see Figure 7.10g); the lift height is approximately 600 mm.

- *High lift carts:* Wheel supported lift trucks; double floored (see Figure 6.55).

6.6.7 Lift trucks

6.6.7.1 Deployment areas

Lift trucks belong to the group of motor-driven industrial trucks. A lift truck is an industrial truck with a lift device, able to carry out vertical movement of the load. The forklift truck is the most significant representative of this group. It has had a lasting effect on manipulation, stacking and warehousing technology. The necessity to create storage units and the effective use of the room height for storing goods, guarantee an economic use of this industrial truck. The forklift carries out transport and stacking tasks. Additional devices take care of a great variety of special tasks and turn it into a specialist tool. Whether to use a lift truck and which type of lift truck should be used depends on a number of factors:

- roadway conditions, route length, maximum gradient of 8 per cent (12.5 per cent);
- load capacity of the floor (screed), ceiling load capacity in multi-storey buildings;
- load capacity and measurements of the lift in multi-storey buildings;
- lift height, stacking height, door measurements;
- cargo and storage features, type of cargo;
- ratio of transport to lifting, forward to backward motion;
- lift truck costs, on costs.

6.6.7.2 Structure, drive

- *Structure*

A lift truck (see Figure 6.24) is a vehicle and consists of a 'tug' as the basic device and lifting equipment. The basic device can have a three-wheel or four-wheel design. In contrast to the tug tractor, the forklift has a fixed front axle and a steered rear axle. Depending on the design of the lifting gear, the load can be taken on with wheel support or self-supporting (see Chapter 6.6.2.1). The lift truck also includes the drive, steering, seat arrangement and tyre components. The steering system (turntable or Ackermann steering), the type of steering (manual or automatic) and the steering control (pedestrian or driver operation) are described in Chapters 6.6.2.2 to 6.6.2.4; for tyres, please see Chapter 4.6.

Figure 6.31   Electric forklift truck, drive with three-phase alternate current technique; DC (direct current) AC (alternating current) (www.jungheinrich.de)

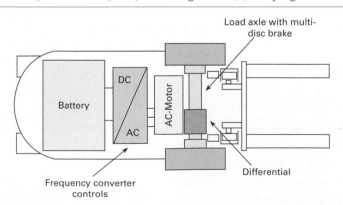

- *Drive*

The drive of a lift truck can occur as combustion engine or hybrid drive with diesel-electric battery electric motor. Electric lift trucks come in three-wheel design with 1 t to 2 (4) t load capacity, in four-wheel design with 1.6 t to 5 t. The drive batteries carry 24-V, 48-V and 80-V tension, depending on the load capacity (see Chapter 4.5.6; Examples 4.3 and 4.4). Diesel lift trucks in four-wheel design have a load capacity of 1.6 to 8 t. Gas forklifts exist with capacities between 1.6 t and 5 (8) t. We distinguish one-wheel drive as rear drive and multiple-wheel drive. For multiple wheels, each wheel can be allocated to a drive or one motor can take on the drive for two wheels.

Lift trucks in three-wheel design are built with front, rear and four-wheel drive. The one-wheel rear drive with turntable steering is a simple and cheap construction with minimal circuitry.

Four-wheel lift trucks only have a front drive with either one motor driving the front wheels via differential gears, or with two motors that impact on the front wheels independently.

For two-wheel front drive the motors have to be steered in line with the curved route. This means that the inner curve motor is switched off from about 30° to 70° turning angle and it is switched back on from 70° in backwards motion.

Increasingly, lift trucks are equipped with three-phase alternating current (see Figure 6.31). A frequency converter converts the direct current into alternating current, in order to then power the drive motor.

Lift cylinders, tilt cylinders and working cylinders for additional devices are powered by a hydraulic drive, ie the combustion engine or separate electric motor emit their performance to a hydraulic pump (usually gear pump), which then transports the hydraulic liquid (oil) to the respective working cylinders via control valves (see Figure 6.32, Chapter 4.5.7, Example 4.2).

Figure 6.32 Hydraulic system of a forklift truck (diagram)

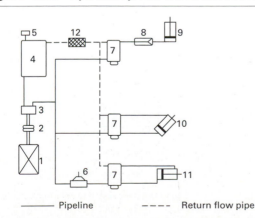

1 Motor
2 Clutch
3 Pump
4 Oil container
5 Air filter
6 Reduction valve
7 Controls
8 Sinking brake
9 Lift cylinder
10 Tilt cylinder
11 Working cylinder
12 Return flow oil filter

———— Pipeline   - - - - Return flow pipe

The hydraulic machine for an electric lift truck has its own drive motor, which carries out the lift, tilt and additional movements. For diesel drive, the hydro pump is directly connected to the diesel motor and is always running (short-circuiting of oil cycle when hydraulic is not in use). For most over-dimensional diesel drives, this construction arrangement compared to battery-electric drive allows for large lift loads with high lift speeds. The lowering speed is controlled and limited via an adjustable valve and based on the weight forces of the load, fork arms, fork carrier and parts of the lifting frame.

6.6.7.3 Stability, load capacity diagram

Lift trucks have to comply with safety regulations. Stability is a measurement to prevent the tipping over of a lift truck. It exists when the sum of the standing moments is larger than the sum of the tipping moments, in relation to the tilting point or tilting axle.

The four-wheel design of a lift truck is characterized by a fixed front axle with the drive wheels and a steerable rear axle, which is hung to swing in the middle of the vehicle longitudinal axle (thus a statically determined system). The suspension of the axle has an impact on the stability of the lift truck. The stand triangle of the lift truck is derived from the axle suspension and the drive wheels.

The three-wheel design has two fixed suspended front wheels and a steered, often also driven, rear wheel. This results in a statically determined system. The connections between the wheel contacts equal the tilting axles 1 to 3 (see Figure 6.33a).

In relation to the front axle of a three-wheel or four-wheel lift truck, the stability v (see Figure 6.33b) is:

$$v = \frac{G \times b}{G_1 \times a} \geq 1.4 \tag{6.9}$$

Figure 6.33 *Stability*

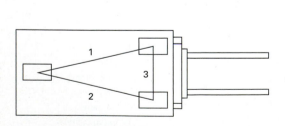

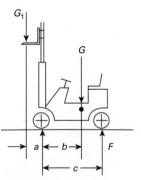

a) Tilting axles of a lift truck.
1 & 2 side stability; 3 longitudal stability

b) Calculation sketch to determine stability

G	in N	Own weight of lift truck
G_1	in N	Weight force of load
a, b	in m	Focal points spacing

The stability of a lift truck depends on the size and location of its own weight and the weight of the load, the track, wheelbase, tyre deformation, the lift frame shape, floor conditions etc. The stability of the lift truck is checked through safety standard tests, set in the ISO 22 915–2 guidelines for counterbalance lift trucks and ISO 22 915–3 for reach trucks as well as DIN EN ISO 3691–1.

Standard safety tests are described in relation to the design and type of lift truck and take into account:

- drive or stack:
  - with or without test load;
  - with or without tilting of the lift frame;
- diagonal drive.

The tests are carried out on an infinitely adjustable platform. During the tests, the lift truck may not tip over on the tilted platform.

The load capacity of a forklift is specified in a load capacity diagram (see Figure 6.34) in relation to the load focus. The load focus corresponds to the horizontal distance from the fork back to the load focus. For forklifts with a load capacity of 1,000 to 4,999 kg (see Example 6.6–12), the load focus is specified at 500 mm; for over 5,000 kg at 600 mm.

6.6.7.4 Lift frame, load handling attachments, other attachments

The *lift frame* is used for vertical movements of the load handling attachments and load. It is powered hydraulically and consists of either just one fixed external mast,

Figure 6.34 Load capacity diagram

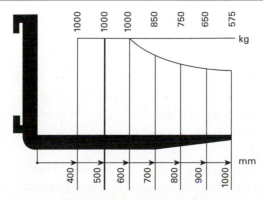

Distances from load focus to fork back

or several telescopic internal masts, in which the vertically flexible load (lift) carriage runs on rollers. In order to facilitate the load intake and discharge, the lift frame tilts forward by 3° as a result of the hydraulic (double effect) tilt cylinder.

A backwards tilt by 8° to 10° prevents the sliding of the load – especially around bends or when driving on gradient stretches. The turning point of the lift frame is usually at the height of the wheel axle.

The *load handling attachments* of a lift truck consist of the load carriage and the load carrier. For forklifts the load carriage is the lift or fork carriage, the load carrier is the fork arms. Other load carriers include different *attachments*. We distinguish between load handling attachments with or without the possibility to take on loads from the floor. Contrary to a telescopic fork, the wing fork can pick up flat pallets or mesh boxes from the floor.

Lift devices are divided by the size of the free lift. The low free lift corresponds to the lift height of the load handling attachment, without changing the overall height of the lift frame. A full free lift is achieved by special lift cylinders and allows for working in low spaces (lorries, containers, train carriages). The internal mast sections only extend from the external mast when the top position of the overall height of the lift truck is reached.

Based on the design of the lift frame, we distinguish (see Figure 6.35):

• single lift frames with single mast or double mast profile;

• double telescope lift frame;

• triple telescope lift frame.

Other designs can be created through equipment or structure:

• with full free lift;

• as free view lift frames, where the view-obstructing components – eg the hydraulic cylinder, hoses and chains – have been moved to other locations in the vehicle.

Single lift frame: Consists of a single mast (Figure 6.35a) or of both external mast profiles, between which the fork carriage is guided. It is lifted and lowered hydraulically, with the ends of the load chain fixed to the fork carriage on the one side and in the vehicle frame on the other. The chain runs over a roller connected to the piston. Lift heights of up to 1.8 m (Figure 6.35a) can thus be achieved.

Double telescope lift frame (Figure 6.35b): This consists of a fixed external mast and a telescopic internal mast, in which the fork carriage of the load handling attachment is guided. We distinguish between standard lift frames with low free lift and those with full free lift.

This is achieved through two integrated cylinders. There are also free view lift frames, either constructed in relevant chain transmissions (Figure 6.35c) or two

Figure 6.35   Lift frame constructions (exploded)

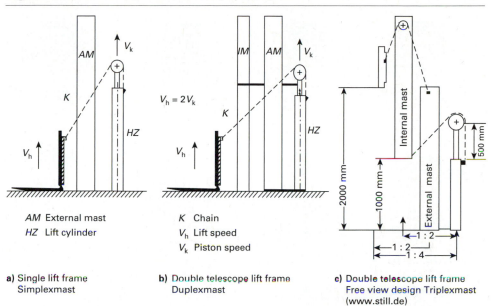

AM External mast
HZ Lift cylinder

K   Chain
V_h Lift speed
V_k Piston speed

a) Single lift frame
Simplexmast

b) Double telescope lift frame
Duplexmast

c) Double telescope lift frame
Free view design Triplexmast
(www.still.de)

parallel lift cylinders (lift height approximately 3.5 m) fixed to the masts. The lift speed depends on the structure ($v_{Load} = 2$ to 4 v_{piston}).

Triple lift frame: This consists of the fixed external masts and two internally flexible mast pairs. The fork carriage is guided in the innermost mast pair. The triple telescope lift frame allows for great lift heights up to 15 m for 6 m overall height.

High-rack forklifts and pickers as well as wheel-supported lift trucks and vertical pickers are equipped with fixed, non-tilting lift frames. Self-supporting and reach trucks are equipped with tilting lift frames.

Aside from the fork as load carrier with both fork arms to take up, carry and set down loads, there are a number of other attachments (Figure 6.36a to d). They complement and expand the standard deployment areas of lift trucks. Even load unit without floor clearance, such as boxes, bales or bulk cargo can be transported. We distinguish between attachments that are fixed to the load carriage of the lift truck and those that are taken on by the lift truck fork via fork shoes or fork pockets.

Attachments and devices can be structured with or without hydraulic drive. They are divided and categorized according to different criteria:

- attachments as load carriers:
  - for bulk cargo:
    * mechanic tilting shovel; hydraulic bulk cargo shovel;
    * snow blade, charging tool;

Figure 6.36 Selection of attachments for lift trucks (www.stabau.com)

Roll clamp

Charger

Timber grab

Scrap iron claw

Load holder

Assembly platform

Double pallet clamp

Side lift swing

Boom
(www.linde-mh.com)

Stone clamp
(www.linde-mh.com)

- for general cargo:
  * forks: folding fork, knife fork, fork extension; telescopic fork and rotating fork;
  * spikes: boom, carpet spike and pallet spike;
  * clamps: bale clamp, appliance clamp, barrel, stone and roll clamp;
  * grabs: scrap iron claw, timber grab and barrel grab;
  * cranes: crane arm, crane arm with telescopic extension;
  * work and assembly platform;
- attachments as movement devices for load carriers:
  - moving device for sideways shifting of load carrier:
    * hydraulic side shift, side shift fork;

- adjusting device to adjust fork tines:

   * tine adjusting device, double pallet clamp;

- rotating device for turning load carrier:

   * pivot (rotating device), pallet rotating device and a mesh box emptier;

- swing device to swing the load carrier:

   * swing device, swing fork and tilt device;

- auxiliary attachments for load carriers:

   - pusher, wipers, clamp pusher, eg for slip sheet: see Example 3.14;

   - pull-push, load holder, container emptier for floor discharge.

Often, there is a combination of an attachment as load carrier with an attachment as moving device:

- double pallet clamp with side shift (see Figure 7.7), rotating roller clamp;

- tilt-charger, barrel tilt clamp and swing push fork.

Negative effects when using attachments can include:

- reduction in lift truck load capacity (calculation of remaining load capacity: see VDI 3578 attachments for forklifts) and increase in floor pressure;

- time lost through assembly and disassembly, deployment checks;

- reduction in stability (counteracted by calculation of remaining load capacity);

- changes to lift truck dimensions (impact on transport route, aisle width and gate width, gate height);

- worsening of visibility;

- checks and/or retrofitting of hydraulics.

The process of choosing attachments can be carried out in line with Example 6.6–3.

6.6.7.5 Transport route, working aisle width, surface area load

Transport route: These are paths designated for the internal pedestrian and/or vehicle traffic, such as walking paths, ramps, roadways, tracks. In line with DIN 18 225 and the workplace regulations (ASR 17/1, 2 'traffic routes') work rooms and storage spaces over 1,000 m² have to incorporate clearly marked traffic routes. There are exclusive pedestrian routes, exclusive vehicle routes and joint pedestrian and vehicle routes. We also distinguish between directional and oncoming traffic. The traffic route width is calculated based on the maximum width of the industrial truck in question or the protruding load, plus double the addition of a 0.5 m for directional traffic and 0.75 m for oncoming traffic.

Figure 6.37   Aisle width for different lift trucks (for the dimensions, see Table 9.1; www.linde-mh.de)

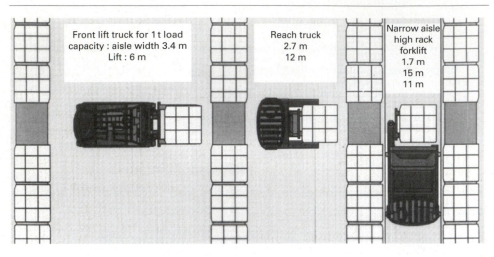

Aisle width: In order to take a load unit from a shelf, a directional change of 90° is required for a forklift, for high shelves the removal occurs without a change in direction. The aisle width is a deciding factor, eg for the efficient use of space and room in a warehouse for floor or shelf storage. The smaller the aisle width, the larger the number of stored load units, expressed in values such as space or room utilization level (see Chapter 9.7).

The aisle width is the distance between the opposing load units and is dependent on:

• industrial truck, eg type of lift truck (reach truck, high rack forklift: Figure 6.37);

• design of the lift truck (three-wheel, four-wheel);

• type and location of the transport aid (lengthwise/across, dimensions, pallet, container);

• safety distance (200 mm according to VDI – 2198, workplace regulations) and pedestrian traffic;

• type of load carrier (fork tine, attachment).

A lift truck's *turning radius* is mostly determined through the constructive design of the steering axle. If lift trucks of the same load capacity but with different steering axles are compared, an electric lift truck with 1.6 t load capacity has a turning radius of:

• with Ackermann steering and floating axle, 2.11 m;

• with turntable axle, 1.88 m;

• with combined axle, 1.92 m.

Floor load: If lift trucks are deployed in a multi-floor building, in a building with a cellar or for loading a lorry/container, the ceiling load capacity of the building or the load capacity of the lorry platform is comparable to the floor load of the lift truck.

$$p_{vorh} = \frac{(m + Q) \times 9.81 \times \xi}{L \times B} < p_{zul} \tag{6.10}$$

p	in N/m^2	Floor load of lift truck according to DIN 2199
m	in kg	Own load (own weight + driver weight)
Q	in kg	Load
ξ		Shock factor
L	in m	External vehicle length including load on forks
B		External vehicle width including load on forks

Measures to reduce the floor load of a lift truck include increasing the tyre contact, such as by changing the type of tyre, reduction of tyre pressure for air tyres or twin tyres.

Point load: This is the ratio of the resulting force to the floor contact in N/m^2. For lift trucks, the point load is hard to determine. Important for rack frames: if the point load is high a metal sheet is placed under the frame to reduce it.

6.6.7.6 Lift truck types

Names and characteristics of industrial trucks can be according to the DIN and VDI information in Example 6.6–13. A categorization of lift trucks can occur based on a number of aspects, distinguishing:

- wheel supported lift trucks (high lift trucks): narrow or wide gauge design;
- self-supporting lift trucks: counterbalance design;
- wheel-supported/self-supporting lift trucks: combined design.

For *wheel-supported lift trucks*, the load is taken on and carried *within* the wheelbase. The wheel arms are either under the load carrier, such as a hollow fork (narrow gauge design) or they go around the loading aid, such as a DIN pallet (wide gauge design or a straddle truck). For the prevalent narrow gauge design, the load carrier hollow fork and load carriage are connected inextricably. The distance between the fork tines corresponds to the insertion apertures of a lengthwise DIN pallet. For the wide gauge design, the wheel arms move around the load, the load carrier fork can be lowered to the ground and is exchangeable. The distance of the wheel arms can be up to 1,400 mm.

Self-supporting lift trucks take on the load *outside* of the wheelbase, so that the load must be counterbalanced by an additional counterweight.

Figure 6.38 Categorization of motor-driven lift trucks for transport and stacking of bulk cargo

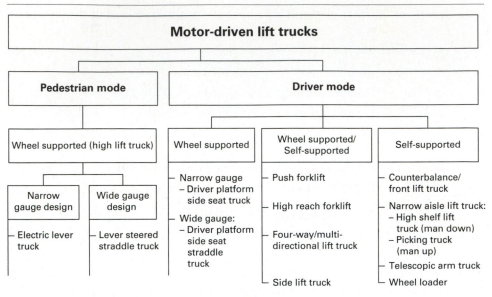

Reach trucks have a movable lift frame that runs within the wheel arms. With a mast pushed forward, they take on the load in a self-supported manner; with the mast pulled back, they transport the load with wheel support. The fork tines lie within the wheel arms, that are approximately 900 mm apart, so that the load can be pick up off the floor between the wheel arms up to a width of 900 mm, such as a DIN pallet with 800 × 1,200 mm. Wider loads must be lifted in self-support in front of the wheel arms and then pulled up over the wheel arms.

Four-way and cross forklifts have to pick up transport and stacking cargo from the floor using the wheel arms and then pull the mast back in order to transport the cargo wheel-supported – for cross forklifts on the platform.

A possible division of motor-driven lift trucks is shown in Figure 6.38.

Pedestrian drive, wheel-supported (high lift truck, also called reach truck)

- *Electric lever lift truck/narrow gauge design*

This type of lift truck is structured like the electric lever forklift (see Figure 6.30a to d) and additionally has a fixed lift frame. The hollow fork is inextricably connected to the lift carriage, is located above the wheel arms and drives under the transverse support for pallets on a shelf. The rollers are placed in the wheel arms and, together with the steered drive wheels, the wheel base. The maximum speed of machines in pedestrian mode is 6 km/h; there are different lift frame designs:

- with single lift frame: consists of *one* mast located in the middle (load capacity 1 t; lift height up to 2,000 mm, Figure 6.39a) or with *two* external masts;
- with one double telescopic lift frame (see Figure 6.86 e/f).

Figure 6.39 Single-mast lift trucks with lift heights of approximately 1.7 m

a) Electric lever forklift
(www.jungheinrich.de)

b) Lever-steered straddle truck
(www.toyota-forklifts.de)

- *Electric lever-led straddle truck / wide gauge* design (see Figure 6.39b)
This type of lift truck moves around lengthwise and crosswise pallets with its wheel arms (floor pick up of pallet) and has a fixed, non-tilting single lift frame or a double telescopic lift frame. The non-powered and non-steered wheels are located in the wheel arms.

Driver mode: wheel-supported (high lift truck)

- *Electric side seat reach truck* (narrow gauge design)
For the standing driver mode, the electric lever stacker is equipped with a foldable lever as well as a folding step. The driver seat design is equipped with a driver's seat. Figure 6.40b shows the driver stand-in version.

- *Electric driver stand-in straddle truck* (wide gauge design)
The driver platform straddle truck is the driver version of the lever-steered straddle. For driver's seat design: see Figure 6.70.

- *Portal stacker* (van carrier, straddle carrier)
Portal stackers are primarily used to transport and stack containers up to 40 feet (see Figure 7.10e and 7.17). They take on the load from above within the wheel base with a spreader. The vehicles drive at high speeds (empty approximately 40 km/h, loaded approximately 20 km/h), have 4 to 16 wheels, often with double tyres and are equipped with all-wheel drive. Each wheel is steered individually.

Figure 6.40   Electric reach trucks: wheel arms drive under transverse support for pallets or drive into the gaps in pallets (www.toyota-forklifts.de)

a) Side seat design   **b)** Driver platform design

Pedestrian mode: wheel-supported / self-supporting

- *Reach truck*

For this forklift with a fixed lift frame, the load is taken on by the self-supported wheel arms with a telescopic fork; the fork and load are pulled back and transported in this position.

- *Reach truck*

For this type of truck, the lift frame can be moved horizontally in the wheel arms (Figure 6.41), ie when the mast is pushed all the way forward it corresponds to a self-supporting stacker. There is almost no need for a counterweight. The load unit is taken off the floor in front of the wheels.

The distance between the wheel arms is approximately 900 mm. This means that a lengthwise DIN pallet can be taken up off the floor between the wheel arms, and that crosswise pallets must be lifted in front of the wheels by approximately 350 mm. This has to be taken into account specifically for pallets that are on the floor of a shelving rack (bottom level). In pulling back the mast, the reach truck shortens the vehicle length (also as a result of the side seat) so that the aisle width is between 2.8 to 3.0 m (see Figure 6.37). The lift height for a triple-telescopic lift frame is 12 m for an overall height of 4.5 m. Maximum speeds are around 9 km/h for driver-standing designs and

Figure 6.41 Reach truck: mast pulled back (www.linde-mh.com)

Figure 6.42 Reach truck: mast moving forward (www.jungheinrich.de)

around 12 km/h for driver-seat designs with a side seat. Figure 6.42 shows a reach truck deployed in a warehouse with mast pushed forward (see Example 11.21).

- *Four-way/multi-directional forklift*

According to their construction, four-way forklifts are reach trucks for long cargo with long cargo fork carriers and with standard carriers for pallets (Figure 6.43). The difference to the reach truck is the rotation of the wheels by 90° so that the four-way forklift can go forwards and backwards as well as sideways to the left or right (see Example 6.6–1). The distance of the fork tines can be changed hydraulically (better support for transport of long cargo). Four-way forklifts only require a small aisle width due to the side-seat arrangement and adjustable wheels.

If the wheel rotation occurs in stages or continuously, the four-way forklift turns into a *multi-directional forklift*.

- *Side stackers (cross-forklifts)*

Side stackers are basically platform trucks that have an integrated reach truck in the middle (Figure 6.44). The driver cabin is very narrow, so that there is a large support area for long cargo. The taking on of cargo is done by moving out the mast and lowering the load onto the platform. The side stacker is deployed in long goods storage for transporting pipes, wooden planks and pressboards, and also in special designs for transporting three pallets at once.

Figure 6.43   Multi-directional forklift trucks

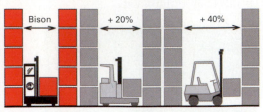

b) Comparison aisle width of multi-directional, reach and front forklifts (www.votex-bison.com)

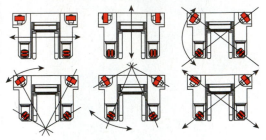

a) Multi-directional forklift with Triplexmast and fully self-supporting lift (www.hubtex.com)

c) Work method: possible wheel positions (www-votex.bison.com)

Figure 6.44   Side stacker deployed in a timber warehouse (www.baumann-online.it)

In order to operate on the opposite side in an aisle, the side stacker has to drive out of the aisle, turn via a turning circle and re-enter the aisle. The aisle width corresponds to the vehicle width (approximately 2.15–2.5 m).

- *Truck-mounted forklift*

The truck-mounted forklift (see Figures 6.57 and 6.58) is a version of the multi-directional forklift but it has a fixed lift frame – often with push fork – as well as telescopic wheel arms and air or super elastic tyres. The load capacity is up to 2.5 t, the lift height up to 4 m.

Driver mode: self-supporting:

- counterbalance forklift (see Figure 6.24);

- narrow gauge forklift; high shelf and order picking forklift (see Chapter 10.4.3);

- telescopic arm forklift, (see Figures 6.51 and 7.16c3);

- wheel loader for bulk cargo.

6.6.7.7 Deployment control, forklift guide system SLS

The deployment control of a forklift can occur decentralized or centralized.

Decentralized means offline operation, one example being a forklift driver who drives to an office (control point) after finishing each assignment and personally picks up more jobs.

Centralized means online operation; the jobs are transmitted via radio data transmission to the forklift in warehousing, order picking or external storage. An SLS is a vehicle disposition and control system, and consists of a control station (computer), radio or infrared data transmission as well as a mobile terminal. It receives assignments from a computer, processes them and passes them to the vehicle via a terminal. The driver fulfils the assignment, fills in an assignment sheet, reports back as 'available', takes on a new assignment and can also communicate with the SLS. The SLS has further operational components, such as manual data radio terminal, scanner and forklift-mounted label printer (see Example 6.6–5; see Chapter 13.3.3).

6.6.7.8 Operational costs of forklifts

In order to provide cost comparisons of industrial trucks, or with other means of transport, the operational costs for a period must be determined (see Chapter 4.8). For an electric forklift with driver seat (1.5 t load capacity three-wheel design; 3.5 m lift height; battery 24 V) the annual operational costs have been determined using VDI 2695 (Table 6.1).

The following applies:

- Item 1.1 to 1.3: Average costs for 2011 without VAT.

- Item 2.1 and 2.2: These are tax rates for one shift operation. Linear depreciation is permitted for forklift and battery over five years (20 per cent per year) and charger over 15 years (6.7 per cent per year), see Table 6.2.

- Item 2.3: Interest corresponding to the annual capital costs. The capital is subject to interest.

Table 6.1 Operational cost calculation of a forklift (2011)

1.0 Investment		
1.1 Electric three-wheel forklift 1.5 t	€	20,000
1.2 Battery (24 V; 800 Ah)	€	6,000
1.3 Charger	€	1,500
1.4 Total investment	€	27,500
2.0 Determining fixed costs		
2.1 Depreciation (20% of 1.1 and 1.2)	€/a	5,200
2.2 Depreciation (6.7% of 1.3)	€/a	101
2.3 Interest (8% of 50% of 1.4)	€/a	1,100
2.4 Fixed costs per annum	€/a	6,401
2.5 Fixed costs per hour (1.470 h/a)	€/h	4.36
3.0 Determining variable costs		
3.1 Maintenance (12% of 1.4; Kal. I)	€/a	3,300
3.2 Energy costs (0.2 €/kWh; one shift)	€/a	1,106
3.3 Variable costs per annum	€/a	4,406
3.4 Variable costs per hour (1,470 h/a)	€/h	3
4.0 Operational costs per annum (2.4 and 3.3)	€/a	10,807
4.1 Operational costs per hour	€/h	7.36
5.0 Personnel costs (One shift operation) (1.2 men per forklift and year at 30,000 € per annum and driver)	€/a	36,000
5.1 Total costs three-wheel forklift per annum	€/a	46,807

Table 6.2 Lifetime value of forklift depending on use

Usual lifetime as basis for depreciation calculation			
	Electric industrial trucks	Combustion engine powered industrial trucks	Battery Charger
Light deployment	12–15	8–12	5–6 15
Medium deployment	10–12	6–8	4–5 15
Heavy deployment	6–10	4–6	4 12

- Item 2.5: We calculate with 1,470 deployment hours per annum.
- Item 3.1: This item encompasses the costs for maintenance: 1) preventative: maintenance, inspection with cleaning and greasing; 2) due to failure: repair with exchange, mending and restoration, eg wages, tyres, oil and parts. These costs depend on the level of use of industrial trucks, which results from the deployment

conditions and the performance requirements, such as environmental influences, roadway condition, external/internal deployment as well as efficient use of the technical performance capability. The level of use is classified as light, medium and heavy, using category (see VDI 2695) I, II and III.

Category I corresponds to use of up to 50 per cent of the technical performance capability, favourable working conditions, even roadways, dust-free air and internal deployment.

Category II: Use of between 50 and 100 per cent of performance capability, internal and external deployment, uneven roadway, track crossing, roadway gradients of up to 10 per cent, constant change in temperature.

Category III: Use of 100 per cent of performance capability, most difficult working conditions, work with attachments, uneven roadways, gradients over 10 per cent, radiation heat, dusty air.

• Item 3.2: The energy cost of a single charge of the battery without electrolyte circulation can be calculated, based on a required remaining capacity of 20 per cent (see Chapter 4.5.6) in line with formula (4.3):

$$E = \frac{24 \times 800 \times 0.8 \times 1.5}{1000} = 23.04 \text{ kWh}$$

For deployment of 1,470 hours per annum and a shift duration of approximately six hours, around 240 charges are required. At an energy cost of €0.20 per kWh, the energy costs work out at:

$$EK = E \times z \times SP \text{ [€/a]} \tag{6.11}$$

EK	€/a	Energy costs per annum
E	kWh	Stored energy
z	a^{-1}	Number of charges per annum
SP	€/kWh	Energy cost per kWh

Here: EK = 23.04 × 204 × 0.2 = €1,105.92 €/a

Note: the energy price in €/kWh is dependent on many factors and must be determined for each individual case. A significant reduction in energy use can be achieved through electrolyte circulation during the charging process: factor 1.15 instead of 1.5 (see Formula 4.3 in Chapter 4.5.6).

• Item 5.0: The driver costs must be included in the operational costs. Holiday and sick leave result in including 1.2 drivers per forklift per annum.

The prices/costs used in this example, such as for the machine, for energy, personnel, depreciation, interest rates, etc depend on business-specific and political factors, so that the methodology to determine costs is decisive, not the cost value.

Currently, many industrial trucks are being leased. For their comparison, the inclusion of part or full maintenance contracts in leasing rates must be taken into consideration (see Example 11.22).

6.6.8 VDI guidelines

Notice: Accident prevention regulations for industrial trucks BGV D27

2198	Technical data for forklift trucks	12.13
2406	Trailers for industrial trucks	11.02
2516	Floor conveyors for storage and retrieval: cycle time calculation in narrow aisles	09.03
2695	Determination of costs for industrial trucks: forklift trucks	03.10
3318	Using freight elevators with industrial floor trucks	09.04
3577	Industrial trucks for high-bay warehouses: specification and operating instructions	09.08
3586	Industrial trucks: terms, symbols, examples	11.07
3589	Selection criteria for procuring industrial trucks	05.07
3641	Mobile data communications systems for internal company material transport	05.88
3643	Self-powered trolley system: suspended trolley system, load 500 kg	11.98
3960	Determination of service hours of industrial trucks	03.98
4462	Industrial truck survey: lorry or trailer-mounted forklift trucks	04.09

6.6.9 Examples and questions

Example 6.6–1: Four-way forklift

Describe how a four-way forklift works in a pallet block warehouse and in a long cargo warehouse.

Answer: Usually, raw materials, semi-finished and finished products, which largely (up to 80 per cent) require interim storage, can only be buffered in two row stacks, as the pallets or containers have to be accessible at any time. The four-way forklift allows four-row stacking for a minimal cargo width of 1 m. The work methodology is shown in Figure 6.45a (see also Figure 6.43).

1 The four-way forklift drives lengthways with a modest aisle width.

2 The storage unit in the first row is taken on or set down through extending or retracting the push frame. The wheels keep their direction.

3 To get to the second stacked row, the wheels have to turn by 90°.

Figure 6.45   Methods of a four-way forklift

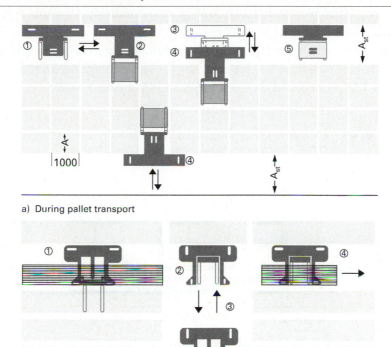

a) During pallet transport

b) During transport of long cargo. ① corresponds to numbers ① and ② in
   a) above. ②, ③ and ④ are identical with movement processes ③, ④ and ⑤ in
   a) above. The sequential stacking of large quantities in a block is unlimited here.
   Each block can be built or taken down from the aisle

4 Now the four-way forklift can carry out its crossway movement and take on or set down the storage unit in the second row.

5 The wheels return to lengthwise position and the transport can occur.

The method of a four-way forklift in a long cargo warehouse (length of long cargo > length of vehicle) occurs in the same way as that of the pallet warehouse and is shown in Figure 6.45b.

Example 6.6–2: Aisle width comparison

Compare aisle widths and level efficient use of space between a four-way forklift, reach truck and front forklift for the same load capacity of 1 t and identical Euro pallet cargo dimensions for lengthways storage.

Answer: The comparison is shown in Figure 6.46a to c. The schematic drawing shows the different required aisle widths of the individual forklift types (17.90 – 2,000; 2,400 – 2,800; 3,110 – 3,400 mm).

The results can also be represented by providing the level of efficient use of space for a four-way forklift as 100 per cent. For the same storage capacity, the reach truck requires 116 per cent and the front forklift 134 per cent of space.

Figure 6.46 Comparison: aisle widths of different forklifts for storage depth of 1 m.
a) Four-way forklift. b) Reach truck. c) Front forklift

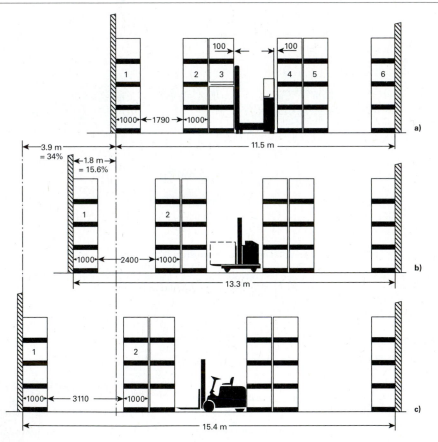

Example 6.6–3: Attachment selection

Describe the method to choose attachment and forklift by creating a flow chart.

Answer: Figure 6.47.

The transport task and type of transport unit are the starting points for selecting attachments.

Figure 6.47 Flowchart for selection of attachment

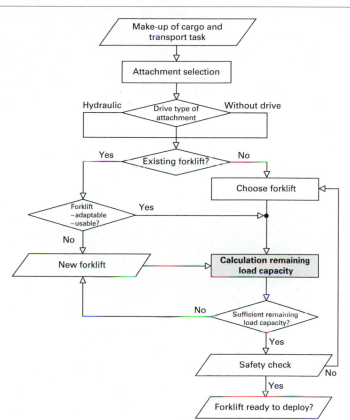

Example 6.6–4: Ergonomic working with tug tractor and trolley

Show two examples of ergonomic working.

Answer: Figure 6.48a shows a low lift truck; Figure 6.48b shows a tug tractor with trailers.

Figure 6.48a Low lift truck with automatic load height adjustment (www.still.de)

The shaft led low lift truck adjusts its driving speed automatically to the shaft angle, which allows for manoeuvring in tight spaces. The top speed is 6 km/h and the fork height only 85 mm, so that it is possible to drive crossways into one-off pallets. The cargo to be loaded or unloaded always remains at working height. This puts less strain on the back and reduces tiredness. A sensor keeps measuring the load height and there is no manual height adjustment necessary.

Figure 6.48b   Tow tractor with trailers (www.still.de) (see Example 12.30)

A tow tractor pulls rolling E- and C-frames, which can take on movable load carriers. In lean production they provide workplaces just in time with manufacturing and assembly parts. Hence, pre-picked load carriers are transported quickly to identified consumption sites based on requirements. The handling time is reduced to a minimum, as the movable load carriers can only be pulled out of the C-frame. Empty runs may be avoided if manufactured parts are taken back on the return journey. There is no heavy handling.

Example 6.6–5: Computer-aided transport management

How does computer-aided transport management (disposition system, transport and stacking system) work for industrial trucks?

Answer: If the transport system is integrated into a holistic logistics system and connected to the production management, warehouse administration and general administration, then a computer acts as the transport control centre (transport control system). On the one hand, the assignments are sent to the control centre via radio transmission, stationary or mobile terminals; on the other, the forklift driver communicates with the control centre via a mobile terminal. The stacking control system's operational units can be seen in Figure 6.49 (see Chapters 6.6.7.7 and 13.3.3).

Figure 6.49   a) Disposition system. b) Data radio terminal. c) Label printer. d) Scanning process (b to d: www.still.de)

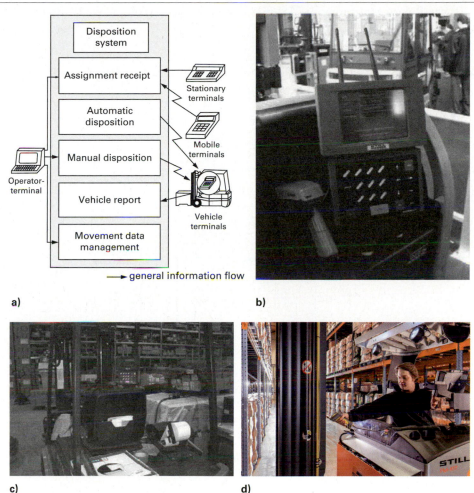

a)

b)

c)

d)

Example 6.6–6: Performance diagram

What is the performance of the electric tow tractor depicted in Figure 6.28a and b?

Answer: The electric tow tractor with 4 t trailer load has the performance diagram shown in Table 6.3. The example given shows that the tow tractor with 2 t trailer load, with a driving speed of 4.3 km/h and gradient of 8 per cent, can manage a distance of 550 m in an hour. If the route is only 55 m long, it can be completed 10 times at the conditions given above (see Example 6.6–7).

The example shows that a vehicle with load of 2,000 kg can manage a maximum gradient of 8 per cent for 550 m at a driving speed of 4.3 km/h.

(If the 8 per cent gradient is 55 m long then it can be completed 10 times in an hour.)

Table 6.3 Performance diagram for electric tow tractor with 4 t trailer load referring to Figure 6.28a and b (www.still.de)

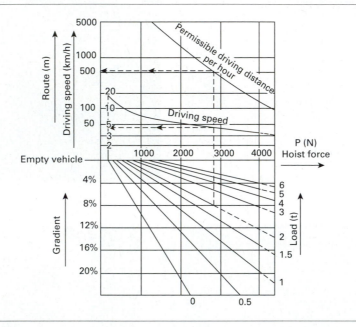

Example 6.6–7: Gradient performance

For the electric forklift depicted in Figure 6.24, calculate the distances achievable in one hour for different gradients, both with and without load.

Answer: The gradient performances can be read in Figure 6.50 for a dry, rough concrete roadway ($\mu = 0.8$) with a 600 Ah battery depending on the tyres (V $\triangleq$ full rubber tyre, L $\triangleq$ air tyres) (see Example 6.6–6).

Example 6.6–8: Economic comparison

Provide an economic comparison for a forklift and tow truck depending on single and double runs as well as the length of the route.

Answer: Table 6.4.

Example (with load of 4,000 kg), gradient 13 per cent, 10 km in length, air tyres. This gradient can be managed 26 times in an hour.

Table 6.4 Economic comparison forklift – tow truck

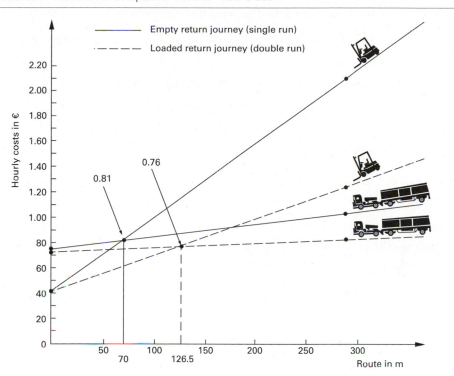

Figure 6.50 Gradient performance of three-wheel forklift (see Figure 6.24) (www.still.de)

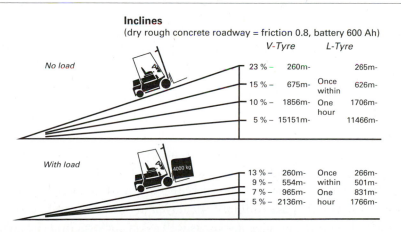

Example 6.6–9: Safety and ergonomic design

Which accident prevention regulation applies to the safe and ergonomic design of forklifts and on which components does it have particular impact?

Answer: With regard to safe and ergonomic design, forklifts are subject to legislation and standards, in particular the UVV 'Industrial trucks' BGV D27. The aim is to ensure that, given proper driving in accordance with regulations, there is no danger to the driver and the environment. The regulations are about:

- wheel protection, driver safety roof, overload protection grid, steering, tyres and driver's space;
- electric equipment, visibility, warning devices, noise and seat design;
- fork carriers, attachments, arrangements and design of display tools.

Example 6.6–10: Warning devices

What warning devices can be used to avoid accidents and to indicate dangerous operating situations?

Answer: We distinguish between optical and acoustic warning devices, which can be installed on the industrial truck as well as along the traffic routes: beacons, hazard lights, horns and sirens, traffic lights, barriers, mirrors, signs for information and warnings.

Warning devices to indicate critical operating conditions at the industrial truck include: battery charge monitor, battery charge indicator, scales to determine loading weights, contour control views, fuel indicator.

Example 6.6–11: Forklift design telescopic arm forklift (reach stacker)

Usually, self-supporting forklifts are equipped with a telescopic lift frame. Disadvantages include the limited visible area, working and control possibilities when the forklift is stationary beyond the tine ends and additional motion function can only be accessed via attachments. What does another design look like, which partly eliminates the above disadvantages?

Answer: Instead of a telescopic lift frame, a telescopic arm is deployed, which can lower the fork or other load carriers hydraulically (Figure 6.51).

Through semi-circular motion of the extendable arm, which is installed at the back of the vehicle, it is possible to transport loads across obstacles and to serve the second line, as well as take on, transport and stack cargo with no floor clearance by using attachments. The telescopic arm forklift requires a wide aisle width, which is why they are ordinarily deployed in outdoor warehouses as rough terrain truck, (empty) container stacker as well as on construction sites with large load capacity (20 t) (see Figure 7.16c (3)). Lift height goes up to 7 m at a reach of 3.8 m.

Figure 6.51　Deployment of a self-supporting telescopic arm forklift

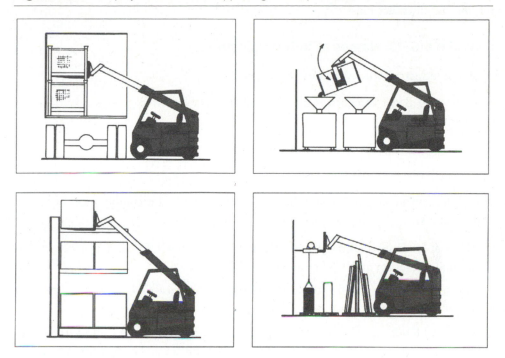

Example 6.6–12: Nominal load capacity/nominal hoist force

Explain the difference between load capacity and nominal load capacity of forklifts, as well as the nominal hoist force of tow tractors.

Answer: The performance description for forklifts occurs through providing the load capacity Q in kg or t. In order to render the load capacities of different manufacturers of forklifts comparable, the type sheets of the VDI standards utilize nominal load capacity.

This nominal load capacity is based on:

- a forklift with double telescopic lift frame;
- a load focus corresponding to the standard distance dependent on forklift type and load capacity;
- a lift height of 3,300 mm.

The real load capacity of a forklift takes into account the structure groups for the forklift and all special vehicle sizes. It is provided on the load capacity sign of the forklift. The nominal load capacity of a tow tractor is determined on dry and horizontal cement floor and results in the hoist force in N at the clutch. The other significant item is the provision of the trailer load (tow load) in t, which results from the sum of all trailer mass.

Example 6.6–13: Names of industrial trucks

How are industrial trucks' names abbreviated?

Answer: VDI 3586 categorizes all industrial trucks into five groups according to these criteria:

- type of drive and lift operation (by hand/motoric);
- steering type and operating type.

The abbreviation used for each industrial truck consists of a combination of letters and numbers.

- The first letter signifies the drive type, such as: D – diesel, E – battery electric, H – manual operation and T – liquid gas.
- The second letter signifies the operating type, such as: G – pedestrian led, S – driver led; F – driver's seat, K – liftable driver's space (picker).
- The third letter signifies the industrial truck design, such as: W – platform truck, Z – double axle tow, N – low lift truck, H – high lift truck, G – forklift, M – reach truck, V – four-way forklift and Q – cross forklift.

In addition, this combination of three letters can be followed by other information in the shape of letters or numbers, eg to describe the line, load capacity, attachment etc. According to the standard, a diesel forklift with 2,000 kg load capacity would have the abbreviation DFG 2,000. The manufacturer abbreviations do not always correspond to the VDI names.

Example 6.6–14: Narrow aisle forklift with large lift height: high shelf stackers

Which components can be automated for a high shelf stacker, in order to facilitate the steering and operating and to increase the handling performance?

Answer: Possible components for part automation are: forced guidance or steering, horizontal and vertical positioning, stacking and unstacking automation, data transmission via radio, infrared technology or induction.

Example 6.6–15: Contactless energy transmission for electric monorails

Sketch the cross section of an electric monorail with contactless energy transmission as well as the principle.

Answer: Figure 6.52. The contactless energy transmission occurs on the basis of inductive energy feed. The advantages compared to sliding contacts are the high driving speed as well as being free from wear and maintenance. This type of energy provision does not cause any dirt and is not sensitive to external contamination.

Figure 6.52 Cross section of an electric monorail with contactless energy transmission (www.eisenmann.com)

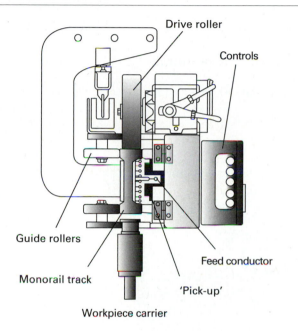

Figure 6.53 shows the principle of contactless energy transmission. It is based on an HF transformer as the energy transmitter. The conductor loop that is fed by the stationary sinus converter forms the primary circuit for this transformer. The secondary circuit is the movable collector coil. The sinus converter feeds highly frequent alternating current to build the magnetic field into the conductor loop. The resulting magnetic field is continuously traversed by the collector and thus induces an equivalent energy.

The Vahle company describes the function as follows:

The 'pick-up' is located in an energized conductor loop of the primary circuit, whose magnetic field penetrates the built in reel system, and creates an output voltage. This fluctuates depending on the primary conductor energy, the load and the magnetic connection. The latter changes through the vehicle movement, the curve situation etc. The downstream electronics processes the 'pick-up' output voltage to a constant voltage level.

Figure 6.53 Principle of contactless energy transmission (www.eisenmann.com)

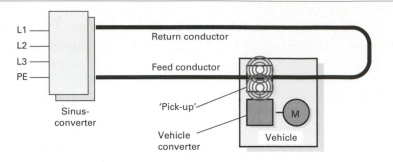

Example 6.6–16: Electric monorail

Provide the technical data as well as a practical example.

Answer: Figure 6.54a and b.

Figure 6.54 Electric monorail

a) Transport of car chassis with heavy load monorail (www.eisenmann.com)

Technical data electric monorail						
System	EHB 625	EHB 635	KHB-F20 KHB-F40	PTS	IMS I	IMS II
Type	Suspended monorail			Drag mono-rail	Floor systems	
Track view						
Max. transport load, double vehicle	500 kg	1.500 kg	10.000 kg	1.500 kg	1.500 kg	4.600 kg
Max. incline (load dependent)	90°	90°	45°	3°	45°	45°
Max. speed	120 m/min	120 m/min	150 m/min	80 m/min	90 m/min	90 m/min

b) Technical data for electric monorail (www.schierholz.de)

Example 6.6–17: Double deck system

What is a double deck system?

Answer: A double deck system is simultaneous loading and unloading with a wheel-supported high lift truck (stacker) with two load-handling devices, as shown in Figure 6.55. The second load-handling device is the load lift of the 'low lift truck'. It is used for non-stackable pallets in lorries, eg for dairy products.

Figure 6.55   Loading/unloading of non-stackable pallets via electric shaft high lift truck (folding step for driver steering) for simultaneous movement and stacking of two pallets: double deck system (www.toyota-forklifts.de)

Example 6.6–18: Safety system for shelf storage with narrow aisle stackers

Which safety systems are used for protecting both personnel and objects when driving in and out of shelf aisles with forklifts, or when personnel are entering shelf aisles? Which standards and guidelines describe the requirements for personnel protection?

Answer: For protection of personnel in shelf aisles stationary and mobile safety systems are used, which work contactless.

The stationary systems, based on light barriers, can either secure single aisle (Figure 6.56a, good but expensive), or a block of shelves (Figure 6.56b, cheaper but not as secure).

Figure 6.56   Safety system for shelving units (www.jungheinrich.de)

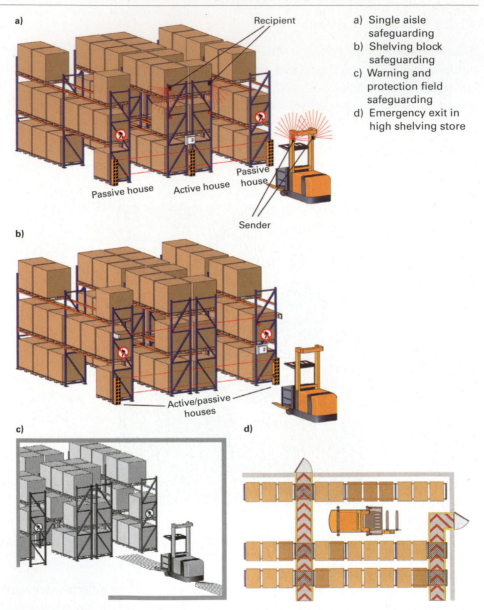

a) Single aisle
   safeguarding
b) Shelving block
   safeguarding
c) Warning and
   protection field
   safeguarding
d) Emergency exit in
   high shelving store

For mobile, laser-scanner-based systems, the components are installed on the forklift (Figure 6.56c) and create warning and protection fields in front of and behind the forklift. If the forklift drives into or out of a shelf aisle, the automatic activation or deactivation of the warning field occurs. If a person enters these fields, or the driver drives in or out too quickly, the speed is automatically reduced or brakes are even applied to stand still. The maximum distance of a point in the warehouse can be

30 m by air, or 50 m on foot to the next fire area or outside space. If an emergency exit is required through the shelves, the exit width has to be at least 0.87 m (for possible arrangements, see Figure 6.56).

The requirements for safety systems are covered in DIN 15 185, part 2, VGB 5.

Cameras are used to achieve quick and safe handling, driving, steering and manipulating, as well as front and back room monitoring to prevent accidents – these are installed in the forks, mast, cabin roof or the back.

Example 6.6–19: Truck-mounted forklifts

The truck-mounted forklift is used in businesses or at construction sites for loading and unloading of cargo with large dimensions and weights without specific handling aids; ie the lorry takes a forklift, a type of multi-directional forklift (see Figure 6.43) at its back. Figures 6.57 and 6.58 show the transport and working method of this type of forklift.

Figure 6.57 Transport of forklift with lorry (www.kooiaap.com)

Figure 6.58 Truck-mounted forklift during stacking (www.kooiaap.com)

Example 6.6–20: Special designs and special forklift equipment

A number of special designs and equipment have been developed for special uses and individual occasions. Show some examples.

Answer: see list below:

1 Free lift heights, see Chapter 6.6.7.4, eg for stacking pallets in a container.
2 Clear vision lifting frames, see Chapter 6.6.7.4, eg for better visibility when driving.

3 Explosion safe forklift design, eg to drive in previously protected spaces.

4 Non-turning tyres (see Chapter 4.6.1.3) when driving on plastic floors.

5 Non-tilting control cabin (Figure 6.59), for better visibility when stacking.

6 Articulated steering for high shelf stackers (Figure 6.61), to minimize traffic area through small curve radius.

Figure 6.59   Tilting control cabin (www.toyota-forklifts.de)

Figure 6.60   Stacker with rotating cabin (www.jungheinrch.de)

Figure 6.61   High shelf stacker with articulated steering (www.toyota-forklifts.de)

Figure 6.62   Reach truck (www.linde-mh.de)

7 Control consoles, eg with PC version for order picking.

8 Reach truck (Figure 6.22): developed from self-supporting forklift, deployed up to 1.7 t; fixed mast, strong manipulation ability and manoeuvrability, high speed, aisle width for lengthwise Europa pallet 2.70 m.

Example 6.6–21: In-floor conveyor

What is the structure of an in-floor conveyor?

Answer: The in-floor conveyor is a floor-supported transport system developed from the electric monorail. The pallet-carrying load carriers run on rollers. Lengthwise and crosswise transport is possible. Single (Figure 6.63) or two-track in-floor conveyors are used.

Figure 6.63   Electric in-floor conveyor (www.eisenmann.com)

Figure 6.64   Push plate conveyor (www.eisenmann.com)

Example 6.6–22: Push plate conveyor

What is the structure of a push plate conveyor?

Answer: See Figure 6.64 – the bodies are transported with push plates as load carriers and are powered through friction or by individual drives. If the plates are chain-mounted, this creates a plate-chain conveyor, part of the group of link chain conveyors.

Example 6.6–23: Lifting gear

What important types of lifting gear are there for bulk and general cargo?

Answer: Figures 6.65 and 6.66. Also, scissor tongs can be used for right-angled and round cargo up to 125 kg.

Figure 6.65   Lifting gear for bulk cargo. a) Scrap metal grabs. b) Clamshell bucket (www. demagcranes.com)

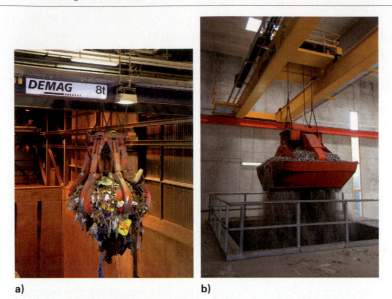

a)   b)

Figure 6.66   Lifting gear for general cargo. a) C-hook, eg for coils (www.demagcranes.de). b) Crane fork, eg for pallets (www.orah.net)

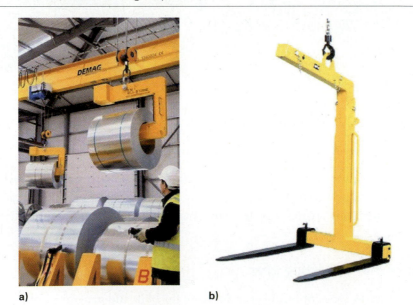

a)   b)

Example 6.6–24: Baggage conveyors

Show a baggage conveyor based on the discontinuous principle.

Answer: Figure 6.67. This shows a flight baggage sorting and distribution system made up of simple static, sensor and drive-free tracks, on which dollies are provided with contactless energy and find their destination automatically through on-board route managers. Data is transmitted via radio. The sorting system transports the baggage with up to 10 m/s and fulfils the functions of conveying, saving and sorting. The loading capacity is between 920 and 1,450 pieces of luggage/h (feeding occurs through retracting the side walls). Extensions can easily be installed.

Figure 6.67   Baggage conveyor with points and transport dollies (www.beumer.com)

Example 6.6–25: Work platforms

Show three different examples of work platforms.

Answer: Figure 6.68.

Example 6.6–26: Container console lift

Show a cardboard box and container lift with fast driving speed and high acceleration for fast-moving machines.

Answer: Figure 6.69 shows a console lift for containers, which can achieve high speed through a belt construction. The acceleration is 3 m/s^2, its speed 2.0 m/s and

Figure 6.68   Work platforms (www.avv-arbeitsbuehnen.de)

a) Moving scissor lift design

b) Stacker design

c) Telescopic stacker design

Figure 6.69   Console lift (www.transnorm.com)

it is built up to 12 m of lift height. The cargo dimensions are up to 1,600 × 900 mm (L × W) and the loading fork can take up to 250 kg. The container lift has a high positioning accuracy. The lift movements occur via the cargo belt and the frictional pulley. Forks, belt or roller conveyor may be used to take on cargo.

Example 6.6–27: Ways to finance forklifts

Forklifts can be financed with borrowed capital as well as capital resources. Both financing methods must be considered in order to find the optimal solution. For borrowed capital, we distinguish between renting, leasing and hire purchase (see Example 11.22). The majority of forklifts today are leased.

Answer. Rent means daily rental, eg for a 2 t forklift worth €30,000 the rental cost is €60 per day + €7 insurance costs (damage cover).

Leasing is a kind of financing which is calculated with or without down payment from 39 months lease period based on the object value, interest rate, salvage value and with or without maintenance contract. For the above type of forklift with €30,000 value without down payment and at 7 per cent interest rate for a lease period of 39 months, the salvage value is 15 per cent (€4,500). Without a maintenance contract the monthly lease payment is approximately €700. This amount is strongly dependent on the type of truck, whether the truck is widely used or not. The maintenance contract, on the other hand, is dependent on many factors including the deployment time of the forklift per year, the level of use and the deployment area.

For hire purchase of a forklift, the monthly hire purchase rate has to be determined depending on duration, down payment, salvage value and maintenance contract. The relevant VAT has to be paid by the buyer upfront.

Example 6.6–28: Driver's seat straddle truck

Show the deployment area for a driver's seat straddle truck in wide aisle design.

Answer: Figure 6.70 shows this type of truck with boom for steel coils in a warehouse with steel tiles. It has a load capacity of 8 t, a single lift frame and special tyres.

Figure 6.70   Heavy load straddle truck (www.jungheinrich.de)

Example 6.6–29: Transport of paper rolls

Show paper roll transport with industrial trucks.

Answer: Paper roll transport with driverless transport system: Figure 6.7.11c and h; with air cushion: Figure 6.85a to c; via stackers and paper roll clamps: Figure 6.71.

Figure 6.71   (Left) Horizontal taking on of paper roll. (Right) stacking in paper roll warehouse (www.jungheinrich.de, www.linde-mh.com)

Example 6.6–30: Column and wall swing crane

Compare column and wall swing cranes in pictures.

Answer: In the workplace, these cranes are used to facilitate handling. The swing area of the wall swing crane is up to 270° and for the column rotating crane it is 360°. The use of these cranes is shown in Figure 6.72.

Figure 6.72   Column and wall swing crane with chain hoist (www.demargcranes.de). a) Wall swing crane. b) Column swing crane

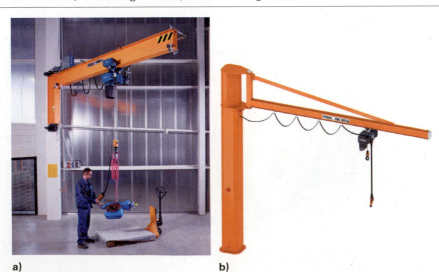

a)   b)

Example 6.6–31: Tilt and refilling devices

What are tilt and refilling devices used for?

Answer: To get across low heights (up to 2 m), lift devices are used to facilitate the loading of machines or the refilling of bulk cargo (Figure 6.73a), or to help with the removal of workpieces for a manufacturing process (Figure 6.73b).

Figure 6.73   Lift and tilt devices (www.ventzki.de). a) Tilt devices. b) Refill devices

a)   b)

Example 6.6–32: Four-way and sideways stacker

Present four-way and side-way stackers in pictures.

Answer: Figures 6.74.

Figure 6.74   Pictorial comparison of four-way and side stackers a) Four-way stacker deployed in long cargo warehouse, driver platform operation (www.hubtex.com)b) Four-way stacker deployed in tyre warehouse, driver's seat operation (www.votex-bison.com) c) Side stacker transporting timber, lying on the platform truck (www.baumann-online.it)

a)   b)   c)

Example 6.6–33: Portal crane

Show a full portal crane being deployed in container storage.

Answer. Figure 6.75.

Figure 6.75 Automatically operated portal crane in container storage (www.terexportsolutions.com) a) Part view of container warehouse; loading and unloading through portal cranes b) Total view of container warehouse

Questions

1 What are the advantages of industrial trucks?

2 Draw up a categorization of industrial trucks according to motor drive type.

3 How can the selection criteria for industrial trucks be divided up?

4 What are the construction features that lift trucks are designed on?

5 What is a pedestrian operation and a driver operation?

6 What values does the drive resistance consist of?

7 What deployment conditions must be known before using a lift truck for a transport task?

8 What is the stability of a lift truck?

9 What is a load capacity diagram used for?

10 Describe lift frame types.

11 How can the attachments for forklifts be categorized?

12 List aisle widths for three forklifts.

13 How is the area load capacity of a lift truck calculated?

14 What are the criteria to differentiate lift trucks?

15 Describe a cross forklift in structure, work method and deployment area.

16 What is the ratio of the operation costs of a forklift to the required personnel costs?

17 Sketch a double telescopic lift frame of a lift truck with a low self-supported lift in an exploded view drawing.

18 What is the remaining load capacity and how do you calculate it?

19 Which hand is used to steer a lift truck and how is this done?

20 Allocate the tyre types of different lift trucks.

21 What is the main deployment area of a multi-directional lift truck?

22 How does a stacker control system work?

23 How does the contactless energy transmission of electric monorails work?

24 What is the double deck system?

25 Describe different personnel safety measures in lift trucks in shelf storage.

26 What type of lift truck is behind the name truck-mounted forklift?

6.7 Driverless industrial trucks: automated guided transport system

6.7.1 Advantages, deployment

About 75 per cent of operational costs of a lift truck (see Chapter 6.6.7.8) are personnel costs. This begs the question, how and under what conditions can the driver of an industrial truck be replaced? One answer is: through automatic operation. If a business has regular or irregular cargo at different locations, with the same transport route, the transport can be automated with an automated guided vehicle transport system (AGVS) on a round course. The computer-aided material flow machines for automatic transport of goods in the internal material flow are equipped with automated guided vehicles (AGVs) and have the following advantages:

- flexible route guidance, simple increase of transport capacity;
- freed up transport routes and free access to machinery;
- automation of material flow, improvement of working conditions;

- simple emergency operation, relatively modest requirements for floor;
- safe, gentle and economic transport, deadline accuracy.

The deployment of AGVs is varied. They take on transport tasks, especially in halls, connect goods entry and procurement storage, manufacturing machines and assembly sites or fulfil tasks in warehousing and order picking as well as in the pre-warehouse zone. AGVS allow for interaction with human beings as mobile workbench, such as in assembly as well as with robots as handling and workstation. There are three AGVS assembly types:

- *Taxi system*: Fulfilment of transport tasks by provision and disposal at assembly sites; the AGV delivers or takes material and leaves the assembly site without waiting time. Advantage: high level of use of the driverless vehicle system is possible.
- *'Mobile workbench' system*: AGVs provide a workplace, the load carrier has the shape of an assembly device and serves as a workpiece carrier for serial assembly. During the assembly at the stationary workplace, the battery can be charged. The long commitment of a vehicle to a workplace is a disadvantage, as it leads to low levels of use as a transport vehicle.
- *'Passenger' system*: No stationary workplace, AGV has a passenger platform for the worker, it moves at creep-speed, is used in assembly, small parts are on the platform, and larger parts are positioned along the route.

6.7.2 Components of an inductive AGVS

An AGVS is made up of the following components (see Figure 6.76):

- vehicle, energy provision, route, load transfer stations, steering system;
- machine management, communication system, personnel protection devices.

6.7.2.1 Vehicle

Designs for AGVs as battery-powered industrial trucks (Figure 6.86a to f):

- tow tractor for trailer transport;
- underrun tow tractor for roller container transport;
- low forklift truck for pallet transport;
- truck as carrier vehicle with chain conveyor for container transport;
- stacker in wheel-supported design for pallet stacking;
- for AGVS designs we distinguish between a *load pulling* AGV, such as a trailer and underrun tow tractor without lifting device, and a *load carrying* AGV, such as a lift truck and carrier vehicle with and without load pick-up from the floor.

Figure 6.76 Components of an AGVS with inductive forced steering

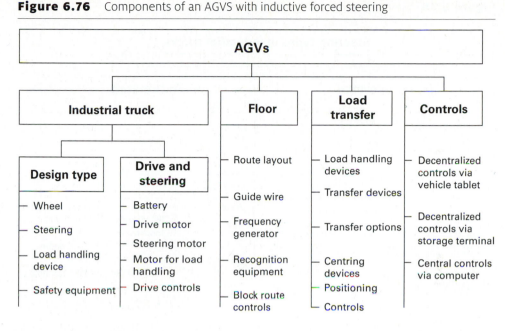

Figure 6.77 Driving gear geometry with three to six wheels (www.ek-automation.com)

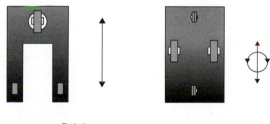

Driving gear geometry

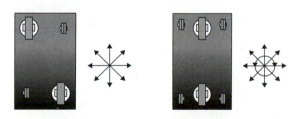

The *driving gear* of AGVs consists of wheels, wheel suspension, drive, steering and brakes. AGVs as carrier vehicles come in three-wheel and multiple-wheel design and are equipped with one-, two- or four-wheel steering. The wheel arrangement can be triangular, rectangular or diamond shaped. If the independent steering and drive wheels are diagonally opposite each other, a particularly manoeuvrable carrier vehicle is created (see Figure 6.78).

Figure 6.78   Steering types of industrial trucks

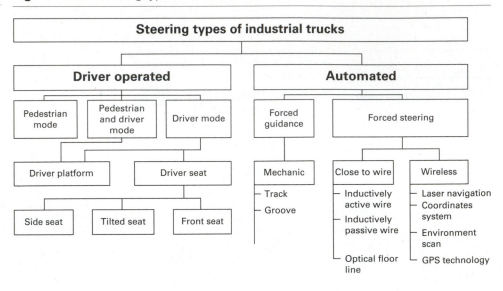

The *energy provision* (see Example 6.7–8) is via batteries, with voltage of 24–48 V and 80 V and capacities of up to 850 Ah, depending on lifting tasks and vehicle acceleration. The most prevalent batteries are lead batteries; the more expensive, maintenance free NiCd batteries are used for three-shift and cycle operation (see Chapter 4.5.6). We distinguish between manual and automatic battery exchange. The battery charge is automatic. Contactless active inductive energy transmission is becoming more and more common for two- and three-shift operation.

The *load handling attachments* of AGVs are dependent on the vehicle type and the type of transport task to be completed. For load carrying vehicles these can be chain conveyors, roller conveyors, lift tables, telescopic tables or forks, roller tables or fixed platforms. For load pulling AGVs it is couplings or driving pins.

AGVs must have special safety devices in order to be used in factory traffic. They include:

- *collision buffers* as mechanic devices, which switch off the engine when touching obstacles, as foam bumpers (difficult to repair) or metal braces (cheap);
- *emergency stop button* for manual operation, *rotating beacon*;
- *horn,* automatically switched on at start-up and at dangerous spots. The start-up occurs delayed by approximately three seconds after the horn beeps;
- *safety switch side panels* generally, and *side feelers* for protruding loads, which are designed as back feelers;
- *contactless laser scanner* with protection and warning fields up to 15 m for high driving speed and gentle braking (see Example 6.6–18).

The driving speed of the AGV is normally 1.1 m/s – the maximum permitted speed is 6 km/h = 1.67 m/s – in bends, at crossings and forks it is approximately 0.5 m/s. The speed is mainly dependent on the type of route, the distance, cargo and whether the route is also used by personnel traffic.

6.7.2.2 Circuit

The circuit determines the route (machine layout) of the AGVS in internal transport, connects loading and unloading sites, serves the provision and disposal of manufacturing and assembly sites as well as the warehouses. The circuit design depends on the local condition, the deployment conditions, the handling amounts at loading sites and the chosen guidance of the vehicle.

Guidance technologies Automatic guidance is forced guidance and forced steering (Figure 6.78).

- *Mechanic forced guidance*: The floor contains grooves or tracks in or on which the mechanic forced guidance occurs.

- *Inductive passive forced steering*: A metal strip of 5 to 10 cm width is stuck to the floor. The AGVS control occurs via magnetic sensors (installed on the underside of the vehicle); these use the magnetic field changes resulting from the steel strip to control the steering motors. Another method sees magnetic strips on the floor instead of metal strips. Advantages: simple process, cheap and fast installation. Disadvantages: hard to extend, prone to disturbances if metal is damaged.

- *Optical forced steering*: Differently coloured marks on the floor of up to 12 cm in width. The recognition of these marks happens using cameras under the AGVS and an image-processing system, which can calculate the steering values for the steering motor. Advantages and disadvantages are the same as for inductive passive forced steering, whereby the coloured marks are subject to damage.

- *Inductive active forced steering*: The in-floor forced steering is structured as follows. An isolated wire is placed in a groove in the floor in closed loops. Subsequently the groove is filled in with artificial resin. This circuit is thus a smooth floor, maintenance free and accident safe in buildings. Outside, it has to be kept free of ice in the winter. A frequency generator delivers an alternate current of a certain frequency (eg 20,000 Hz, 100 mA), which creates a concentric, electro-magnetic alternating field in the wire. The sensor head of the AGVS contains two search coils, in which the electro-magnetic alternating field induces voltage. This is dependent on the distance of the coils to the wire. Different voltages of the two coils, such as the result of bends, are used as steering information during the directional comparison and are transmitted via an amplifier to the steering motor as steering impulses (Figure 6.79).

Figure 6.79 Components of an inductive steering system (www.jungheinrich.de)

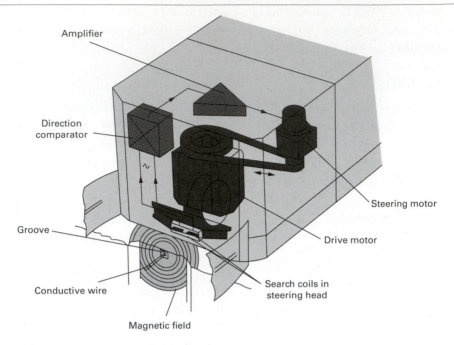

It is possible to place an additional wire for contactless energy transmission into the groove. Advantages: more sophisticated technology, simple vehicle steering. Disadvantages: obsolete technology, difficult and cost-intense layout, change of layout expensive.

Wireless forced steering is also called navigation, using marks on the floor on one hand and laser or GPS on the other hand. For active recognition the AGVS looks for the path independently based on the specification of a 'point zero'. For passive recognition, it uses fixed features of the environment to steer the vehicle (see Example 6.7–9). We distinguish:

- *Point navigation*: The conductive wire is replaced by permanent magnets in the floor arranged as points between 1 and 10 m. Advantages include a simple floor installation compared to the passive indicative process. Disadvantages include the floor type and expenses when changing routes.

- *Grid navigation*: A grid of magnets or transponders (or colour marks on the floor) is installed in the floor along the route. The transponders are installed through use of reading devices. These transmit their identification signal and register accurately to the millimetre. Thus, the AGV can determine its position lengthwise and crosswise. The advantage is flexible navigation within the grid area and the disadvantage is the high outlay when preparing the floor and installing the grid.

Laser navigation   The conductor wire in the floor for the active inductive steering significantly limits the flexibility of the AGVS. Wireless steering systems (free navigation) bring great advantages: for frequent changes to machinery in manufacturing and assembly; when changing loading and unloading sites; for large vehicles; for frequent exchanges of vehicles; when extending; for tight bends; for floors with strong iron reinforcements.

With laser navigation the AGV (Figure 6.80a) has a laser unit that transmits a laser beam, running around the vehicle much like a radar beam. The working space of the AGVS has fixed points to aim for, such as reflective foils (foil strips approximately 3 cm wide and 50 cm long, length is required for unevenness) on walls, columns or objects. The laser scanner (Figure 6.80b) calculates the angle to the reflective strips, and determines the position and direction in the space exactly.

Three or four registered reflective strips suffice for an exact determination of position. Faulty reflexes can occur due to stained steel surfaces. AGVS speeds of up to 2 m/s result in the same accuracy for positioning of approximately 10 mm as for inductive steering. The higher the speed, the smaller the accuracy for positioning.

Advantages: free navigation; no floor installation; layout changes can be implemented easily. Disadvantages: reflectors required on columns, walls and machinery; laser head is located above load and personnel; no outside deployment.

- *GPS (global positioning system):* Advantages include flexibility, and a non-location-specific installation. Disadvantages are that it can only be deployed outside and, to a limited degree, between buildings, and the large outlay for desired high positioning accuracy.

Figure 6.80a   System representation laser navigation (www.goetting.de)

Figure 6.80b   Manual destination entry (www.ek-automation.com)

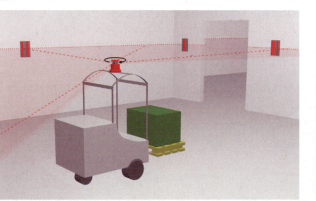

Obstacle recognition systems, block route steering for inductive steering systems   Floor magnets, transponder, optical object recognition (camera) and radar are used for route and point recognition, to open and close doors or to mark stops. If there are multiple DTA on a circuit, then the principle of *block routes* can help prevent collisions. The circuit is divided into block circuits and it is specified that only one vehicle can drive into the next block route, if no other vehicle is within (smallest block route section approximately twice the vehicle length), in order to avoid vehicle collisions.

The circuit contains areas with certain tasks: battery charging station, block routes, points, crossings, stations (magazine) to take in unused AGVs, transfer stations, workstations, lifts, gate entries.

The machine layout of a mineral oil business is shown in Figure 6.82. Driverless transport vehicles connect the bottling lines with the high shelf warehouse, the order picking area and the shipping area. The AGVs are equipped with three-stranded chain conveyors, provide the bottling lines with empty pallets from the empty pallet store and take full pallets with barrels and canisters to be stored in the high shelf warehouse. In the order picking area, provided by AGVs from the high shelf warehouse, order-based mixed pallets are put together. AGVs deliver finished pallets to the stretch machine, where they are covered in foil for transport safety. They eventually get to the shipping area. Batteries are charged automatically in the charging station.

Data transmission   Data transmission between the AGVs and the control centre usually happens with radio data transmission. For large facilities with narrowband lines of 456 MHz, only one aerial is required, for medium and small facilities on broadband of 2.4 GHz (radio, Wi-Fi) multiple aerials are needed. Shelves, steel supports and power lines can cause disturbances.

6.7.2.3 Load transfer stations

For *load pulling* AGVs, the load intake or load transfer for trailer tractors occurs through the clutch and for underride tractors through locks   For *load carrying* AGVs, forklifts can take on or transfer loads using forks from the floor or at a certain transfer height.

Figure 6.81a   Different navigation systems (www.goetting.de) based on a) transponder, b) GPS, c) radio

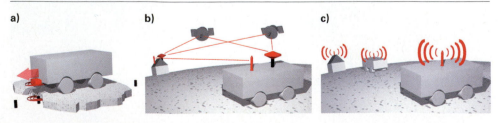

Figure 6.81b   Different navigation systems (www.mlr.de)

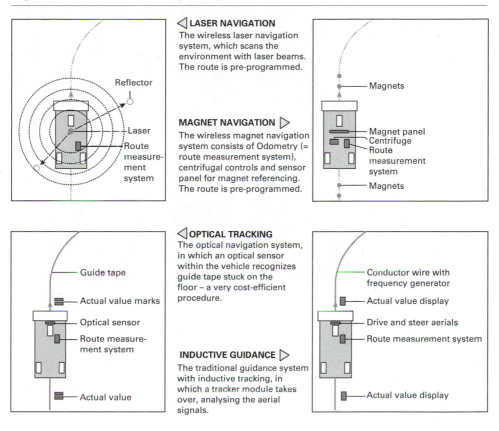

◁ **LASER NAVIGATION**
The wireless laser navigation system, which scans the environment with laser beams. The route is pre-programmed.

MAGNET NAVIGATION ▷
The wireless magnet navigation system consists of Odometry (= route measurement system), centrifugal controls and sensor panel for magnet referencing. The route is pre-programmed.

◁ **OPTICAL TRACKING**
The optical navigation system, in which an optical sensor within the vehicle recognizes guide tape stuck on the floor – a very cost-efficient procedure.

INDUCTIVE GUIDANCE ▷
The traditional guidance system with inductive tracking, in which a tracker module takes over, analysing the aerial signals.

For carrier vehicles, the load transfer depends on the load unit/crates, containers, pallets, the load handling attachment (chain/roller conveyor, lift table, telescopic fork), the type of transfer device as well as specific restrictions (fine positioning of workpiece or tool carriers using cones). For the load transfer of load handling devices there are these options:

1 AGV active, such as lift table – transfer station passive, such as static device.

2 AGV passive, such as platform – transfer station active, such as telescopic fork.

3 AGV and transfer station active, such as driven roller conveyor.

6.7.2.4 Facility management

The facility management for vehicles depends on a variety of factors, such as environment, tasks, deployment, such as opening doors, gates, dire gates, lift etc. This has

Figure 6.82 Facility layout of an AGV facility (www.dematic.com)

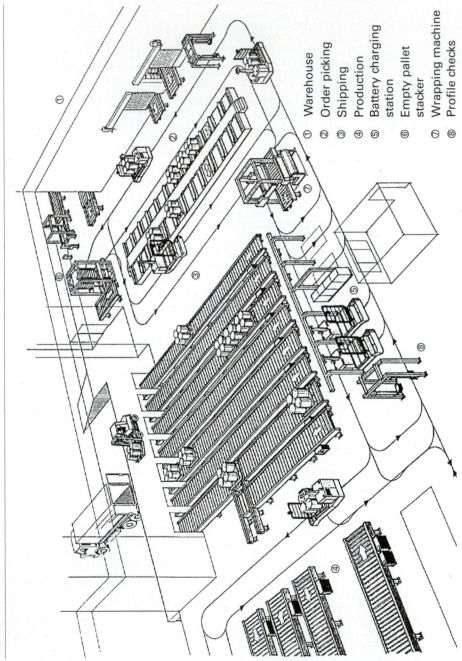

① Warehouse
② Order picking
③ Shipping
④ Production
⑤ Battery charging station
⑥ Empty pallet stacker
⑦ Wrapping machine
⑧ Profile checks

resulted in the multitude of controls available on the market. Driving and steering the AGV is carried out independently by the AGV; it only receives the commands, which activities have to be done. Generally, the automatic steering as a deciding factor of an AGV must cover:

- traffic control;

- managing the loading and unloading of the AGV using load-handling devices;

- deployment management of the AGV to process transport assignments.

For stationary deployment of the guidance system, we distinguish between centralized and decentralized guidance. For central guidance all functions reside in the control centre, such as assignment administration, vehicle disposition and traffic control.

Each AGV communicates with the control centre, reports before points, crossings or transfer stations (responder) and is directed centrally. The AGVS guidance as part of the material flow management is shown in Figure 6.83.

Figure 6.83   Visualization of AGV management (www.ek-automation.com)

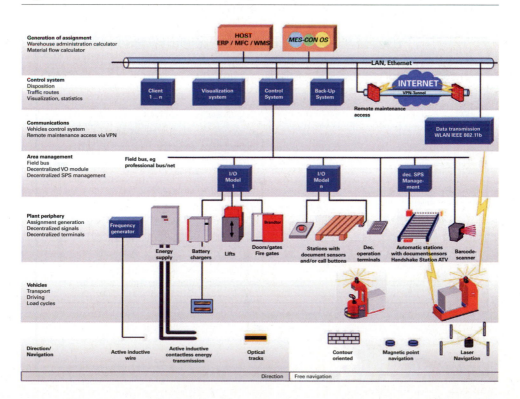

VDI 2510 provides details about an AGVS facility and particularly about the facility management. The most important regulations to be adhered to for operating a AGVS facility is EN 1525.

The *block route guidance* of a floor facility (inductive AGVS) is part of the circuit management. We distinguish between physical block division and logical block guidance. For the physical block division, a responder is placed on the floor to signify the start of a block. If the block is not clear, drive and steering energy is reduced and the vehicle halts. When the block becomes free, the block route guidance reconnects drive and steering energy, which the vehicle recognizes as a command to drive.

An AGV facility mostly receives a circuit tablet for graphic visualization, representing the circuit as a model. It is used for dynamic status announcements of the AGV, shows the individual areas, such as transfer stations and block route, and provides information about the availability of AGVs (status bar). Thus, the circuit tablet can be used for disposition and control of transport processes (Figure 6.84).

The circuit is entered into a computer (CAD program), in which each point of the building's layout is divided into and determined as X–Y-coordinates. These points can then be measured with the reflectors.

Figure 6.84   Visualization of AGV management (www.goetting.de)

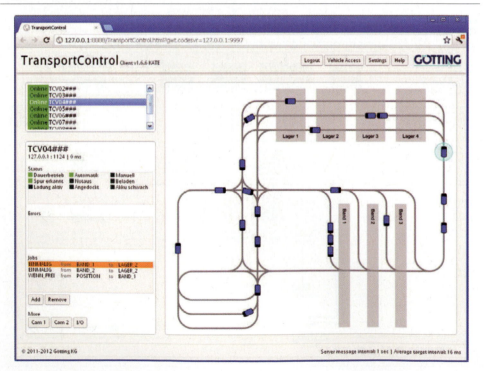

6.7.3 VDI guidelines

2510	Driverless transport systems	10.05
2710	Holistic planning of AGVS	04.10
4451	Compatibility of driverless transport systems (AGVS)	07.03

6.7.4 Examples and questions

Example 6.7–1: Planning example for a transport task

For a fixed operation route of 1,000 m 300 pallets or mesh boxes have to be transferred in 6 hours at 15 stations. Taking into account the operational conditions, an automatic transport system should be selected between the warehouse and production area. Which means of transport are possible and how many transport units can be transported in one shift?

Answer: Options for transport systems are:

1 Underfloor conveyor.

2 Power and free conveyor.

3 Stackers and tractors.

4 AGV tractors.

As we are looking for a continuous transport system with a pre-determined circuit, which is flexible and reliable, and allows for easy and cost-effective capacity increase, the following are not suitable based on operational considerations (rough selection):

Conveyor 1: Too inflexible.

Conveyor 2: Too great a constructive outlay (ceiling not capable of carrying load).

Conveyor 3. Too personnel intense.

For transport system 4, the number of transport units in eight hours is roughly calculated. Coupled pallet movers are used as trailers for the tractor and for transporting pallets.

Circuit	1,000 m
Average speed	3.8 km/h = 63.3 m/m
Number of stops per round	4 (average stops)
Stay at each stop (roller track transfer)	0.5 min
Pure driving time $t_f = 1,000 / 63.3 = 15.8$ min	(for one round)
Total stop time $t_h = 0.5 \times 4 = 2.0$ min	(for one round)
Time for one tractor round	$t_u = 17.8$ min
Number of tractors	$n_s = 6$ (selected)

Number of trailers per tractor (pallet movers) $\qquad n_a = 2$

Operating hours per day $\qquad t_h = 8$ h

The theoretic minimum number of transport units per eight hours is:

$$q = n_s n_a t_h \times (1/t_u) = 6 \times 2 \times 60 \times 8 \times (1/17.8) = 323.5$$

Example 6.7–2: Economic comparison lift truck – AGVS

Forklifts can be replaced economically for simple deployments by an AGVS facility (see Chapter 6.7). In the simplest case, a vehicle is operated through direct commands. If multiple vehicles are used, a control computer serves to manage the facility. Compare lift trucks and AGVs as part of an economic comparison.

We can use an AGVS facility with driverless transport vehicles as an example. The circuit is 400 m and contains 10 transfer stations. These consist of powered roller conveyors, and the load handling device is also a roller conveyor. Euro pallets with cargo are being transported. If a master computer is used, then all transfer stations have input devices to request the vehicles and to enter the destination. As economical duration for use, five years are allocated for a lift truck and eight years for an AGVS facility. The pallet load unit weighs 1.2 t.

Answer: First, answer the question of how many vehicles in an AGVS facility are required to replace one forklift in terms of transport performance. The basis of this comparison is:

- driving speed:
  - forklift: 6 km/h;
  - AGV: 3.5 km/h;
- duration of load exchange:
  - forklift: 5 s;
  - AGVS: 20 s;
- personal distribution time of driver: 10 per cent.

This results in the required time for one round of 400 m including load exchange:

- forklift: 270 s ((240s + 5s) + 0.1× 245 s = 269.5 s);
- for AGV: 431 s, ie 1 forklift is replaced by 1.6 AGVs.

If the facility is only run with forklifts, the following operating costs per year apply (see Table 6.1):

- Number of forklifts $\qquad$ 1 $\quad$ 2 $\quad$ 3
- Operating costs in €T $\qquad$ 46 $\quad$ 93 $\quad$ 140

If the facility uses AGVS, the operating costs have got to be calculated. The fixed costs, when using a system director (more than one AGVS) consist of:

- Facility management   € 71,100
- Round circuit (€97/m)   € 39,200

  Total   € 110,300

The operating costs per year depending on the number of used vehicles can be taken from Table 6.5.

The operating cost comparison results in:

- number of forklifts   1   2   3
- operating costs T€/a)   46   93   140

Corresponding to:

- number of AGVs   2   4   5
- operating costs T€/a   6.26   84.4   95.3

Table 6.5 Determination of operating costs

Operating costs	Number of AGVs with roller tracks	1	2	3	4	5
1.0 Investment						
1.1 Vehicle, batteries, chargers	€T	26.9	73.8	110.7	187.6	184.6
1.2 Facility fixed costs	€T	43.9	110.3	110.3	110.3	110.3
1.3 Stations	€T	29.0	29.0	29.0	29.0	29.0
1.4 Input panels	€T	–	5.0	5.0	5.0	5.0
1.5 Total investment	€T	109.7	218.1	55	291.9	328.9
2.0 Determining fixed costs						
2.1 Depreciation (12.5% of 1.5)	€T/a	13.7	27.2	31.9	36.5	41.1
2.2 Interest (8% of 50% of 1.5)	€T/a	4.4	9.0	101.2	11.7	13.1
2.3 Fixed costs per annum	€T/a	8.1	36.0	42.1	48.6	54.7
3.0 Determining variable costs						
3.1 Repairs (12% of 1.5; Cat. I)	€T/a	13.2	26.2	30.6	35.0	39.4
3.2 Energy costs (0.30 €/kWh)	€T/a	0.3	0.6	0.9	1.2	1.5
3.3 Variable costs per annum	€T/a	13.4	26.8	31.5	36.2	40.5
4.0 Operating costs AGV per annum	€T/a	31.6	62.7	73.6	84.4	95.2

(rounded values)

Result: The comparison shows that AGVs, thanks to the significantly longer life-time and comparatively modest personnel requirements (maintenance, repairs), are already a real alternative to forklift transport using two forklifts, without taking into consideration additional conditions, Such conditions may be training of forklift drivers and the partially required electrician for the AGVS facility.

A further question is, how many forklifts, for simple cycle strategy (see Chapter, 9.7), are required to process 200 pallets ($\triangleq$ 200 rounds) in an eight-hour shift?

Answer:

Number of possible transports in 8 hours	$(3{,}000 \times 8) / 270 = 107$	transports/8h
Number of forklifts	$200 / 107 = 1.87$	2 forklifts

Example 6.7–3: Air cushion transport

What principle is the air cushion transport based on and how can it be used for AGVS facilities?

Answer: The principle for air cushion technology is described in Figure 6.85. The floor make-up is the deciding factor for using air cushion technology. It is decisive for the air consumption as well as the required force to move the load.

Figure 6.85   Principle of air cushion technology (www.solving-gmbh.de)

Functionality
When the air flow is switched on, the following happens:

The ring-shaped rubber bellows expand and fill the distance between the load carrier and floor.

When the rubber bellows have sealed the floor, the air pressure in the space restricted by the bellows increases. The air cushion element with the load lifts up.

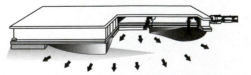

If the internal pressure is higher than the counter-pressure of the load, the air streams out under the bellows and forms a thin air film. On this air film the load practically floats without any friction.

The smoother, more even and air tight the floor, the lower is the air consumption. Other than the floor make-up, the air consumption is also dependent on the air system material, the air system itself and the load and air pressure.

The load capacity of a system is determined by the liftable area of the air cushion and the air pressure. One air cushion can lift between 250 kg and 400 kg.

Transports of up to 400 t are possible (see Figure 5.70b).

The air film on which the load slides almost without friction has a thickness of approximately 0.1 to 0.2 mm. The motor noises are under 68dB (A), the air flow is low, so that little dust is swirled up. For transport, and thanks to the low friction, only a little force is required, approximately 0.001 – 0.003 times the weight of the load.

Friction wheel drive is most prevalent. Air cushion transport is used to move large loads, such as for machinery exchange or for heavy goods transport in an internal area, and for AGVS facilities (Figure 6.86). The guidance can be manual, direct or remote.

Figure 6.86   Layout of an AGV system with airbag AGV: coil transport (www.solving-gmbh.de)

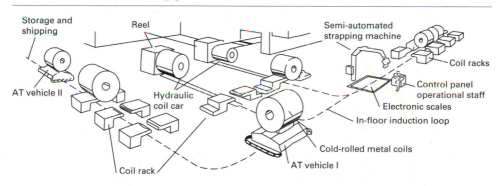

Example 6.7–4: Pitch bend

Whenever industrial trucks have to overcome differences in height, eg for inclined routes, ramps or transfer bridges, a pitch bend is created when crossing from the horizontal to the inclined level, and vice versa. What has to be considered in this case?

Answer: For all industrial trucks check whether there is enough floor clearance, so that the vehicle does not hit the ground. For forklifts, also check to ensure the load carrying device does not hit the ground. One solution for the problem of loading and unloading lorries via transfer bridges (especially for the first row of pallets) can be the use of a pedestrian pallet truck with ramp lift.

Example 6.7–5: Forced steering for AGVS/energy concept

a) Which additional wireless forced steering systems are there, other than laser navigation (see Chapter 6.7.2.2)?

Answer – navigation: The wireless forced steering systems, also called free navigation, includes magnet navigation with or without centrifuge. Floor magnets are installed 'with centrifuge' approximately 10 m apart, without centrifuge 1 to 2 m apart. No directional change can happen between the magnets.

Each of the following technologies, some still under development, has its specific features with special requirements in the relevant deployment situation. Wireless forced steering comes with less outlay in terms of installation than the performance based version. However, a greater outlay for managing the facility and vehicle occurs. The deployment of wireless (free navigation) forced steering makes sense for frequent changes to the circuit and extension:

- Coordinates system: Floor fixed system, for which the operating area is divided into coordinates (floor grid) and is created using programmable plates or optical patterns (magnets, colour and transponder).

- Global positioning system (GPS technology): Technology is under development, which to date is only usable for outdoor navigation. Disturbances can occur through buildings and other constructions. Positioning accuracy is in m.

- Environmental scan technology (under development): To scan the environment, cameras or ultrasound are used. The AGV can avoid obstacles.

b) Which guidance technologies are preferably used for AGVS facilities?

Answer – deployment: Free navigation is in first place with approximately 35 per cent, closely followed by active inductive forced steering with 30 per cent – laser navigation, active inductive forced and passive inductive forced steering.

c) What data transmission systems are options for AGVS facilities and which energy concepts are used?

Answer – data transmission: The data radio transmission technology is preferred. The communication does not require eye contact and the process covers whole areas. Only one aerial is needed for narrowband 456 MHz, often it is used with broadband 3.4 GHz.

Answer – energy concept: See Chapter 4.5.6. We distinguish between one-, two- and multiple shift operation. For one-shift operation usually lead armour-plated batteries are used, which can be charged with night power (capacity-based operation), or contactless energy transmission is used.

For two-shift operation either exchange batteries or NiCd batteries, which can be charged while halted at transfer stations or workstations through fast charge with high charging energy using contact loops (clock operation), are used. The latter process is also used for multiple shift operation.

Example 6.7–6: Driverless transport systems

Show examples of AGVS in pictures.

Answer: Examples of AGVS can be seen in Figure 6.87 a to g.

Costs for an AGVS facility as in Figure 6.86f with two electric shaft stackers at €45,00 each for 25 destinations with laser navigation including assembly: €180,000

Figure 6.87 Driverless transport vehicles AGVS (www.ek-automation.com)

a) AGVS as mobile workbench for motor assembly

b) Carrier vehicle with powered roller conveyor

c) Above: vehicle with lift table under-riding large load transport. Below: carrier vehicle for paper roll transport

d) Coil transport 32 t, lift mast with boom, laser navigation, area moving driving gears

Figure 6.87   *(Continued)*

e) Manual storage in an aisle with wheel-supported AGVS electric shaft stacker

f) Automatic storage of a pallet with AGVS stacker in Figure (e)

g) Tractor with trailer

h) Paper roll transport with AGVS high lift truck

i) Diesel AGV (265 kW; v = 22km/h, turning radius 11.5 m) as carrier vehicle outside for container transport (www.hhla.de)

Example 6.7–7: Inductive guidance

How does a narrow aisle stacker enter into an aisle?

Answer: Using inductive guidance, which guarantees extremely high accuracy, the smooth entry into the aisle is achieved. The steering continuously corrects the course with the help of AC technology. Advantages include short tracking times with driving angle of up 90°, high driving speeds, little space requirements (Figure 6.88).

Figure 6.88 a) Getting closed and drive on conductive wire b) Recognition of wire and start of automatic tracking process c) Completion of tracking and active inductive guidance in narrow aisle (www.jungheinrich.de)

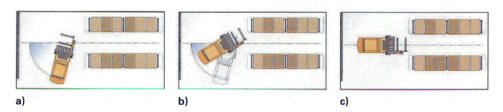

a) b) c)

Example 6.7–8: Battery exchange and battery charging types

The following must receive energy in an AGVS: all mechanical vehicle movements including load intake and discharge; steering; electrics; electronics. Which types of battery exchange and battery charging can be used depending on the deployment and which other features apply?

Answer: Figure 6.89 answers the questions, and Figure 6.90 shows a central battery charging station.

Figure 6.89 Comparison of battery exchange and charging types (www.ek-automation.com)

	Manual battery change	Automatic battery change	Automatic battery charge PzS	Manual battery change NiCd	Contactless energy transmission
1-shift operation	−	−	−	−	o
2-shift operation	+	−	+	o	+
3-shift operation	++	+	++	+	++
Cycle operation	o	o	o	++	++
Capacity operation	++	++	+	−	++
Costs: Maintenance, staff	o	+	+	+	++
Investment costs	++	−	+	o	−
Supplier diversity	++	++	++	−	−
Demands on flooring	++	+	+	+	−

++ Very suitable, optimal solution + Suitable O Limited suitability, average − Tends to be unsuitable −− Unsuitable, at least 1 KO crtierion

Figure 6.90   Central automatic charging station for AGV tractors (www.ek-automation.com)

Example 6.7–9: Features of steering and navigation systems

What ratings do different steering and navigation types get in terms of accuracy, flexibility, size and sensitivity to dirt?

Answer: Figure 6.91.

Example 6.7–10: Contactless energy transmission for AGVS

How does contactless energy transmission work for an AGV?

Answer: The electric energy is inductively transmitted into one or more AGVs from floor-based wires in a contactless manner. The primary circuit consists of a double wire (winding) in the floor along the route. About 2 cm above ground is the secondary circuit in the AGV. It is through the air gap that the electromagnetic coupling occurs. The transmission frequency is about 20 to 25 kHz. The system requires little maintenance and has little wear, but it is only suitable for simple AGVS facilities (see Example 6.6–15).

Example 6.7–11: Container handling site using AGVS

Show a picture of the handling site for containers with AGVS.

Answer: Figure 6.92.

Figure 6.91   Rates comparison of features and characteristics of AGVS steering
and navigation types (www.goetting.de)

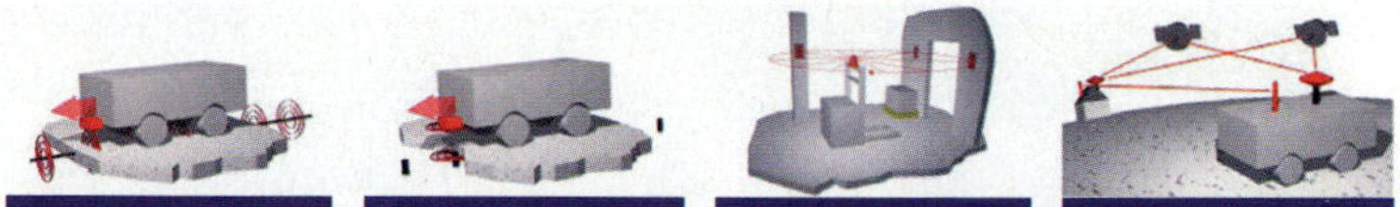

		Physical guidelines		Floor markers		Off-the-floor markers		Actively trans-mitting markers	
		Conductor	Optical line (bar)	Passive transponders	Magnets	Artificial markers (reflectors)	Natural markers (Land markers: objects, walls)	GPS (Realtime)	Radiolocation
Accuracy		****	****	****	***	***	**	**	*
Flexibility		*	**	**	**	***	***	***	***
Build size (small)		****	****	**	***	**	***	*	*
Reliability		****	**	***	***	***	**	**	**
Breakdown sensitivity	Wear of labels	***	*	****	****	**	**	**	**
	Impervious-ness (to dirt)	****	*	****	****	**	**	****	****
	Rain, snow	****	*	****	****	*	*	****	****
	Glare	****	**	****	****	**	**	****	****
Costs	For vehicle	****	****	**	***	**	**	*	*
	Infrastructure	*	**	*	*	**	***	***	*
Suitability	Indoor	****	****	****	****	****	***	*	**
	Outdoor	****	*	****	***	*	*	***	**
Sensor height above floor (m)		< 0,5	< 0,5	< 0,2	< 0,1	> 2	> 2	> 2	> 2
Accuracy of repetition at low speed (cm)		<1	<1	1	1	2	5	3	20
Signal recognition and processing time (ms)		<10	20	15	10	100	100	100	100

Figure 6.92   Container handling with AGVS in container port
(www-terexportsolutions.com)

Questions

1   What are the deployment areas for AGVS?

2   Which three AGV assembly principles are there?

3   What components make up an AGVS facility?

4   What safety equipment can be found in AGV?

5   What guidance technologies are possible for AGVS facilities?

6   How is the active inductive steering structured?

7   What automatic load transfer can be distinguished?

8   What possibilities are there for facility management?

9   Which VDI guideline provides details about AGVS?

10 What are the advantages of wireless forced steering and how does laser
steering work?

Handling logistics 07

7.1 General

The following modes of transport are part of external goods transport: road transport; rail freight transport; shipping; and air traffic. Except for air traffic, businesses have internal transport connections.

Goods receipt is the business interface with the procurement market, while goods issue is the interface with the sales market. This is where the goods turnover happens between the external goods flow and the internal material flow. Handling (see Figure 1.3) means the exchange of the load from an external mode of transport to an internal means of transport, or from the latter to a mode of transport, and leads to time delays in the material flow chain.

Handling logistics considers material and goods turnover holistically and across businesses. Its goal is to plan, manage and optimize the operational material and goods flow with the accompanying information flow, as well as the relevant administrative and dispositive functions. The consumption-synchronous delivery of material according to the just-in-time principle (see Example 2.15) leads to a decentralization of the goods receipt and changes to the traditional handling structures.

The objectives of dispositive handling logistics are to:

- increase handling performance;
- shorten rest times of vehicles;
- reduce personnel costs;
- avoid damage to goods;
- optimize organizational process design while considering structural device-related equipment.

Strategies and dispositive functions are used to achieve these objectives, including:

- strategies for loading and unloading;
- packaging and transport safety strategies;
- delivery and shipping strategies;
- buffer strategies;
- disposition for freight space, fleet and tours.

The immediate tasks for unloading processes at goods receipt are:

- determining handling point (gate or ramp);
- provision of handling means and aids;
- releasing cargo;
- carrying out unloading;
- identification (cargo papers);
- buffering of cargo.

Through standardization of loading aids (pallets), as well as through automated means of handling, handling speed and performance can be increased.

The handling speed corresponds to the working speed for the handling function. The handling performance is calculated from the quotient of volume, mass or quantity and the time unit, or it can be expressed through giving a median transport route based on the number of work cycles. It is used to evaluate the handling of goods.

7.2 Bulk handling

For bulk handling, discontinuous and continuous handling technology is used on the operational level. Depending on the type of bulk cargo (see Chapter 3.1.2), the type of transport (ship, self-unloading truck, dump truck train, tanker or tipper) and the required handling performance ($\dot{m}$, $\dot{V}$), the handling for storing and removing can occur using continuous conveyors in silos, bunkers or in buildings (see Chapter 5):

- belt conveyors;
- bucket conveyors;
- screw conveyors;
- swing conveyors;
- pneumatic conveyors and chutes.

Usually, a bulk cargo handling plant consists of a combination of different continuous conveyors to achieve an optimal line for the transport route from source to sink (see Figure 7.1). Discontinuous conveyors are used in the immediate handling care, particularly to bridge small distances:

- unloading of ships or train carriages;
- loading of belt conveyors, with hopper cars (see Figure 7.1).

Discontinuous conveyors for this are bridge, rotating and portal cranes with double-clamshells as well as industrial trucks, such as excavators, graders, wheel loaders, tippers, stackers and dump trucks.

Figure 7.1 Handling facility with storage and filling areas for bulk cargo (www.linde-mh. de) 1 Bulk cargo receipt, 2 Bulk cargo distribution, 3 Discharge car, 4 Hopper car, 5 Bulk cargo distribution, 6 Bulk cargo loading into road vehicles, 7 Bulk cargo loading with wheel loader into rail vehicles, 8 Drop bunker, 9 Drop plant, 10 Drop belts with closing device, 11 Bag synchronization, 12 Bag loading onto rail vehicles, 13 Bag loading onto road vehicles, 14 Additional loading zone for road vehicles, 15 Additional loading zone for rail vehicles, 16 Palletizer, 17 Wrapping machine, 18 Shrink oven A: Bulk cargo storage, B: Packing station (incl. staff areas), C: Full bag storage, D: Bag labelling operation (not shown), E: Energy provision and transformer, F: Workshop and magazine, G: Container outdoor storage (not shown)

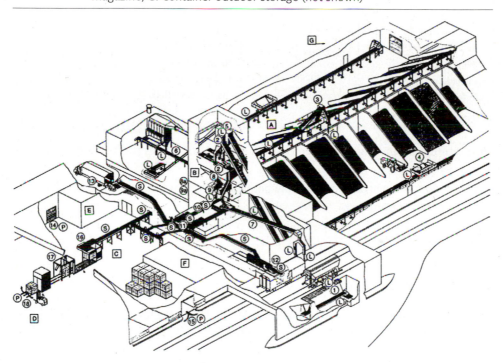

7.3 General cargo handling

7.3.1 Handling equipment

Continuous and discontinuous handling equipment is used for handling (Figure 7.2). Continuous handling equipment includes:

- for bag loading and unloading: belt and telescopic belt conveyors;

- for crates, packages and multipacks: small rollers and roller tracks;

- for pallets: chain and roller conveyors.

Figure 7.2 Division of handling equipment for general cargo

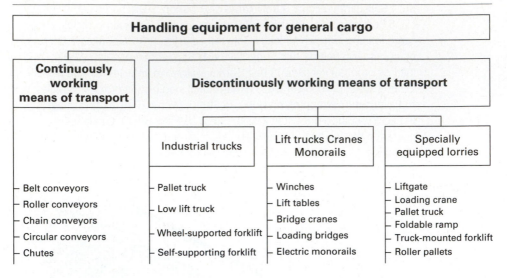

Discontinuous handling equipment includes the use of cranes for heavy pieces, forklifts or low lift trucks for palleted loading units.

Depending on the transport volume per time unit, handling can be manual, mechanized or fully automated.

Definitions for handling frequency, rate, performance and duration can be found in Chapter 9.7.

7.3.2 Handling area

The technical design of the handling area and type of handling equipment for loading and unloading of cargo are determined by:

- handling area buildings: with or without ramp;
- type of means of transport: lorry, rail carriage or container;
- type and features of cargo: pallets, crates, weight and dimensions;
- type of loading and unloading process: rear handling and side handling;
- size of handling performance: piece transport $\dot{m}_{st}$ (number of pallets per hour);
- distribution of supply and handover: regular and irregular.

The handling area includes:

- loading zones including ramps and loading gates;
- safety equipment such as proximity sensors;
- manipulation area for forklifts; courtyard for vehicles.

The loading and unloading of vehicles can occur as:

- rear handling for lorries and containers;
- side handling for freight carriages and lorries;
- roof handling for hood carriages and lorries.

Handling can be carried out:

- from the courtyard or roadway (low floor handling);
- using ramps;
- in a continuous or discontinuous process;
- manually, or mechanized with handling equipment, such as forklifts;
- automated (fast loading) with roller tracks;
- with onboard tools at the lorry such as liftgate (lift loading platform), loading crane, truck-mounted forklift (see Figure 6.57), on-board pallet truck or shaft led electric forklift.

7.3.2.1 Ramps

The ramp can be used to carry out direct cargo handling for lorries, rail carriages or elevated containers. Ramps support the handling process with adjustable bridging of the height difference and an additional handling surface. We distinguish between mobile and stationary ramps (Figure 7.3; Pitch bend: see Example 6.7-4).

Mobile ramps are used where the building floor and courtyard are on the same level. These are mobile ramps that can be driven on with a forklift and usually have a loading table. The loading ramp allows for rear and side handling, and can be placed lengthwise, ie parallel to the mode of transport, or at a right angle to it (Figure 7.4a).

Figure 7.3 Structural components of cargo handling via ramps

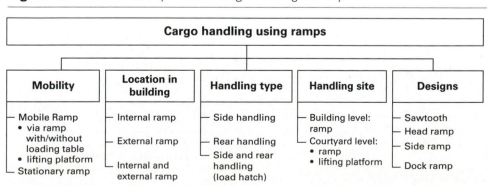

Stationary ramps are fixed equipment, arranged in buildings or outdoors. The internal ramp and the loading ramp located along the building wall allow for draught-free handling regardless of weather conditions with little loss of energy. Outdoor ramps often have roof covers, but staff are exposed to draughts and the weather. Stationary ramps bridge the height difference between the wheel centre line and the loading platform. The ramp level is usually at 110 cm above courtyard or building level for a lorry, 120 cm for a carriage (see VDI 2360; Example 9.5).

Figure 7.4   Ramp designs a) Mobile ramp designs b) Internal ramp lengthwise
c) Loading ramp with sawtooth ramp d) Loading ramp with head ramp
e) External ramp lengthwise or a head ramp (not sketched). Side loading
and unloading f) Dock ramp in gradient and head version.

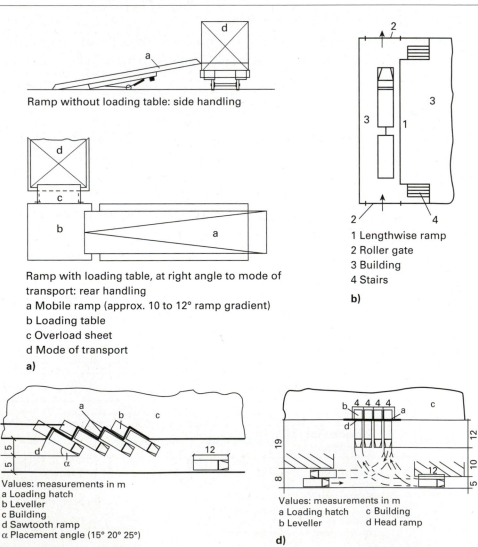

Ramp without loading table: side handling

Ramp with loading table, at right angle to mode of
transport: rear handling
a Mobile ramp (approx. 10 to 12° ramp gradient)
b Loading table
c Overload sheet
d Mode of transport

a)

1 Lengthwise ramp
2 Roller gate
3 Building
4 Stairs

b)

Values: measurements in m
a Loading hatch
b Leveller
c Building
d Sawtooth ramp
α Placement angle (15° 20° 25°)

c)

Values: measurements in m
a Loading hatch   c Building
b Leveller   d Head ramp

d)

Figure 7.4   *(Continued)*

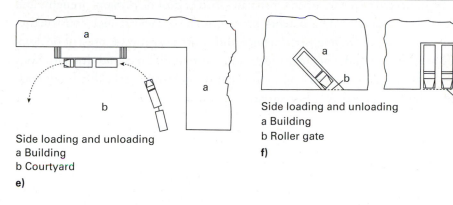

Side loading and unloading
a Building
b Courtyard
e)

Side loading and unloading
a Building
b Roller gate
f)

Designs of stationary ramps include:

- *Internal ramp*: Ramp located in building, usually used lengthwise but also designed as a dock ramp, making it suitable for side handling of articulated vehicles and freight wagons (Figure 7.4b).

- *Loading ramp* (loading hatch): Internal ramp along building wall can be designed as a head, sawtooth or deep ramp; rear handling only. Equipped with a leveller, gate and gate closure (little loss of energy). The integrated leveller has to have floor clearance in order to load and unload lorries with a liftgate (Figure 7.4c and d).

- *Deep ramps* are used if courtyard and hall floors are at the same level. They are created by forming a trough with a sloping access road.

- *External ramp*: Usually designed lengthwise (Figure 7.4e) for rear and side handling.

- *Dock ramp*: In inclined or head design (Figure 7.4f), sometimes equipped with a lifting platform for the entire articulated lorry for level compensation.

The lorry must have lifting equipment for the loading platform in order to level out the spring deflection for loading and unloading. For the dock ramps, lorry handling from the ramp is possible with self-supporting forklifts for lengthwise loading of DIN pallets.

For floor clearance of ramps, see Example 7.21.

7.3.2.2 Levellers, gates and gate sealing

Ramp adjustable levellers (with fold lip or adjustable feed) are used for levelling between the mode of transport and the ramp, in addition to providing a bridge for any gaps. If the ramp height and loading area are nearly identical, such as for a rail carriage, it is sufficient to use a simple leveller sheet. Outside ramps normally require externally mounted levellers, stationary, swivelling or mobile rails.

For bad weather protection, external ramps have a roof, although some workers will still be subjected to the weather. Open gates lead to dust dispersion, draughts and energy loss. Nowadays loading hatches prevail, because they: reduce construction costs; guarantee high handling performance and short downtimes; present docking options for all lorries and container types; allow for continuous and discontinuous loading of containers and swap bodies; prevent draught-related health conditions; save approximately 80 per cent lost energy.

Figure 7.5a   Loading hatch with leveller and gate sealing: emergency stop in both lifting cylinders, internal and external light, sensor technology and safety chock (www.crawfordhafa.de)

Figure 7.5b   Loading hatch with sawtooth ramp (left), and with head ramp (right) (www.crawfordhafa.de). The figure on the right shows the cavity for lorries with tail lift, visible below the leveller (see Example 7.21)

Figure 7.5c   Different sectional gate designs (www.crawfordhafa.de)

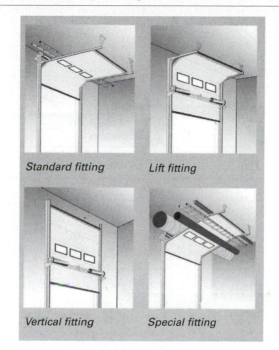

Standard fitting   Lift fitting

Vertical fitting   Special fitting

Industrial gates come as roller, sectional, push, lifting, circulating, folding, swing or revolving gates. For loading hatches or loading gates, sectional or roller gates are used in the main. Sectional gates are much quicker than roller gates and may include window segments (see Example 7.3 and 7.4). The selection of industrial gates is based on structural and operational conditions, opening and closing frequencies, weather requirements, sound insulation and the type of opening and closing controls.

Gate sealings at loading hatches come in slats, plain and bead design as well as in inflatable design. For externally installed lengthwise ramps, extendable air locks are used as gate sealing, such as for rail loading. For air curtains, an air jet blows from the top down to achieve climatic separation.

Safety equipment includes the need for approach bumpers at the leveller, pipes installed on the floor to facilitate positioning, good lighting of the handling area and distance sensors between lorry and ramp.

7.3.3 *Handling systems for loading units*

Distinguishing between manual, mechanic and automated handling systems depends on the number of loading units to be loaded within an hour. The capacity of these systems decides which handling method is used.

Bag or package handling: Telescopic belt conveyors are used as loading and unloading tools for lorries, carriages and ships for general cargo such as bags,

Figure 7.6a   Bag loading machine – lorry side loading: spiral chute, mobile belt conveyor, swivelling, rotating and height adjustable telescopic cargo conveyor (side view and top view) (www.beumer.de)

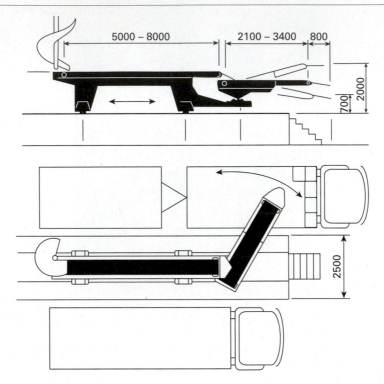

packages, boxes etc. We distinguish single and double telescopic belt conveyors (4 to 8 m in length) with belt widths of 500 to 1,000 mm, $v = 0.5$ m/s and load capacity up to 50 kg per metre (Figure 7.6a, see Chapter 5.2.2). Short distances for the stevedores and little manipulative effort can achieve high handling performance.

Automatic bag loading for lorries is shown in Figure 7.6b. Here, bags of cement, plaster, fertiliser, flour etc are not just loaded but simultaneously packed in bonded stacks. The hourly rate of performance can be up to 3,000 bags.

Pallet handling: For handling systems with pallet loading units, there are different possibilities to increase lorry handling levels. For each of the following, the collation of the pallets for mechanized systems is required beforehand:

- In order to facilitate pallet handling and to reduce loading time, forklifts with *pusher*s are used. These push pallets to the middle of the lorry. Wire harnesses the pushing of the load and protects the platform floor.

- Self-supporting forklifts can be equipped with special attachments, depending on appropriate load capacity (see Chapter 6.6.7.4), and can take on (transport and side load) 2 to 5 or 4 to 12 pallets simultaneously onto the lorry platform (Figure 7.7).

Figure 7.6b   Automated bag loading of a lorry (www.beumer.de)

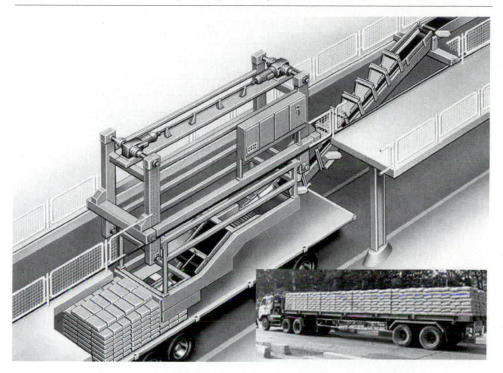

- A mobile handling system in portal design is able to simultaneously take on and load four or six pallet units for side loading of a lorry or elevated container using forks from a roller track (Figure 7.8).

The shortest loading and unloading time, and thus the highest handling performance, is achieved with *automated* handling systems.

Principle: All pallet units are collated as a loading block and transported into the lorry or container at once. The loading and unloading times are under 10 minutes. This usually requires a lorry equipped with roller or chain conveyors. The following automatic handling systems can be distinguished:

- handling system with roller pallets (Figure 7.9b);
- handling system with ball roller carpet;
- handling system with roller or chain conveyor (Figures 7.9a and 7.13);
- handling system with lift chain conveyor (no lorry installation necessary);
- handling system with belt conveyor (Example 7.19);
- handling system with load carrier (installation of guide rails).

Figure 7.7   Left: Forklift with sixfold or fourfold fork as well as integrated single and total side shift (www.linde-mh.com/www.still.de)

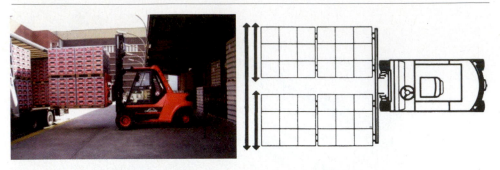

Figure 7.8   Lorry side loading with mobile portal bridge and multiple forks

Figure 7.9   Automatic rear loading for pallet units. a) With roller conveyor. b) With roller pallets

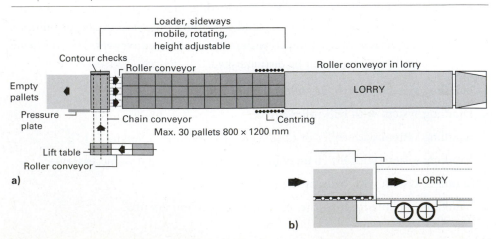

When assembling loading blocks on roller or chain conveyors, three pallets can be transported step-by-step by laying them lengthwise.

The use of this system only makes sense for a radius of 100 km around the factory, as the return journey with the company-owned lorry is usually without load, and the time saving is particularly noticeable for short distances. Typical occasions for deployment are for companies whose central distribution store is located 20 km from the factory, or for which the provision of regional storage plants has to happen with goods from the main factory, such as breweries (here, the return journey carries empties).

In summary, these are some of the prerequisites for an economical use of automatic handling systems:

- *Load*:
  - high and consistent transport volume;
  - collation of cargo in units with the same loading aid equipment;
  - modular structure of loading block on loading area, such as DIN pallet (2×1.2 m or 3×0.8 m for a lorry/container with 2.43 m width);
  - guarantee of even strain on loading area (see Chapter 3.3.6);
  - create loading concept (see Figures 3.18 and 3.19).
- *Means of handling*:
  - space requirement for handling system on factory grounds for goods issued for the automatic assembly of a load.
- *Automated loading in lorry*:
  - lorry dimensions;
  - matching loading block with lorry capacity;
  - own fleet;
  - installation of means of transport in lorry (chain or roller conveyor);
  - positioning of equipment for automatic docking of lorry.
- *Transport route*:
  - suitable for short routes only (approximately 30 km);
  - for return journey with empties, such as beer crates, up to 100 km;
  - automatic unloading at destination;
  - possibly automatic empties removal.

7.3.4 Container and swap body handling

As part of the logistical process, handling of containers can involve the change from one mode of transport to another: ship – rail – lorry. Special means of handling are

Figure 7.10 Handling means for container a) Loading bridge (container bridge) in portal design with hanging trolley for loading and unloading ships with foldable boom b) Loading bridge with fixed boom and trolleys for handling, for ships and storage site c) Mobile portal crane on tracks with trolley, loading onto lorries and carriage d) Mobile portal crane for container handling and stacking e) Portal stacker f) Crossways forklift g) Portal lift truck; additional means of handling: cranes and telescopic forklifts, see Figure 7.16

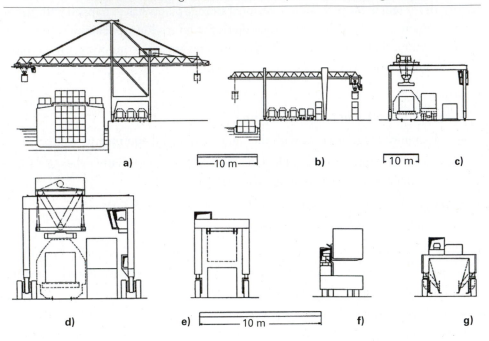

used for this (Figure 7.10), such as loading bridges, container cranes, portal stackers, equipped with loading tools such as hydraulic grabbers, grippers or spreaders (Figure 7.11) – spreaders and grippers are often combined.

Empty containers are often stored four to six times high (lengthwise or crosswise with self-supporting stackers) with the load handling attachment, which can be a spreader partly combined with a fork (Figure 7.16; see Chapter 3.1.4.3).

Swap bodies are usually used for the disposal of waste and refuse, such as a multiple chamber container, exchange tipper or press container (see Chapter 3.2.3 and Figure 3.9c).

Swap bridges are used to take on different cargo for transport by lorry or flat train cars (see Example 7.9).

Roll-off tippers transport roll-off containers, which are taken on and off by using chains or double articulated hooks. *Skip loaders* take on containers by using transport rollers and a winch for transport (Figure 7.12).

Figure 7.11 Spreader (gripper) for container handling. a) Single spreader. b) Universal telescopic spreader (side and top view)

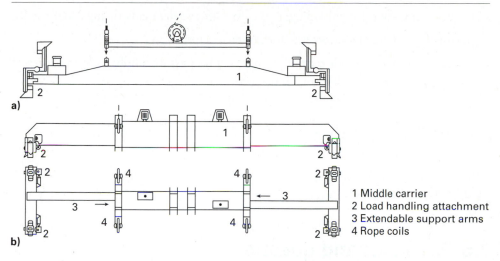

a)

b)

1 Middle carrier
2 Load handling attachment
3 Extendable support arms
4 Rope coils

Figure 7.12 Means of transport for swap bodies: skip loader (offloading process)

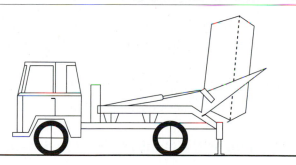

7.4 Aspects of planning the handling area

The JIT principle (see Example 2.15) moves the delivery point from the traditional centralized goods receipt in the procurement store, to many decentralized sites in the company – such as assembly. For planning an interface between external goods flow and internal material flow, a wealth of data is required:

- means of transport for delivery: type, size, loading height and turning radius;
- scope of delivery/frequency of delivery: average to maximum delivery amount, timing, number and distribution of deliveries across the day, regular or irregular delivery;
- shape of delivered cargo: single piece of cargo, on pallets, in containers, packages and load units;

- features of good and transport aids: sensitive, stackable and a type of load handling with means of transport (see Chapter 4.9.1);
- means of transport for unloading: crane, forklift and manually (using roller track);
- personnel and area requirements for goods receipt;
- structural design of goods receipt: with or without ramp; number, type and size of gates, gate sealing, levellers and courtyard size.

7.5 VDI guidelines

2409	Gateways in industrial buildings	07.03
3968	Safety of load units: Stretching Bl5	12.09

7.6 Examples and questions

Example 7.1: Automatic loading and unloading

Sketch a schematic for the material flow of a loading ramp for automated loading and unloading of a lorry. The transport units are DIN pallets. The lorry is equipped with chain conveyors.

Answer: Figure 7.13. Note that the rear of the lorry and the loading ramp include a centring device in order to achieve quick docking and the correct vehicle position.

Example 7.2: Calculation of the number of required loading gates

Answer: Assembling and loading a shipment (12 m articulated lorry with 28 pallets, see Figure 3.18) takes, on average, 1.7 hours. Per workday (AT) a maximum of 330 pallets have to be loaded.

$$\frac{330 \text{ Pal/AT}}{28 \text{ Pal/Lkw}} = 11.8 \text{ Lkw/AT} \approx 20 \text{ loading hours}$$

10 per cent is added to account for distribution time, and this comes to a rounded figure of 26 loading hours. The loading occurs over six hours a day, so the number of required loading gates is:

$$\frac{26 \text{ h loading for 1 gate}}{6 \text{ h loading time}} = 4.33 \text{ gates}$$

Five loading gates were selected; this equals a capacity use of 87 per cent.

Figure 7.13 Automatic rear loading for Euro pallets with chain conveyors (www.dematic.com)

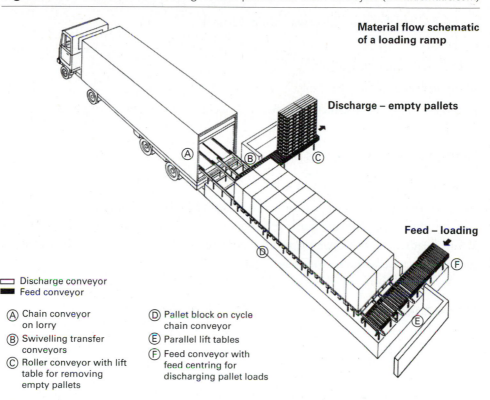

Material flow schematic
of a loading ramp

Discharge – empty pallets

Feed – loading

▭ Discharge conveyor
■ Feed conveyor

Ⓐ Chain conveyor
on lorry

Ⓑ Swivelling transfer
conveyors

Ⓒ Roller conveyor with lift
table for removing
empty pallets

Ⓓ Pallet block on cycle
chain conveyor

Ⓔ Parallel lift tables

Ⓕ Feed conveyor with
feed centring for
discharging pallet loads

Example 7.3: Industrial gates

How can industrial gates be operated through the forklift or driver, and what features are significant to their use?

Answer: Gates can be operated by pull or push lever, radio controls, remote control, light barrier, motion sensor, induction loops and ultrasound (Figure 7.14a).

Figure 7.14a Different controls for industrial gates (www.crawfordhafa.de)

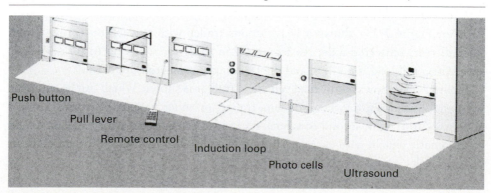

Push button

Pull lever

Remote control

Induction loop

Photo cells

Ultrasound

The following features should be considered for use:

- opening mechanism: sideways, swing, vertical;
- speed;
- heat and sound insulation;
- transparency; controls;
- special requirements, such as individual opening of one wing, colour, etc.

Example 7.4: Speed gates

What is the structure of a speed gate?

Answer: Two double-walled gate sections open without swinging to the side, and roll into the sideways framework in a space-saving manner. The gate is immediately at full headroom. The opening speed is approximately 2 m/s. A forklift can drive through the gate without stopping (Figure 7.14b).

Figure 7.14b   Industrial speed gate (principle) (www.butzbach.com)

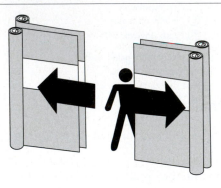

Example 7.5: Internal heavy goods transport

Show a heavy goods trailer and transport options for a universal vehicle.

Answer: Figure 7.15a shows a heavy goods trailer with turntable steering (front: steered; rear: unsteered axle; see Figure 6.25a to d) for loads up to 63 t. The top speed for a full load is 6 km/h, and the trailer can be steered up to 180°.

Figure 7.15b shows a universal vehicle. A tractor is shown, which can be equipped with an adjustable fifth wheel for semi-trailers or roller pallets (platforms) using a gooseneck (top right; second row, left). It can also be equipped with a ballast weight or automatic clutch, with carriage shifting plate or with hydraulics for attachments or tow hook.

Figure 7.15 Heavy goods vehicles

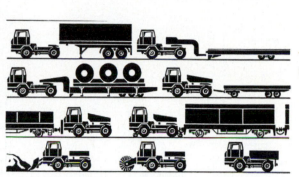

a) Heavy goods trailer
(www.mafi.de)

b) Universal vehicles (www.planindustrie.de)

Example 7.6: Container transport with lift trucks

What are the options for container transport with lift trucks?

Answer: We have to distinguish between a loaded container and an empty container. A loaded container can only be taken on and transported crossways over the gripper by a lift truck. These lift trucks have a capacity of 20 to 50 t. For empty transport, containers can be taken on from the front by a spreader, or lengthways and from above. Special empty container lift trucks with higher driver's seat and clear view lifting frame can stack four to six empty containers on top of each other. Their load capacity is 8 t. Figure 7.16a and b show two fundamentally different stacking methods: a) the lift truck has a telescopic lift frame; b) the truck has a telescopic extendable arm in driving direction. Device 7.16b has a rotating spreader so that a container can be taken on and put down lengthwise, crosswise or from the top, and even rows two and three can be served. Figure 7.16c demonstrates different transport and stacking possibilities of containers using lift trucks.

Example 7.7: Portal lift truck

Portal lift trucks (van carrier) are used for transport and stacking. Double stacking can be achieved with devices that are approximately 7 m high and can transport a 40 00 container (30 t payload) at about 40 km/h and 20 t at about 28 km/h. The diesel motor has about 140 kW, in which the wheels are individually spring-suspended from shock-absorbent and lengthwise steering. Each wheel can be powered individually. The bend radius is 9.5 m (approximately) and a diagonal movement with crab steering is possible up to 40°. The lift speed is approximately 9 m/min. The spreader, which can be

Figure 7.16 Transport and stacking options for containers (Figures c (1) to c (3): www.kalmarind.de)

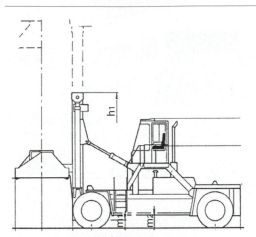

a) Counterbalance forklift (front lift truck) with spreader: top intake

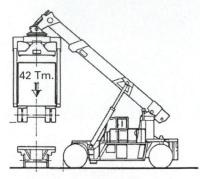

b) Telescopic arm lift truck with gripper

c) (1) Front lift truck: lengthwise side intake (side pick)

c) (2) Front lift truck: top intake (top pick)

c) (3) Telescopic arm lift truck: top intake (top pick)

c) (4) Front lift truck: Front lift truck (side pick)

extended for the various container sizes, can be turned by 6° in either direction and can be moved by 300 mm crossways in order to grab the container as quickly as possible.

What does a portal lift truck look like?

Answer: Figure 7.17 shows a portal lift truck transporting a container.

Figure 7.17   Portal lift truck for threefold stacking: container loading bridges (www.hhla.de) as tandem bridge for 2 × 40 ft container, or 4 × 20 ft container for loading or removal process. Increase of handling performance especially for large ships, which can stack up to nine containers. In Wilhelmshaven (deep sea harbour), container loading bridges are used with 69 m booms for ships up to 59 m in width, that is 22 containers next to each other with a total of 18,000 TEU units. The track-based loading bridges are 83 m high and weigh 1,750 t. With hoisted booms, they have a height of 126 m

Example 7.8: Lorry loading and unloading with low lift truck

To calculate handling times and handling performance for loading and unloading of lorries, the values for different low lift truck need to be determined.

Answer: For a lorry with 14 DIN pallets and in line with a pre-determined loading pattern, the average times can be taken from Table 7.1 for a simple trip of 30 m under certain conditions. The time it takes for intake and putting down, as well as other processing times, is taken into account in the time requirement per work cycle. The handling means are shown in line with the table order in Figure 7.18 (for load safety, see Chapter 3.3.6).

Table 7.1 Value for loading and unloading a lorry with different low lift trucks

Vehicle type	Ø Speed km/h	Time for 60 m min	Loading time for 14 pal/ min	Value handling performance Pal/h
Pallet truck	1.5	2.4	42	20
Electric shaft-led lift truck	3	1.2	25	34
Electric shaft-led lift truck with platform	3.5	1	21	40
Electric lift truck with driver platform	5	0.7	15	56
Electric three-wheel lift truck	6	0.6	14	60

Example 7.9: Combined traffic

Combined traffic was created to make use of the respective advantages of traffic modes for lorries and rail (see Chapter 4.3). The flexible lorry collects cargo in loading units across short routes and the environmentally friendly freight train transports it across larger distances. The loading units are containers (see Chapter 3.1.4.3), swap bodies with swap containers or swap constructions and semi-trailers.

What is the structure of the handling area road/rail (handling station)?

Answer: Mobile portal cranes carry out the handling tasks. Figure 7.19 shows such a portal crane with a gauge of 46, spanning four handling tracks, four storage tracks for loading units (interim storage), two loading and unloading tracks for lorries and a lorry track in the middle. The portal crane is equipped with a combined spreader-gripper-loading device. For container handling, the four grippers are retracted, so that the spreader can be extended in line with the relevant container size. The grippers are used for handling semi-trailers on/in pocket wagons, as well as swap bodies on the freight rail carriages. There is no locking of swap bodies and containers with the carriage. There is, however, a form fit using a pivot. The portal crane has a load capacity of 41 t; the loading gear can rotate the loading unit by 180°.

Figure 7.18 Handling equipment (industrial trucks) in use (www.linde-mh.de)

a) Pallet truck

b) Electric shaft-led low lift truck

c) Electric shaft-led low lift truck
with foldable driver platform

d) Electric low lift truck with driver platform

e) Electric low lift truck with driver seat

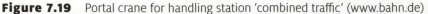

Figure 7.19 Portal crane for handling station 'combined traffic' (www.bahn.de)

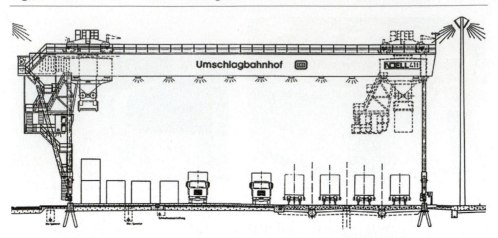

Example 7.10: Container handling

Divide up industrial trucks for container handling (transport, stacking).

Answer: Features for a systematic division may be: load intake; design of industrial truck; transport process. The following industrial trucks are for stacking containers only (Figure 7.16):

- self-supporting lift trucks: front lift trucks (top, lengthwise and side pick); telescopic arm lift trucks (top and lengthwise pick);

- wheel-supported lift trucks: portal lift trucks (top pick); portal cranes (top pick);

- self-supporting/wheel-supported lift trucks: side (cross fork) lift trucks (top and lengthwise pick).

Example 7.11: Added value through external goods transport

Under what circumstances can external transport add value to the transported goods?

Answer: Chapter 4 gives details on added value for internal transport, Chapter 9.1 for storage. Added value can be achieved with the external goods flow if the good is taken from a site where it is superfluous (low demand), to one where it is scarce and in short supply (for example tropical fruit, coffee and tea). This will lead to a higher price.

Example 7.12: Automatic lorry-pallet loading system

In what conditions can an automatic lorry-loading system be used economically? What different automatic loading systems do you know?

Answer: The conditions are described in Chapter 7.3.3.

Automatic lorry-loading systems for pallets can be divided into two alternative systems:

- with additional transport means installed in the loading area;
- without additional transport means in the loading area, but with means outside of the lorry.

For the first option, the following means of transport or devices are installed in the loading area:

- electrically powered *roller conveyors* (see Figure 7.9);
- electrically powered *suspension chain conveyors* (see Chapter 5.3.2);
- three parallel apron conveyors as plate belt conveyors (see Chapter 5.2.3): *apron floor*;
- rolling belt conveyors, partly pulling (see Chapter 5.2.2): *roller floor*;
- three parallel u-tracks for roller cars, roller frame or roller pallets, installed in or on the loading truck bed;
- *shuttle floor* (walking floor), where the loading area is divided into sliding beams moving forwards and backwards independently of each other.

The second group includes:

- lift chain conveyors: telescopic conveyance of pallets through pneumatic lifting of chain and transport on built-in track;
- slide bar conveyors: working similarly to the lift chain conveyor through pneumatic lifting and telescopic to and fro movement of the slide bars;
- mobile portal crane on tracks, with fork pairs for simultaneous double or four-fold pallet transport – side loading for lorries only;
- loading area palletizer to load bags or pallets onto lorries, or bags onto pallets in the loading area for cement, cereal or fertilizer.

Examples 7.13 and 7.14: Manual and automatic loading system

What are the possibilities to transport heavy loading units (up to 2.5 t), such as paper rolls or pallets, manually and automatically in the rear of a trailer?

Answer: Manually through lorry equipment of non-powered rollers for different cargo types (Figure 7.20a). Mechanically or automatically with lorry equipment of powered chain or roller conveyors for palleted cargo (Figure 7.20b and c), as well as with a walking floor for non-palleted cargo (Figure 7.20d).

Figure 7.20 Loading system for lorries (www.joloda.com)

a)   b)

c)   d)

Example 7.15: Loading with ramps

Show the different possibilities for ramps at the interface of goods receipt and goods issue with the different modes of transport.

Answer: Figure 7.21.

Figure 7.21 A selection of ramp designs (www.crawfordhafa.de)

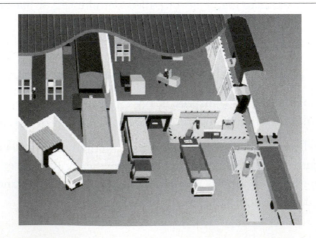

Example 7.16: Ramp designs

Show different ramp designs for a factory hall.

Answer: Figure 7.21 shows various ramp designs: from left: sawtooth ramp with thermal lock; rear loading of a rail carriage; two loading hatches with two internal levellers; external ramp with mobile leveller and rear loading; side loading of a rail carriage with rain-proof, extendable lock; carriage loading using a mobile ramp.

Example 7.17: Hub/spoke cross-docking

What is hub/spoke cross-docking?

Answer: Hub is the term for a turnstile, a distribution centre in a network, a junction with distribution function where a redistribution of packages occurs at all times of the day and night. Within 24 hours, the tasks of a package hub can change as follows:

- traffic: many depots deliver packages to be distributed in this depot (area);
- system traffic: many depots deliver to the hub for redistribution to these depots;
- combination traffic: interim handling, collation of packages in low quantities for forwarding to another hub.

A hub or spoke system (Figure 7.22) is built from the various manual and automatic sorting systems within the building (see Example 5.11).

Cross-docking is goods handling without storage. It is a material flow concept in which the goods are delivered by many companies in large quantities, such as on pallets at one side of the building The customer orders are then picked in the building, with orders already made for the items. On the other side of the building, the picked orders are immediately loaded into a lorry. Often prepacking is used to create complete pallets as transport units, which are then transported directly from goods receipt to goods issue. The *advantages* are a reduction in delivery times, stock and costs, bundling of transport and no goods storage.

Example 7.18: Industrial gates, energy saving

What technical options exist, depending on the building construction, to integrate gates? What causes energy loss, and how can this be minimized?

Answer: Figure 7.23a shows different designs of roller gates. The causes of energy loss are as follows: draught; negative pressure at the gate (high air speed); chimney effect in the building; warm air leakage as a result of excessive pressure and flow conditions in the building; pressure discrepancies between the internal and external atmosphere. These factors all affect the amount of heat.

Figure 7.22   Hub and spoke system (www.habasit.ch)

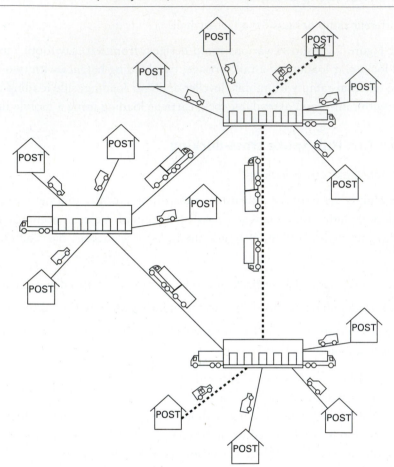

In order to reduce the amount of warmth lost, or to achieve energy savings, it makes sense to use high-speed gates. Compare a high-speed roller gate and a normal roller gate (size 3×3 m = 9 m², with the opening and closing of the high-speed gate of 2 s = 4 s (work cycle) each, and 20 s = 40 s each for the roller gate). We assume the following conditions:

- internal and external temperature discrepancy: $t = 10°C$;
- air stream $v = 5$ m/s;
- number of gate openings: 59 per workday;
- number of days per heating period: 6 months at 20 days each = 120 workdays;
- gate passage takes 1 minute.

The degree of warmth in 1 m³ of air depends on temperature and humidity. The specific warmth is calculated at $0.31 \times t$ in kcal °C/m³. There is a loss of warmth of

Figure 7.23   Roller gates. a) Designs. b) High speed gates. c) Roller gate
(www.efaflex.com)

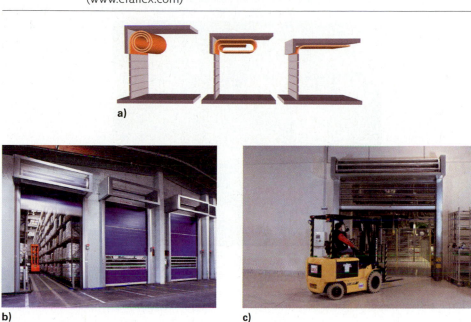

a)

b)   c)

0.31 kcal °C/m^3 × 10°C × 5 m/s × 9 m^2 = 139.5 kcal/s. For gate opening of 1 minute
and taking into account that the gate is open from 0 to full and vice versa, the loss of
warmth is calculated at 50 per cent: 139.5 × 60 × 0.5 = 4.185 kcal. The comparison of
the two types of gate is:

- high-speed gate: 4 × 139.5 × 0.5 = 279 kcal/work cycle and per workday: 279 ×
  50 = 13,950 kcal/workday;

- roller gate: 40 × 139.5 × 0.5 = 2,790 kcal / work cycle and per workday: 2,790 ×
  50 = 139,500 kcal/workday.

The difference: 139,500 – 13,950 = 125,550 kcal/workday.

During the heating period, the high-speed gate saves approximately 20 × 6 ×
125,550 = 15,066,000 kcal. This corresponds to approximately 2,760 l of fuel oil,
at a price of €0.80 per litre, resulting in an approximately saving of €2,200 per heating period. The savings made from using a refrigerated warehouse are considerable!

Example 7.19: Automatic lorry loading

What additional option for automatic lorry loading is there in Chapter 7.3.3?

Answer: Automatic loading with a belt conveyor (Figure 7.24). The load is put
together on a belt conveyor and passed on to the belt conveyor on the lorry.

Figure 7.24 Belt conveyor loading systems external and on the lorry as well as different trailer systems (www.westfaliaEurope.com)

Example 7.20: Container loading

What is the process for container loading, and what has to be taken into consideration?

Answer:

Step 1: Order, delivery with lorry and checks of container: condition report; location of container for loading (with/without ramp).

Step 2: Cargo checks: creation of a stowage plan; stowage regulations.

Step 3: Loading in line with regulations with/without transport aid, such as slip sheet, see Example 3.14. Load securing with air bag, pallets, wooden frame.

Step 4: Create shipping papers; provision and pick-up of container.

Example 7.21: Tail lift/platform lift

What types of platform lifts are there?

Answer:

a) *Standard platform*: Fixed platform that can be lowered to the floor, and which also functions as rear closure for the lorry in a vertical position – these platforms are prevalent in Europe.

b) *Slide-out platform*: Consists of two parts connected with hinges that can be unfolded manually. An advantage is based on the disadvantage of the standard platform: it does not require a ramp with floor clearance when loading using ramps.

c) *Foldable platform*: Also a split platform under the lorry, but does not run in rails under the lorry like the slide-out platform.

Example 7.22: Load handling attachments for bulky general cargo

Show four examples of load handling attachments for bulky and heavy general cargo.

Answer: Figure 7.25 a to d.

Figure 7.25   Load handling attachments for heavy general cargo (www.kalmarind.de) a) Gripper for timber beams using a telescopic arm lift truck b) Spreader for 40 inch container using a portal lift truck c) Special gripper for steel slabs using a telescopic arm lift truck d) Spreader with trusses to load wind turbine part onto lorry

a)

b)

c)

d)

Questions

1 What are the objectives of dispositive handling logistics?

2 How do you define the logistical function *handling*?

3 What modes of transport make up a bulk handling plant?

4 Which factors determine the technical design of the handling area?

5 How can goods handling be carried out?

6 Show the systematics for the categorization of ramps.

7 Describe a handling hatch together with the relevant equipment.

8 What pallet handling systems are there?

9 Which prerequisites and conditions have to be fulfilled in order to use automatic loading and unloading?

10 What are roller tippers and skip loaders used for?

Handling 08

8.1 Definition and task

VDI standard 2860 (Assembly and handling; handling functions, handling units; terminology, definitions and symbols) explains handling as the creation, defined changing or temporary maintenance of a predetermined, spatial arrangement of certain bodies relating to a reference coordinate system, whereby additional conditions may exist, such as time, quantity and direction. As part of the planning of material flow technology, operations for the purpose of this chapter shall be the execution of a change of location or direction of the cargo without a long transport route. Some of the required operational tools are shown individually or in interaction with a system. In this way, individual and team workplaces in manufacturing and assembly form part of this chapter. Likewise, equipment and devices are to facilitate easier, quicker or automated stacking, or to change the location for general cargo. Robots of any kind can play a big role here, which includes the previously described continuous and discontinuous conveyors.

The reasons for a handling function for goods vary. The following functions may be carried out:

- checking, turning and swivelling;
- positioning and piecing together;
- branching, forming units, separating and buffering.

Handling means and devices are used to achieve these functions.

8.2 Means of handling

Handling tasks are usually personnel intensive, so there are many devices and equipment to automatically carry out handling tasks, such as palletizers to move packages into the location determined by the packing pattern (see Chapter 3.3.3). Devices and equipment are selected from the wealth of handling devices offered by the industry:

- to create units, separation, order picking and for sorting;
- to lift, lower, rotate and position.

Often, devices in one group may also fulfil tasks of the other group.

8.2.1 Handling devices to change quantity

Palletizers and depalletizers, consisting of a robot for automated execution, are used to change quantities. The handling robot can be stationary or mobile. The most important difference of the stationary, floor-based handling robot is the workspace required. This includes cylindrical, spherical or toroidal.

Articulated arm robots for palletizing and depalletizing are shown in Chapter 3.3.3.

Portal robots can be divided into line and area portal robots. A stationary robot with cylindrical work area is shown in Figure 8.1. It is used as a palletizer robot to create pallet units. The CIPS (Computer Integrated Packing System) program measures and weighs each individual package and reports the data to the control system. Then the package is taken to one of the six spaces in the crossways provisioning area. A requested package is pushed to the transfer site using pushers, taken on by the robot and set down on the determined location on the mixed pallet. The order of the packages on the belt conveyor is not important in this process. Figure 8.2 shows an example of depalletizing and palletizing. The unit consists of the receipt box, the pallet handling device and the discharge box. The transport truck with the loaded pallets is accurately placed in the receipt box. The handling device lifts the pallet from the stack with the tong gripper and transports it to the workstation. The empty pallet is stacked by the handling device on the transport truck in the issue box. The height of the pallet stack is monitored.

Figure 8.1   Palletizing robot with horizontal articulated arm for package palletizing

Figure 8.2   Depalletizer and palletizing station (www.gepowercontrols.com)

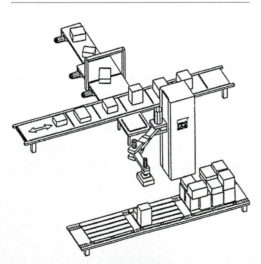

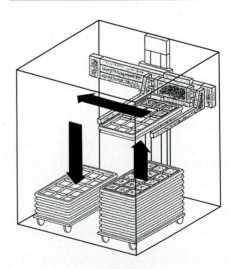

8.2.2 Handling devices to change location

A handling manipulator can be used to carry out functions such as lifting, lowering, rotating, gripping etc. It has a boom in a rhomboid design. The load handling attachment depends on the cargo type and is, thus, interchangeable. The control head has a control lever. The device is equipped with nine degrees of freedom and comes in a number of different stationary designs such as column, wall or ceiling device, as well as mobile ceiling device (Figure 8.3). Additional designs include the manual or battery-powered pallet truck with relevant pneumatic or hydraulic gripping devices. Equipment to empty a container to simplify loading a lorry, rotating a part or lifting a pallet to unload without bridges can all be called handling devices. Examples are Figures 6.6.4g, 3.11, 8.4 and 8.5. In order to accurately place parts in assembly sites, machines or a part conveyor such as the sorting bowl are used (see Figure 5.66).

Different manipulators can be attached to the handling arm:

- to take on, rotate, move or empty barrels by picking from the top, edge or around;

- for simultaneous gripping of multiple containers via mechanical or pneumatic equipment for palletizing or loading a truck;

Figure 8.3 Installation options of a manually operated handling device. 1 Mounting stand, 2 Ceiling mount, 3 Wall or carrier mount, 4 Fixed cantilever column, 5 Swivel cantilever column, 6 Ceiling suspension

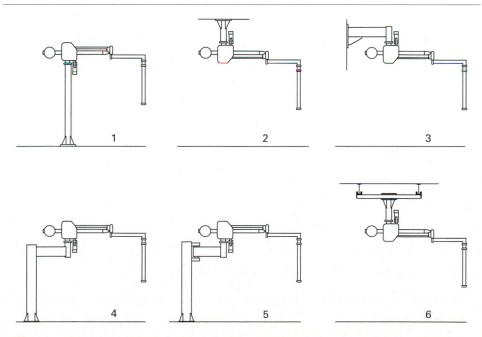

Figure 8.4   Rotating an oven with the help of handling equipment

Figure 8.5   Handling devices

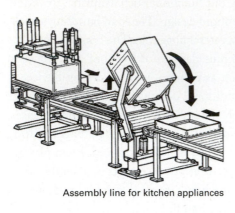

Assembly line for kitchen appliances

a) Container lifting and tilting device

b) Device to lift and empty barrels

c) Lifting and rotation device

d) Equipment to empty containers

- for intake of workpieces and semi-finished products such as cylinders, film roll, wheels, discs etc to support operations of tool machinery in manufacturing or assembly work.

8.2.3 Handling devices in integrated deployment

For assembly lines, many different handling devices are used as a result of the coming together of individual parts of different shapes, dimensions and weight in order to create the finished product (see Figure 2.21).

VDI 2860, which covers assembly and handling technology, deals with the handling functions (see Example 3.2).

8.3 Handling processes

The handling process is made up of:

- its object and the pre-determined features and characteristics;
- the primary functions, such as storing, changing quantity, moving and securing;
- the device that is able to fulfil the handling task.

For part and full automation, first a number of questions have to be answered, partly through analysis:

- The handling object:
  - What are the dimensions, weight, special features and shape of the general cargo?
  - What is the dimensional stability of the general cargo (box, bag and packaging)?
  - What supporting surfaces are there and what do they look like?
  - Does the general cargo contain information that has to be read?
- The handling device:
  - What are the quantities and cycles of the general cargo?
  - How much stowage or clamp pressure can the cargo bear?
- The handling functions:
  - What transport routes (source to sink) are required?
  - What quantities are taken on?

8.4 Handling system and material flow

When designing a handling system that has to be integrated into the operational processes, upstream and downstream material flow, as well as the relevant interfaces, have to be taken into consideration. We distinguish a reversing, continuous and circumventing material flow, as well as a material flow working with and without cycles. The *cycle-based* material flow has a defined and usually unchanging rhythm and is structured in a linear function. This material flow is fixed; disruption leads to a total standstill because there are no buffers.

The *non-cycle-based* material flow runs continuously, and can be selected and used in both line and cell structure. This type of material flow is less prone to disruption because it works with buffers and disruption, and does not result in all of the material flow standing still.

The components of a handling device can be seen in Figure 8.6, and we have to note that each axle requires such a position sensor. If we look at an articulated arm robot, the gripper is a significant component. The gripper must be selected according to the type and features of the handling object. The gripper works along the following operating principles (Figure 8.7):

- magnets: permanent/electric magnets such as battery/permanent magnets or magnet traverses;
- surface hooks;
- pneumatic: suction pads;
- mechanical: force or form-fitting.

Figure 8.6   Block diagram for controls of handling device

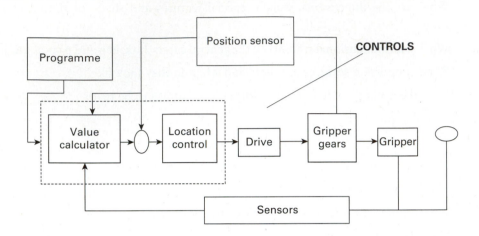

Figure 8.7   Handling devices a) Sheet metal transport with travers magnet without slack (www.dematic.com). b) Bag transport with vacuum tube lifter (www.tawi.com). c) Removal of porous and airtight plates with vacuum gripper in cantilever arm; this gripper allows plates to be moved horizontally and vertically, swivelled or turned over (www.schmalz.com). d) Mechanic handling device to transport drinks crates (www.tawi.com). e) Mechanic gripper for handling rolls (www.tawi.com)

Figure 8.8   Left: Simultaneous gripping of four barrels (capacity load 140 kg) (www. schmalz.com). Right: Multiple suction gripper for handling fragile boxes, plastic bags etc for high loads

The robots used in handling technology can be divided into:

- cartesian, cylindrical, spherical and parallel robots according to workspace;
- articulated or portal robots according to mechanical structure;
- assembly, palletizing and order picking robots according to deployment area.

Vacuum handling devices: Ergonomic operational components, delicate movements in horizontal and vertical directions as well as exact positioning for one- and two-handed operation ensure optimal effectiveness and economy. This is achieved through a selection of ergonomic operational components for vacuum tube lifters (Figure 8.9).

Figure 8.9   Vacuum handling devices (www.smi-handling.de) a) Removal of a cardboard box from a shelf using a vacuum lifter b) Swivel and tilt travers of a vacuum lifter

Figure 8.10   Different parallel gripper systems with adjustable size (www.demagcraenes.
com) a) Mechanic clamp gripper and system graphics for cuboid cargo
b) Various container grippers and systems graphic for diverse container types

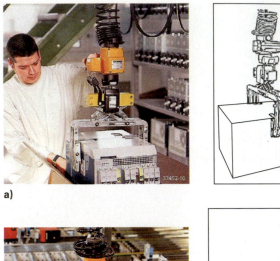

a)

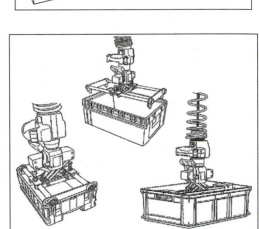

b)

Figure 8.11   Vacuum tube lifter (www.schmalz.com) a) Creation of pallet loads
b) Handling of packages in goods receipt and goods issue

a)

b)

Figure 8.12 Handling barrels (Bauer GmbH, Südlohn) a) Barrel turning tongs. b) Barrel lifter. c) Barrel gripper

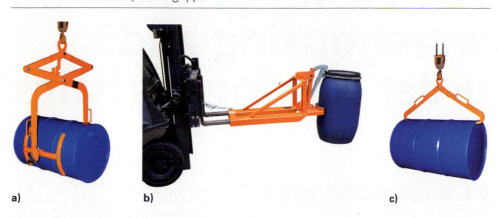

a) b) c)

Mechanical parallel gripper systems often rely on the friction principle using the transport weight. Gripper surfaces connect with the workpiece or container surface, such as steel, cardboard, wood. Figure 8.10 shows some parallel gripper types.

The basics of warehousing and order picking logistics

9.1 Warehousing, stock

In a manufacturing business, we distinguish between unwanted warehousing (delay) and wanted warehousing (see Chapter 2.1). Whenever goods are stored, for whatever reason, then this commits capital, occupies space and uses resources. One would have to try to avoid storage, so that the materials required for manufacturing and assembly are only procured and delivered when needed. This *consumption-based materials delivery* (for JIT, see Chapter 1.3.1) can save costs of capital commitment and warehousing. Disadvantages can occur through delayed delivery (due to weather, accident, strike action, etc) as this disrupts the production processes. This type of warehousing principle can be executed for long-term production programmes provided the effective organization is in place, such as for sections of the automobile industry (see Example 9.12).

In manufacturing, the *stockpiling principle* tends to be used for several reasons:

- to secure materials provision for production;
- to secure the ability to deliver to the market;
- to balance the chronological and quantity-related fluctuations in demand between procurement, production and sales;
- to allow for sorting of stored goods and to assemble manufacturing, assembly or customer orders (order picking);
- to enhance goods, such as through maturing or drying processes (beer, wine, cheese, wood);
- for speculative investment in goods in anticipation of increased prices, feared shortage, threatened strike action or seasonal deliveries, such as coffee, paper, tobacco.

Stocks in a warehouse allow for:

- continuous, smooth production;
- exact timings;
- bridging of disruptions;
- economical manufacturing with high utilization;
- independence from the procurement market;
- high delivery performance;
- low cost procurement of raw, excipient and operational materials;
- appropriate storage of materials that are presently not required.

Stockpiling, however, causes capital commitment and warehousing costs, creates organizational and disposition problems and brings diverse risks, such as ageing, theft and loss.

Stocks can also cover up:

- disruption-prone manufacturing and assembly processes;
- lack of punctuality;
- lacking or uncoordinated capacities;
- rejects.

Stockpiling occurs in a warehouse. It represents a time buffer (long-term storage) for incoming and outgoing goods, from the procurement and sales side as well as the manufacturing side. Storage (see Chapter 2.1) can be defined as planned disruption of the material flow.

A holistic storage system consists of *warehousing* (an umbrella term for all tasks of storage management), the *warehouse organization* with *warehouse administration* and *warehouse management*, as well as the *storage of goods*. The warehouse administration regulates the stocks, orders and personnel. The warehouse management oversees the warehousing processes, such as the material flow, warehouse storage and stock swap, as well as order picking. A continuous exchange of information and constant communication occurs between warehouse administration and management using various IT systems. The storage of goods occurs on the floor or on the shelves.

Stocks are the critical factor in storage costs as a result of capital and space commitment. Thus, low stocks should be aimed for. Depending on the storage function, this objective faces the opposing demand of:

- high reliability, high delivery performance and degree of service;
- low purchasing prices and short order processing times;
- high flexibility, high availability, high utilization and high productivity.

Thus, the stock factor is always a compromise, based on which influencing factors are given the highest priority. The question arises, which measures can result in a lowering of storage costs? The general answer: technical and organizational measures derived from the warehousing costs (see Chapter 9.3), such as:

- increase of turnover rate and order cycle;
- clear out of stored goods and streamlining of range;
- stock reduction for individual items;
- deployment of standardized storage means: unit creation and reduction of manufacturing depth;
- centralization of storage areas: mechanization and automation;
- storage and retrieval devices with small aisle width: utilizing height of building.

Stock can be reduced through stock management (see Example 9.11 and Chapter 9.6). First, we must distinguish between safety stocks and production-based work in progress.

Safety stocks in the procurement warehouse are dependent on purchasing goals (price reduction and speculation), in the production warehouse on production goals (utilization, batch size) and in the distribution warehouse on sales goals (delivery performance).

Production-based work in progress is dependent on order processing times, added value, turnover and material deployment.

For stocks serving a safety function, it is possible to try to manage the insecurities through agreements and contracts using the developments in the environment and the behaviour of market partners. If stock behaves in the way depicted in Figure 9.1, a reduction in stock will happen simply through lowering the upper stock limit.

Figure 9.1   Stock movement for an item over six months

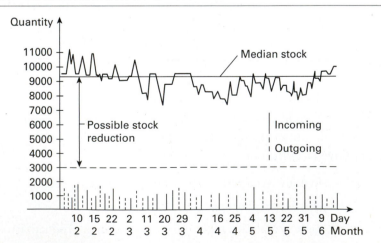

This does not reduce delivery performance in any way. The upper limit is above the storage and retrieval factors.

Production-based stock movement (for the calculations, see Example 2.19), which can also influence the stock, can be reduced by:

- shortening product processing times;

- introduction of manufacturing management;

- orders at shorter intervals;

- new provisioning strategies (see Example 2.15);

- changes to the manufacturing processes (standardization of individual parts; creation of parts families; permissibility of fluctuations in quality; changes to the manufacturing depth);

- new product creation.

9.2 Warehousing terminology, definitions

A warehouse can be named and categorized in line with a variety of criteria, such as the function in the value-added process, which is distinguished between the following (see Figure 9.7):

- A *procurement warehouse* is for providing production with material as required by the manufacturing orders (other names are raw material warehouse and goods receipt warehouse).

- A *production warehouse* buffers the interim products in line with the manufacturing and assembly stages (other names are semi-finished product warehouse and interim warehouse).

- A *distribution warehouse* stores the company's products and serves customers (other names are finished product, goods issue, sales and shipping warehouse).

There are also different kinds of warehouses, which depend on the type of function and activity, for their distinction:

- *Unit warehouse* (Figure 9.2)
  If the warehouse is made up solely of load units (logistical units), which can be taken out in the same way they were put in, the warehouse is called a unit warehouse. It serves as a *reserve warehouse* for an order picking warehouse. If an order only consists of units, a unit warehouse can become an order picking warehouse. This is also the case for dynamic provisioning (see Chapter 11.1.1). A unit storage warehouse is easily automated and can be a high, flat or compact warehouse for pallets, containers or crates (see Chapter 9.4.3). The presentation

Figure 9.2   Unit warehouse for pallet loads: storage; pre-storage zone (see Examples 9.14 and 9.15; Figure 11.22b) serves the management and arriving and departing load units with large conveyor technology (www.dematic.de)

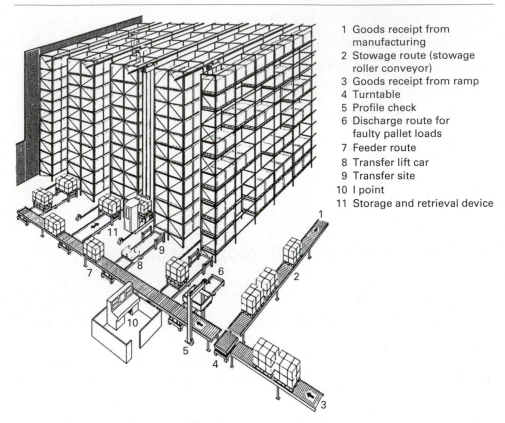

1 Goods receipt from manufacturing
2 Stowage route (stowage roller conveyor)
3 Goods receipt from ramp
4 Turntable
5 Profile check
6 Discharge route for faulty pallet loads
7 Feeder route
8 Transfer lift car
9 Transfer site
10 I point
11 Storage and retrieval device

of the pre-storage zone in Figure 9.3 is obsolete, but still shows the relevant processes – which are taken care of by IT (see Figure 9.19).

- *Order picking warehouse* (Figure 9.3)

  If partial quantities, such as pallet or container units, are removed from a provided total quantity based on fixed requirements, and assembled for an order, the warehouse is called an order picking warehouse. The order picking warehouse is usually very personnel-intensive, but can be automated if certain conditions are fulfilled. It can be run as a high, flat or compact warehouse.

Depending on the number of warehouses in a company, we can distinguish:

- *Central warehousing*

  If the storage activities of a small/medium-sized company, or the procurement or distribution warehouses of a larger company, are combined, this is called a central warehouse. An example is a central procurement warehouse.

Figure 9.3 Manual order picking warehouse for frequently handled items: gravity container with continuous racks for boxes, order picking container on non-powered roller track and an inclination angle for empty boxes, eg 5–6% corresponds to 3.5 to 4.5° (www.bito.com)

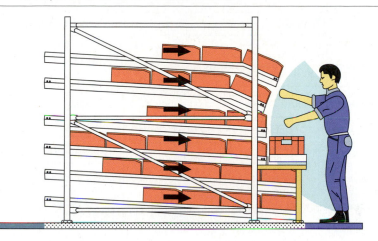

Advantages are: no multiple storage; low capital commitment; automation possible; concentrated storage; good stock monitoring; good utilization of storage and retrieval devices; good transparency of storage; low personnel deployment; low commitment of working capital; little storage space; low disposition effort. The site selection is of particular importance for a distribution warehouse (see Figure 1.7). *Disadvantages* of a central warehouse are: low degree of flexibility for urgent orders and changes; high costs; destruction of many goods if fire occurs; high requirements on warehouse organization (see Example 9.3).

- *Decentralized warehouse*
  If the warehouses are allocated to consumption sites, this is called decentralized warehousing. The disadvantage of multiple storage is offset by these advantages: low organizational effort; short routes; specifically adapted warehousing technology; fast processing of urgent orders; low material flow costs. If a disaster or fire occurs, often only a part of the warehoused goods are destroyed. Production warehouses, sometimes also procurement warehouses, are often located at decentralized storage sites (see Example 9.3).

The warehouse site depends on the two following factors:

- the *building design* (Figure 9.4): buildings, storeyed buildings, purpose-built warehouse buildings (silo warehouses) and high-shelf warehouse buildings;
- the *construction type*: flat stores up to 6 m, high flat stores 6 to 12 m high, warehouses more than 12 m, multi-storey warehouses and multiple flat warehouses on top of each other.

Figure 9.4   Warehousing possibilities for general cargo

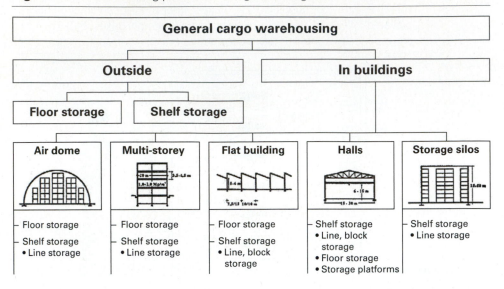

Static storage means that from storing to removing the load unit, it resides in the same place, such as a pallet shelf. With dynamic storage, the load unit changes site during the storage duration, in a continuous shelf.

Other distinguishing and identification criteria are:

- type of stored goods: bulk storage; general cargo storage;
- reasons for storage: buffer storage, reserve, maturation storage;
- location: external warehouse ≙ free storage; internal warehouse ≙ warehouse building;
- operation type: manual, mechanical, crane, storage and retrieval device, forklift;
- type of storage: floor storage, shelf storage;
- stored objects: raw material, tool, packaging aid and parts warehouse;
- movement of stored goods: static storage, dynamic storage (see Example 9.13);
- load unit: pallet warehouse, container warehouse, cassette warehouse;
- type of business: industrial warehouse, trade warehouse, third party warehouse;
- management type: automated warehouse, manual warehouse;
- warehouse structure: line or block storage;
- accessibility: directly/indirectly accessible;
- shelf type: pallet shelf, continuous shelf, narrow aisle warehouse.

In order to clearly define a warehouse, different features or criteria have to be examined. To categorize the types of warehouse, a combination of different features can help.

9.3 Warehouse organization, storage site allocation

Warehouse organization has a great influence on the profitability of the warehouse, and consists of process, structure and information organization. It has to fulfil provisioning, management and safety tasks. Warehouse organization is dependent on the goods' turnover frequency (order cycle) and the warehouse administration system (see Chapter 13.3.3). Additional tasks for warehouse organization are:

- statistics, inventory and controlling: monitoring of processes and conditions;
- operator's requirements;
- manufacturing method (single, serial, order manufacturing);
- type of storage site and stock administration.

Warehousing costs can be reduced through smart warehouse structure organization. In particular, low stocks mean low capital and space commitment (see Chapter 9.1). The warehouse structure and process organization must fulfil the warehousing objectives and demands, such as:

- highest possible degree of area, space and height utilization (see Chapter 9.7);
- fast and safe identification of stored goods; eliminating mistakes;
- highest possible flexibility, such as when range structure changes;
- high utilization of personnel and storage facilities;
- maximum protection of stored goods from damage and theft;
- simple and effective inventory accounting/administration.

For *storage site allocation*, we distinguish between fixed storage site allocation and free storage site selection (chaotic warehousing), as well as the creation of storage zones.

Fixed storage site allocation   This principle sees each item being allocated a specific fixed storage site. Fixed storage site allocation has the advantage of simple space organization (storage site number = item number). When used in shelving racks, this also leads to a number of disadvantages:

- utilization of shelving of only approximately 20 per cent;
- utilization of number of storage spaces of approximately 60 to 80 per cent;
- space size or number of spaces to be determined for largest item quantity;

- warehouse size to be planned for largest storage volume;
- effort for change when refilling spaces is high;
- empty spaces are created when items discontinued.

Fixed storage site allocation is used for large ranges with small quantities per item and low volume. This principle is applied in tool warehouses, spare parts warehouses, model warehouses, order picking warehouses and food warehouses. Items are stored on shelves according to specific preferences, such as:

- turnover frequency, retrieval frequency and FIFO within a storage space;
- weight, volume, dimensions, route length and value;
- complementary items, neighbourhood problems and construction groups.

Free storage space selection (chaotic storage place allocation)   The disadvantages of fixed storage space allocation can be avoided through free storage space selection. Each free storage space can be taken up by any item (unit). The individual storage space is defined in a system of coordinates, and the item is allocated to this particular space on the shelf. Thus, utilization of the number of storage spaces can increase to almost 100 per cent. A disadvantage is increased organizational efforts. The storage space of an item can be found in a database. Free storage space selection is used in unit warehouses (reserve warehouse), where a large range is stored in large quantities, or in an order picking warehouse (as unit warehouse) with dynamic provisioning. A prerequisite for this principle is, first, the unique labelling of individual storage spaces (see Figures 9.5, 3.32 and 9.6). This forms the basis for a manual or IT-supported warehouse management system.

Creation of storage zones   Zone creation often makes storage space allocation easier and is particularly found in order picking warehouses. It can be structured in a customer- or component-based way, specific to countries or businesses, according to turnover frequency, dimensions, value of stored goods or serial order picking. We distinguish between single-zone and multiple-zone structures when it comes to order picking (see Chapter 11.2.3).

Shelf space coordinates 01 02 10 01 in Figure 9.6 signify:

01   : Storage area number 1 in a business
02 (z) : Shelf aisle number 2
10 (x) : Row 10; even number corresponds to storage space on right side of aisle
01 (y) : Level 1

Figure 9.5   Warehouse and storage space numbering. a) Shelf row numbered in double pallet shelving unit. b) Shelf space numbered numerically and with barcode. A: storage type, such as procurement warehouse; 10: shelf row; 0: shelf column; 3: shelf level; arrow: top shelf space (www.jungheinrich.de)

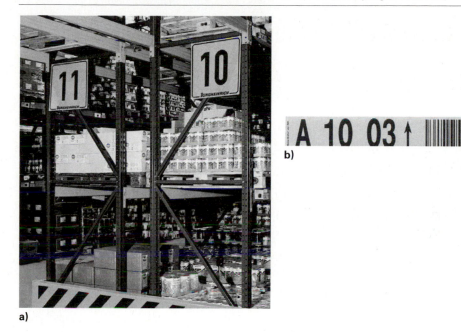

Figure 9.6   Coordinates of a storage space. They are placed in a coordinate system x–y–z. The shelf space is determined by the x–y–z coordinates

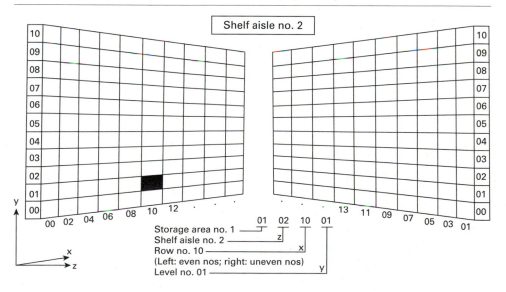

The visual determination of storage (shelf) spaces occurs with the help of shelf aisle number signs, printed plastic plates, writeable magnetic tapes, self-adhesive label holders as well as storage in a computer-based storage space database.

9.4 Warehouse structure

Upon examination of the structure of a procurement, production or distribution warehouse, it becomes obvious that it can have the same subsystems (Figure 9.7):

- goods receipt system;
- feeding transport system;
- unit or order picking warehouse with:
  - storage system;
  - warehousing system as floor or shelf storage;
  - goods retrieval system;
- discharging transport system;
- shipping system.

Figure 9.7   Warehousing structures in an industrial business

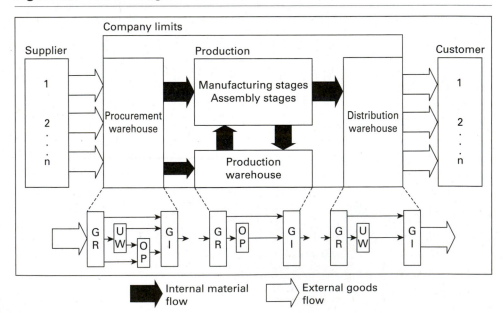

9.4.1 *Goods receipt (GR)*

The tasks of goods receipt is to carry out technical and organizational work, such as unloading, buffering, unpacking, sorting, repackaging, preparing for storage (such as pallet units, as well as provisioning). Information functions are also part of goods receipt, such as entering or scanning incoming goods into the warehousing management system (see Chapter 13.3.3), quantity checks and quality checks. The inspection process can take different forms: qualitative or quantitative checks; chemical checks; colouring, material or surface checks.

Once checks have come back positive, the goods are allowed to move on to the storage process. These controls and checks can last an entire day, so that the goods are buffered in goods receipt for the duration. The goods receipt area must be big enough to allow for all these activities and functions to take place. The space calculation considers the largest possible delivery quantity. Additional demands on goods receipt are the optimized design of the interface for the external goods flow with the internal material flow, in order to obtain short unloading times for lorries or rail carriages by appropriate design, such as a ramp, and by using appropriate handling tools, such as a low lift truck, as well as to minimize the number of unloading gates (see Chapter 7.3.2).

The goods receipt area can be large, and goods are usually located on the floor and taken up for transport by industrial trucks. It can be a complex system, with roller tracks, belt conveyors, feeders and discharge mechanisms, which move and sort goods automatically and put them together as units.

When planning a goods receipt area, one must also consider operational spaces such as the warehouse office, control centre, charging stations for industrial trucks, CO_2 or sprinkler systems as well as sanitary facilities. Accelerated data capture can be achieved by using mobile data capture (see Example 9.9).

9.4.2 *Transport systems*

Feeding and discharging transport are structured manually, part or fully automatic as an independent system. A forklift is capable of simultaneously being a feeding and discharging means of transport, as well as the means of storing and retrieving. Each individual function can also be carried out using its own means of transport, such as roller, chain or belt conveyors, carts, forklifts or storage and retrieval devices. Depending on the local and business-specific conditions, the feeding and discharging, the means for storage and for retrieval can be structured as a self-sufficient system (see Chapter 10.4).

9.4.3 Unit warehouse (UW)

The storage process of a unit warehouse consists of the chronological arrangement of functions:

- unit put into storage;
- continued storage of unit;
- retrieval of unit.

Means of transport and storage can be allocated to these storage process functions:

- storage transport system, such as forklift, storage and retrieval device;
- storage system, such as floor or shelf storage;
- retrieval system, such as lift crane and a high shelf lift truck.

Unit warehouses of a certain size can be automated relatively easily and without problems. The specific features of goods (see Figure 3.2), the type of storage unit made up of aid and goods, as well as the transfer at relevant interfaces, can cause problems (see Figure 9.2).

9.4.4 Order picking warehouse (OP)

The storage process of an order picking warehouse consists of the chronological arrangement of these functions:

- put into storage: feed and provide replacement;
- store: corresponds to static provisioning;
- retrieve: collect and pick order.

Just as in the unit warehouse, individual functions in the order picking warehouse also correspond to function carriers, with people being the function carrier during the storing process, and particularly, the retrieval process (see Figure 9.3; Chapter 9.2).

9.4.5 Goods issue (GI)

Goods that were order picked for goods issue have to be checked, packaged, addressed and labelled. The orders are assembled on specially labelled sites. Consignments for rail or lorry (carriers) have to be placed near the loading bay.

Relevant areas are required to fulfil this function. Prepackaging and packaging capacities in the shape of packaging stations (Figure 9.16), fully automated strapping or gluing machines have to be considered for the division of the area, and for shipping the number of loading gates also have to be determined (see Example 7.2).

The design and size of the courtyard – this applies to both goods receipt and goods issue – has to be planned depending on (see Chapter 7.3.2):

- delivery and shipping modes of transport such as rail and lorries (turning radius);
- structural design of the handling area (with/without ramp);
- type of handling (side/rear handling);
- type of handling goods and means of handling.

The location of the goods issue warehouse should be near the goods issue gate. The goods issue warehouse has nothing to do with the production operation. For small and medium-sized businesses, goods receipt and goods issue are joined up due to personnel and space reasons.

9.4.6 Warehousing structure designs

9.4.6.1 Variants

The designs for procurement, production and order picking warehouses depicted in Figure 9.7 with physically separate unit and order picking warehouses, as well as a unit or order picking warehouse only, can be structured in an integrated way (Figure 9.8). For the last design, we address the differences between the two-aisle and main aisle system.

Figure 9.8 Warehousing structure with spatial integration of unit and order picking warehouse

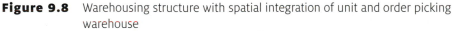
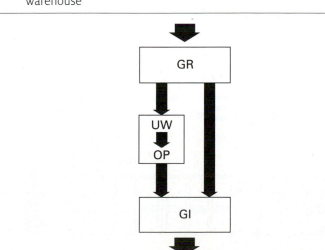

9.4.6.2 Main aisle system

This type of warehouse system (Figure 9.9) consists of an order picking warehouse on the first and second level with double shelves (lengthways storage; multiple location system) of Euro pallets and a unit warehouse on the third to the nth level. The main aisle is a wide aisle, used by the order picking vehicles as well as the forklifts for storage and retrieval of whole loading units in the third to n^{th} level. A forklift implements the loading of the order picking warehouse (first and second level). The wide aisle must be wide enough so that the order picking vehicles and forklifts can pass each other by.

The advantage of the main aisle is the saving of one single aisle, which means lower costs. A disadvantage is the simultaneous order picking and stacking. This can be avoided, or at least reduced, through separating the activities chronologically.

9.4.6.3 Two-aisle system

This warehousing system (Figure 9.10a) consists of single shelf rows (lengthways storage of pallets). The forklifts run in *separate* aisles, one for the operation of the unit warehouse of the third to n^{th} level, and the other for order picking vehicles on the first and second level. These are narrow aisles: order picking aisles, which are 1,000 mm wide, and a high reach truck, which is 1,500 mm wide. The advantages of this system are the separation of order picking and storage, as well as the securing of continuous replenishment.

Other designs for a two-aisle storage system are shown in Figures 9.10b and 11.36.

Figure 9.9   Layout of main aisle system. a) Horizontal order picker. b) Reach truck (www.jungheinrich.de)

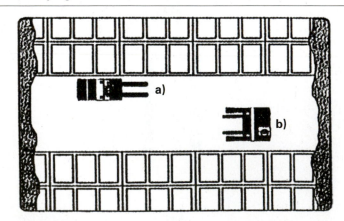

Figure 9.10   Layout of two-aisle system a) Order picking warehouse (first and second level): operation through horizontal order picker in aisle 1; storage in level three to nth level; operation through narrow aisle forklift in aisle 2 (www.jungheinrich.de) b) Order picking warehouse: manual order picking from continuous shelf with order picking truck; ground level: 'order picking tunnel'; above: loading units from push back racking (see Figure 11.48) for pallets with forklift operation from both sides (www.bito.com)

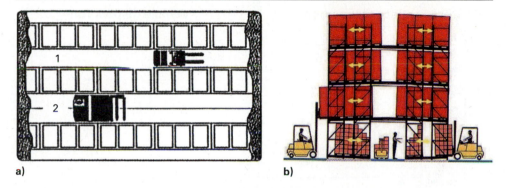

a)   b)

9.5 Warehousing logistics

If a warehouse is examined from a logistical perspective, warehousing logistics encompass administrative systems, disposition systems and operational systems.

A warehousing system consists of the following: analogue to the transport system (see Figure 4.2); the components loading units; warehousing technology and warehouse organization (see Figure 10.6); conveying technology for the pre-storage zone; packaging technology (handling technology, palletizer); safety technology (shrink machine); building construction.

Figure 9.11   Components of operational warehousing and order picking logistics

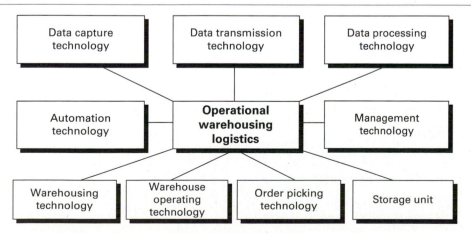

Figure 9.12 Logistical perspective of the material and information flow in a warehousing system

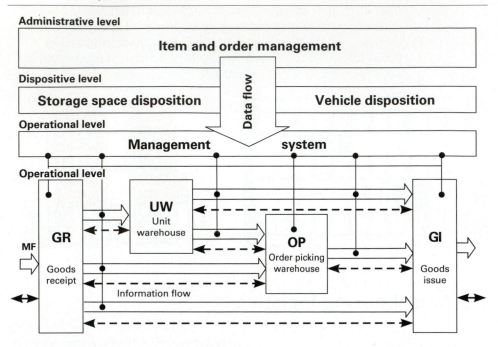

9.6 Warehousing costs

The warehousing process, which does not add any value to stored goods (except in enhancement or speculative warehousing (see Chapter 9.1)), makes the stored items more expensive through costs in procurement, production and distribution warehouses.

These are made up of:

- *inventory costs*:
  - capital commitments costs;
  - insurance against fire and theft;
- *personnel costs*:
  - storing, retrieval and removal, personnel training and transport operation;
  - warehouse management;
  - inventory;
- *operation costs of resources*:
  - warehouse furnishings;
  - storage aids;
  - transport;

- *building costs* (area costs for storage outside):
  - depreciation, interest, heating, ventilation and lighting;
  - upkeep: inspection, maintenance and repair;
  - insurance and building management;
- *other costs*: loss in value due to ageing, damage and theft.

The operating costs of resources correspond with the depreciation and interest on capital for warehouse furnishings and means of transport, as well as the costs for energy and maintenance.

Technological and organizational measures can reduce warehousing costs. Savings are won for:

- inventory costs through:
  - decrease in the stored quantity per item;
  - removal of slow-moving items, streamlining of range;
  - increase in the turnover rate, stocking according to ABC analysis;
  - modular principle for products, stocking strategy of just-in-time;
  - introduction of on-demand orders, checking small customers for effectiveness;
- personnel costs through:
  - increasing mechanization;
  - decrease in order picking and repackaging;
  - reduction in order picking times: short routes, less downtime;
  - reduction of warehousing management system, IT-supported demand and consumption-based stock management and inventory;
- operating costs through:
  - reduction in storage aids, changing of storage operating devices;
  - creation of load units, deployment of standardized storage aids;
  - fulfilment of demands through relevant storage systems;
  - achievement of high utilization;
- building costs through:
  - reduction in building area, dissolution of rented warehouse space;
  - lowering heating costs, reduction of downtime;
  - centralization of warehousing areas, storage operating devices with small aisle width;
  - high usage of area, height and space;
  - introduction of continuous loading, achievement of high handling performance.

The building costs are recorded more easily and quickly through determining rental costs in € per month and m². These are made up of area, heating, electricity and repair costs (for more on calculation of costs per pallet space, see Examples 1.7 and 11.15).

If you calculate the percentage of capital commitment costs from the individual cost ratios, and relate them to the value of the average stored goods, the warehousing costs in the metal processing industry in 2013 are approximately 19 to 30 per cent of the average value of stored goods.

Take note when using figures without knowing what they are based on (see Chapter 1.5.1 and 9.7; for costs when outsourcing a distribution warehouse, see Example 1.7).

9.7 Terminology, key figures

To calculate, assess, compare, plan and continuously monitor a warehouse, key figures (see Chapter 1.5.1) are used. In order to work with them, it is necessary to clearly define each key figure and to determine its basis and related figures.

Cycle time   A storage or retrieval cycle in a warehouse is a closed process of movement to fulfil the logistical function storage or retrieval. The storage cycle is made up of the load intake, horizontal and vertical loaded journeys, load discharge and empty return journey. The process of the storage cycle depends on the vehicle type, operation and type of positioning. The duration of the storage process' cycle is determined as cycle time in minutes. In practice, we calculate with median cycle times.

The following defines the differences between single and double cycles:

- single cycle as storage or retrieval cycle;
- double cycle as combination of storage and retrieval cycle (see Chapter 9.8).

Gross warehouse area (Figure 9.13)   This is the warehouse area without those areas taken up by office, staff room, provisioning for warehouse goods, feeder and discharge stations, loading and unloading sites.

Net warehouse area   This is the gross warehouse area (without the traffic and manipulation areas) for storage operating devices. The net warehouse area corresponds to the area taken up by shelving.

Aisle width   This encompasses the distance between storage units or shelves, and is determined by:

- design and type of storage operating devices (such as forklift, storage and retrieval truck);

Figure 9.13 Representation of gross warehouse area. a) Empties. b) Battery charging station. c) I-point (www.jungheinrich.de)

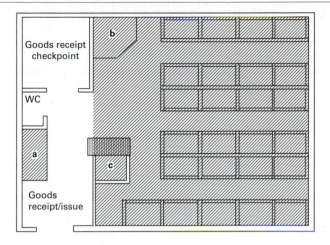

- load unit and loading aids (such as pallets, containers);
- storage method for storage unit (such as lengthways or crossways storage, see Chapter 10.3.1.2);
- safety distance.

Benchmarks for aisle width depend on the utilized storage operating device; total capacity load of 1 t for lengthways storage of a DIN pallet can be found in Table 9.1 (for more on aisle widths of forklifts, see Figure 6.37).

Table 9.1 Benchmarks for aisle widths

Storage operating device (approx. 1 t load capacity)	Aisle width in m
Pallet truck	0.9–1.2
Shaft lift truck	1.9–2.3
Front forklift	3.2–3.5
Reach truck	2.6–2.8
Four-way forklift	2.2–2.5
Cross forklift	2.2–2.5
Order picking forklift	1.6–1.8
Stacking crane	1.5–1.7
Narrow aisle lift truck	1.5–1.8
Shelf operating device, on tracks	1.4–1.6

Key figures in warehousing are:

$$\text{Degree of area utilization} = \frac{\text{Net warehouse area}}{\text{Gross area}} \times 100 \, [\%] \qquad (9.1)$$

If the degree of area utilization only relates to the different shelving types (Table 9.2), then shelving racks have to be taken off the defined gross warehouse area.

Example: A shelving rack with a shelf depth of 40 cm, aisle width of 1 m, this will be:

Net warehouse area $2 \times 0.40 \times$ shelf length L
Gross warehouse area $2 \times 0.40 \times L + 1.0 \times L$

Results in:

$$\text{Degree of area utilization} = \frac{2 \times 0.40 \times L}{L(2 \times 0.40 + 1.0)} \times 100 = \frac{0.80}{1.80} \times 100 = 44.44 \, [\%]$$

The net warehouse area corresponds to the area taken up by shelving, the gross warehouse area in this example merely corresponds to the aisle area.

$$\text{Degree of height utilization} = \frac{\text{Utilized height}}{\text{Usable height}} \times 100 \, [\%] \qquad (9.2)$$

$$\text{Degree of space utilization} = \frac{\text{Storage unit volume} \times \text{Number of units}}{\text{Gross warehouse space}} \times 100 \, [\%] \quad (9.3)$$

Table 9.2 Degree of area utilization of different storage systems

Storage system	Degree of area utilization in % *
Pallet block storage (floor storage)	80
Standing shelves for long materials (manual op)	40
Shelving racks (Aisle width 1 m)	45
Drive-in racks (6 to 7 pallets back-to-back)	70
Pallet shelving (with front forklift)	40
Pallet shelving (with shelf operating device)	60
Continuous shelf (shelf operating device)	65
Mobile rack (8 shelves with one aisle)	75

Reference values depending on:
– weight, dimensions and volume of cargo;
– shelving depth and transport aid;
– manual or mechanical operation (on foot, with truck, type of lift truck, shelf operating device)

Terms like turnover frequency and handling time as economic key figures are interconnected like this:

The *turnover frequency* (*handling ratio, warehouse turnover*) shows how often stock is turned over during a defined period, whereby we distinguish by quantity or value. The turnover frequency is calculated from the ratio of the turnover and stock.

Turnover frequency

$$= \frac{\text{Warehouse turnover } [\text{€/year}]}{\phi \text{ Warehouse stocks } [\text{€}]} \text{ such as } \frac{400}{1000} = 4 \text{ times per year} \qquad (9.4)$$

The turnover time is the ratio of the observation period to the turnover frequency. It provides an average storage time for a product in the warehouse.

$$\text{Handling duration} = \frac{\text{Number of days per year}}{\text{Turnover frequency per year}} \text{ such as } \frac{360}{4} = 90 \text{ days} \qquad (9.5)$$

$$\text{Average warehouse stocks} = \frac{\text{Initial stock} + \text{final stock}}{2} \qquad (9.6)$$

The average warehouse stock derives from the ratio of warehouse sales and turnover ratio based on one item, a product group, the entire warehouse, in quantity or value. The turnover ratio (Formula (9.4)) is calculated from the annual sales amount/median stock value or quantity based.

The inventory range is the reciprocal value of the turnover frequency.

$$\text{Inventory range} = \frac{\phi \text{ Inventory } [\text{€}]}{\text{Warehouse turnover } [\text{€/month}]} \text{ [months]} \qquad (9.7)$$

Items with high turnover frequency are called fast movers, best sellers or top sellers; those with low turnover frequency are called slow movers or duds.

The handling performance is shown by the quantity units per period, such as number of stored/retrieved pallets per period and per handling device.

The pallet space costs in €/pallet/month are calculated from the area, the number of pallet spaces in shelves and the area costs in €/m²/month (see Example 11.15).

$$\text{Pallet space costs} \frac{\text{Storage area } [\text{m}^2]}{\text{Number of pallet spaces}} \text{ area costs } [\text{€/m}^2\text{/month}] \qquad (9.8)$$

Capacity calculations (volume, mass and piece stream), cycle calculations: see Chapter 2.3.2, Example 11.1.

Order processing time: see Example 2.14.

Profitability calculation (amortization time): see Example 4.8 and Figure 4.20.

Operating costs of forklifts: see Chapter 6.6.7.8.

Premises key figures (basic areas, floor areas and cubic index): see Chapter 12.10.2.

9.8 Warehousing strategies

Strategies (see Chapter 1.5.2) for warehousing are used to determine the flow for storing and retrieving, the control of the order of removals and the storage space. Such strategies are:

- *FIFO* (first in – first out): the item that was stored first is the first one to be retrieved. Continuous shelves fulfil this strategy automatically; in pallet shelves this strategy is implemented by organizational measures.

- *LIFO* (last in – first out): the item that was stored last is the first to be retrieved, automatically in drive-in racks or with block floor storage.

- *Cross-distribution strategy*: this consists of evenly distributing the same item in different shelving aisles in order to be able to still fulfil orders fully – if without FIFO – in case a shelf operating device breaks down.

- *Double cycle strategy*: combined storing and retrieving.

- *Connecting aisle strategy*: reducing walking distances when order picking 'man to item' through connecting aisles at right angle to main aisle for small to medium sized product range.

- *Stripe strategy*: see Figure 11.19; process of accessing item storage spaces in two-dimensional order picking with the vertical order pickers, in order to reduce distances.

- *Order picking strategies*: see Figure 11.8.

- *Distributions strategies*: see Figure 1.7.

VDI guidelines (see Chapter 11.7)

9.9 Examples and questions

Example 9.1: Degree of volume utilization

When analysing a timber warehouse, the degree of utilization for the existing floor storage was calculated at 0.2 m^3/m^2. This degree of volume utilization can be improved.

Answer: Depending on the number of stored timber types and dimension per type, floor storage should be changed. Cantilever and standing shelves are suitable shelving types. By using the height up to 2 m, the degree of volume utilization increases to 1.2 m^3/m^2. During such an analysis and planning, additional valuable storage space can be gained through removing shelf warmers.

Example 9.2: Degree of area utilization

Calculate the degree of area utilization for a shelving rack system.

Answer: See Chapter 9.7 on key figures with formula (9.1).

Example 9.3: Centralizing or decentralizing warehouses

We often have to consider whether a central warehouse or a decentralized system of warehouses is economical for a business. The decision mainly depends on the assessment of the advantages and disadvantages, and on business-specific influencing figures. What are the general advantages and disadvantages for centralization and decentralization?

Answer:

Centralization: We distinguish between horizontal and vertical centralization. Horizontal centralization features a number of warehouses on one level, such as three central warehouses, while vertical centralization is determined by the number of warehousing levels, such as one level.

- *Advantages*:
  - not enough specialist staff in business;
  - easier administration;
  - cost savings and simplified warehouse.
- *Disadvantages*:
  - subordinate positions receive commands: less enjoyable work;
  - contact between management and staff is lost.

Decentralization: This transfers decision-making authority to subordinates.

- *Advantages*:
  - increase in feelings of responsibility, which would result in quicker reaction to problems;
  - smaller management body at the top.
- *Disadvantages*:
  - larger number of trained staff;

- lack of holistic overview;
- streamlining advantages are lost that prevents creation of specialists.

Example 9.4: Management of a distribution warehouse

What are the possibilities in managing a distribution warehouse for finished products with the smallest possible stock?

Answer: A distribution warehouse can be managed by using a safety or minimum inventory and maximum item stocks. This should be represented by using the example of a product (Figure 9.14), with a manufacturing batch, three working days and the maximum item stock at 100. For purchased items, it is the relevant order time and quantity. For each item, determine the batch size, manufacturing time, maximum item stock, order time and quantity.

The minimum inventory is the smallest inventory of an item, in order to guarantee a delivery that includes demand and replacement fluctuations.

This management system is a fixed disposition system based on being set up through a controller with constant future values, constant demand as well as constant batch sizes, stored quantities and manufacturing time.

In a fixed disposition system, the controller can be replaced by a PPS system, in which batch sizes, manufacturing times and maximum inventories can be entered. The control plan can then be carried out through chain observation for six days.

Figure 9.14   Graphic representation of the inventory of an item over a period with maximum quantity of 100, safety inventory of 20 items and the batch size order (order amount) of 80 items with a replacement time of three working days and constant demand (order point process)

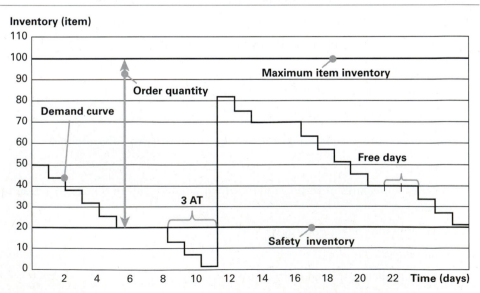

Example 9.5: Goods receipt/goods issue of a procurement and distribution warehouse

What are the advantages of the design of goods receipt/issue for a distribution warehouse as head, sawtooth or deep ramps and levellers (see Chapter 7.3.2), as opposed to outdoor loading through a loading gate (also applied to the goods receipt of a procurement warehouse)?

Answer: The *advantages* are:

- short stand times for lorries through flat rear loading; high handling performance;
- docking options for almost all lorry types;
- continuous loading of containers, swap bridges;
- hardly any energy loss, closed building prevents draught: no dust, less illness due to cold and less damage to goods.

Example 9.6: Order/item/product range structure

How do the structure of items, product range and orders determine warehouse design?

Answer: The *order structure* is described through the following order-related data: number of orders/year; number of positions/order; number of pocks/position; number of shipping packages/order; order weight; order volume. Additional figures are: weekly distribution of orders; annual fluctuations; revenue/order.

The *item structure* is a division of a product range in line with classification criteria. An item is the smallest unit of a range. To describe the item structure we use: weight; dimensions; volume; turnover frequency; number of item groups; dangerous goods; expensive goods; type of packaging (such as cardboard, container and pallets). The item structure is a decisive influence on the production programme in a business for the design of order picking systems (for more on item features, see Chapter 3.1.3; for a definition of an item tree, read Example 11.25).

The product range structure is the summary of items in the production programme of a business. To plan warehousing, the range is placed in ABC classification, or divided in line with the turnover frequency of components, or in line with other criteria such as weight, volume or other features.

This data is important for making *enquiries* or requesting a quotation:

- *goods receipt* with information about how often a good is delivered and in what form (pallets, container, varietal purity, mixed, daily, weekly, lorry, rail, container, origin of goods, with quality checks, number of suppliers and barcode identification);
- *storage and order picking* with figures on average stay, inventory/storage spaces, regulations, size of handling area, storage requirements, order picking type, structure and process organization (see Chapter 11.2);

- *shipping* with information about number of shipped packages per day, time requirements, average shipping weight/volume, packaging regulations, shipping type (express shipping), type of documents, additional work such as assembly, labelling and information systems.

Example 9.7: Warehouse planning

What are the components of warehouse planning and which comparison criteria can be used for assessment?

Answer: Components of a warehouse for structure and process organization:

- storage good: general cargo, bulk cargo, storage aids; pallets and containers;
- loading unit: type, dimensions and weight;
- storage system: unit storage and order picking warehouse;
- storage methods: floor and shelf storage;
- shelving type: pallet shelves or continuous shelving;
- storage arrangement: fixed storage space arrangements and free storage space selection;
- storage organization: storage space/warehouse inventory administration, order picking and warehousing management system;
- operation: manual, mechanical and automated;
- storage operating devices: forklifts and aisle width;
- environment, safety equipment and fire safety.

Comparison criteria are:

- investment;
- operating costs;
- storage space costs/pallet/month;
- turnover costs/pallet/month;
- area and space requirements;
- degree of automation;
- warehousing strategies:
  - flexibility;
  - number of operation staff;
  - expansion options.

Example 9.8: Capacity

How can capacity be defined and what are the key figures?

Answer: Capacity is the full use of a system's or technical equipment's ability to perform. The entire performance of a system depends on the technical and human performance. Capacity can be related to load, order picking and warehousing. Capacity is measured by the degree of utilization (see Chapter 6.6.7.8, 3.1).

A forklift has a degree of utilization of 50 per cent – in an observation period of eight hours, it is used for four hours. If the figures are captured by a counter for operating hours, the recording type has to be considered, as well as what activity the recording was for: in assembly, to hold building components or when transporting and stacking. In a pallet shelf, the capacity is calculated by the ratio of stored pallets to the total number of pallet spaces.

In manufacturing, capacity is calculated from the sum of manufacturing and support hours, and the gross working hours. Productivity comes as a result of the manufacturing and support hours put in.

Example 9.9: Goods receipt with mobile data capture

Show one solution.

Answer: Mobile data capture equals a mobile workplace that can carry out data capture for IT such as using radio technology, independent of the electric grid (ie the computer is connected to the host system using wireless LAN).

Figure 9.15 Trolley for mobile data capture in goods receipt and order picking (Eberhardt + Partner GmbH & Co KG)

The trolley in Figure 9.15 for storing and order picking contains a battery, computer, barcode scanner and a printer. For product-oriented, receipt-free order picking, 14 orders can be processed simultaneously. The items for order picking are shown using a pick-by-light, which is collected per item and placed in the relevant order container. It can carry out up to 200 picks/h, and has a fault rate of <0.1 per cent through scanning and counter checks.

Example 9.10: Components of a packaging station in goods issue

What are the components of a packaging station and in which arrangement?

Answer: Figures 9.16, 9.17 and 9.18.

Figure 9.16   Packaging station and normal arrangement of components (www.huedig-rocholz.de) 1 Packaging and worktable, 2 Drawer, 3 Roller container, 4 Additional table for scales, 5 Back board, 6 Workplace lighting, 7 Double socket, 8 Space with monitor, 9 Bracket for display device, 10 Fixing pillar, 11 Form tray, 12 & 13 Magazine for folding boxes, 14, 15, 16 & 17 Under-desk cutting stations, 18 Shelf for keyboard, 19 Clamps for display device, 20 Cabinet

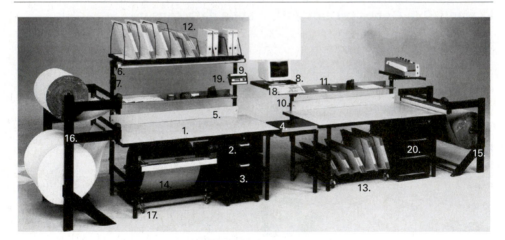

Example 9.11: Stocks

How do you achieve low stocks?

Answer: By using stock management. It consists of:

- stock classification;
- planning and management of stock;
- stock control;
- delivery times (see Chapter 1.5);
- IT support.

Figure 9.17 Fixed packaging station – tilting table to push the package onto roller conveyor – with fall waste hole, to work on both sides (symmetrical strain on body, left-handed staff); right and left of the packaging table are shipping envelopes; (right) cardboard box trolley with relevant range; in the middle of the picture, there is a mobile clipboard with the order list and address label; (left) in the chutes there are the items to be packed for the order. A packer can operate several packing desks. (www.otto.de)

Figure 9.18 Cardboard box trolley (www.jungheinrich.de)

Example 9.12: Warehousing principles

What warehousing principles are there?

Answer: *Consumption-based procurement* with low capital commitment, but weaknesses as a result of transport downtime; *stockpiling* with continuous provisioning ability but high capital commitment as well as organizational and disposition efforts; *combination* of consumption-based procurement and stockpiling, with stock calculations and optimization of costs but higher organizational and disposition effort.

Example 9.13: Shelving types

What are static storage and dynamic storage?

Answer: Static storage includes floor, shelf rack, pallet and drive-in shelving; dynamic includes continuous, push-back, mobile and automated storage, such as the automatic small parts warehouse. The investment for static storage is lower than for dynamic storage. Transport costs and volume utilization have to be considered.

Example 9.14: Pre-storage zone

Show pre-storage zones in pictures.

Answer: Figure 9.19 shows a pre-storage zone consisting of pallet conveyor technology of a high shelf warehouse. This conveyor technology is made up of roller and chain conveyors, lift tables and empty pallet depot. Based on requirements, the pallets from production can be directly forwarded to goods issue or buffered in the high shelf warehouse.

The schematic picture in Figure 9.19b shows different combination options of components in the pre-storage zone: forklifts, contour checks, automatic layer palletizing using robots, manual order picking and repackaging in containers.

Figure 9.19   Pre-storage zones of pallet high shelf warehouses with storage and retrieval machines. a) Pallet conveyor technology in pre-storage zone. b) Combination options for components in the pre-storage zone (www.dematic.com)

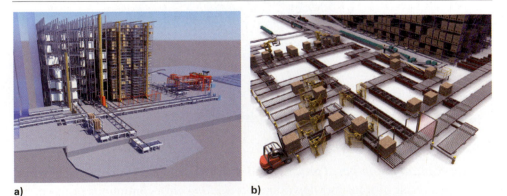

a)   b)

Example 9.15: Task and means of transport in pre-storage zone

What means of transport can be found in the pre-storage zone and what is its task?

Answer: The pre-storage zone is the interface with other warehouse areas, such as the small parts warehouse and goods receipt for stored goods prior to manufacturing, assembly, order picking and external businesses, as well as shipping.

Depending on the type of storage unit, roller and chain conveyors are used for pallets in goods receipt and goods issue, as well as transport trucks and electric monorails. For containers and cardboard boxes, roller and belt conveyors are used. Often this is followed by sorting systems or order picking stations.

What is important is a well thought out plan of the optimal configuration, in order to save investment and to optimize the performance of the entire system. A quick material flow prevents bottlenecks in provisioning, buffering, loading and unloading, manufacturing and shipping.

Questions

1 What is the use of stock and what are its disadvantages?

2 What measures can be used to lower warehousing costs?

3 What are unit warehouses and order picking warehouses?

4 Name the categorization criteria for warehousing types.

5 Define fixed storage space order and free storage space selection.

6 What subsystems are used in an entire warehousing system?

7 Sketch four versions of warehouse structures.

8 What components belong to operational warehousing logistics?

9 What costs are warehousing costs made up of?

10 What is the definition of the degree of area utilization?

Warehousing and shelving types 10

10.1 Bulk warehousing

Depending on the type and quantity, bulk cargo can be stored outside or in special containers, such as silos. These can be outside or inside buildings (see Figure 10.1).

10.1.1 Bulk cargo floor storage

Floor storage is used in both external warehouses and indoor storage. In external warehouses, heaps are built for weather-resistant goods, such as coal, ore, sand etc. Storing and retrieval is done with loading bridges, cranes, belt conveyors, diggers etc. The embankment angle of the resting stored good (see Chapter 3.1.2) creates the required storage area for the storage volume and height. The floor of the storage area must be suitable for the heap operating devices and must be well drained.

Most bulk cargo that must not get dirty and is not weather-resistant, such as fertilizer or salt, is stored in buildings. Storage areas in buildings are covered in an abrasion-resistant, dust and dirt repellent coating, which is also suitable for the operating devices (such as floor load capacity of screed). Machines for the storing and retrieval of bulk goods are continuous conveyors, such as belt conveyors, swing conveyors, pneumatic conveyors, and discontinuous conveyors, such as diggers or forklifts with an attached shovel.

10.1.2 Bulk container warehousing

Large containers, such as bunkers or silos, can be outside or in a hall. Silos are bulk good storage made of wood, concrete, metal or plastic for storing cereals, fertilizers, plastic granules, coffee, sand, cement etc. Silos are built on the ground (high silo) or in a pit (deep silo). Usually a silo has a cylindrical shape and stands vertically.

Bunkers store bulk goods and are made of steel, steel concrete, light metal, plastic-covered steel or plastic. Their shape can vary and depends on the bulk materials and the local conditions (see Figure 10.2):

- prismatic bunkers have a circular cross section (outlet: truncated cone);
- pocket bunkers consist of a row of prismatic bunkers.

Figure 10.1   Warehousing types for bulk cargo

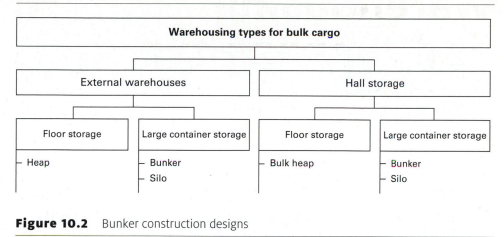

Figure 10.2   Bunker construction designs

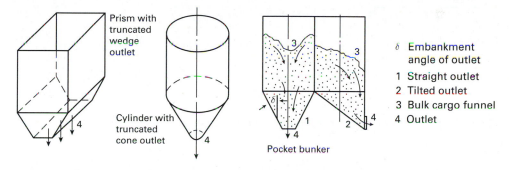

10.1.3 Filling and emptying of bunkers/silos

Filling a silo can be done with continuous and discontinuous conveyors, or directly with a shuttle vehicle through tipping of the entire vehicle or just the loading area. The intake of the cargo occurs with a funnel, the transport to the silo with continuous conveyors. Emptying a silo can be done continuously through bunker locks using gravity in combination with continuous conveyors for removal.

Silo locks are flat or rotating pushers, flaps or accumulative locks (see Figure 10.3), which can be moved using a pressure cylinder, aerator or gear motor. Emptying of the silo can occur continuously through continuous conveyors, but also in smaller doses. Continuous conveyors that are used are belt, screw, swing conveyors or rotors (see Figure 10.4). The removed quantities are regulated by adjusting the silo locks, or through changing the following:

- belt conveyor speed;
- rotation speed of the rotor or screw;
- frequency of swing trough.

Figure 10.3   Bunker locks

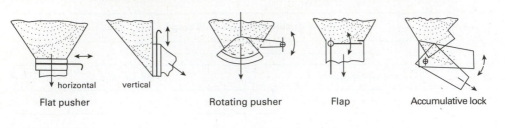

Figure 10.4   Means of transport for emptying bunkers

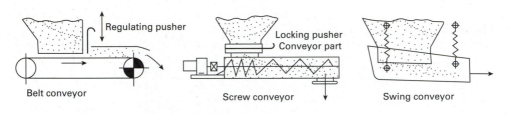

10.2 General cargo warehousing

Warehousing in a business can be found outdoors or in buildings. Only weather-resistant general cargo can be stored outdoors, such as containers, cast parts and cable drums. Sheet metal, sectional steel and pipes are stored in buildings these days to prevent adverse impact on the quality. The following chapter will deal with different options for storing general cargo in buildings (see Figure 9.4).

10.2.1 Storage methods, storage system, shelving types

The storage method of procurement, production and/or distribution warehouses for general cargo can be *floor storage* (see Chapter 10.2.2) or *shelf storage* (see Chapter 10.3). We distinguish storage methods between the following two types of warehousing:

- unit warehouse;
- order picking warehouse.

Floor storage: For floor storage we distinguish between *line or block storage*, stacked or unstacked; for shelf storage between *line and compact storage* and access methods for different types of shelving (Figure 10.5 a/b).

Figure 10.5 Systematic division of shelving types according to two possibilities a) and b)
(LE = storage unit)

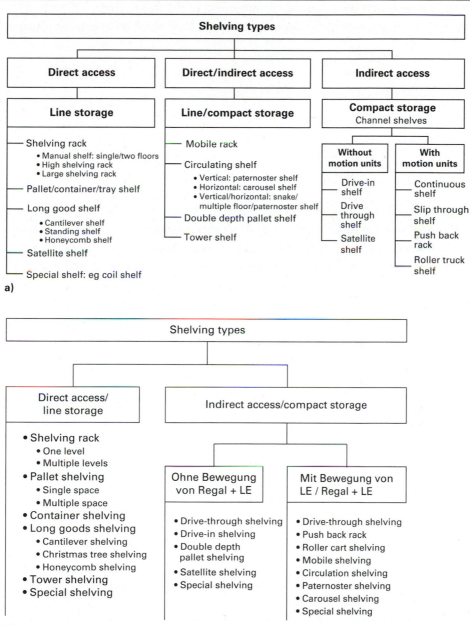

a)

b)

Shelf storage: Strictly speaking, a unit warehouse is also an order picking warehouse, if an order picking assignment either only consists of whole storage units or the order picking occurs with dynamic provisioning of the storage unit.

For bridging short distances (provisioning and buffering), the means of transport used, include:

- continuous conveyors:
  - circular conveyors, power & free conveyors;
  - belt conveyors, roller and level roller conveyors;
  - transfer tables, floor conveyors;
- discontinuous conveyors as ATS machines (see Chapter 6.7), such as low lift truck, carrier vehicles and lift trucks.

Components of a storage system are made up of the *storage unit* (storage goods with or without storage aids), the type of *storage technology*, consisting of shelving type and relevant storage operating methods (storage and removal devices), as well as the *warehouse organization* with storage space administration and warehousing management (Figure 10.6). Shelf storage is only possible with transports, which means shelf storage includes means of transport or personnel to execute the storing or removal processes. The storage system also consists of storage goods, storage and transport technology, as well as the warehousing administration system.

Warehousing management depends on several factors, such as fixed storage space order or free storage space selection (see Chapter 9.3). Examples of different shelf storage systems can be found in Chapter 11.6, for warehousing administration systems in Chapter 13.3.3.

Figure 10.6   Components of a storage system

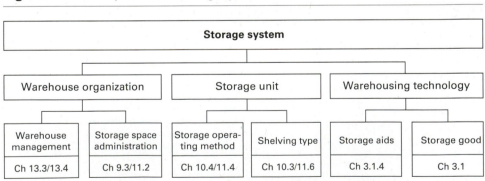

10.2.2 Floor storage

The goods are either stored on the floor or on storage platforms, in line (row) or block storage. What is missing, as seen in Figure 10.6, is the shelving type. The stored goods can be stacked or unstacked, with or without storage aids such as bars, rungs, containers, frameworks, pallets, with or without stacking frames or mesh box pallets (Figure 10.7).

The order of stacks is usually vertical to the aisles (parallel stacking). It can also be at an angle for narrow aisle widths (30° to 45° stacking) (Figure 10.8). Depending on the storage goods, the stack itself can contain multiple stackable units on top of each other, such as pallets, containers, boxes or paper rolls. Floor storage is usually managed using forklifts equipped with attachments, depending on

Figure 10.7 Floor storage a) Floor block storage of drinks pallets; forklift handling (www.linde-mh.com) b) Floor block storage of paper rolls; operated by double-carrier hanging trolley with vacuum lift for 6.5 t (www.demagcranes.com) c1) Principal sketch, block storage (www.ohra.de); c2) Principal sketch, line storage ([16])

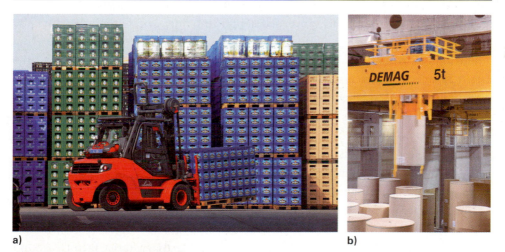

a)

b)

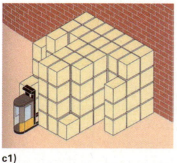

c1)

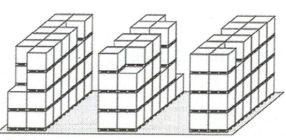

c2)

Figure 10.8   Stacking methods for floor storage

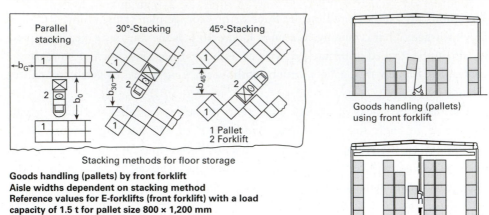

Stacking methods for floor storage

Goods handling (pallets) by front forklift
Aisle widths dependent on stacking method
Reference values for E-forklifts (front forklift) with a load
capacity of 1.5 t for pallet size 800 × 1,200 mm
Normal aisle width b_G ≈ 1,950 mm
Aisle width for parallel stacking b_0 ≈ 3,250 mm
Aisle width for 30° stacking b30 ≈ 2,400 mm
Aisle width for 45° stacking b45 ≈ 1,900 mm

the storage goods (see Figure 6.36a to d), such as roller or cardboard clamps. For storage goods with floor clearance, self-supporting and wheel-supported forklifts can be used.

Advantages of floor storage are flexible storage space, no shelving costs and the fact that it is a modest investment. *Disadvantages* include: usually hard to mechanize; limited stacking height; only the top layer can be removed; a lot of restacking for non-separate goods, as there is no direct access to the individual load units, such as DIN pallets.

Floor storage is used as a unit warehouse (reserve/buffer warehouse) in stacked form with a high degree of area and room usage. Block stacking is used for storing large amounts of the same item without FIFO fulfilment. The required area and height are only used 100 per cent for storage of a single item. For a small range, such as the storing of 500 pallets with 15 items, the degree of height usage (stacking factor) is around 80 per cent and the degree of area usage (area factor) around 75 per cent.

10.3 Shelf storage

The categorization of shelving types can be as line or compact storage in line with Figure 10.5a. Both methods have a lot of different designs. Line storage is characterized by the access to each item or each unit at a time without restacking (see Chapter 10.3.1). For compact storage, the units are stored behind each other and on top of each other in a shelving rack. Access to one item is not necessarily possible. Compact storage is used both for items with high quantities per storage unit (continuous shelf), as well as for many items with small quantity per storage unit (roller cart shelf). Significant restacking occurs when order picking. Line and compact storage are used for both unit and order picking warehouses (see Chapter 10.3.3).

Both types of shelf storage method can also be combined, which results in shelving types that use line storage depending on the required activities, such as opening an aisle for a transfer shelf (see Chapter 10.3.2).

The labelling of shelving types is based on the type of goods or storage aid, the shape or construction method, or the movement from shelf and storage unit. Only once the individual shelving type is more closely observed is it possible to distinguish between the many sub-categories.

10.3.1 Shelving types for line storage

Access to the storage goods is possible at any time, without restacking.

10.3.1.1 Shelving rack

- *Structural build*: It consists of a basic and extension shelf with supports between (square posts, corner pieces, H-bars). The shelves (steel sheets: lacquered, galvanized, or plastic: coated) are set on strengthening elements and there may be accessories, such as back, side or separating walls, as well as front panels. Designs include screw-in or stacking shelves, shelf depth: 0.4 to 0.6 m; shelf width: 1 m; shelving height: 2 m; bay load capacity: up to 1.5 t; shelf load: up to 330 kg, height adjustable shelves at a 25 mm distance.

  Advantages: low investment; simple and quick assembly for stacking shelves; manual storing and removal.

  Disadvantages: limited removal at top and bottom of shelf (distances and bridges); large traffic area proportion (for more on the degree of area usage 45°, see Chapter 9.7). For small and medium-sized parts with or without light boxes, as an order picking warehouse in drawers for small and tiny parts with fixed storage place allocation, such as a parts warehouse, tool and model warehouse, assembly warehouse or production warehouse.

Design types:

- manual and shelving rack (see Figure 3.3b);
- wide-span shelving rack: shelf width 1.5–2.5 m; shelf depth 500–800 mm;
- two-floor shelving rack (Figure 10.9) approximately 4 m high with stairs and mesh;

Figure 10.9 Two-floor shelving rack (www.ssi-schaefer.de)

Figure 10.10 High shelving rack with storage and retrieval device as order picking warehouse (www.ssi-schaefer.com)

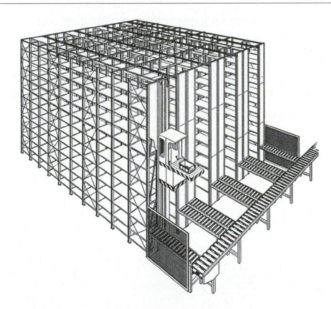

- high shelving rack up to 12 m high (see Figure 10.10); operation: manual storing and removal using a storage and retrieval device for order picking. For a whole unit of crates, boxes or small containers, also automatic operation with storage and retrieval device (see Figure 11.22).

Advantages include: good access to each item; relatively good overview; shelving rack: low investment and manual operation:

- *Large shelving rack* made of steel with wood, steel or mesh shelves for storing steel plates, press boards, carpet, fabric and art tolls on pallets and loading frames; for different sized storage aids, usually as a unit warehouse; operation using forklifts.

- *Drawer system* is a clipboard rack with telescopically extendable floor.

10.3.1.2 Pallet shelf, container shelf

Structural construction – we distinguish:

- Pallet shelf in *one-space design*: The shelf stands (point capacity, see Chapter 6.6.7.5) are a pallet width apart and contain angle profile in shelf depth direction for the intake of load units: *crossways* storage of pallets (see Figures 10.11a, 10.12a and c), support column distance level of shelf depth for pool pallets approximately 800 mm.

- Pallet shelf in multiple space design: Shelf stands are far apart and are connected through support beams (traverses). Up to five pallets can be stored next to each other on the support beams: lengthways storage (Figures 10.11b and 10.12b). For crossways storage of the pallets or for storing containers (feet), support brackets are required (poor use of space). Support column distance at depth level for pool pallet 1,100 mm (for more on names/cross section representation, see Figure 11.41).

Shelf compartment heights are variable through whole profiles in the support stands. Safety clamps prevent unintentional unlinking of the support beam through the forklift. Shelves are available in galvanized or lacquered design. For storing containers in a multiple space system, support brackets are required (Figure 10.11b).

Utilization: prevalent storage method of small and large quantities of pallets per item and wide range.

Single space design usually as order picking warehouse with fixed storage space allocation.

Multiple space design usually as unit warehouse with free storage space selection.

Operation: depending on shelf height – with forklift types, with storage and retrieval devices as well as stacking crane. High shelf warehouses can be operated up to 13 m in height with a high shelf forklift. Fully automated storage and retrieval with storage and a device of up to 50 m in height.

Advantages: good access to each item; good utilization of height; pressure free storage of goods; rational construction; good degree of area utilization with track-led storage and retrieval device.

Figure 10.11   Pallet shelves

a) Single space design operation with storage and retrieval device (www.bito.com)

b) Multiple space design operated by forklift (www.ssi-schaefer.com)

Disadvantages: dependent on certain storage aids, such as a pallet; degree of area utilization about 40 to 65 per cent (aisle width depending on storage and retrieval device as well as location and dimension of load unit); poor utilization of space (Figure 10.12); lost height for pallet unit made up of: set manipulation height 100 mm, support beam 100 to 200 mm, pallet height 150 mm equals approximately 250 to 400 mm of lost height, multiplied with pallet area approximately 1 m^2 equals 0.35 to 0.45 m^3 in lost volume; FIFO only possible through organization; same shelf compartment heights for multiple pallets; floor anchor required, if height and width of shelf exceed ratio 4:1 (double shelves better than single shelves); impact protection, corner deflector for forklift operation and push through stops required for single shelves; support bracket for crossways storage of pallets, mesh boxes or mesh grills for pallets with variable dimension; barrel support for barrels with drip tray.

Designs: in buildings up to 7.5 m high (Figure 9.4): shelf rack installation; above 7.5 m high: pallet shelves in high shelf or high space warehouse (sprinklers usually required). Special shelves: storage silo: only for large quantities of pallet units for which shelves have roof and side panels, in steel or steel concrete construction, maximum height up to 45 m; pallet shelving (large shelving rack) made of wood, sheet metal or mesh for simultaneous storage of different pallets (for more on cost per pallet space, see Example 11.21).

Figure 10.12   Calculation sketch for space utilization pallet and tray shelves

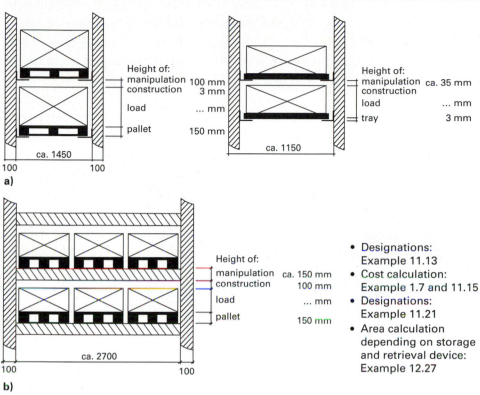

Pallet shelf:
a) Single space system, crossways storage, shelf depth DIN pallet 0.9 m
b) Multiple space system, lengthways storage for DIN pallet 800 × 1,200 1.3 m; designations, see Figure 11.41
c) Tray shelf, extendable tray (900 × 650 mm); crossways storage

10.3.1.3 Shelving for long goods

For definitions of long goods, see Chapter 3.1.3; for systematics see Example 11.32.

Cantilever shelves   These consist of a middle support column and floor bars, as well as the one-side or two-side cantilevers. These supports are set up at a certain distance to one another and connected using diagonal bars. Cantilevers can be height adjustable or have special designs, such as a telescopic cantilever. The long goods (also sheet metal and panels) can be placed on the cantilever individually or in bundles in a long goods trough, pallet or cassette. Up to 200 t are possible per shelf support (Figure 10.13 a/b). Operation is manual, mechanized with four-way forklift or automatic using a portal crane over the sides.

Cantilever or high cantilever shelves are used for long goods as well as hanging storage units, such as motor blocks, coils or paper rolls. Operation is mechanic with four-way forklift (see Figure 11.26), or automatic with storage and retrieval device. *Advantages*: clear and professional storage, usually 4 to 6 m long; one- or two-sided design, and combination: one-sided sheet metal. *Disadvantages*: oddments can only be stored in a long goods trough or standing up in partial storage.

Stacking cradle shelves   Long goods can be located next to and on top of each other in cradles, which do not allow for direct access, so that restacking is necessary. They have good space utilization, and use uncomplicated storage technology, and are suitable for long goods with modest turnover. Special traverses are allowed for simultaneous transport of multiple cradles. Crane operation.

Honeycomb shelves   For a small to large range of long goods, whereby the long good is stored in cassettes in the chambers. For small quantities per item, individual storage is often used. Operation is at the front, implemented by storage and retrieval devices. For large range and high turnover, automatic storage and retrieval for opposing arrangement of two shelves is sensible (see Figure 11.25). To 15 m high shelving, up to 3 t per cassette.

Advantages: compact storage; for small storage quantities installation of a storage platform is possible; high degree of utilization of space and area for opposing arrangement; optimization of turnover through two adjacent extraction roller conveyors.

Disadvantages: a large manipulation and operating area is required in front of shelves; awkward operation via travelling crane for heavy profile, when turnover is low.

Standing shelves   When long goods are leaning at an angle on a shelf that is made up of several individual stands, connected through diagonal bars (Figure 10.13c; Figure 11.44a).

Advantages: little space requirement. *Disadvantages*: only suitable for small storage quantity and low weights.

10.3.1.4 Special shelves

Depending on the shape, dimensions and weight of the storage goods, existing shelves are usually converted, or shelves are used that are specially constructed for the particular storage goods, eg converted pallet shelves for cable drums or cantilever shelves for coils (Figure 10.13d).

Figure 10.13   Cantilever and standing shelves

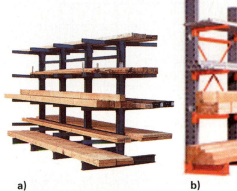

a)   b)   c)

a) Double-sided cantilever shelves (www.ohra.de)
b) One-sided cantilever shelving (www.galler.de)
c) Cantilever shelves for coils, crane operations using
   a c-hook (www.ohra.de)
d) Standing shelves (www.ohra.de)

d)

10.3.2 Shelving types for line/compact storage

After the transport process, access to storage unit without restacking at all times.

10.3.2.1 Mobile shelving

Structural construction: when addressing structural construction, we distinguish between the following (Figure 10.14):

- extractable shelf (lengthways): extraction cabinet;
- parallel mobile shelf: mobile rack.

Figure 10.14   Mobile shelving principle

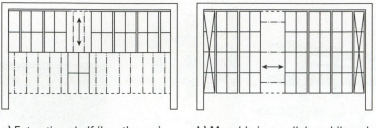

a) Extraction shelf (lengthways)   **b)** Movable in parallel: mobile rack

The extraction cabinet is made up of shelving units arranged side by side – usually shelving racks – which can be pulled out and operated from both sides (Figure 10.15a).

Use: for small tools, press moulds and pharmaceutical goods.

Advantages: good area and space utilization. *Disadvantages*: only for small quantities, blocked when storing/retrieving.

Mobile shelving (Figure 10.15b) consists of mobile undercarriages, on which all shelving types, such as racks, pallet or cantilever shelving, can be installed as double shelving. The undercarriage moves with rollers on tracks on the floor or the wall (see Figure 11.51). The individual carriages with their shelving can be moved closer to each other. Depending on size and load capacity of a shelving carriage, either a manual (transmission, rotary drive) or a motor-driven (single or group drive) drive is used, which is up to approximately 8 m high (ratio of shelving height to width 4:1).

Usually, 8 to 10 shelving units are furnished with one operating aisle. The outsides create fixed single shelves. Speed for single operation is 0.06 to 0.08 m/s, for group operation (with magnetic clutch) 0.15 m/s. Safety equipment in the shape of limit switch bars on the mobile shelves switch off drive immediately when touched. Selector switches for opening the aisle increase time of access. Operation of mobile shelving: for small shelves manually with forklifts, automatically with stacker crane (Figure 10.16).

Use: for B and C products, when operating aisles are only modestly utilized, also for models, tools, equipment, books, files; as procurement warehouse for raw materials, such as long goods and sheet metal for cooler storage.

Advantages: high degree of area utilization; good space utilization (Figure 10.17). *Disadvantages:* low storage and retrieval frequencies; high investment; difficulties for retrospective installation, as shelf heights are increased by the height of the tracks (this is not the case when tracks are wall-mounted).

Figure 10.15 Mobile shelving

Figure 10.15 Mobile shelving

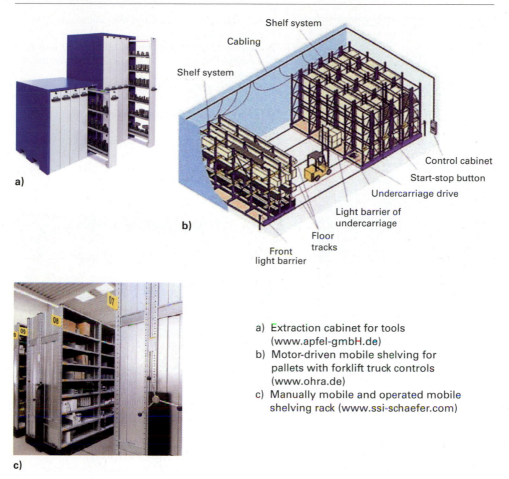

a) Extraction cabinet for tools
(www.apfel-gmbH.de)
b) Motor-driven mobile shelving for
pallets with forklift truck controls
(www.ohra.de)
c) Manually mobile and operated mobile
shelving rack (www.ssi-schaefer.com)

10.3.2.2 Circulating shelving

Structural construction: when discussing circulating shelving, we must distinguish between the following:

- vertical circulating shelves: paternoster shelving;

- horizontal circulating shelves: carousel shelving;

- combined circulating shelves: levelled or snake paternoster shelving.

Paternoster shelving   Paternoster shelving is made up of two parallel, continuously circulating chains, connected through bars. Depending on the goods, load-handling attachments are used such as gondolas, compartments, cassettes or drawers. In order to have the quickest possible access, the paternoster shelving (Figures 10.18 and 10.19)

Figure 10.16   Automated mobile shelving with stacker crane operation

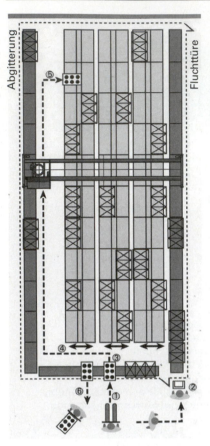

1 Storage pallet transported to transfer site with pallet truck
2 Pallet data entered manually using keyboard or a manual scanner in warehousing management system
3 Stacker crane picks up pallet after profile check for storage
4 Mobile shelf opens simultaneously with pallet intake
5 Stacker crane drives into open aisle and transfers pallet at the storage space
6 Retrieval happens in the opposite direction from storage (www.kardex-mlog.com)

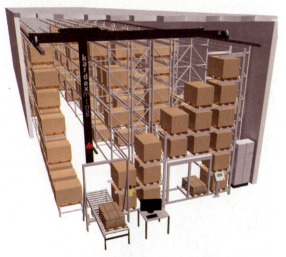

a) Layout for automated mobile shelving with three double shelves

b) Built-in mobile shelving in a building with goods receipt and goods issue sites

Figure 10.17   Area comparison: pallet shelving – mobile shelving

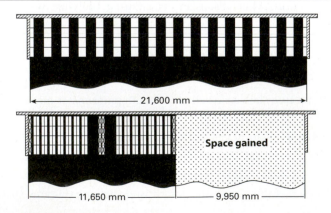

Figure 10.18 Paternoster shelving: principal representation

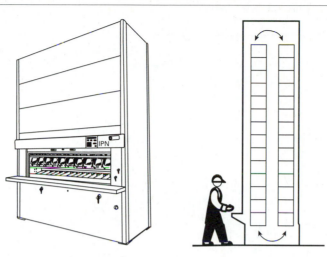

Figure 10.19 Order picking from paternoster shelving (www.haenel.com)

is reversible and can be controlled by selection (shelving height up to 12 m; width: 2.25 to 4.5 m; depth: 1.3 to 1.8 m; usable depth compartment: 400 to 600 mm; load per shelving unit up to 23 t, 600 kg per shelf). Unloading safety is achieved through overload protection and prevents one-sided overloading. If the paternoster stands over multiple levels, a storage space can only be installed on one side per level (fire protection requirement due to chimney effect).

Operation: manually with the right work height and ergonomically correct as well as fully automated, such as for entering an order picking assignment using a

Figure 10.20   Automated paternoster set up with order picking site: good to man principle (www.haenel.de)

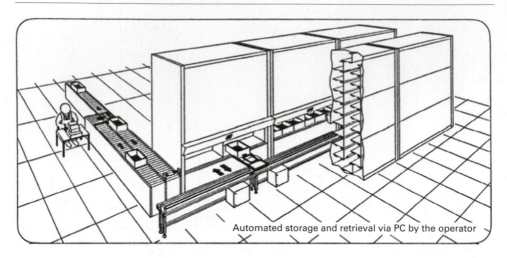

Automated storage and retrieval via PC by the operator

barcode, automatic successive delivery of items with route minimization (comprehensive management options with storage management system or ERP systems), manual retrieval and confirmation. Fully automated storage and retrieval of storage crates for dynamic provisioning at an order picking site is shown in Figure 10.20.

Use: for B and C products; widespread as order picking warehouse for small material such as tools, equipment, assembly material, lever arch files etc as procurement, production and distribution warehouse as well as in offices; as unit warehouse with fixed storage space allocation for automatic storage and retrieval.

Advantages: dynamic provisioning: goods delivered to staff at grab height and, thus, less time; low space requirements; high area and space utilization; theft proof; protected from dirt; search aids through positioning bar on work surface; integration in work processes; quick access; can be automated. *Disadvantages:* high investment; no direct access to all stored goods; certain waiting times for retrieval process; load handling attachments (Figure 10.23); all stored goods are continuously moved; energy requirements; slow circulating speed of approximately 0.16 m/s; costs: 3.5 × 1.5 × 4 m (w × d × h) with 25 trays approximately €35,000.

Multi-level and snake paternoster shelving (Figures 10.21 and 10.22)   Variable designs in vertical, horizontal and combined construction for bulky loads, long goods, cable drums, cylinders, barrels, rollers etc. Utilization of room height, savings in floor space, flexible adjustment of load carrier to storage good (see Figure 10.23). Circulating speed up to 12 m/min, load capacity of load carrier up to 3.5 t. Filling and retrieval possible at multiple sites.

Figure 10.21 Multi-level paternoster (www.hubtex.de)

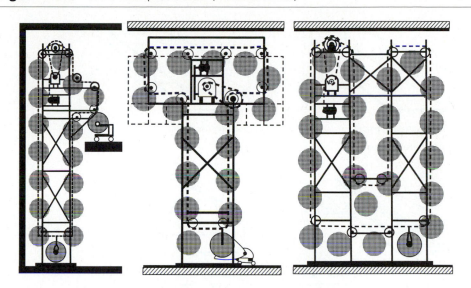

Figure 10.22 Snake paternoster: line layout (www.hubtex.de)

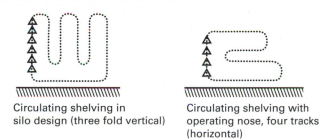

Circulating shelving in
silo design (three fold vertical)

Circulating shelving with
operating nose, four tracks
(horizontal)

Carousel shelving is built as a horizontal circular conveyor, whose hangers are shelf compartments, and are guided on floor tracks. Its operation takes part in a defined location, so that dynamic provisioning can occur as with the paternoster shelving (Figure 10.24a). High performance carousels are shown in Example 11.12 and Figure 10.24b.

Used for B and C products as order picking warehouse in low spaces with high turnover and paperless order picking. By combining multiple shelves, waiting times can be reduced to a minimum (Figure 10.25).

Management can occur manually with buttons for start and stop, turnover performance of up to 120 order items per person and hour. By using a control panel and partly automated management, turnover performance can increase to 180 items per person, per hour. By using IT-supported management and display devices, as well as paperless order picking (see Chapter 11.2) the turnover performance can be increased to 300 items per person, per hour. In high rooms, it is possible to construct carousel shelves up to 7 m in height.

Figure 10.23 Designs of load handling attachments (www.schwab.de)

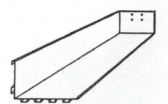

Carrier with floor, empty

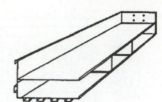

Double carrier with floor, empty

a) For paternoster

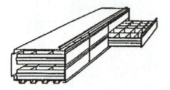

Carrier with three rows, drawers adjacent, 1–3
drawers on top of each other per row

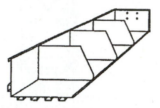

Carrier with variable separating panels,
15 : 15 mm adjustable

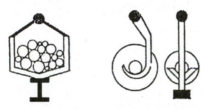 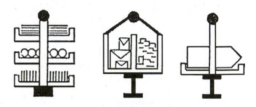

b) For multi-level and snake paternoster

Figure 10.24 Carousel shelves

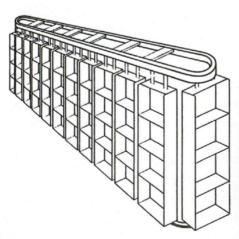

a) Principal sketch

b) Carousel shelves protection against
contamination with window components
(www.dematic.com)

Figure 10.25   Possible arrangement of carousel shelves (top view) (www.dexion.de)

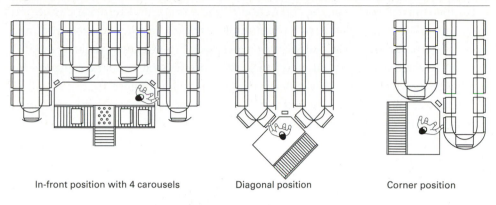

In-front position with 4 carousels   Diagonal position   Corner position

Figure 10.26   Schematic representation of a double-depth pallet shelf

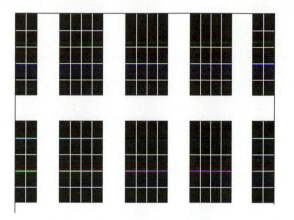

10.3.2.3 Double depth pallet shelving

The structure is represented schematically in Figure 10.26. These are pallet shelves in a multiple space system, in which two pallets are always stored behind and three next to each other. Storage and retrieval devices are required for operation, equipped with telescopic forks. The manipulation height can be increased through greater fork deflection.

This type of shelving is particularly suited for an item range with a larger quantity of pallets per item and for expensive storage space, such as cooling warehouses.

For a simple pallet shelf, an increased storage capacity of 30 per cent is the result.

10.3.2.4 Tower shelving

A tower shelf (also called lift, shuttle or vertical shelf) has the following structure: two opposing single shelves are constructed in line with single space design. The operation (storage and retrieval of trays) is carried out by a vertical moving lift (extractor with a chain, rope or tooth-racked hoist) between the shelves using a pulling technique. There are devices with a feed and discharge location, which guarantee the transfer conveyor the connection to the storage and retrieval device, but there are also devices which can have multiple retrieval instances on the front and back. The storage aid is a self-supporting tray/cassette (up to approximately 4,050 × 864 mm), which rests in the support brackets in the shelving unit, and is pushed for storage or retrieval. The trays can be arranged as required (Figure 10.27).

The tower shelf works fully automated, for storage, the height of the load unit (item) is scanned and a suitable storage space is selected. The storage process can be time and space optimized (item-to-man principle). The controls can be operated optically or language-based. Economic deployment occurs from approximately 6 m in height.

Features:

- short access times; high compartment utilization, especially through adjusting compartment height to stored tray (Figure 10.27c);

- high area and space utilization;

- shelving height up to 10 (35) m, modular structure;

- stored good is only moved during storage and retrieval processes;

Figure 10.27a   Tower shelf with preventative fire protection (N_2) (www.kardex-remstar. de; www.wagner.de)

Figure 10.27b   Storage and retrieval opening (www.haenel.de)

Figure 10.27c   Comparison of storage compartments with same height and adjusted in height to storage unit; top: carrier for intake of gliding trays (www.megamat.com)

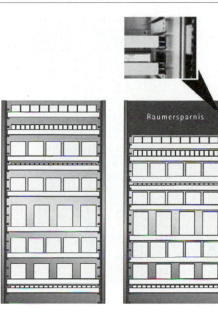

Figure 10.27d   Three-dimensional tower shelf with two openings for goods receipt/issue (www.kardex-mlog.com)

Figure 10.27e   Automated tower shelf for sheet metal (www.kasto.com) 1 Chain lift for shelf operation, 2 Shelf block, 3 Pallets, 4 Storage and retrieval station, 5 Protective equipment, 6 Controls

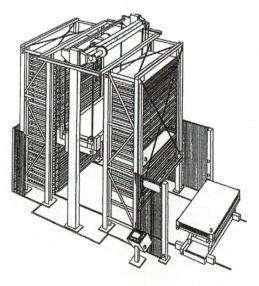

Figure 10.27f   Tower shelf for sheet metal with sideways storage/retrieval operated using a vacuum lift or forklift (www.largerlogistik.ch)

Figure 10.27g   Different storage and retrieval arrangements for tower shelves (www.kasto.com)

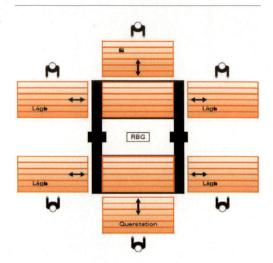

- protection against dust, contamination and theft;
- computer-controlled storage and retrieval, as well as programmed provisioning; integration to host, simple control via touchscreen;
- simple transfer to continuous conveyor;
- fixed storage space or free storage space selection;
- limited number of cycles: tray speed up to 2.2 m/s, individually adjustable;
- load up to 700 kg per tray and 70 t per machine;
- costs including freight and assembly for machine with outside dimensions 3 × 2.5 × 6.5 m (W × D × H) approximately €65,000.

Deployment possibilities: for tools, assembly and manufacturing parts; usually used as order picking warehouse.

A further development is the three-dimensional tower shelf (Figure 10.27d), a combination of two to five tower shelves. Operation occurs using a horizontally moving truck, which is installed onto a lift. The big advantage is the high storage capacity and the two openings, so that order picking and storage/retrieval can happen simultaneously, of which the order picker can work at both openings without loss of time.

An automated version of the tower shelf for sheet metal is shown in Figure 10.27e. Deployed for a punching machine or nibbling machine for buffering unprocessed and processed sheets.

10.3.3 Shelving types: compact storage

Load units or pallets can only be retrieved by restacking. Shelving types with multiple storage units behind or on top of one another are often called channel racking (Figure 10.5).

10.3.3.1 Drive-in shelves, drive-through shelves

Structural construction: a pallet shelf in single design construction with multiple storage spaces behind, next to and on top of one another. A drive-in shelf is a type of shelving that is only accessible from one side, and a drive-through shelf for operation from both sides. The operating device is a forklift, which must lift the load to a certain height before driving into the aisle (Figure 10.28) and for long channels is guided on tracks. This should not be confused with a push-back shelf (Figure 11.48).

Use: for non-stackable goods with modest turnover (B and C products) and large quantities per item and a modest range, such as seasonal items, eg camping equipment or plastic granules in bags or pallets. Usually channels are single origin.

Advantages: high area and space utilization (approximately 70 per cent). *Disadvantages:* no FIFO, but LIFO (see Chapter 9.7); storage and retrieval not entirely simple; compartments in one level have same height; individual drive-in channels not optimally used, such as due to single origin storage maximum of 80 per cent utilization of channels.

Figure 10.28a Drive-in shelf; forklift drives into storage channel; channel stocked from the back to the front (www.bito.com)

Figure 10.28b Drive-through shelf: shelves can be used from both sides (www.jungheinrich.de)

Figure 10.29   Pallet flow-through shelf (gravity drive) (www.ssi-schaefer.com)

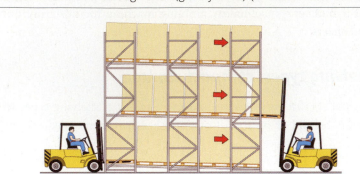

10.3.3.2 Flow-through shelving, slide-through shelving

Structural construction:

- small container flow-through shelves;
- pallet flow-through shelf;
- slide-through shelf.

The basic principle is a compact shelf block made up of channels lying next to and on top of each other. The flow-through shelf is filled from one side with small containers or pallets, and units are retrieved from the other side. The channels are equipped with carrier rollers (see Figure 5.36), are tilted by 3 to 8° (the goods run through the channels automatically through gravity), or are equipped with a horizontal single drive.

Designs, advantages and disadvantages

- *Small container flow-through shelving*

A small container flow-through shelving consists of a compact shelf with small dimensions for a large range of small parts, with high turnover as order picking warehouse, such as in mail order businesses. Depending on the weight of the container unit, it can have plastic rolls, steel rolls, rolls with side bearing and flange.

Advantages: simple shelf; low investment for manual operation; gravity drive; little space requirement; FIFO principle necessary; large item diversity in tight space; separation of storage and retrieval. *Disadvantages*: single origin channels are only filled partially; storage space utilization < 80 per cent; crates collide with each other when stored.

Designs: they are designed as manually-operated shelves (see Figure 9.3), but also contain automated storage and retrieval for relevant size; sometimes they can be moved manually.

- *Pallet flow-through shelf*

The front of a channel cross section of a pallet unit approximately 2 m² for load unit of 1.8 m. This means it is only suitable to be deployed for a *small range* with *high turnover* and a *large quantity of pallets per item*.

Designs for pallets: gravity pallet flow-through shelf (heavy goods roller conveyor); horizontal pallet flow-through shelf (accumulating roller conveyor). *Designs for roller pallets*: gravity flow-through shelving (tacks for roller pallets).

- *Gravity flow-through shelf for pallets*

Equipment and separation devices on retrieval side, deceleration of storage pallets through centrifugal brake rolls, eddy current brakes or, usually, through motoric drive of carrier roller in order to move storage goods at a steady pace of 0.07 to 0.2 m/s over the carrier rollers. Channel length up to 40 m.

Advantages: FIFO necessary; separation of storage and retrieval; good overview; easy stocktake; access to each item on retrieval side; high degree of area utilization; mechanical or fully automated operation with forklifts or storage and retrieval devices; storage and retrieval device with tilting powered roller conveyor as load handling device; low energy use; storage space utilization less than 80 per cent. *Disadvantages*: volume loss through tilt corresponds to one pallet level; high investment; requires perfect pallets; brakes and separating function.

Operation: dependent on degree of automation, often different storage and retrieval devices.

- *Slide-through shelving*

Flow-through shelf without carrier rollers, equipped with sliding sheets for cardboard boxes, packages; gravity transport through tilting of sheets greater than 35° for only few units after one another; good value for money and can be found in mail order businesses.

10.3.3.3 Push-back shelving

A push-back shelf is a gravity flow-through shelf with only one storage and retrieval location per channel at the front (see Example 11.27). Storage occurs in line with LIFO principle. The channels are equipped with slightly tilted roller tracks so that the forklift has to press the pallet against the incline and the stored pallets. Usually two to four pallets one after the other.

Advantages: compact storage; only one operating aisle; space saving; good value for money; all items are at front of shelf. Used only for a small amount of pallets, (such as buffer warehouse in goods receipt/goods issue) to maintain short loading and unloading times for lorries.

10.3.3.4 Satellite shelving

A storage and retrieval device requires two to three minutes on average per single cycle for storing or retrieving a unit in a high pallet shelf. In order to increase the number of pallets per hour, and to achieve an even higher degree of space utilization, satellite and roller cart shelves were developed.

High utilization of space is achieved through storing up to 10 pallets behind each other by reducing aisles. Larger turnover is achieved through exchanging the storage and retrieval device with track-led distribution trucks on each storage level. The vertical motion occurs with one or more lifts. The distribution truck has a satellite vehicle, which drives into the storage channels under the pallet, lifting it and transporting it back to the distribution truck. The satellite vehicle is connected to the distribution truck with a trailing cable. This type of shelving can easily be expanded. There are three designs:

Single space storage   Pallets can be stored without restacking (line storage). This is achieved by satellite tracks between the pallets in low degree of space utilization. Figure 10.30a: The storage and retrieval machine moves down the connecting shelf aisle and positions itself in front of the connecting aisle. The satellite vehicle

Figure 10.30   Satellite shelving (www.westfaliaEurope.com) a) Single space storage: layout of a satellite shelf; satellite with telescopic fork, drives into connecting aisle to take on a pallet b) Compact storage: satellite shelf with 6 pallets behind one another, and with storage and retrieval operation

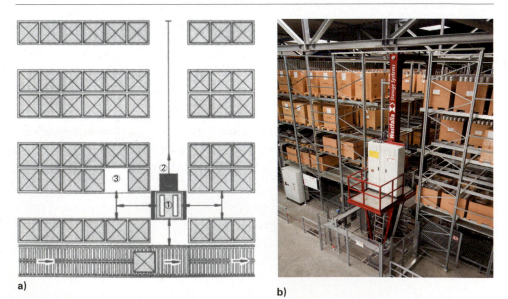

a)

b)

(1) is equipped with a telescopic fork, moves away from the storage and retrieval device and positions itself in front of the single space (3). Storage and retrieval occurs using the telescopic fork. Turnover performance: 50 to 60 pallets per hour. Area utilization as pallet shelving.

Compact storage with storage and retrieval device   A storage and retrieval device drives into the shelf aisle (Figure 10.30b), is equipped with a satellite vehicle and operates five levels. Once positioned in front of a channel the satellite vehicle moves away from the storage and retrieval device, drives in a channel, under the pallet and achieves storage/retrieval by lifting it. In order to get to pallet '3', the pallets in front '1' and '2' have to be moved. Turnover performance is up to 70 pallets/h. The speed of the storage and retrieval device and satellite vehicle are 200 m per minute or 60 m per minute. High area and space utilization as well as simple pre-storage zones are features of this warehouse. Pallets are built up in the storage channel from back to front. Empty spaces are on the inside of the channel front. The work process is similar to a drive-shelf.

Compact storage with transfer truck (shuttle system)   The storage and retrieval device is replaced on each storage level with a distribution (transfer) truck (shuttle) (Figure 10.31), which is equipped with a satellite vehicle. Vertical transport occurs with lift and high turnover performance: 70 pallets/h × number of levels. Satellite vehicles also suggest quite high costs. The storage space is allocated at the back of the transport channel, with empty spaces at the front. One lift per storage and retrieval pallet.

Figure 10.31   Satellite and roller cart shelving (level structure) a) Principal sketch of satellite shelving with distribution truck and integrated lift b) Principal sketch of roller cart shelf, satellite with connected roller panels

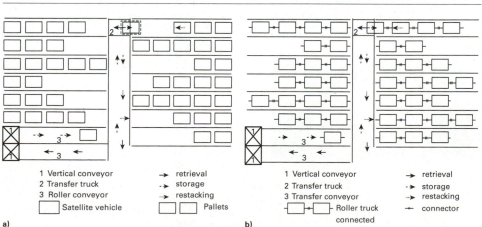

1 Vertical conveyor	→ retrieval
2 Transfer truck	-→ storage
3 Roller conveyor	⇢ restacking
▫ Satellite vehicle	▫▫ Pallets

a)

1 Vertical conveyor	→ retrieval
2 Transfer truck	-→ storage
3 Transfer conveyor	⇢ restacking
⊢▫⊣ Roller truck connected	⊶ connector

b)

10.3.3.5 Roller cart shelving

The roller cart shelf (Figure 10.31) allows for block allocation, with the storing and retrieving occurring without a satellite vehicle. The pallets are roller pallets, are placed on roller carts or are mobile loading frames with fixed castors and run on tracks in the storage channel. Each storage level is served by a transfer truck. The connection technology of up to 10 individually hung units is the deciding factor. The connection is energy saving, using a horizontal insertion technique. The roller cart always stands at the front of the channel, the empty spaces in the back, which results in shorter turnover times. The difference in structure and method of the roller cart and satellite shelf with distribution truck is compared in a simplified schematic way in Figure 10.31.

Advantages: high turnover frequency; high degree of space utilization; quick access times. *Disadvantages*: restacking when aisles are not of single origin or to maintain FIFO principle; roller frame required for DIN pallets (additional roller cart handling: returns and storage); connection technology; LIFO.

10.3.3.6 Satellite shelf with forklift operation

See Example 11.26.

Figure 10.32a/b   (www.westfalia-Europe.com)

b)

a) Distribution truck with satellite in a satellite
    shelf, driving on one level
b) Three levels with distribution truck

a)

10.4 Means of transport for storage and retrieval

In order to achieve storage of goods for floor and shelf storage, the goods must be transported to the storage site. This is done with discontinuous conveyors, which carry out the storage and retrieval in unit warehouses and the filling of an order picking warehouse with units. Storage and retrieval devices are components of a storage system (Figure 10.6). These can be storage and retrieval devices or forklifts, carrying out additional tasks, such as supplying and taking away the storage unit, or manipulations in goods receipt or issue. Figure 10.33 summarizes the possible discontinuous conveyors for storage and retrieval in a unit warehouse.

10.4.1 Cranes

Cranes used for storage and retrieval are basically:

- *bridge* and *hanging crane* for operation floor storage, such as long goods, or with special load handling attachments for pallets (automated crane). C-hooks only for occasional pallet transport (see Chapter 6.4 and Figure 6.66a and b);

- *mobile crane* for activities in outdoor warehouses;

- *portal crane* and portal stacker: see Chapter 6.4.3, as well as Figures 7.10a and 7.17;

- *stacker crane*: see Figures 6.20, 10.8: floor storage of mesh box pallets with stacker crane operation.

Figure 10.33 Means of transport for storage and retrieval in a unit warehouse

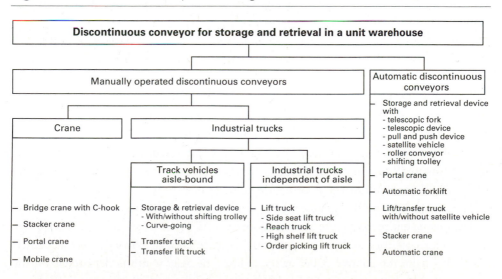

10.4.2 Track-bound industrial trucks

In the pre-storage zone, transfer and transfer lift trucks are used for transport and lifting but also for storage in satellite and roller cart shelves: see Figure 6.22.

For work in the shelf aisle for storing and retrieving in the unit or order picking warehouse, the aisle dependent, track-bound storage and retrieval device is used. It is made up of drive frame (floor traverse), column, lift truck, chassis, hoist, load handling attachment and controls. Depending on the design of the device, these can be equipped with or without a cabin (usually only an emergency platform). Storage and retrieval devices are track-guided on the floor, rarely on shelving units, and get support from the shelves. They are used for manual or automated storage and retrieval of load units into or from storage areas.

A categorization of storage and retrieval devices can be done based on a number of aspects:

- manually operated storage and retrieval devices for order picking tasks: 'man to item';

- manual or automated storage and retrieval devices for loading units: for order picking of entire load units or provisioning based on principle 'item to man';

- automated storage and retrieval device for small part storage based on principle 'item to man'.

We also distinguish between one- and two-column devices with builds of up to 45 m.

The energy supply for the drive, lift and load handling motor mainly occurs via conductor lines (see Chapter 4.5.4.3). Drive and lift movements always overlap.

For fully automated devices, data transmission to the device from warehousing administration and material flow computers occurs on straight routes optically using data transmission light barriers, such as infrared, slotted hollow conductors on an inductive basis or radio data.

Depending on the type of device, such as automated small parts warehouse and an aisle length up to 30 m, a cable connection can be used for data and energy transmission.

The route measurement happens absolutely with angle encoders or with laser distance measurement devices. According to the ruling standards (DIN EN 528 storage and retrieval devices safety) 'people must be protected from risk of injury as a result of moving devices, through limiting access to the work area'. This means the aisles of manual and automated storage and retrieval devices have to generally be secured against unauthorized access with suitable measures.

The *manual and automated storage and retrieval device* (Figure 10.34) for storing and retrieving entire load units, such as goods on pallets or in containers, is equipped with a telescopic fork and is (automatically or manually, or partially automatically) controlled from the control panel in the cabin. The aisle width is dependent on the

Figure 10.34 Storage and retrieval devices (www.dematic.de) a) One-column and
two-column storage and retrieval devices for units and order picking
warehouse b) Pre-storage zone of a pallet warehouse with storage and
retrieval device operation

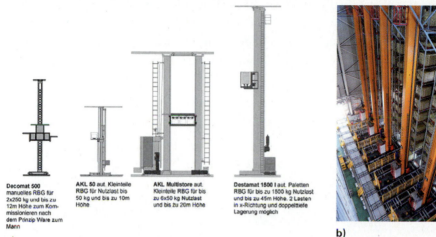

Decomat 500
manuelles RBG für
2x250 kg und bis zu
12m Höhe zum Kom-
missionieren nach
dem Prinzip Ware zum
Mann

AKL 50 aut. Kleinteile
RBG für Nutzlast bis
50 kg und bis zu 10m
Höhe

AKL Multistore aut.
Kleinteile RBG für bis
zu 6x50 kg Nutzlast
und bis zu 20m Höhe

Destamat 1500 l aut. Paletten
RBG für bis zu 1500 kg Nutzlast
und bis zu 45m Höhe. 2 Lasten
in x-Richtung und doppelttiefe
Lagerung möglich

a)

b)

dimensions of the loading aids and their location to the driving direction of the storage
and retrieval device. For lengthwise storage of a Euro pallet the aisle width is approximately 1.5 m. The load weighs up to 1,500 kg, has a speed of up to 140 m/min and
an acceleration up to 0.5 m/s^2. Load handling attachments are for single and double
depth storage, such as a telescopic fork and table, whereas the satellite is for storage
of multiple depth. The working method is either single or double cycle. For safety, the
operating aisles have to be barred. A basic prerequisite for a smooth operation is a high
quality of pallets as well as uniformity and dimensional tolerance of pallet and load.

Storage and retrieval devices (SRD) used as *manually operated order picking
devices* can be equipped with a variety of load handling attachments, such as fixed
load table, roller track, roller table and fixed fork, which can usually take up to
500 kg of load. To facilitate order picking activities, the load handling attachment
can carry out lift and lowering movements itself. The design of an open cabin is
based on ergonomic aspects and can be equipped with an order picking platform.
Operation of the storage and retrieval device is done manually from the control
panel in the cabin (two-handed operation). The height of the device is usually 12 to
16 m (see Figure 10.10).

Automated storage and retrieval device for small part warehousing; see Chapter 11.6.

Shifting and curve-going storage and retrieval device Usually only one storage
and retrieval device works in one aisle and is thus fully utilized. In cases of low
goods turnover, a storage and retrieval device can also work multiple aisles. There

are two possibilities: the device drives onto a shifting truck, perpendicular to the aisle (transfer truck: Figure 10.35), which takes it to the required aisle, or it can reach the aisle itself using the tracks as curve-going storage and retrieval device (Figure 10.36; see Chapter 6.5.2). The heights of shifting and curve-going storage and retrieval devices usually go up to 30 m. The driving and lifting speeds depend on the cargo, lifting height and turnover performance. Driving speeds can be up to 200 m/min, lifting speeds go up to 63 m/min and the telescoping speed of the load handling attachment up to 50 m/min. Load securing is required due to the high speed (see Examples 11.7 and 11.8).

Shifting widths: For shifting storage and retrieval devices, we have to note that the higher the hall warehouse, the larger the volume loss, which is caused by shifting

Figure 10.35 Shifting truck for SRD (www.dematic.com)

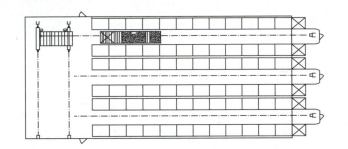

Figure 10.36 Curve-going SRD: automatic, entering another aisle (www.koettgen.de)

widths. Depending on the shelf operating device, the following shifting widths are calculated for a storage and retrieval device load capacity of 1 t:

- self-supporting forklift: 4.0 m;
- reach truck: 3.0 m;
- order picking forklift: 4.0 m;
- vertical order picker: 3.5 m;
- curve-going SRD: 4.0 m (Figure 10.36);
- SRD with shifting truck: 4.3 m (depending on construction length).

10.4.3 Industrial trucks

Different types of lift trucks can be used for storing and retrieving for floor and shelf storage (Figure 6.38). For high shelving with shelf heights of over 7.5 m specific forklifts were developed called reach trucks (see Figure 6.41) and narrow aisle forklifts. The features of a narrow aisle forklift are: high shelf forklifts as man-down version, and order picking forklifts as man-up version.

High shelf forklift   High shelf forklifts are self-supporting forklifts with a fixed mast, which have a telescopic or swing-push fork. They are mechanically guided on tracks in the shelf aisle, or force-steered (see Figures 6.78, 6.87a to c), with an aisle width of approximately 1.6 m and no 90° turning. They can be used for stacking work up to 14 m.

The storing and retrieval process of the load unit into or out of the compartment is automated, as is the height selection and positioning of the forklift in front of the compartment (see Example 6.6.14). The load capacity is usually 1 t, the height of the high shelf forklift is approximately 4.5 m and the lift height up to 13 m (fourfold telescopic lift frame). Its own weight is over 6 t. The operating platform is fixed and always down, also known as a man-down version.

The telescopic fork allows for the load unit to be stored or retrieved in both directions in the shelf aisle. A floor pick-up of the load is not possible.

The swing-push fork can be swung 90° from the middle setting of the fork to the left/right, and can be moved sideways along the fork carrier for the storing or retrieval process. It intakes the load from the floor and three sides. A rotation of 180° in the shelf aisle is only possible when both movements are synchronized.

Special prerequisites for the deployment of narrow aisle forklifts have to be fulfilled. This includes floor requirements for evenness DIN 16202, tolerance DIN 15 185 and load capacity DIN 1045 of the levelled floor. Assembly tolerances and reliable shapes of the shelves, aisle safety and personnel protection have to be adhered to in line with regulations (see Example 6.6–18).

Figure 10.37   High shelf stacker (www.jungheinrich.de) a) High shelf stacker with three-fold telescopic lift frame and swing-push fork as load handling attachment b) High shelf stacker in action; operating platform always down

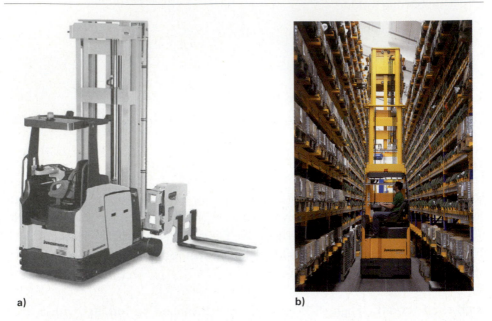

a)   b)

Order picking forklift   An order picking forklift is both a vertical order picker as well as a high shelf forklift. It is equipped with a lifting operating platform for order picking and for storing and retrieving of load units. The operating platform is integrated with the load handling device as a driver's cabin, and moves upwards (man up version). The controls of the order picking forklift are also of significance: mechanically guided or inductively steered. The load handling attachment is a telescopic form or a swing-push fork. The aisle width for a telescopic fork is 1.5 m, and it requires more time for positioning than a swing-push fork, whose aisle width is 1.75 m, taking less effort to position.

An integrated height measuring system ensures accurate positioning of the load, route measuring sensors for all movements increase the functional comfort, safety and system availability. Figure 10.38a shows the operating stand of an order picking forklift.

Usually these machines are equipped with:

- vehicle diagnosis system with fault storage, motor running time checks or start-up diagnosis;
- electric steering with automatic straightening in aisles;
- energy reclamation when braking; combination instrument with lift controls; freeview construction of lifting frame; comfortable driver's seat; steering wheel position display through LED; electric lift stop; abseiling equipment; rotating light; cabin lights; two working headlights; battery: electrolyte transmission.

Figure 10.38a Order picking forklift (www.jungheinrich.de) Operating stand of an order picking forklift with integrated lifting frame for reaching higher storage height

Figure 10.38b Order picking forklift in action; operating stand moves up with the lifting frame (www.toyota-forklifts.de)

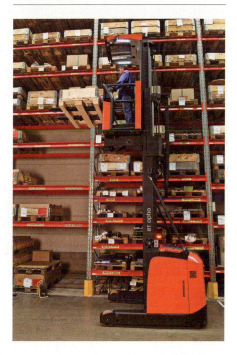

When operating an order picking forklift in a high shelf warehouse, a personal protection system is required (see Example 6.6–18). The load carrier often has a secondary lifting frame in order to save energy during manipulation, to work fast, to reach the order picking pallet without bridges, and to set down a pallet in the top shelf compartment. The working height is up to 13 m (see Figure 10.38b). The components include: lifting frame, driver protection roof, control panel, load handling attachment, fork, driver's cabin, battery and a load chain.

The lift truck management system is used so that storing, retrieving and order picking in a warehouse can be done quickly and effectively (see Chapter 13.3.4). It provides the forklift driver with information in real time, using the data transmission devices installed on the forklift. The different data about empty storage spaces, distribution of items in storage aisles and sorting of the storage goods in line with FIFO can be accessed, or when order picking, the required items can be shown in a route optimized list, in order to shorten order picking time. A dialogue with the computer is provided, in order to receive information of what do to in case of missing items.

Special attention has to be given to the *guiding technologies of narrow aisle fork-lifts*. When storing or retrieving, the forklift driver cannot take care of steering, so this has to be done automatically. This can occur mechanically or inductively:

- *Mechanic:* a) High guidance track filled with concrete, for large lift heights. Pallet stands on the floor. b) With guidance track on the floor, for small and medium lifting heights. Pallet lies on crossbeam.

- *Inductive:* Via inductive guidance, safety distance between load when/load and shelf a minimum of 100 mm; pallet stands on floor (see Chapter 6.7.2.2).

VDI guidelines and examples (see Chapter 11)

Questions

1   What storage possibilities are there for bulk cargo?

2   What storage methods are there for general cargo?

3   What are the advantages and disadvantages of floor storage?

4   Sketch a schematic division of shelf storage.

5   What pallet shelf systems do we distinguish?

6   What long goods shelves are there?

7   List the advantages and disadvantages, the construction and deployment prerequisites for a gravity pallet flow-through shelf.

8   What circulating shelves are there?

9   Sketch the schematics behind the transport for storing and retrieving.

10   Sketch the potential designs of a storage and retrieval device.

11   What is the difference between a satellite and a roller cart shelf?

12   What advantages does the roller cart shelf have compared to a satellite shelf?

Order picking systems

11

Order picking is the retrieval of specified items to put together an assignment, which can consist of one or more order items, and which details the quantity of each item. The order picking function is the collation of a customer order of specific subsets from a provided total quantity in line with prescribed requirement details. The subsets consist of items collected from a range (= total quantity) for an order (= requirement details).

Here are some examples:

- In a procurement warehouse, the required raw materials in line with a manufacturing order have to be order picked.
- In a production warehouse, the required semi-finished products and purchased parts have to be order picked for an assembly order.
- In a distribution warehouse, finished products have to be collated for a customer order.
- In an order picking warehouse of a mail order company, items purchased by the customer have to be order picked.

Order picking is the transition from single origin warehousing to mixed order and contains the following basic functions (Figure 11.1):

- provisioning of items;
- moving the order picking;
- retrieval of items;
- delivery of items.

11.1 Functions of the order picking process

11.1.1 Provisioning items

Provisioning as an order picking function means to take the item in its provisioning unit to the retrieval location in the warehousing area. Provisioning can be based on two principles (Figure 11.2):

Figure 11.1   Functions in an order picking warehouse

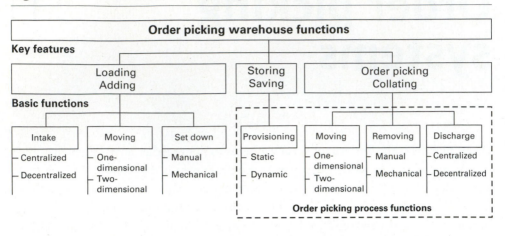

Figure 11.2   Static and dynamic item provision

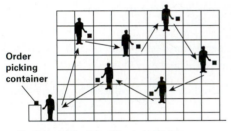 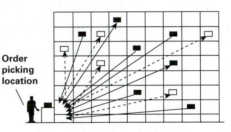

Order picking container

- Static provisioning of items in shelving rack machine
- Order picking principle: man to product
- Two-dimensional movement using a storage and retrieval machine
- Order picking warehouse with fixed storage space allocation

Order picking location

- Dynamic provisioning of items in front of pallet shelf through automatic storage and retrieval
- Order picking principle: product to man
- One-dimensional movement at order picking location
- Unit warehouse with fixed or free storage space allocation when returning containers

● *Static provisioning*

Items are located at a fixed storage location in the order picking warehouse, in line with the principle of fixed storage space allocation, which the order picker must get to. Static provisioning of items is called 'man/robot to product'.

● *Dynamic provisioning*

Items are transported from a unit warehouse to a pre-determined order picking location outside of the shelving area, to retrieve the item according to the order details. This happens manually by the collector or automatically through a robot. Dynamic provisioning is called 'product to man/robot'. Dynamic provisioning occurs in continuous shelves and automatic small parts warehousing.

Figure 11.3   Moving an order picker with horizontal order picking machine: low lift truck, driver platform version with long fork for two pool pallets (www.jungheinrich.de)

Figure 11.4   Moving an order picker using a vertical order picking machine (www.toyota-forklifts.de)

11.1.2 Moving the order picker

Moving the order picker encompasses all motions to take the collector from the location of order receipt to the retrieval sites and to transport the order picked items to the discharge site. Movement only occurs for static provisioning and can be distinguished as a one-dimensional or two-dimensional method:

- For *one-dimensional movement*, the collector moves within a coordinated direction within a shelving aisle, either on foot (Figure 9.3), or faster by using a horizontal order picker (Figure 11.2).

- For *two-dimensional movement*, the collector moves in two coordinated directions within a shelving aisle using a storage and retrieval machine, or using a vertical order picker (Figures 11.4 and 10.38).

11.1.3 Removing items

Removing includes all activities to retrieve the articles from the provisioning unit as required by the order. Retrieval can occur manually or automatically:

- *Manual* retrieval corresponds to the retrieval by the collector directly by hand or with a mechanic aid, such as a grabber. The handling area of a person is significantly limited as a result of their physiology (bending down, stretching up).

- *Automatic* retrieval corresponds to retrieval through an order picking machine/ robot (Figure 11.19).

11.1.4 Discharging items

Discharging of collated items encompasses all transfer activities. It can happen centralized or decentralized. Centralized discharge is the transfer of the order picking container or pallet as unsorted load unit at a checkpoint or packaging location. Decentralized discharge means the order picked items are transferred to multiple locations (Figure 9.3).

11.2 Organizational structure and workflow management for order picking

11.2.1 Workflow management

When collating orders (item order picking), we distinguish between the following workflow strategies:

- *Order-focused order picking* works successively through all processed items on a collection list (pick list) by removing the goods from the provisioning containers. At the end of this process, the order has been completely collated, which is known as single-stage order picking.

- *Item-focused order picking* first collates the items for multiple orders, and then allocates the items to the respective orders.

- For big orders, different item structures or large order picking warehouses, the order list is divided up into several parts. This leads to a *zonal division* of an order picking warehouse. The order can now be processed in **parallel** or **serial** through multiple order pickers (Figure 11.5).

During parallel order picking, part orders are processed simultaneously in the order picking zones, either order- or item-focused. For serial order picking, they are processed successively, either order- or item-focused.

Aside from the four options above, other variants are created by combining order-focused order picking (A items) and item-focused order picking (B and C items), as well as by increasing the number of stages.

11.2.2 Order picking techniques

If multiple orders are processed by an order picker simultaneously, we call this *multi-order picking* (see Figures 11.7a(ii), 11.15 and 11.16). Goods are often retrieved from the provisioning units in an item-focused manner and then discharged into the respective order container, such as a K-trolley, in an order-focused way (see Examples 11.24 and 13.4).

Figure 11.5   Serial order picking
K_n Order picker
1 & 2 Transfer points

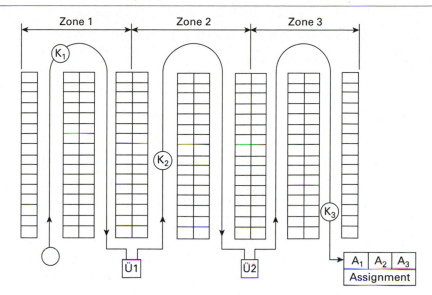

If the items are order picked directly into a shipping box and packaged, we call this a *pick-and-pack system*. This requires an order and item-focused volume calculation in order to determine the shipping box.

A variety of information is processed when order picking: *pick lists, paperless order picking and automatic order picking machines* (see Chapter 11.5). For order processing the following activities apply: information intake; access; acknowledgement or confirmation.

A *pick list* (paper order picking) provides the order picker with instructions in the shape of an order picking list, such as in a shelving rack (collation of retrieval positions). From this mostly route-optimized list, the order picker collects the relevant items in the given order. The pick list is the most prevalent method of information sharing, and is often sufficient, but has the disadvantage of resulting in reading errors and low order picking quality (especially for lots of pick positions).

Paperless order picking is a partly automated order picking system. The main difference from the pick list is the online communication as operator guidance. This is shown through the following features:

- mobile data capture with data terminal (see Chapter 13.3.3 SLS);
- pick-by-light system;
- pick-by-voice system;
- pick-by-balance system.

Paperless order picking consists of the following components:

- main terminal;
- senders and receivers, numbers depending on size of warehouse;
- stationary or mobile terminals with keyboard or wand;
- codes on the items, such as barcodes.

Paperless order picking can achieve:

- high order picking performance through direct display of retrieval quantities per item at each retrieval station;
- low fault rate, as pick lists cannot be mixed up, nor reading mistakes be made through getting rows mixed up;
- a current, transparent order monitoring method through online connection to a warehouse management terminal.

Mobile data terminal   Here, the sender or receiver machine of a vehicle is connected to the main terminal (see Chapter 13.2) using infrared or radio transmission. The main terminal, which contains information on quantities and storage data of existing items, takes over the order picking assignments, arranges them optimized for time and route, and transmits them online through infrared/radio transmitters to the terminal displays or a handheld machine with keyboard, scanner and display (Figure 11.6). The data is read by the order picker in the display or dialogue system that has been implemented and the completed pick/order confirmed.

Pick-by-light system   In a shelving rack, each storage space is equipped with an alphanumerical or numerical display (Figure 11.7a), which is placed above or beneath the provisioning location and connected to a server. This display consists of a unit, which provides the order picker with the quantity, and a confirmation button. The retrieval quantity can be adjusted either up or down through a correction button. Personnel and disruption data can also be requested. When an order picking assignment is entered using a barcode into the shelving rack, all compartment displays of the relevant items for order picking light up. Once the retrieval has been confirmed by the order picker, the light goes off again. This guarantees a simple check on order picking.

Two-tone displays are used, when two order picking assignments are processed simultaneously by one or two people in parallel.

Pick-by-voice system   Transmission of picking and confirmation by voice command. It consists of the Talkman with strap, headset and charger. The order

Figure 11.6 Data radio terminals for paper free order picking

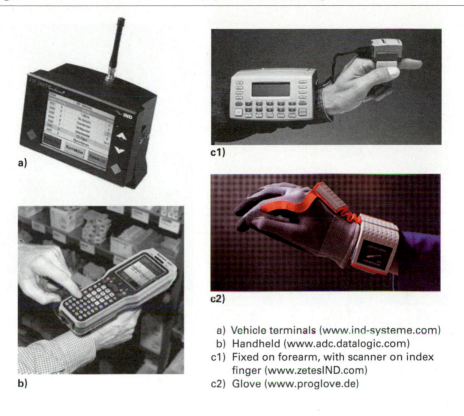

a) Vehicle terminals (www.ind-systeme.com)
b) Handheld (www.adc.datalogic.com)
c1) Fixed on forearm, with scanner on index
    finger (www.zetesIND.com)
c2) Glove (www.proglove.de)

picker is voice-led (Figure 11.7b), and voice picking keeps both hands and eyes free, multiple order pickers can work simultaneously in one aisle without paper. Voice recognition has reached an advanced level, is quick and reliable, independent of dialects or accents, filters sources of noise and supports the vocabulary.

This system is used in areas of order picking, such as cold stores, where thick gloves are used for work, making it hard to operate keyboards. LCD displays also face limitations of radio transmission at temperatures below −28°C.

Pick-by-balance system This order picking system is a combination of pick-by-light and precision scales with counter function, which are situated under each storage container (Figure 11.7c). For incorrect retrieval (too little or too much), the weight discrepancy is noted and a red light, as well as the remaining quantity, is shown on the display. An automatic confirmation goes through if the weight of the retrieval is correct. This continuous monitoring guarantees exact stocks, prevents mistakes and reduces inventory checks (see Chapter 11.4.2 and Figure 11.16).

Figure 11.7a   Pick-by-light order picking

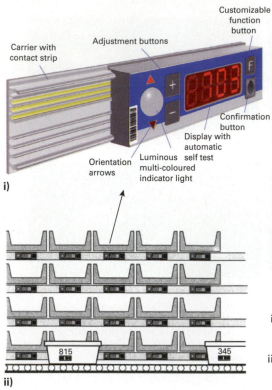

i)

ii)

iii)

i) Compartment display (www.luca.eu)
ii) Shelving rack with compartment light
and roller track for order picking
container (www.zetstIND.com)
iii) Order picking truck for multi-order-
picking (Ehrhardt + Partner GmbH &
Co. KG)

Figure 11.7b   Pick-by-voice order picking
(www.dematic.com/de/pick-by-voice)

Figure 11.7c   Pick-by-balance
order picking (www.kbs-gmbh.de)

Summary Machines used for scanning and order picking in logistics are sophisticated, usually in practical ergonomic sizes, and are relatively lightweight (approximately 300 to 500 g). They also reliably and quickly (approximately 36 scans/s) capture complex information. The reading distance is up to 1 m, the frequency is between 400 MHz to 2.4 GHz.

Each machine has individual strengths and features:

- reach truck with manual scanner: Figure 6.49a to d;

- goods receipt and order picking truck with data radio terminal: Figure 9.15.

11.2.3 Organizational structure

The organizational structure of the order picking system can have single or multiple zones. It is based on structural and workflow strategies summarized in Figure 11.8.

An example of an organizational structure strategy is shown in Figure 11.9. The placement of an item on a shelf can follow the preferences shown in Chapter 9.3. If there is an ABC division of items according to turnover or handling frequency, the items can be used to allocate storage spaces in line with organizational structure I, II and III in Figure 11.8. This happens for both fixed storage space allocation, as well as free storage space selection.

An example of workflow strategies is shown in Figure 11.10a. According to these three strategies, it is possible to execute an order picking assignment in a high shelving warehouse with an order picking forklift.

Figure 11.8 Division of order picking strategies

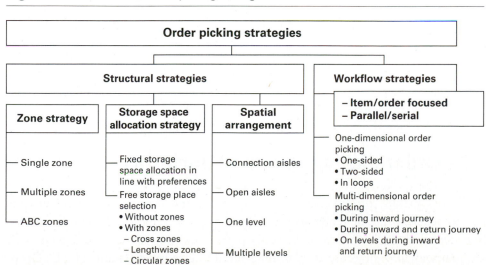

Figure 11.9 Order picking organizational structure strategies with ABC division in line with Figure 2.9

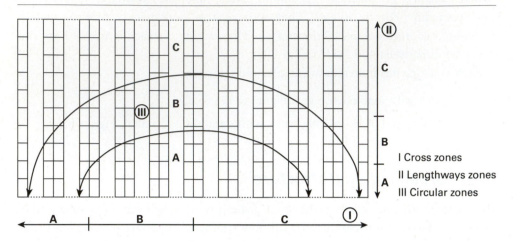

I Cross zones
II Lengthways zones
III Circular zones

Figure 11.10a Order picking – workflow strategies of storage and retrieval machine in high shelving warehouse a) Order picking during inward journey only b) Order picking during inward and return journey c) Order picking on levels during inward and return journey

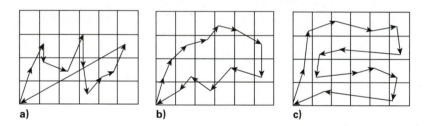

a)   b)   c)

Another example for optimizing order picking is shown in Figure 11.10b. With the aid of heuristic algorithms, optimized order picking tours are created from the entire pool of assignments, where up to 50 per cent of order picking routes can be saved compared to traditional route creation.

11.3 Order picking time and performance

The order picking process can be a complicated and personnel-intensive process due to business-specific requirements, as well as a time- and cost-intensive activity. In order to work economically, the order picking location has to be designed in an optimal way and the order picking time should be reduced (Figure 11.11). Order

Figure 11.10b   Traditional and heuristic order picking tours (www.dresden-informatik.de)

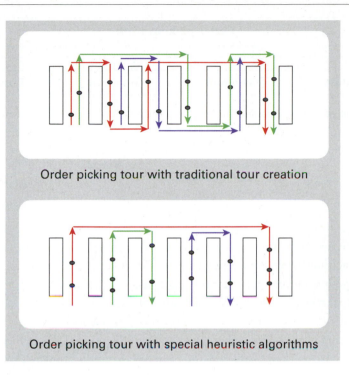

Order picking tour with traditional tour creation

Order picking tour with special heuristic algorithms

Figure 11.11   Reduction of order picking time by: a) Left: order picking and packaging location with dynamic provisioning (www.stoecklin.com) b) Right: order picking truck with multi-order-picking (www.knapp.com)

a)   b)

Figure 11.12 Structure of order picking time

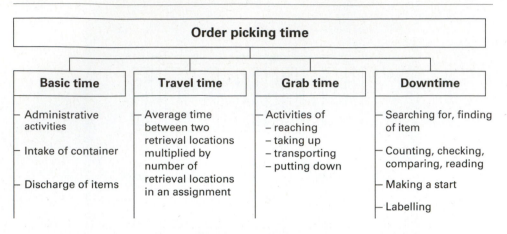

picking time is the time it takes to collate an order. Order picking time can be divided up into basic time, travel time, grab time and downtime (Figure 11.12).

The *basic time* for manual order picking consists of the time used for receiving the assignment, sorting the paperwork, intake of information, intake and discharge of the order picking container and/or passing on of paperwork. The basic time is about 5 to 10 per cent of the order picking time and can be reduced through effective work preparation (streamlining and good design of organization), through trained personnel and optimized provisioning, such as of order picking containers.

The *travel time* consists of slices of time for basic route, order picking route and gear change, and is the biggest part of order picking time at 30 to 50 per cent. Through streamlining of the range, reducing stock/items, and removing shelf warmers, this time can be shortened:

- for static provisioning through:
  - arrangement in line with turnover frequency, customer and component-related, ABC analysis;
  - IT route optimization; sequence of order picking;
  - movement of order picker on order picking vehicles (one-dimensional);
  - two-dimensional movement of order pickers (storage and retrieval machine);
  - front surface reduction of storage areas (item concentration), such as continuous shelf;
  - item-focused order picking, such as multi-stage process;
- for dynamic provisioning through:
  - item to man, with the aid of paternoster, carousel and tower shelving, automatic small part warehouse, unit warehouse + order picking space outside of warehouse (travel time ≈ zero).

The *grab time* is made up of reaching, taking in, transporting, putting down in the order picking container. It makes up between 5 and 10 per cent of the order picking time, is often hard to determine and depends on the following:

- shape, dimension and weight of items;
- grab height (0.2 to 1.8 m), ideally 1 to 1.2 m;
- grab depth (0.3 to 0.8 m), ideally up to 0.4 m;
- retrieval unit quantity per position and access;
- skills and physiological characteristics of the order picker.

Two-dimensional motion in the shelving racks (see Figure 10.10) reduces grab time compared to a one-dimensional motion, as does a change of the storage space for goods in shelving racks, which includes items with high turnover within grabbing distance.

Downtime represents between 10 and 35 per cent of order picking time and is made up of the positioning and checking processes required for the processing of an assignment. It can be reduced by information and search aids, good working conditions, suitable equipment, trained and experienced personnel and replacement of the order picking list with paperless order picking (Figure 11.6).

The *order picking performance* corresponds to the quantity retrieved per time unit, related to the average assignment scope, and is expressed in grab units per hour, container per hour or positions per hour. It is also defined by the number of average assignments per time unit. The order picking assignment can either come from internal customers (production, assembly) for the procurement or production warehouse, or from an external customer order for the distribution warehouse. The division of an order picking assignment into partial assignments is called batch assignment. The assignment is specified by:

- number of positions;
- number of retrievals per position;
- average drive and lift route from position to position.

The order picking performance depends on a number of factors, such as:

- whether the motion of the order picker is on foot or by order picking vehicle;
- whether orders are picked manually or automatically;
- which strategies (static or dynamic provisioning) are chosen;
- which workflow (item or order focused, paperless) is applied;
- what the dimensions and weight of the items in the range are;
- what the order structure is.

The working environment, the type of order picking shelving as well as the physiology and motivation levels of the order picker also play a role in the order picking performance.

The following list (from the Bito catalogue) provides experiential and average values for order picking performance per hour:

- shelving rack with one-dimensional motion   35 –   90 access occasions;
- shelving rack with two-dimensional motion   40 –   90 access occasions;
- pallet shelving with one-dimensional motion   30 –   50 access occasions;
- pallet shelving with two-dimensional motion   40 –   90 access occasions;
- continuous shelving with one-dimensional motion   140 –   250 access occasions;
- continuous shelving with paperless order picking   350 –   480 access occasions;
- automatic container warehouse   40 –   250 access occasions;
- circular shelving with one-dimensional motion   100 –   160 access occasions;
- shelving rack with robot operation   100 –   350 access occasions;
- automatic order picker   5000 –   10,000 access occasions.

Through analysis of the individual order picking times, these can be represented in a pie chart (Figure 11.13; downtime is divided between basic and grab time), and the resulting order picking performance can be compared with standard values for assessment or visually displayed with the help of an evaluated strengths and weaknesses profile (Figure 11.14).

11.4 Manual order picking

In a car parts warehouse, a customer assignment is fulfilled through manual order picking by a member of staff without aids. The assignment consists of a small number of items, then the order picker goes to the storage spaces on foot, retrieves the items by hand and completes the assignment. In order to finish the process quicker and more economically, aids such as transport or paternoster shelving may be used.

11.4.1 Order picking using transport

If it is not a sporadic or irregular assignment, as is the case in a car parts warehouse or in a tool warehouse, but is many different assignments (eg in a mail order

Figure 11.13 Pie chart of the picking time analysis with calculation of picking performance

Order picking time per assignment	Ratio
Basic time	27%
Route time	49%
Grab time	25%

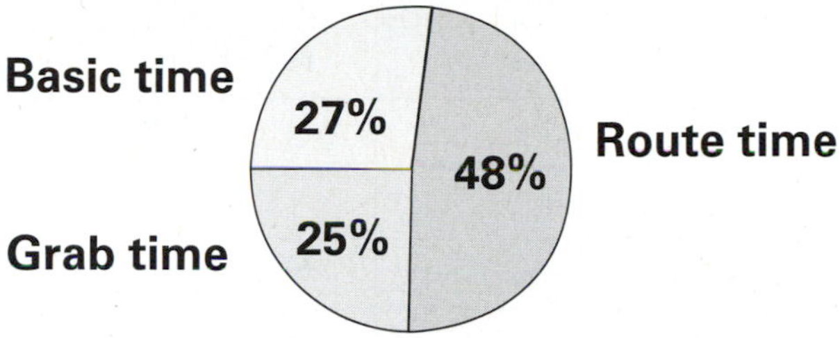

Total time of recorded time (without packaging time)	130 minutes
Sum of picks (= access)	196 picks
Sum of quantities	398 pieces
Networking time per shift (per shift and person) (Mon–Wed)	438 minutes

Order picking performance per shift and person (196/130*438)	660 picks per shift and person
Order picking performance per shift and person (196/130*60)	90 picks per shift and person
Order picking performance per shift and person Comparison value from practice-focused literature	90–170 picks per hour

company or a food warehouse), then this must be done in an economical way. This requires:

- reduction of travel time;
- minimizing tiredness of order picker;
- increasing order picking performance.

This is done by deploying a means of transport, which either transports the items to an order picking site (Figure 11.11), or transports the order picker to the items (Table 11.1). Examples of this are:

- horizontal order pickers for carrying out one-dimensional motion;
- vertical order pickers for carrying out two-dimensional motion.

Order picking is supported through non-powered transport, such as roller tracks, which are used to move containers (see Figure 9.3) or trucks (see Figure 9.10b), and through motor-powered transport, whereby discontinuous conveyors form the largest percentage.

Figure 11.14   Strengths and weaknesses profile of an order picking area

Area	Review Feature	Weak	Medium	Strong
Order picking	Order picking per person	●		
	Total performance per person		●	
	Basic time – average	●		
	Travel time – average	●		
	Grab time – average		●	
	Dead time – average		●	
	Order picked item quantity	●		
	Quality of order picking	●		
	Existing warehouse equipment		●	
	Warehouse housekeeping		●	
	User friendliness of radio terminal		●	
	Base data maintenance	●		

Table 11.1   Division of means of transport for order picking

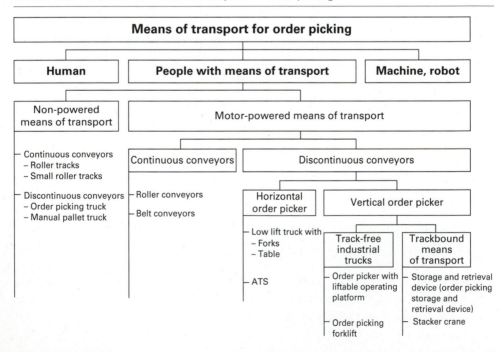

11.4.2 Horizontal order picker

These order picking vehicles have no platform, or one that can only lift up to 1 m. They are used for one-dimensional motion, with the grab area corresponding to the natural grab height of approximately 1.75 m (Figure 11.3). By using a foldable step as well as a step platform, the vehicle's grab height area can be extended (for more on order picking on a second level, see Chapter 9.4.6). This can also happen through an operating platform that lifts up to 1 m. Horizontal order pickers have forks or load handling attachments with low lift equipment for taking on order picking pallets or containers with floor clearance.

A specially designed version of the horizontal order picker is called a data mobile. It is an induction or track-led, manually operated electric truck consisting of four to six levels, with two adjacent order picking containers each (of different size depending on assignment volume) resting on electric scales. It also includes a visual display unit, scanner and keyboard, an infrared data transmission unit and a platform stand for the order picker. *For static provisioning and paperless order picking, collation is item-focused and the items are then put into the container* (for more on multi-order picking, see Figures 11.15 and 11.16).

The orders are then transmitted to the machines from the processing computer, which uses infrared data transmission and is route-optimized. Position after position is displayed on the monitor (item, quantity and container). Mistakes are eliminated through the automatic filing display, automatic positioning and electronic weight checks, with an error rate of less than 0.05 per cent. An order picking warehouse structure with two-aisle system consists of a separation between storage and order picking. It is used for large range, large order volume, short order processing times and a high number of orders per day, such as pharmaceutical products in a pharmaceutical warehouse. Pharmaceutical warehouses have an order picking performance of 200 to 400 picks/h.

11.4.3 Vertical order picker

We can distinguish between track-bound transport and industrial trucks for these order picking vehicles through the following features:

- Track-bound transport as vertical order pickers are storage and retrieval machines and stacker cranes (for more on storage and retrieval machines, see Chapter 10.4.1; Figure 10.10 and for stacker cranes see Figure 6.30a to d).
- Industrial trucks as vertical order pickers are:
  - order picker forklifts (see Figure 10.38) which are used for order picking and are also capable of storing and removing palleted load units in shelves;

Figure 11.15 Tug as order picking vehicle for order picking light goods, either equipped with a trailer or a rear docking system (www.toyota-forklifts.de)

Figure 11.16 Data mobile (www.pp-systeme.com)

– vertical order pickers with a lifting enclosed driver's platform, along with an integrated load area (Figure 11.4), whose lift height can be up to 8 m. Additionally, it is only possible to store or retrieve small storage units, such as storage bins or boxes, mobile (Figure 11.49).

11.5 Automatic order picking

Order picking is a labour-intensive process. As personnel costs are on the increase, the search is on for processes requiring little labour. They result from part- or fully automated order picking, ie when an assignment is processed without personnel. A step towards part-automated order picking is paperless order picking (see Chapter 11.2).

Order picking machines are available for items with similar shapes, such as packaged shirts, medicine boxes, packages, etc. The items have certain features, and machines grab and transport them using grabbers, tongs or pneumatic suckers. The heart of such an order picking machine is the management system. It must have information on the items, such as geometric shape and measurements, weight, storage location for static provisioning and location of items on the partial pallet for dynamic provisioning. The order picking management system has to administer and process the order, managing the transport to the storage locations in order to order pick the required items in the respective quantities.

The management of motion and grab processes of the order picking robot occurs with commands. The grabbed items have to be put into provided containers or certain locations, such as a pallet. The management system has to remember the packing pattern of an order picking pallet in order to be able to set down another item on it at a relevant location. The designs of robots and order picking machines comply with the shape, weight and dimensions of the items and also aim to produce as high as possible an order picking performance.

Automatic shelving rack order picking   This order picking system (Figure 11.17) is made up of modular shelving racks, whose shelves are at an angle to the operating aisle and the track-led storage and retrieval machine with the order picking robot. The storage consists of B and C items with small to medium dimension, packed in boxes. The order picking robot consists of finger-like small belt conveyors, which move sideways under the angled boxes, lifting them up slightly over the edge and transporting them forward. They then fall into the coded order container. The storage and retrieval machine is order-focused when collating the items, and are refilled manually from the rear of the shelving. The system can manage up to 1,200 picks per hour.

Automatic A-frame order picking   Construction: Single origin items (A items), such as medication, cosmetics, music or video software (hard packaging) are manually stacked in two opposing and angled allocation shafts. Underneath the roof-like allocation shafts is a belt conveyor. Automatic order picking is *order-focused for static provisioning*.

Designs:

- *Order picking on belt conveyor within the shelving*

A scanner reads the order barcode on the container and the main warehouse computer activates the pushers in the relevant allocation shafts. All items are thrown simultaneously (*parallel order picking*) onto the belt and reach the belt at the front

Figure 11.17   Order picking system a) Robot with two-sided order picking shelving
b) Retrieval of item from the shelf and transport using a belt conveyor
going into order trough (www.pp-systeme.com)

a)   b)

of the machine, or fall into a funnel (not depicted in the figure). The management programme ensures synchronization between the container and the packaging units onto the belt (Figure 11.18a).

For one version of this high-performance order picking machine, the belt is divided into successive sections for one order each that take on the items as the belt passes (*serial order picking*). The transmission technology can manage up to 2,400 orders/hour. The error rate is around 0.01 per cent.

Order picking directly into the container within the shelving: The barcode on the container is read, identified and accepted by the main warehouse computer when it runs into the order picking machine and is then 'married' with an order. The management programme controls the allocation of the items, so that the retrieval equipment transports the items into the container passing on the belt simultaneously (for more on *serial order picking*, see Figure 11.18b).

- *Order picking onto belt conveyor outside the shelving*

As shown in Figure 11.18c, the items are gently ejected from the shaft shelf onto the external belt conveyor with curve belt conveyor. This is used for small items such as music, video or software ranges with system performance up to 9,000 pieces/h at an error rate < 0.05 per cent.

Figure 11.18   Automatic A-Frame order picking: one level design up to 10,000 positions/ hour (www.dematic.com) a) Discharge onto belt: discharge rate 2 to 5 pieces/s/item, performance dependent on belt speed and length of the belt section reserved for the order: ⌀ 800 containers/h, v ≈1 m/s b) Order picking directly into container c) A-frame order picker with external belt conveyor, for provision of pharmacies and hospitals with fast moving goods (www.knapp.com)

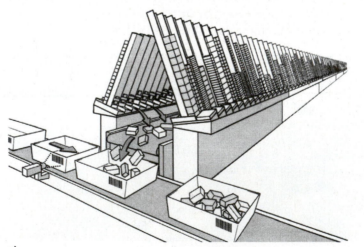

a)

Figure 11.18 *(Continued)*

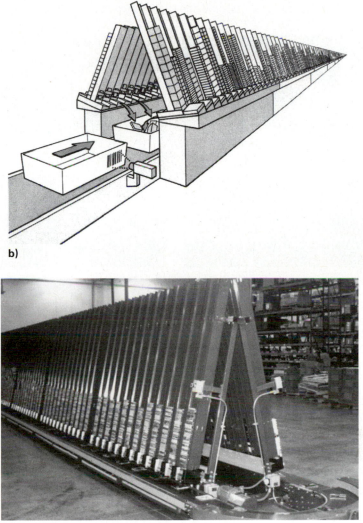

b)

c)

Automatic multi-order picking

Construction:

- two-sided shelving rack, manual filling from rear;
- robot designed as storage and retrieval machine with mast up to 7 m high and load handling attachment in the shape of a telescopic arm, mobile on a track in the shelving aisle;
- grab system (Figure 11.19a) at end of telescopic arm to pick individual items: suction elements, with infrared sensors (optical location recognition of items);

Figure 11.19   Order picking robot on storage and retrieval machine with grab arm.
a) Grab arm, item is discharged into carousel storage, on an order-focused basis. b) For shirts, only one shelf shown (www.kht-online.de)

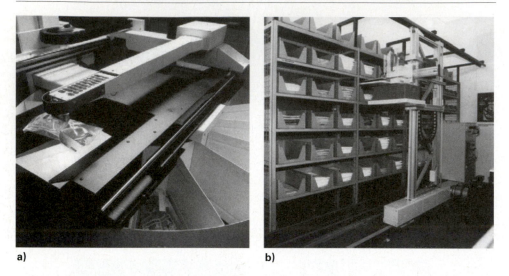

a)   b)

- carousel storage (Figure 11.19a) of items for up to eight orders (segmented division of rotating cylinder; items fed in from top, items fall into stationary cylinder – carousel storage – by moving floor area);

- stationary carousel storage for passing over order picked assignments into order picking containers running on roller conveyors.

The items must have a suitable packaging surface for uptake with suction pads. The suction pad retrieves an item and puts it into the respective segment on the order picking carousel.

During retrieval, the storage of the item on the shelf can be sorted or unsorted. The robot is moved by a computer to the relevant storage shelves, because the computer knows both the storage locations of the items as well as the composition of the order. *Retrieval of items is item-focused, discharge is order-focused.*

Order picking robots for shirts (the same dimension of all items): for one order container (Figure 11.19b) item-focused order picking; for multiple containers multi-order picking.

Automatic order picking and storage system   In Figure 11.20, a compact automated order picking warehouse is shown in silo design for small parts, which has been secured with cladding against unauthorized access and dirt from all sides. The small parts are in small containers. These will be grabbed by a centrally located storage and retrieval machine and placed in the opening. The order picking performance is around 300 picks/h, the shelving has a height of 3.6 m.

Figure 11.20   a) Automatic order picking and storage system (www.knapp.com). b) Order picking robot (www.viastore.com) (see Figure 3.11)

a)   b)

11.6 Examples for unit and order picking warehouse systems

According to Chapter 10.2.1, Figure 10.6, a shelving storage system consists of the subsystems storage unit, storage technology and storage administration, as well as other components. By combining subsystems and components, a variety of shelving storage versions can be created, all with their own advantages and disadvantages. When looking at the chosen division in unit and order picking warehouses we determine that a unit warehouse can also fulfil the tasks of an order picking warehouse when:

- the order picking assignment only consists of entire units;
- order picking is carried out in front of the shelving aisle at a special order picking location (dynamic provisioning).

For the intake of containers, trays or other load handling attachments, there are a number of construction methods.

Figure 11.21   An automatic small parts warehouse system block without screen

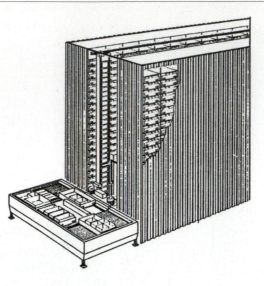

- pull technology: cassette pushers;
- drive-under technology: telescopic;
- grab technology: sideways retrieval grabber.

11.6.1 Automatic small parts warehouse

An automatic small parts warehouse (Figure 11.21) is an enclosed, automated warehousing system for storing items of small volume and consists of:

- two opposing single shelves in a one-place system;
- an automated track-led storage and retrieval machine (see Figure 10.34);
- different load handling attachments;
- storage aids such as containers, trays and cassettes;
- a pre-store order picking area.

This results in small part warehouse versions in one-place or multiple-place design for trays and containers.

Small parts warehouse with trays   The shelving is 14 m high and constructed in line with the one-place design, is completely covered externally and is operated by a storage and retrieval machine. According to Figure 11.21, the storage and retrieval machine usually pulls the tray from the shelf onto the load handling attachment, transports it to the order picking area, picks it up again and takes it back to the same storage location, pushing the tray back into the shelf. As a result of high acceleration when driving, lifting and telescoping, the applied double cycle strategy (see Chapter 9.8) achieves high turnover performance: up to 120 double cycles per hour with high speed (v up to 7 m/s) and high acceleration (v up to 4 m/s). The load capacity of the fully automated storage and retrieval machine is between 50 and 300 kg, the aisle width, depending on the tray length, up to 1.8 m. The trays are usually simple, sheet metal troughs with different wall heights of approximately 8 to 20 cm and possess handles or handle bars for pulling/pushing along the narrow sides. The pulling technique in connection with the sheet metal tray results in a minimum in lost height and, thus, lost volume (see Figure 10.12).

The small parts warehouse works according to the principle 'item to man' (see Chapter 11.1.1), so that the travel time of the order picker is nearly zero. The order picking area can be designed in different ways, in Figure 11.21 as an order picking U-shape. The trays, which usually run anti-clockwise (width approximately 65 cm, length approximately 160 cm), run past the order picking location in lengthwise direction and are order picked there and then. The location of the item on the tray is predetermined, so that the computer will show it when the tray is called up on the monitor. The monitor facing the order picker shows items by highlighting their storage or retrieval location. The tray has a fixed storage space with a barcode. This is read during the storage process so that the tray is always stored at the fixed location. An order picking assignment is read into the warehouse computer using the barcode and the items to be order picked are automatically provided to the order picking location.

The small parts warehouse with trays (known as a tray warehouse) can be described as follows:

- as a unit warehouse: trays (units) are stored and retrieved in their entirety;
- with fixed storage space allocation: trays have a fixed storage location;
- as an order picking warehouse with dynamic provisioning: item to man and item collation in front of shelving;
- with high order picking performance through high turnover of trays;
- little travel time for order picker;
- little downtime through order picking aids, such as optical guidance and fully automated processing;
- secured against theft and dust;
- with maximum use of space through pulling technique, tray shape and different shelf space heights;
- for use with small and medium-sized parts, integrated with manufacturing and assembly (Figure 11.23) through immediate allocation.

Small parts warehouse with containers   The shelving in small parts warehouses with plastic or cardboard containers (300 to 400 mm wide, 400 to 600 mm long, 2 or 4 times depth) are built up to 20 m high. The aisle width is about 850 mm, the approach dimensions are approximately 580 mm at the top and 450 mm at the bottom. The load handling attachment drives under or around the side of the storage crate, lifting it up and moving it onto the storage and retrieval machine, in order to discharge it in the pre-storage zone. This can be constructed in different ways, especially when it is a small parts plant with multiple small parts warehouses. The operation occurs with high performance storage and retrieval machines. The pre-storage zone usually contains multiple order picking sites (Figure 11.22).

Special designs   Small parts warehouses store containers of boxes in double or quadruple depth. In order to achieve as high a turnover as possible of containers

Figure 11.22   Small parts warehouse (www.viastore.com)

a) Small parts warehouse storage and
    retrieval machine
b) Pre-storage zone with automatic order
    picking
c) Storage and retrieval machine for
    storing and retrieving
d) Pre-storage zone with roller and chain
    conveyors

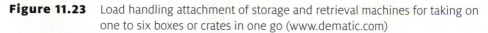

Figure 11.23 Load handling attachment of storage and retrieval machines for taking on one to six boxes or crates in one go (www.dematic.com)

per time unit, two or more containers are retrieved simultaneously, or the storage and retrieval machines access multiple storage places in one cycle. This is why storage and retrieval machines have multiple load handling attachments, which are either arranged next to or on top of each other (Figure 11.23). Storage and retrieval machines are high performance machines made from aluminium, in order to achieve high acceleration and speeds. For a storage and retrieval machine with one mast the additional load is 50 kg/load handling attachment, the driving and lifting speed 6.3 m/s, the relevant acceleration 5.3/3.9 m/s^2, the aisle width 1.06 m and the machine height 10 m. For a double mast version with the same aisle width, the height is up to 20 m, the driving/lifting speeds 5.0/3.0 m/s for acceleration values of 3.3/3.9 m/s^2.

11.6.2 Extra-long goods storage

The storage and transport of extra-long goods often cause problems for companies due to the bulky, heavy and unstable dimensions of the goods. If possible, extra-long food and manufacturing machines, such as cutting and separating equipment, are placed in close vicinity in order to keep the routes short. Different storage methods are possible, such as floor and shelf storage in line and blocks, manually, mechanically or automatically operated. The storage technique used for a storage case depends mostly on the business-specific conditions (workflows, quantities, room dimensions, turnover etc). In Chapter 10.3.1.3, manually and mechanically operated long good shelves were shown, such as floor storage with post demarcation, cantilever arm shelves and honeycomb shelf storage. In the following, examples of the same shelving types shall be shown for automated storage systems. One objective of compact storage systems is to always gain valuable production space by using the height of a building (see Example 11.32). **Investment in automation technology costs only a third of the costs of constructing a new building.**

Floor storage in blocks   In a storage block, storage is created by use of long good stacking frames or special load carriers, such as racks on the floor, placing the stack unit next to and on top of one another. It is operated – storing and retrieving – with travelling or hanging cranes, which are equipped with special traverses for taking on stacking units. An anti-swing system and positioned steering help the crane to set down the load accurately and transport it without swinging. Operation is part or fully automated (Figure 11.24). Pipes of 6 m in length are usually packed in bundles with hexagonal shape.

Figure 11.24   Floor block storage; operating a travelling crane and traversing (www.demagcranes.com)

a)   b)   d)

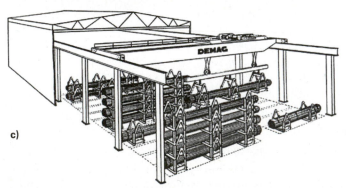

c)

a) Load handling of square bundle of steel pipes using magnets
b) Mechanic load intake of grain bundles
c) Stacking cradle frames as load handling devices for hexagonal pipe bundles
d) Load handling via vacuum lift for round bars from racks (for paper rolls, see Figure 10.7b)

Floor storage *advantages*: no fixed storage construction; flexible space use; adaptable to length of long good. *Disadvantages:* restacking efforts; slow; for B and C items.

Honeycomb warehouse   Automatically operated honeycomb shelving warehouses consist of one or two opposing honeycomb shelving units (see Chapter 10.3.1.3) with two storage and retrieval machine, or a stacking device. This has a lift truck with a push or pull attachment in order to push the cassettes into the compartments equipped with plastic gliders from the front, or to pull them out (Figures 11.25 and 11.52).

The cassettes can be simply adapted to the goods, so that even long metal sheets can be stored. The manufacturing equipment can be arranged around the block. The cutting and separating machines are fed by long goods cassettes *through* the honeycomb shelf, by equipping the storage compartments on the manufacturing level with roller tracks to pass through the cassettes.

Honeycomb warehouse *advantages*: high cassette turnover performance through short routes; can be fully automated; different cassette dimensions in one warehousing system; provisioning principle item to man; high degree of area and room use. *Disadvantages:* expensive, economic for high item quantity and high turnover; only for warehouses with high storage capacity.

Cantilever shelving warehouse   The operation of a cantilever shelf happens from the long side of the cargo. It consists of cantilever shelving for the intake of individual long goods or long good cassettes. The operation is automatic via a transfer bridge crane with lift travers (see Figure 10.14) or via a portal crane with lift equipment as well as four-way forklift (Figure 11.26).

Figure 11.25   Honeycomb warehouse (lengthways storage), operating a two-mast storage and retrieval machine (www.dematic.com)

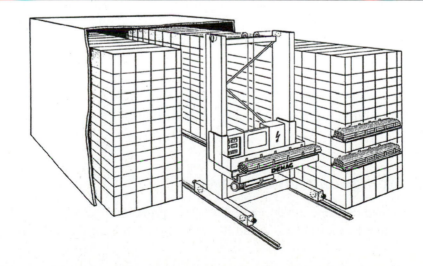

Figure 11.26 Crossways storage of timber with four-way forklift in a cantilever shelf (www.jungheinrich.de)

Advantages of cantilever shelving: provisioning principle – cargo to man; high degree of area and room utilization; can be installed in spaces of any dimension; it is possible to build over transport routes (tunnel solution). *Disadvantage*: only suitable for small to medium handling performance.

Cantilever arm high bay warehouse A high bay warehouse for long goods is made up of cantilever high shelving, in order to take in the long goods. It is operated from the long side with a two-mast storage and retrieval machine. Both provisioning principles apply. For low turnover, a storage and retrieval machine can operate multiple shelf aisles by using a transfer bridge. The load capacity of the storage and retrieval machine is up to 5 t with driving, lifting and telescoping speeds of 160/30/48 m per minute. Long goods lengths up to 7 m, storage height up to 40 m and turnover performance up to 25 double cycles per hour are possible (Figure 11.27).

11.6.3 *Storage and retrieval levels*

If each item had the same turnover frequency, the optimal storage and retrieval point of a pallet high bay warehouse would be at the intersection of the shelf diagonals.

Figure 11.27 High bay warehouse with crossways storage, operating a two-mast storage and retrieval machine (www.dematic.com)

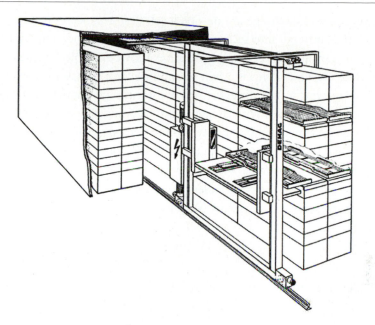

This would only be feasible for a warehouse consisting of two single shelves (see section on small parts warehousing). However, the storage goods have different turnover frequencies (A-B-C items), so that each item area has to be created in a warehouse for certain turnover frequencies in order to optimize routes and performance. It makes sense to have the goods receipt and discharge installed separately along the front of the shelving. It would be ideal to determine the storage and retrieval points in the middle of the storage height. For cost reasons (lift and lowering heights), the storing and retrieving occurs at floor height, so that no vertical conveyors are required. The disadvantage of this arrangement is the long and empty journeys between the storage and retrieval points.

Nowadays, goods receipt and discharge are placed along one front of the shelves. This allows for two designs:

1 Goods receipt and discharge are on different levels, whereby the goods receipt is above the goods discharge, the reasons being:

- retrieval always has priority;
- retrieval conveyors do not have vertical conveyors: less prone to disruption;
- the timing of goods receipt is usually not as important.

This design is usually prevalent in practice and it results in higher storage and retrieval performance.

2 Goods receipt and discharge are on one level. Performance in pallets per hour is lower, such as through intersections, right of way rules and simultaneous use of a means of transport for storage and retrieval. An example for such a design is shown in Figure 11.28. This is a unit warehouse with free storage space selection (limitation of weight and different heights of storage compartments), which is used in a unit warehouse with dynamic provisioning. The pallet high bay warehouse has approximately 4,000 pallet storage spaces, two shelf aisles and can take in approximately 10,000 items through shelf and compartment pallets. The order picking space has a turntable with roller conveyor, which guarantees simple and quick order picking of the shelf pallets in particular, which is usually carried out through an item-focused workflow (see Figure 11.29).

Figure 11.28   Floor plan of the pre-storage zone of a unit warehouse (two aisles) with storage and retrieval; I-point and order picking sites

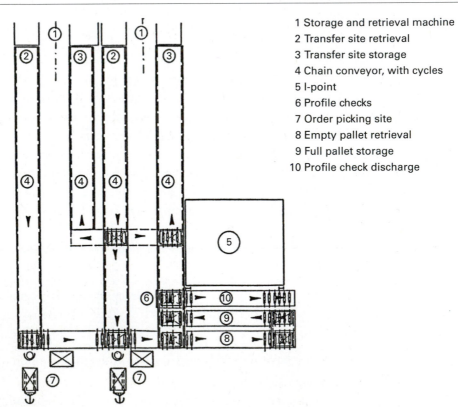

1 Storage and retrieval machine
2 Transfer site retrieval
3 Transfer site storage
4 Chain conveyor, with cycles
5 I-point
6 Profile checks
7 Order picking site
8 Empty pallet retrieval
9 Full pallet storage
10 Profile check discharge

Figure 11.29 Order picking space with order picking pallet

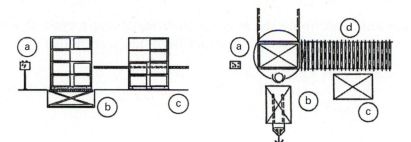

a) Control panel
b) Rotating scissor lift table with roller conveyor

c) Empty goods shelf pallet
d) Stowage roller conveyor

11.7 VDI guidelines

2493	Conveyance and storage of long goods	09.03
2516	Floor conveyors for storage and retrieval cycle time calculation in narrow aisles	09.03
2694	Bins and silos – feed, storage and extraction of bulk materials	07.12
2690/1	Material and data flow in high bay warehouses	11.94
2699	Storage and transport of small coils	03.95
3311E	Paperless order picking	09.15
3577	Industrial trucks for high bay warehouses – specification and operating conditions	02.09
3581	Availability of transport and storage systems including subsystems and elements	12.04
3584	Flow storage systems for piece goods	09.03
3590	Order picking systems practical examples	08.02
3612	Incoming goods/outgoing goods	12.96
3626	Checklist for planning and implementation of high bay warehouses	07.93
3629	Basic organization functions in warehousing	03.05
3630	Automatic mini load warehouses	08.06
3657	Ergonomic design of packing workstations	07.93
4415	Automated order compilation	10.99
4490	Operational logistics key figures from goods receiving to dispatch	05.07
BGR 234	Storage equipment and devices	09.06

11.8 Examples and questions

Example 11.1: Determine the average time for a single cycle of a high bay stacker when deployed in a pallet high bay warehouse

The average time for a single cycle is required in order to calculate the number of high bay stackers needed when the number of storage and retrieval units (pallets) per day are known (see Equations 2.6 and 2.9).

Answer:

$$z = \frac{\dot{m}_{St}\, t_{ges}}{3,600\, t_a} \qquad \text{Number of high bay stackers} \qquad (11.1)$$

$\dot{m}_{St}$	quantity/day	Number of pallets to be stored and retrieved
t_{ges}	in s	Average time for a single cycle of a high bay stacker
t_a	in h/day	Daily operating time for a high bay stacker

To solve this task, an understanding of t_{ges} is required. t_{ges} is determined with the help of the diagram in Figure 11.30.

In the diagram, the route is given in metres (m) on the left hand side of the coordinate plane. The travel time (t_1) for the journey there and back is shown on the top vertical axis. The total of driving and lifting time (t_1 and t_2) on the right horizontal axis, in addition to the lifting process (t_3), results in $t_1 + t_2 + t_3$ shown on the bottom of the vertical axis. In parallel to this is the cycle scale (t_{ges}), which also contains the times for intake and setting down, as well as for manipulating the load handling attachment. When determining the average time, we assume the route is two-thirds of the shelf aisle length and the storage height is two-thirds of the maximum lifting height. The example below showcases the average time for a single cycle of a high bay stacker, with a working route of 75 m (maximum shelf aisle length) and a maximum storage height of 12 m, which is t_{ges} = 130s.

Lifting time straight for medium lift height	(2/3 × 12 = 8 m)
Lowering time straight for medium lowering height	(2/3 × 12 = 8 m)
Driving route 2/3 × 75 = 50 m	

For transferring the stacker to another shelf aisle, we have to calculate 20 s.

Example 11.2: Warehouse floor area comparison

How much built-up floor space is required to store 5,000 pallets for a storage height, including pallets, of 1,300 mm? Determine the respective floor area for operating the pallet shelving with:

a) a high bay stacker or storage and retrieval machine of the same height;

b) a reach truck;

c) a forklift.

Figure 11.30 Diagram for single cycle times for high bay stacker

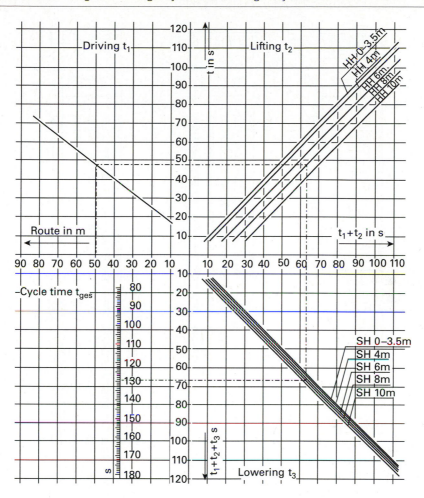

In order to save space, lengthwise storage was chosen (shelf depth 1,200 mm).

Answer: To solve this question we assume variable aisle widths, the possible lift heights of transports a to c, and the total height of a loaded pallet. For determining the height of the building, consider the free height in shelf compartments (100 mm) and construction height of traverses for resting the pallets on (approximately 120 mm) for determining the width of the building:

Width per double shelf = 2 × pallet length (2,400 mm) plus 100 mm construction width.

To compare data, all values were compared in a table in the order they were determined for all three means of transport (Table 11.2). A visual representation can be seen in Figure 11.31. The required floor area can be calculated as follows:

Figure 11.31   Representation of floor area comparison

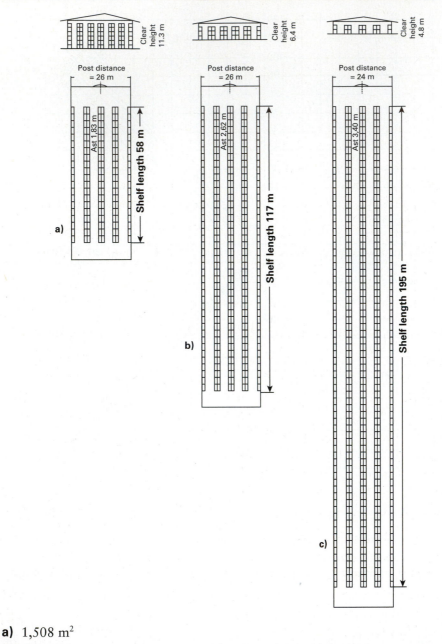

a) 1,508 m²

b) 3,042 m²

c) 4,680 m²

The required installation of a sprinkler plant in case 'a' accounts for the large difference between row 7 and 8 in Table 11.2.

Table 11.2 Listing and comparison of data for floor area comparison

		Means of conveyance		
No.	Planning data	a	b	c
1	Aisle width in m	1.83	2.62	3.40
2	Number of shelf aisles	6	5	4
3	Post distance (hall width) in m	26	26	24
4	Shelving length in m	58	117	195
5	Lift height of conveyor in m	9	4,5	3
6	Number of stacked pallets	7	4	3
7	Height of stacked pallets in m	10.3	5.8	4.3
8	Required height of hall in m	11.3	6.4	4.8
9	Number of stored pallets	5,040	5,040	5,040
10	Required floor area in m² (for shelf area only)	1,508	3,042	4,680

Example 11.3: Calculating amortization time for warehousing planning

In a manufacturing hall with a height of 6 m, there is a warehouse for castings on a floor area of 325 m² consisting of shelving with a height of 2 m and floor storage. Calculate how saving (rationalization success) can be achieved through a shelving rack (5 m high) and operation using a storage and retrieval machine, and after how long the investment will have been amortized. The planning resulted in a new storage area of 65 m². Two out of three warehousing staff can be saved as a result of the new design. Assumption: medium capacity use of the storage and retrieval machine.

Answer: The answer to this task is found by using a cost comparison calculation (Table 11.3). The annual operating costs of the old warehouse are €121,100, those of the planned warehouse would be €51,371. This results in an annual saving of €69,789. For the relevant investment of €85,000, the amortization time would be 1.29 years. It is the difference in values that are of most interest in Table 11.3.

Such a rationalization also results in:

- lowering of wage, rental and interest costs;
- increase of turnover performance; shorter access times;
- reduction of fatigue through safe and comfortable working; improved orderliness and better overview, greater degree of space utilization.

Table 11.3 Tabular determination of operating costs for existing and planned warehouse

	Old answer	New answer
	€/a	€/a
1 Personnel costs		
Wage and on costs		
(251 workdays per year; 8 h per workday)		
Number of staff x 251 days x 8 Std.	9,360	30,120
2 Depreciation		
10% pa linear:		
a) Storage and retrieval machine		
€40,000 / 10		4,000
b) Shelving		
€45,000 / 10	1,000	4,500
3 Capital interest		
10% pa of half the average capital committed		
a) Storage and retrieval machine		
€(40,000 x 10)/(100 x 2)		2,000
b) Shelving		
€(45,000 x 10)/(100 x 2)	1,000	2,250
4 Maintenance costs		
5% pa of investment amount		
Storage and retrieval machine		
(5% x €40,000) / 100		2,000
5 Calculatory rental costs		
€180 per square metre pa (incl. heating,		
maintenance, repairs and cleaning)		
€180 x 325 (65)m^2	58,500	11,700
6 Operating costs		
Electricity costs for connection values of:		
2.0 kW per hoist and		
0,5kW per drive motor		
2.5kW for a price of 0.10 €/kWh		
and 30% ED (251 days x 8 h x 0.3 = 602.4 h)		
2.5 kW x 0.10 € x 301.2 h		151
Total €/a	121,110	51,371

Example 11.4: Key figures

Determine key figures for block and high bay warehouses (see Chapter 1.5.1 and Example 1.2). A new warehouse containing 20,000 pallets is planned, and two versions have been designed: a block and a high bay warehouse.

The investments have been calculated, for the block warehouse at €2.9 m, and for the high bay warehouse at €6.65 m. The following key figures must be calculated for comparison purposes using the operating costs:

a) warehousing costs in € per pallet and month;

b) turnover costs in € per pallet storage and retrieval.

Answer: The results were determined in a table (Table 11.4). For key figure a, the costs for the block warehouse are €0.97, for the high bay warehouse they are €2.19 per pallet per month. The turnover costs for storing and retrieving a pallet are €1.86 for the block warehouse and €0.90 for the high bay warehouse. In order to decide which warehouse should be built, these key figures, amongst others, can be used as criteria to determine the pallet turnover quantities per annum, warehousing and manipulation costs.

Table 11.4 Determining key figures for warehousing and turnover costs via operating costs for block and high bay warehouse

Estimate of operating costs including determining key figures for two warehousing types

Investment amount: Block warehouse €2.9 m — Number of stored pallets: 20,000
High bay warehouse €6.65 m — Number of pallets for turnover pa: 145,000

No	Operating type costs	Block warehouse	High bay warehouse
		Values in €/a	
1	Building maintenance 1% of investment amount	29,000	66,500
2	Maintenance means of transport 5% of investment amount	–	110,000
3	Maintenance and replacement of pallets 5.5% of investment amount	15,500	15,500
4	Maintenance and replacement push on frames 4% of investment amount	44,000	–
5	Operating costs E-stacker	30,000	10,000
6	Personnel costs €15 per h	240,000	120,000
7	Subtotal	358,500	322,000
8	Interest 5% of investment amount	145,000	332,500
9	Subtotal	503,500	654,500
10	Depreciation buildings 3%	87,000	199,500
11	Depreciation means of transport 20%	22,500	295,000

(continued)

Table 11.4   *(Continued)*

No	Operating type costs	Values in €/a Block warehouse	High bay warehouse
12	Depreciation transport plant 10%	–	29,000
13	Depreciation pallets and push on frames 20%	276,000	56,000
14	Depreciation shelving 7%	3,500	–
15	Total depreciation	392,000	475,000
16	Total of annual costs	895,500	1,129,500
17	Warehousing costs €/pallet and month [(row 9-5-6) : 20,000 : 12]	0.97	2.19
18	Turnover costs €/pallet storing and retrieval [(row 5 = 6) : 145,000]	1.86	0.90

Example 11.5: Warehouse planning for predetermined building

The following values must be determined for a building with a gross warehousing space of 4,100 m³, comparatively and in dependence of different means of transport: a) forklift; b) stacker crane; c) storage and retrieval machine determined in comparative format:

- the number of stored pallets;
- the net storage space;
- the degree of space utilization.

Answer: Figure 11.32 and Table 11.5.

Table 11.5   Comparison of forklift, stacker crane and storage and retrieval machine in respect of warehousing space

	Warehouse operation		
	Forklift	Stacker crane	Storage and retrieval machine
Gross warehouse space in m³	4,100	4,100	4,100
Storage capacity in %	100	150	265
Number of stored pallets	424	636	1,120
Net warehouse space in m³	825	1,238	2,180
Degree of space utilization in %	20	30	53

Example 11.6: Storage and retrieval machine data

What data characterize a storage and retrieval machine for pallets or containers?

Answer:

1 Technical data, such as capacity load, machine height, aisle width, machine length, deepest and highest setting, driving and lifting speeds, size of driver's platform and transfer speed.

2 Type of load handling attachment and capacity load.

3 Type of steering.

4 Additional equipment, such as fine positioning and height pre-selection.

Figure 11.32 Comparison of storage capacity dependent on warehouse operating device for pallets storage. a) Forklift. b) Stacker crane. c) Storage and retrieval machine

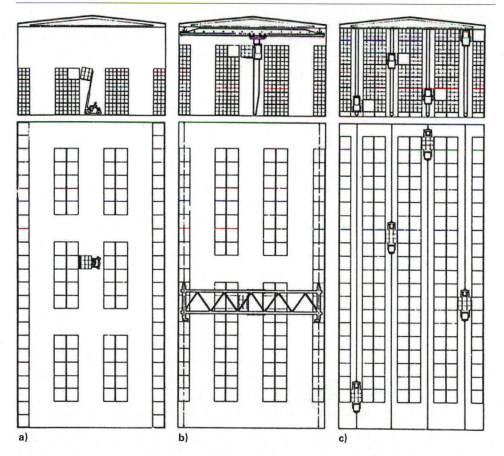

a)   b)   c)

Example 11.7: Storage and retrieval machines

What transport can be used for storing and retrieving pallet units in a unit and order picking warehouse (up to 15 m height), if the degree of utilization of the six existing shelf aisles is less than 25 per cent per shift each?

Answer: Based on the degree of utilization and the number of shelf aisles, there are 1.5 means of transport per shift. Two devices can be used as means of transport, which can both operate in multiple aisles. The options are:

- narrow aisle stacker: high bay stacker or order picking forklift;
- stacker crane (2 × 3 aisles after one another);
- storage and retrieval machine: with transfer truck or curve-going design.

Example 11.8: Order picking high bay warehouse

In a parts warehouse for forklifts, 12,000 items are stored in boxes with 30 kg load weight in a shelving rack. Up to 500 incidences of storage and up to 2,000 retrievals must be carried out per shift with a storage and retrieval machine. Sketch the warehouse floor plan and the order picking machine.

Answer: Figure 11.33. The feeding and removal of containers with unit and order picking products are carried out with roller conveyors. The platform of the storage and retrieval machine contains a scale in order to allow for quicker order picking of the small materials.

Figure 11.33 Floor plan shelving rack, view of order picking storage and retrieval machine (www.dematic.com)

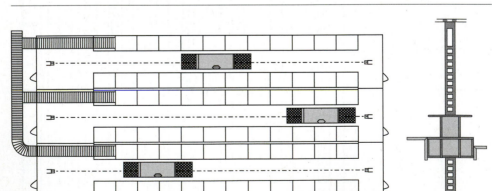

Example 11.9: Order picking warehouse

Show different designs of order picking warehouses with one or more levels.

Answers:

- Figure 11.34:

    - continuous shelf: separation of storage and retrieval;

    - retrieval of larger units from pallets on bottom, smaller items from boxes higher up;

    - order picking on one level.

Figure 11.34   Combination of container and pallets continuous shelf for order picking on one level (www.bito.com)

- Figure 11.35:

    - continuous shelf: separation of storage and retrieval, order picking tunnel;

    - order picking on one level – units on pallets;

    - order picking truck for assignment.

Figure 11.35   Combination of unit and order picking warehouse via two continuous pallet shelves with gravity drive on top of one another (www.bito.com)

- Figure 11.36:

  - continuous pallet shelf; flow through of crossways pallets for better order picking;

  - separation of storage and retrieval;

  - availability guaranteed through successive pallet units, one-dimensional order picking;

  - operation unit warehouse and refilling order picking warehouse with storage and retrieval machine (also possible with order picking or high bay stacker);

  - order picking on three levels;

  - order picking warehouse for large quantities per item, high item number and high level of replacements.

Figure 11.36   Spatial allocation of high bay shelving as unit warehouse, operation of order picking warehouse on three levels with storage and retrieval machine (www.bito.com)

- Figure 11.37:

  - horizontal continuous pallet shelf with stowage roller conveyor for pressure-free stowage of pallets (unit warehouse, FIFO);

  - two-sided operation through storage and retrieval machine with roller track as load handling device;

  - high turnover performance of up to 100 pallets/hour and machine through short distances;

  - lowest level: order picking warehouse as continuous gravity shelf, manual order picking on order picking truck in order picking tunnel.

Figure 11.37   Order picking warehouse with unit warehouse on top as horizontal continuous pallet shelf (www.westfaliaEurope.com)

Example 11.10: Floor area comparison

Conduct a comparison of floor areas (see Chapter 10.3.3.2) for the shelving racks and continuous shelves sketched in the floor plans (Figure 11.38).

Answer: The result is a floor area saving of 25 per cent. The travel time of the order picking process is reduced by approximately 40 per cent.

Figure 11.38   Comparison of shelving rack and continuous container shelving

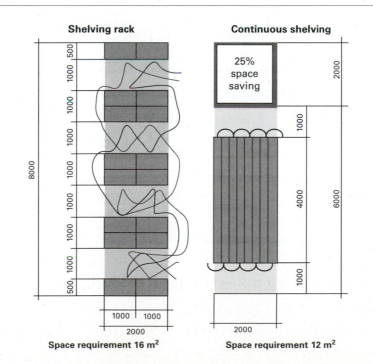

Example 11.11: Honeycomb shelving

What are the retrieval options for long goods storage in a honeycomb shelf?

Answer: Figure 11.39 shows the following retrieval options, top to bottom:

- crane with traverse;
- forklift with attachment;
- storage and retrieval machine;
- mobile support;
- mobile lift table.

Figure 11.39   Retrieval options for honeycomb shelf (www.lagerlogistik.ch)

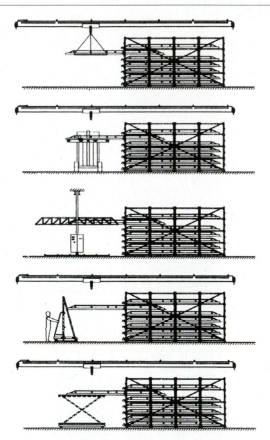

Example 11.12: High bay storage for sheet products

We are looking for a high bay warehouse with tower shelving for sheet products with direct connection to processing machines (nibble, punch and cutting machines).

Answer: Figure 11.40; single sheets are removed for processing from the units, which are stored sideways. Remaining pieces and open pallets are returned to the warehouse and stored with storage and retrieval machines.

Figure 11.40   Fully automated tower shelving for sheet products with separate storage and multiple retrieval places along the side of the tower shelf (www.kasto.com)

Example 11.13: Pallet shelving

What terms are used for a pallet shelf with multiple storage places? What is shelf load and bay load?

Answer: Figure 11.41; shelf load = maximum load weight of all pallets in a shelf; bay load = total of all shelf loads on all shelving levels between two posts (= post weight).

Example 11.14: Determining master data

What is the purpose of determining master data and how is this done?

Answer: Master data can serve the determination of the shipping box size for an assignment, of its weight and, thus, the optimization of shipping costs using the fee charges of the post office, so that, dependent on the dimensions, two small parcels may be chosen by the computer instead of one large package. Item weights are also needed for manual and automatic order picking, in order to spot errors.

Measuring the item profiles, their volume and weight, as well as determining the stock requirements of an item is done with a so-called space requirement measuring device (Figure 11.42) using integrated infrared transmission and receiving modules. Disruptive extraneous light is suppressed. Infrared light is not dangerous for the eyes. Modules for maximum compressing of textiles also exist.

Figure 11.41   Labels on a pallet shelf

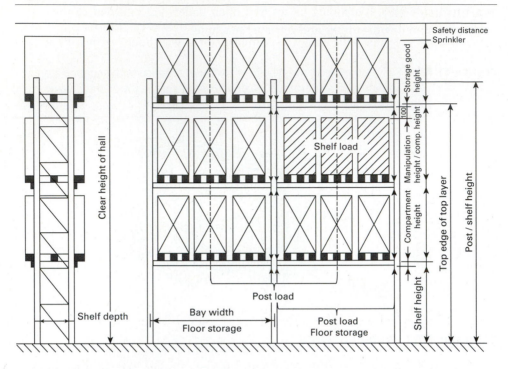

Figure 11.42   Mobile space requirement measuring device with weight determination on a transport truck with self-sufficient energy source and a battery with power inverter. We distinguish: multi-volume and profile scanner (see Figure 5.34c) (www.kht-online.de)

Example 11.15: Calculation of costs per pallet space in a pallet shelving warehouse

Calculate the cost per pallet space and month for a warehouse with a floor area of 7,000 m² and 6,500 pallet spaces, based on the rental costs (€4.00/m²/month), the heating expenses (€0.40/m²/month), electricity costs (€0.20/m²/month), and the maintenance costs (€0.50/m²/month). Storage and retrieval costs are approximately €2–3/pallet.

Answer:

The floor area costs per month are: 4.00 + 0.40 + 0.20 + 0.50 = €5.10/m²/month

The costs for one pallet space can be calculated as per (see Example 1.7):

7,000 m² × €5.1/m²/month: 6,500 pallet spaces = €5.49/pallet/month

Example 11.16: Storage of box pallets

What options are there to line store DIN box pallets?

Answer: There are three solutions, for which both crossways and lengthways storing of box pallets is possible:

- pallets/container shelving as one space system;
- pallet shelving in multiple space system with support brackets;
- large shelving rack.

Example 11.17: Pallet shelving: lengthways and crossways storage

What are the percentage differences for costs and floor area for a pallet shelf, on the one hand for lengthways storage, on the other for crossways storage?

Answer: Crossways storage causes 13 per cent additional costs and uses approximately 17 per cent more space than lengthways storage.

Example 11.18: Long goods storage

Show examples of standing shelves.

Answer: See Chapter 10.3.1.3. Figures 11.43 and 11.44 show standing shelves for long goods and cable drums.

Figure 11.43 Standing shelf for long goods (www.dexion.de)

Figure 11.44 Standing shelf for cable drums (www.dexion.de)

Example 11.19: Automatic order picking

What criteria determine automatic order picking and the type of utilized automatic order picking systems?

Answer: These are the criteria:

- geometric, physical and chemical features, such as shape, and surface finish (see Figure 3.2);
- specific characteristics, such as recognizable features and stackability (see Figure 3.2);
- packaging status of order picking items, such as packaged or unpacked;
- provisioning of items: see Chapter 11.1.1;
- storage type: see Figure 10.5;
- order state of items, such as sorted or unsorted;
- retrieval unit as a single package: box, container, tin or multipack;
- retrieval option, such as with grabber (mechanic, magnetic, pneumatic), telescopic fork/table, discharger and handling attachment;
- refilling options and organization.

For automatic order picking (see Chapter 11.5) there are available: cantilever arm robots, area portal robots, palletizers, special order picking robots, shaft order pickers, storage and retrieval machines for unit and order picking warehouses, such as storage and retrieval machines in small parts warehouses.

Example 11.20: Entire warehouse system

Outline an entire warehouse system, representing all its main features.

Answer: Figure 11.45.

Figure 11.45 Representational depiction of fully automated satellite shelving with storage and retrieval machine for pallet with corrugated cardboard. (www. hoermann-gruppe.de)

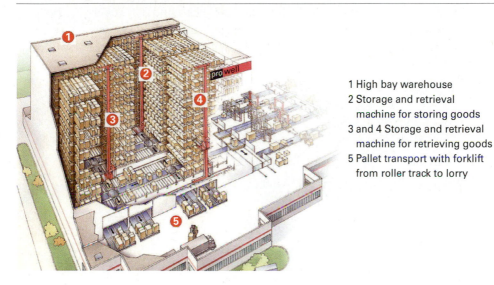

1 High bay warehouse
2 Storage and retrieval
  machine for storing goods
3 and 4 Storage and retrieval
  machine for retrieving goods
5 Pallet transport with forklift
  from roller track to lorry

Example 11.21: Key figures for planning a pallet warehousing system

Calculate the warehouse capacity for an existing building with known dimensions and weights of storage unit with DIN pallets 800 × 1,200, as well as the investment for different alternatives.

What key figures are required for this?

Answer: See Table 11.6 and Example 12.27. The values in the table assume a multiple space principle for the pallet shelving: maximum sag of the traverse minus one length L/200. For the shelving, 8 per cent of the investment can be allocated to freight and assembly costs for the pallet shelving; these are then included in the values. Premiums of approximately 5 per cent are for safety equipment and accessories, such as push-through protection, crash barriers for posts and corner buffers, as well as filler plates under the posts and wall plugs.

The provided leasing rate for the forklift is calculated with a duration of use of 1,210 hours per year – this corresponds to a shift a day: 220 days/year × 5.5 hours/day – and a legally prescribed depreciation period of eight years, and a lease time between 39 and 84 months. For a lease of five years, a remaining value of €3,000 based on experiential data and an interest rate of 6 per cent, the monthly leasing rate for the front forklift (price: €19,000) is €325 per month. Added to that is machine insurance, such as for fire or flooding, so that the total is approximately €332 per month per forklift (as of 2007, see Example 6.6-27).

Table 11.6   Summary of planning data for shelf storage of DIN pallets

No	Shelf storage/ shelf type	Storage and retrieval machine (SRM)	Investment approx. €/SRM[1]	Leasing approx. €/month	Aisle width mm	€[2] pro pallet space, approx.
1	2	3	4	5	6	7
1	Pallet shelf	Front fork- 3-wheel	19,000	350	3,200	25
		Forklift 4-wheel	25,000	450	3,600	25
2	Pallet shelf	Reach truck	30,000	450	2,800	25
3	Pallet shelf	Narrow aisle forklift	65,000	1,300	1,600	30
4	Pallet shelf	SRM on tracks[3]	70,000	–	1,400	40
5	Mobile shelf	Reach truck	30,000	450	2,800	100
6	Continuous shelf[4]	Front forklift	25,000	450	3,600	200
7	Large shelving rack grate	Front forklift	19,000	350	3,200	50
8	Drive-in shelf	Front forklift	19,000	350	Pallet crossways	55
9	Pallet shelf	Front forklift	19,000	350	Pallet crossways	50
10	Moulded shelf[5]	Front forklift	30,000	450	3,500	60

[1] with reference to 1.2 t load capacity for 3-wheel, 1.6 t for 4-wheel design; Lift height approx. 5 m; [2] for approx. 500 pallet spaces, incl. freight and assembly; [3] without steering, for which approx. €150,000 are calculated; [4] with gravity drive; [5] for 2.5 t load capacity/pallet space

Example 11.22: Comparison of offer for order picking forklift with operating costs calculation

The 11-year-old order picker in an existing warehouse with high bay pallet shelving should be replaced. Carry out a comparison of the offers of three suppliers by conducting an operations cost comparison for purchase and lease. Also list additional figures and forklift features that are significant for the selection. Carry out a cash value comparison for the cheapest forklift and answer the question of whether a purchase or leasing is more economical.

Answer: See Table 11.7. Additional figures for the selection assessment can be found in Chapter 10.4.3 'Order picking forklift', as well as additional equipment, payment and delivery conditions, delivery time and warranty. The information in Table 11.7 shows that manufacturer B with order picking forklift Y means the lowest investment. Should the forklift be purchased or leased?

Table 11.7 Operating cost comparison for order picking forklift

Lfd	**Offer comparison**			
	Manufacturer	**A**	**B**	**C**
Nr	**Order picking forklift type**	**Type X**	**Type X**	**Type X**
1	**2**	**3**	**4**	**5**
1.1	Purchase price net €	69,747	64,800	67,400
1.2	Assembly costs €	incl.	incl.	3,450
1.3	Guide rollers €	incl.	incl.	810
1.4	Investment net €	**69,747**	**64,800**	**71,660**
2.0	**Operating costs for purchase €**	**17,257**	**16,524**	**18,898**
2.1	Depreciation pa €	8,718	8,100	8,425
2.2	Interest pa € at 9%	3,139	2,916	3,033
2.3	Maintenance contract pa	5,400	5,508	7,440
2.4	Parts	incl.	incl.	incl.
3.0	**Operating costs for lease €**	**26,772**	**20,316**	**22,933**
3.1	Leasing rate €/month	2,231	1,203	1,291
3.2	Costs for full service € pa	incl.	5,880	7,440
3.3	Remaining value €	0	1,450	2,020
3.4	Operating hours pa €	800	1,200	1,200
3.5	Lease type	**Full service/ (60 months)**	**Full service/ (60 months)**	**Full service/ (60 months)**

The operational cost comparison calculation can ignore wage, energy and maintenance costs, as these are irrespective of the financing option. The operating costs result from depreciation and interest costs in line with Table 11.8. The big difference is the period of use of eight years for purchase and five years for lease.

Table 11.8 is a static comparison. Using the capital value method, it is possible to apply interest to all income and payments from a point in time. This application of interest from a point in time is called cash value. For constant annual payments, a dynamic comparison can be limited to the total of all cash values. If this is applied to the current case, the results are as found in Table 11.9.

Table 11.8 Cost comparison calculation for order picking forklift

Operating costs for purchase pa	**10,206**
Linear depreciation pa for 8 years	8,100
Interest pa at 6.5%[*]	2,106
Total costs for purchase after 8 years	81,648
Operating costs for lease pa	**14,436**
Lease costs pa [€] for 5 years	14,436
Remaining value payment t_5 [€]	1,450
Total costs for lease after 5 years	73,630
* internal reference value	all prices in €

Table 11.9 Cash values for purchase and lease

Cash value of payments for purchase [€]	**62,142**
Annual costs k [€]	10,472
Int. interest i [%]	6.5
Remaining value R_8 [€]	0
Period of use n [a]	8
Cash value of payments for lease [€]	**61,049**
Annual costs k [€]	14,436
Int. interest i [%]	6.5
Remaining value R_5 [€]	1,450
Period of use n [a]	5

The comparison shows that a lease is advantageous. One prerequisite is that the order picking forklift is purchased for the remaining value at the end of the lease period and used for another three years.

Example 11.23: Operating costs comparison pallet shelving and mobile shelving

For storing 1,500 Euro pallets with a total height of 1,800 mm and a weight of 800 kg per load unit a pallet shelving or a mobile shelving unit can be used, as the capacity use of 10 aisles is at about 10 per cent per aisle. The design shows a required floor area of 1,000 m² for a pallet shelving with five levels and operation by reach truck (aisle width 3,000 mm). For the mobile shelving, approximately 45 per cent of the floor area = 450 m² can be saved. Depreciation is linear and is 10 years for the pallet shelving and eight years for the mobile shelving. Carry out an operating cost comparison for the two shelving types.

Answer: First, determine the investment (see Table 11.10). The operating costs are listed in a table (see Table 11.11), design: see Figure 10.19.

The investment is:

Table 11.10 Summary of investment (based on DIN pallets)

No	Size	Stationary pallet shelving (€)	Mobile pallet shelving (€)	Note
1	Pallet shelving	30,000	–	25 €/pallet space
2	Mobile shelving	–	120,000	100 €/pallet space
3	Reach truck	40,000	40,000	
4	10% contingency	7,000	16,000	
5	Total	77,000	176,000	

The above information can be used to calculate the operating costs. The operating cost comparison results in lower operating costs but a much higher investment for the mobile shelving.

Table 11.11 Operating cost comparison

No	Size	Euro pallet shelving (€/a)	Mobile Euro pallet shelving (€/a)	Notes
1	Rent (6 €/m²/month)	72,000	39,600	
2	Lease reach truck	7,200	7,200	
3	Depreciation	3,000	15,000	No contingency
4	Interest (8%)	1,200	4,800	No contingency
5	Personnel costs 1.2 employee/a	36,000	36,000	€30,000/a/empl
6	Total	119,400	92,600	

Example 11.24: Multi-order-picking with tractor and horizontal order picker

What systems are on offer for multi-order picking with industrial trucks?

Answer: Trailers constructed for multi-order picking can be pulled by a tractor (Figure 11.15), and may have a type of shelf truck. For horizontal order pickers, vehicles are used with and without a liftable operating platform. Shelf parts with or without scales but mostly with IT connection have load handling options, such as for fork tines (see Figure 11.46).

Figure 11.46 Horizontal order picker with order picking shelf a) With liftable operating platform up to 1 m (www.pp-system.com) b) Without liftable operating platform (www.still.de)

a)   b)

Example 11.25: Item names, item identification, item group and order volume

What are they and what figures are part of it?

Answer: Item names are a part of the item group (see Example 11.14). The item identification happens using plain text, item number, barcode or transponder.

The item group (item group file) is a part of the warehouse administration and consists of features, characteristics (see Chapter 3.1) and data to describe all items, such as item name, item number, storage location and storage space. The order volume is characterized by the total of orders with item quantity, number of positions per item, weight, volume and value.

Example 11.26: Satellite shelving with forklift operation

Answer: Figure 11.47 shows a drive-in shelf with reach truck operation, whereby the satellite (powered load sledge) can move down the aisle independently of the carrier vehicle once unlocked, driving under the first pallet in the channel and lifting and returning it to the forklift. Once locked again, the pallet and forklift drive to the predetermined destination. By separating pure order picking and stacking aisles, small aisle widths can be implemented in the order picking aisle. Steering of the satellite is carried out using a radio signal.

Figure 11.47 a) Schematic representation of satellite movements (arrows). b) Satellite leaves the reach truck (www.jungheinrich.de)

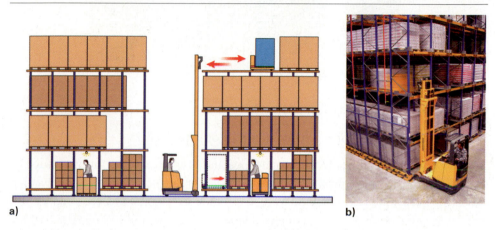

a)   b)

Example 11.27: Push-back shelving

How has this shelving type been constructed and how is it operated?

Answer: Figure 11.48 represents this shelving type. It works in line with the LIFO principle, is used when a few pallets are required and when space is tight. Usually it stores five pallets behind one another, which are pushed into the shelf channel by the forklift (low incline of approximately 2 per cent).

Figure 11.48 Push-back shelving (www.ssi-schaefer.com)

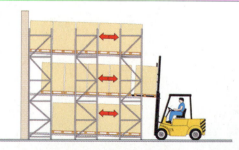

Example 11.28: Vertical order picker for small assignments

How can small assignments up to a height of 5 m be order picked?

Answer: Figure 11.49.

Figure 11.49   Mobile vertical order picker (www.crown.com)

Example 11.29: Paper roll transport

What options are there for mechanic transport of paper rolls?

Answer: Transport can occur with continuous and discontinuous conveyors, such as drag chain conveyors (Figures 5.19b and d). For low frequency, forklifts and travelling cranes are mostly used (for more on travelling cranes, see Figures 11.24b, c and 11.50).

For more on automatic transport, see Figure 6.7.11e, as well as Figure 6.7.10 for air cushion transport.

Figure 11.50   Paper roll transport with cranes (www.demagcranes.com) a) Mechanical gripper with six gripper jaws and up to four paper rolls per cycle b) Mechanical using a tambour traverse from machine, approx. 100 t to rewinder c) Pneumatic with two trolleys and vacuum lifts: turnover increase in paper roll block warehouse, different roll diameters

a)   b)   c)

Example 11.30: Mobile shelf

How can a mobile shelf be constructed without the disruptive tracks on the floor?

Answer: One option is the mobile shelf in Figure 11.51, for which the individual shelf trolleys are guided on a floor track fixed to the wall.

Figure 11.51   Manually operated mobile shelf for tyres, wheels and exhaust units: detailed sketch: guidance of shelf trolley on a profile fixed to floor and wall (www.ssi-schaefer.com)

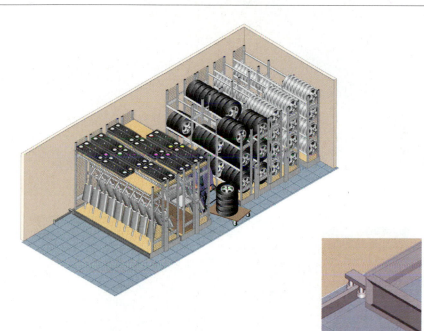

Example 11.31: Honeycomb shelving

Provide a pictorial representation of a honeycomb shelf.

Answer: Figure 11.52.

Example 11.32: Long and sheet goods storage

Construct a systematic division for long and sheet goods shelving in a table.

Answer: See Figures 11.53 and 12.29.

Storage and retrieval can occur from the side or front, manually through pushing or pulling, or mechanically or automatically with transport aids, such as a long

Figure 11.52   a) Honeycomb shelf for long goods; furthest left: storage site; right: retrieval locations with processing machines; in the middle between the honeycomb shelf blocks: storage and retrieval machine with extension roller conveyors for long goods cassettes (www.kasto.com) b) Honeycomb shelf for small range and small quantities. Right: adaptor for fork tines to retrieve long goods troughs (www.bartels-germany.de)

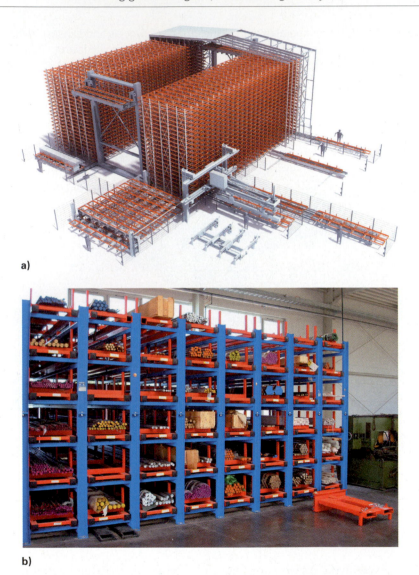

a)

b)

goods cassette. The shelves can be fixed, mobile or on rolls, as well as constructed with one or two sides. Single or clock storage is possible.

Options for transport are shown in Figures 10.13, 10.27, 11.24 to 11.27, 11.39, 11.40, 11.43 and 11.52.

Figure 11.53 Systematic representation for storage of long and sheet goods in shelves

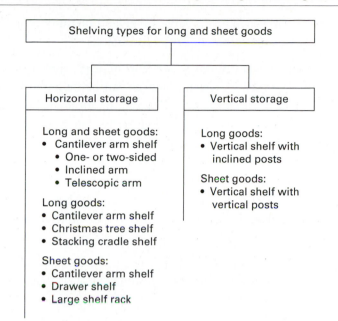

Example 11.33: Long goods storage with front operation

Show options for storing small quantities with small range.

Answer: The figures in Example 11.32 show options for light and heavy long goods for front operation. Another option is offered by the constructions in Figure 11.54. Storage can occur with or without long goods cassette (see Figure 3.5s). Such cassettes are used for bendable material, rest pieces or for feeding cranes with multiple individual pieces (see Figure 11.25).

Figure 11.54 Long goods warehouse with front operation (www.bartels-germany.de)

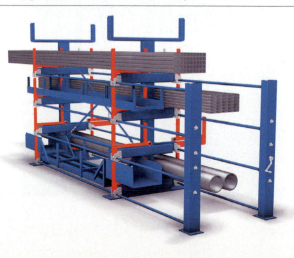

Example 11.34: Small parts warehouse and satellite warehouse

What storage is recommended for a large range and quantity of goods with small volume, such as plastic containers or cardboard boxes?

Answer: There are different options as single or multiple space system with single, double or multiple storage in shelves. Shelves can be operated with storage and retrieval machines or with shuttles. Load handling attachments can take one or more storage units simultaneously (see Figure 11.23). Small parts warehouses and satellite storage systems offer high storage density and best space efficiency. All storage and retrieval processes are controlled and monitored by a warehouse management system (for more on this, see Figures 13.14 and 13.15), in order to ensure energy saving, error-free and transparent processes. Figure 11.55 shows parts of the pre-storage and storage zones of multiple adjacent small parts storage systems.

Figure 11.55   Pre-storage zone (www.viastore.com) Pre-storage zone of a small parts warehouse

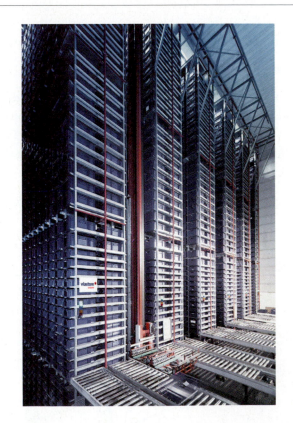

Example 11.35: Double-depth pallet shelving

What designs can a double-depth pallet shelf have for a compact goods issue warehouse?

Answer: In a goods issue warehouse and depending on production processes, products are regularly and irregularly passed on for storage in the goods issue warehouse.

Figure 11.56   Double-depth storage of pallets with sorting function (www.kardex-mlog. com). Pallet storage using a forklift or automated connection to existing high bay warehouse

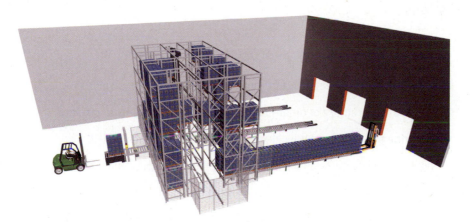

Figure 11.57   Double-depth storage (www.kardex-mlog.com) and a schematic top view of Figure 11.56 with goods receipt and goods issue with automated or forklift storage connection and forklift loading

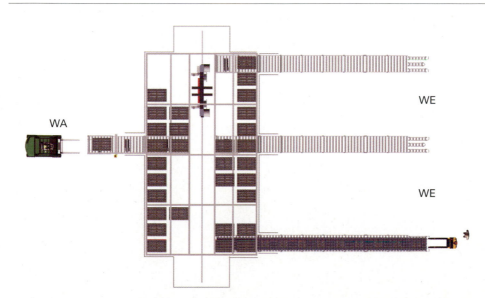

It is the task of goods issue to put together assignments in the shortest possible time and transport them to provided lorries. In order to carry out this process as effectively – and thus fast – as possible, a warehouse with double-depth storage can be used. For pallets, the storage and retrieval performance can be significantly increased through double-depth storage when pre-sorting in line with a delivery plan. Figures 11.56 and 11.57 show a warehouse design for 184 Euro pallet spaces with dimensions of 8 × 10 × 16 m (W × H × D) with a retrieval performance of 106 pallets p/h with up to 64 double cycles p/h.

Questions

1 What is the basic function of the order picking process?

2 Which storage systems/shelving types have dynamic provisioning?

3 What is the structure of order-focused and item-focused order picking?

4 Describe paperless order picking.

5 What time units make up the order picking time of an assignment?

6 How can the time units for travel time, grab time and downtime be reduced?

7 Sketch out the division of horizontal and vertical order pickers.

8 What is the workflow for automatic shaft order picking?

9 Show different storage options for long goods.

10 Describe the advantages and deployment of small parts warehousing systems.

11 What are the options for automatic long goods storage?

Planning systematics and project management

12

12.1 Planning basics

12.1.1 Tasks and meaning

Over the last few years all industrial businesses have made significant investments in material flow for transport, warehousing and information systems. The degree of mechanization and automation has reached a high level. Extensive planning is required so that these long-term investments are technically, economically and organizationally correct and sound. Factors such as goods, capacities, space, personnel, time and capital are subject to price increases and shortages, and they must be deployed in a rational manner. This can be achieved through planning.

Planning will improve existing operational structures, develop future structures, avoid erroneous investment and, thus, actively influence the future. According to Wöhe, planning is 'the mental anticipation of future actions through consideration of different action options and deciding on the most cost effective way' (Wöhe *et al*, 2016). In order to achieve this, planning needs to be *forward looking, systematic, methodical, dynamic, iterative, flexible, adaptable, exact, complete, unambiguous, continuous and economical.*

Planning is a tool used to achieve the objectives of the business. It is a logistical function (see Chapter 1.2). In this regard, business planning must have a certain position within the organization. A useful division is to allocate long-term planning as strategic planning by the business leaders (staff function) and to establish medium- and short-term planning within the logistics department.

12.1.2 Planning reasons

Planning can be required for internal causes, such as range expansion, production quantity increase, streamlining measures, or new manufacturing processes, as well as external requirements such as safety regulations or changes in the procurement or sales market.

Internal reasons for warehouse planning are:

- high warehousing costs, large numbers of staff, large stocks and a complex organization;
- obsolete warehousing technology, confusing organization and disruptions;
- low use of transport and warehousing means capacity;
- saving of rental, warehouse and provisioning space;
- increased level of mechanization and automation.

12.1.3 Types of planning

The term planning is ambiguous and was defined in Chapter 12.1.1. The different types of planning are represented through terminology related to goods, tasks and planning, which can also inform about the level of planning commitment. We differentiate in line with commitment level and task of planning, such as consulting, statement, study, investigation or report. A factual and task specific statement can be planning terms such as *new build, expansion, renovation* or *streamline planning*. Terms such as *structural, system, execution, rough* or *fine-tune planning* give information about the planning stage as well as about the accuracy of planning. The planning area is expressed through warehouse, transport or material flow planning (see Chapter 2.6). The timing aspect in planning finds expression in short-term, medium-term and long-term planning with the relevant levels of detail going from high to low.

12.1.4 Influencing factors

The influencing factors for planning can be divided into internal and external factors. External factors come from the business environment such as financing, customer and supplier requirements as well as influencing factors from technology, examples being new processes and machinery as well as environmental conditions (see Figure 1.1).

Legislation, regulatory requirements as well as regulations are limiting factors in planning, but cannot be ignored. They have great influence on planning solutions. Contacting the relevant authorities at the earliest stage is required, when considering the potential difficulties that arise when planning permission with building authorities or a trade supervisory office. For material flow planning, these external influencing factors have to be complied with:

- *Regulations to protect workers*
  Such as workplace regulations, accident prevention regulations and work consti-tutional legislation.

- *Regulations to protect resources*
  Such as recommendations for fire protection in high bay warehouses, areas for the fire service, fire-resistant doors and water mains.

- *Regulations to protect the environment*
  Such as pollution control, regulations to prevent noise, keeping the air clean, emission protection as well as the Flood and Water Management Act 2010.

Internal influencing factors are requirements, objectives and strategies by management (Figure 12.1), but there are also marginal conditions, benchmarks and restrictions within a business, such as building dimensions (ceiling load capacity, support grids and door heights), or large machine foundations.

12.1.5 *Planning principles*

Planning principles are used to show up general objectives for the planners and to provide evidence that the planning is compliant with the principles. Such planning principles include:

- check the necessity for planning;
- view partial plans as components of holistic planning;
- process stages;
- check alternatives and solutions for flexibility;
- carry out planning in a product and function-focused and economical way;
- design simple, clear, complete, comprehensible and accurate planning.

Planning objectives (see Chapter 1.5.2) include:

- simplifying manufacturing and assembly processes;
- minimizing transport;
- utilization of space volume;
- taking into account humanized workplaces;
- minimizing human labour;
- keeping investments small;
- achieving high utilization of equipment and plants;
- economic planning.

For developing and identifying objectives the following points are significant:

- transparency of objectives – shared understanding by all planners and participants;
- ranking of objectives;
- determining key figures for savings, planning success and profitability.

Thus, the lean production process tries to eliminate all non-value adding times (see Chapter 2.5.5), through optimization of success factors time, quality and costs. Another objective of the planning process is also the optimal utilization of business resources. These are:

- Optimization of time: short order processing times (see Figure 2.23), clear processes (see Example 2.18) and preventing waste (see Chapter 2.5.5).
- Optimization of quality: minimizing errors, increasing quality standards and developing reliable processes.
- Optimization of costs: prevention of waste (see Example 12.27); increasing value-adding times, lowering general costs, saving personnel and space costs.

12.2 Planning data

Binding and correct data form the crucial basis on which structures, systems and processes are developed, determined and identified. Thus, a lot of attention should be given to them. When planning, the compiling, calculating and determining of planning data during the analysis stage of system planning is the most time-intensive part, which can take up to 60 per cent of total planning time. The entirety of planning data represents the target data profile (framework). Target data can be calculated from current data and prognosis data.

The data used during planning can be divided according to different criteria (information is often called data; people process information; machines process data). We distinguish the following:

- static, dynamic, specific data;
- short-, medium- and long-term data;
- basic data/business-specific data;
- objectives, strategies, requirements;
- past, current and future data;
- current and target data, prognosis, trend data;
- provisions, benchmarks, marginal conditions, restrictions, requirements, master data;
- key figures, ratios;
- external – internal data;

- seasonal data, median – maximum values;
- value, priority and weighting of data;
- representative data.

Data quantity and data quality can be very different for long-, medium- and short-term planning. Figure 12.1 shows how objectives, strategies and requirements can develop, what factors they are influenced by and what schedules apply. The data framework for planning an order picking warehouse contains the following data, amongst others.

Static data:

- *item structure* (see Example 9.6): item range, quantity structure of item, dimensions, weights, volumes, weight per retrieval unit, turnover frequency of items, ABC analysis;
- *storage units*: pallets, containers, crates, dimensions, weights, quantity of warehouse units;
- *storage capacity*: storage space quantity, storage space dimension, storage volume.

Figure 12.1   Development of business-specific data

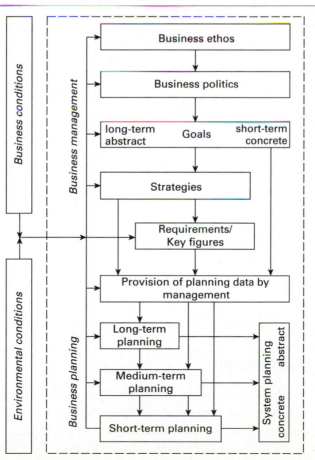

Dynamic data:

- *storage and retrieval machine movements*:
  - number of storage incidences during business hours;
  - number of retrievals during business hours;
- *order structure*:
  - number of orders during business hours;
  - number of positions/order;
  - number of retrieval units/position;
  - order volume.

Specific data:

- for tools/pallets warehouse, small container warehouse, cold store/long goods warehouse: such as climatization, stackability and perishable nature.

Restrictions:

- area and space values;
- hall heights, location of goods receipt/issue;
- degree of automation;
- specifications, key figures, strategies and marginal conditions.

12.3 Planning systematics

12.3.1 Iteration process

The results of planning are multiple alternative solutions, which must be assessed in line with quantitative and qualitative criteria, in order to determine the optimal alternative, ie to filter the solution, which best fulfils the planning criteria.

The multitude of solutions for planning result in combining different solution figures and the wealth of industrial systems on offer. If the solution is not in line with a predetermined degree of fulfilment, then the planning process has to be carried out again with the results from the initial planning.

This iteration process has to be carried out until the required degree of fulfilment has been achieved, or planning is aborted due to economic reasons (Figure 12.2).

12.3.2 Planning process

The planning process happens systematically in planning stages, from the objective setting to the implementation. The number of planning stages depends of the planning task, the planning scope, type of planning and the time aspects, such as for long

Figure 12.2 Iteration process for planning

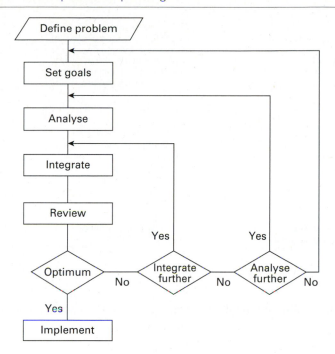

term planning the determination of guidelines and frameworks (see VDI 3637). The stages consist of, amongst others, systematic and implementation planning.

The planning process happens methodically through dividing each stage in successive phases, and is divided into *preparation, analysis of current status, development of system alternatives* and *review*. Each planning phase in turn is divided into successive sections. Thus, the analysis phase is divided into *collation, assessment, representation* and *review of data*.

Planning systematics built on the factual, time and methodical aspects is represented in Figure 12.3. The planning process goes from the abstract to the concrete, from system to detail.

The planning process can refer to functions and processes, such as analysis = identifying processes (identify); developing concepts = developing processes (innovate); realizing the best alternative = implementing processes (implement); working with implementation = running with new processes (run).

12.3.3 *Project management*

A project has a clearly defined and temporary task. Through external and internal dependencies and influencing factors, it is complex and must fulfil a number of different requirements.

Figure 12.3   Project organization (www.lischke.com)

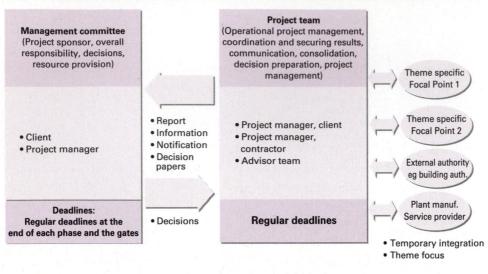

Businesses, institutions and planning firms participate in a project and their, at times, hierarchical allocations are determined by the organization (Figure 12.3). Project management is at the centre of the organization.

In line with VDI 69901–5, project management is the totality of management tasks that includes the interaction of planning, operating and controlling. Projects have technical and organizational interfaces, are future-oriented through using prognosis data, often have long planning and implementation times (as well as high costs), and have divergent objectives (see Chapter 1.5.2). A project consists of many subtasks, which are described in work packages with activities and responsibilities.

Project management tasks include:

- coordination and monitoring of costs and deadlines;
- team management;
- steering and controlling project process;
- task allocation on behalf of client;
- invoicing.

The decision-making (steering) committee may be a body directly reporting to management, representing management, or a member of the management team with decision-making authorization (for more decision-making committee tasks, see Chapter 12.5.6, and for team structure, see Chapter 12.9.1).

12.4 Preliminary study

There will be further discussion about short-term planning. The preliminary study, also called the feasibility study, is used to clarify the need for planning by estimating the planning success. To do this, the planning task has to be worded by:

- defining, structuring and demarcating the problem;
- determining priorities and planning objectives.

Furthermore, rough examination of planning measures, relevant figures, requirements and decision-making criteria have to be worked up in the form of analysis, rough solutions and cost framework in order to come to a conclusion about the planning success. The results from the preliminary study are used to make a decision for or against planning.

A feasibility study assumes the objectives and checks their achievability and compliance with requirements. It must answer questions, such as whether qualified personnel are available in the required numbers, whether required machinery and transport exist, whether free hall space is available for manufacturing, assembly and storage, and whether the costs and deadlines can be guaranteed.

12.5 System planning

System planning can be called rough planning. Its task and objective is to identify solutions to problems. For this, system planning is divided into the following rough planning phases (see Figure 12.4).

12.5.1 Preparation for planning

This planning phase should prepare all relevant work to carry out the actual planning and can be called 'planning for planning'.

These tasks include:

- formulating planning objectives and tasks;
- demarcation of planning scope;
- deciding on in-house delivery or for a planning firm;
- appointing planning team and determining methodology;
- creating a schedule;

Figure 12.4   Planning systematics

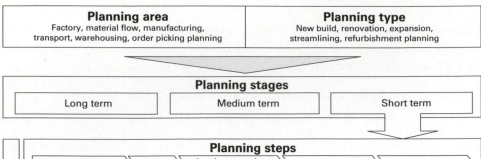

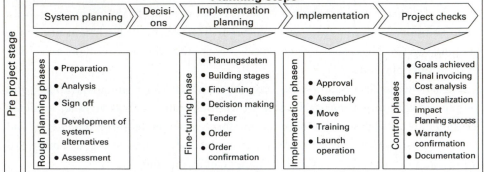

- determining monitoring process, degree of accuracy and representative monitoring period;

- informing participants.

12.5.2 Analysis

This serves the monitoring, evaluation, representation and assessment of relevant current data, identifies weak points and prognosis data and creates the target data framework for the system identification phase. The methodology of the status quo analysis (Figure 12.5) includes:

- development of questionnaires and survey documents, determining of marginal conditions, restrictions, benchmarks, provisions and requirements;

- recording current data through questioning, observing, recording; studying documents;

- showcasing interesting figures using visual methods;

- assessing results through comparison, contrasting with key figures, assessment measures and requirement criteria, benchmark; determining weaknesses, strengths and bottlenecks;

Figure 12.5 Methodology for carrying out an analysis

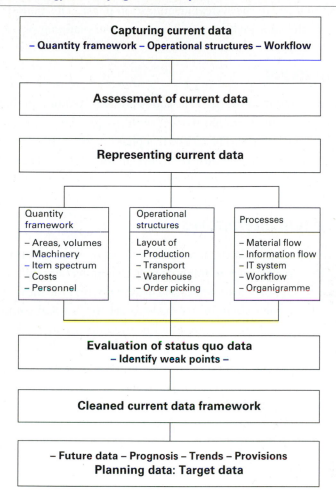

- creating the status quo data framework;

- determining future data through prognosis, trend calculation and creating the target data framework (see Example 12.3).

If the shipping volume or the shipping carton size is to be calculated for an order using relevant software, the master data has to be known.

To capture master data for warehousing administration and shipping volume calculation, a previse cargo survey and weight measurement is required. A space requirement measuring device with weight measurement is used, which is directly connected to the warehousing administration system and which captures the barcode (see Example 11.14). The measuring system is located on a truck, as a data capture system stationed independently from the network. The cleaned data is used to calculate the target data using trend figures, and, as a result of the analysis phase, these form the input to the system identification phase. The analysis represents over 50 per cent of the allocated time, the longest system planning phase.

12.5.3 Approval

The analysis is presented to the client and is documented in a preliminary report, in order to show how the team has worked with the problem, as well as how the data was recorded and assessed. The aim of this phase is to establish a concrete approval of the investigation so far, because only once an analysis has been approved can the planning team carry on working effectively.

12.5.4 System alternatives

Working up alternatives is the most creative and most important phase of system planning. The requirement is to translate target planning data into technical concepts as solutions. To support the identification of systems, first the ideal functional process is determined and then attempts are made to get to the ideal solution as closely as possible, despite marginal conditions and restrictions. Requirements have to be met and different systems may be suitable. For these system alternatives, the requirements for resources, floor space, personnel and costs, as well as for transport and warehousing capacities, have to be determined.

The following activities are part of the phase to identify system alternatives (Figure 12.3):

- checks and potential changes to the target planning data with regard to quantities, capacities, workflows and carrying out system investigations;
- developing the ideal functional processes;
- optimizing allocation of departments;
- determining manufacturing and assembly principles of warehousing;
- identifying partial systems and systems for load unit, transport, warehousing and manufacturing;
- rough dimensioning of concepts;
- drawing of rough/block layout;
- calculating investments and operational costs as well as key figures, such as degree of height utilization;
- collating alternative system solutions;
- making contact with regulatory authorities;

- checking compliance with legal requirements, such as preventative fire safety;
- showing expansion options.

The result of the system alternatives phase is the representation of different possible solutions, which are sketched in rough layout with dimensions 1:2,000.

12.5.5 Assessment

In the assessment phase (Figure 12.3), a profitability, benefit and risk analysis, or a simple comparison, helps to determine the optimal alternative from amongst the possible solutions. This looks for the solution, which comes closest to the weighted requirement criteria. This solution acts as a proposal, which has to be approved by the business management team.

Possible assessment criteria, such as for the material flow area, can be:

- flexibility, adaption to production fluctuations;
- allocation from warehouse to manufacturing;
- degree of mechanization, degree of automation;
- order processing times of workpieces;
- clarity, disruption potential;
- investment and operating costs, personnel requirements;
- interface creation;
- crossings and oncoming traffic;
- floor space, height and space utilization;
- capacity utilization of means of transport;
- expansion possibilities.

The assessment phase process might be:

- collation of assessment criteria;
- determining assessment process;
- weighting of criteria;
- comparison of advantages and disadvantages;
- carrying out technical-economical system comparison;
- development of an assessment matrix for qualitative and quantitative criteria;
- determining ranking of alternatives;
- comparison of current key figures with target key figures of alternatives.

The assessment of system alternatives is carried out by planners based on technical, economic and organizational aspects. The results of the assessment determines the optimal alternative, ie the alternative that fulfils the requirement criteria and objectives of the tasks to the greatest degree.

12.5.6 Decision

During the planning step 'decision', the decision-making committee (Figure 12.4) must approve the chosen alternative and decide on the continued planning, or terminate planning. The decision is not only taken based on the planners' aspects, but is also drawn with a business focus in mind.

12.6 Implementation planning

Once the decision has been taken to continue planning, the first step of implementation planning is to check whether the entire system plan can be implemented in one or multiple building stages. Criteria for this include affordability and necessity.

The tasks of implementation planning are, on the one hand, the fine-tuning of the initial building stage in layout dimension 1:50, taking into consideration marginal conditions, regulations and restrictions, and on the other hand, the execution of the tender and order process. Often, longer periods of time pass by between system and implementation planning, during which initial situation and marginal conditions may have changed. The procedure of implementation planning can be summarized as follows:

Planning data

- checking if planning data is still up to date;
- collation of all data for the chosen alternative;
- listing floor space figures and costs of individual subsystems.

Building stages

- planning and calculating the number of building stages based on necessity and affordability;
- decision to plan the first building stage.

Fine-tuning

- detailing the first building stage with regards to transport, warehousing, manufacturing and assembly systems, management and organization;
- planning building design (building, foundations and support grid);

- developing the establishment of departments (interior planning and layout);
- checking compliance with any regulations;
- determining foreign and internal labour;
- considering interfaces;
- listing control and approval processes;
- checking expansion options.

Tender and quote comparison

- create specifications and enquiries;
- choose providers through manufacturer comparison:
  - sub-suppliers, references;
  - parts provision and service offers;
  - manufacturer reputation, reliability and goodwill for returns;
- sending enquiries (tender);
- comparing and evaluating quotes;
- determining best three providers for contract negotiations;
- rejecting remaining providers.

Order

- execution of contract negotiations with selected providers based on technical, economic and organizational aspects (financing and delivery deadlines);
- clarifying all details;
- ranking three providers;
- create order documents with:
  - list of technical (mechanic, electric, control-related) minimum requirements, throughput, performance and availability;
  - determine hand over modalities, such as throughput investigation;
  - compliance with legal regulations;
  - assembly process, personnel training;
  - completeness, functionality and warranty;
  - deliver and payment conditions;
  - contractual penalties;
  - schedule order confirmation;
  - delivery and assembly deadlines;
  - parts list, drawings and operating instructions;

- award order (= award of contract, purchasing contract) to the first provider with scheduling of order confirmation;
- order confirmation;
- rejection of remaining providers.

Once the order has been confirmed the planning step 'implementation planning' is concluded.

12.7 Implementation

The *implementation* of the project is not really part of planning, in the strict sense, but has mostly to do with coordination, monitoring and checks. Thus, this planning step is concerned with the build and assembly of all plants and equipment, which then have to be checked, controlled and taken over.

In order to prevent difficulties, it is recommended to produce meeting protocols for each project team meeting with the client and suppliers, and to work on the acceptance report early on (Figures 12.3 and 12.26). The tasks of implementation are:

General tasks

- make and maintain contact with the manufacturer;
- check and sign off drawings for approval;
- facilitate building meetings;
- apply for and obtain permits.

Assembly

- coordination of foreign and internal labour;
- checking interfaces and junctures;
- monitoring deliveries for quality and quantity;
- checking assembly and build;
- monitoring adherence to deadlines.

Acceptance (equals transfer of risk)

- comprehensive testing programme including execution of preliminary acceptance, partial acceptance, function and performance controls;
- completeness and availability checks, test runs;
- acceptance of plant through authorities and using acceptance protocols.

Move and training

- planning move;
- training and induction of personnel.

Launch

- start operations of plant, taking over of plant;
- determining maintenance works.

The project is concluded with the taking over of the plant by the client and their personnel. Project monitoring has to happen retrospectively.

12.8 Project monitoring

Once the taking over process has been completed, project monitoring (evaluation) is tasked with determining the costs and planning success, as well as producing a review document and related documentation. However, it is important to note that the streamlining effect can only be effectively determined once personnel have been trained and any occurring issues of the plant have been alleviated. This is, at the earliest and depending on the project, three to twelve months afterwards. Individual activities to be carried out as part of project monitoring are:

- checks if objectives, requirements and criteria have been met;
- execution of final invoicing/cost analysis and monitoring of warranty promises;
- determining streamlining effects, planning success and improvements;
- documenting planning and production of review report.

The structure of a documentation or planning report may be:

1   Introduction

1.1 Purpose and objectives of planning

1.2 Demarcation, methodology

1.3 Theoretical basis, glossary

2   Status quo analysis

2.1 Capture, analysis and representation of data

2.2 Identification of weak points, assessment of status quo analysis

2.3 Prognosis figures, target data framework, catalogue of measures

3   Solutions proposals/development of alternatives

3.1 System planning, target concept

3.2 Profitability observations, assessment, results

3.3 Fine-tuning

4   Implementation planning (see Example 12.6); implementation

The planning processes of a short-term plan shown here can be used for factory planning, but also in segmented areas such as workshop or material flow planning, regardless of industry branch. The procedures just have to be adapted to the respective task, and supplemented or amended accordingly. It is possible to carry out individual actions in parallel to one another; the order of the steps cannot be switched.

Following the takeover of the plant, the optimization of plant segments commences, as it is not possible to take into account a range of marginal conditions during planning.

12.9 Planning tools

Planning tools are the tools a planner uses in the shape of aids for information and coordination and which also include processes and methods used for data capture, data processing and visualization as well as for system identification and the preparation of decision-making processes.

The task and purpose of planning tools are:

- avoiding repetition through standardization;
- supporting individual planning phases through tried and tested techniques;
- reducing training periods in processes and methods through simplification and clarity, as well as saving planning time through methods and organization, through clear arrangements and streamlining.

12.9.1 Coordination and information tools

Coordination tools The planning team is considered to be the most important 'coordination tool', as well as the network plan, Gantt chart (as process and scheduling tool) and the project log (for filing and file notes).

- Planning team: the teams are divided into internal, external and mixed. The planner from an external planning firm has the following advantages compared to internal planners, who carry out planning in addition to their normal job:
  - used to working in teams;
  - experience from many projects;
  - trained in methodological and systematic processes;
  - has tried and tested organization and planning aids available;
  - independent;
  - no difficulties in recording data.

Figure 12.6   Structure of a planning team

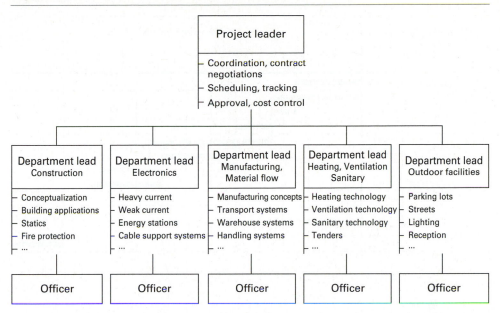

A planning team has a hierarchical structure (Figure 12.6). It is made up depending on the task, planning scope and the available planning time.

- *Network plan*: this is usually used for complex, large planning processes and serves for planning workflow and schedule. Its advantage is its formality, which forces in-depth thinking and reduces the possibility of forgetting activities. The disadvantage is the relatively high costs of creating it, which can be significantly reduced by using IT software.

- *Gantt chart*: Scheduling and workflow planning can be built easily and quickly for rough and detailed overviews using a Gantt chart (Figures 12.7 and 12.28). Using target and current representation, it provides a good overview of the planning status.

- *Project log* in digital form: It represents the guidelines for planning. All required and important planning documents are contained therein, such as tables, questionnaires, institutions, authorities, providers, costs, file lists etc.

- *Filing:* In order to enable quick access to documents, all existing paper documents and drawings should be filed according to certain aspects.

- *File notes:* As part of the planning framework, each meeting should have a file note as a results protocol; these should be numbered and e-mailed to all participants. This prevents issues, lack of clarity and errors, or allows for their quick resolution. By creating proforma or paper with a consistent header (date, location, number, participants, distributor, topic), the amount of work can be reduced and harmonized for the appropriate staff.

Figure 12.7   Gantt chart for scheduling and monitoring in weekly overview

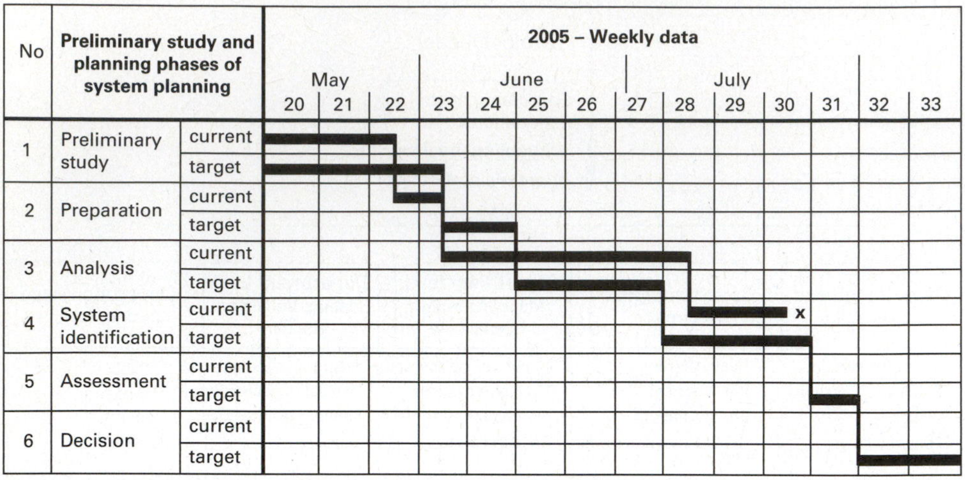

No	Preliminary study and planning phases of system planning		2005 – Weekly data												
			May			June				July					
			20	21	22	23	24	25	26	27	28	29	30	31	32	33
1	Preliminary study	current														
		target														
2	Preparation	current														
		target														
3	Analysis	current														
		target														
4	System identification	current											x			
		target														
5	Assessment	current														
		target														
6	Decision	current														
		target														

(x today)

Information tools Planning forms offer a range of information tools for their employees, in order to be able to obtain information for a prospective planning process quickly and thoroughly. They use documentation in books and periodicals, collate internal project and experience reports, possess image files and have all kinds of information readily accessible on their computers.

This reduces parallel and duplicate work, the time required to obtain information is reduced, planning quality increased and it takes into account the latest technology. By visiting seminars, fairs and exhibitions, the planner expands their knowledge, and uses factory visits and discussions with specialists to obtain specific knowledge for project work.

12.9.2 Methods for analysis

Analysis deals with the development of planning data. For this purpose, data must be identified, assessed and will be presented. Many of the methods to record data also contain an option to assess the respective figures. We have to distinguish between past, current or future data.

It is important for selecting the investigative method to know if it is average values or top values that have to be recorded, whether it is about capturing individual items or item groups, how to treat seasonal fluctuation and which figures can be seen as representative. Possible and frequently used investigative methods are summarized in Figure 12.8 and are divided into *direct* and *indirect* analysis. Surveys can refer to either current or past data. Prognosis and trend values are usually determined

Figure 12.8 Division of analysis methods (without prognosis procedure)

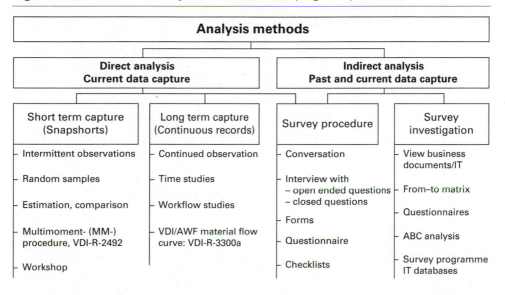

by business management through market analysis and provided to the planner. The most universal and adaptable data recording method is the survey or questionnaire.

Upon creation, the following points should be considered:

- always have the goal in mind;
- check if required data are available in the required format;
- work with questions, such as for transport and warehousing: who, what, how much, where from, where to, when, how long for, with what, how should it be transported and stored (see Chapter 4.9.1);
- when determining the questionnaire header, row and columns should be numbered and don't forget dimensions of data;
- pay attention to logical structure and process of recorded and assessed data;
- run tests with questionnaires and amend if necessary;
- include a complete sample questionnaire with the survey.

To obtain specific times, such as rest, distribution and planning time, usually long-term data capture is used for capacity utilization and figures, and short-term data capture for weak points and bottleneck analyses. Direct analyses of current data are carried out with:

- multi-moment procedure: Chapter 2.5.3.1;
- value stream design: Chapter 2.5.5;
- surveys and questionnaires: Chapter 2.5.3.4.

Indirect analyses of past and current data are carried out with:

- from–to matrix: Chapter 2.5.3.3;
- ABC analysis: Chapter 2.5.4.

12.9.3 Optimization processes

In order to meet the objectives, processes are used for quantifiable figures. We distinguish between the maximization and minimization process. They are used for allocation problems, in order to minimize transport routes and, thus, transport costs, for weaknesses, in order to achieve maximum utilization and/or for bottleneck investigation for transport systems, in order to determine redundancies.

12.9.3.1 Allocation process

Depending on the production workflow, an industrial business must allocate the individual's business areas, such as warehousing, manufacturing, assembly etc in line with organizational, technical and economic aspects. This also applies for *resources* in one department, such as manufacturing. The main objective is to minimize material flow costs by keeping the product ton × km as small as possible. All allocation processes are aimed towards this objective.

Now let's begin to understand the differences between circular and triangular processes.

Circular process: this is a simple method to quickly allocate the department. First, the transport frequency and transport quantities are determined by using a from–to matrix (see Chapter 2.5.3.3) and these are determined for the units and quantity of transport incidences between the departments (triangular matrix). The numbered departments are drawn into a circle with the same distance apart. Connecting lines represent transport units per time unit between the departments. This results in a disorderly circular diagram (Figure 12.9a). This diagram is then changed into an orderly circular diagram, so that those departments between the largest transport streams are situated next to each other. Subsequently, and maintaining any fixed points, an allocation layout can be produced, which has the lowest t × km (Figure 12.9b).

Triangular process: the time-consuming triangular process is a constructive method in which departments or resources are captured as points. Based on a from–to matrix, this is transformed in to a triangular matrix, then it is about identifying those department pairs with the deepest relationships. The calculation happens in a table and the results are entered into a schematic with equilateral triangles. For this process, it is best to use an Excel table, which can determine the most economical allocation by using an optimization program for the different solutions.

Figure 12.9   Circular process.

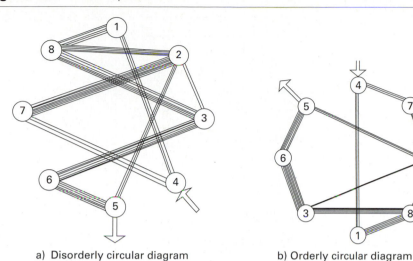

a) Disorderly circular diagram   b) Orderly circular diagram

12.9.3.2 Simulation

Following VDI guidelines 3633, a simulation is the copy of a real or planned system, or a dynamic process, in a model with sensible simplifications. The objective is to obtain findings, key figures and detailed information about the system which can be transferred to a real setting – making simulation a tool for the preparation of decisions. The results have a direct impact on the planning and execution. The importance lies in the fact that a decision is not based on factual knowledge or a static system planning, but on a dynamic planning model. A simulation does not deliver the optimal solution like a solution development process would, but it is used to identify weaknesses, highlight bottlenecks, determine throughput and utilization, expose connections between motion cycles as well as find capacity limits for movements. Simulation is used to test components in plants, to determine processing times and to obtain knowledge about reducing them, to investigate disturbances in a system or recognize capacity utilization and waiting times, secure investments and achieve shorter operation times. Complex planning processes can be tested by using simulation and optimization.

A prerequisite for successful simulation is the careful and accurate capture of analysis data (see Chapters 12.5.2 and 12.9.2), about data of the material and information flow, management and organization as well as performances and processes.

The steps of a simulation occur in three phases: preparation, execution and evaluation (Figure 12.10), creating a cycle as the result of successful modelling: simulation – assessment – optimization – modelling – simulation.

Despite reducing software, the *disadvantages* of simulation include: high costs (approximately 0.4 to 0.8 per cent of investment); time required for data capture

Figure 12.10   Simulation process

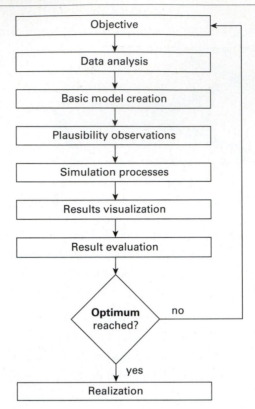

and modelling, learning programming language; potential error sources; model, data, calculation, system and interpreting mistakes; no guarantee for optimal results.

Advantages of simulation can be seen in: shortening of planning time; increase in planning quality and security; use for complex system; planning results can be presented clearly visually and in animated form; weaknesses in processes can be assessed accurately.

We distinguish the following simulation types:

- time or event focused;
- discreet or continuous;
- stochastic or deterministic;
- static or dynamic;
- open or closed;
- prescriptive or descriptive.

Once the objective has been accurately determined and a detailed current data analysis has occurred, the model is defined, created and validated during the preparation phase. Key figures define the measurements, such as times and quantities in processes. For material flow simulation, the following tasks may be processes: for planning the workflow strategies, for change planning the controls and for expansion planning the plant analysis with operations and disruptions. As part of validation, the simulation programme is implemented and the model tested for contradictions, exceptions and processes.

During the execution phase, the simulation takes place. Input parameters are changed and the model might be improved. Repeated simulation runs with either one or when multiple variables are carried out.

During the execution phase, the obtained data for decision making is included in the planning. Thus, the unwanted creation of warehousing areas or occurrence of bottlenecks can be recognized in the material flow.

Simulation software is available from many companies. The investment is only worth it if they are used consistently, as one-off use planning firms prove to be more economical. With regards to the material flow, there is the software program WITNESS for graphic modelling, and programs such as iGrafx Process, Enterprise Dynamics or EM-Plant, SimPlan, Fastdesign, Pl@Net for real time, expansion, adaption and integration tasks.

Requirements for software tools are: flexibility, performance, 3D animation, interfaces, process management, buffer optimization, machine utilization, static evaluation (see Example 12.24).

12.9.4 Assessment and decision-making methods

Assessment methods aim to implement planning, based on the objective and using weighted qualitative and quantitative requirement criteria. This is a version for which the requirement criteria have the highest degree of fulfilment. All methods aim to achieve a subjective assessment. This is implemented amongst the team, paired criteria comparisons and two-stage procedures.

12.9.4.1 Morphological process

In order to only examine those solutions that make sense out of a multitude of combination options of diverse figures, the morphological box is used. This corresponds to a two-dimensional matrix, and filters out those solutions that are roughly worth examining (Figure 12.11). The use of the morphological box occurs during the system identification phase in order to limit the number of solution alternatives, so as to only obtain those solutions that are useful.

Figure 12.11   Morphological box

Operating system / Storage type	Forklift	Stacker crane	Storage and retrieval machine	Continuous conveyor
Floor storage in blocks	●	◐	○	○
Fixed shelving	◐	◐	●	○
Mobile shelving	◐	●	○	○
Continuous shelving	◐	◐	●	◐

● Solution for examination   ◐ Technically possible but not fit for purpose   ○ Technically impossible

12.9.4.2 Qualitative process

When there are quantitative and qualitative criteria for assessing alternatives, evaluation methods will determine the best solution out of the existing alternatives. This includes:

- benefit analysis;
- decision table technique;
- two-stage scoring;
- risk analysis.

The two-stage scoring is used frequently because it is reliable and quick, as well as easy to understand. It is described in the following paragraphs. Its procedure occurs in the following steps:

- determine and list assessment criteria (see Example 12.4);
- select assessment criteria and limit to 8–12;
- create weighting matrix;
- weight assessment criteria using weighting matrix;
- build a scoring system with point, eg 10 points from badly resolved (1 point) to satisfactory and good to very well resolved (10 points);
- build scoring matrix;
- carry out assessment by scoring individual criteria for the individual alternatives;
- calculate matrix;
- determine optimal alternative using ranking.

Table 12.1 Weighting matrix

		A	B	C	D	E	F	G	Weighting in Points (Sum)	Weighting in Percentage (%)	Rank
	Criteria	**A**	**B**	**C**	**D**	**E**	**F**	**G**	**Points (Sum)**	**Percentage (%)**	**Rank**
No	**1**	**2**	**3**	**4**	**5**	**6**	**7**	**8**	**9**	**10**	**11**
1	Flexibility A		1	0.5	0.5	1	0	0	3	~14	4
2	Clarity B	0		0.5	0.5	0	0	0	1	~5	7
3	Degree of automation C	0.5	0.5		0.5	0	1	1	3.5	~17	3
4	Allocation D	0.5	0.5	0.5		0.5	0	0	2	~10	6
5	Expansion E	0	1	1	0.5		0.5	0	3	~14	5
6	Floor area requirements F	1	1	0	1	0.5		0.5	4	~19	2
7	Personnel requirements G	1	1	0	1	1	0.5		4.5	~21	1
8	Total points	–	–	–	–	–	–	–	21	100	

The structure of the *weighting matrix* is shown in Table 12.1. The criteria are entered horizontally and vertically, each criterion is compared to all the others and assessed, to decide if it is worth more (1 point), worth less (0 points) or equal (0.5 points). Only the right-hand side of the triangle matrix is assessed, as the value in the left half results from mirroring along the diagonal axis ($0 \rightarrow 1$; $1 \rightarrow 0$; $0.5 \rightarrow 0.5$). The points or percentage weighting of the criteria is achieved through horizontal addition and percentage division.

In the assessment matrix (see Table 12.2), their weighting and the degree must meet the criteria for each alternative, and has to be determined in line with the set scoring system. Multiplying the score (column 3) with the weight (column 2) results in the points (column 4). The total of columns 4, 6 and 8 provides the total points and utility value, of the individual alternatives. The alternative with the highest number of points represents the optimal solution. Should this two-stage process fail, it must be supplemented with a cost comparison calculation, in which the point totals of the best solutions should be close to one another.

12.9.4.3 Quantitative process

When we have quantifiable data, such as incurred costs for wages, energy, maintenance, depreciation and interest then the processes of an investment calculation can identify the most economical solution for the existing alternatives.

Table 12.2   Assessment matrix

No	Assessment criteria	Weighting G	Alternative I		Alternative II		Alternative III	
			N	N × G	N	N × G	N	N × G
	1	2	3	4	5	6	7	8
1	Flexibility	3	5	15	7	21	7	21
2	Clarity	1	6	6	6	6	5	5
3	Degree of automation	3.5	4	14	6	21	9	31.5
4	Allocation	2	6	12	6	12	7	14
5	Expansion	3	5	15	7	21	7	21
6	Floor area requirements	4	6	24	10	40	8	32
7	Personnel requirements	4.5	6	27	8	36	10	45
8	Total points	–	–	113	–	157	–	169.5
9	Rank	–	–	III	–	II	–	I

The first group is based on a cost, profit and profitability comparison, whereby the factor time is practically negligible. Static processes are:

- cost comparison calculation (see Example 11.4);
- profit and operating costs comparison calculation (see Examples 11.3, 11.22 and 11.23);
- profitability comparison calculation, economic comparison (see Examples 1.9 and 6.7–2);
- amortization calculation (see Examples 4.8, 11.4).

If we start out from the payment and expense streams during the economic utilization period, dynamic processes can be used, such as:

- capital value method;
- annuity method;
- method of internal rate of return;
- amortization calculation (see Examples 4.8, 11.22 and 12.10).

Dynamic methods assume that there is a time difference for investments where incoming payments and expenses are concerned. Capital that may be available in future is calculated for the current value through discounting. A simplification can be achieved by calculating the equal annual returns during these periods. For the investment, the interest is calculated for the lifetime of the object through the incoming payment and expense streams. The return on investment is the interest rate, used to calculate the cash value of all returns through discounting. The cash value corresponds to the costs paid for the investment. All relevant business management literature provides key information about prerequisites, methodology and application of the individual methods.

12.9.5 Presentation

The analytical data must be assessed, calculated and presented. This happens both in the analysis phase, as well as during the system identification phase (see Chapter 12.5). The type of presentation plays a significant role. It is used to highlight, clarify and design characteristic, relationships and processes, in order to use the percentage comparison of the figures to show conditions, facts or weak points, and to facilitate their assessment. There is a large number of ways to present them, divided into *graphical* and *concrete* (Figure 12.12) and three-dimensional (Figure 12.13).

The following figures show examples of:

- process plans depicted using a Sankey diagram (Figure 12.14);
- bar chart plan (Figures 12.7 and 12.26);

Figure 12.12 Division of presentation methods

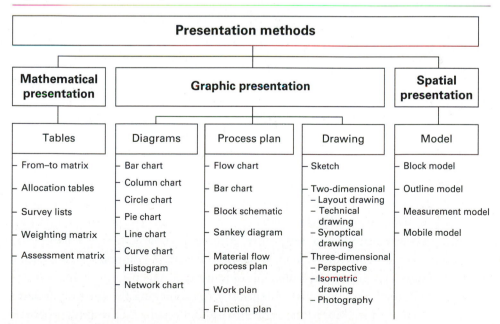

Figure 12.13 Three-dimensional presentation of repackaging efforts in goods issue

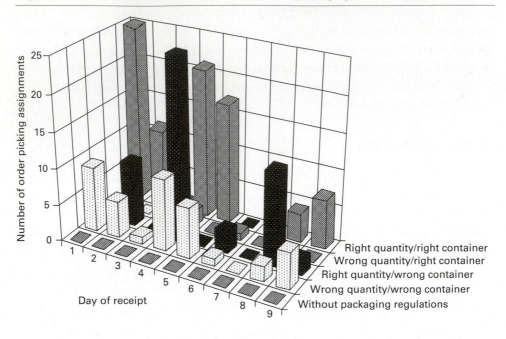

- material flow plan (Figure 2.10);
- column diagram for target–current comparison (Figures 12.27 and 2.22);
- network diagram (Figure 1.15);
- process chart (Table 2.7 in Example 2.19);
- fishbone diagram (Figure 1.14);
- decision-making matrix (Figure 1.13).

12.9.6 Presentation techniques

Interim analysis reports as well as project results are not just provided in the form of a written report, but are normally presented in a presentation.

Report: A report lives on its design, format and graphic presentation (see Chapter 12.9.5). The cover is just as important as the representation of the relevant findings and results using sketches, drawings, structure images, photos and pasting layout in two-dimensional and perspective. Although coloured design is expensive, this option should be used for the most important facts. A computer with relevant text and graphics programs offers all kinds of tools, which deliver quick and impactful support. Reports are often just skimmed by those making the decision because they are short of time. More time is spent reading summaries, results, proposed

Figure 12.14 Sankey plan, process plan for loading units

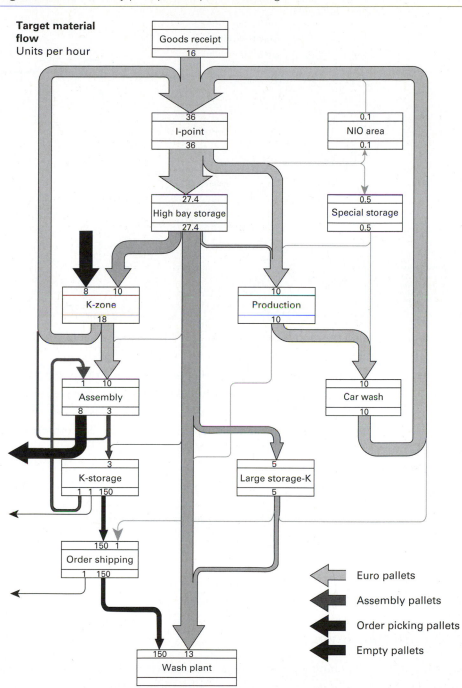

Target material flow
Units per hour

Goods receipt — 16

36 — I-point — 36

0.1 — NIO area — 0.1

27.4 — High bay storage — 27.4

0.5 — Special storage — 0.5

8 | 10 — K-zone — 18

10 — Production — 10

1 | 10 — Assembly — 8 | 3

10 — Car wash — 10

3 — K-storage — 1 | 1 | 150

5 — Large storage-K — 5

150 | 1 — Order shipping — 1 | 150

150 | 13 — Wash plant

Euro pallets

Assembly pallets

Order picking pallets

Empty pallets

Figure 12.15   Interior layout of a machine factory with material flow representation (www.fastplan.de)

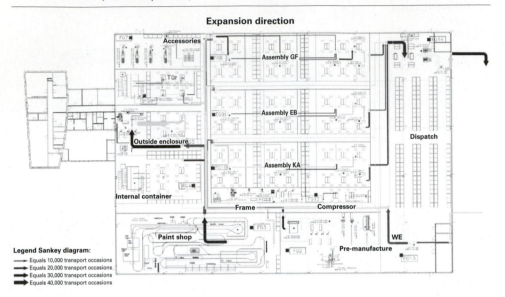

solutions and profitability calculations, so that special attention should be given to the design and development of those.

Presentation: A presentation should be well prepared, only refer to the most important points or present the most important conclusions. A range of options is available to visually support the presentation, such as planning aids like pin boards, magnetic boards, flipcharts, models and perhaps a short video. The number one presentation tool is the projector with a PowerPoint presentation.

Design characteristics for slides are:

- legibility: font and font size;
- clarity: structure, not too much information in texts and figures;
- appeal: table and image design, colours.

12.10 Factory planning basics

12.10.1 Interior layout

The result of interior planning is presented as interior layout (Figure 12.16). It is the graphic representation of the arrangement and allocation of departments, machines, warehouses, transport, workplaces, traffic routes and supply lines. The qualitative and quantitative rough material flow is presented in lines and arrows, the different material streams in colours. A legend provides information on the meaning of symbols. Figure 12.16 only shows the qualitative MF relationships. For tender documents, a scale of 1:50, or at least 1:100, is required.

12.10.2 Development plan

The land development plan (general land use plan) presents the mandatory use of land. Each business should own such a plan for its premises, in order to carry out expansions, changes and restructuring within the plan's framework. Building regulations have to be adhered to in creating such a plan. The plan indicates the following:

- the ways in which the land can be used (retail park, industrial park);
- which other land the premises are adjacent to;
- to what degree the land can be used (number of floors, ground floor area and other floor areas) and what the soil bearing capacity is;
- where and what expansion is possible;
- where traffic routes for material and people have to be allocated and where car parks can be created;
- where supply and refuse lines for the business can be placed for energy, water and waste water;
- where interfaces should occur internally and externally (connection to roads).

The land development plan is used to better utilize the land, for optimization of building investments and to provide building data. For business management, it represents a planning tool for long-term planning, in order to turn the business into a holistic production and administration business, based on provision of route and building grids, building sections, building heights, etc. Management can use the land development plan to refer to for all expansion, renovation and extension measures (Example 12.2), and also:

- to show the infrastructure for the traffic and supply areas;
- to determine the allocation of buildings based on material flow-related aspects;
- to present the external connection to roads, railway, energy and water.

The production of a land development plan has to occur in compliance with building regulations, whereby a number of directives and laws have to be complied with. The most important figures for a planner to consider are the provisions of the land utilization ordinance, represented in the following equations:

1 Size of plot × basic area number = area of all building plants

2 Size of plot × floor area number = floor area

3 Size of plot × cubic capacity number = cubic capacity

It also includes information about the number of full floors (Z). Depending on the building area, the following values are provided in the land utilization ordinance: Z, basic area number and other floor space for retail areas and ground floor space and the cubic index for industrial parks. If the ground floor space is GRZ = 0.8 and if the premises size is 4,000 m², then the maximum permissible ground floor space of all buildings is:

$$GR = G \times GRZ = 4,000 \times 0.8 = 3,200 \text{ m}^2$$

If the cubic index is BMZ = 9 m³ / m² then the permissible cubic mass for all buildings is:

$$BM = G \times BMZ = 4,000 \times 9 = 36,000 \text{ m}^3$$

If the number of floors is GFZ = 2, then the permissible floor space total is:

$$GF = G \times GFZ = 4,000 \times 2 = 8,000 \text{ m}^2$$

If it is a two-floor building, it is 4,000 m² per floor. The smaller value has to be adhered to.

If a business consists of a structure that has grown over decades of work halls and administration buildings, its premises floor plan would be an irregular polygon (Figure 12.16a). If the management wants to do away with this shortcoming without moving the business, then it might be an option to try to straighten the premises' edges, in order to achieve right angles, and on the other hand, to allocate departments to other appropriate buildings.

At first, a land use plan for the premises is produced, as if it was concerned with a new build plan on a greenbelt, taking into consideration the inevitable restriction. Then the overall planning would be divided up into building stages (see Figure 12.16b), in order to implement a modern factory on the old premises without disruption to production and in line with financial feasibility in 5, 10 or 15 years (Figure 12.16c).

12.10.3 Site investigation

If a business is moving, a branch factory is being built or a new company being formed, it is also important to carry out a site search. The decision for a site is just another long-term investment decision. The investigation happens by assessing a variety of site factors (see Chapter 12.9.4.2). These can be divided into pan-regional, regional and local factors.

Pan-regional factors include:

- political stability;
- taxes;

Figure 12.16 Restructuring of a factory without moving the business (www.agiplan.de)

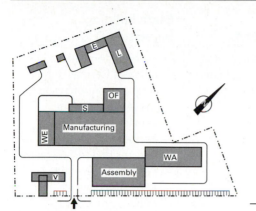

Historically grown business

a)

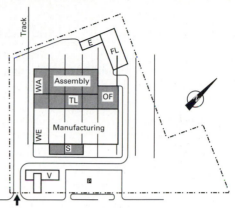

Successive adaptation to future
process-appropriate structures

b)

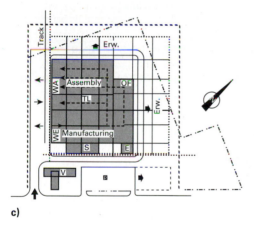

c)

a) Evolved business structure of an
   Industrial business

b) Building stage I

c) Implemented general land use plan
   (building stage II)

- economic system;
- economic policy;
- contracting partners;
- language;
- education system;
- wage on-costs.

This division can reduce the level of effort for the investigation, as potential sites might not fulfil pan-regional or regional factors; this means they can be excluded

Table 12.3   Extract from regulations for land use planning (Germany)

Building code GB	Land use NVO	State building regulation O
– Land use planning – Floor space utilization plan – Building plan – Building method – Coverable areas – Building and other appendices – Above ground facilities – Public access and pipeline rights – Protected areas – Planting of trees and bushes	– Premises utilization – Number of full floors – Ground floor space – Floor space – Cubic mass – Building method (open/closed) – Building line/boundary – Building depths – Type and dimensions of building utilization	– Different regulations in different German states – Arrangement of building measures (lighting/ventilation) – Space to move for fire engines and rescue teams – Escape route length – Minimum distance of buildings from neighbouring premises' boundaries – Distances between buildings

(knock-out criteria). Labour markets, wage costs and taxes are cross-sector, pan-regional and regional site factors.

Additionally, there are these *regional* factors:

- transport costs;
- delivery service;
- infrastructure;
- communication networks;
- labour costs;
- procurement markets;
- economic business support;
- investment support;
- climate.

Local factors encompass:

- economic support: cost of premises;
- premises quality: location, size, soil load capacity, ground make-up, groundwater level, topography, level of development, previous use, public access and supply lines, clearance areas, type of use on adjacent premises, legally binding land use plan and development plan by the local council;

- traffic connections: type and width of road, lorry storage surfaces, possibilities for turning, location and connection options for railway tracks and waterways;

- supplies and waste disposal: water, gas, electricity, waste water, refuse;

- environmental regulations: noise, clean air limits, waste water make-up.

Prior to commencing a site investigation, certain planning data are required for guidance, such as:

- space requirements, personnel requirements, requirements on traffic network;

- specific data (such as for an aluminium hut: energy supply, electricity price, waterways).

It has to be assumed that, due to necessary free space for parking lots, traffic routes, distances between buildings etc, only 60–70 per cent of the premises area can be built on. The calculated required space for the business has to, therefore, be multiplied by 1.4 to 1.6, especially when the building design is single-floor. Moreover, a space reserve for future expansion (free space or optional space) should be considered for the size of the premises. Thus, the total size for the premises increases to 1.7 to 2.0 times the space requirements for the internal space. The premises size is the first knock-out factor for land on offer when searching for a site. Once the short-listed premises have been investigated during the site search, the optimal premises are determined through a two-stage scoring system (see Chapter 12.9.4.2).

12.10.4 Identifying solutions

The most creative system planning phase is the identification of solutions. An ideal functional process plan, independent of all marginal conditions and restrictions, can be a great help. Identifying solutions often includes the task of alleviating weaknesses. For this, solutions can be identified by using the procedure outlined in Figure 12.17a. Figure 12.17b shows a procedure for developing and assessing improvement measures.

12.10.5 Computer-aided factory planning

Computer-aided planning systems are used in order to carry out factory planning, as well as planning for component parts such as warehouse, transport and material flow or the interior layout (see Chapter 12.9.3.2). These not only take the strain of routine activities, but, through standard programs and relevant databases, they also enable support for creative planning processes.

The basis for computer-aided factory or material flow planning is the description of data for resources, processes, products and personnel. First, the object groups of the project have to be collated. For factory planning these include:

Figure 12.17a   Procedure to identify solutions

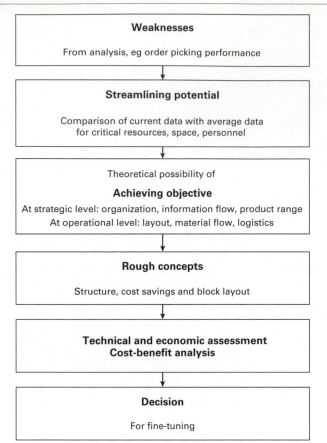

If we are dealing with material flow planning, transport and warehousing systems are decisive factors, which are divided into:

- means of transport: continuous conveyors/discontinuous conveyors;
- warehousing facilities: shelving and warehouse operating devices;
- transport aids: pallets, crates and containers;
- operational structure: centralized or decentralized.

Each of these resources can be modelled on the description of its characteristics.

- buildings, halls, structural installations;
- resources for manufacturing and assembly;
- heating, ventilation and sanitary facilities.

Figure 12.17b Procedure for development and assessment of measures (www.lischke.com)

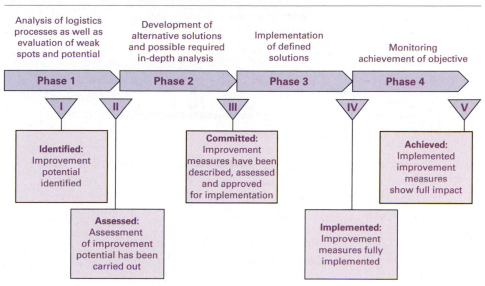

In order to clearly define the resources, a wealth of information (attributes) and two- or three-dimensional visuals have to be produced and connected to one another (Figure 12.18).

In order to allow for administration and activation of the created resource models, a model library has to be created. This is structured based on clear aspects. Each planner can use those models from the resource/symbol library that are required for their project (Figure 12.19). The implementation of real objects into models is managed with the help of CAD systems, such as CATIA (Computer Aided Three Dimensional Interaction Application) by the Dassault Company.

The next step is about the generation of the factory or material flow layout with all relevant resources, and their connection through the operational structure by considering process-focused, time-bound values. It is important that investigations, such as simulation or animation, are carried out in order to identify bottlenecks, collision potential and danger spots, as well as to carry out improvements and optimizations. The results of generating the layout are two- or three-dimensional representations, which can be rotated into different layers and viewed from a number of sides (Figures 12.20 and 12.21).

12.10.6 Fire prevention

The goal of fire prevention in industrial buildings is to avoid fire, as well as to prevent or limit the spread of a fire when it happens. The people working in the buildings are

Figure 12.18   Allocation of visual and alphanumerical data

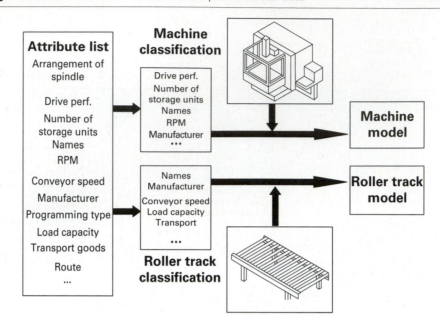

Figure 12.19   Strategy for model description and administration

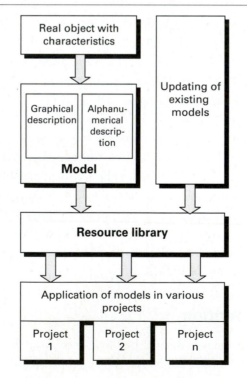

Figure 12.20   Representation of computer-aided interior planning (www.tarakos.de)

Expansion direction

a) Goods issue area

b) Packaging area

Figure 12.21   Example of computer-aided factory planning (www.tarakos.de)

considered as greatest priority, before the material assets. The required type of fire prevention measures are legally provided in the respective country's building regulations, on which the authorization by the responsible building authority for use of an industrial building is also based. The basis for building fire prevention are outlined in DIN 12 230 part 1, and for goods these are determined in the guidelines of the association of property insurers (VdS in Cologne).

In line with DIN 12 230, the *fire prevention class I to V* is determined for components and buildings based on the respective duration of fire resistance. The duration of fire resistance is calculated based on fire load, building structure, type of use for space and influencing factors on the duration of the fire, in order to obtain a reliable figure for each of the firefighting sections. The fire protection equipment for a building with fire alarms and fire extinguishing systems has to comply with these requirements. Preventative fire protection considerations have to be carried out in parallel with the planning sections, as is shown in Figure 12.22 for warehouse planning.

The most important components of a fire alarm system are the fire alarms, based on different physical and/or chemical triggers. There are smoke, heat, light, spark or pressure detectors. For smoke suction systems, a minute amount of smoke particles is enough to recognize a fire in its very early stages. The quicker a fire is detected, the faster the firefighting measures can commence.

Fire extinguishing equipment includes sprinkler, spray, water mist, foam, CO_2 and powder systems. Each of these systems has particular deployment areas and restrictions, such as for the extinguishing agent based on its impact on people, material assets and the environment.

Sprinkler systems are used to limit and extinguish the source of the fire. A sprinkler component is usually a glass vial filled with a liquid, which expands with heat to the extent that the vial explodes and makes way for the pressured (up to 2 bars) extinguishing agent. The escaping extinguishing agent hits a toothed spraying disc and is distributed as with a watering can across a larger area. Shelving consists of various levels, so the spraying disc is located above the glass vial, or the spraying disc would keep the liquid cool during fire sources lying high up. The temperature that triggers the spraying depends on the chosen liquid in the glass vial (the colour of the liquid corresponds to a certain trigger temperature). The nature of the extinguishing agent is a matter of what goods have to be extinguished; usually it is water. The extinguishing process has to be maintained until the fire brigade arrives. The amount of extinguishing agent stored, type and size of the sprinkler system, and the required water amount per time unit are determined by the relevant fire hazard classification of the goods and the period until the fire brigade arrives (for more on components of sprinkler systems, see Figure 12.24).

Figure 12.23a shows a sprinkler control centre, controlling the fire extinguishing process. For areas prone to frost in unheated warehouses, the water mains for

Figure 12.22 Allocation of different fire prevention measures as part of planning steps (Fire brigade access road from building 5,000 m²)

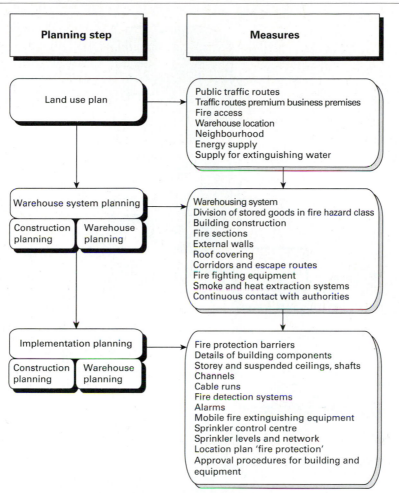

sprinkler systems are under air pressure (dry systems). Loss of pressure triggers the extinguishing process and supplies the pipes with water.

CO_2 extinguishing systems are based on the fact that CO_2 is heavier than air as well as colourless and odourless. CO_2 is not conducive, is neutral and dissolves without a trace. Its extinguishing effect is in displacing oxygen. Special safety measures have to be taken for humans, such as warning signals before opening high-pressure systems.

Powder systems are seen as quick extinguishers for liquids or flammable metals. They are based on a sudden extinguishing stream of propellant and powder.

The association of property insurers (VdS) divides goods in a warehouse in fire hazard classes BG1 to BG4. An important distinguishing factor is the type of

Figure 12.23a Functional schematics of a sprinkler system with monitoring (www.info@minimax.de)

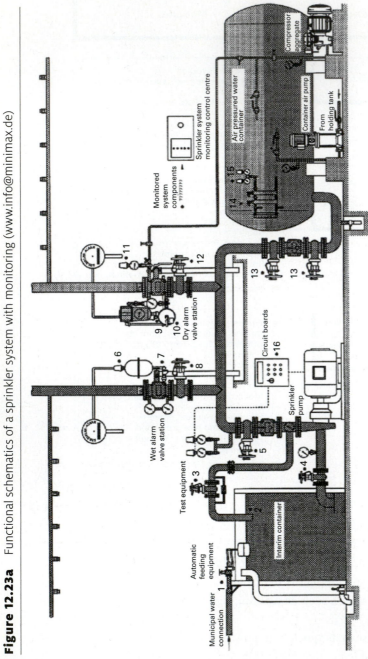

Monitoring equipment for:

1 Pressure and isolation valves in pipe
2 Fill level in interim container
3 Isolation valve in pump test pipe
4 Isolation valve in pump extraction pipe
5 Isolation pipe in pump pressure pipe
6 Alarm off-switch
7 Isolation valve
8 Shut-off

9 Alarm pressure switch
10 Alarm stopcock
11 Pressure in dry pipe network
12 Isolation valve
13 Isolation valve air pressured water container
14 Fill level air pressured water container
15 Pressure in air pressured water container
16 Energy supply and operating status of sprinkler pump

Figure 12.23b   Equipment for nitrogen production for protection space, see Figure 10.27a (www.wagner.de)

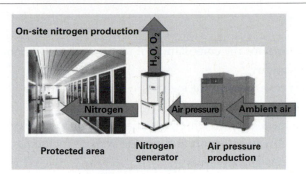

manufacturing business. For instance, a producer of foamed materials, whose goods are classed in fire hazard class 3 due to the high fire load and high flammability, is classed as fire hazard BG 3.2. The relevant fire prevention regulations have to be met.

VdS guideline 2341 provides an index of all existing guidelines, and can be obtained free of charge. VdS guideline 2095 is concerned with automated fire detection systems in high bay shelving.

Large buildings are divided into fire sections of 1,600 m² in size. It must be guaranteed that the distance to the next fire section is no further than 40 m from any location in this area, and that there are always two escape routes. However, there are plenty of exceptions to the rules for this regulation. The insurance side looks a little different. If the rules aren't complied with, you lose bonus points, or there is no insurer.

Another active fire prevention system makes use of the material's characteristics to only catch fire at a certain level of oxygen. No sustained combustion is possible if the level of oxygen volume in the air is less than 15 per cent for paper, less than 15.5 per cent for corrugated cardboard and less than 16 per cent for timber. In order to achieve this, nitrogen is blown into the protection area with equipment as depicted in Figure 12.23b. Application happens in spaces with little public traffic, such as IT equipment areas, archives, libraries, hazardous materials warehouses, telecommunications rooms or in tower shelving (see Figure 10.27a).

When the O_2 concentration in the air is lowered to 17 per cent, humans can still work without regulations; this corresponds to a height of approximately 2,500 m: from 17 per cent to 18 per cent they can work for four hours, followed by a half hour break; from 15 per cent to 13 per cent they can work for two hours, followed by a two hour break.

A complete factory planning includes plans for: fire bridge, escape and rescue, hazardous goods, key management and locking, waste disposal systems, controls, emergency power systems.

12.11 Guidelines

VDI guidelines

2519	Procedures for the compilation of tender and performance specification	12.01
2523	Project management for logistics systems in materials handling and storing	07.93
3564	Recommendations for fire protection in high bay warehouses	04.11
3581	Availability of transport and storage systems including subsystems and elements	10.06
3595	Methods for the layout of operational areas and resources in terms of optimum material flow	06.99
3633	Simulations in materials handling, logistics and production	12.13
3637	Data collection for long-term factory planning	09.96
4414	Renewal and expansion of logistics systems	12.95
4499	Digital factory – fundamentals	05.11
6600	Project engineer – requirements for qualification	01.09

DIN Standards

276	Cost planning for high builds	12.08
14 096	Fire prevention regulation	01.14
14 090	Areas for fire brigade access on premises	05.03
4102	Flammable behaviour of building materials and components, see DIN EN 1365	09.05

Additional guidelines and legislation include: workplace regulations and guidelines (ArbStättV); Working Conditions Act (ArbSchG); regulation about fire prevention (VVB). Accident prevention regulations include: GUV-R 133: Fire extinguisher equipment in workplaces; VDE 0123 is a leaflet for firefighting in electrical systems.

12.12 Examples and questions

Example 12.1: Planning causes

How can external and internal planning causes be categorized?

Answer: External causes (see Chapter 1.1) are:

- business move;
- new technologies such as CAD, CIM, automating options and RFID;

- market-bases, such as competing products, product faults;
- legal regulations such as environmental regulations, work safety;
- procurement market, such as material costs, personnel costs.

Internal causes (see Chapter 2.5.1) are:

- business objectives such as expansion of the business and new products;
- operational circumstances such as costs, long order processing times and operational chances;
- organization such as team work;
- technology such as manufacturing, warehousing or transport systems;
- organizational structure such as paperless order picking or a mobile data carrier.

Example 12.2: Land use plan

What kinds of land use plans are there?

Answer: We distinguish:

1 Preparatory land use plans, called area usage plans.
2 Legally binding land use plans, called building plans.

Example 12.3: Prognosis process

What are the most common prognosis processes?

Answer: In order to take into consideration future business developments when planning, the quantity of products and product groups, as well as future products, must be predicted. Prognosis processes deliver probable values, with which the current data framework from the analysis can be calculated to the target data framework.

Such prognosis processes include:

- time series analysis (averaging, exponential equalization and trend extrapolation);
- Delphi method and scenario technique.

Example 12.4: Assessment criteria

What are the options for identifying assessment, evaluation and requirement criteria?

Answer: Methods to identify criteria and ideas are:

- brainstorming;
- morphological box (see Figure 12.10).

Example 12.5: Availability and reliability

What do the terms availability and reliability mean, and what are they used for?

Answer: Availability and reliability for transport and warehousing systems are key figures and are used for:

- determining contractually agreed key indicators;
- obtaining comparable values in quotes;
- defining demonstrable values;
- capturing changing values over time.

Availability and reliability identify the ratio of downtime or repair time for discontinuous working means of transport and systems, both current and predicted. For this, a ratio is calculated of expected or measured downtime and theoretically possible deployment times.

With the help of disruption statistics (for more on disruption protocol, see VDI 3580) the reliability and availability can be calculated according to VDI 35801.

Availability is a measurement of the probability of finding a system in a disruption free and functioning condition.

Reliability (see VDI 3581) is a measurement for the probability that a function can be run without disruption. Both figures are linked together functionally.

Availability for a system component is calculated as:

$$\eta = \frac{(T_\mathrm{E} - T_\mathrm{A})}{T_\mathrm{E}} = 1 - \frac{T_\mathrm{A}}{T_\mathrm{E}}$$

T_E Operating time; T_A Downtime

Availability of serial system components is calculated as: $n_\mathrm{gesamt} = n_1 \times n_2 ... n_\mathrm{n}$ and for parallel components: $n_\mathrm{gesamt} = u_1 \times u_2 \times ... u_\mathrm{n}$ with $u = 1 - n$ = non-availability.

Depending on the serial or parallel structure of the system, the individual availabilities have to be multiplied or added up.

Example 12.6: Implementation planning

Show the development of a building layout in a sketch and an implementation plan example.

Answer: Figures 12.24 and 12.25.

Example 12.7: Representative project processes

Draw the process from analysis to implementation for a project in another form from that shown in 12.7.

Answer: Figure 12.26.

Figure 12.24 Process for layout planning: interior planning of a building

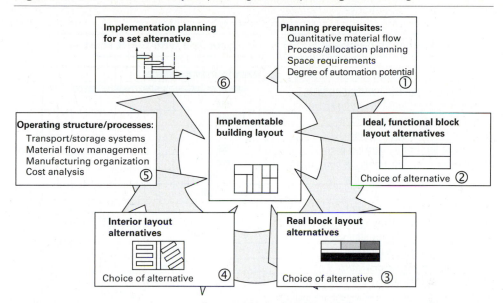

Example 12.8: Representation of warehousing costs/summary logistics costs

After carrying out the analysis (current status) and system planning (target status), visually show the saving for warehousing costs, as shown in Figure 12.27.

Answer: The summary of logistics costs is shown in Figure 12.28.

Example 12.9: Continuous improvement processes, quality management

How can an implemented plan be realized further?

Answer:

a) By continuous comparison of current and target data and relevant adaptation.

b) With the help of continuous improvement processes and/or quality management.

Both methods try to engage staff and use their experience and simultaneously transfer additional responsibilities, in order to achieve greater commitment to the business. Continuous improvement processes and quality management are options to achieve constant optimization of processes, products and organization. Both result in an improved quality of products, increases in productivity and lower costs. This leads to satisfied customers and clients.

Continuous improvement activities in manufacturing for increased productivity through minimizing search times and better work safety commence with sorting items that are no longer needed, a systematic order of ergonomic work equipment,

Figure 12.25 Implementation plan for new warehousing technology in existing warehouse

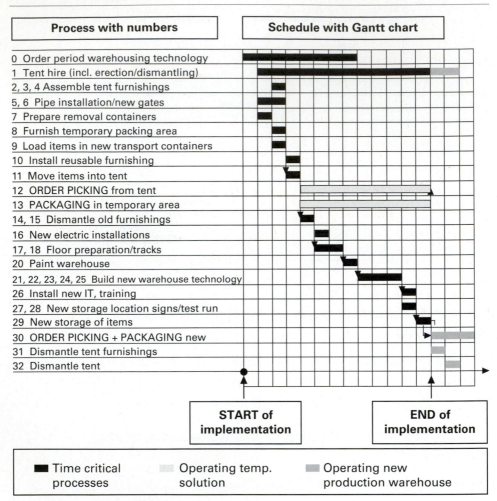

standardization of processes, as well as the discipline to maintain set standards and continuous checks and controls.

A continuous improvement of the quality management process is visually represented in Figure 12.29. The requirements and satisfaction of customers are the basis of the improvement system.

Common quality management processes include:

- Process-supporting checks (IPC = in-process control).

- Alignment to standards: based on the technical committee ISO/TC 176, quality series ISO 9000. This standard does not represent a method for quality management, but contains internationally applied standards, which a business has to fulfil in order to comply with the quality standard.

Figure 12.26 Gantt chart for project process

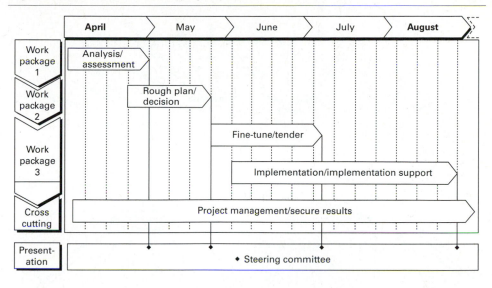

Figure 12.27 Current/target comparison of warehousing costs for system planning

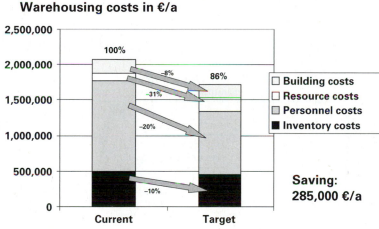

- Total quality management (TQM).
- Six sigma.
- Lean management.
- Business process re-engineering.

Example 12.10: Dynamic amortization calculation for a warehouse extension with goods receipt

A warehouse extension shall be expanded with goods receipt including ramp and transfer bridges. The extension, the earthworks, heating and electrical installation will cost

Figure 12.28   Summary of logistics costs (www.lischke.com)

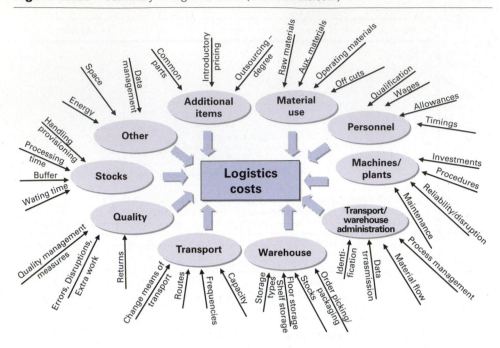

Figure 12.29   Process-focused quality management according to DIN 9001

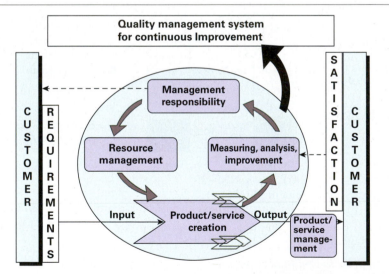

€210,000, the ramps and transfer bridges €99,100 and the IT connections €15,600. The calculated savings through dissolving a rented warehouse, for personnel and transport, come to €232,200. What is the dynamic amortization time for concept X?

Answer: Table 12.4.

Table 12.4   Calculation of dynamic amortization time for a building concept

Dynamic amortization calculation for concept X: $t_{dyn} = 2.39$ years				
No		**Year 1**	**Year 2**	**Year 3**	**Year 4**
1	Capital commitment (–) (out of 7)		–212,328	–119,046	40,990
2	Payments (Investment in Euros)	–99,100 –210,900 –15,600	–68,100 0 –1,800	–58,000	
3	Interest 8% (of total 1+2)	–26,048	–22,578	–14,164	0
4	Total (1+2+3)	–351,648	–304,806	–191,210	40,990
5		Only 60% of incoming payments apply in year 1	Only 80% of incoming payments apply in year 2	100% of incoming payments apply in year 3	100% of incoming payments apply in year 4
6	Savings (in Euros)	139,320	185,760	232,200	232,200
7	Transfer to next year (6–4)	–212,328	–119,046	40,990	273,190

Contrary to static amortization calculations, the dynamic amortization calculation includes the annual interest of the investment. The calculated amortization time is 2.39 years. Table 12.4 shows that after three years the return on investment is 121 per cent. Total savings of €232,200 are only achieved in full after three years, as delivery times, preliminary work and implementation time require a certain start-up time. The achievement of 60 per cent and 80 per cent of savings in years one and two are estimated values.

Example 12.11: Creating alternatives

Departments VI, VII and VIII in a business have been streamlined and should now be optimized. For each individual department, develop two or three planning options. Alternatives are then created through combining different options for individual departments (see Figure 12.30).

Example 12.12: Specifications and customer requirements

What is the difference between specifications and customer requirements?

Answer: Specifications contain a qualitative, quantitative and functional requirements profile by the client. With regards to the delivery and service scope, such as

Figure 12.30 Systematics for creating alternatives by combining options

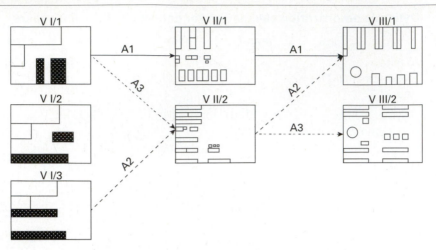

for a warehousing management system, the specifications describe the hardware and software components. *Specifications* should cover the content to answer the questions 'What?' and 'What for?' They serve as a basis for a tender, a quote and award of contract and form part of the customer requirements.

Customer requirements are worked up once the contract has been awarded by the customer and they describe how the system should be implemented based on the information in the specification. They answer the questions 'how' and 'with what' the specification will be implemented. Customer requirements must be signed off by the client, making them binding for the implementation of the project (see VDI 2519).

Example 12.13: Planning process

How can planning for Figure 12.3 and Figure 12.17a also be carried out?

Answer: Depending on the planning task – improvement, optimization, planning – the following steps can be distinguished:

1 Analysis: Listing and assessment of internal and external figures and requirements.

2 Structuring areas of activity and prioritization of activity areas.

3 Planning with profitability verification.

4 Implementation and evaluation of optimization measures through checks.

Example 12.14: Regulations for operating licence

Due to business closures, changes to production, sale and insolvencies of businesses, factory premises are on offer, whose use requires compliance with a number of regulations, causing costs. List some of these regulations for the purpose of operational licences.

Answer:

1 On premises, outside buildings:

- fire access, parking lots, safety measures, video monitoring;
- loading/unloading sites for goods receipt/issue;
- waste collection points;
- transfer sites for electricity, water, waste water, gas, surface water.

2 Interface road/premises/building:

- mains/cables cross sections for water, waste water, gas, electricity and transformers.

3 Near and within buildings:

- external lightning protection system, rain water drains, energy saving regulations;
- safety technology (belongs to area electro technology): fire detection systems, such as smoke alarms, fire extinguishing systems, sprinkler systems;
- building services (technical equipment in buildings): electric systems: main distributor, location of switch cabinet; heating/cooling; ventilation/climate control: air supply/extraction, air circulation; telephone;
- sanitary technology, drinking, waste, rain water, grease/oil separator;
- production and warehousing technology; layout material flow, machine layout plan, machine lists with weight, connections for electricity, air pressure, cooling liquid.

4 Surveys, evidence, regulations for operating licensing:

- Fire safety surveys, based on statutory building regulations in land use regulations; implementation of land use regulations (LBauO); industrial building regulation standards. To produce a survey the following documents are required: floor plan, number of staff, machine layout with machine list, production and warehousing buildings; cross sections, social and office space, warehouse dimensions, materials, fire sections, energy control centre.
- Emission control legislation application (BIschG): whether this legislation applies to a business depends on the categorization of the business as an *operation requiring licensing* or an *operation not requiring licensing*. This categorization can be found in the appendices of the fourth regulation for the emission legislation and is based on emission protection and building planning legislation. The application contains the following documents: raw materials, products, environmental impact; extracted air treatment, noise, water supply, waste water, water protection; waste, amounts of household and production waste, requirements for waste sites, such as materials requiring monitoring: roofing; heating systems.
- Production of the following is required: schedule; safety concept, locking concept; lighting concept; drainage application.

- Evidence for the following is required: insurability; industrial safety regulation for pressured containers; compliance with accident prevention regulations; work safety legislation (workplace regulations; work safety legislation); waste management cycle legislation (AfallwiKrG); water management legislation (WHG); chemical substances legislation (ChemG) with hazardous materials regulation, such as water endangerment; explosion protection; noise insulation.

- The following have to be put in place: landlord insurance; builder's risk insurance; health and safety inspector (SIGEKO).

Example 12.15: Reasons for an investment

What might be the reasons for an investment?

Answer: First, the short- and long-term consequences of an investment have to be considered and viewed depending on the current and future marginal conditions. Questions will always be about follow-up costs and operational costs. The higher in the hierarchy the investment has to be carried out, the more the future consequences have to be taken into account and relevant strategies developed and decided.

First, we need to distinguish between reasons for a) constant turnover and b) increasing turnover.

Reasons for:

a) offset investment against saving, decreasing personnel requirements, quality improvement, error reduction;

b) results of increasing turnover.

Example 12.16: Building materials for a warehouse

What has to be taken into account when selecting building materials for a warehouse?

Answer: A warehouse can be built from steel or steel concrete. Usually this makes a difference in the costs. If steel is good value, a steel structure will be built, which also has the advantage that many mains/cables of building services can be located in the gaps between the girders and surfaces. However, a steel building is made more expensive as a result of preventative fire regulations, as the steel has to be covered in a fire-retardant layer. The fire resistance should hold out for as long as possible: 30, 60, 90 or 120 minutes. Paints such as S30, S60 or S90 are based on this. These layers foam up in heat. Steel/concrete buildings have the disadvantage that large pipes, such as ventilation and air extraction pipes, are located under the roof girders, as large-scale drilling weakens the concrete, thus the building has to be of a certain height.

For normal standards, (industrial) warehouses cost approximately €500 to €600 per m²; office buildings cost approximately €800 per m². If the cost calculation is based on building volume, a standard building will cost approximately €100 to €130 per m².

The costs for external areas for lorries are between €80/m² and €150/m², whereas higher values apply depending on sewers, drainage, lighting and painting work.

When furnishing a building with a travelling crane, the reach and load capacity must be taken into account, for a reach of 20 m and load capacity of the crane of 5 t, the costs, including crane tracks, mains connections, freight, assembly and acceptance are approximately €26,000 to €30,000 (guide price). The travelling crane is box-shaped, approximately 900 to 1,000 mm high and the hook height is approximately 250 mm, so that the usable hall height is reduced by approximately 1.25 m. Put differently, the hall must be built higher by approximately 1.25 m.

Example 12.17: Reducing waste

How can waste reduction be included in planning?

Answer: First, waste has to be analysed and, second, it must be quantified (monetary determination); further steps should deal with developing, comparing and assessing solutions. The last steps are to make a decision, develop implementation planning, maybe a pilot solution, and the implementation.

Example 12.18: Process representation

What is the iteration process for planning in Figure 12.2 and how can it be presented as a general control cycle?

Answer: Figure 12.31a shows a possible representation for a functional process.

Figure 12.31a   Control cycle for a process

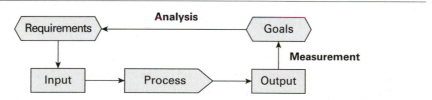

The start of a process is depicted in Figure 12.31b. Often one more component/ column has to be added with document flow. The steps of the process should be structured in core, main and partial processes.

A process system can be divided up as shown in Figure 12.31c:

Figure 12.31b Functions of a process start

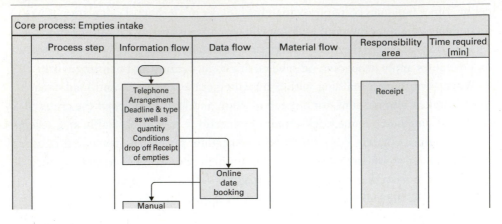

Figure 12.31c Schematic representation of a process system division

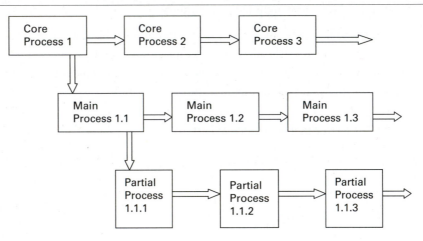

Example 12.19: Process optimization

What possibilities are there for process optimization?

Answer: Optimization options can only be carried out after a weakness analysis; this is usually about capturing current processes and identifying and assessing weaknesses. Once this process analysis has been concluded, strategies are developed to eliminate weaknesses based on optimization options. These optimizations include: avoiding process loops, duplicating work and repetition. Other options can be examined for optimization potential: elimination, standardization, integration, parallelization, moving, substitution, prevention iteration, cooperation, reduction of versions, decreasing deployed quantities.

Example 12.20: Kaizen method

What is the Kaizen method to increase efficiencies and how is a Kaizen workshop structured?

Answer: Kaizen means 'changing to improve' and is a work philosophy with the aim of achieving continuous improvement and optimization of work processes with increases in quality and usefulness for the customer, as well as creating an optimal work environment for employees.

A Kaizen workshop first examines the current situation on site, then searches for improvement options and tries to implement them. Processes are analysed and evaluated on site, in order to eliminate unproductive, unnecessary and wasteful procedures and to optimize everything that is productive and necessary. The workshop team is led by a coach, while employees from the relevant areas are participants (see Examples 12.9 and 12.17).

Example 12.21: Methods–time measurement (MTM)

What is MTM?

Answer: MTM is a method to determine required times for work processes. The work process is captured on video and is then analysed externally in an institute and divided into individual elementary basic movements – of which there are 11. The basic movements have normal time periods allocated to them. The prescribed time results from the total of normal time periods and is used to calculate wages per work unit. Larger activities are divided into multiple work processes, whose prescribed times have to be added up.

Example 12.22: Mezzanine storage, warehouses with silo structure

How can floor space be save or gained, and what factors does this depend upon?

Answer:

a) Mezzanine platforms (Figure 12.32 can increase storage space and height utilization. Suitable for B and C items in limited quantities with medium to low turnover; stairs and possibly lift required.

b) Silo warehouse construction (see Figure 9.4) is economical for large quantities with the same storage device, high turnover and limited size of premises (see Figure 12.33).

c) Through certain use of relevant shelving and operating devices with the aim of saving space through small aisle width and utilization of room height.

Figure 12.32   Mezzanine storage construction for two additional levels (www.ohra.de)

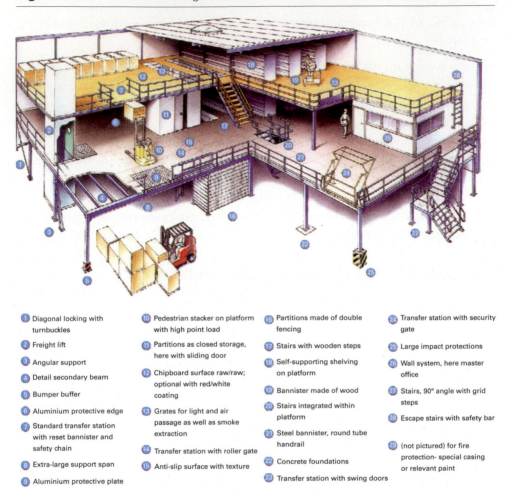

① Diagonal locking with turnbuckles	⑩ Pedestrian stacker on platform with high point load	⑯ Partitions made of double fencing	㉔ Transfer station with security gate
② Freight lift	⑪ Partitions as closed storage, here with sliding door	⑰ Stairs with wooden steps	㉕ Large impact protections
③ Angular support		⑱ Self-supporting shelving on platform	㉖ Wall system, here master office
④ Detail secondary beam	⑫ Chipboard surface raw/raw; optional with red/white coating	⑲ Bannister made of wood	㉗ Stairs, 90° angle with grid steps
⑤ Bumper buffer		⑳ Stairs integrated within platform	
⑥ Aluminium protective edge	⑬ Grates for light and air passage as well as smoke extraction		㉘ Escape stairs with safety bar
⑦ Standard transfer station with reset bannister and safety chain		㉑ Steel bannister, round tube handrail	㉙ (not pictured) for fire protection- special casing or relevant paint
	⑭ Transfer station with roller gate	㉒ Concrete foundations	
⑧ Extra-large support span	⑮ Anti-slip surface with texture		
⑨ Aluminium protective plate		㉓ Transfer station with swing doors	

Example 12.23: Structure of workplaces

Build a process with roller conveyors for packing, labelling and tagging of finished products as well as packaging and palletizing of items.

Answer: Figure 12.34.

Example 12.24: Simulation of complicated storage system, procedures

a) What questions does simulation for warehousing systems help to answer?

Answer:

- Does the order picking area need expanding by additional workspaces?
- Can developments within the organization lead to an increase in productivity, and by what percentage?

Figure 12.33 Silo construction design (www.ohra.de)

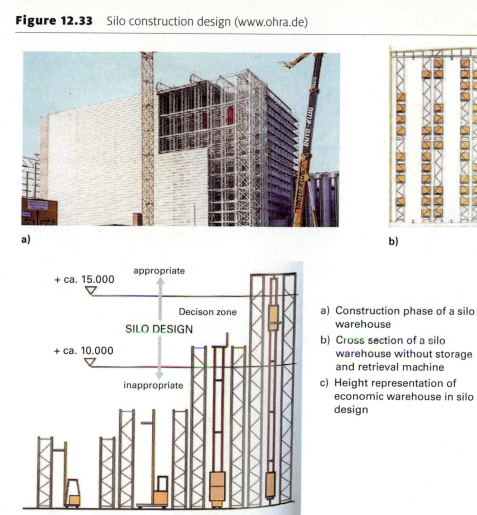

a)

b)

a) Construction phase of a silo warehouse

b) Cross section of a silo warehouse without storage and retrieval machine

c) Height representation of economic warehouse in silo design

c)

- How does an increase in the item quantity and number impact on storage capacity?
- What are the effects of item structure changes?
- How long are order processing times?
- What are the capacity limits for a storage and retrieval machine for a storage system?
- Are the existing storage and retrieval strategies the correct ones?
- Does an existing storage system have to be expanded or newly built?

Figure 12.34   Depiction of work and packing spaces; transport by roller conveyors with ejector function (www.transnorm.com)

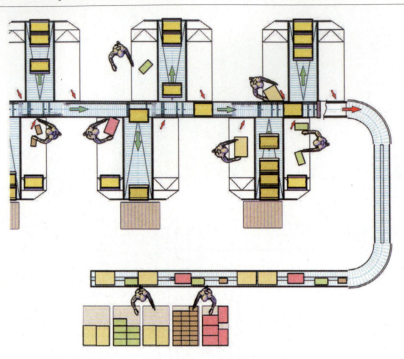

- Where are the bottlenecks in a warehouse, and has the workflow been put together in the optimal way?
- What is the utilization of a small parts warehouse, a tower shelving warehouse or another component?
- How high is the number of on time or delayed packages per shipping?

b) What is simulation used for in storage systems?

Answer: Storage systems consist of the components storage unit, warehouse technology and warehouse organization, as well as order picking, storage furnishings and building and can be seen holistically in material and information flow. Simulation is used for simultaneous observation of the storage systems as well as its components.

The objectives are:

- identify weaknesses;
- make bottlenecks visible;
- determine key storage indicators;
- achieve transparency for processes;
- shorten time until operation starts.

c) What might the approach to a simulation for a goods transport system look like?

Answer: Figure 12.35.

Figure 12.35   Representation of an approach to a warehouse transport system simulation (www.simPlan.de)

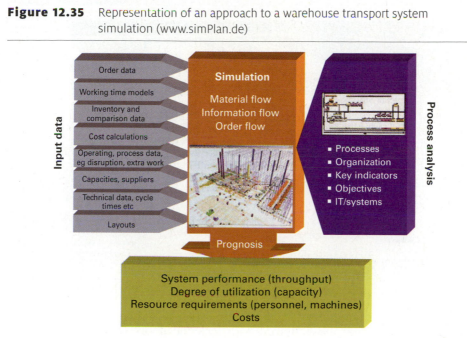

Example 12.25: Computer-aided factory and material flow planning

What does a partial impression of a computer-aided factory and material flow planning look like?

Answer: Figure 12.36.

Example 12.26: Sprinkler system for pallet shelving

What are the components and costs for a sprinkler system?

Answer: From a storage height of 7.5 m, a pallet warehouse with flammable goods requires a sprinkler system. Components are a control centre, pump house, water basin, ceiling sprinklers and shelf sprinklers. Sprinklers are usually placed every 90 cm between double shelves, for single shelves on the rear, with a sprinkler covering two pallet spaces. If one sprinkler costs €60, €150,000 is needed for 5,000 pallet spaces and another €50,000 is required for assembly and planning.

If a warehouse is built directly at the production hall, a steel/concrete wall is required (costs approximately €100 to €150/m²); openings in this wall for pallet

Figure 12.36   Representation of a working interface for a factory and MF planning showing a library of user elements; software program taraVRbuilder (www.taraVRbuilder.com)

transport to production are equipped with lockable doors (costs approximately €10,000 per opening).

Example 12.27: Floor space calculation of pallet warehouses

What is the ratio between floor space of Euro pallet warehouses to possible operating devices?

Answer: Figure 12.37. The warehouses examined contain reach truck operation, manual operation with small aisle forklift and automatic storage and retrieval machines.

Figure 12.37   Sketch of a pallet shelving section for lengthways storage of three Euro pallets next to each other and opposite with aisle width of 1.5 or 3.0 m (perspective view)

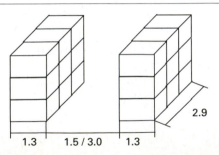

2.9

1.3   1.5 / 3.0   1.3

a) *Warehouse with reach truck:*

5 levels with 1.5 m high compartments at 7.5 m height, requirement 3,600 pallet spaces

Number of pallets for fivefold stacking = 30

Floor space: 2.9 m × 5.6 m = 16.25 m^2 at warehouse height 7.5 m

Calculation of total storage space for 200 m^2 goods receipt floor space and 200 m^2 for forklift

For 3,600 pallets: 3,600 / 30 × 16.25 = approx. 2,000 m^2 + 400 m^2 = 2,400 m^2

b) *Warehouse with narrow aisle forklift*

9 levels with 1.5 m high compartments at 15 m building height; requirement 3,600 pallet spaces

Number of pallets for ninefold stacking = 54

Floor space: 2.9 m × 4.1 m = 11.89 m^2 at warehouse height 15 m

Calculation of total storage space for 200 m^2 goods receipt floor space and 250 m^2 for forklift

For 3,600 pallets: 3,600 / 54 × 11.89 = approx. 800 m^2 + 450 m^2 = 1,250 m^2

c) *Automatic warehouse with shelf operating device*

12 levels with 1.5 m high compartments at 20 m building height; requirement 3,600 pallet spaces

Number of pallets for twelvefold stacking = 72

Floor space: 2.9 m × 3.9 m = 11.31 m^2 at warehouse height 15 m

Calculation of total storage space for 200 m^2 goods receipt floor space and 250 m^2 for forklift

For 3,600 pallets: 3,600 / 72 × 11.31 = approx. 570 m^2 + 450 m^2 = 1,020 m^2

We have to take into consideration that with two-shift operation for solution a) and b) 2.5 employees, for c) only approximately 0.5 employees are required. Moreover, for flammable goods a sprinkler system must be installed for solutions b) and c) (see Example 11.26).

Ready to occupy halls (including heating and lighting) cost approximately €700 to €800/m^2 at 7.5 m height and for 15 m height approximately €800 to €900/m^2 of floor space.

Example 12.28: Loading frames for rolled goods

What are the options for transporting and manipulating pressure sensitive rolls of aluminium, foil or paper?

Figure 12.38   Reach truck transporting a loading frame for rolled goods (www.still.de)

Figure 12.39   Electric lift truck for rolled goods, such as for placing rolls in laminating calendars (www.besco.it/de)

Answer: These rolls have a core drill hole, through which an axis can be driven in order to take them into stackable loading frames, or for hanging transport as well as storage. The dimensions of the loading frames are approximately 1,000 mm in width with lengths of up to 1,800 mm; the weight is between 500 and 1,000 kg. The loading frames (see Figure 12.38) have feet at four corners with dimensions of 100 × 100 mm that means they can only be conveyed continuously by chain conveyors (duplex/triplex chain ISO 606).

Special trucks have a tray for taking on the rolls (see Figure 12.38), they are constructed with a battery-electric lift of approximately 600 mm for short transports or to hang the rolls in press or laminating machines. For low turnover, there is manually operated equipment in order to lift rolls out of the frames using axes. Depending on how sensitive to pressure the rolls are, they can lie on pallets on wedge pads, which are stored like loading frames in single space shelves or in large shelf racks, or, via axes, in paternoster shelving or cantilever shelving. Transport options are AGVs, forklifts with rotating roller clamps, cranes or high lift trucks (Figures 6.36a to d, 6.66a and b, 6.70, 6.71, 6.87a to i, 10.13 and 11.50).

Example 12.29: Shelving space and shelf operating device costs

What are the planning costs of a storage space of a Euro pallet including freight and assembly, depending on the shelving type and shelf operation?

Answer: We distinguish lengthways and crossways storage:

a) Lengthways storage:

- pallet shelving with forklift operation: approximately €25–30;
- pallet shelving with automatic storage and retrieval operation: approximately €60–65;
- large shelving rack (grid/wooden beams) with forklift operation: approximately €60–65;

b) Crossways storage:

- drive-in shelving with forklift: approximately €50–55.

Operating devices including chargers: electric shaft forklift approximately €18,000; forklift €30,000, reach truck 7.0 m storage height approximately €50,000, narrow aisle forklift 11 m storage height approximately €110,000.

Example 12.30: Operation of manufacture and assembly with tugger trains

Show options to provide manufacture and assembly with material from the warehouse.

Answer:

1 See Figure 6.48a and b in Example 6.6–4 tug vehicle with trailers for intake of pallets, mesh boxes and a forklift required for operation.

2 See Figure 12.40: Tug vehicles with tugger trailers, which can be loaded and unloaded from both sides: by lowering the trucks no forklift is required. This type of trailer can be deployed particularly in narrow aisles.

3 See Figure 12.41.

Figure 12.40   Tug with trailers (www.still.de)

Figure 12.41   Tug with trailers (www.linde-mh.com)

Example 12.31: Industry 4.0

What does 'industry 4.0' mean?

Answer: The term 4.0 stands for the 4th industrial revolution, corresponding to the steam engine, assembly line and the computer. 4.0 describes all intelligent machines that can be digitally networked, work autonomously and solve tasks independently.

This requires two systems:

1 machines in logistics are means of transport or transport systems that intelligently transport material of any kind to the warehouse and shipping areas, manufacturing and assembly areas;

2 software and control systems with information and communication technologies that intelligently, effectively and quickly adapt individual processes.

4.0 means that men, machines, materials, software and services directly communicate to one another and cooperate with each other across the entire value chain of a product. Information and material flows have to be organized and controlled. In particular, this means that all processes, starting with the first idea about planning, development, production and hand over to the client, and after use up to recycling, are part of the value chain. In this way, men, machines, software and services are connected in cyber-physical systems. Hence, the flexibility and performance of production and distribution are increased. Moreover, optimization of networks are carried out, such as in terms of costs, resource utilization and availability.

4.0 requires devices and software for:

Autonomous systems: pre-stage: Tug, stacker and low lift truck as order picking vehicles, that find the order picking space, store and retrieve and drive to the intake and offload sites independently during automatic order picking of entire units.

It is more difficult when individual pieces are to be order picked instead of entire crates or pallets. For partly autonomous systems, the order picker no longer needs to mount the machine to carry on, but at a hand signal or other signal it drives to the order picking site independently: this saves time.

The goal is an **autonomous navigation of networked mobile systems**, e.g. for ATV or order picking vehicles, such as with 3D object and site recognition and with flexible grabbers.

Virtualization of reality, eg in support of service activities.

Networking and data security in order to combine different systems, achieve compatibility of networks, eg a container with screws sits on a scale and, when empty, triggers a means of transport to refill or exchange the container.

3D-print results in a significant time and work saving, as the data from the CAD model a part can be immediately produces, thus making redundant supply chains and the manufacture of individual pieces. For small quantities, 3D printing is cost-effective.

Figure 12.42   Connections for 'industry 4.0' (www.viastore.com)

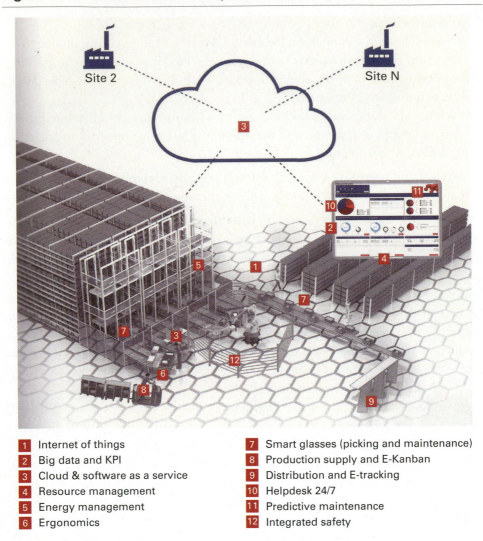

1 Internet of things
2 Big data and KPI
3 Cloud & software as a service
4 Resource management
5 Energy management
6 Ergonomics
7 Smart glasses (picking and maintenance)
8 Production supply and E-Kanban
9 Distribution and E-tracking
10 Helpdesk 24/7
11 Predictive maintenance
12 Integrated safety

Questions

1   How can 'planning' be defined and what are its characteristics?

2   What reasons might there be for planning?

3   Which factors can restrict planning?

4   List six planning principles.

5 What criteria can be used to divide up planning data?

6 List a possible data profile for planning an order picking warehouse.

7 Sketch the schematics of a planning system.

8 What are the tasks of project management?

9 What are the tasks of system planning? What is the objective of a preliminary study?

10 Show the schematics of an analysis process.

11 How do you carry out 'implementation'?

12 Which factors are part of a planning toolset?

13 How is a planning team made up?

14 How can data acquisition methods be categorized?

15 Describe a process cycle as allocation method.

16 What are the objectives of simulation?

17 What is the process of two-stage scoring?

18 What representation methods are there? The answer should be given as a schematic representation.

19 What are the tasks of the land use plan?

20 What regulations of the land use plan determine the floor space and volume-related building on premises?

21 List pan-regional site criteria.

22 What is the process for computer-aided factory planning?

23 What preventative fire protection measures have to be carried out in the planning steps land use planning, warehouse system planning and implementation planning?

24 How does a sprinkler system work?

Reference

Wöhe, G, Döring, U and Brösel, G (2016) *Einführung in die allgemeine Betriebswirtschaftslehre*, 26th ed, Munich: Verlag Franz Vahlen

Information logistics

13

The goal of information logistics is to provide the right information at the right time, and in the right place. The most important prerequisite for this is a synchronization of material and information flow. The operational functions of information logistics include the capture, storage, processing and provision of data required for the management and monitoring of the material and information flow in transport and warehousing systems. We can distinguish between pre-, post- and supporting material flow information.

Identification is the exact recognition of an item and consists of components capture, transformation and storing of data. An information system is made up of these components:

- network;
- hardware: server, computer;
- software: databases, programs (processing logic), operating system (management logistics) and interface logic.

An information system encompasses all components and elements for storing, gaining, processing, backing up and optimizing data. A logistical information system must provide materials and items in the right quantity and quality at the right time, and in the right place, observing business-specific restrictions, and must also provide information about the existing processes.

The order of successive information is called information flow and contains all pieces of information concerned with planning, management and monitoring of business processes. Information and document flow are the two main types of information flow that can also be receiptless. Data is quantifiable information that can be represented by symbols.

The information flow results from the hierarchical level structure of information systems. The organization of the information flow can be visualized through the different levels with their tasks:

- Administrative/dispositive level: Main server – host/PPS. Customer management, production planning, material management, sales and order processing and summary inventory management.

- Inventory management level (main logistics level): Warehousing management system – process computer. Storage space focused inventory management, storage space allocation, goods receipt processing, storage, retrieval, replenishment, order processing, order picking, packaging and loading.

- Transport management level (main MF and management level): Transport/forklift management system, material flow optimization, transport order management, material tracking and status information.

- Operational level (process level): Device and drive control. Status capture and display of information through sensors, radio data, terminals and scanners.

Data capture of identification occurs through manual or automatic recognition of direct or indirect features, such as colour, shape, which is transformed into information in barcodes or identification numbers.

13.1 Identification labels for general cargo

In production, warehousing and order picking systems, general cargo (products, packages, containers, pallets) are transported unaccompanied in the warehousing and shipping areas, or sorting and order picking tasks have to be fulfilled. Such material flow tasks ensure that the goods are clearly labelled. An identification system recognizes the object in the material flow or in production using information labels or sensors with the help of suitable data processing devices. Information technology is based on different basic physical principles:

- *Mechanical* information labels such as ticker tape, pens and metal flags are cheap, robust, easy to handle, only have low information density, can only be written on once and are of little significance nowadays. They can be read with the help of mechanical and inductive elements, as well as with light barriers.

- *Magnetic* information labels such as strips or cards use magnetic fields or layers to store information that can be read contactless using magnetic heads of reed contacts. Magnetic information labels are characterized by high data receptivity, can read data well and are not sensitive to dirt. They have a small reading distance and tracking tolerance.

- *Optical/electronic* information labels use marking on the transport cargo, or its silhouette, and are read with pens, laser scanners or CCD cards.

- *Electronic/electromagnetic* information labels are now the most prevalent codes. Contactless electromagnetic waves transmit the information into electronic memory. We distinguish hard coded and freely programmable data labels. Hard coded labels cannot be changed, but read indefinitely. Freely programmable data labels, on the other hand, can be changed at any time.

Figure 13.1 Basic structures of identification technology

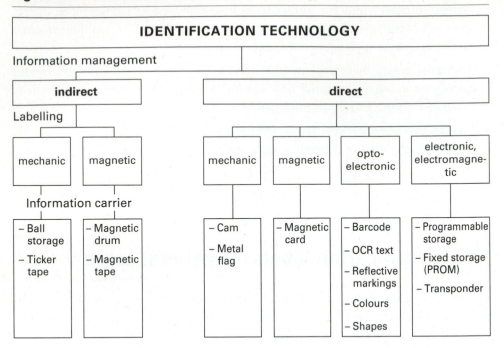

There are different automatic identification systems (auto-ID processes). The most important ones are biometric systems (voice recognition, fingerprint scan), smartcards, barcode technology (eg EAN 128), RFID (radio frequency identification) and optical systems such as OCR (optical character recognition). In logistics, the following contactless processes are used:

- optical processes (barcode, infrared and optical analysis);
- radio based processes (RFID);
- magnetic processes (magnetic cards).

13.1.1 Barcode technology

Identification is the connector between transport and warehousing processes and the general cargo. Universal product data labels (one-dimensional/1D code, barcode) and mobile data storage (MDE) are the most frequently used machine-readable information labels for labelling items, loading aids and storage spaces. Automatic identification is of great significance and occurs with tried and tested barcode and RFID technology.

Barcode technology consists of barcode printers and reading devices (decoding and testing equipment). The barcode data carrier belongs to this group of opto-electronic

Figure 13.2   Barcode make-up (from Arnold, *Material Flow Teachings*, p. 265, Figure 7.5)

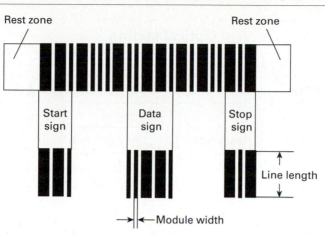

information labels and is made up of parallel dark lines on light background, whereby the code for a piece of information is achieved through lines and/or gaps with different thicknesses. Both lines and gaps are used to record information. A one-dimensional barcode is characterized as follows (Figure 13.2):

- line: dark element and gap: light element;
- line length;
- module width x: width of narrowest element in a code;
- start and stop signs, in front of where code starts and after where code ends one rest zone r;
- separators as gap between the lines of two signs;
- plain text zone below barcode: plain text of encoded information;
- information density: number of signs per mm of width.

The barcode structure is represented in Figures 13.3 to 13.7. For a two-width code the lines and gaps only appear in two different widths, for multiple width codes in more than two widths. The barcode type used depends on the task requirements of:

- the amount of information;
- the space available for code on the cargo;
- the space shape of the mounting location: flat, round, uneven (box, container, tube, roll, tin and bag);
- environmental factors: dirt, damage and temperature;
- the type of reading device (resolution ratio);
- the material of the barcode base (receipt, PVC and polyester).

Figure 13.3 Overview of coding structure with code types

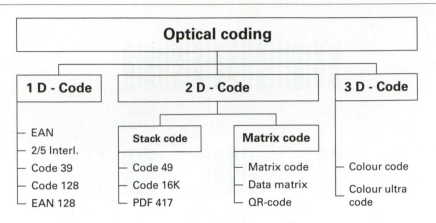

Figure 13.4 Example of a combination of an EAN code for the book trade (price, ISBN) and a two out of five interleaved code for internal material flow (tax code, storage space data). EAN (European article number) is used to clearly identify an item and is placed as barcode on the packaging by the manufacturer. The numbers from left to right signify: manufacturer country, manufacturing number, item number of manufacturer and verification code

Advantages and areas of use for inexpensive barcode technology:

- 100 per cent recognition accuracy and worldwide use;
- user friendly, universal use, reliable and efficient;
- reduction in time, effort and typos during data capture;
- check and confirmation of additional data capture and high work speed;
- fully automated material flow management through automatic identification;
- processing of entire work processes.

Additional advantages of barcodes are: high standardization; low costs; high acceptance; good integration; information immediately on site. Disadvantages result from:

Table 13.1 Description of different barcode types

Code type	Features	Design	Information density	Areas of use
2 out of 5 interleaved	Numerical code (0–9), each sign is made up of 3 narrow and 2 wide lines or gaps	Wide and narrow lines or gaps/signs	High	Conveyance technology
	Continuous code	A sign is made up of 5 lines, the following sign of the 4 intermittent gaps and the gap after the fifth line	The print ratio is between 1:2 and 1:3. Example: for $x = 0.3$ mm and $V = 1:3$ the information density is 2.7 mm/digit. As all gaps contain information, the tolerance is very small (+/– 10 %)	
	Self-checking			
	Two-width code			
EAN	Numerical (Digits 0–9)	7 modules/signs, divided into 2 lines and 2 gaps which are 1, 2, 3 or 4 modules in width. All lines and gaps contain information	High	Trade (POS)
	Continuous code		2.1 mm/digit for $x = 0.3$ mm	
	Only 8 or 13 signs can be represented	Tolerances have to be very small		
	Multiple-width code			

direct sight connection; sensitivity to dirt; no flexibility to change; no possibility to read multiple barcodes simultaneously, they are captured one after the other by the scanner; direct alignment is necessary; short distance between barcode and reading device; barcode cannot be reused or rewritten; as an optical process, it is too uncertain and too slow for complex logistic processes due to low data processing capability.

Figure 13.5   Different two-dimensional barcodes

Figure 13.6   Arrangement possibilities for barcodes

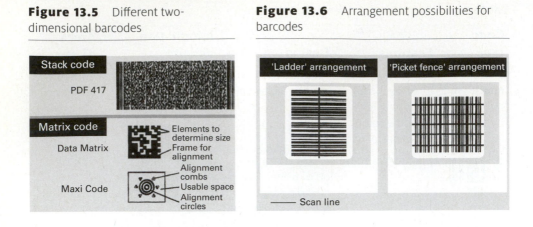

13.1.2 Multi-dimensional barcode

In order to include larger amounts of data per space unit, two-dimensional (2D code) and three-dimensional colour code (3D code) were developed. They consist of groups of data cells that are often arranged in rectangles, and have a typical information symbol for the special 2D code (see Figure 13.5). Stack and matrix code are two main types of image processing systems that are capable of reading two-dimensional code.

Barcodes are assessed on space usage, density, capacity, quick identification and decoding, as well as the number of sign sets. The 'data matrix' code has a square/rectangular shape, large packing density and a capacity of approximately 10 to 2,300 signs. It is used for product marking for small parts. The 'Aztec code' is used to sort packages and for online ticket printing. It can contain up to 100 signs.

For this 2D code, there are also combinations, such as between 1D and 2D codes for the composite code UCC/EAN Composite. For 3D code, the third dimension is created through colour, so that 1D, 2D codes do not refer to geometric figures, but to data content.

The QR (quick response) code was developed as a two-dimensional square code for automobile industry logistics. It usually consists of black and white dots and can have varying sizes. What is important is a contrast with the environment. Within the square there are at least 21×21 and a maximum of 177×177 elements. The code contains preliminary information and the utilized data format. Alignment is based on marking on three of the four corners. 2D technology can possess more than 400 signs or approximately 7,000 numbers and approximately 3,000 bytes – very large amounts of data can be stored. Information can still be read even when the code is damaged by up to 30 per cent. The code is licence and cost free. Further developments include the Micro-QR code and the iQR code.

13.1.3 Arrangement of data labels

What are the arrangement options for barcodes used in industry for fixed scanners?

Two basic transport directions-based arrangement options can be distinguished from barcodes (see Figure 13.6):

1 Ladder arrangement: lines of the barcode run parallel to the transport direction, and it is scanned along a scan line.

2 Picket fence arrangement: lines of the barcode run parallel to the transport direction, called 'picket fence'. For security reasons, the scan is carried out by multiple parallel scan lines, offset to one another.

13.1.4 Reading devices

These capture data on a data carrier optically. For 1D to 3D codes, there is a multitude of reading devices, structured along different physical principles, or divided in line with different features. Manual and stationary handling are two main types of optical identification. Handheld reading devices are wireless or mobile. Stationary devices read the code semi-automatically or automatically. The scan technology of reading devices is based on their lights (LED, laser), on the utilized sensor (photoiode, line sensor) and the type of scanning process – sequential or parallel – as well as the assessment basis (line or image). The combination of these different values results in the designs for the reading devices (see Figure 11.6).

Laser scanner (scanner = device to read an area line by line, such as barcode): point and line scanner; sensor scanner; line and matrix scanner.

Reading devices with an omnidirectional mode can also read the line code when it is not moved by at a right angle and not on one level past the reading device, so that they radiate grid-like and allow the barcode to be read independent of direction and radiation.

For handheld reading devices, up to 70 scans/s can occur depending on the system, up to 600 scans/s for stationary devices. The reading distance is up to 3 m depending on the device.

13.1.5 Mobile data storage

Mobile data storage means electronic storage devices. Electronic/electromagnetic information labels include freely programmable data labels, which can be used as mobile data storage (MDS). Writing and reading devices (programming unit = writing unit) are capable of capturing and storing data and information during the material flow and give access to these at any time. MDS belong to the group of direct identification technology.

Mobile data storage is active, which means its data can be held centralized or decentralized. The mounting of the MDS occurs directly or indirectly on the cargo.

Figure 13.7   Schematic structure of an identification system with mobile data storage
Legend: MDS: mobile data storage; WR: writing/reading device; AU: assessment unit; PH: periphery host

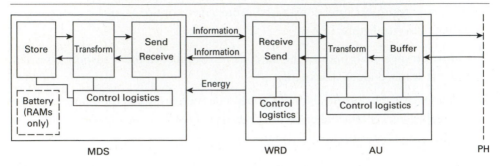

Indirect mounting is used for either very small or very cheap cargo; the MDS is fixed to the transport aid (container, roller truck, loading frame) and can be used again and again. When using an active MDS, the relevant cargo can be controlled without the help of the warehouse control system through decentralized data storage.

The energy supply for data storage, controls, information processes and communication for programmable MDS happens either via battery (MDS type RAM) or using the electromagnetic field of the writing/reading device (MDS type EEPROM = electrically erasable programmable read only memory).

An identification system with mobile data storage, which can take many pieces of cargo to a predetermined destination, consists of:

- mobile data storage devices (MDS);
- writing/reading devices (WRD);
- assessment units (AU).

An identification system is made up of the components MDS, WRD and AU, these components in turn consist of different elements that are systematically represented in Figure 13.7.

In a material flow system the WRD controls the communication between the cargo (equipped with a mobile data memory) and the superordinate control system, eg. a master computer. The WRD converts the data received from an AU into electromagnetic waves to read or write data. The AUs represent the interface between the WRD and the master computer. Upon meeting a WRD, it is equipped with all data necessary for processing, transport or storage, depending on the task. The data can be read at each decision stage and, based on it, data can be transmitted, decisions made or data changed.

13.1.6 RFID technology

Structure: The RFID system (tag) consists of the following components:

- RFID transponder: fixed to identifiable object and aerials;

- reading device (reader): contains transceiver and recorder to control communications interface;
- computer: data processing.

The transponder can be electronically programmed and contains data for clear identification of the tag (object). It consists of a coupling unit and a microchip (for more on information carriers, see Figure 13.8a). Either a coil or an aerial is used as a coupling unit. The transponder is embedded in plastic and, thus, is resistant to contamination. Different tag designs are on the market (see Figure 13.8b). The tag requires energy, which it is supplied with through different procedures:

- passive RFID transponder: are fed into the reader from the field;
- semi-active transponder: possess an internal battery to provide for the microchip; the field energy of the reader is used to send the data;
- active RFID transponder: possess a battery for the microchip and mobile radar.

Figure 13.8a   Transponder system (www.ind-systeme.com)

Sending transponder data

RFID transponder
(Radio chip or RFID tag)
Electronically stored
Ident-number

RFID reader
with aerial, connected
to computer and
communicating with
transponders

Computer/server
with application

Figure 13.8b   Features and characteristics of four transponder types [16]

Name	Omni-ID Flex	Confidex Steelwave Micro	Sontec Hummingbird II	Marubeni TAGAT81
Dimensions	77 × 15 × 2 mm	38 × 13 × 3 mm	25 × 9 × 3 mm	9 × 9 × 3 mm
Reading reach on metal	2 Metre	1.5 Metre	1 Metre	0.5 Metre
Reading reach on plastic	2 Metre	1 Metre	0.3 Metre	0.5 Metre
Weight	2.9 Gram	2 Gram	3.8 Gram	3 Gram
Costs	2.25 Euro	0.88 Euro	1.73 Euro	2.25 Euro

The reader can read data into or from the transponder. The reach is dependent on the transponder type. Passive transponders have a reading reach of 10 cm to 6 m, active ones up to 100 m. We distinguish stationary and mobile readers.

While with a barcode information can be optically read through a scanner, the information is read electromagnetically by a reader for the transponder. The electromagnetic principle allows reading of data without visual contact. If the transponder is located inside an item, packaged against moisture, heat, damage or contamination, all information can still be read nevertheless. Anti-collision technology makes it possible to read multiple transponders at the same time.

Advantages and *features* of a transponder are:

- simultaneous reading of multiple transponders, bulk reading and high processing security;
- identification of products without visual connection with data exchange in seconds;
- variable data storage, high storage volume and high data security;
- full automation of item tracking possible;
- rewritable;
- transparent exchange of information in real time;
- faster than barcode, thus higher data processing time;
- not as sensitive as barcode, plain text or labels;
- hidden mounting of transponder on containers, crates or boxes.

*Disadvantage*s of transponders:

- product features such as high percentage of water (cooling fluids), high density or existence of metal parts (car parts) can adversely affect data transmission;
- data protection concerns;
- low levels of standardization;
- connection to IT systems;
- problems in data transmission.

In connection with labels, the transponder can be affixed to almost any base permanently or removable, visible or hidden. Its use is for product labelling and tracking, processing management and controls as well as item protection. One example for use of transponders is for reusable packing systems (see Example 3.8). A manufacturer sends his products in expensive foldable reusable containers (see Figure 3.3g) to the customers. The transponder label affixed to the reusable container includes all important data, such as recipient, date, contents, quantities, weight etc. The customer sends the empty reusable container back to the sender, who compares the transponder data with his merchandise management system, documents the shipment as received and deletes the data. The container is once more available for further transport. The *frequency area* with which the reader communicates is one selection criterion for the RFID system.

These are divided into four areas:

- low frequency (LF) < 135 MHz;
- high frequency (HF) < 13.56 MHz;
- ultra-high frequency (UHF) < 860–930 MHz;
- miwaves = 2.45 GHz.

Other selection criteria include:

- reading reach;
- data transfer rate;
- susceptibility to failure;
- costs of transponder and readers;
- recognition speed of transponders;
- influences in the usage area by other users on same frequency.

13.2 Data transmission technology

When transmitting data we distinguish between a simple binary signal and the exchange of data telegrams. Simple elements for binary data transmission are light barriers, magnetic switches, reed contacts and limit switches. The exchange of data telegrams occurs contactless using *induction, radio* and *infrared technology*. Inductive and infrared technology are usually used for a point and route-related data transmission (building); for covering a larger area (outdoors) radio and infrared technology (see VDI 3641) are used. The data transmission system connects the operational level of internal logistics, such as of forklifts and order picking devices, to a superior control centre, which takes on dispositive and administrative tasks.

13.2.1 Data transmission with induction technology

Inductive data transmission (see Figure 13.9a) makes use of alternative fields in the area of 20 to 100 kHz. The data transmission reach is up to approximately 0.5 m. It is called pathway technology or linear supported technology and occurs with

Figure 13.9   Schematic representation of different data transmission technologies in a warehousing management system with mobile data communication

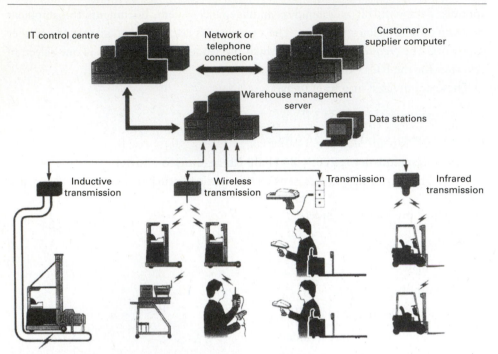

data transmission loops with point-related transmission. A secure data transmission occurs at a rate of 10 Mbits/s.

The route-related data transmission can occur through:

- the string line by modulating the digital frequency;

- a wire separately installed to the string line in the floor joints with its own carrier frequency.

13.2.2 Data transmission with radio technology

We distinguish between narrow band radio data (for more on narrow bands, see Figure 13.9b) and broadband radio data (spread spectrum). Electromagnetic fields in frequency areas 433 MHz to 466 MHz are used for narrow band and 2.4 GHz for broadband with transmission rates of 4.8 to 19.2 Kb/s or 2 to 11 Mb/s. The reach is vice versa: 1 m for narrow band and up to 100 m for broadband. As a result of the high data transmission rate for broadband radio data, this radio technology is used for receiptless order picking, in stacker control systems and in wireless systems in manufacturing, where multiple aerials are usually necessary. The advantage of narrow band radio data is the large transmission reach of up to 1 km, so that the area of use is particularly in outdoor warehouses, courtyard areas or container terminals, but also in halls. Often only one aerial is required; this is determined by testing, which also recognizes radio shadows. Narrow band radio data systems are subject to authorization. The broadband area is used in two procedures: direct sequence procedures and frequency hopping procedures. For the first, the frequency area I divided into many channels, working in parallel, so that a large transmission rate can be achieved: 11 Mb/s. For the latter procedure, there is a constant change between channels, leading to a lower transmission rate: 2 Mb/s. This procedure is less sensitive to radio disturbances and is, thus, used more often.

The use of radio data for mobile terminals allows for current and secure information, such as about stocks and material requirements, and, thus, also increases capacity use and profitability of resources. Radio data is used for receiptless order picking and stacker control systems.

13.2.3 Data transmission with infrared technology

With infrared technology it is possible to transmit data via points, route or areas, the transmission speeds are between 300 and 19,000 baud. The transmission rate is around 56 Kb/s to 1.5 Mb/s, the frequency area around 950 nm. A prerequisite for transmitting data is a visual connection between sender and recipient, whereby the transmission reach is up to 100 m. These systems are used in hall areas, for medium distance and data processing rates. Disruptive influences are sunlight, lighting types with high infrared content, infrared remote controls and light barriers. Authorization for data transmission is not required.

Data transmission is used in warehousing and order picking areas:

- for *goods receipt* to capture items, determine storage locations for fixed storage strategies, for executing storage via a stacker control system, etc;
- for *warehousing* for accurate inventory management, administration of storage locations, storage arrangement with free storage space selection;
- for *order picking* for receiptless order picking, creation of order picking assignments, execution of refilling;
- *for goods issue* for creating loads, for checking delivery, for communicating connection between transport vehicle and control station, for generating invoices.

13.3 Material flow management and administration

Aside from the 'hardware components' load unit, shelving and storage and retrieval machine of a shelf warehousing system (see Figure 10.6), the software component 'warehousing processes' plays a significant part in the profitability of a warehouse. Unit warehouses are usually managed in line with free storage space selection, whereby certain storage strategies have to be complied with, such as FIFO, cross-distribution of items or short route for storage and retrieval devices for goods with high turnover. The management of the workflow is dependent on the size of the warehouse. As hardware and software for warehouse processing computers are available at low cost, unit warehouses are mostly automatically managed.

13.3.1 Offline operation

Offline operation is a discontinuous data transmission between a central computer and a periphery device. The coupling of this system management between process and process computer can occur via a line, such as a keyboard, or without a line, using disc or radio data. Hence offline operation is also called coupling. The computer assesses the input data and information and subsequently directs the transport vehicles as well as the storage and retrieval machines to the pre-storage zone (see Figure 9.2).

Figure 13.10 shows manual management of the material flow in a business through manual booking, administration and synchronization.

13.3.2 Online operation

Online operation is system management whereby information and data for input and output are continuously transmitted and constantly checked between process and processing computer (periphery devices and computer) using a fixed connection. We call this direct *closed* coupling.

As an example, the system management in offline operation is executed with a centralized punch card control system and related to the pallet shelving storage shown in Figure 9.2. Although this method of operation is obsolete and no longer used today, the activities of the operator, which are carried out by computer or software in online operation, can be seen clearly. The input and output of data occurs at the control panel at the I-point (identification point) of a storage shelving system (see Figure 9.2). At this point the worker retrieves two of the three pallet dispatch notes fixed to the pallet during the storage procedure and looks for an empty space in the

Figure 13.10 Offline material flow management (www.still.de)

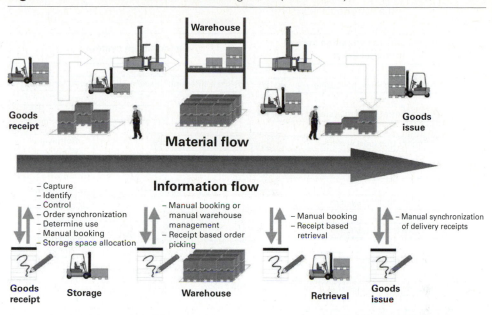

punch card index based on requirements, such as turnover frequency, cross distri-bution principle, etc, and takes out a punch card. This punch card, once read into the punch card reader, is placed into a sleeve together with the pallet dispatch notes (storage goods) and filed according to the item number of the index for full storage spaces. When reading into the punch card reader, the coordinates of the storage space are read and the management for pallet storage is activated (see Figure 13.11).

In the full storage space index, the FIFO principle can be achieved through a simple arrangement. Newly stored items are placed in the back of the item stack, retrieval receipts are taken out at the front. The retrieval procedure occurs in reverse order. Receipt '1' is collected and passed at regular intervals to IT in order to revise the inventory correctly. The same happens during the retrieval procedure with receipt '2'. The I-point is the only point in the warehouse where information flow and mate-rial flow physically converge. Instead of working with punch cards, nowadays this data transmission is carried out with barcodes and scanner or with magnetic card and reading direction.

The objective of online operation is always to make transport faster, error free and more cost effective. This is achieved through:

- *online booking*: replaces time-consuming manual offline booking, achieves docu-mentation and statistics;
- *adherence to schedules*: is achieved through timely processing of tasks;

Figure 13.11   Schematic representation of offline information and receipt flow in a warehousing system

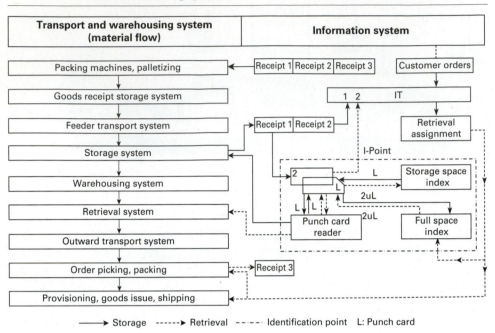

→ Storage   ----→ Retrieval   -·-·- Identification point   L: Punch card

Figure 13.12   Online material flow operation (www.still.de)

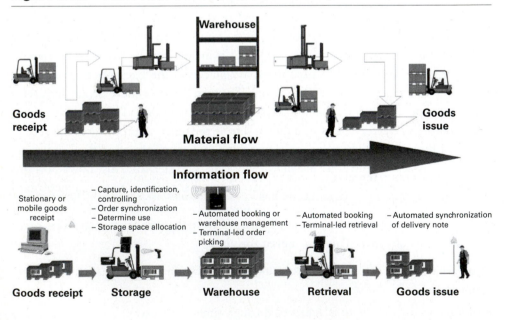

- *system overview*: provides information of past, current and future transports as well as the current status of resources, transparent material flow;

- *throughput increase and reduction of errors*: reduces logistics costs, increases capacity use; better fulfilment of requirements.

13.3.3 *Warehouse management system WMS/stacker control system*

Warehousing management is about administration of inventory and storage locations and can be carried out manually, or nowadays usually with a warehouse management system. The WMS supports the processes for planning, management, coordination and control in a warehouse and takes over:

- warehouse master data management (see Example 11.14), warehouse movement data;

- goods receipts and goods issue management;

- goods movements for storage, re-storing and retrieval.

For warehouse and material flow management, software components are available, used for the execution and optimization of individual processes:

- storage location management; online inventory;

- paperless order picking; shipping management;

- means of transport management, barcode management;

- connection to subordinate control and management systems;

- stocktake as well as one-off inventory.

The tasks of the WMS are the coordination and management of material and information flows. The WMS is the interface between material flow and information flow (see Figure 1.3), such as when goods arriving in goods receipt trigger processes for quality control, unit creation and storage. To execute activities, it is required that information about the goods must be provided at the I-point (warehouse control centre). In summary, the tasks of the EMS (see Examples 13.6 and 13.7) are:

- monitoring of goods receipt and goods issue (see Chapter 9.4);

- optimization of storage and retrieval;

- determining warehouse strategies for order processing, order picking, redistribution;

- warehouse management, inventory, monitoring and management of documentation;

- net requirements calculation, stocktake, locking down spaces, bypass optimization;
- division of warehouse on the computer into spaces, areas, aisles, shelving rows;
- management of items via storage location, space, compartment, storage unit and storage aids;
- automated storage space allocation in ABC zones with storage space optimization;
- personnel management, bottleneck recognition.

The WMS is often integrated into an ERP system, but can also be separate. The WMS has subsystems, such as means of transport, storage and retrieval machine and robots, so that the warehouse management computer is organized hierarchically and is located between the ERP system and the material flow calculator. The server is used in the background for data maintenance, centralized processing and bookings.

A stacker control system (SCS) manages industrial trucks, mostly forklifts. For processing a transport or order picking assignment without SCS, the order picking papers are printed first, and passed to the forklift driver. The driver chooses the route, carries out the task, and returns the papers to the control centre. The results are then entered into the IT systems. When using an SCS all these activities are done automatically.

Figure 13.13   Architecture of a warehouse management system (www.prologistik.com)

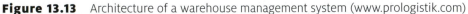
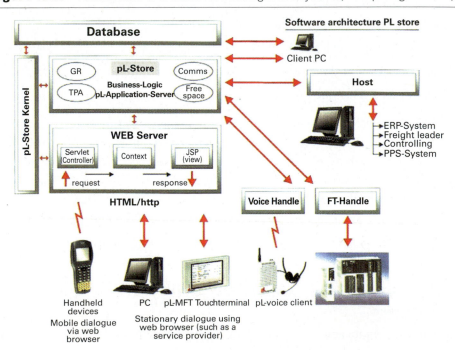

It is the goal of an SCS to ensure capacity use of the forklift as well as to optimize its routes through preventing empty and search journeys. An SCS can operate independently or is part of a warehouse management system. The components of a WMS are (in general from www.ifdag.de):

- transport management for an automatic transport assignment and for paperless capture and transmission of transport tasks, recording and checks for urgent assignments and their processing;

- route finding for an optimal route avoiding empty journeys, locating forklifts;

- business intelligence for producing statistics and images of transport processes in real time, transport per forklift and driver, empty journey ratio, transport times, assignment peaks and pool as well as maintenance management and management of control centre for stacker fleet;

- resource management with independent management and mobile monitoring, management of stacker fleet.

An enterprise resource planning (ERP) system is an integrated business planning and management system for processes and resources. By integrating administration, disposition and management functions this creates a holistic system for business activities in a company, whereby internal business processes are at the forefront. ERP systems aim to lead to an efficient deployment of internal resources and encompass models and subsystems for all business tasks such as inventory management, disposition, bookkeeping, controlling, manufacturing and personnel management. Subsystems are independent. They have open interfaces on both sides. If modules and subsystems are fully interconnected, a holistic information flow in the business can be guaranteed.

Information derives from a database common to all subsystems and modules. It is made up of long-term master data, such as customer, supplier, item and resource master data. Master data can, in turn, be divided into:

- identification and order data;

- calculation, construction and production data;

- procurement, disposition and sales data.

Identification data recognize the items using the item number. Order data summarize items (data sets) and allow assessment of all items in one group.

13.3.4 Configuration of a material flow–information flow system

Two different options for structuring a material flow–information flow system in warehouse and pre-storage areas are shown in Figures 13.14 and 13.15.

Figure 13.14 Configuration of a warehouse management system for tower and paternoster shelving (www.haenel.de)

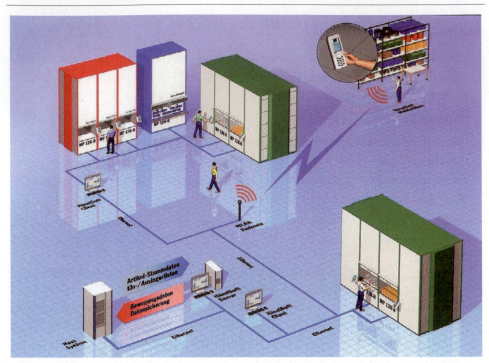

What is important is a security concept for the material flow–information flow system so as to prevent emergencies, such as by using a secure server, duplicating power supplies and having parts for terminals and scanners in reserve on site. Emergency scenarios have to be considered during planning, such as downtime of the entire system (install backups and work with paper records), for radio downtime, for downtime of a terminal/scanner (use replacement).

The material flow management and inventory management are carried out according to a number of principles, such as the push principle, pull principle, JIT, Kanban, order point and order quantity procedures.

13.3.5 Connecting a warehouse to IT

If an existing warehouse area is to be optimized through radio data and connected to an existing IT system, the first decision to make is whether to work with narrow band or broadband technology. Narrow band technology has a wider reach at a lower transmission rate, whereas the opposite applies to broadband technology: it has a high transmission rate but low reach (see Chapter 13.22).

Figure 13.15   Hardware structure of an information and management system (www.kasto.com). The system has the following components: automatic order processing, material master data, inventory, permanent stocktake, SQL database; host interface to a.o. SAP R/3, modem remote diagnosis and teleservice; visualization of system status; maintenance intervals, batch management, data back up

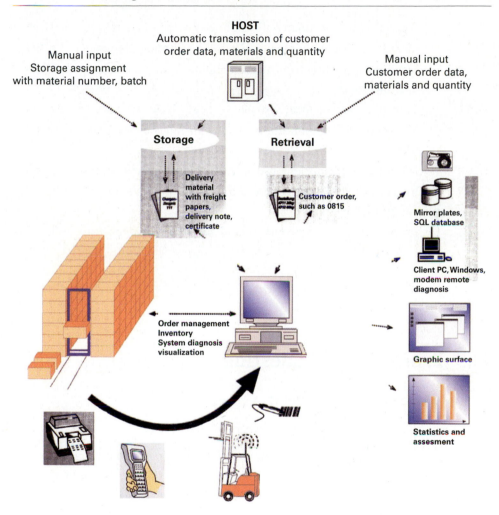

When connecting a warehouse area to IT or to a merchandise management system (MMS: computer-aided system to capture and track accurate quantities of items) there are two possible options: direct connection to IT via end user devices, or an indirect system like a separate warehouse management system (WMS). The advantages of a WMS are: taking the strain of the MMS, only order and inventory data have to be transmitted between WMS, and MMS and there are a number of possibilities to carry out business-specific workflows by management via radio data. When connection is directly to a SAP MMS, all dialogues have to be carried out on the radio data terminal, which has a negative impact on the reaction times of the MMS.

13.4 VDI guidelines

2339	Operating unit for material handling systems	05.99
2515/1	Identification labels for material handling systems – barcode	12.94
2515/2	Identification labels for material handling systems – mobile data memories	05.98
3591	Transport management systems	01.03
3641	Mobile data communication systems for internal company material transport	05.88
3964	Mobile data memories, product performance specifications	10.93
3969	Interfaces of the warehouse administration system with subordinate systems	12.03
4416	Production data acquisition and identification – identification systems	05.15
4428	Mobile data terminals	08.99

13.5 Examples and questions

Example 13.1: RFID print systems

What creation and print possibilities are there for RFID tags?

Answer: See Figure 13.16. RFID is used for identifying products and transport labels. A transponder is a small computer chip, which stores the EPC code. There is no need for visual contact between the reading unit and the data label during the reading process. To process RFID labels, label printers and applicators are equipped with a reading device, and the data is transmitted from the computer via an interface onto the label printer. The label can be printed and the transponder is programmed at the same time.

- Portable slap and ship: Barcode content is transformed into an EPC code and the information is written onto a tag without printer.
- Mobile slap and ship: An RFID printer is located on a truck, and this prints smart labels. The barcode content is transformed in an EPC code, the label is manually affixed.

Figure 13.16 Overview of possible RFID applicator and print systems (www.bluhmsysteme.com)

Portable Slap & Ship	Mobile Slap & Ship	Print, Code & Apply	Print, Code & Apply Flag Tag
Task			
• Transportable solution to get to different locations and tag existent packaging units without printing • Transform from NVE to EPC • Additional fixing of EPC tag to existing label	• Mobile solution to get to different locations and tag existent packaging units and label with additional information • Transform from NVE to EPC (standalone) • Print current data via WLAN (online)	• Fully automated RFID labelling of pallets and boxes • Removal of erroneous Smart labels	• Fully automated RFID labelling of pallets and boxes with hard to read products (metals or fluids) • Automatic folding of Flag tag • Removal of erroneous Smart labels
Operation type			
portable	mobile	fixed	fixed
Connection			
Stand-alone	Stand-alone, Online	Stand-alone, Online	Stand-alone, Online
Process			
Read barcode, create EPC code, write in tag by press of button approx. 5 sec. per pallet/box	Read barcode, create EPC code, write in smart label by press of button approx. 5 sec. per pallet/box	Data are sent to print applicator using customer system and 1:1 applied onto product	Data are sent to print applicator via customer system and 1:1 applied onto product
Labelling			
Manual, selective Smart label on demand	Manual, selective Smart label on demand	Automatic, selective Smart label on demand	Automatic, selective Smart label on demand
Tag			
Handy Tag, Handy Flag Tag	Smart Label, Handy Flag Tag	Smart Label	Auto Flag Tag

- Print code and apply: Tags are printed and applied in one procedure via pneumatics with vacuum and pressure measurement.

- Print, code and apply flag-tag: Automatic writing, printing and application, the flag-tag application folds the label part with the RFID tag automatically before affixing it. This guarantees good legibility.

Example 13.2: Packaging marking

Packaging should be marked on one side with text, graphics and barcode at high transport speed. What does the relevant device for this look like and how many nozzles does the writing head have?

Answer: See Figure 3.27; the writing head can possess 96, 192 or 352 nozzles, which are supplied by 32 ink channels.

Example 13.3: MMS and SMS structure

Visually illustrate the structures for a merchandise management system (MMS) and a stock management system (SMS).

Answer: Figure 13.17.

Figure 13.17 Overview of possible RFID applicator and printer systems (www.ifdag.de)

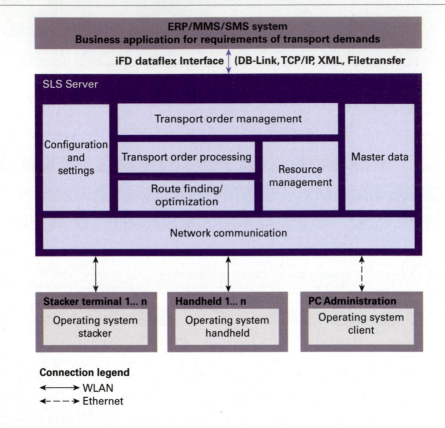

Connection legend
→ WLAN
← – – → Ethernet

Example 13.4: Transport and warehousing services

What components belong to transport and warehousing services?

Answer: For both values, information logistics is a decisive component.

Transport services include: *loading* (time window or deadlines, safety regulations); *load security* (dependent on loading cargo): general/bulk cargo, hazardous cargo; climate dependent; loading plans; loading concepts; regulations, such as VDI 2700; maybe toll processing); *transport* (transport route, shipping size as complete or part load, transport speed); *unloading* (time window deadline, self-pick up; tail lift, pallet truck, truck mounted forklift; means of handling on site).

Warehousing services include: *goods receipt* (means of handling, data capture, quantity and quality controls, creation of storage unit; removal of waste); *storing* and storage (storage space allocation); maybe *packaging* (pre-assembly, removal); *order picking* (order picking system, such as pick-by-voice, pick and pack, multi-order picking; *packaging* (packaging regulations, creation of load units); *goods issue* (provisioning, removal, cross docking).

Example 13.5: Control centre

What are the tasks of a warehouse control centre?

Answer: The control centre is a centralized point in the warehouse system, taking over the management of the entire system and also the following tasks:

- information about the status of order picking for an order;
- provide order-picking order; results of order picking, multi-stage order picking;
- approval of order picking for urgent and special orders; retrieval of entire pallets;
- order picking management system, such as using radio data or barcode; sorting and printing order picking lists;
- automatic refill management, execution of retrieval strategies, such as FIFO;
- order release; order monitoring, order and load completion;
- order processing, inventory management; automatic and permanent stocktake;
- storage space management, stacker control system, optimization of routes;
- interface monitoring and realized interfaces, such as SAP, Navision, JDEdwards;
- data exchange with customers; route planning; personnel deployment management;
- integration of warehouse control; automatic redistribution; optimization of capacity use stackers;
- point out critical situations and process, such as open deliveries, critical stocks, transport orders without receipt, non-executed transports, personnel bottlenecks.

Example 13.6: Warehouse management software

Create a checklist of the performance potential of warehouse management software that might be purchased, with a view to the requirements in the business.

Answer: A checklist is shown in Table 13.2.

Table 13.2 Comparison of requirements for and performance of warehouse management software

			Performance software	Assessment requirements		
No	Function, process step	Additional functions		Necessary	Desirable	Not needed
1	2	3	4	5	6	7
1	Goods receipt	Online capture goods receipt	X	X		
2		Synch delivery/order quantities	X		X	
3		Deduction from stocks			X	
4		Display goods receipt for dept.	X			X
5		Controlling, invoice checks				X
6		Creation of storage units	X		X	
7		Processing of returns	X	X		
8		Identity checks		X		
9	Storage	Control storage ability				X
10		Selection warehouse area				X
11		Selection storage space	X	X		
12		Monitoring storage				X
13		Transport selection				
14		Storage strategy	X	X		
15	Retrieval	Management, retrieval orders			X	
16		Order picking strategies			X	
17		Creation goods issue zones	X		X	
18		Return storage units			X	
19		Transport selection				X
20		Retrieval checks				X

No.	Category	Function			
21	Administration	Storage space inventory		x	x
22		Inventory updates	x	x	x
23		Release/lock storage space		x	x
24		ABC structuring of warehouse		x	x
25		Warehouse master data	x	x	x
26		Management storage locations, spaces	x	x	x
27	Item management	EAN barcode management		x	x
28		Item reservations		x	
29		Minimum stock management		x	x
30		Item master data	x		x
31	Customer/ supplier data			x	x
32	Inventory	Permanent inventory		x	x
33		Sample stocktake	x	x	x
34		One-off stocktake	x	x	x

(continued)

Table 13.2 (*Continued*)

No	Function, process step	Additional functions	Performance software	Assessment requirements		
				Necessary	Desirable	Not needed
1	2	3	4	5	6	7
35	Interface	PC	x	x		
36		Printer	x	x		
37		Barcode scanner	x	x		
38		Transponder (RFID)	x			x
39		Mobile handheld terminal	x	x		
40		Vehicle terminal				x
41		Pick-by-light	x		x	
42		Pick-by-voice	x		x	
43		MMS	x	x		
44		Shelf operating devices				x
45		Till	x			x
46	Statistics (key indicators)		x	x		

Example 13.7: Functional scope of a warehouse management system (WMS)

What additional functions to Chapter 13.3.3 and what advantages might a WMS have?

Answer:

- quality control, such as applying signs for items that require checks or unusual suppliers;
- returns, such as processing returns checks;
- cross-docking, such as synchronizing received goods with partly missing items of retrieval assignments;
- packaging and shipping, such as printing of pack and delivery notes, checking shipping boxes;
- expiry data management, such as management of expiry data for stocks;
- statistics and reporting, such as visual and tabular evaluation;
- consignation management, such as allocation of goods, warehouse and storage space for one client;
- warehousing charges calculation, such as automatic calculation of warehousing services in line with different methods.

Some advantages are: complete traceability, decrease of intra-logistical costs, improvement of workflows, increased transparency, shortening of processing times, optimization of order picking accuracy.

Example 13.8: Automatic label printer

How can products with different shapes be labelled in a fully automated way?

Answer: A fully automated labelling machine is shown in Figure 13.18. Figure 13.19 shows the different product shapes that can be labelled with the same machine. The process of labelling occurs in this order:

1 Alignment: The product shape affects which module is used to align the product. The exact alignment is an important factor for the accuracy of the label.

2 Customizing: Depending on the machine performance, there are different modules. Without additional tools it is quick to switch to other products and sizes.

3 Two-sided: From top to bottom, from right to left, it is possible to label both sides.

Figure 13.18 Fully automated labelling machine (www.bluhmsysteme.com)

Figure 13.19 Different product shapes for labelling (www.bluhmsysteme.com)

4 Wrapping: This is done with wrapping modules – the product is set in motion and the label is taken on during the movement.

5 Rotating: This occurs with the three-roller unit. Oddly shaped containers can be labelled without a spiralling effect. The label is accurately positioned and aligned.

Example 13.9: Network structure for an automatic transport vehicle

What does a network structure look like for an ATV system with WLAN communication?

Answer: The network structure with the necessary components is shown in Figure 13.20. WLAN communication means that all orders can be passed by the control centre via WLAN to the controls of the ATC. The control centre coordinates the traffic for multiple vehicles between the ATV and the destination, stop, go and release commands. Also:

- The ATV reports to the control centre when passing checkpoints using WLAN, so the control centre always knows where the ATV is at any moment.

- The ATV reports the completion of the assignment to the control centre.

- There is no communication between the ATVs.

Figure 13.20   Network structure of a STV system with WLAN communication (www.stoecklin.com)

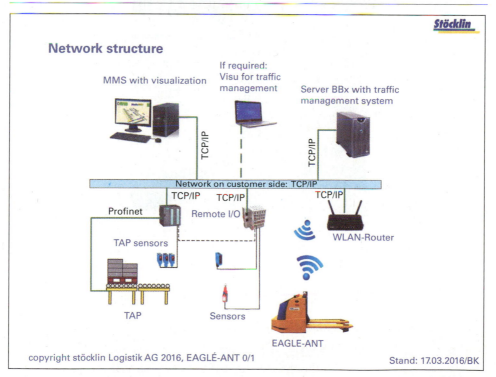

Example 13.10: Visualization of automatic transport and warehousing systems

How can the operating status of automatic transport systems and storage and retrieval systems be represented?

Answer: The status of systems, whether free or occupied, operating and control conditions, as well as disruptions, can be visually displayed by graphics (Figures 13.21 and 6.7.8).

Figure 13.21   Visualization of transport systems and five storage and retrieval machines on a route image (www.kardex-mlog.com)

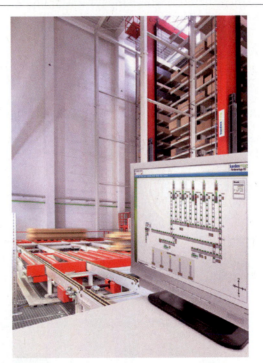

Questions

1   What identification labels are there for general cargo?

2   Describe optical coding options.

3   How does a one-dimensional barcode work?

4   What is a mobile data store?

5 What are the advantages/disadvantages of a transponder?

6 Where can data transmission with radio data be used?

7 What are the tasks of a warehouse management system?

8 What are the subsystems that the architecture of a material flow–information flow system is made up of?

9 What are the tasks of a label printer? When are automatic systems used? How is a box labelled?

INDEX

Note: Pages with figures or tables are indicated in *italic*